MEDICAL LAW

FOR THE
ATTENDING PHYSICIAN

A Case-Oriented Analysis

SALVATORE FRANCIS FISCINA

SOUTHERN ILLINOIS UNIVERSITY PRESS
Carbondale and Edwardsville

Copyright © 1982 by the Board of Trustees
Southern Illinois University
All rights reserved
Printed in the United States of America
Edited by Beatrice R. Moore
Designed by Quentin Fiore
Production supervised by John DeBacher

Library of Congress Cataloging in Publication Data

Fiscina, Salvatore Francis, 1941–
  Medical law for the attending physician.

  (Medical humanities series)
  Includes index.
  1. Physicians—Malpractice—United States.   I. Title.
II. Series.   [DNLM: 1. Jurisprudence—United States—
Cases. W 32.5 AA1 F5m]
KF2905.3.F57   344.73′041   82-5559
ISBN 0-8093-1045-7   347.30441   AACR2

CONTENTS

PREFACE

The law attempts to define societal expectations for a physician's professional conduct under varying clinical circumstances. It examines, characterizes, and analyzes that conduct in the clinical context of the practice of medicine. This legal task is accomplished by reflecting what society would consider reasonable conduct under the circumstances.

The impact and effect of law on medical practice have created suspicion and confusion among physicians concerned with their professional legal obligations. This book is intended to guide the practitioner through a journey which highlights medicolegal landmarks by illustrating professional conduct in the clinical context. Written primarily for the attending physician, this volume demonstrates the process used in the judicial system to analyze and measure the reasonableness of professional conduct. An effort has been made to develop acceptable principles of professional behavior through indicative and deductive use of clinicolegal cases. In addition, specific standards of expectation have been applied to a physician's conduct. Legal facts of cases which are primarily procedural in nature have been omitted. The rationale for this exclusion is that legal elements of "causation" and "damages" are usually quasi-scientific determinations, and are largely unrelated to the propriety of professional conduct; therefore, they are emphasized only indirectly.

Organization and presentation of material are arranged so as to focus on the roles, tasks, and events which are part of an attending physician's clinical practice of medicine. The format used is the clinical illustration or "clinicolegal case study." Each group of cases addresses a significant point in the medical encounter, such as acceptance of patients, diagnosis, treatment, and consultation.

In medical training, clinicopathologic correlations provide experience in clinical discrimination of states of disease and illness. Drawn from actual case studies, this selection presents landmarks of clinicolegal correlations by overlaying basic variations of the physician-patient encounter with legally commendable conduct.

ACKNOWLEDGEMENTS

I acknowledge with special gratitude Ted LeBlang, Associate Professor and Director of the Law and Medicine Program at Southern Illinois University School of Medicine, whose skill, foresight and perseverance made the publication of this volume a reality; Dave Sharpe, Professor of Law and Legal Medicine at George Washington University National Law Center, who provided valuable time and legal expertise in ways not readily apparent; Janet B. Seifert, who spent much time and effort in reviewing material and suggesting approaches; James G. Zimmerly, President of the American College of Legal Medicine, who as a partner and fellow physician-attorney provided strong support; and Terry Furlow, another physician-attorney, who assisted me in selecting and refining the clinicolegal teaching cases presented in the second section.

To credit the people responsible for putting the manuscript into its final form, I owe many thanks to Jane King, for the innumerable hours she spent rewriting, editing, and refining the manuscript; to Lynne Cleverdon, who performed the invaluable service of coordinating all the technical aspects of getting a book ready for publication; and to Glen W. Davidson, who as Series Editor kept this seemingly unending task in perspective.

Shirley Boker, Eileen Wilson, Ann Wallington, Jo-Ann Porter Lewis, Marilyn Flanigan, and Ann Clough deserve special thanks for typing various parts of the manuscript. I also acknowledge the extensive assistance of the staff at the George Washington University National Law Center Library.

PART I
CASE STUDIES

1

THE PHYSICIAN-PATIENT RELATIONSHIP

When a patient asks a physician to diagnose and treat a specific condition and the physician agrees to do so, an express verbal contract is formed. In the absence of such an express agreement, an implied contract may be created from the conduct of the physician and patient. In both situations, once the physician-patient relationship has been established the physician becomes obligated to provide proper medical attention and may be liable for breach of the contractual obligation. In addition, independent of a contract between the parties, a physician also has certain duties toward a patient which are imposed by law—the violation of which may also result in liability.

The physician-patient relationship can be established under many circumstances. It may result when a physician responds to the aid of a seriously ill or injured person, or from the request for services by a family member for another family member. Usually a physician is not obligated to enter into a contractual relationship with a patient. However, some preexisting contractual arrangements with a third party, such as a hospital, may require the acceptance of a patient under certain circumstances. A patient's expectations of the initial physician-patient encounter and physician conduct in undertaking to provide care for the patient may be important factors in determining whether or not a relationship has been formed. Even a telephone conversation may suffice under some circumstances.

Once a physician-patient relationship has been formed, many questions arise as to the requirements of and acceptable limitations on the physician's attendance of the patient. For example, a physician has a special duty to use care in advising those in contact with an infectious patient. There are also various requirements and limitations within emergency situations. In addition, because the physician-patient relationship is a consensual one, a physician has the right, after agreeing to accept and attend an individual as a patient, to place reasonable limitations on the relationship.

Limitations imposed by a physician, however, are subject to certain re-

3

quirements. For example, a physician has an obligation to refer a patient elsewhere if necessary; a duty not to abandon a patient by withdrawing attendance while the patient still requires medical care; and a responsibility to stay abreast of medical developments and advances.

SECTION 1: FORMATION OF THE PHYSICIAN-PATIENT RELATIONSHIP

The complex nature of medical care may result in disputes as to whether a physician was, in fact, responsible for the care of a certain patient, or whether a physician-patient relationship actually was formed.

Under some circumstances, the physician may deny the existence of an intention to undertake responsibility for treatment and may attempt to uphold this position by referring to the contractual nature of the physician-patient relationship. In the following case, the physician argued that because he neither treated the patient nor intended to treat the patient, no physician-patient relationship was formed. The court, however, did not accept the argument in this particular case.

Smart v. Kansas City. The patient was being treated for a leg injury at a university-affiliated hospital. A clinical professor, who was at the clinic seeking case histories to present at a teaching conference, stopped to look at the patient's right leg and remarked to the resident physician who was examining her for treatment that it looked to him as if the leg should be amputated. He then went on his way and did not use the patient in his lecture. The leg was not amputated at that time. Ten months later, the woman fell on a sidewalk, injuring her right knee. When she subsequently underwent an above-knee amputation of her right leg, she claimed that the amputation was required because of the injury to her knee, and she sued the city. The city attempted to introduce the professor's testimony as to the condition of the woman's leg ten months prior to the accident. The woman, however, contended that the professor was her physician at the time of the examination and therefore was precluded from disclosing confidential matters at issue.

The court concluded that if the physician had examined the patient with her knowledge and consent, and the patient believed that the examination was being made for the purpose of treating her, then the physician-patient relationship was created by implication.

Smart involved an actual, albeit cursory, examination of a patient; however, when a physician has merely the appearance of being an attending physician but without direct contact with the patient, it is unlikely that a physician-patient relationship will be formed.

Ranier v. Grossman.   A gastroenterologist who was a professor of medicine at a medical school was invited to lecture to a group of physicians at a continuing medical education meeting at a hospital. During the session, various gastrointestinal cases and x-rays were presented to him for discussion. A physician in the audience, who at the time was treating a patient for ulcerative colitis, presented the facts of his patient's history and x-rays. The professor opined that in such a case surgery was indicated. Subsequently, the inquiring physician made his recommendation to the patient. Surgery was performed, but serious complications resulted.

The patient later sued for malpractice, alleging that the professor had served as a consultant and that he had negligently recommended surgery which was in fact unnecessary. The professor contended that he had never met, seen, or treated the patient for any condition and that he had not been called in for consultation by any physician concerning the care or treatment of the patient. The court consequently determined that no physician-patient relationship existed on which to base a duty of care on the part of the professor to the patient. There had to be more contact than existed between the professor and the patient to establish a legal physician-patient relationship.

The *Ranier* case lacked, among other requirements, an intent to establish a physician-patient relationship. However, as was indicated in *Smart*, circumstances may lead to a reasonable inference that the physician intended to accept the person as a patient and to render professional services to that patient. As indicated by the following cases, an appointment for a specific treatment or a telephone conversation with a prospective patient may be sufficient to establish a relationship between a physician and patient if the substance of the contact warrants that particular result.

Lyons v. Grether.   A blind woman, accompanied by her four-year-old son and her guide dog, arrived at a physician's office to keep an appointment for treatment of a vaginal infection. She was told that the physician would not treat her unless the dog were removed from the waiting room. She insisted that the dog remain because she was not informed that any steps would be taken to assure the dog's safety or its availability to her after treatment.

The physician refused to treat her vaginal infection or to assist her in finding other medical attention. The physician's conduct humiliated the woman in the presence of other patients and her son. For another two days while she sought other medical assistance, her infection became aggravated and she endured pain and suffering. She sued the physician, charging that he had breached his duty to treat her. The physician contended that he had no duty to treat the woman because he had not accepted her as a patient.

The court pointed out that, in the absence of a statute, a physician has no legal obligation to accept as a patient everyone who seeks his services. A physician's duty arises only upon the creation of a physician-patient relationship. Ordinarily, that relationship springs from a consensual transaction. If a patient entrusts his treatment to a physician and the physician accepts the case, a physician-patient relationship is created. In this case, reasonable inferences could be drawn to establish a physician-patient relationship and a duty to treat. The court noted that, standing alone, the woman's allegation that she had an appointment with the physician would not establish a physician-patient relationship because it connoted nothing more than that the physician had agreed to see her. However, the appointment she had been given was for treatment of a vaginal infection. The implication was that the woman had sought and the physician had granted an appointment at a designated time and place for the performance of specific medical service, the treatment of a particular illness. This was a consensual transaction giving rise to a physician-patient relationship and a duty to perform the service contemplated. The court did not address whether the woman's refusal to part with her dog without the assurances she sought constituted a circumstance justifying the physician's withdrawal from her case, or whether the woman was denied a reasonable opportunity to acquire the services she needed from another physician.

O'Neill v. Montefiore Hospital.   A man went to an emergency room at 5:00 A.M. complaining of anterior chest pain and shortness of breath. When his wife related that her husband was a member of a prepaid medical group, the nurse replied that the hospital did not treat the group's members. The nurse then called one of the medical-group physicians and discussed the patient's complaints with him. She then gave the telephone to the patient and he related his symptoms directly to the physician. The physician told the man to go home and come back to see the medical-group physician who would be available at 8:00 A.M. that day. Shortly after the couple arrived home the man died as a result of a myocardial infarction. When the widow sued, the medical-group physician contended that the man had not been his patient.

The court concluded that the physician had accepted the man as a patient because he had discussed his problem with him on the telephone. However, additionally, the court was influenced by the patient's contractual affiliation with the group of which the physician was a member.

In contrast to the *O'Neill* situation, the court may determine that the contact necessary to form a physician-patient relationship between a physician and a person seeking medical attention is insufficient to constitute an "undertaking" to provide medical care. This "undertaking" is a prerequisite for a physician-patient relationship.

Fabian v. Matzko.　Mrs. Fabian developed a sudden and intense headache, neck stiffness, and nausea. Her husband brought her to their family physician who diagnosed her condition as a viral infection. Later that day, when the medications prescribed by her physician did not improve his wife's condition, Mr. Fabian called the community hospital. He could not reach his physician; therefore, he asked to talk to an available physician. He was connected with Dr. Cahill who asked Mr. Fabian what his wife's problem was. Mr. Fabian recited his wife's symptoms and also noted that she dragged her leg when she walked. Dr. Cahill than asked Mr. Fabian who his wife's doctor was. Mr. Fabian replied, "Dr. Matzko." Dr. Cahill asked, "Well, what did Dr. Matzko say?" Mr. Fabian replied, "Well, Dr. Matzko said it was the virus." Dr. Cahill then said to Mr. Fabian, "Well, you are not a doctor to make a diagnosis; if your doctor said it is a virus, it is a virus." Mr. Fabian told Dr. Cahill that he wanted his wife admitted to a hospital for a check-up. Dr. Cahill replied that the hospital's standard procedure required that the family physician, if a patient had one, had to admit that patient to the hospital. Therefore, Mrs. Fabian could not be admitted unless the arrangements were made by Dr. Matzko. After the conversation ended, Mr. Fabian attempted but was unable to contact Dr. Matzko. He called the hospital again, but was told that Dr. Cahill had left for the day. Subsequently, it was determined medically that Mrs. Fabian had sustained a subarachnoid hemorrhage with serious and permanent neurological damage.

Mrs. Fabian sued Dr. Cahill for failing to render proper medical assistance to her. She contended that a physician who undertakes to render services to a person which are necessary for the protection of that person, is liable for physical harm resulting from his failure to exercise reasonable care to perform his undertaking. She alleged that Dr. Cahill "did something" in response to Mr. Fabian's questions and concerns about his wife's health when he confirmed the family physician's medical diagnosis. This was a legally sufficient undertaking to provide professional medical services.

The court pointed out that, even under a broad view of what constitutes medical services to a patient, the facts in this case were insufficient to establish such a physician-patient relationship. The only meaningful contact between the husband and Dr. Cahill was a telephone call in which Dr. Cahill informed the husband of the hospital's policies. This did not constitute an "undertaking," and therefore no physician-patient relationship ever arose.

To illustrate further the point at issue, the court in *Fabian* distinguished an earlier decision in which the physician-patient relationship also began by a telephone call (*Hamil v. Bashline*). However, in *Hamil* the contact was more substantial in that the caller was told to bring the patient to the hospital. At the hospital, the physician on duty ordered an electrocardiogram, but an unsuccessful attempt was made to obtain a satisfactory and diagnostic one. Based on these facts, the *Fabian* court found that the substance of the relationship in *Hamil* was significantly greater than in *Fabian* and could thus serve as the basis for liability.

SECTION 2: THE CONTRACTUAL NATURE OF THE PHYSICIAN-PATIENT RELATIONSHIP

Bases for Suit

Once the physician-patient relationship has been formed, express and implied warranties as to the physician's care of a patient take effect. A breach of contract may occur, for example, if a physician materially fails to perform a duty imposed by express agreement; or, under special circumstances, the contractual nature of the physician-patient relationship may encompass the physician's obligation to provide competent and careful services. A legal cause of action for a breach of contract, however, is distinguishable from a legal action for professional negligence. In contrast to contract actions in which duties have been established pursuant to agreement between the parties, professional negligence involves a violation of a duty imposed by law and is a wrong, independent of contract.

Professional negligence may be committed by a physician who also has contracted with a patient to provide services. Thus, a physician theoretically may be submitted to liability both for violation of duties to this patient imposed by law (negligence) and for violation of duties arising by virtue of an express agreement between his patient and himself (contract). Nevertheless, courts usually determine that a physician's breach of certain obligations imposed by law supersedes promises implicit, but not clearly expressed, in a contract for professional services which may have existed between the patient and the attending physician. This point is illustrated in the following case in which the court determined that the substance of the patient's legal complaint against her physician was based upon a duty imposed by law rather than a contract.

Malone v. University of Kansas Medical Center.   A patient went to a hospital for diagnosis and treatment of lower abdominal pain. She was examined by several full-time salaried physicians at the hospital. One of them gave her a prescription for a urinary tract infection and discharged her to return home. On the following day her fallopian tube ruptured as a result of an ectopic pregnancy. During the ensuing emergency surgery, additional complications occurred which necessitated the performance of a hysterectomy.

She sued the hospital. Under a state statute the hospital was immune from liability for professional negligence. Therefore, the patient attempted to characterize her legal action against the hospital as a breach of an express contract, a legal cause of action not barred by statute. She contended that when she presented herself as a patient at the hospital she entered into an express contract with the hospital in which the hospital agreed to provide "complete, competent, and necessary medical treatment" for her; and the hospital breached that contract by releasing her without providing the promised medical treatment.

The court pointed out that the mere allegation that a contract for professional services has been formed is not sufficient to substantiate a legal cause of action for breach of contract. The court noted that although the patient's contention was couched in terms of breach of contract, it in substance presented a legal cause of action for professional negligence. The contention was that the professional services furnished were "incomplete and incompetent"; in other words, the physicians failed to exercise the reasonable skill, care, and diligence which the *law* requires of hospitals and physicians, regardless of the existence of any contract between the parties.

Breach of Contract Actions

In contrast to the above case, in which the court would not allow professional negligence to be characterized as a breach of contract, the following cases exemplify situations in which breach of contract issues may arise between physicians and their patients.

In *Alexandridis*, below, an obstetrician who expressly contracted to deliver a gravid patient, but who negligently failed to be present at the time of delivery, was held liable for injuries to his patient caused by a less qualified substitute on the basis of a breach of contract.

Alexandridis v. Jewett.   Because Dr. Jewett, an experienced obstetrician, had successfully delivered the patient's first child, the patient engaged him to deliver her second child. Later she agreed to accept either his services or those of his partner, Dr. Driscoll. The expected date of confinement was May 16. Dr. Jewett's office records dated April 28 indicated that the patient's cervix was "very soft, indicative of rapid delivery after onset of labor." On May 7 at approximately 3:30 A.M., the patient's husband called Dr. Jewett at his home and told him that his wife was in labor. The husband reminded the physician that his wife was a nurse and "she must know what she is talking about." Dr. Jewett told the husband to take the patient to the hospital immediately. It was Dr. Driscoll's night on duty, therefore Dr. Jewett called the hospital and told the obstetrical nurse to call Dr. Driscoll after the patient had been evaluated by a resident and any necessary medication had been administered. Dr. Driscoll lived about twenty minutes from the hospital.

A first-year resident in obstetrics was waiting for the patient when she came off the elevator at 4:45 A.M. His examination disclosed that the patient's cervix was fully dilated and fetal heart rate was irregular, indicating fetal distress. The resident concluded that the patient should be delivered without delay. He negligently performed an episiotomy. The child was delivered at 4:59 A.M. Dr. Driscoll entered the delivery room at 5:15 A.M., while the resident was in the process of placing superficial sutures to complete his episiotomy repair. As a result of the episiotomy the patient sustained injury to her anal sphincter which resulted in persistent rectal incontinence. She sued Dr. Jewett and Dr. Driscoll for breach of contract in failing to deliver her child.

The court observed that Dr. Jewett anticipated that the patient would have a rapid delivery after the onset of labor. He knew the patient was a nurse who reported herself to be in labor near her expected delivery date. Therefore, he should have known that birth could be imminent. Having in mind that it would take Dr. Driscoll at least twenty minutes to reach the hospital the court concluded that Dr. Jewett's instruction to delay calling Dr. Driscoll pending further evaluation or administration of medication was unreasonable. As a result, no call was made to Dr. Driscoll until after the patient had been examined at the hospital and determined to be ready for delivery. By this time it was too late for him to personally attend the patient. Therefore, Dr. Jewett's conduct was a breach of his promise that he or Dr. Driscoll would personally deliver the patient. This promise was not fulfilled by the resident physician's delivery because the patient had contracted for delivery of her baby by one of two highly skilled and experienced obstetricians. In effect, she only received the undertaking of a partially trained physician. Thus, the contract had been breached.

Another basis for a breach of contract claim may be a patient's allegation that a physician promised a particular service which the physician subsequently failed to provide as promised. However, courts are usually skeptical about imposing contractual liability on an attending physician because the uncertainty of medical science, the unpredictability of medical results, and the differences in individual patients make it unlikely that a physician of integrity would, in fact, promise a particular outcome. Moreover, courts recognize that some patients are subjectively prone to transform hopeful expressions of opinion into hard promises, particularly following an undesirable result. Thus optimistic statements of opinion by the physician, which may have therapeutic value, usually are distinguished from promises. However, the law also recognizes that to preclude contractual liability altogether would foreclose accountability of the physician who enters expressly or by implication into a special agreement for a certain result, and fails to achieve it.

As indicated by the following cases, courts recognize that physician and patient are at liberty to contract with respect to their relationship as do other parties entering into a consensual relationship, with breach thereof giving rise to a legal cause of action. The courts also recognize, however, that the physician-patient relationship has certain qualitative differences because a physician's therapeutic reassurance to the patient that he will be all right must not be converted by the disappointed or quarrelsome into a binding promise. Loose or exaggerated language, however, when presented in a manner that a patient would reasonably accept at face value, may be sufficient to establish a binding promise. Further, where a physician expressly or implicitly enters into a special agreement for a certain result, he may be liable under a breach of warranty theory if the specified result is not effected, even if the physician exercised extraordinary skill and care. The trier of fact, usually the jury, determines whether a physician's statements to a patient were merely therapeutic reassurances or constituted a warranty to produce a certain result.

Guilmet v. Campbell. The patient experienced recurrent hemorrhage from a peptic ulcer; the latest episode had been associated with shock. His family physician admitted him to the hospital and obtained consultation with two surgeons. They told the patient: that there was "no danger at all" in the operation; that the operation "takes care of all your troubles"; that he could "throw his pillbox and Maalox away"; and that he would be able to return to work in "approximately three to four weeks at the most." A gastrectomy and vagotomy were performed several months later, but the surgery was complicated by a perforated esophagus and a resultant mediastinitis. Three subsequent reparative operations were required, necessitating prolonged hospitalization.

The patient sued the surgeons. He charged that they had promised to cure him and, because the operation was unsuccessful, they had breached their promise. The surgeons denied they had promised a cure. The court noted that the determination of whether the parties had entered into a "special agreement to cure" depended upon the factual intent and characterization of the words which were spoken, and the circumstances under which they were spoken. The court stated that, as in all contract cases for personal services, in order to find for the plaintiff, the jury must have found from the evidence that the physicians made a specific, clear, and express promise to cure or to effect a specific result which was in the reasonable contemplation of both themselves and the patient, and which promise was relied upon by the patient. In this case the court found that the jury could reasonably have inferred that such a promise had been made.

Hawkins v. McGee. The scar tissue on the patient's hand was the result of a severe electrical burn which he had received nine years before he consulted the physician about treatment for the hand. On several occasions, the physician recommended an operation which involved the removal of the scar tissue from the palm of the patient's hand and the grafting of skin from his chest.

Before the operation was decided upon, the patient's father went to the physician's office and asked, "How long will the boy be in the hospital?" The physician said, "Three or four days, not over four, then the boy can go home and it will be just a few days when he will go back to work with a good hand." The physician also said, "I will guarantee to make the hand a 100 percent good hand."

The grafting procedure went poorly and produced a dysfunctional hand. As a result of the complications of the procedure the patient also was required to stay in the hospital well beyond four days. On behalf of his son, the father sued the physician, charging a breach of contract both in terms of the hospitalization period and the functional result of the operation.

The court determined that the assurance the physician made to the father that the patient would be out of the hospital in four days and back at work soon thereafter would not justify a finding that the physician contracted to complete the hospital treatment in four days or that the patient would be able to go back to work within a few days thereafter. The court pointed out the statement could only be construed as an expression of opinion or prediction as to the probable duration of the treatment and the patient's resulting disability. The fact that these estimates were exceeded did not impose contractual liability upon the physician.

However, the court concluded that if the patient could prove that the physician had said that he would make the hand "100 percent good," the patient would establish the issue of warranty and would then be allowed to sue the physician for breach of contract. The physician contended that even if he did utter these words, no reasonable person would understand that they were used with the intention of entering into a contractual relationship. Therefore they could reasonably be understood only as the physician's expression, in strong language, that he believed and expected that the operation would give his patient a good result. Thus, the physician contended that before the legal question of whether a contract for a special result had been made should be submitted to a jury, the court had to determine whether the words could possibly have the meaning imputed to them by a patient whose case was founded upon a certain interpretation of the language. The physician further argued that common knowledge of the uncertainty which attends all surgical operations and the improbability that a surgeon would ever contract to make a damaged part of the human body "100 percent perfect," in the absence of countervailing considerations, should be decisive in this case.

The court observed that there was another circumstance in this case which tended to support the patient's contention. The physician repeatedly solicited from the patient's father the opportunity to perform the operation. This raised the inference that the physician sought an opportunity to "experiment with skin grafting," to enhance his clinical experience in skin grafting procedures. Thus, if the physician, in fact, spoke the words attributed to him, the court indicated that it may be reasonably inferred that he did so with the intention that the words should be accepted at face value as an inducement for the granting of consent to the operation by the patient and his father. The court concluded that ample evidence was presented that the statements were accepted at face value by them. Under these circumstances the court held that the legal question of the making of the alleged contract was submitted properly to the jury.

Stewart v. Rudner. Because of two previous stillbirths, the patient insisted that a caesarean section be performed when her current pregnancy came to term. Her family physician promised to see to it that the attending surgeon would perform the operation. A caesarean section was not performed and she delivered another stillborn. Thereupon, she sued her family physician. The court held that the circumstances in this case indicated that the physician made a clear and unambiguous promise to insure that she receive a specific procedure. Therefore his promise was legally binding and subjected him to liability for its breach.

Noel v. Proud. Although the patient had bilateral partial hearing loss, he was able to hear and understand normal conversation with either ear. He consulted with a physician regarding his hearing loss. After an examination of the patient, the physician informed him that he was a good candidate for a stapes mobilization operation. Although he told the patient that the operation might not have any beneficial effect on his hearing, he said the operation would not "make his hearing any worse." In reliance upon, and in consideration of, the physician's promises and warranties, the patient accepted the proposed surgical services. As a direct result of the operation, the patient experienced a 50 percent decrease of hearing in the ear that was operated on. He could no longer discriminate sounds, including normal conversation, either with or without the use of an artificial hearing aid. The patient sued the physician. The court ruled that, under the circumstances presented, the physician's statement constituted a promise to obtain a specific result.

SECTION 3: ATTENDANCE OF PATIENTS—REQUIREMENTS AND LIMITATIONS

This section focuses on the various requirements of, and limitations on, the physician's attendance of patients. Included is discussion of the physician's duty to others in contact with the patient the physician is attending, the physician's duty to a patient in an emergency situation, and limitations the physician may place on the physician-patient relationship.

Duty to Those in Contact with the Patient

A physician who informs those in contact with a patient that an illness is not contagious, when with proper skill and care the physician should have known better, may be liable for negligence when others rely upon the physician's assurances and suffer injury.

Edwards v. Lamb.   The wife of a patient was advised by the physician that there was no danger in helping dress her husband's infected wound. She did so and, as a result, she contracted a staphylococcal infection. She sued the physician. The court pointed out the physician's conduct was one of positive action, not merely of failure to act. When he informed the wife that there was no danger of infection he voluntarily assumed certain obligations. Although his obligation to her was merely to advise and not to administer treatment as to a patient, when he advised her he assumed the obligation to use care in so doing. The gratuitous character of the services rendered to the wife would not excuse the physician's failure to exercise such care as the circumstances demanded.

Duty in Emergency Situations

When a legally recognized physician-patient relationship is formed, it is usually assumed that a mutual agreement has been reached between patient and physician about the need for and the provision of services. In an emergency, however, conditions and circumstances often preclude such a clear understanding between a physician and the person in need of urgent medical attention. Although the societal assumption is that an imperiled person who is in urgent need of medical attention would seek competent attention and care from one capable of providing it, this assumption places no legal responsibility on a physician to attend and assist injured persons at the scene of an accident. An apparent exception to this rule is the Vermont "Duty to Aid the Endangered Act" which purports to establish such a duty for all citizens by providing that

> A person who knows that another is exposed to grave physical harm shall, to the extent the same can be rendered without danger or peril to himself or without interference with important duties owed to others, give reasonable assistance to the exposed person unless that assistance or care is being provided by others and . . . shall not be liable in civil damages unless his acts constitute gross negligence or unless he will receive or expects to receive remuneration.

As mentioned above, a physician is not generally required to render aid to another in peril; and therefore could, with legal impunity, refuse to aid a stranger in need of immediate medical care. However, a physician, by undertaking to give assistance, may establish a physician-patient relationship and consequently assume a legal duty to act with reasonable care. If the volunteering physician fails to use reasonable care under the circumstance, regardless of humanitarian motives, liability for the negligent conduct may be established.

Under the exigent circumstances of providing emergency care, the quality and quantity of a physician's treatment often necessarily is reduced. As a result, the chances of medical failure are increased, in spite of a physician's best efforts. Thus, a physician who renders emergency care is only required to exercise the degree of care that other reasonable and competent physicians would have given under similar circumstances. In an emergency a physician is not held to the same standard of judgment and performance as under normal conditions for delivering health care. Although this standard for emergency care reduces the chances for a patient's success at litigation, it may fail to discourage the commencement of malpractice actions against the physician who gratuitously attends an injured victim in good faith. As a result, physicians have been reluctant traditionally to aid accident victims because of concern about consequential professional liability. To overcome such reluctance, states have enacted statutes known as "Good Samaritan" laws, which are designed to alter certain traditional legal rights and obligations. Although these laws vary widely in scope and coverage, their general import is to establish some form of immunity from liability for ordinary negligence which may occur at the scene of an accident or emergency. However, these statutes have limited application in the area of malpractice litigation, given that their basic purpose is to encourage physicians to provide unscheduled emergency care.

Colby v. Schwartz. A man who sustained serious injuries from an automobile accident was taken by ambulance to the emergency room of the community hospital where he was treated and then transferred to an intensive care unit. After arriving at the hospital at 1:00 P.M., the emergency on-call surgeon examined the patient and ordered him prepared for an exploratory surgical procedure which commenced at 3:00 P.M. During the course of the operation, at approximately 4:30 P.M. the patient died. The cause of death was attributed to hemoperitoneum which was due to multiple intra-abdominal lacerations caused by the blunt force of the automobile accident. The patient's estate sued the surgeon for negligent care.

In an effort to have the case summarily dismissed, the surgeon sought the immunity of the state "Good Samaritan" statute. He claimed eligibility for protection of this statute by virtue of the fact that he had rendered "emergency medical care" upon the patient.

The court concluded that the legislative purpose of the statute was to induce physicians to render medical aid to individuals in need of such care who might not otherwise receive it. This purpose was to be effected by limiting the patient's legal remedy against a physician who treats him in an emergency situation, thereby discouraging even the commencement of suit. The court noted that the legislation was directed toward physicians who, by chance and on an irregular basis, come upon or are called to render emergency medical care. Under these circumstances, the medical needs of the individual would not be matched to the expertise of the physician and facilities would be severely limited. The general practitioner might well find himself treating an individual for needs outside general medical training or the specialist asked to practice in an unrelated specialty.

The court pointed out that the surgeon operated upon the patient as part of the normal course of practice as a member of the hospital "emergency call" plan. The court concluded that, acting in this capacity, he did not render the type of physician care which constitutes "emergency medical care" as it is used in the statute. Therefore, the statutory provisions were inapplicable and unavailable to the physician as a defense.

Colby should be distinguished from the following case in which a hospital physician who was not part of the "emergency team" responded in good faith to an emergency within the hospital and was subsequently granted immunity pursuant to the state's "Good Samaritan" statute.

McKenna v. Cedars of Lebanon Hospital.   The patient underwent a therapeutic abortion and a tubal ligation sterilization. In the recovery room she had some difficulty breathing, but later she felt much better and had lunch on the gynecology ward. Approximately two hours later, she started making involuntary movements. A patient sharing the room with her called for assistance. When the nurse arrived, she determined that the patient appeared to be having a type of seizure activity, and called the page operator for any physician available on standby basis. When his beeper sounded, Dr. Warner, the chief resident on obstetrics was on the floor above performing a routine pelvic examination. He spoke to the page operator and dashed to the floor below where the nurse guided him into the patient's room. There he observed the patient having a grand mal seizure. He asked the nurse for Valium and injected five milligrams into the patient's intravenous tubing in order to control the zeisure. The seizure activity stopped, but shortly thereafter the patient was noted to be pulseless. Dr. Warner began external cardiac massage and called for a cardiopulmonary resuscitation team. Despite the efforts of the cardiopulmonary resuscitation team, the patient remained comatose and died several days later.

Thereupon, the patient's estate sued Dr. Warner for malpractice, and produced an expert medical witness who opined that Dr. Warner's response to the patient's seizure fell below the standard of care. Dr. Warner contended that he was protected by the state's "Good Samaritan" statute which stated that "No licensed physician, who in good faith renders emergency care at the scene of the emergency, shall be liable for any civil damages as a result of any of his acts or omissions in rendering the emergency care."

In addition, the state's Health and Safety Code exempted from civil liability various health facilities and personnel for acts or omissions "while attempting to resuscitate any person who is in immediate danger of loss of life." The plaintiff contended that the policy behind the "Good Samaritan" statute prohibited application of the law's protections to hospital emergencies.

Dr. Warner established that: he was not "on call" for emergencies; he was not a member of the hospital cardiopulmonary resuscitation team; and he had rendered emergency care in good faith at the place where her emergency occurred. He also established that he did not have a previous physician-patient relationship with the patient.

The court pointed out that the statute applied to "emergency care at the scene of the emergency," and concluded that the "scene of the emergency" did not preclude a hospital setting. It reasoned that whether a physician's response to an emergency in a hospital should be protected under the "Good Samaritan" statute depends on whether the physician already owed a duty to respond; if he did not, the need to encourage physicians to render emergency medical care, when they otherwise might not, prevailed over the need to uphold the right of a victim of malpractice to sue for damages.

The court held that because the physician involved was not "on call" for emergencies and was not a member of the hospital team whose job it was to respond to emergencies,* and did not have a previous physician-patient relationship with the patient, his response to the emergency situation was as a volunteer and the protection of the "Good Samaritan" statute thus applied.

Limitations on the Physician-Patient Relationship

The physician-patient relationship is a consensual one. Therefore a physician has the right, after agreeing to accept and attend an individual as a patient, to place reasonable limitations on the relationship. An attending

---

* The court concluded that the fact that Dr. Warner was chief resident did not necessarily, or as a matter of law, make him an ex officio member of an emergency team, which might be expected to deal with emergencies as its normal function.

physician is not required to do everything a patient asks. There is no obligation to make house calls or treat a patient wherever that patient wishes to be treated, except perhaps in an emergency, where a physician who refuses to make reasonable concessions to circumstances might be considered to have abandoned his patient. When a physician imposes practice restrictions, these should be explained to the patient at the formation of the physician-patient relationship. This point is illustrated in the following case which also establishes the rule that a physician has the right to determine the environment in which professional services will be provided.

Vidrine v. Mayes.   The pregnant patient asked her obstetrician to deliver her baby at home. He responded that home deliveries were unwise because of the lack of appropriate and necessary facilities if complications occurred, and he indicated that he would not do it. The patient withdrew from the professional relationship and consulted a midwife for further prenatal care. After the woman went into labor at home, complications developed and the midwife advised her husband that a physician should be called. The husband called her former obstetrician who told the husband that he would be glad to see the patient, but insisted that she be immediately transported to the hospital. The husband called other physicians and they all told him the same thing. More than six hours elapsed before the husband called the obstetrician and again and agreed to bring his wife to the hospital. The obstetrician delivered a stillborn. The patient and her husband sued the physician.

The court dismissed the action and pointed out that the dangers of a home delivery were so obvious that the obstetrician was justified in having refused to deliver the baby at home. The court also noted that the husband was repeatedly and explicitly told, after his wife went into labor, that the physician would care for her if she would come to the hospital and thus the delay in receiving care was attributable to the patient and her husband.

Transfer of Patient Care

Although a physician may place reasonable limitations on the physician-patient relationship, he is not expected to ignore a patient's complaints simply because the physician is not qualified to treat the patient. Ordinarily such inattendance to a patient's complaint would not be an acceptable limitation. The law recognizes a duty on the part of a physician to advise the patient to consult a specialist or another practitioner qualified in a method of treatment which the physician is not qualified to give.

The physician's duty to advise the patient as to the need for referral arises when the physician knows, or should know, that the requisite skill, knowledge, or facilities to treat the patient properly are not within the physician's resources.

Furthermore, when an attending physician refers a patient to a specialist for a specific problem, the physician should notify the patient of the plan and obtain consent for the referral; under such circumstances, the referring physician is ordinarily relieved of the ongoing responsibility for attending the patient for that problem. The following case illustrates an acceptable referral situation.

Brandt v. Grubin.   A young man had consulted a general practitioner because of anxiety, loneliness, and insomnia. The physician prescribed fifteen Thorazine tablets to take the "edge off" the patient's anxiety. He then recommended psychiatric care directly to the patient and referred him to a psychiatric clinic for further treatment. He also made a similar recommendation in a note which the patient took home to his family. Thereafter the general practitioner was repeatedly called for assistance by the man and his family, but did not respond to their requests. Several days later the patient was treated at an emergency room. Two days afterwards, he was admitted to the hospital and placed in a psychiatric ward. There he committed suicide. The patient's mother sued the physician claiming that he had improperly withdrawn from care of his patient.

The court concluded that the physician's treatment of the patient had terminated when he recommended to the patient and his family that the patient seek psychiatric help. The court pointed out that a general practitioner, when faced with a specialized problem, should not be "faulted" because he referred his patient to a specialist. The court said that a physician employed for a specific service was ordinarily under no duty to continue treatment after the service had been rendered. The patient visited the physician only one time; the physician determined that he was incapable of providing the requested services. He explained this to the patient and his family and referred him to a proper care facility. He had no further obligation to treat the patient.

SECTION 4: ATTENDANCE OF PATIENTS—ABANDONMENT

Abandonment, when used in the context of the physician-patient relationship, generally refers to the unilateral severance by the physician of his professional relationship with the patient, without reasonable notice, at a time when the necessity for continuing medical attention remains. Abandonment, as the following materials indicate, may include failure to notify the patient of the physician's impending absence and/or failure to provide reasonable medical attention, or other improper withdrawal by the physician from the physician-patient relationship.

Absence and Substitution

Anticipated absence from a physician's practice obligates the physician to provide patients with due notice and to arrange for a competent substitute. The same obligation would apply if a physician is ill and unavailable to patients, except for a sudden illness beyond the physician's control. Even in the latter situation, however, the physician should attempt to provide adequate substitution. If a substitute with similar qualifications cannot be provided, notice should be given to the physician's patients of the impending unavailability of medical care so that the patients can obtain care elsewhere. The legal adequacy of notice to the patients and whether the substitute is, in fact, qualified are usually questions of fact for determination by a jury.

The following cases illustrate that if a physician fails to give notice to the patient and fails to provide for a competent substitute, and the absence subsequently affects the patient adversely, the physician may be held to have abandoned the patient.

The first case illustrates that a physician who is discontinuing a practice must properly withdraw from providing medical attention to his patients. Subsequent notification usually requires a notice mailed to a physician's active patients, informing them of the discontinuation of the medical practice on a specific date and advising the patients to make other arrangements for continuation of medical care.†

Lee v. Dewbre. Two physicians practiced in partnership. One of them was attending a patient during her pregnancy, but prior to delivery he sent out notices that he was closing his practice, and he moved away. His patients, including the pregnant woman, were taken over by his partner. After the partner delivered the baby, the patient had a postpartum hemorrhage and sued her original physician for abandonment. The court pointed out that the patient had reasonable notice of the withdrawal of her attending physician from practice and that the partner possessed the same general qualifications as her original physician. Under these circumstances the court decided that no actionable abandonment had occurred.

Livingston v. Portland General Hospital Association. The physician set a patient's fractured arm. She complained from the outset that the cast was too tight, but the physician did not examine it or have it bivalved. He went on a two-week vacation and did not designate a substitute to care for the patient. She went to the hospital almost daily and complained, but no other

†The patient's records maintained by the physician should be made available to the patient's new physician under circumstances which do not necessarily imply that the patient has a right to these records. Oral notification and public announcement should supplement this process.

physician saw her because she already had an attending physician. When the cast was removed it was discovered that a large piece of plaster was embedded in her arm. As a result she sustained permanent injury and sued her physician for improperly withdrawing necessary care from her. The court held that under the circumstances of the case the physician had abandoned his patient.

The degree of attention that the physician must provide to a patient is governed by the patient's medical needs. Therefore, in determining the adequacy of a substitute's qualifications, factors in addition to the physician's education, training, and experience are taken into account. Substitution involves a transfer of responsibility. If this is made during a crisis, for example, the substitute should be a physician who is both generally familiar with the type of clinical crisis and also specifically familiar with treating the particular crisis before sole responsibility is assumed.

Ascher v. Gutierrez. The patient was scheduled for a dilation and curettage under general anesthesia. Within two or three minutes of induction with Pentothal by the anesthesiologist, the patient developed laryngospasm which compromised her ventilation. Manual attempts to adequately ventilate her failed. Drugs were injected to relax the laryngeal muscles. After approximately thirty-five minutes of attempting to overcome the laryngospasm and intubate the patient, the anesthesiologist left the operating room to attend another operation. He was replaced by an anesthesiologist who had been providing anesthesia in an adjacent operating room. After approximately fifteen minutes this anesthesiologist was finally able to intubate and properly ventilate the patient. By that time, however, she had suffered permanent brain damage as a result of prolonged hypoxia. The patient and her family sued the original anesthesiologist for abandoning his patient. The jury determined that the anesthesiologist's departure to attend another patient had constituted a form of abandonment. It had been an improper withdrawal because it involved the transfer of care and responsibility to another physician who was not familiar with the patient's critical medical status.

A physician who arranges for a second physician to act as a substitute ordinarily is not responsible for the substitute's negligence if due care was used in the selection process. The following case illustrates that a physician may be vicariously liable in certain cases for the wrongful acts of another physician he has selected as his agent for the purpose of providing care to his patients. Where a substitute physician is the appointed agent of the physician who had contracted to render specific services to a patient, the physician-principal may be liable for the negligence of the substitute physician-agent.

Wilson v. Martin Memorial Hospital.   Dr. Ashby was engaged to treat a patient during the course of her pregnancy and childbirth. He had instructed her that when her pains began, she was to go to the hospital. When Dr. Ashby had to go out of town, he arranged for Dr. Telle to cover his practice and perform necessary services for his patients. Dr. Telle was previously unknown to Dr. Ashby's pregnant patient. When she experienced abdominal pains she went to the hospital where Dr. Telle evaluated her condition, and sent her for an x-ray examination. He then told the patient that "it is going to be a case of an operation. This baby is so large you cannot give a natural birth to it." He also told her husband, "Your wife is going to have a baby and it is a caesarean case because the baby is too large for a natural birth, however, I am handicapped. I can't use my own judgment. Dr. Ashby left his patients in my care but I still don't have authority to do what I want to do." Dr. Telle did nothing, and did not perform a caesarean section. The next morning, Dr. Telle told the husband that they "had to take the baby from below." The baby weighed 12 pounds. As a result of pelvic dystocia and a difficult delivery the child sustained a permanent scalp injury. The patient sued both Dr. Telle and Dr. Ashby because of negligent delay in the delivery of her baby.

The court found that Dr. Ashby in this situation appointed Dr. Telle his agent for performance of the necessary services to the patient which Dr. Ashby had contracted to render; therefore, he would be vicariously liable for injury to the patient which resulted from Dr. Telle's negligent management of the patient's care.

In the hospital setting, a substitute who is a resident physician usually is considered to be an inadequate substitute for an attending staff physician. Thus, a staff physician is required to exercise a greater degree of supervision and control over the selection of a resident physician who is being asked to provide treatment on a patient of the attending physician. Where the sole role of the physician is to instruct and teach the resident staff and not to act as a patient's attending physician, however, the physician would ordinarily not be liable for the negligence of the resident physician. Likewise, a private attending, supervising physician is not liable for negligence in the performance of routine duties by resident physicians. However, the physician may be expected to monitor patient care matters in which superior skill might prevent injury to the patient.

Moeller v. Hauser.   On June 6 a young boy who was visiting a friend was involved in an accident in which he fractured the middle third of his femur. He was taken by ambulance to a medical center. The medical staff bylaws and regulations at this hospital provided that patients shall be assigned to a specific service and final responsibility for the care of each patient was to rest with the attending physician to whom the case was assigned. Dr. Hauser, a staff member of the Fracture Service, was assigned as the attending physician for the care of this patient. He advised the resident physician assigned to the service to place the patient in Bryant's overhead traction. Between June 7 and June 30, Dr. Hauser saw the patient six or seven times. At the end of this period he felt that the patient's condition was satisfactory. On July 1 the residents rotated to other Services in the customary manner. The new resident who came on the Fracture Service examined the patient and determined that the traction had slipped; he therefore reapplied traction, and continued to see the boy daily. Although he knew Dr. Hauser was the staff attending physician, he did not discuss the case with him between July 1 and July 10 because he felt there was no reason to call him. On or about July 6, however, the patient developed a fever, secondary to a pressure sore which had developed on the dorsum of his foot. This ultimately resulted in ulceration, necrosis, and permanent tendon injury. The patient sued the staff attending physician claiming that he had negligently cared for the patient.

Expert testimony established that pressure sores are common in cases where the patient is in traction. The main purpose of daily examination was the early detection and treatment of such lesions. The testimony concluded that the injury to the foot was caused by the failure to make a proper examination at a time when the pressure sore was still superficial and readily treatable. Dr. Hauser testified that he was surprised that the patient was still in the hospital since he thought he had been discharged. He claimed that on June 30 he had left word with the charge nurse who accompanied him at the time that the traction be removed, a splint applied, and the patient be sent home. He recalled that the patient's parents were anxious that the boy be discharged so they could return to their home in another city. Since he thought these instructions had been carried out he had not inquired whether these instructions had been followed, nor did he talk about discharging the patient to either of the two residents who were on the Fracture Service. The order to discharge the patient did not appear in the order book.

The court pointed out that, although an attending physician supervises the activities of the residents, responsibility for this supervision does not necessarily extend to duties which residents perform as part of the general hospital routine. The mere fact that Dr. Hauser was on the hospital staff and certain residents were subject to his general supervision did not make him liable for their conduct. However, the attending physician has final responsibility for the care of his patients. Dr. Hauser was under a duty to see the patient and to inspect his foot during the time when pressure sores developed because, at that time, the patient was still receiving medical care at the hospital. Thus, he had a duty to check on whether the patient had, in fact, been discharged. If he had done this, his superior knowledge could have properly guided the resident assigned to his clinical service in a manner that would have precluded or minimized the eventual injury.

Capps v. Valk. The patient's family physician diagnosed ureterolithiasis and told his patient that her condition necessitated special treatment. He recommended Dr. Valk, a professor of urology at a university medical center. He telephoned Dr. Valk concerning the patient's condition and told him he was referring her to him for treatment. The patient was advised to go to the medical center where Dr. Valk would personally treat her. Dr. Valk operated on the patient and removed the impacted stone. He left in place a ten by one inch rubber drain. Two inches of the drain extended beyond the skin surface. He gave instructions to the resident physician to remove the tube on the tenth postoperative day. On that day the resident removed the sutures and clipped the tube off even with the skin surface. The remainder of the tube was never removed. Dr. Valk visited the patient daily and monitored her status by checking her chart. At the time of discharge, he personally billed the patient for his services. After the patient returned to her home, her incision continued to drain. She was in pain and was unable to sleep. Six weeks after the operation she went to her family physician's office. He examined the incision, discovered the drain and removed it. The patient sued Dr. Valk for negligently allowing the drain to remain in her body.

Dr. Valk testified that when a patient engages the services of a specialist and enters the hospital for surgery, the duty of the specialist does not end with the performance of the surgery, but extends to aftercare of the patient including the duty of visiting the patient, making sure the patient is convalescing satisfactorily and finally, discharging the patient. If complications arise during the time the patient is in the hospital, the surgeon should immediately become aware of the problem and take appropriate steps to correct it. However, Dr. Valk contended that he had no duty to check and make sure the drain was removed prior to the patient's discharge.

The court determined that Dr. Valk was not acting as a professor and clinical instructor when he performed surgery on the patient. His employment was not special and limited to surgery only, but he was acting as the attending physician. As such, he owed a duty to the patient to provide aftercare, to visit her regularly and make sure she was convalescing satisfactorily, and to discharge her from the hospital. The court pointed out that the physician-patient relationship continues until it is ended by the consent of the parties, revoked by the dismissal of the physician, or until the physician's services are no longer needed to treat the patient's condition. Therefore, the court held that Dr. Valk had a duty to see that the drain had been properly removed.

Thomas v. Corso. A man was scraping freezing rain from the windshield of his car, which was parked on a highway shoulder. He was struck by a passing car. An ambulance took the injured man to a community hospital. The emergency room nurse recorded that the man was hit by an automobile and that he complained of numbness of the right thigh. She noted that the patient was able to move the right leg and the leg did not appear deformed, although his pants were not removed. She further noted that at 11:10 P.M. his pulse was 84 and his blood pressure was 80/60. Emergency room coverage was provided by private staff physicians who were "on call" at home on a voluntary, rotating basis. The physician on duty was called about the patient at 11:25 P.M. and was told the history and that the blood pressure was 100/60. The physician told the nurse to admit the patient and to administer 100 mg of Demerol intramuscularly. By 12:15 A.M. the patient was perspiring, asking for water frequently, and his skin was cool. The nurse noted a "strong odor of alcohol." At 12:30 A.M. his blood pressure was 90/70. The nurse paid little attention to his abnormal vital sign and his requests for water because he had been given Demerol and had been drinking. At 2:00 A.M. she found the patient in Cheyne-Stokes respiration and without pulse. The physician was notified and cardiopulmonary resuscitation was begun immediately but proved unsuccessful. When the physician arrived he observed that the patient's leg appeared foreshortened and externally rotated. Autopsy disclosed a comminuted fracture of the femoral neck, comminuted fractures in the pelvic area with jagged fragments penetrating the peritoneal cavity, and fracture and separation of the coccyx from the sacrum with extensive hemorrhage around these fractures. The patient's estate sued the physician for not coming to the hospital to attend the patient.

The court said that once the physician-patient relationship is established the physician has a duty to attend the patient. Expert evidence was not required to demonstrate failure to attend a patient when common sense indicated that, without medical attention, the consequences may be serious. When a patient has been struck by an automobile with possible life-threatening internal injuries, even a layman is able to conclude that the physician ought to be in attendance to make an informed and professional judgment of his patient's condition rather than rely on the observations of someone else, especially someone with less training.

Physician's Withdrawal from the Physician-Patient Relationship
Unless specific arrangements to the contrary are made, once a physician undertakes to provide treatment to a patient, in the absence of an agreement limiting the physician's employment, the physician is required to continue attendance of the patient as long as the case requires attention. When a physician prematurely and improperly withdraws from the relationship, liability may arise for breach of the contractual relationship. The following

cases indicate the scope of the physician's potential liability in terminating a physician-patient relationship.

When a physician hospitalizes a patient, the implication is that the patient's medical condition requires more than the usual degree of attention. Under these circumstances the failure to provide careful and close monitoring would ordinarily constitute improper medical inattention.

Levy v. Kirk.   The patient had been treated by his physician on several occasions for chronic congestive cardiac failure. When he became ill again, his wife called the physician and related the patient's problems to him. The physician hospitalized the patient, but did not write any medical orders or visit him for several days, even though he was in the hospital on several occasions during this period. When he finally saw his patient, he immediately ordered oxygen and administered medication and other life support measures, but the patient died shortly thereafter in acute pulmonary edema. The wife sued the physician for failing to medically attend her husband. The court held the physician's inattentive conduct was sufficient to establish a legal cause of action for abandonment.

McGulpin v. Bessmer.   A patient underwent varicose vein stripping. His postoperative course was complicated by vascular gangrene of the foot. The surgeon told the patient that an amputation of his foot was immediately required. The patient consented. However, the surgeon did not return to the hospital nor did he communicate with the patient in any way over the next four days. The patient was then transferred to another hospital where another surgeon performed the amputation, with more extensive surgery necessitated by the delay. The patient then sued the original surgeon, charging that the surgeon had improperly withdrawn from the case.

The court pointed out that the surgeon's own statement regarding the urgent need for amputation indicated that the patient required immediate and close attention. Because the surgeon did not provide this type of attention, his inattention constituted abandonment.

Collins v. Meeker.   The patient injured his groin while at work. His employer sent him to a surgeon who detected an inguinal hernia and performed a hernioplasty. Subsequently the patient experienced pain in the groin which radiated into the scrotum. When the groin pain persisted he consulted a Dr. Mastio who recommended a period of "watching and waiting." Several months later he returned to Dr. Mastio with the same complaint at the site of the hernioplasty. Dr. Mastio operated through the old incision site and "rebuilt the external inguinal ring." Postoperatively the patient continued to experience groin pain. After his discharge from the hospital his complaints continued and Dr. Mastio finally rehospitalized him. While the patient was in the hospital, Dr. Mastio became frustrated by the patient's incessant complaints and discharged him as his patient by telling him that he "was sick of the whole deal," and that the patient "was sick in the head and no medicine would do him any good." Shortly thereafter the patient consulted another physician who performed a third operation in which he discovered that the rebuilding of the external inguinal ring had been constructed so tightly that it compromised the circulation and the flow of secretions to and from the testicle. The patient then sued Dr. Mastio.

The court held that Dr. Mastio's manner of withdrawing from the physician-patient relationship by informing his patient that there was nothing wrong except that "he was sick in the head," when in fact the patient was experiencing a complication of surgery, was improper, and constituted abandonment.

Morrell v. Lalonde. The physician operated on the patient for a strangulated hernia. He made an abdominal incision, observed extensive bowel damage, and closed the incision without attempting to relieve the obstructed bowel. He then informed the patient that she was going to die and immediately discharged her from the hospital to "die at home." Thereafter the physician neglected to call on his patient, stating that he was too busy at the hospital. The patient sued the physician. The court said the physician's duty required him to have his patient remain in the hospital in order to avoid the risk to her life that might result from a premature discharge. Failure to do so constituted a form of abandonment.

Ricks v. Budge. A patient developed a postoperative hand infection and complications after his physician had discharged him from the hospital. He returned to the operating physician but the physician refused to treat him because he had not paid his bill for care rendered during the first hospital stay. The patient sued for abandonment. The court held that the surgeon had improperly withdrawn his attendance to his patient's medical needs.

In order for improper withdrawal of medical attention to become the basis for liability of the physician, it must be demonstrated that the withdrawal occurred at a time when further medical attention was needed but not received. If the necessary care is rendered from another source without detriment to the patient, a legal cause of action for abandonment against the physician is unlikely to be established.

Meiselman v. Crown Heights Hospital. The physician performed an incision and drainage on his patient's infected thumb. Later the patient's wife telephoned the physician and reported complications. During the conversation the physician established that the patient was unemployed. On that basis he refused to continue to treat him or see him again. However, he told the wife to take her husband to the county hospital. She followed his advice and another physician was in charge of the case within a half hour of the telephone call. The court conceded that, although a technically improper withdrawal of medical attention may have occurred, the patient's medical needs were not jeopardized and there was no damage to the injured thumb occasioned by the physician's sudden withdrawal.

A situation may arise where withdrawal of medical care is required of the physician by circumstances beyond the physician's control; this situation is exemplified by the following case.

Clark v. Wichman. A patient sustained a leg fracture in an automobile accident and was taken to a general hospital. There an orthopedic surgeon reduced the fracture and instructed her not to bear any weight on the leg. Prior to being dismissed from the hospital the patient developed a traumatic psychosis, and therefore was transferred to a mental hospital. All her medical records, including orthopedic reports, were sent with her. The orthopedic surgeon did not medically attend her while she was in the mental hospital. He resumed care of the patient when she was transferred back to the general hospital. While in the mental hospital she claimed she was forced to walk on her injured leg thereby allegedly causing additional injury to her leg. Thus she sued her orthopedist for abandoning her. The court held that the orthopedic surgeon was not obligated to follow his patient to the mental hospital. Moreover, he had no right to do so because he was not a member of the mental hospital staff. He had made all records and instructions available to the physicians at the mental hospital and was not liable for their failure to follow them.

Patient's Withdrawal from the Physician-Patient Relationship

The patient may terminate the physician-patient relationship at any time by unilateral withdrawal from the relationship. Because such withdrawal is often unexpressed or unannounced by the patient, disputes may arise as to whether a physician has an ongoing or continuing responsibility to medically attend the patient in a proper manner. As long as the relationship of physician and patient continues for the particular condition which the physician is employed to treat, and the physician continues to attend the patient in relation thereto, a continuing physician-patient relationship will be presumed. In the absence of these conditions, however, it is not necessary that there be a formal discharge of the physician or formal termination of employment. If there is nothing more medically to be done for the particular injury or illness which the physician was employed to treat, or if the physician properly withdraws from attending the patient for it, the relationship ordinarily ceases without any formality.

Fleishman v. Richardson-Merrell, Inc. In July 1960, the patient's physician diagnosed hypercholesterolemia and gave her a prescription for MER/29 (Triparanol). She spoke to her physician again only once after the time he gave her the prescription. This contact occurred the following week when he checked her condition and took a blood test. The prescription itself authorized only two refills. However, the patient continued to obtain and take the MER/29 beyond the expiration of the prescription. The physician did not attend or see her at any time between July 1960 and December 1961, nor did he consult with her about her continuing to take the drug. Moreover, she did not notify him that she was experiencing problems of visual acuity which she subsequently claimed were side-effects of the drug. In December 1961 she immediately stopped taking the drug when a radio program reported that cataracts were side effects of MER/29. When she was informed that she had sustained permanent injuries to her eyes as a result of the prolonged use of the drug, she sued the physician on the theory that he had a continuing duty to make periodic calls to follow her progress and to notify her of the dangerous propensities of a drug which he had prescribed as soon as he knew or should have known of them.

The court declared that, even assuming the existence of such a continuing duty by a treating physician to a patient under his care, no such duty arose under the facts in the present case. Such a duty is owed only to a patient who actually remains under the physician's treatment and who follows the course of treatment provided. The court held that although the physician had the duty of following his patient's progress while she was consulting him and taking the drug pursuant to his prescription, this duty terminated shortly after her last visit to his office in July 1960. She continued to take the drug after that time, not as a part of his treatment or under his prescription, but of her own volition and by her own procurement. The physician had no duty to continue to follow her progress after the prescription expired because she had withdrawn from his supervision and treatment; he had no knowledge or reason to know that she was continuing to use the drug. Moreover, the court concluded that the patient herself dispensed with the physician's services and thus terminated the physician-patient relationship many months before December 1961, when it first became known that the prolonged use of the drug could have dangerous side effects.

Where a patient fails to keep a post-surgical appointment with the physician *and* declines to see the physician again, the physician-patient relationship is usually terminated on the day of the appointment which the patient failed to keep.

Millbaugh v. Gilmore. On January 8, the patient underwent surgery for alleviation of symptoms associated with benign prostatic hypertrophy. On March 27, he saw his surgeon for a postoperative evaluation and was instructed to return in one month for further evaluation. The surgeon gave him a prescription for antibiotics. Without his surgeon's knowledge, the patient continued to have the prescription refilled and took the medicine over the next year until he sought the services of another physician.

The patient did not keep his scheduled April appointment nor did he see the operating surgeon thereafter. Subsequently the patient sued his surgeon for alleged negligent performance of the surgery. In order to avoid the statute of limitations, the patient had to demonstrate that the physician-patient relationship continued during the time he was taking the medication previously prescribed by the surgeon. He contended that the taking of medicine prescribed by his physician during the physician-patient relationship continued the physician-patient relationship indefinitely, or until the patient consulted another physician.

The court held that there was not a continuing course of treatment which would have precluded termination of the physician-patient relationship. It pointed out that the patient's conduct terminated the physician-patient relationship. Although the patient was "acting under his surgeon's advice" in taking the medicine, he was, by his own conduct, no longer his surgeon's patient at that time. The taking of the medicine prescribed by the surgeon after that termination of the relationship did not constitute a "continuing course of treatment" because it was done in an unsupervised manner which neither afforded the surgeon an opportunity to correct any errors on his part, nor provided a basis for the full treatment contemplated in a physician-patient relationship. Therefore, the court concluded the refusal of a patient to submit to further treatment by an attending physician terminated, by necessary implication, the physician-patient relationship.

SECTION 5: ATTENDANCE OF PATIENTS—MAINTAINING MEDICAL
EXPERTISE

A physician may "abandon" his professional discipline by not keeping pace with medical advances and developments. The obligation to "keep up" is incorporated in the standard for medical attendance of a patient. A physician is expected to possess the knowledge necessary for the effective practice of medicine. Implicit in this expectation is that a physician is keeping abreast of pertinent medical developments so that he might adopt and apply those techniques and advances which have become recognized as standard in his specific type of practice.

Reed v. Church. The physician diagnosed syphilis in his patient and administered medicine for its treatment. The patient began to experience visual difficulties and eventually lost the sight of one eye. It was determined that his vision had been affected by the medication. The patient sued the physician for using that medicine for his condition. The court indicated that a physician should have been familiar with the current literature about the prescribed medication which indicated that the medication should be terminated at once if any vision problems occurred.

Naccarato v. Grob. A small-town pediatrician failed to administer tests for phenylketonuria to an infant. Eventually the child was discovered to be irreversibly retarded as a result of the disease. The child sued the pediatrician. At trial, testimony established that these tests were not routinely performed by pediatricians in the locality where the infant was born because of the rarity of the disease. Several pediatricians from other geographical areas, however, testified that good medical practice would require them. The court pointed out that although small-town physicians did not have the means to keep up with their fields as well as urban physicians, the law increasingly recognized that even general practitioners are not necessarily excluded from the medical mainstream. The present advanced state of communication makes isolation rare for professionals. They have access not only to medical literature but to all manner of continuing education seminars, conferences, and conventions. The legal expectation is that the attending physician will, as part of his obligation to his patients, read journals, attend meetings and make an effort to keep up with general developments of patient care.

A specialist is expected to know more than a nonspecialist about the care and treatment of specific conditions within the specialty; one reason for specializing is to narrow the focus of knowledge in favor of depth. Proper diagnosis and treatment of a physician's patient includes an obligation to use current knowledge of appropriate treatment for a condition which the specialist routinely undertakes and should be competent to provide without consultation with another specialist.

To determine if a specialist is keeping abreast, courts look at what is generally accepted as proper care in the specialty. Therefore, a patient who can demonstrate that the illness was treated by an outmoded method (even if due skill and care were used in its application), probably has a legal cause of action if an untoward or unsatisfactory result occurs. Under certain circumstances, a specialist may not rely upon a general community standard if it is outmoded to the extent that it inadequately protects patients from injury associated with the treatment of a condition within his specialty.

Toth v. Community Hospital at Glen Cove. A woman had premature twins who experienced respiratory distress syndrome. The attending pediatrician gave orders to the nurses to have the twins placed in incubators and to have oxygen administered in a manner which involved a delicate clinical titration of oxygen concentration with the respiratory distress of the neonate. Although his orders comported with the prevailing community standard of care, his instructions as to the amount of oxygen to be administered were not properly followed. He did not check on the nurses and thus did not discover their noncompliance. As a result of excessive oxygen administration, the twins developed retrolental fibroplasia and resultant blindness. The mother sued the pediatrician on behalf of her twins for failing to adequately monitor the treatment he prescribed.

The court suggested that a general practitioner probably would not have been liable if he had failed to check to see if his explicit orders had been properly carried out, because such personal monitoring was not the community standard. However, the court pointed out that a specialist may be liable when a general practitioner is not, if the customary practice itself is inadequate. The court concluded that the specialist should have known enough about the care of a premature neonate to realize that the standard practice was insufficient to adequately protect his patient. Thus, the court held it was negligent for the pediatrician not to have discovered the impropriety in oxygen administration.

VARIATIONS OF THE PHYSICIAN-PATIENT RELATIONSHIP

This chapter presents those situations which vary from the traditional physician-patient relationship, as discussed in chapter 1. These variations may occur because the physician is employed by a hospital, by a third party to the relationship (such as a patient's prospective or actual employer), by an insurance company or by a nonpatient (such as a spouse or relative who arranges for the care of a patient). In each of these situations, the traditional physician-patient relationship is modified. For example, a physician's affiliation with a hospital or an employer may limit or otherwise affect the relationship, thereby establishing the physician's primary duty to the third-party employer, and not to the patient.

Other variations in the traditional physician-patient relationship involve duties to others which develop from a physician's treatment of a patient, such as the duty of a physician to refrain from outrageous conduct in the treatment of a patient. In the latter situation, a physician may be liable not only to the patient but also to a relative of the patient who witnesses the physician's conduct.

SECTION 1: THE PHYSICIAN'S RESPONSIBILITY TO AN EMPLOYER

The physician-patient relationship and its attendant requirements and limitations may be conditioned by special circumstances. This section presents and discusses how employment of the physician by a third party affects the physician-patient relationship.

Hospitals as Employers of Physicians
A physician's affiliation with a hospital may substantially affect that physician's right to choose initially whether to form a physician-patient relationship. Some courts have stated that physicians employed by public or private hospitals enter the relationship of physician and patient as soon as the pa-

tient is brought to a hospital. Additionally, a physician who contracts to provide emergency services for a hospital, or who is designated as "on-call" to an emergency room, ordinarily is obligated to evaluate a patient who seeks medical care in the emergency room of the hospital. As an "on-call" physician for the hospital, the physician is required to evaluate the need for immediate medical treatment of a patient who comes to the emergency room. In such a case the physician-patient relationship is presumed, based upon public expectations of emergency care. Thus, the physician who refuses to evaluate the patient may later be precluded from denying in court that a physician-patient relationship existed, if a reasonably careful physician under the same circumstances would have medically attended the patient.

As the following cases illustrate, a physician, who has agreed with a hospital to staff the emergency department on an "on-call" basis, ordinarily has a duty to render emergency care to all patients coming into the emergency department in need of such care.

Hiser v. Randolph.   The patient, a diabetic, had been examined by her private physician because she was feeling lethargic. The following evening, the patient became unconscious as a result of diabetic ketoacidosis, and was brought to a hospital emergency room. The hospital maintained an emergency department staffed on a rotating "on-call" basis by eight physicians who composed the entire complement of physicians with clinical staff privileges at the hospital. Under state law, any hospital providing emergency department services was obligated to provide emergency services to everyone who was in need of them. When the emergency department contacted an "on-call" physician, he refused to come in and treat the patient. Instead, he referred the emergency department nurse to the patient's private physician, who was also a member of the hospital staff. The private physician insisted that the "on-call" physician respond to the patient's emergency situation. When the emergency department nurse again telephoned the "on-call" physician and asked him to see the patient, he again refused. The hospital chief of staff was then notified of the situation. Approximately forty minutes later, he came into the hospital and attended the patient. Despite his therapeutic efforts, the patient died as a result of complications of ketoacidosis. The estate of the deceased patient then sued the "on-call" physician for failing to treat that patient.

Expert testimony established that the delay in initiating treatment contributed to the patient's death. The court pointed out that even though a physician is generally free to refuse to treat a patient, the "on-call" emergency physician had a contractual obligation to treat the patient, based on his agreement with the hospital. Because the hospital was obligated to treat all patients who present themselves in the emergency room, the physician was obligated to do so also.

New Biloxi Hospital v. Frazier.   A man sustained a gunshot wound in his chest and was brought into an emergency room. The "on-call" physician, a private attending staff member, was called by a nurse and came to the emergency room to look at the patient. Although he was aware that the patient was in shock, the physician did not institute life support measures or attend to the patient's medical needs. Instead he ordered him transferred to a Veterans Administration Hospital after learning that the patient was a veteran. Shortly after the patient arrived at the Veterans Administration Hospital, he died. A suit was filed by his estate based on the physician's failure to provide proper medical care of the patient after he was brought into the emergency room.

The court concluded that the hospital undertook to render emergency medical service to the patient; he was recorded as an emergency room patient and remained there two hours. Under such circumstances a duty arose to use reasonable care in protecting the patient's life and well-being. The court thus held that a therapeutic relationship with the patient had been established. The formation of the physician-patient relationship was governed by the physician's third-party arrangement with the hospital.

As indicated in the preceding case, the physician's relationship with a hospital may determine whether a physician-patient relationship has been formed. If the hospital may refuse to treat a patient, a physician, as an agent of the hospital, may also refuse to form a therapeutic relationship with the patient. As the following case suggests, once a patient is rightfully refused admission to a hospital because of hospital policies, a physician-patient relationship may not be recognized even though the physician may have administered emergency services.

Harper v. Baptist Medical Center-Princeton.   Mr. Harper was injured in an accident and taken by ambulance to the nearest emergency room which was that of a private hospital. The physician who examined him ascertained that he had a severed popliteal artery and administered medication for pain. Harper was explicitly told that he had not been admitted to the hospital because he did not have health insurance that would reimburse the hospital for its charges. Shortly thereafter, Harper was transferred to a charitable hospital where he underwent surgery. As a result of the accident he sustained a permanent foot drop and filed suit against the private hospital and the emergency room physician because of their refusal to treat his injuries.

The hospital and the physician contended that they were under no duty to accept Harper as a patient. The court held that the facts did not show that the hospital or the physician had accepted Harper as a patient before sending him to the other hospital. Therefore, the court concluded that the physician did not owe Harper a duty to provide him with medical care.

Not only may a physician's affiliation with a hospital determine many of the contractual aspects of the physician-patient relationship, but also the affiliation may operate to limit a physician's liability for negligence. For example, a physician who at the time he treated the patient was employed as an intern on the staff of a state hospital is an agent of the state and therefore covered by a sovereign immunity statute. However, if the physician in treating a person did not meet the definition of agent in the statute which established immunity of a state and its agents, he could lose the benefit of its protections.

Even though a patient is admitted to a hospital, and a physician is contractually obligated to attend the patient by virtue of an arrangement with the hospital, special facts and circumstances of the situation may make the physician not responsible for the care of that patient.

Ruth Easter, Administratix of the Estate of Bobby Lee Easter, Deceased v. Lexington Memorial Hospital, et al. A man was brought to a hospital emergency room after he had sustained second and third-degree burns, lacerations, abrasions, and a fractured arm in a hotel fire. Several other victims of the fire were also brought to the emergency room for treatment. There was only one physician on duty in the emergency room at this time. A specialist on the private staff of the hospital, who had experience in the treatment of burns was present in the hospital. When he saw the victims of the fire arriving on stretchers, and realized there were too many patients for one physician to handle, he offered his services to the emergency room physician, who was then treating a patient. The emergency room physician pointed at the injured man and suggested, "Why don't you see that one over there," but never told the physician to do anything. The staff specialist told the injured man he was not working in the emergency room, but had volunteered to help. The man replied, "Thank you." The staff specialist was under the impression that the emergency room physician had already seen the patient, even though he had not actually observed the physician and man together. When the specialist asked the man if he had received tetanus shots before, the man replied that he was not sure, but he "thought he had." He told the specialist that when he had been in the army, he had suffered a traumatic amputation of his arm. Learning that, the specialist ordered tentatus toxoid, which he felt was sufficient immunization. After rendering the emergency treatment, the specialist asked the emergency room physician what was to be done with the patient. The emergency physician responded that the man was to be admitted to the hospital under the supervision of the "on-call" surgeon. Five days later the patient developed tetanus. He was transferred to another hospital where he subsequently died as a result of the infection.

The man's estate sued, among others, the emergency room physician, charging that he had a duty to treat the patient or, if overwhelmed by the patient load, declare an emergency and call in more physicians to assist him in treating the people involved in the accident who were brought to the emergency room.

The court declared that no physician-patient relationship existed between the emergency room physician and the injured man; therefore, the emergency room physician was not obligated to leave a patient he was treating to see the injured man when another qualified physician offered to evaluate him and there were several other patients in the emergency room needing medical attention at that time. The court also pointed out that bringing in more physicians would not have helped the injured man, who already had a specialist attending him. Thus, the court concluded that no act or omission of the emergency physician was the legal cause of the man developing tetanus. Moreover, the court indicated that under the circumstances of this case, there was insufficient evidence to characterize the specialist as an agent of the emergency physician, thereby making him vicariously liable for the specialist's alleged negligence.

Leathers v. Serrell.   Mrs. Leathers went to a state operated medical center to visit her seriously ill brother. While she was in a waiting room she was approached by Dr. Serrell, an intern who had been treating her brother. He informed her that her brother had died. She became upset, whereupon Dr. Serrell offered her a sedative. At the request of Dr. Serrell and in his presence, the nurse administered an intramuscular injection of Valium to Mrs. Leathers. In administering the injection into Mrs. Leathers's right arm, the nurse was hindered by Mrs. Leathers's long-sleeved sweater. As a result the injection administered by the nurse penetrated Mrs. Leathers's radial nerve, causing permanent neuropraxic injury to her arm and hand.

Because the hospital was governmentally immune, Mrs. Leathers sued Dr. Serrell personally for negligence in supervising the injection. Dr. Serrell was unlicensed. The scope of Dr. Serrell's duty as an intern was determined by a state statute which stated in part:

> Unlicensed or licensed practitioners may be employed as interns or residents in a legally established and licensed hospital *provided their practice is confined strictly to persons who are bona-fide patients within the hospital or who receive treatment or advice in an organized outpatient department of the hospital* to which ambulant patients regularly come for professional services rendered under supervision of licensed members of the hospital staff, provided further, that such employment is a

part of a regularly established course of instruction for such interns or residents. Such intern or resident shall be responsible and accountable at all times to a licensed member of the staff. (Emphasis added)

The court found that although a contractual physician-patient relationship had not been established, Dr. Serrell chose to treat Mrs. Leathers even though he could have sent her to the hospital's emergency room. In treating a nonpatient for whatever practical or humanitarian motivations or reasons, Dr. Serrell lost the cloak of sovereign immunity. He was only permitted to practice medicine in conformity with statutory provisions; he exceeded the scope of his authority in treating Mrs. Leathers and, therefore, was personally liable for his negligence.

Companies as Employers of Physicians

(1) Physician's Primary Responsibility

As the preceding materials indicate, the physician-patient relationship may be affected by a physician's affiliation with a hospital. It may also vary whenever the physician is hired to examine a job applicant or employee by the prospective or actual employer, or when the physician is hired to examine a person by a prospective or actual insurer. Generally, in these situations a physician's primary duty is to the employer and not, as in the traditional physician-patient relationship, to the patient. The physician assumes the role of examiner rather than therapist; and is expected to report the state of the person's health directly to the third party, and is not expected to treat the person for any condition discovered during the course of his examination. Under these circumstances courts generally have held that a physician-patient relationship does not exist between the physician and the examinee. Thus, the physician's duty of care to the examinee is not the same as that which is owed to patients.

As the following cases illustrate, because these types of evaluations do not establish a physician-patient relationship, and consequently no traditional duty of due care to the examinee, the latter usually has no legal cause of action against the examining physician for negligent misdiagnosis of a medical condition.

Lotspeich v. Chance-Vought Aircraft. At the time of her preemployment examination, the applicant's chest x-ray clearly documented the presence of tuberculosis. Nevertheless, she was not advised of this condition and was hired. Three years later, while still employed, she developed military tuberculosis, the treatment of which required protracted hospitalization. As a result, the employee sued the physician. She claimed that proper diagnosis and treatment at the time of the physical examination would have materially shortened her recovery period. The court held that because the physician's obligation at the time of the preemployment examination was to the employer and not to the applicant, he owed her no duty of careful diagnosis nor any obligation to report her condition to her.

Rogers v. Horvath.   An employee of General Motors Corporation received Workmen's Compensation benefits for a shoulder injury. When the benefits were terminated she filed a claim for continuation. Pursuant to its rights under the Workmen's Compensation Act, General Motors had the claimant examined by an orthopedic surgeon. After the examination, the surgeon reported to General Motors and testified at the Workmen's Compensation hearing that the claimant was a malingerer. On the basis of this testimony, the referee decided that the claimant was not disabled. The claimant then sued the physician, alleging malpractice in his examination of her. She asserted that he had a duty to examine her in accordance with the standard of orthopedic practice and she alleged that he willfully or negligently failed to conduct a proper examination, and thereby failed to properly diagnose her condition.

The court held that no physician-patient relationship existed between the employee/claimant and the orthopedic surgeon. The examination of the claimant was performed on behalf of her employer in preparation for testimony before the Workmen's Compensation referee. The examination was not performed for the claimant's benefit to diagnose or treat an ailment. Therefore, the claimant had no legal cause of action for malpractice.

The following case exemplifies a variation in these third-party employer situations. In this case a woman was examined by a physician not for employment reasons but because she sustained an injury in the store which employed the physician. Despite the variation in facts, the court reached the same conclusion; that is, the physician was not liable because a physician-patient relationship was not established by the examination.

Quarles v. Sutherland.   A woman sustained an injury in a department store. She was taken by store personnel to an office where she was examined by a physician who had been retained by the store. After evaluating the woman, the physician determined that she was not seriously injured. The woman was not charged for the physician's services. The woman did not know and was not advised that he was employed by the store. Subsequently, the woman filed a personal injury claim against the store. Her attorney wrote to the physician who had examined her in the store and requested a medical report. The attorney cautioned the physician not to give information of the patient's condition to anyone without notifying him. In spite of this admonition, the physician sent a copy of his medical report to the store's attorney. The report indicated that the injury was inconsequential. On the basis of the report, the store refused to compensate the woman for her alleged injury. When the woman discovered that the physician had sent a report to the store's attorney, she sued the physician. She charged that the physician's disclosure had prejudiced her claim against the store. She contended that if the physician disclosed any confidential information he had obtained from her, she would have a legal basis for a breach of an implied contract.

The court concluded that a physician-patient relationship did not exist and, therefore, the woman had no contractual rights owed to her by the physician and thus she had no basis for her suit. It rejected the theory of implied contract and concluded that the woman had merely accepted and received medical treatment from the store's physician. By acceptance of such treatment, however, the store physician did not become her physician also.

(2) The Physician's Responsibility to Examinee

A physician who is employed to examine a person for the benefit of a third party is primarily responsible to that third party. Although a traditional physician-patient relationship usually does not exist under these circumstances, the physician may still owe the person examined a duty to perform the examination with reasonable care. Notwithstanding such a duty, courts recognize that the physician's duty to examine a prospective employee carefully is limited by the goals and needs of the employer.

Beadling v. Sirotta. A company radiologist reported to the company that the chest x-ray of a job applicant strongly suggested that the applicant had active tuberculosis. As a result, the personnel manager turned down the applicant for a job and advised him to consult his physician to determine whether he had tuberculosis.

The next day, the applicant's own physician referred him to another radiologist who performed a chest x-ray and reported "infiltration of the apical segment of the right upper lobe with small cavity." The applicant was then hospitalized for extensive testing. On the advice of the second radiologist, the applicant's family physician treated him for tuberculosis pending the outcome of definitive tests.

Four months later, a pulmonary specialist evaluated the applicant and diagnosed minimal pulmonary tuberculosis. Although the specialist indicated that the applicant was employable subject to continuation of the antituberculant medication for at least a year, he could not classify the lesion as clearly inactive. The company still refused to hire the applicant on the basis of this latest report. When the applicant's own radiologist subsequently determined that his chest x-ray was normal, the applicant sued the company radiologist who had first diagnosed active tuberculosis. He contended that the radiologist's unqualified report to the employer resulted in his initial failure to obtain employment. The report should have indicated that there was only a possibility of tuberculosis, not that he definitely had tuberculosis.

The court reasoned that the examining physician's duty to discover physical impairments in the examinee is limited by the needs of the employer. The court stated that this limitation on the physician's duty is in part supported by the public's interest in denying employment to those whose health may endanger other workers.

The court pointed out that in this case it made no difference to the employer whether the company physician had diagnosed active or possible tuberculosis because the radiologist was employed to provide medical information on an applicant's health status to the company. If the radiologist had hedged and used "possible" tuberculosis rather than "active" tuberculosis, the employer would still have denied the applicant employment.

As illustrated by *Beadling*, the physician's duty of exercising reasonable care in evaluating the examinee is conditioned by his duty to the employer. However, an exception to this rule may exist in situations where a prior physician-patient relationship existed between the physician and the examinee.

Dowling v. Mutual Life Insurance Company of New York.   A physician was paid by an insurance company to complete an "attending physician's statement" on one of his patients who had applied for insurance. One month prior to this time, the patient had complained to his physician about chest pains and was sent to a radiologist for a chest x-ray. The next day a messenger delivered the radiologist's report which indicated that a follow-up x-ray was advisable because there was a suggestion of an infiltration of the left lung. The report was filed in the patient's clinical records without the physician being made aware of its existence. Thus, when the physician filled out the insurance forms, he reported to the insurer that he had no knowledge of anything in the patient's medical history that would affect his insurability.

When active tuberculosis was diagnosed nineteen months later, the patient sued his physician, claiming that his failure to inform him of the finding caused his tubercular condition to progress to such an extent that a long period of hospitalization and major surgery was necessary by the time his condition was finally detected. The physician contended that he had been employed by the insurance company to evaluate the applicant's status; and although he had been negligent in that regard, he owed no duty to the examinee and thus was not liable for negligence.

The court held that, even though the physician was hired to examine his patient by the company, he was still personally liable to the patient for the negligent delay in diagnosis because of the past physician-patient relationship.

The following cases in this section more fully develop the physician's duty of care to the examinee. For example, although a company physician usually owes no duty to a job applicant to discover a disease during preemployment examinations because there is no duty on the company's part to discover the presence of disease, a company physician may owe an employee of the company a duty to exercise due care not to injure him physically or otherwise. A negligently made, inaccurate report of the state of the employee's health which injures the employee's chances of promotion, might be sufficient injury for liability to result from the physician's negligence.

Armstrong v. Morgan. Mr. Armstrong was employed by Zale Corporation. Upon being promoted to a vice-president position he was requested to undergo a physical examination. He was examined by Dr. Morgan, who was employed by Zale to perform examinations and report the results to the appropriate corporate officers. Dr. Morgan's report indicated that Mr. Armstrong was in poor physical condition. When the report was received by his employer, Mr. Armstrong lost his employment, plus the benefits which he had accrued by virtue of his position with the company.

Mr. Armstrong sued Dr. Morgan, contending that the report contained false and inaccurate statements and conclusions regarding the condition of his health, and that Dr. Morgan was negligent in his diagnosis because he did not exercise reasonable skill in conducting the physical examination. Mr. Armstrong further contended that the inaccurate and improper diagnosis resulted in damages to him because he lost his job.

The court pointed out that in the absence of a contractual physician-patient relationship, the physician usually owes no duty of due diagnostic care to a person he has examined for the benefit of a third party. The court concluded, however, that notwithstanding the absence of a contract between Mr. Armstrong and Dr. Morgan, the physician owed the employee a duty not to injure him physically or otherwise. If Dr. Morgan negligently performed the examination and, as a result, gave an inaccurate report of the patient's health which damaged Mr. Armstrong, the physician would be liable for the damage caused by his negligence.

A physician-patient relationship is not formed under circumstances in which the physician's sole role is an examiner for a third party. There is, however, a more fundamental rule under which a physician may incur an obligation to the person examined: a physician who performs a professional activity, even though gratuitously, may thereby become obligated to act carefully. Thus, some courts have held that a physician examining a person at the request of a third party may owe that person the duty of reasonable care even in the absence of a physician-patient relationship. Notwithstanding this, a physician acting as a "company doctor" need not necessarily disclose findings to the person examined. However, if the physician elects to discuss findings with the person referred for examination, the physician must not mislead the person about the actual condition.

Hoover v. Williamson.   Mr. Hoover had been exposed to silica dust during the years he worked at General Electric. Annual chest x-ray examinations of certain employees of General Electric Company were required by the company under the direction and supervision of Dr. Williamson, a physician who was paid for his services by the company. After such an examination clearly revealed to Dr. Williamson that Hoover had silicosis, Dr. Williamson advised Hoover that he had a "little infection on the lungs" and referred him to a consultant. Dr. Williamson subsequently concealed from Hoover the recommendation of the consultant that Hoover minimize exposure to silica dust. Instead, Dr. Williamson allowed him to return to a job with silica exposure. Five years later, when Hoover first learned of the seriousness of his condition, he sued, claiming that Dr. Williamson's breach of a professional duty to him caused him to sustain serious and permanent pulmonary disease.

The court pointed out that if Dr. Williamson had done no more than direct or supervise the x-ray examination of Hoover, his only duty would have been to General Electric. However, Dr. Williamson undertook to advise Hoover of his health; referred him to a consultant; and after his consultation, undertook to advise Hoover again. Contrary to his professional obligation, he affirmatively misrepresented the nature and seriousness of Hoover's condition and deliberately concealed from him the recommendations of the consultant. He was, therefore, negligent for not exercising due care in relating the information to Hoover, and thus was liable to him for damages.

A physician who is employed to examine a person solely for the purpose of obtaining medical evidence for use in a proceeding challenging the person's claim of injury, and who neither offers nor intends to benefit the person examined, is presumed to have no reason to believe that such a person will rely on his report. Thus, the physician is not liable to that person for a negligently prepared report which causes injury. Under these circumstances the physician's duty to meet the requisite standard of care in the preparation of the report runs to the employer requesting it.

Keene vs. Wiggens.   Mr. Keene sustained injuries compensable by his employer under Workers' Compensation. Two months after the injury he was rehospitalized and underwent a laminectomy. Following surgery he experienced chills, fever, nausea, and low back pain radiating to his right leg. The condition persisted and at the request of the Workers' Compensation carrier of his employer, various surgical consultants were called in to verify the need for additional surgery. Several months later he was rescheduled for surgery; however, on the advice of the consultant surgeons, this operation was cancelled. This action prompted Keene to call the carrier to complain that he needed further treatment or surgical repair to relieve the pain. The carrier then sent Keene to a consultant for examination. The consultant advised Keene that the studies were not satisfactory and that another evaluation was needed to determine whether Keene was in need of further treatment. Therefore, Keene was sent for examination to Dr. Wiggens. The carrier wrote to Dr. Wiggens and asked him to examine Keene, review the entire record, and give his opinion as to the extent of permanent disability and what it might be should Keene undergo surgery. Dr. Wiggens examined Keene, but did not treat or give him advice. Dr. Wiggens then reported to the carrier that Keene had arachnoiditis not amenable to surgery and recommended no further medical treatment or surgery. Keene received a copy of the report. Subsequently, when Keene was unable to work, he sued Dr. Wiggens claiming he relied on Dr. Wiggens' opinion to his detriment.

Dr. Wiggens contended that he conducted an examination of Keene solely for the purpose of rating the injury to settle the claim and not for care or treatment of the examinee. Thus, he argued that he had no physician-patient relationship with Keene and hence he owed him no duty of care in preparation of the report.

The court pointed out that an essential element of Keene's suit alleging medical malpractice on the part of Dr. Wiggens was the establishment of a duty owed to him by the physician. The determination of this duty is established by law, taking into account the fundamental principle that all persons are required to use ordinary care to prevent others being injured as a result of their conduct. A physician owes a duty of care to persons who are foreseeably endangered by his conduct with respect to material risks that make the physician's conduct unreasonably dangerous to a person who the law determines is entitled to protection. The court noted that any departure from this principle involves the balancing of a number of considerations, namely: the foreseeability of harm and the degree of certainty that the person will be injured; and the closeness of the connection between the physician's conduct and the injury suffered by the person. In addition to these factors in the balancing process, the court declared that consideration must be given to the extent to which the transaction between physician and a person was intended to affect the person's welfare.

When a physician-patient relationship exists (either expressed or implied), the patient has the right to expect the physician will care for and treat him with proper professional skills and will exercise reasonable and ordinary care and diligence. However, the nature and scope of the duty a physician owes to each person varies with the relationship he has to the person; the foreseeability of harm that may be expected to flow from his conduct; and the reliance which the person may reasonably be expected to place on the opinion he received from the physician.

In some states, a physician is liable for malpractice only where there is a relationship of physician-patient as a result of a contract (expressed or implied) that the physician will treat the patient with proper professional skill, and there is a breach of professional duty to the patient. No such duty may be established when the physician does not examine the person as a part of, or for the purpose of, medical treatment. Where no physician-patient relationship exists, the physician's only duty is to conduct the examination in a manner not to cause harm to the person being examined. Under those circumstances the physician acts as an agent of the person requesting the examination and, absent special circumstances, his duty to observe good standards of professional skill in reporting the results of the examination runs only to the person employing him. In some states, however, courts have not used status (the physician-patient relationship) alone as a means of determining liability in the evaluation of a patient.

In this case, the court concluded that it was not reasonably foreseeable that Dr. Wiggens' conduct would injure Keene. Dr. Wiggens was hired solely to conduct an examination for purposes of rating disability compensation benefits. Dr. Wiggens did not offer or provide medical treatment to Keene, and thus he could not reasonably expect the claimant to rely on his opinion. Such a report was initiated by, arranged for, and forwarded directly to Workers' Compensation carrier for the carrier's own best interest. Keene was seeking benefits from his employer's carrier and his dissatisfaction with the benefits being offered by the carrier suggested that he was pursuing a claim adverse to the interests of the employer.

Although the law expects the physician to be objective in these matters, the court pointed out that a claimant cannot assume the insurance company's physician will be as generous as his own physician when assessing the injury to be rated. If a matter of opinion is requested of the physician by the insurer, the claimant should not expect the most advantageous conclusions. That expectation would be altered, however, if the carrier's physician *treats* the claimant or otherwise seeks to provide a benefit. That situation was not involved in this case.

The court held that no physician-patient relationship (express or implied) existed which would give rise to a duty of care owed to the examinee in connection with the medical report. Keene went to Dr. Wiggens' office at the request of the carrier because he was required to submit to examination as a claimant. Dr. Wiggens did nothing more than examine Keene and make his report to the carrier as he was hired to do. The carrier requested this examination to verify the opinions of the other consulting physicians who had stated no operation or treatment was called for and to rate the disability. Dr. Wiggens' opinion was needed to properly rate the case for settlement of the claim; as such the opinion was solely for the carrier's benefit in the adversary Workers' Compensation proceedings. The examination was not part of Keene's care or treatment. Dr. Wiggens did not voluntarily offer Keene any advice and counsel or otherwise intend to benefit Keene personally. Had Dr. Wiggens volunteered care or treatment or otherwise intended to serve or benefit Keene in a direct manner, and if it was reasonable for Keene to rely on such benefit, a duty to Keene of due care would have been established. However, in this case, Dr. Wiggens owed Keene no duty of professional skill in connection with the report.

Section 2: The Physician's Responsibility to Nonpatients

Variations in the physician-patient relationship may develop when the interests of persons other than the patient are affected by encounters which occur in the context of the physician-patient relationship. These situations may include circumstances in which: medical care for a patient is arranged by a spouse or other family member; a physician has a duty to a nonpatient to warn of the patient's condition; a nonpatient is adversely affected by a physician's negligent treatment of the patient; or a physician's duty to the public overrides his responsibility to his patient.

Duty to Nonpatients Who Engage a Physician's Services

When a relative arranges with a physician to care for a person, a physician-patient relationship with the person is established by the relative's act. The usual situation is one in which a spouse calls a physician for suspected illness of the other spouse. Under such circumstances the physician must give primary consideration to the patient's interests even if those interests conflict with those of the spouse because the relationship is with, and the consequent duty of providing proper care is owed to, the patient and not to the spouse who engaged the physician's services.

As exemplified by the following case, when a physician relies on the spouse or relative in making a determination as to treatment of the patient, he should determine whether the spouse or relative's motive in arranging for care may be improper.

Maben v. Rankin.   At her husband's request, Dr. Rankin came to the patient's home in order to evaluate and treat her. The husband related that she was acting strangely and needed to be hospitalized. The patient appeared upset and refused hospitalization. Therefore, Dr. Rankin forcibly administered an injection to her. The next thing the patient remembered was finding herself in the hospital where she remained against her will for fifteen days. Despite her protest during this time, she received electroshock treatment. She subsequently sued Dr. Rankin for false imprisonment.

Expert testimony established that the patient had not been mentally ill, but instead was upset because of her husband's infidelity and other objectionable conduct. Dr. Rankin testified that his observation of her symptoms, together with information he received from her husband and other physicians who had previously examined her, indicated to him that she was mentally ill and needed hospital care and electroshock treatment. He indicated that it was his medical opinion that she was not competent to exercise the best judgment for her own welfare and was potentially dangerous to her husband and herself.

The court pointed out that a physician is usually not required to investigate whether the consenting spouse or relative has a malicious or ulterior motive in seeking to have a physician hospitalize a spouse or relative. Although good faith on the part of the requesting person is presumed, it may be overcome by a set of circumstances such as in this case. If circumstances alert a physician that the requesting relative is acting in bad faith, he must investigate the matter further before taking action which would deprive his patient of rights in an unauthorized manner. However, the court stated that proving that the physician was, or should have been, on notice that the relative may be acting in bad faith is the burden of the patient/plaintiff.

Although a physician's primary duty of care is to the patient, a physician may also be responsible to the spouse or other relative arranging for medical care of the patient. For example, where a nonpatient arranges with a physician for the care of a spouse or a relative, the physician has a duty to attend the patient as agreed.

Maltempo v. Cuthbert.   An incarcerated young man had a history of brittle "juvenile" diabetes mellitus requiring insulin therapy. Over the course of days, while he was in jail, he developed ketoacidosis and became sluggish and unresponsive. Family members visited him at the jail and became alarmed at his condition. His mother immediately called her family physician, but was referred to another physician who was taking "call" for him. She informed the covering physician that her son was a "diabetic in very bad shape" and that the jail personnel did not believe that he was sick. The physician assured the mother that he would look into the matter and call her if there were any problems. He then called the jail. Upon being told that the young man was being treated by the jail physician, he did nothing further. He neither went to the jail nor called the jail physician nor contacted the mother.

The next morning, while being transported from the county jail to the state prison where he was to serve a sentence, the young man aspirated his vomitus and died. His mother brought a multiple-party suit. Her claim against the sheriff and the jail doctor was settled. She also sued the covering physician for failure to care for her son. The physician contended that the young man was already attended by the jail physician and it would have been a breach of ethics for him to interfere with that care.

The court pointed out that the physician had entered into a professional relationship on behalf of the mother; therefore, the mother had a right to rely on his assurances. His agreement to act allowed the mother to believe that her son was being cared for and effectively prevented her from seeking other medical care.

A variation of a physician's responsibility to nonpatients in the spousal arrangement of care area is shown in the following case in which a spouse did not arrange for the care of her ex-husband; but the arrangement she made for the welfare of her child resulted in the diagnosis of her husband's behavior, which harmed him; yet the physician may owe no duty of due care to the husband because a physician-patient relationship had not been formed with the husband.

Chatman v. Millis.   The mother of a two-year-old child was divorced from the father of the child. Her ex-husband had visitation privileges with the couple's son. Partly because of actions of the child, she became concerned that her ex-husband had subjected the child to homosexual conduct. In the matter of terminating the father's visiting privileges, she sought the aid of her family physician to determine whether the child had been molested by his father and, if so, the implications on her son's psychosexual development. After talking with the mother and the child, her physician wrote the mother's attorney a letter in which he detailed a comment made by the child and concluded his letter by stating:

> while it will be the court's decision and not mine, I feel that it would not be a good idea to allow the child to continue to visit his father at all. If it is necessary that visitation rights be continued, I would strongly urge that the presence of a third person, preferably a relative, be in their presence at all times. As I mentioned in our prior telephone conversation, I would be willing to testify in court about my interview or the statements made in the letter above.

When the father discovered the letter, he instituted suit alleging malpractice against the physician.

The court held that to permit the father to bring a malpractice action against the mother's physician, there would have to be a physician-patient relationship or some similar relationship between the father and the physician. It concluded that no relationship existed in this case because the physician did not even know nor had he ever examined the father. Moreover, the diagnosis reached was not for the benefit of the father; therefore, even if the physician's finding was negligently made, the father did not rely upon this diagnosis to his detriment. The father was not damaged by the allegedly negligent diagnosis, but by the alleged defamation. The court pointed out that physicians, like all persons, owe a duty to refrain from defaming others. However, that duty does not result from, nor is it derived from the physician-patient relationship.

Duty to Avoid Injury to Nonpatients

Another variation derived from the physician-patient relationship is the physician's duty to avoid injury to nonpatients who may be foreseeably harmed by the conduct of his patient. The following cases illustrate the scope of this duty.

A physician is obligated to provide pertinent and accurate information as to the nature of the patient's disease where such knowledge is necessary for the safety of others. Thus, a physician may be obligated to advise a patient (with, for example, cerebral arteriosclerosis, diabetes mellitus, or a seizure disorder) of aspects of the illness that the physician professionally should realize would endanger a third party.

Lemmon v. Freese.   Mr. Lemmon had consulted Dr. Dieckmann to diagnose the cause and treat a convulsive disorder. Dr. Dieckmann was unable to determine the etiology of the seizure disorder. When Lemmon asked about driving, Dr. Dieckmann told him that he could drive an automobile. He did not forewarn Lemmon of the dangers involved in driving an automobile. Approximately three months later, Lemmon had a seizure which rendered him unconscious while operating his automobile. As a result, he struck and injured a pedestrian who then sued Dr. Dieckmann charging that the physician negligently had advised Lemmon that he could drive an automobile. Dr. Dieckmann contended that he owed a legal duty to his patient Lemmon only, and not to any third party.

The court pointed out that a physician who negligently gives information to a patient is subject to liability if action taken by the patient in reasonable reliance upon such information results in harm to persons which the physician should expect to be put in peril by his negligent action. The court noted that Dr. Dieckmann should have anticipated that members of the public would be put into jeopardy if Lemmon had a recurrence of his seizure while operating an automobile.

In addition to a physician's duty to warn the patient of hazards inherent in the patient's condition or treatment, a physician, by virtue of his relationship with the patient, may have a derivative duty to warn a reasonably identifiable third party who may be harmed foreseeably by the patient's action.

Tarasoff v. Regents of University of California. While receiving outpatient psychotherapy at a college health service, a college student disclosed to his psychotherapist that he wanted to kill his girl friend who lived nearby with her parents, but who was at that time away on a summer trip. The therapist with the concurrence of two psychiatrists, reported the matter to the campus police and then sent them a letter requesting detention of the student and his commitment for observation to a mental hospital. The campus police picked up the student for questioning. Satisfied that he was rational, they released him on his promise to stay away from his girl friend. When the police reported their action to the chief psychiatrist, he asked for the return of the psychologist's letter to the police, and directed that all copies of the letter be destroyed. The student did not return for psychotherapy. Subsequently, the student persuaded his girl friend's brother to share an apartment with him which was located near his girl friend's residence. Two months later, shortly after his girl friend returned from her trip, the student went to her home and killed her.

The victim's parents brought suit against the psychiatrists for negligence in failing to warn their daughter or them of the impending danger. The parents contended that since the physicians knew the patient was at large and dangerous, their failure to warn his intended victim or others likely to apprise her of the danger constituted a breach of the physician's duty to exercise reasonable care to protect the victim. The physicians contended they owed no duty to the victim or her parents.

The court pointed out that a legal duty is only an expression of the "sum total of those considerations of policy which lead the law to say that the particular person is entitled to protection." Thus, a physician may owe a duty of care to persons who are foreseeably endangered by a physician's unreasonably dangerous conduct. In order to avoid foreseeable harm to a third party, a physician may be required to control the behavior of his patient or to warn another of such conduct. This affirmative duty for the benefit of third persons may arise because of a physician's special relationship to his dangerous patient. The physician-patient relationship alone may be sufficient to support a physician's duty to exercise reasonable care to protect others against dangers emanating from his patient's illness. By entering into a physician-patient relationship, a physician becomes sufficiently involved in the management of his patient to assume some responsibility for the safety not only of the patient himself, but also of a third person whom the physician knows to be threatened by the patient. The court pointed out that physicians cannot escape liability for negligence merely because a victim was not their patient. When a physician determines, or should determine, that his patient presents a serious danger to another, he incurs an obligation to use reasonable care to protect the intended victim against such danger. The discharge of this duty may require that he take reasonable and necessary steps, depending on the nature of the case, to warn the intended victim or others likely to apprise the victim of the danger. In this case, the court concluded that the victim's interests were entitled to legal protection. Therefore, the physicians, once having decided that their patient presented a danger to his eventual victim, were negligent in failing to warn her or her parents.

A physician may have a duty to take whatever steps are reasonably necessary to protect an intended victim of his patient when he determines, or should determine, in accordance with the standards of his profession, that his patient presents a probable danger to that identified person. The relationship giving rise to that duty may be found in the broadly based obligation a physician may have to protect the welfare of the community.

McIntosh v. Milano. Dr. Milano first began treatment of his adolescent male patient, then age 1 5, after the latter's school psychologist had given the patient's parents Dr. Milano's name because of the patient's involvement with drugs. Dr. Milano treated him on a weekly basis for what was initially diagnosed as an "Adjustment Reaction of Adolescence." During the course of therapy over a two-year period, the patient related many fantasies involving fear of other people, and the use of a knife to threaten people who might intimidate or frighten him. The patient also related experiences and emotional involvement with Kimberly, a girl who was five years older than he was and who lived with her parents next door to the patient. Dr. Milano initially considered all these revelations as fantasies, but he came to accept that some of the experiences were true. The patient "didn't spend a lot of time describing in detail what he and Kimberly did," but Dr. Milano felt that fit the patient's character in that "he thought that nobody would believe him." When the patient repeatedly expressed anxiety to Dr. Milano over his relationship with Kimberly, Dr. Milano advised him to break off the relationship because of his possessive feelings toward Kimberly, and because he was "overwhelmed" by the relationship. He talked to the patient's parents about the relationship between their son and Kimberly, but never attempted to contact Kimberly or her parents. The patient had confided in Dr. Milano that he had fired a BB gun at Kimberly's or her boyfriend's car when he was upset because she was going on a date with her boyfriend. The patient also told Dr. Milano that he carried a knife to show to people to scare them away if he felt threatened. He brought the knife to a therapy session to show Dr. Milano.

Although Dr. Milano denied that the patient ever said that he intended to kill Kimberly or inflict bodily harm, the patient had indicated that he wished Kimberly would "suffer" as he did; had expressed a jealous and possessive attitude toward her; was jealous and hateful toward her boyfriends; had difficulty convincing himself that fights or things were really over or finished; and was very angry that he had not been able to obtain Kimberly's phone number when she moved from the family home.

During a therapy session when Dr. Milano briefly left the room, the patient stole a prescription form from the physician's desk. Later that day he attempted to obtain 30 Seconal tablets from a pharmacist with the stolen prescription form. The pharmacist became suspicious and called Dr. Milano, who instructed him to retain the unauthorized prescription form, not to fill it, and to send the patient home. The patient left the pharmacy upset. Dr. Milano tried to reach the patient at home. Later that afternoon the patient took a pistol that he had kept hidden at his home, and knowing Kimberly was expected to visit her parents, got her to go with him, wittingly or unwittingly, to a local park area where he fatally shot her. The patient was tried for homicide.

At the criminal trial Dr. Milano indicated that when he felt that a patient was endangering himself or someone else, he would "look into it and contact his patient's parents, school, or people like that." He stated also that the patient's powerful reactions of anger and jealousy, ambivalent feelings of affection, and desires for retaliation emerged, accentuating prior conflicts, and centered primarily on fantasies of revenge for Kimberly's dating and sexual experiences with other men. Although the patient was able to share some of his feelings with his parents and received their support, he did not develop a flourishing social life independent of Kimberly.

After the completion of the criminal trial, Kimberly's parents instituted a wrongful death action, based in large part on the trial testimony of Dr. Milano and a report of a psychiatrist retained as an expert witness that expressed the opinion that Dr. Milano had a duty to warn Kimberly, her parents, or appropriate authorities that the patient posed a physical threat or danger to her. The parents asserted that Dr. Milano breached that duty.

Dr. Milano contended that a physician did not owe a legal duty to potential victims, and that such a theory should not be applied because it would impose an unworkable duty on physicians to warn another of a patient's dangerousness when that condition cannot be predicted with sufficient reliability; would deter therapists from treating potentially violent patients in light of possible malpractice claims by third persons; and would result in increased commitments of patients to mental or penal institutions.

There was expert medical testimony that Dr. Milano had deviated from accepted medical practice by failing to warn or protect Kimberly, the object of the patient's dangerous aggression. The expert opined that in this case dangerousness of the patient was not a prediction, but a known fact. This conclusion was based on the findings that the patient had exhibited evidence of his dangerousness by firing a weapon at Kimberly's car; exhibiting a knife to Dr. Milano; forging a prescription; verbalizing threats toward Kimberly and her boyfriends; and fantasizing violent retribution.

The court pointed out that whether a duty exists for a physician to warn against an injurious event by a patient to a third party depends on questions of fairness, involving a weighing of the relationship of the parties, the nature of the risk involved, and the public interest in imposing the duty under the circumstances. A physician may have a duty to control the conduct of a patient to prevent the patient from harming a third person if a special relationship exists giving the third person a right to protection. Absent a special relationship, a physician's recognition that action on his part is necessary for another person's aid or protection does not impose a duty to take such action.

The court pointed out that the concept of such a legal duty for the medical profession is not new. Disclosure is required in numerous situations. A physician-patient relationship places a duty to warn others against possible exposure, for example, to contagious or infectious diseases, and state statutes require physicians to report such patient conditions as gunshot wounds and epilepsy to the authorities. In the state where this case was tried, there was a statute providing that any person who has knowledge of actual commission of certain crimes, such as threatening to take the life of another person, but who fails to report or disclose the fact, is himself guilty of a crime. The statute made no exception for a physician. The Principles of Medical Ethics recognize that confidentiality gives way where "it becomes necessary in order to protect the welfare of the individual or of the community."

The court acknowledged that an accurate prediction of dangerousness cannot be made in all cases, nevertheless it concluded that rendering an opinion and a prognosis should be based on the history of the patient and the course of treatment. Where reasonable men might differ in their opinion, a physician is only held to the standard for a physician in the particular field and community. The court suggested that to an admittedly uncertain, but nevertheless sufficient extent, "dangerousness" is identifiable, and although not a "disease," as that term is commonly used, may affect third persons in much the same sense as a communicable disease. The court decided that Dr. Milano knew or should have known that the patient's desires for retaliation presented a clear danger or threat to Kimberly. The court concluded that the obligation imposed on Dr. Milano was similar to that already borne by the medical profession, and that he recognized such a duty when he stated that if he felt a patient was endangering himself or others, he would "look into" the matter or contact appropriate persons.

Where a victim was not known or identifiable, but rather a member of a large amorphous public group of potential targets, no affirmative duty exists to warn a segment of the population inclusive of the victim.

Thompson v. County of Almeda. A juvenile offender had been institutionalized under court order. During the offender's incarceration, the county officials became aware of his latent, dangerous, and violent propensities regarding young children. Thus violent, sexual assaults upon young children were a likely result of releasing him into the community. The county also knew that the offender had indicated that he would, if released, take the life of a young child residing in the neighborhood. However, he gave no indication which young child he intended as his victim. In spite of this knowledge, the county released the offender on temporary leave into his mother's custody at her home, and did not advise or warn the mother, the police, or the parents of young children living within the immediate vicinity of the offender's house of the known facts. Within twenty-four hours of his release, the offender murdered in the garage of the home of the offender's mother a five-year-old boy who lived with his parents a few houses from the residence of the offender's mother. As a result, the parents of the murdered child sued the county, contending that it negligently failed to warn neighbors of the juvenile offender's dangerous propensities and of his release to the custody of his mother.

The court declared that a therapist is obligated to determine whether his patient poses a serious threat of violence, in order to protect the foreseeable victim of that danger. Generally, a physician owes a duty to control the dangerous conduct of his patients where there is a known and specifically foreseeable and identifiable victim of the patient's threats. Under such circumstances, liability may be imposed on a physician for failing to take reasonable steps to protect the victim. The warnings required were directed at making those individuals aware of the danger to which they were uniquely exposed. Although, as a precondition to liability, the intended victim need not be specifically named, he must be readily identifiable.

The court pointed out that in cases that impose a duty upon those who create a foreseeable peril (not readily discoverable by endangered persons) to warn the endangered of such potential peril, involved situations where the conduct of a person having responsibility for another placed the specific victim in a position of clearly foreseeable danger. A potentially dangerous offender incarcerated in the custody of county officials, who has made a *generalized* threat to a segment of the population, does not create an affirmative duty by the county to warn someone of the latent, dangerous qualities arising from the offender's release.

As the preceding cases illustrate, an attending physician may be liable to nonpatients who are foreseeably injured by the conduct or condition of the patient, if the physician has negligently failed to take precautionary action to lessen a patient's danger to third parties, or to warn certain endangered third parties about the potential peril of his patient's condition that poses a reasonably foreseeable threat to them. However, if the threat does not *emanate* from his patient's conduct, the physician is not required to warn third parties, even though his negligence in treating his patient may have effectively precluded a warning to a third party to take action to avoid a foreseeable injury.

Soto v. Frankford Hospital. On November 3, Mrs. Soto became unconscious as a result of inhaling carbon monoxide from a defective gas heater in her home. She was hospitalized in the intensive care unit, with an incorrect admission diagnosis of drug overdose, and treated with supportive measures. She signed herself out prior to being discharged. On November 30, her husband became unconscious and died as a result of carbon monoxide intoxication from the defective heater.

Mrs. Soto sued her attending physician for the wrongful death of her husband, contending that his negligent diagnosis of her condition caused him to fail to warn her and her husband of the ongoing hazard of the defective heater. In support of her case, she cited legal decisions holding that a physician may be liable to nonpatients who are foreseeably injured by his patient. These cases involved circumstances in which an attending physician has negligently diagnosed an infectious disease or seizure disorder; or has failed to warn the patient of a drug side-effect; or has failed to warn a person of the threats made against him by a patient during psychotherapy. The court noted, however, that in the situations cited by Mrs. Soto, the *patient's*, not the physician's, conduct directly caused the injury to the third party. The court pointed out that even if the attending physician had been negligent in misdiagnosing Mrs. Soto's condition on November 3, the injury to her husband was "one step removed" from those situations and cases in which the *patient's* conduct injures a third party. Under such circumstances, the attending physician is not under a duty to control the conduct of his patient. This court declared that where the threat or hazard does not emanate from some conduct by the patient, but instead from a defective object, the attending physician who treated the patient owed no duty to a third party such as her husband.*

Renslow v. Mennonite Hospital. When his patient was thirteen years of age, a physician negligently transfused her with incompatible Rh-positive blood which sensitized her Rh-negative blood. Although the physician discovered he had administered the incompatible blood and was aware of its deleterious effects, he did not disclose his error or notify the patient or her family. The patient first discovered her condition many years later after a routine blood screening was performed in the course of prenatal care. As a result of the negligent transfusion, her child was born with erythroblastosis foetalis. The child sued her mother's physician who had been responsible for the negligent transfusion.

The court pointed out that it was reasonably foreseeable at the time of the negligent transfusion that the teenage patient later would bear a child that would be injured as the result of the improper blood transfusion. Thus, the physician could be charged with the knowledge of what this future child would encounter as a result of the physician's negligent transfusion of her mother. Although the negligent force which had its impact upon the infant in its prenatal state was set in motion prior to the child's conception, the court found no reason to deny a legal cause of action to a person simply because she had not yet been conceived at the time of the wrongful conduct.

The performance of a test on a person ordered by a physician, does not necessarily establish attendant duties to the person. If the purpose of the test is for the benefit of the public, rather than the treatment of the person, a traditional physician-patient relationship with its attendant responsibilities is usually not formed.

Collins v. Howard. A man was involved in an auto accident. The police took him to a hospital where the "on-call" physician ordered a blood sample which was taken by one of the nurses on duty. The blood was sent to the laboratory and analyzed for alcohol content. Although the man did not give the hospital authority to disclose to anyone the results of the analysis, the hospital disclosed the report of the blood alcohol to his employer, thereby causing the man's dismissal from his job. The man sued the hospital, contending that his confidential relationship with the hospital was breached.

The court pointed out that the state did not recognize a confidential relationship between physician and patient or hospital and patient. None ex-

---

* The court did not discuss whether it would have reached a different conclusion had the physician correctly diagnosed Mrs. Soto's condition as carbon monoxide poisoning and still failed to warn her husband.

isted at common law and no state statute had been enacted establishing the relationship. Thus the court concluded that none existed that would automatically preclude the disclosure of results of a blood alcohol determination.

The court further stated that even if the state recognized the existence of a confidential relationship, such a doctrine could not be invoked in this case because no treatment of the man was given or contemplated in taking a sample for blood alcohol determination. The purpose of obtaining a blood specimen for alcohol concentration determination was the state's public policy that persons who operate vehicles on the highways must be amenable to reasonable examinations and tests to determine sobriety, in order to decrease the incidence of traffic fatalities. The court therefore concluded that if taking blood samples for alcohol content will act to protect the public, then there may be a limited intrusion of an individual's rights and privileges.

SECTION 3: OUTRAGEOUS CONDUCT OF THE PHYSICIAN

A physician is also obligated to prevent reasonably foreseeable emotional injury to patients and others that is likely to directly result from the physician's outrageous conduct. This obligation may require a physician to take into consideration during the treatment process the emotional state of the patient and others. The deliberate inflicting of mental suffering on patients or on a closely related third party may be determined to be outrageous conduct in these cases: if the physician's conduct was intentional or reckless and so socially intolerable that it offended generally accepted standards of decency; or if the physician knew, or should have known, severe emotional distress would likely result. In these situations, a physician may be found liable for the "outrageous conduct" itself, or such conduct may establish legal causes of action for assault, false imprisonment, or fraud, each of which is illustrated in the following cases.

Outrageous Conduct Toward Patients

Inderbitzen v. Lane Hospital. The patient was in labor and hospitalized for the purpose of receiving medical attention necessary in the delivery of her child. When a medical student attempted to examine her to determine the stage of labor, she demanded a physician. The young man left the room and returned with a staff physician who subjected the patient to a rectal and vaginal examination. A similar examination was then performed by the student. She was then taken to the delivery room where several other medical students performed vaginal and rectal examinations. As these students rolled her over and "poked and prodded about her body," she screamed and protested repeatedly at this treatment. Whenever she protested, the students laughed and told her to be quiet. The patient sued the hospital claiming that she suffered mental anguish as a result of the physician's and students' conduct.

The court stated that decent and respectful treatment is implied in the physician-patient contract for treatment because a patient necessarily is required to expose his or her self in connection with the provision of medical services. Therefore, the court held that the levity and rudeness displayed by the young physicians constituted an assault which violated the physician-patient agreement. Thus the patient's distress of mind, evidenced by her repeated screaming and protesting, was compensable.

Improper and unacceptable conduct on the part of an attending physician within the context of the physician-patient relationship may also occur as a result of unlawful restraint of liberty or freedom of motion. If such restriction is imposed against a patient's will it may constitute false imprisonment. Although actual forceful restraint is unnecessary, the patient must experience a threat and reasonable apprehension of force. Such apprehension may result from a physician's words or acts.

Marcus v. Liebman.   A woman was having difficulty sleeping and had become "completely overwrought." On the recommendation of her clinical psychologist, Dr. Bass, she agreed to enter a hospital for several days of rest. Therefore she submitted herself for voluntary admission at a general hospital. She was placed on the psychiatric ward and introduced to the psychiatrist, Dr. Liebman. During her first session with Dr. Liebman she threw things at him because she did not want him as her physician. She was then placed in restraints after which she began screaming and singing in order to annoy people. After that, a drug was administered to calm her down, and she was removed from restraints. On her fourth hospital day, she informed Dr. Liebman that she wanted to sign a release paper which made her release mandatory within five days of signing the form. Dr. Liebman gave her the form and she signed it. Several days later, Dr. Liebman told her to rescind her request for release. He instructed her to sign the rescission form or she would be committed to the state hospital. Although she told Dr. Liebman that she wanted to be released and that he had no right to force her to sign the rescission form, she was frightened and believed that Dr. Liebman actually could have her sent to the state hospital, so she signed the paper. While a patient, she took trips outside the hospital to see movies and to bowl. When she was released from the hospital several weeks later, she sued Dr. Liebman for unlawfully restraining her freedom against her will.

Dr. Liebman admitted that he had told the patient that if she persisted in her request to leave, a court order could be sought to keep her in the hospital, but he denied telling her that he would seek such an order. Dr. Bass, the patient's clinical psychologist, testified that when he visited the patient during her hospitalization she told him she wanted to be released from the hospital and from Dr. Liebman's care.

The patient admitted that she knew she could be released from the hospital within five days, but she believed Dr. Liebman could have her committed to the state hospital if she did not sign the paper rescinding her request to leave. The court pointed out that the patient's apprehension of coercion was reasonable, considering her mental condition and her incarceration in a hospital. The court declared that the fact that the patient received telephone calls, had visitors, and even made trips outside the hospital during her weeks of hospitalization may be relevant to a determination of whether the patient's apprehension was reasonable, but was not determinative of the issue. Dr. Liebman argued that the threat which gave rise to the alleged false imprisonment was of a future action, and therefore the patient's apprehension was unreasonable. However, the court concluded that the threat to have a patient committed was a present threat because Dr. Liebman could have initiated commitment procedures immediately. The fact that these procedures could not have been concluded immediately did not change the threat to one in the future. At the time the alleged threat was made the patient was already confined. It was reasonable for her to believe that before her release, commitment procedures could have been concluded. Thus the present threat was sufficient to establish a legal cause of action for false imprisonment.

As the following case illustrates, a physician's conduct may be considered outrageous when the physician intentionally and recklessly inflicts mental distress upon a person whom the physician should know would be especially vulnerable to such professional misconduct.

Chuy v. Philadelphia Eagles Football Club.   Don Chuy, a member of the Philadelphia Eagles, sustained a severe shoulder injury in a professional football game. Several weeks later it was discovered that his condition was complicated by an acute pulmonary embolism. After hospitalization and treatment the embolus was dissolved.

After Chuy had recovered from the acute phase of his injury and had been examined by Eagles' physicians to determine his ability to play again, there was some question in the minds of the Eagles' medical consultant whether Chuy might have stress polycythemia, a condition sometimes observed in active, anxiety prone individuals. His medical condition was a matter of interest to Philadelphia sports writers because he had been the subject of a prominent trade the previous year under the terms of which he had been brought to the Eagles and an All-Pro lineman had been sent to the Los Angeles Rams. Accordingly, a Philadelphia sports writer interviewed the Eagles' team physician on the matter. This resulted in a nationwide newspaper account reporting that the team physician had stated that Chuy was suffering from polycythemia vera, a serious blood disorder, which would prevent him from playing professional football again. The team physician knew the nature of the disease, and had not inadvertently confused the benign with the serious condition. He also knew that Chuy did not have polycythemia vera. Chuy read the article while he was at home in California and became panic stricken. He consulted his personal physician who explained the serious nature of polycythemia vera. Although he counseled Chuy that in his opinion he was not suffering from the disease, his physician suggested tests to rule it out conclusively. Chuy was inconsolable because he anticipated death. As a result, he experienced prolonged extreme emotional anguish.

Chuy subsequently sued on the theory that a physician whose extreme and outrageous conduct intentionally or recklessly causes severe emotional distress to another is subject to liability for such emotional distress. He argued that the team physician knew that Chuy did not have polycythemia vera; nonetheless he told the press that Chuy had the disease and that he must, therefore, leave professional football. Chuy contended that the team physician publicized that Chuy was suffering from a disease unrelated to football because that might enhance the Eagles' leverage in dealing with Chuy's contract claim.

The court pointed out that Chuy's distress was reasonable and justified under the circumstances, and resulted from the physician's knowledge of the athlete's special susceptibility to such distress. The court held that there was sufficient evidence to infer that the team physician intentionally or recklessly inflicted upon Chuy mental distress. It concluded that such conduct was outrageous and the harm caused was compensable.

Outrageous Conduct Toward Nonpatients

The preceding cases have involved the physician's outrageous conduct toward patients. The manner in which a physician attends a patient may also establish legal liability to certain nonpatients who observe the outrageous conduct. Under special circumstances, the law may provide compensation for the mental anguish of close relatives of a patient which is intentionally or recklessly caused by a physician's intolerable behavior. For example, as the next case illustrates, a physician who accepts a patient, especially in an emergency situation, has an obligation to respect an accompanying relative's peace of mind, at least to the extent of making a good faith attempt to render adequate treatment to the imperiled patient.

Rockhill v. Pollard.   A mother and her baby daughter were injured in a wintertime automobile accident. A passing motorist stopped at the scene, took them to a nearby town and made arrangements for them to be seen at a physician's office at 9:00 P.M. The physician met the mother and child at his office and was overtly hostile and discourteous to the mother, especially when she asked him several times to examine the infant who appeared lifeless. Finally, the physician took the baby into the examining room, listened to her heart and lungs with his stethoscope. The child vomited as she was being dressed. Despite this, and without further examination, the physician told the mother that there was nothing wrong with the child. He then told her that he could not permit her and the baby to wait in his office until her husband could pick them up. Although the temperature was below freezing and the baby's clothing and blanket were wet with vomitus, the physician told them to wait outside by a streetlight until someone came to pick them up. When the father arrived he took them to the emergency room in a nearby town. The baby was hospitalized and operated on for a depressed skull fracture. The mother sued the physician because of his outrageous conduct toward her, which she claimed caused her extreme suffering.

The court stated that ordinarily, without showing that the mother suffered physical harm as a result of the physician's conduct, no legal damages for emotional harm could be awarded to her. However, the court pointed out that, when a physician's extreme and outrageous conduct is directed at a member of the patient's immediate family who is present at the time, and causes severe emotional distress, a physician may be subject to liability to that third person if the physician's conduct is outrageous in the extreme. In this case the court held that the physician's utter rudeness was evidence of his intention to cause the mother severe emotional distress. The court pointed out that the statement that there was "nothing wrong with the child" represented more than a mistaken diagnosis. It concluded that the physician refused to give or suggest any treatment even though he must have known that there was a strong possibility that the infant had been injured seriously. This was conduct outrageous in the extreme.

The court cautioned that liability for emotional harm to someone who was not a patient nor the subject of a physician's act is imposed only where the physician's conduct has been so outrageous in character and so extreme in degree as to be regarded as intolerable in a civilized society. Patients and their relatives necessarily are expected to be hardened to a certain degree of rough language, unkindness, and lack of consideration on the part of an attending physician.

The precise boundaries of a physician's conduct beyond which such conduct would be considered "outrageous," are unclear. Although liability for outrageous conduct does not extend to mere insults, indignities, or annoyances; as the following cases illustrate, the fact that the physician knows that close relatives are peculiarly susceptible to emotional distress may be an influential factor in determining the scope of outrageous conduct.

Johnson v. Women's Hospital.   Mrs. Johnson delivered a premature infant that expired shortly after birth. Her attending physician told a hospital nurse to advise Mrs. Johnson that the hospital could handle the disposal of the body or arrange for burial. The nurse did not relate this information, but simply told Mrs. Johnson that the hospital would "probably take care of everything." The hospital retained the infant's body in its Pathology department.

While at her physician's office for her six-week postpartum check-up, Mrs. Johnson was given her medical chart by the nurse for delivery to her physician. She noted a report in the chart from the hospital pathologist which stated that the body could not be disposed of as a surgical specimen. When she confronted her physician about these circumstances, he instructed one of his nurses to accompany Mrs. Johnson to the hospital in order to look into the matter. When Mrs. Johnson inquired as to the manner of disposition of her infant, a clerical employee in the Pathology department presented Mrs. Johnson with her infant's shrivelled body in a large glass jar filled with formaldehyde. Shocked by this event, Mrs. Johnson sued the hospital, as the employer of the clerk.

The court held that the hospital's conduct was "outrageous." It went beyond the bounds of decency in that it recklessly disregarded the sensitivities of Mrs. Johnson, even though it should have known that such conduct would cause severe emotional distress.

Conduct which is so grossly and wantonly negligent as to constitute intentional infliction of suffering on certain nonpatients may be considered to be legally outrageous.

Muniz v. United Hospital Medical Center-Presbyterian Hospital.   A woman gave birth prematurely to a baby at the hospital. The baby manifested symptoms of respiratory distress and was immediately transferred to a medical center where the necessary neonatal facilities for intensive treatment of the baby were available. The mother remained at the hospital where she delivered the baby. The next day the mother telephoned the medical center and was advised that the infant was in good condition. On the same day, however, when the baby's father visited the medical center to check on the baby's condition, he was not permitted to see the baby. The evening of the following day the mother received a telephone call in her hospital room from an employee of the medical center where her baby had been taken, stating that the baby was dead. The mother became hysterical and required extended hospitalization. Over the next two weeks, the parents made repeated personal inquiries of the medical center to establish the veracity of the telephone report, but were not given specific information that would establish this fact, leaving them uncertain whether the baby was dead. On telephone inquiries by the mother, the different people she spoke to told her that they did not know whether the baby was alive or dead or why its body had not been made available to the parents. Finally, three weeks after the baby's death, a medical center employee told the mother that he had ascertained the baby was dead, but was not able to locate the baby's body. The next day this employee advised the mother that the baby's body had been located "upstairs" and asked her to come in and claim it.

The parents sued the medical center claiming that it negligently failed to advise the parents of the baby's death as expeditiously and humanely as possible. Instead it delivered a callous, offhand announcement of the baby's death by an unidentified telephoner to a hospitalized mother.

The court concluded that the hospital's conduct violated all bounds of humanity and was a gross deviation from all accepted behavior in connection with such medical incident. The court pointed out that the hospital was negligent because it failed to invoke any humane follow-up procedure by personal or even written contact with the parents to advise them as to the factual background leading to the baby's death, or to formally notify them of the child's death. In addition, the court faulted the hospital's "callous failure to maintain a system of identifying and locating corpses of patients who expire while hospitalized." It described such conduct as wantonly negligent and outrageous. Consequently, it held the hospital liable for the emotional and mental distress which it inflicted upon the baby's parents.

DeCicco v. Trinidad Area Health Ass'n.   A woman suddenly became comatose at home. Her husband called the family physician who came to her house, examined her, and diagnosed a cerebrovascular disorder. The physician called the local community hospital for an ambulance to take her to a medical center in another city that had facilities to treat her condition. Even though the husband also made an independent request of the hospital, the administrator would not grant the use of the ambulance unless the patient's attending physician, who had resigned from the hospital staff, consented to having the patient brought to the hospital first to be examined by staff physicians to determine if further transportation was necessary. The attending physician then requested an ambulance from a town twenty miles away. The patient died an hour after arriving at the medical center. The husband brought a suit against the hospital administrator, seeking punitive damages on the theory that his conduct was outrageous.

The court pointed out that the recovery for outrageous conduct is permitted where the recitation of the facts to an average member of the community would arouse his resentment against the actor and lead him to exclaim, "outrageous!" The court concluded that this test was met when the hospital administrator refused ambulance service to a critically ill patient on grounds irrelevant to her need for, or the availability of, the service.

Ferrell v. Chesapeake & Ohio Railway Emp. Hosp. Ass'n.   While eating dinner, a man swallowed a chicken bone. His wife took him to a hospital where a thoracic surgeon examined his larynx and esophagus with a laryngoscope but was unable to locate a foreign body. The surgeon could get only a brief glimpse of the throat because the patient was uncooperative. The surgeon attempted to obtain a barium swallow study, but the patient would not swallow enough liquid to enable the surgeon to perform an adequate examination. The patient was irrational, and at times seemed to be hallucinating. Not considering the ailment to be an emergency, the surgeon instructed the patient's wife to bring her husband back in the morning at which time he hoped he could get a satisfactory barium swallow. The wife took her husband home, but then took him to a different hospital where the physician who examined him was unable to establish the presence of a chicken bone in his throat. Because he was of the opinion that there was no immediate danger, he instructed the wife to bring her husband back to the hospital at 9:00 A.M. the next morning.

The next morning the patient did not return to the hospital as requested, but instead his wife took him to see her family physician who made arrangements to have the man examined by a thoracic surgeon who attempted but was unable to accomplish bronchoscopy because the patient would not cooperate. Thus the patient was hospitalized. The admission work-up indicated that the patient was suffering from delirium tremens. Consultation with an otolaryngologist was obtained. A soft tissue x-ray disclosed a foreign object in his throat. The otolaryngologist administered Probanthine to reduce muscle spasm in the throat, and Sparine was administered to ease the patient's restlessness and confusion, but the patient became more confused and unmanageable and had to be restrained. The otolaryngologist did not recommend surgery to remove the chicken bone because he did not regard the chicken bone as a danger to the patient's life at that time and because of the patient's unstable physical and mental condition. Instead, he called in an internist to investigate the possibility of delirium tremens. When the internist consulted with the patient's wife, she insisted that the diagnosis of delirium tremens was incorrect. The follow-up soft tissue x-ray of the neck taken one week after admission did not disclose a foreign body. Therefore, the attending physician told the wife that the bone apparently had passed. Shortly thereafter, the patient died and a small chicken bone in his throat was noted at autopsy. The causes of death were bilateral bronchopneumonia and cerebral edema. It was later established that the patient had a history of schizophrenia and excessive alcohol use.

The wife sued all the involved physicians charging that their careless refusal to remove the chicken bone from her husband's throat was improper, and had subjected her to the mental anguish of witnessing the agonizing demise of her husband for lack of proper medical treatment and attention.

The court pointed out that there has been a trend in the law to allow for emotional distress which results from a physician's outrageous conduct which is especially calculated to cause, and does cause, mental distress of a serious nature. If a physician's conduct creates the probability that mental disturbance would follow to his patient, or a close relative, and the physician proceeds in deliberate disregard of this consequence, he may be liable for such distress. In addition, a physician may be liable if his vindictive conduct toward a patient causes emotional distress to a person close to a patient when the emotional distress is a foreseeable result of such conduct. Moreover, if a close relationship exists between the person suffering the emotional distress and the patient against whom the conduct is directed, harm to the former is likely to be forseeable.

After a review of all the clinical facts and interactions, the court concluded that it was unable to find any acts on the part of the physicians involved in this case that constituted willful, wanton, or vindictive conduct.

A physician may be liable for abusive comments about another person, made in the course of his medical practice, if the comments are false and uttered in an intentionally malicious manner designed to cause the person loss of esteem or employment.

Barry v. Baugh. A registered nurse went to the office of Dr. Baugh, her husband's physician, to have her husband examined and certified that he was mentally ill and committable to the state hospital as an alcoholic addict. She explained her purpose to Dr. Baugh, who responded in a voice loud enough to be heard by persons in the waiting room, "There is nothing wrong with your husband, other than he is an old drunk and should be in jail instead of in the hospital, but if you insist I will call the county." Dr. Baugh then telephoned a county official and said, again in a voice capable of being heard by persons in the waiting room, that Mrs. Barry wanted her husband committed to the hospital, and that he would sign committal papers if Mrs. Barry would also agree to be committed, as both she and her husband were crazy.

Thereafter Mrs. Barry sued Dr. Baugh, charging that his intentionally wanton and malicious statement that she was crazy caused her humiliation, embarrassment, and mental anguish because she knew that if word got out that Dr. Baugh said she was crazy, her livelihood and reputation would be in jeopardy. As a result of this fright, she claimed she could not sleep or digest her food. She did not allege that she lost her employment as a result of Dr. Baugh's remarks.

The court pointed out that Mrs. Barry, who was a nurse, could recover damages from slander if Dr. Baugh's words constituted charges made against her in reference to her profession that were calculated to injure her in that capacity. However, the court concluded that Dr. Baugh's words were not spoken in reference to, or in the context of, her professional competence. For Mrs. Barry to recover damages, Dr. Baugh's words had to relate to something that would affect Mrs. Barry's character as a professional. Dr. Baugh must have had Mrs. Barry's profession in view and uttered the words in reference to it (as if he had said of a lawyer that the lawyer will not pay his clients the money he collects for them). Neither the words spoken nor the colloquium indicated that Dr. Baugh was alluding to Mrs. Barry in her capacity as a nurse; on the contrary the conversation dealt with Mrs. Barry's concern over the mental incompetence of her husband.

The court pointed out that even if Dr. Baugh's words did not amount to slander, his oral abuse of a person may be actionable if the abuse is false, malicious, and intentionally or wantonly designed to injure the person it is uttered against. They declared, however, that Dr. Baugh's mere oral abuse of Mrs. Barry was not necessarily a violation of a legal right. Nevertheless, a person who is verbally abused, generally would be upset, especially where the speaker is a physician whose position is such that his statements are likely to harm the person attacked by causing loss of esteem or employment. Such abuse in connection with other factors disturbing to the tranquillity of the average person, such as misjudging character, intelligence, ability, or sanity, is a moral wrong that is often punished by society through adverse public opinion and avoidance of a person known to display such conduct. In addition, under certain circumstance and situation, society punishes such conduct through legal means, by providing the person attacked a private right against the malicious opinion and judgment of a physician that is intended to injure the person attacked and that is expressed in abusive words made known to a third person. The court recognized, however, that life would be intolerable if a person had to be constantly on guard to avoid anything that might be expected to offend the sensibility of another. It concluded, therefore, mere insult and contemptuous language such as expressed by Dr. Baugh, which was not designed to, and did not cause special injury to Mrs. Barry, was insufficient to provide her with a legal cause of action against him.

A close relative's legal cause of action for injury from emotional trauma must be the result of the shock of a direct emotional impact upon the relative from the sensory and contemporaneous observance of the physician's misconduct.

Justus v. Atchison. A father was allowed in the delivery room during his wife's labor and observed the nurses and physicians ministering to her and the fetus. In particular he observed the monitoring of the fetal heart tones; the decrease in those tones and the resulting anxiety of the nurse; and the prolapsing of the umbilical cord at the time of delivery. In general, he observed the pain and trauma to his wife. He was present at the time the physician advised that the baby would not live. Sometime after the delivery and subsequent resuscitative efforts, he was told that his son was born dead. At that point he experienced great emotional shock. The father subsequently sued the physicians for the injury he sustained from the emotional trauma of witnessing their alleged malpractice.

The court declared that there was no doubt that the father observed the allegedly negligent delivery of his stillborn son and that such observation induced increasing fear and anxiety on his part. However, the shock from such observation did not occur until the father was informed that his son had been born dead. He did not know that the death had occurred until he was so informed. There was, therefore, no direct emotional impact upon him from his sensory and contemporaneous observance of the allegedly negligent delivery itself. Thus, his claimed injury was not legally compensable.

3

DIAGNOSTIC CONSIDERATIONS

A physician is expected to evaluate a patient in a manner that will make possible the formulation of effective treatment. Ordinarily, this requires that the physician *possess* adequate medical knowledge (education, training, and experience) and *apply* clinical skill, in a manner designed to arrive methodically at an accurate diagnosis.

From a legal standpoint, a physician is given latitude in determining the *method* of diagnosis. However, the physician's *application* of diagnostic procedures must be consistent with the degree of diligence and care exercised by similarly situated physicians under similar circumstances.

Although a physician is not expected to insure the correctness of a diagnosis, a patient is entitled to as thorough and careful an evaluation as attending circumstances will permit, with utilization of diagnostic methods approved by and implemented by similarly situated physicians. The availability of facilities, the degree of specialization possessed, the proximity of specialists and special facilities, together with other relevant considerations, are circumstances taken into account in assessing the reasonableness of a physician's evaluation.

A physician is expected to detect disease by diagnostic methods ranging from screening to comprehensive diagnostic work-ups. This task is ordinarily accomplished by establishing an adequate basis for diagnosis of the disease which is reflected by the manner in which the physician collects medical information and the effectiveness in which he selects salient diagnostic data. The physician may rely upon customary diagnostic tests and procedures to confirm the clinical impression that has been developed from the history and physical examination, so long as such reliance is not in conflict with the clinical presentation of the patient's illness or injury.

SECTION 1: THE PHYSICIAN'S DUTY TO PROVIDE A SKILLFUL AND CAREFUL DIAGNOSIS

If in seeking to make a proper diagnosis of a patient's medical problem, the physician fails to use the required degree of skill or care and an incorrect diagnosis results, liability may be established if the patient is harmed thereby. The required degree of skill or care for a physician who undertakes to diagnose a patient's condition is that which ordinarily is possessed and exercised by other physicians in similar circumstances.

Facts and Circumstances of Patient's Condition
Essential to the physician's responsibility to provide a skillful and careful diagnosis is the physician's duty to become aware of the facts and circumstances surrounding the patient's condition. Generally, the physician should collect the necessary data in a careful, thorough, and organized manner and must avoid going off on a diagnostic tangent. The following cases illustrate the application of this standard.

Landeros v. Flood. On repeated occasions during the first year of the patient's life, she was beaten by her mother and the latter's common-law husband. On April 26, 1971, when the infant was eleven months old, her mother took her to the hospital for diagnosis and treatment. A comminuted spiral fracture of the right tibia and fibula was diagnosed. The injury gave the appearance of having been caused by a twisting force. The mother had no explanation for this injury. The child also had contusions and abrasions on her body. Undetected was a nondepressed linear fracture of the skull, which was then in the process of healing. The child demonstrated fear and apprehension when approached and, in general, exhibited "the battered child syndrome." The physician released her from the hospital without diagnosing "battered child syndrome," and returned her to the custody of her mother and her boyfriend who thereafter intentionally inflicted traumatic contusions, puncture wounds, severe bites, and second and third-degree

At fourteen months of age the patient was brought to a different physician and hospital for medical care. "Battered child syndrome" was immediately diagnosed and reported to local authorities. She was taken into protective custody, hospitalized and placed with foster parents. Her mother and her boyfriend were convicted of child abuse.

Through a guardian the patient sued the physician, alleging that diagnosis of the patient's condition should have included skeletal x-rays and that such a diagnostic procedure would have disclosed her fractured skull. Because the physician did not take such x-rays, he did not diagnose the cause or severity of her condition. If he had applied the required diagnostic methodology, he would have suspected that the patient's injuries were associated with the "battered child syndrome." This would have resulted in an investigation by concerned agencies and placement of the patient in protective custody until her safety was assured because the physician had a duty to comply with the law requiring the reporting of child abuse.

The court noted that a physician who undertakes to diagnose a patient's condition is required to manifest the knowledge and skill which ordinarily is possessed and exercised by other physicians in similar circumstances. This standard of care includes a requirement that the physician know how to diagnose the "battered child syndrome." The court concluded that a reasonably prudent physician examining this patient in 1971 would have suspected she was a victim of the "battered child syndrome" from the injuries and circumstances presented to the physician, and if so he would have confirmed that clinical impression by ordering skeletal x-rays. If such diagnostic studies were suggestive of "battered child syndrome," he would have promptly reported his findings to appropriate authorities to prevent a recurrence of the injuries.

A physician is expected to reasonably inform himself of all salient facts and circumstances that may be germane to formulating a clinical diagnostic impression.

Rostron v. Klein.   Mr. Elrod fell over backwards and struck his head on the concrete floor of a service station. By the time an ambulance arrived he had regained consciousness. He was taken to the hospital where he was examined by Dr. Klein, a physician who had examined him a year before in connection with a syncopal episode. Dr. Klein had a record of this past medical history before him. He conducted a neurological evaluation related to the syncopal episode, but he neglected to inquire into the possibility of injury in connection with the fall. Dr. Klein discharged Elrod from the hospital even though there was evidence that Elrod was confused and unable to move his right hand. Within hours after his discharge Elrod was taken to another hospital where x-rays disclosed a skull fracture and an epidural hematoma was diagnosed. Decompression surgery was performed but he died the following day. Elrod's widow sued Dr. Klein for negligence in the diagnosis of her husband's condition.

The court found that Dr. Klein's evaluation of Elrod's condition was insufficient legally to satisfy the standards of practice in the community because of his failure to inform himself of the facts and circumstances surrounding Elrod's injury.

A physician must conduct as thorough and careful examination as is required by the facts and circumstances surrounding the case in order to meet the duty to provide a skillful and careful diagnosis.

Cooper v. Sisters of Charity.   A sixteen-year-old boy was struck by a truck while riding a bicycle. Later that afternoon he told his mother he had hurt the back of his head and had vomited. The mother observed a red area on the back of his head, and took him to an emergency room. He was able to enter the hospital unaided. While waiting to be attended, he vomited again. The mother related the history of the accident, vomiting, and headache to Dr. Hansen who examined the top of the boy's head, tested his reflexes and grip, examined his eyes with a light, looked in his ears, and ordered x-rays, the results of which did not disclose a skull fracture. The mother stated that her son was lying down on a stretcher throughout the examination and, although she called Dr. Hansen's attention to the fact that it was the back of the boy's head that was hurt, he did not examine that area of her son's head. Neither Dr. Hansen nor a nurse determined the boy's vital signs. Dr. Hansen did not test the boy's gait, balance or coordination; nor did he conduct any other diagnostic procedures. Concluding his examination Dr. Hansen advised the mother that the patient should be taken home, put to bed, and awakened frequently during the night. The mother was told that if she were unable to awaken him, or if he vomited more than twice, or if she recognized any other change in his condition, she should bring him back to the hospital.

When the mother and her son returned to her apartment the boy went to bed. He remained awake with no apparent change in his condition until early in the morning when he became restless and died. The cause of death was intracranial pressure secondary to an epidural hematoma that was the result of a basal skull fracture. At autopsy, the prosector noted an area of trauma over the occipital aspect of the scalp. The mother sued the physician and hospital for negligent diagnosis.

Expert testimony established that the swollen and discolored area of the scalp would have been apparent to observation and sensitive to palpation. Thus it should have been discovered on examination at the emergency room. It was also established that the vital signs were important parameters in assessing the seriousness of head injuries.

Dr. Hansen testified that, although he had no personal knowledge whether vital signs were taken at the hospital, taking such signs is mandatory procedure in the emergency room. He testified further that, at present, he did not know what the patient's vital signs were that night, but that he was sure that he had known them at that time. When questioned by the plaintiff's attorney his testimony regarding the vital signs was as follows:

PLAINTIFF'S COUNSEL: What were the vital signs?
DR. HANSEN: I don't know, sir.
PLAINTIFF'S COUNSEL: Did you ever know on that evening . . . what
                   the vital signs were?
DR. HANSEN: I am sure that I must have.

PLAINTIFF'S COUNSEL: I am asking you if you knew, not what you think.

DR. HANSEN: I would say yes, sir.

PLAINTIFF'S COUNSEL: Did you ever make a notation of his blood pressure?

DR. HANSEN: No, sir. . . .

PLAINTIFF'S COUNSEL: In other words, Dr. Hansen, you relied upon the nurse at the hospital to take all the vital information?

DR. HANSEN: That's right. . . .

PLAINTIFF'S COUNSEL: Doctor, let's see if we can agree. Is it important for somebody to find out what the boy's blood pressure was?

DR. HANSEN: That's right.

PLAINTIFF'S COUNSEL: And what his temperature was?

DR. HANSEN: Yes, sir.

PLAINTIFF'S COUNSEL: And what his pulse was?

DR. HANSEN: That's right.

PLAINTIFF'S COUNSEL: And what his respiration was?

DR. HANSEN: Yes, sir.

PLAINTIFF'S COUNSEL: I am asking you, Doctor, when you went in to see him that evening what was his temperature?

DR. HANSEN: I don't remember.

PLAINTIFF'S COUNSEL: You mean you don't know what was his blood pressure on that evening in the emergency room?

DR. HANSEN: I don't remember.

PLAINTIFF'S COUNSEL: What was his rate of respiration on that evening?

DR. HANSEN: I don't remember.

PLAINTIFF'S COUNSEL: What was his pulse on that evening?

DR. HANSEN: I don't remember.

PLAINTIFF'S COUNSEL: Now, the reason these notes are taken or these reports are kept is so that the doctor can refresh himself on what he observed, what conclusions he made, or what treatment he prescribed, and similar information; is that not so?

DR. HANSEN: That's right, sir.

PLAINTIFF'S COUNSEL: Yet on this evening that he came in you have no record of that information, Doctor, did you ever yourself make a record of what those vital signs were?

DR. HANSEN: I did not.

PLAINTIFF'S COUNSEL:	To your knowledge did anyone ever make a record of what those vital signs were?
DR. HANSEN:	Not a permanent record, no, sir. . . .
PLAINTIFF'S COUNSEL:	Have you ever discussed this matter with the nurse prior to submitting yourself to deposition?
DR. HANSEN:	I think that I did once, yes, sir.
PLAINTIFF'S COUNSEL:	Was the discussion, "Did you take the blood pressure that night"?
DR. HANSEN:	No, I was not aware that the blood pressure was not recorded on this chart at that time.
PLAINTIFF'S COUNSEL:	You have no knowledge, if it was ever taken, of your own, do you?
DR. HANSEN:	I have no knowledge of my own. I have no written report of it.
PLAINTIFF'S COUNSEL:	You have no personal knowledge that it was done, do you?
DR. HANSEN:	It was a mandatory routine that should be done in the emergency room.
PLAINTIFF'S COUNSEL:	I will agree with that, but I am asking you, sir: You have no personal knowledge that it was done, do you?
DR. HANSEN:	I would answer that the same way, sir.

The court held that a physician, who was evaluating a patient with a history of head injury, but who did not examine the site of injury nor gain knowledge of the patient's vital signs did not satisfy the standard for the professional conduct that a physician in the community should observe under like circumstances.

In contrast to the preceding case, when a physician is not told of pertinent diagnostic facts and circumstances, and has no reason to suspect their existence, liability will usually not result for a mistaken diagnosis. If the patient or family member is apparently capable of telling the physician about the illness, but omits relevant and pertinent information, the physician cannot be expected to surmise that an entirely different set of circumstances may, in fact, be in operation.

Johnson v. St. Paul Mercury Insurance Co. A mother found her two-year-old son playing with an empty aspirin bottle and assumed he had ingested the contents. Nineteen hours later he became ill, the father took him to the hospital and told the nurse's aide on duty about the aspirin. The aide told him to be sure to tell the examining physician. The father, however, did not tell the physician about the aspirin when the child was being examined, even though the physician asked if the child had eaten any medicine. The diagnosis of "croup" was made and the child was taken home. Shortly thereafter the child died as a result of salicylate poisoning. The parents sued the physician, alleging that he had conducted an improper examination and, therefore, failed to discover the possibility of aspirin ingestion. They contended that whether the father had alerted the physician of that possibility was irrelevant in assessing the attending physician's duty to discover relevant data on which to formulate a clinical diagnosis.

The court nevertheless held that because the father had failed to advise the physician about the child's aspirin ingestion, the physician had not been negligent. Under the circumstances the physician could not have been expected to have utilized information that the father had never revealed.

As *Johnson* indicates, when matters material to the diagnosis are not disclosed to the physician, a physician's subsequent misdiagnosis ordinarily is not considered to be the result of his negligence. However, if the clinical presentation of the patient indicates, or should indicate, to a diligent and careful physician that the information received is either inaccurate or incomplete (that is, if the physician's observation does not "square" with the information provided), a duty arises to make further diagnostic investigation in order to reconcile the disparate findings. Thus if elucidation of the signs and symptoms establishes a clinical presentation that should alert the physician to the existence of other, or more serious, problems beyond the exposition of the patient or the patient's family, the physician is required to further investigate these circumstances.

Rewis v. U.S.   While the mother was ill in bed with the "flu," her fifteen-month-old daughter ingested an unknown quantity of adult aspirin tablets. Without knowledge of this fact, the husband took his wife to the hospital. Upon his return home he was told that his daughter had eaten her supper, but then had immediately started vomiting and had experienced a bad case of diarrhea. The father also observed that the child was "blue around the eyes and lips" and "deep breathing." He took the child to the hospital, and saw the same physician who had treated his wife. The physician noted the findings and recorded that the child was "hyperventilating." Her temperature and the remainder of the examination was normal. Because the child's mother had just been found to have a viral infection, the physician diagnosed the child's condition as the "flu." He prescribed a decongestant and one baby aspirin every four hours. The father then took the child home and administered the dosages prescribed. During the night the child was extremely restless and crying. The father took the child back to the hospital the next morning. The physician who evaluated her immediately called a pediatrician who took a blood sample which demonstrated a markedly high salicylate level. Heroic measures were undertaken to save the child, including transfer to a facility for renal dialysis. However, she died en route. Her parents sued the initial treating physician.

At the trial, expert medical testimony established that because the child had been hyperventilating to such an extreme degree when she was examined, the symptoms presented to the physician should have alerted him to the existence of some other problem in addition to the "flu." He then should have investigated further the cause of the problem. His failure to do so resulted in liability for the harm caused.

Collection and Consideration of Historical Data

In addition to the duty to become aware of the facts and circumstances surrounding a patient's condition, a physician has an ancillary duty, to consult when necessary, prior accessible medical records before or during the evaluation of a patient. If the present illness necessitating diagnostic evaluation is related to the patient's former sickness, the physician is expected to become informed of this aspect of the patient's medical history.

O'Neil v. State.   A patient had been treated for some time with Nembutal. Because her psychiatrist felt she was becoming addicted to barbiturates, he advised her husband to take her to a general hospital for evaluation. The physician who admitted her diagnosed that she was psychotic. He did not ask any questions about drug use, even though the patient told him she took Nembutal. He did not review available records from her previous admissions and refused to talk to her husband. Although he was given the name of her psychiatrist who had recommended that she seek evaluation, the admitting physician made no effort to contact him. During her hospitalization the patient died of barbiturate withdrawal reactions that went unrecognized.

Her husband sued the attending physician for negligent evaluation and misdiagnosis of his wife's condition. The court held that the attending physician's failure to take an adequate history of her drug use or to check her records for indications of the same thing fell below the requisite standard of care under the circumstances of this case.

When the patient's present illness is unrelated to past medical history, prior records would be required only if, under the circumstances, a reasonably careful physician would consider it necessary to obtain and review them. Thus where it is the customary practice of duly careful physicians to consult such records, as in the following case, negligence may result for failure to do so.

Mulligan v. Wetchler.   A fifty-two-year-old patient was examined at a private hospital by a physician who felt that the patient should be hospitalized in order to rule out appendicitis. However, the patient could not be admitted at the private hospital because the hospital was fully occupied. Therefore, the patient was transferred by ambulance to a city hospital where he arrived moaning, twisting, and complaining of severe abdominal pain. The examining physician did not request or review the transfer certificate which accompanied the patient, and indicated that the diagnosis at the first hospital was "Acute gastroenteritis. R/O appendicitis?" Forwarding such certificate with the patient was not only accepted practice but was required by the city health code. After briefly palpating the patient's abdomen and taking his temperature and blood pressure, the physician prescribed a sedative and an enema and sent the patient home. Several hours later another physician examined the patient at his home, and diagnosed appendicitis. The patient was taken to a hospital where surgery was performed. However, the appendix had perforated. The patient died several days later as a result of complications of the perforation. The patient's family sued the city hospital.

Expert medical testimony established that it was common and accepted practice for the physician at the receiving hospital to ascertain the diagnosis made at the remitting hospital and the reasons for transfer of the patient. Thus the court concluded that the city hospital physician should have determined both the reason for transfer and the prior diagnosis, and then should have given the patient a complete evaluation to rule out appendicitis. The court held that the physician was negligent in failing to review the transfer sheet or to ask questions of the patient or those persons with him about prior diagnosis.

When circumstances permit, an adequate medical history is required if the use of reactive drugs is planned for the treatment of a patient. If a physician does not inquire about pertinent facts referable to drug therapy, and if the results of treatment are adversely affected because such facts were not obtained, liability may result. Generally, however, the physician may rely on the information provided by the patient. If the patient does not disclose obvious information, or gives misleading responses, the physician is not liable for an untoward result, provided the patient could reasonably have been expected to understand the physician's inquiries.

Sanzari v. Rosenfeld.   In preparation for dental surgery a dentist injected into the patient's mouth a solution containing lidocaine for anesthesia and epinephrine for hemostasis. The patient had a history of hypertension. The dentist "guessed" that he might have asked how the patient's general health was before administering medication containing an ingredient that he knew may have been contraindicated in hypertensive patients. Following the injection, the patient experienced an incapacitating cerebrovascular accident, and subsequently sued the dentist.

The court stated that it is within the common knowledge of laymen that a reasonable person who knows a drug is potentially harmful to a certain type of patient should take adequate precaution before administering the drug. Although the dentist said that it was his "guess" that he asked her how her general health was, his chart contained no notations about her hypertension or medical status in general. The court found that the dentist's lack of assurance about what he did, plus the absence of any record, would support a legitimate inference that he did not make pertinent inquiries before he used the drug. Thus, the court concluded that the dentist had not taken adequate precautions before injecting the medication into the patient.

Duty to Use Customary Tests

Another duty of the physician in forming a diagnosis involves the obligation to use screening methods customarily used in the profession. The following cases exemplify this rule.

As a first example, although a physician does not have a duty to conduct an exhaustive genealogical profile on patients, he is required to take a rudimentary genetic screen or history to detect well-known and serious genetic diseases, especially for patients who are at higher risk.

Howard v. Lecher. Dr. Lecher confirmed that Mrs. Howard was pregnant and consequently agreed to provide prenatal care and deliver her child. Although the physician knew, or should have known, that the Howards were of eastern European Jewish background, and thus were potential carriers of Tay-Sachs disease, he did not take a genealogical history, nor did he properly assess the history that he did take. Even though tests were available to determine whether the Howards were carriers and whether the fetus was afflicted with the disease, Dr. Lecher did not advise the Howards of the possibility of performing these tests.

In 1972, Mrs. Howard gave birth to a child who two years later succumbed to the inevitable effects of Tay-Sachs disease. The parents sued the physician, charging that he had failed to take an adequate genetic screening history. They contended that the physician had a duty to compile adequate data so that related genetic screening, serum assays, amniocentesis, and other confirmatory tests on the fetus could have been conducted. They further contended that, upon being advised of the results of those tests, Mrs. Howard should have been given the option to eugenically terminate the pregnancy or to proceed to childbirth. They sought reimbursement for medical expenses resulting from their child's condition and for the pain and anguish of watching their child deteriorate and die from Tay-Sachs.

The court noted that Tay-Sachs disease is an inherited, incurable disorder caused by the absence of a vital enzyme, which results in early progressive neurological degeneration and death. When two carriers of the enzymatic deficiency produce offspring, there is a 25 percent risk that their child will be afflicted with the fatal disease. By 1972, a relatively simple, inexpensive, and accurate medical procedure had been developed to identify the irregular enzyme.

The court pointed out that genetic counseling, involving communication between physicians and patients in an attempt to deal with the occurrence or the risk of genetic disorders in a family, has become widespread in the provision of health care. Given this medical background, the court concluded that the physician's evaluation was negligent because he had taken an incomplete history and had failed to perform accepted procedures for screening a Tay-Sachs carrier. The court concluded that because the nature of the child's condition makes it likely that parents will suffer grave emotional harm, it is reasonable that a pregnant woman might have expected her physician to ascertain the facts of her background and once having done so, to conduct appropriate confirmatory tests.

A physician is obligated to carefully and competently collect data customarily compiled to advise the patient of the probability of procreating a child with a well-recognized congenital abnormality.

Park v. Chessin.   Mrs. Park gave birth to a child with polycystic kidneys who died shortly after birth. After the death of her child Mrs. Park continued to be treated and advised by her obstetrician. When she inquired about the advisability of future pregnancies, the physician told Mrs. Park that she did not have any reason to fear that a future pregnancy would result in the birth of another congenitally defective child. Even though there was some genetic likelihood that pregnancy would again result in a child being born with polycystic disease, the physician did not perform tests to ascertain the genetic makeup of the patient or her husband in order to rationally ascertain the probability that a subsequent child would be so afflicted. Instead, he told the parents that polycystic kidney disease was not hereditary, thereby reassuring them without having researched or investigated relevant and available medical information concerning the hereditary nature of polycystic kidney disease. Relying on this advice, Mrs. Park became pregnant and delivered a child who was also born with polycystic kidneys. As a result, she and her husband sued the obstetrician.

The Parks contended that the physician made representations with the pretense of knowledge and with reckless disregard for the facts because he did not ascertain or inquire as to the correct factual circumstances of the patient's case. In addition, they contended that had they been properly advised of the risks of abnormality, they would have elected to terminate the pregnancy. They claimed that because the physician failed to advise them of the risk, they were denied the opportunity to take the additional steps to obtain an abortion.

The court pointed out that a physician who provides prenatal care to an expectant mother may be liable if, during prenatal examination, he negligently fails to evaluate and detect the probability of occurrence of a well-recognized genetic defect in the child. The court analogized this situation to cases in which the physician has failed to make a timely diagnosis of a curable disease. If the physician had advised the parents of the risk of bearing a genetically defective child, and of the availability of tests for detecting the disorder, such tests would have revealed the defect, and the mother would have decided to have an abortion in order to avoid serious hardship to themselves and their child.

If a diagnosis is in doubt, a physician is required to perform as definitive a diagnostic investigation as is necessary to arrive at a reasonably effective treatment plan. The physician must, therefore, be aware of the limitations of diagnostic data, and be familiar with the accepted methods of arriving at a definitive diagnosis.

O'Brien v. Stover. On May 10, the patient visited Dr. Stover, an oral surgeon, on referral from her regular dentist. An abcess surrounding a mandibular molar was noted and the tooth was extracted. X-rays disclosed partial destruction of the bone underlying the tooth. On May 26, Dr. Stover observed that the tooth socket was not healing properly. On June 9, when the patient complained that the tissue within the extraction site bled easily, Dr. Stover ordered tests to determine if a blood dyscrasia might be affecting her healing. These tests turned out to be negative. He did not perform a tissue biopsy of the extraction site.

Over the next two months the patient periodically was examined by Dr. Stover. The tooth next to the extraction site became loose and required extraction. That tissue also did not heal properly and bled easily when probed. Additional x-rays disclosed bone destruction; additional blood tests and a bone marrow aspirate were normal. On August 22, the patient complained to Dr. Stover that her gums bled spontaneously. Dr. Stover took a cytological smear of the affected area. The pathologist reported that the cytological smear was negative, but that no definite conclusions concerning the pathological nature of the tissue could be drawn without a tissue biopsy. Dr. Stover did not order a tissue biopsy because he feared that the biopsy incision might possibly cause the infection to spread if the patient's condition were osteomyelitis.

During the next few weeks the patient was treated twice by Dr. Stover for serious hemorrhaging from the base of the socket, once requiring hospitalization. On September 26, Dr. Stover observed a gingival mass and referred the patient to a hospital where a biopsy of the lesion disclosed poorly differentiated epidermoid carcinoma. Surgical and radiation treatments were unsuccessful, and the patient died of the cancer ten months later. The patient's estate sued Dr. Stover for negligent misdiagnosis of the patient's cancer.

Dr. Stover contended there was no obvious evidence of a gingival tumor prior to September 26 and therefore it was unreasonable to expect him to have diagnosed the cancer earlier. However, the court pointed out that there were other signs of cancer much earlier, and thus the absence of a visible tumor in and of itself did not relieve him of negligence. Dr. Stover should have suspected cancer because there were sufficient clinical findings present. Although Dr. Stover was aware that some underlying condition was causing the patient's extraction site not to heal properly, he made no diagnosis of the cause of this continuing abnormal condition, even though he suspected a systemic illness as early as June 9, at which time a tissue biopsy would have disclosed the cancer.

The court pointed out that the method chosen by Dr. Stover for diagnosis was inadequate. Although a cytological smear may be a good screening device, it is not a definitive diagnostic method under circumstances in which other clinical findings are suggestive of cancer. Compared to a tissue biopsy, a cytological smear has a greater chance of failing to detect cancer. Therefore, in order to arrive at a definite diagnosis, a tissue biopsy should have been done.

Dr. Stover testified that he did not do the tissue biopsy because he belonged to a school of thought which advocated a more conservative approach to the treatment of osteomyelitis initially, because the more aggressive surgical approach involved a risk of spreading the infection into other sensitive areas, which could have serious consequences. The court, however, found this contention was irrelevant because the "two schools of thought," come into play only when a definitive diagnosis of osteomyelitis is made.

The court noted the real issue dealt primarily with proper methods of making the diagnosis. Although there was a school of thought which advocated the more conservative treatment of a known case of osteomyelitis, where cancer was suspected as the underlying condition, the fear of spreading infection was an insufficient reason for not making a tissue biopsy in order to make a definitive diagnosis. In addition, the court noted Dr. Stover did not begin treatment for osteomyelitis until two and one-half months after he knew there was some underlying cause for delayed healing. Had he embarked upon a "therapeutic trial" or course of treatment for osteomyelitis earlier, his patient's lack of response to this treatment would have been highly suggestive of the need to reevaluate the diagnosis and would probably have led to an earlier discovery of the cancer.

Physicians often establish a data profile on a patient to monitor and detect sentinel developmental deviations early enough to prevent permanent morbidity. If this screening data has become by custom and usage a professional standard, the physician is required to carefully assess this collected information. Thus if methods such as growth charts are utilized in the routine evaluation of the development of a patient, the data pattern generated by this method must not be ignored, but should be analyzed as an aid to diagnose the patient's problems.

Hansen v. Bussman. The child was the product of an uneventful pregnancy and delivery. No abnormalities were noted by her family physician on her "six-week check-up." Between five and eight months of age, her parents became concerned that she was not developing properly. She "seemed listless and slow in growing, wasn't trying to sit up, and she was real pale."

At tens months of age the infant was examined by a pediatrician. The mother told both the nurse and the physician that she wanted a "complete physical" for her baby because of her concern over the baby's lack of growth. The nurse recorded the child's height and weight on a growth chart. The pediatrician noted that the growth lag that he observed he attributed to the family growth pattern because the mother was a small person. He diagnosed iron deficiency anemia, prescribed oral iron, and told the mother that the hemoglobin should be checked again in six weeks.

On the next visit the hemoglobin count had risen from 8.8 to 9.1 grams. On the third visit it was 8.6 grams. Assuming that the baby was not absorbing iron adequately, the pediatrician prescribed several iron injections to be given by his nurse to the infant on subsequent visits. On the sixth and last visit at fourteen months of age, the infant's hemoglobin level had risen to 9.9 grams. He told the mother that although the infant's blood had not come up to normal yet, she should keep feeding the baby and the blood would be back to normal. He did not indicate that the infant was in need of further examination or tests.

At sixteen months of age the infant's condition was diagnosed as congenital hypothyroidism or cretinism. Appropriate treatment restored her to normal physical development, but it was then too late to restore her mental development. As a result, she will be mentally retarded and will never be able to live independently. The parents sued the pediatrician on behalf of the child.

Expert testimony established that although this child did not have the classic symptoms and stigmata of cretinism, she did have retarded growth and development. The court noted that the pediatrician's growth chart should have confirmed a "growth deficiency." This created an obligation to undertake an investigation for the cause of deficiency, including tests which would disclose a thyroid deficiency before irreversible effects on mental function occurred. Either the physician did not properly keep the chart or else he did not properly interpret its significance as a guide to diagnosis. In both cases such conduct was indicative of negligence.

When a patient is injured and a possible fracture is suggested even to a lay person, it is common knowledge that x-rays would aid in the diagnosis of the injury. However, simply ordering an indicated x-ray is an insufficient shield from liability for negligent misdiagnosis, unless adequate and proper x-rays for the condition under diagnosis are ordered.

Betenbaugh v. Princeton Hospital.   The patient was taken to a hospital following an injury to her lower back. Her physician directed that an x-ray be taken of her lumbosacral area. A lateral view was not taken. The physician found no evidence of a fracture and his negative finding was confirmed by the hospital's radiologist. When the patient's pain did not subside, she consulted her family physician who determined that the x-rays taken at the hospital were inadequate, in that they did not include the entire lower portion of the spine. He sent her to a radiologist for further study. On the basis of the new x-rays, a fracture was discovered. She sued her initial physician for negligent misdiagnosis.

The radiologist who took the second set of x-rays testified that it was customary to take a lateral view when performing a radiological examination of the lumbosacral area. Thus the court held that the failure of the hospital radiologist to include a lateral view that would have disclosed the fracture was negligent because it constituted a failure to meet the established standard for making an adequate radiological examination of the spine.

Duty to Use Tests Not Customarily Performed

As indicated in the previous subsection, a physician may be liable for misdiagnosis if the correct diagnosis is dependent upon the performance of customary and routine screening tests and procedures which are not performed. Where a disease can be definitively detected and successfully arrested at an early stage, liability may also be imposed under certain circumstances, for failure to perform a test not customarily performed by most physicians. This is particularly so when the test involves the utilization of screening procedures to detect a disease by a simple, accurate, harmless, and inexpensive means; and early treatment can successfully arrest otherwise irreversible effects of the disease if it is left undetected over a substantial period of time.

Helling v. Carey.   In 1959, when the patient was twenty-one years old, she first consulted an ophthalmologist because of myopia and was fitted with contact lenses. She next consulted him twice in 1963 concerning irritation caused by the contact lenses. She was subsequently evaluated for visual complaints three times in 1967 and four times in 1968. The ophthalmologist considered the patient's visual problems to be related solely to irritation associated with her contact lenses. In October 1968, however, he tested her orbital pressure and visual field for the first time. These tests indicated that the patient had primary open angle glaucoma, and disclosed loss of her peripheral vision and reduction of her central vision. The patient sued the ophthalmologist and charged that she sustained severe and permanent damage to her eyes as a result of his negligence.

Medical testimony established that the standards of the profession for ophthalmology did not require routine pressure tests for glaucoma for patients under the age of forty because the disease rarely occurs in that age group, unless the patient's symptoms reveal to the physician that glaucoma should be suspected. The court pointed out that, in most cases, reasonable care is, in fact, customary care. Nevertheless, the court cautioned that customary care is never strictly the measure of reasonable care. The court reasoned that the medical profession may have unduly lagged in the adoption of new and available devices; and therefore it may not set the legal standard of its own tests, no matter how persuasive its custom and usages may be. In this case, reasonable care required giving the pressure test to the patient. The court concluded that the consequences of the disease undetected are so great that the precaution of giving this test to detect glaucoma in patients under forty years of age becomes so imperative that, in spite of absence in the standards of ophthalmology, it is the duty of the courts to say what is required to protect patients under forty from the damaging results of glaucoma. The court held that the standard of care for ophthalmology was inadequate to protect this patient from the early detection of glaucoma, and the ophthalmologist was negligent in failing to perform a relatively simple and harmless tonometric examination at an earlier point in time, which would have averted the resulting substantial loss of her vision.

Section 2: The Physician's Liability for Mistakes in Diagnosis

If the physician uses the proper degree of skill and care in diagnosing a patient's condition, he will not be liable for a simple mistake or error. However, a physician's failure to utilize available diagnostic means and facilities for the collection of an adequate diagnostic data base may suggest that a resultant misdiagnosis is more likely to be negligent than simply an error of judgment.

Misdiagnosis of a patient's condition may be an innocent error in judgment, or it may represent negligence in the collection of information essential to a proper diagnostic conclusion. Negligent collection of medical data impairs a physician's ability to make an informed judgment as to the nature of the patient's illness. Although an "honest" error of judgment based upon the findings of appropriate test results is excusable, failure to obtain adequate data from which medical judgments can be correctly made is negligent. The following cases illustrate where legal lines are drawn between acceptable and unacceptable diagnostic errors.

Clark v. U.S. The patient had a history of chronic pelvic inflammatory disease and had been hospitalized several times for treatment of this condition. Finally she underwent a total hysterectomy. The disease process had so distorted the location and position of her genitourinary organs that the two gynecological residents who performed the hysterectomy were unable to locate and protect the right ureter. As a result the ureter was inadvertently sutured in two places during the surgery.

On the second postoperative day the patient was febrile and complained of right flank pain and tenderness. One resident recorded that these symptoms indicated either a kidney infection or a blockage of the ureter and noted that an intravenous pyelogram (IVP) might be indicated. Instead, the two residents decided to treat for kidney infection with antibiotics. They did not consult a urologist or have the IVP performed until the sixth postoperative day. At that time an IVP and right retrograde urogram were performed and disclosed the compromised right ureter. By that time, however, the ureter was so degenerated that it separated when the sutures were removed and it became necessary to rebuild it. Two months later the ureter had become blocked and it was necessary to perform a nephrectomy. The patient subsequently brought suit.

The court stated that the fact that the diagnosis was erroneous did not furnish a basis for liability. However, the court drew sharp distinction between an error of judgment and negligence in the obtaining of factual data essential to arriving at a proper diagnostic opinion. If a physician does not use available scientific means and facilities for the collection of reasonable factual data upon which to formulate a diagnosis, the result is not an error of judgment, but negligence.

Once medical data has been collected, a physician must then select data which support a proper diagnosis. Again, a fundamental difference exists between mere errors of diagnostic judgment and negligent selection of data with which the physician may execute diagnostic judgment.

Hicks v. U.S. Late at night, a woman was brought to an emergency room after she experienced an hour-long history of intense abdominal pain and vomiting. After briefly questioning the patient about her symptoms, the emergency room physician simply palpated her abdomen and listened for bowel sounds. Recording his diagnosis as "gastroenteritis," he told her she had a "bug" in her stomach, prescribed medication for pain, and told her to return in eight hours for reevaluation. The patient went home and continued to vomit. Shortly thereafter she became unconscious and was taken back to the hospital. Efforts to revive her were unsuccessful. Autopsy disclosed a high intestinal obstruction, secondary to internal herniation of loops of small intestine into a congenital malformation. Death was caused by a massive hemorrhagic infarction of the intestine as a result of strangulation of the bowel.

The patient's husband sued alleging that the physician did not meet the requisite standard of diagnostic skill and care. The physician contended that the symptoms of high bowel obstruction and "gastroenteritis" are so similar that his misdiagnosis was not negligent, but rather an error of judgment.

The court pointed out that where the clinical presentation of an illness is consistent with either of two possible conditions, one lethal if not attended to promptly, a physician must do more than perform a cursory examination and release the patient. The fact that an intestinal obstruction is a relatively rare occurrence, and that "gastroenteritis" is statistically more probable, does not excuse the physician's failure to make further pertinent inquiries and perform additional diagnostic tests that might have served to distinguish the one condition from the other. The court held that in this case the accepted standard called for further diagnostic differentiation of the patient's condition, if only to rule out the more serious illness. The failure to do so constituted a negligent lack of due diligence and care.

If a physician has peformed tests which generally are recognized as approved standard diagnostic aids, in view of the clinical presentation of the patient, liability probably will not be established, even though the physician's diagnosis proves to have been erroneous, if the diagnostic procedure selected is one among several accepted alternatives.

Ball v. Mallinkrodt Chemical Works. Although the patient had severe hypertension, even after long and extensive evaluation, her attending physician was unable to determine the cause of this condition. In the course of evaluation, the physician recommended that a translumbar aortogram be performed to determine if her hypertension was caused by renal artery stenosis. Almost immediately after the radiologist injected the radiopaque medium, sodium acetrizoate, the patient experienced severe pain in her chest and abdomen, and neurological loss in both legs. The angiogram confirmed the suspicion that contrast medium had extravasated and migrated to the area of the spinal cord. As a result of this complication the patient sustained paralysis of her legs and impairment of her bowel activity, and she sued the radiologist.

Expert testimony indicated that for several years prior to the performance of the aortogram, sodium acetrizoate was the contrast agent chosen for such tests because it provided the best radiographic picture, even though other agents were considered by some physicians to be less toxic. The court concluded that the radiologist exercised his best judgment in choosing a proper contrast agent, the use of which was approved by competent medical authorities. The court further stated that where the treatment or procedure is one of choice among competent physicians, a physician is not negligent if he selects the one which, according to his best judgment, is best suited to the patient's needs.

The physician's diagnostic thinking is a reflection of his degree of knowledge and skill. Courts examine the mental process a physician uses in patient evaluation to determine if he has met the requisite legal standard of care. Inconsistencies and incongruities between a physician's mental process and his overt professional behavior that make it difficult to reconcile his thought and action to discredit his professional capacity.

Smith v. Shankmkan.   The patient visited her physician because of abdominal pain and fainting. After taking a cursory medical history and briefly palpating her abdomen, the physician diagnosed salpingitis and administered penicillin and Demerol and sent her home. He did not perform a pelvic examination. Despite several return visits to the physician, he continued to use a regimen of antibiotics and analgesics. Finally the patient was taken to a hospital in acute distress. She died soon after admission due to exsanguination as a result of a ruptured tubal pregnancy. The patient's estate sued the physician for negligent diagnosis.

The court held that the physician had not used proper and fundamental diagnostic methods, such as a complete history and physical exam in the evaluation of this patient's problems. Moreover, his tentative diagnosis of salpingitis should have alerted him to the possibility of types of tubal problems, such as an ectopic pregnancy, especially when the patient did not respond to treatment for salpingitis. This should have caused him to perform a more thorough clinical investigation of her problems, utilizing standard methods to rule out such a serious condition.

A difference of professional opinion as to diagnostic methodology is not enough to establish negligence in the choice of method. The law recognizes that physicians customarily differ as to the diagnostics tests they prefer to use, and in their opinion of the reliability of such tests. Thus a misdiagnosis which results in an operation properly undertaken on the basis of the diagnosis does not necessarily establish liability.

Hoglin v. Brown. On March 27, 1967, Mrs. Hoglin consulted Dr. Brown, a general practitioner, for advice and treatment for chronic pelvic pain. The patient indicated that her last menstrual period was on February 14, 1967. Dr. Brown performed a pelvic examination and diagnosed "retroverted, moderately enlarged fibroid type of uterus and probable cervical stenosis." To help rule out the possibility of pregnancy, he prescribed hormone tablets (Gestest) for two days. If menstruation was not induced within two weeks, pregnancy would be presumed. However, Gestest was regarded as less reliable than various other tests to determine pregnancy. Therefore when Mrs. Hoglin took the Gestest tablets as directed on March 28 and 29 and no menstruation occurred, Dr. Brown was reluctant to conclude that she was pregnant.

On March 31, Dr. Brown again performed a pelvic examination, dilated the cervix, and obtained an endometrial biopsy. One reason he performed the biopsy was to rule out pregnancy, even though there were other reasons for performing the procedure as well. In obtaining the biopsy, Dr. Brown observed a stenotic cervix. The tissue that was submitted for pathological analysis was diagnosed as "late secretory endometrium," a diagnosis which usually indicates the absence of pregnancy.

Mrs. Hoglin continued to have pelvic and back pain and her menses did not begin. Relying upon the results of the endometrial biopsy, Dr. Brown suggested that she undergo a hysterectomy. He also suggested that she seek consultation with a specialist, but she declined.

On April 24, a hysterectomy was undertaken. After the midline incision was made and the cavity explored, the uterus appeared to be pregnant. Accordingly, the incision was closed and the hysterectomy was not performed. A urine test was subsequently performed, which confirmed the pregnancy. Mrs. Hoglin later spontaneously aborted and sued Dr. Brown, claiming physical injury by reason of an unnecessary exploratory laparotomy.

The patient contended that there were three tests available, namely the hormonal Gestest, the urine test, and the bimanual palpation, and that when the Gestest indicated pregnancy, Dr. Brown should not have commenced the operation without administering one of the other two tests to eliminate the possibility of pregnancy. Dr. Brown contended that he used the bimanual palpation on two occasions and also used a fourth test, an endometrial biopsy, a standard test which he relied on as a means of determining pregnancy. In this case, the endometrial biopsy test demonstrated a condition associated with nonpregnancy.

The court pointed out that it was Dr. Brown's duty prior to performing a hysterectomy to utilize tests recognized as standard to rule out pregnancy. There was conflicting medical testimony as to whether the endometrial biopsy test was an acceptable determinant of pregnancy. Evidence was also

submitted that physicians differ as to the tests they prefer, and that the reliability of the diagnostic tests varies. The court found that because the evidence was conflicting, the jury had a right to choose the evidence it would
believe, and thus had a right to find that Dr. Brown complied with the applicable standard of care by using and relying upon the endometrial biopsy
and bimanual palpation to rule out pregnancy. Therefore the jury could find
that his misdiagnosis of pregnancy was not arrived at negligently.

A physician is not required to use or exhaust all diagnostic procedures in
caring for the patient. However, when a potentially beneficial procedure is
not used, the physician is expected to be able to explain why its use was
unwarranted under the circumstances, or why alternative means of managing the patient's condition were reasonable.

Delaune v. Davis.   A college student was injured in an automobile accident
and taken to a hospital where he was attended by a surgeon for fractured
ribs and sternum. A chest tube was inserted to drain the fluid that had accu-
mulated in his thoracic cavity. Although his initial chest x-ray suggested a
widening of the mediastinum, subsequent daily x-rays disclosed no progression of this finding. Therefore, the surgeon felt that the probability of
serious mediastinal injury was so minimal that he could not justify subjecting the patient to invasive diagnostic studies, such as an aortogram. In addition, the patient's clinical condition had improved such that he insisted on
being allowed to return to college. At the time of discharge his surgeon told
him to select a physician in his college town and have that physician call the
surgeon.
    After returning to college, the patient did not consult a physician even
though he continued to experience chest pain. Approximately seven weeks
after the accident, the progression and persistence of pain caused him to
consult a physician who examined him and referred him to a radiologist.
Chest x-rays disclosed a soft tissue density in the aortic zone indicative of a
traumatic thoracic aortic aneurysm. The radiologist referred him to a cardiovascular surgeon who admitted him to a medical center for immediate
surgery. During the operation the aorta ruptured, resulting in uncontrollable hemorrhage and death.
    The patient's mother sued the surgeon who attended her son imme-
diately after the automobile accident. She contended that an aortogram
should have been performed during her son's hospitalization to diagnose the
traumatic aortic aneurysm. The court pointed out that when a physician
makes a judgment relative to the manner in which he chooses to treat his
patient, he must consider the condition of the patient, and his clinical progress or lack of it, as manifested by subsequent diagnostic tests. The court
noted that although an aortogram may be the most definitive diagnostic

procedure to detect an aortic aneurysm, it is inherently hazardous and should not be performed unless other clinical findings warrant it.* Under the circumstances of this case, the court concluded that an aortogram was not essential.

A diagnosis which turns out to be erroneous will not be considered a negligent misdiagnosis if a physician carefully and diligently performs and relies upon appropriate standard tests in arriving at the diagnosis. A physician may even rely on a "false positive" result of a test if other aspects of the patient's case makes such reliance reasonable.

Stephenson v. Kaiser Foundation Hospitals. The patient had known for several years that she had a uterine fibroid, but because it was asymptomatic, she did nothing about it. In January, when Dr. Lelich examined her, he recommended surgery. The patient indicated that she wanted to wait until April. When she was examined by Dr. Lelich on April 23, he took x-rays and read them as normal. She entered the hospital on April 28 for the scheduled surgery. The size of the tumor imposed certain limits on the clinical examination, and because he was aware that the tumor could mask evidence of an early pregnancy, which would not be evident on the x-ray, Dr. Lelich ordered a pregnancy test. The test was reported as "positive," therefore, he postponed the surgery and discharged the patient from the hospital. He told her to report back in two weeks. At that time she reported menstrual bleeding and indicated that she did not feel pregnant. On June 19, Dr. Lelich reexamined her, and because he could not hear any fetal heart tones, he ordered another pregnancy test. Again the result was positive. The patient insisted that she could not be pregnant as she was bleeding regularly. Dr. Lelich told her she had to wait several months until the diagnosis of pregnancy could be verified. On October 29, Dr. Lelich ordered another x-ray. When no evidence of fetal skeleton was detected, he informed the patient that his earlier diagnosis of pregnancy had been erroneous. The patient sued the physician because of the negligently misdiagnosed pregnancy which, she claimed among other things, caused her to lose work time.

Expert testimony established that, under the circumstances of this case, the physician's approach of waiting for several months was in accord with the proper standards of practice. It was pointed out that an early pregnancy could not be easily detected by clinical examination or by x-ray because of the patient's tumor, and because some women continue to bleed regularly throughout their pregnancy. The pregnancy test chosen by the physician was customarily used, properly administered, usually accurate, and rarely

---

* The case occurred prior to the advent and refinement of effective noninvasive diagnostic techniques for defining a thoracic aortic aneurysm.

falsely "positive." It was also established that the fetal skeleton would not show up on an x-ray until four or five months, and that it was not good practice to x-ray a pregnant woman before that time because of the radiation danger to the fetus. In addition, there were no other reasonable means for confirming the pregnancy.

The court pointed out that a physician is not required to warrant his diagnosis. Although in this case the physician mistakenly had diagnosed pregnancy, the facts and circumstances of the case indicated that his mistake was not due to failure to exercise ordinary care, diligence, and skill in making the diagnosis; therefore, it was not a negligent misdiagnosis.

If a physician performs and reasonably relies on tests that are approved standard diagnostic aids in view of the symptoms presented, ordinarily he is not liable if his diagnostic conclusions turn out to be wrong.

Ries v. Reinhard. A woman consulted the physician because of vaginal pruritis. After taking her history, the physician examined the patient. He then made a gram stain of the vaginal discharge, microscopically examined the smear, using the methylene blue technique, and then told his patient that she had gonorrhea, in all probability contracted by sexual contact. Because the pruritis had occurred shortly after coitus with her husband, the physician told the patient to talk with her husband or, if she preferred, he would talk to him. He then treated the patient for gonorrhea. Two days later, the husband consulted the physician. When he was unable to obtain a smear from the husband's urethra because of the absence of a discharge, the physician expressed doubt as to whether the husband had gonorrhea. Nevertheless, he told the husband that he was convinced that his wife had the disease, and therefore he advised him to commence treatment immediately. The following day, the couple consulted another physician who performed gram stain examination on vaginal and urethra smears. When the laboratory reported that the tests were negative for gonorrhea, the physician told the couple that neither one of them had the disease.

Subsequently the couple sued the initial treating physician. When he was notified of the suit against him, he sent the slide containing the vaginal smear from the wife to two laboratories. Both laboratories reported evidence of gonorrhea. At the time the lawsuit was filed, expert testimony established that it was the ordinary community practice of physicians to use either the methylene blue test or the gram stain test in making diagnoses of gonorrhea.

The court pointed out a physician is not required to make a perfect diagnosis, but is only required to have that degree of skill and learning ordinarily possessed by similarly situated physicians. In this case the physician relied on the methylene blue test which was at the time a standard diagnostic aid for diagnosing certain types of gonorrhea. His interpretation of the test was confirmed therefore, even though his conclusion may have been in error, he was not liable to the patient.

If the physician knows, or should know, that the accuracy of the results of a diagnostic test are highly suspicious because they are at odds with the clinical presentation, he is obliged to investigate and to reconcile the discrepancies by repeating the test or ordering a more definitive test.

Price v. Neyland. A baby was born to an Rh-positive homozygous father and an Rh-negative mother. Before the baby was born, the mother had a positive Coombs test indicating her sensitivity to her Rh-positive fetus. This information was recorded in the mother's chart which was available to the pediatrician. Although the baby appeared healthy at birth, within two days of life she developed jaundice. The pediatrician diagnosed the neonatal jaundice as "physiologic." This diagnosis was based primarily on laboratory tests made a few hours after the baby's birth, which reported that the baby's Rh-factor and Coombs test were negative. In fact, these tests were erroneous. A test, which would have proved the presence of bilirubin in the baby's brain, was not performed. Moreover, in spite of the fact that the second blood count, made on the fourth day postpartum, showed a significant drop in the hemoglobin no follow-up hemoglobin test was ordered. Relying on the mistaken laboratory tests, the pediatrician ignored the jaundice, ordered no further tests, and allowed the baby to be brought home. The jaundice persisted, the baby developed kernicterus and permanent brain damage. On behalf of the child, the parents sued the pediatrician.

Expert testimony established that a baby of an Rh-positive homozygous father and a sensitized Rh-negative mother would encounter a serious blood incompatibility at birth. In addition, it was established that when laboratory tests are unexpected, unlikely, or inconsistent with clinical findings, the laboratory tests should be repeated. The court pointed out that where a baby of an Rh-positive homozygous father and an Rh-negative mother developed jaundice in the first few days of life, diagnostic monitoring and follow-up testing was required. The court held that if the tests had been repeated, pathologic jaundice would have been established and an exchange transfusion would have been performed to avert brain damage. On the basis of what the physician knew, or should have known, about the blood incompatibility and the clinical findings presented by the baby, he should have realized that the tests were in error or incompatible and should be investigated further. Under these circumstances, he was liable for his mistaken diagnosis.

The failure of a physician to effect a cure or bring about a patient's complete recovery is not necessarily evidence of negligence because negligent professional conduct cannot be presumed solely because the patient has an untoward or unsatisfactory result.

Hawkins v. Ozborn.   A nine-year-old boy experienced intermittent abdominal cramping, vomiting, diarrhea, and fever. The next morning his family physician's examination disclosed hyperactive bowel sounds, generalized abdominal tenderness, but no rigidity or rebound. The physician's clinical impression was "acute infectious gastroenteritis." He prescribed an antibiotic and antiemetic. During the night the nausea, vomiting, and diarrhea progressed. Therefore, the next day his physician hospitalized him and ordered intravenous fluids and medication. His admission white blood cell count was 18,000. There was no vomiting after admission and the abdominal findings remained the same for twenty-four hours. Although he considered other diagnostic possibilities, including appendicitis, the physician's working diagnosis remained acute infectious gastroenteritis. The next day the white blood cell count was 16,800 and the abdominal findings were unchanged.

During the late night hours of his second hospital day the child's condition materially worsened. He vomited bile and complained of increased abdominal pain. For the first time his abdomen became distended. Early the following morning the physician observed the patient's condition to be significantly changed from the previous evening. Now the patient had a distended, rigid abdomen, severe generalized abdominal tenderness, and absent bowel sounds. The physician diagnosed an "acute abdomen," and requested immediate surgical consultation with Dr. Booth, a general surgeon.

Dr. Booth ordered x-rays, which demonstrated distention of the small bowel with air-fluid levels. He diagnosed a perforated appendix complicated by small bowel obstruction. A laparotomy disclosed a ruptured appendix and peritonitis. The child remained critically ill for several weeks. The parents, on behalf of their child, sued the family practitioner for negligent misdiagnosis.

At trial, Dr. Booth expressed the opinion that if the case had been referred to him earlier, the most likely diagnosis, considering the patient's age, would have been appendicitis. This view was based upon clinical findings of fever, nausea, vomiting, abdominal tenderness, and elevated white blood cell count. Dr. Booth testified that it was difficult to determine rebound pain, and he did not regard the presence of hyperactive bowel sounds, or the absence of abdominal rigidity or distension, as findings not suggesting appendicitis. Dr. Booth conceded, however, that symptoms of gastroenteritis would be the same as those noted by the family practitioner.

All other expert medical testimony contradicted Dr. Booth's opinions. Two surgeons affirmed that the diagnosis of acute infectious gastroenteritis was the correct working diagnosis. One surgeon opined that the patient probably had infectious gastroenteritis from the time of the initial examination until two days later when he developed acute appendicitis, secondary to the original infection. Both surgeons testified that this was an atypical case of appendicitis. They also testified that peritonitis rapidly develops following rupture of the appendix, and noted that the peritonitis which was found at the time of surgery was approximately ten hours after abdominal distention was first noted.

The court decided from conflicting medical evidence that the clinical findings manifested by the patient during his first two days of hospitalization clinically presented a case of acute gastroenteritis. Later in the clinical course and secondary to the gastroenteritis, an acute appendicitis developed, which ruptured. The court concluded that as the symptoms usually associated with appendicitis became apparent, surgical consultation for the treatment of an acute abdomen was obtained. Therefore, the physician was not negligent for mistaken diagnosis.

4
COMMUNICATIONS ABOUT TREATMENT

An attending physician who undertakes to diagnose and treat a patient's condition has a responsibility to disclose to the patient the nature of the diagnosed disorder, hazards of and alternatives to treatment, and proper instructions needed for continued treatment and follow up. The physician may also have an obligation to disclose errors made in treatment, or those made by another physician of which the physician becomes aware in subsequently treating the patient.

In addition, a physician is expected to communicate properly to other involved personnel, information necessary for the proper care and safety of the patient. The information required to be communicated is that data which is germane to diagnosis or treatment of the patient's condition. However, when a patient's condition and/or treatment would not have been changed even if pertinent information had been communicated, a legal course of action will usually not be established for failure to transmit it.

As the generator and custodian of the patient's medical information, a physician may be requested to disclose it to third parties. In doing so, a physician should not disclose confidential information arising from the physician-patient relationship, except under special circumstances. If disclosure is permitted or required, the physician must present the information in an objective manner, and must also avoid, if possible, conflict of interest situations.

SECTION 1: DISCLOSURES RELATING TO A PATIENT'S CONDITION

Generally, a physician has a duty to make proper disclosures as to a patient's condition. As the following cases indicate, this duty may include cautioning a patient as to future activities, advising a patient of potential hazards involved in a course of therapy, or of the adverse effects of a particular disease.

A physician who does not tell a patient about a known injury and does not warn a patient to be cautious about stresses that would aggravate the injury, may be found to have been practicing below the standard of care. If the physician's failure to advise the patient caused subsequent injury, liability would be established.

Martisek v. Ainsworth. A man sustained serious injuries as a result of a fall while working. He was hospitalized and the attending physician diagnosed fractures of the elbow and calcanus. The following day, x-ray examination disclosed compression fractures of two vertebrae, but the physician did not tell the patient about the back injuries and prescribed no specific treatment for them. He told the patient that there was nothing wrong with his back and did not instruct him to limit his activities.

After the patient was discharged from the hospital, he returned to his job and performed only light work for some time because of persistent back pain. Gradually, he began working an eight-hour day. Although he suffered back pain, he was not aware that his back had been injured. Several months later, he reinjured his back as a result of helping a fellow employee lift a sixty-pound weight. The injury ultimately required an orthopedic operation and he was further disabled. The patient brought a malpractice suit against the first physician for failing to inform him of the extent of his injuries and failing to advise him of his physicial limitations as a result of those injuries.

The orthopedic surgeon who operated on the patient's back testified that the injuries sustained in his original accident rendered the patient's back vulnerable to the subsequent back injury. The court concluded that the physician's conduct was negligent in failing to inform the man of the extent of his back injury and in failing to instruct him to limit his activities. The court pointed out that a layman, drawing on general experience and common sense, could determine the relationship between the physician's failure to advise the man about his condition and the subsequent injury.

When serious side effects are known to be associated with a medication, a physician is obligated to advise a patient, or those responsible for the patient, of the hazards involved in a course of therapy.

Sharpe v. Pugh. The family physician of a two-year-old child gave her a prescription for Chloromycetin on three occasions for viral infections and tonsillitis within a six-month period.

Literature prepared by the manufacturer of Chloromycetin contained the following information:

"WARNING"

Serious and even fatal blood dyscrasias (aplastic anemia, hypoplastic anemia, thrombocytopenia, granulocytopenia) are known to occur after the administration of chloramphenicol (Chloromycetin). Blood dyscrasias have occurred after both short-term and prolonged therapy with this drug. Bearing in mind the possibility that such reactions may occur, chloramphenicol should be used only for serious infections caused by organisms which are susceptible to its antibacterial effects. Chloramphenicol should not be used when other less potentially dangerous agents will be effective, or in the treatment of trivial infections such as colds, influenza, or viral infections of the throat, or as a prophylactic agent.

Precautions: It is essential that adequate blood studies be made during treatment with the drug. While blood studies may detect early peripheral blood changes, such as leukopenia or granulocytopenia, before they become irreversible, such studies cannot be relied on to detect bone marrow depression prior to development of aplastic anemia.

On the last occasion of treatment, the physician advised the continuation of therapy with the drug, even after the parents informed him that the child had developed extensive "red spots" (petechiae) on her body. Thereafter, the child developed aplastic anemia and sustained a secondary fatal intracranial hemorrhage. The parents sued, charging that the physician had a duty to warn the parents that taking the drug might produce side effects including aplastic anemia. They contended that they would not have permitted use of the drug in treatment of the child had they been advised or warned of the known danger. The physician contended that he was under no legal duty to explain to the parents the properties of the drug which he, in the exercise of his professional judgment, prescribed. He also argued that he had no duty to warn them that the taking of Chloromycetin might produce dangerous side effects.

The court declined to define precisely the extent and limits of a physician's legal duty to disclose the possible adverse effects which may arise from the use of a prescribed drug, because such a determination would invade the province of the physician's professional judgment. Nevertheless, it stated that a physician would be negligent if he prescribed, as a remedy for illnesses for which it was neither necessary nor suited, a drug which he knew or should have known had dangerous side effects without advising and warning the child's parents of the possible injurious effects related to its use.

A variation of the preceding situation involves therapeutic hazards which become known only after initial treatment was properly provided. A physician whose nonnegligent therapeutic efforts subsequently places a patient at serious risk of harm may be required to warn and advise the patient of these developments. To simply ignore the potential harm to the patient by taking no action to preclude or minimize it, may represent a passive act of negligence.

Tresemer v. Barke.   In 1972, a physician inserted a Dalkon Shield in the uterus of his patient. At that time it was one of the most popular and acceptable intrauterine devices on the market and it was believed to be one of the safest and most effective. Approximately two years later, serious question as to its safety was raised and was acknowledged in the general medical community. Shortly thereafter the device was withdrawn from the market.

Although the physician had become aware of the newly discovered hazards of the device, he made no effort to so inform patients whom he had previously provided with Dalkon Shields. One of these patients became pregnant with the device in place. The device caused her to have a septic abortion that was fraught with complications. The patient sued the physician. She contended that he had failed to warn her that the Dalkon Shield was a potential health hazard, even though he had acquired actual knowledge of the danger.

The court stated that the duty to warn patients of newly discovered dangers of treatment arises by virtue of the trust and confidential relationship between the physician and the patient. Where the danger grew out of an act that was performed in the context of the physician-patient relationship, the continuation of that status imposes a duty to warn. However, where such a duty is recognized, it only requires the physician to take some reasonable action under the circumstances to warn his patients. Failure to make a reasonable effort may be construed to be a passive act of negligence.

If medical treatment is administered as part of a mass health program in which physicians are not expected to assess the medical risks of the treatment in light of their knowledge of each patient's needs and susceptibilities, an involved third party may have a duty to warn participants of the risks involved in the treatment.

Cunningham v. Charles Pfizer & Co., Inc.   In 1963 a medical society and health department sponsored a polio immunization clinic, using Sabin oral polio vaccine. Pfizer furnished the vaccine, which was produced and manufactured in accordance with U.S. government specifications. Physician members of the medical society sponsoring the program were available at each distribution point to answer questions about the vaccination, and were aware of information concerning the relationship between ingestion of the vaccine and the onset of polio. However, Pfizer made no effort to furnish this information to participants in the mass immunization program. A 15-year-old boy took Type I vaccine as part of this program. Pfizer gave no direct warning to him or his parents concerning possible untoward effects of the vaccine. Within five weeks after he took the vaccine, the boy contracted a paralytic disease.

On behalf of the child, his parents sued Pfizer, contending that Pfizer failed to warn the boy, or his parents, of the risk of contracting polio from the vaccine. Pfizer countered by contending that they had no duty to warn ultimate consumers of the risks involved in taking the vaccine, but only had a duty to warn physician members of the medical society sponsoring the program.

The court pointed out that, generally, in cases involving prescription drugs, a drug manufacturer has only a duty to warn the prescribing physician because in such cases the choice involved is essentially a medical one, which involves an assessment of medical risks in the light of the physician's knowledge of his patient's needs and susceptibilities. Further, it is difficult under such circumstances for the manufacturer, by label or direct communication, to reach the consumer with a warning. A warning to the medical profession is in such cases the only effective means by which a warning could help the patient.

With reference to a mass immunization program, however, the court declared that although the drug was denominated a prescription drug, it was dispensed to all comers at mass clinics without an individualized balancing by a physician of the risks involved. In such cases (as in the case of over-the-counter sales of nonprescription drugs), warning by the manufacturer to its immediate purchaser will not suffice. Thus the court concluded that in certain circumstances, such as mass immunizations, a drug manufacturer may have a duty to ensure consumers are warned of known risks involved in taking a drug, and failure to fulfill this duty would then make the manufacturer absolutely liable for injuries caused by the drug. At the time the boy took the vaccine, Pfizer was aware of a report of the special advisory committee on oral poliomyelitis vaccine that indicated that the committee had reviewed a number of cases of polio associated with administration of Type I vaccine. Therefore, Pfizer had a duty to warn participants by available means of communication, such as posters, releases to be read and signed by recipients of the vaccine, or prescribed oral warnings.

A physician is obligated to inform patients of the probability that they or their children will be adversely affected by a disease if such information is likely to be important to them for decision-making.

Gleitman v. Cosgrove. On April 20, Mrs. Gleitman was examined by Dr. Cosgrove and determined to be two months pregnant. When she informed Dr. Cosgrove that on or about March 20, she had had an illness diagnosed as German measles, he responded that Rubella would have no effect on the child. Her next visit was in July, at which time she saw Dr. Cosgrove's associate, Dr. Dolan. Mrs. Gleitman repeated her inquiry about the effects of German measles and again received a reassuring response. Similar inquiries and responses occurred on each of her subsequent monthly visits. A few weeks after her baby's birth, multiple congenital defects of Rubella syndrome became apparent.

Mrs. Gleitman and her husband sued. Their medical expert testified that a physician, knowing that Rubella had occurred during the first trimester of pregnancy, should have informed the patient of the likelihood of birth defects because women who have Rubella in the first trimester of their pregnancy have a 20 to 50 percent chance of producing infants with birth defects. Dr. Cosgrove testified that some physicians would recommend and perform an abortion for this reason, but he did not think it proper to "destroy four healthy babies because the fifth one would have some defect."

The court held that the physician had a duty to inform his patient of the possibility of birth defects. It concluded that Mrs. Gleitman's physicians negligently failed to inform her of the effects which Rubella might have upon the infant then in gestation. Had she been so informed, she might have sought other medical advice and obtained an abortion.

A physician's obligation to advise patients as to various health hazards and matters must be performed as carefully and accurately as circumstances will allow. This does not mean, however, that the physician must be perfectly correct in the prognostication.

Greinke v. Keese.   After evaluating his patient, the physician diagnosed "progressive exogenous obesity, hypercholesterolemia, cirrhosis of the liver and gout." The physician had treated the patient for some time and was familiar with his life-style and general health status. On this basis he advised the patient that he had "about 12 to 18 months to live." Relying upon this information the patient decided to take an early retirement from his employment. This resulted in a substantial detrimental change in his financial status. After the patient's survival exceeded the physician's prediction, the patient sued the physician charging that the prognosis was improperly made and the advice was negligently given. He did not charge that the physician had given him wrong advice as to treatment of medical conditions.

The court noted that prediction of the length of a patient's life under any circumstances is difficult and somewhat speculative. The court concluded that the physician had expressed his opinion based on his knowledge and experience. It was not possible for the physician to undertake an investigation that would have established the inaccuracy of his prediction. The court pointed out that a physician's opinion of longevity, based on his knowledge of the patient's physical and mental condition, if proven erroneous, should not form the basis of a legal cause of action for recovery against the physician, unless the physician had given the wrong advice as to *treatment.*

SECTION 2: THE PHYSICIAN'S INSTRUCTIONS TO THE PATIENT

In addition to the requirement that a physician make proper disclosures as to the patient's condition, a physician is required to instruct a patient as to the hazards of a particular course of therapy, the hazards of future activities, or the need for future care. Instructions often are required for the care of an illness, for follow-up therapy, or the occurrence of complications. The following cases explore and illustrate these situations.

In instructing the patient as to matters concerning the care of an illness or injury, the attending physician's instructions must be as specific as the situation warrants, taking into account such factors as the nature of the condition and the capacity of the specific patient to comprehend and comply.

Crosby v. Grandview Nursing Home.   A woman who worked at a nursing home fell while engaged in her employment and fractured the fifth metatarsal bone of her foot. Her physician applied a walking cast and instructed her to refrain from walking on the cast until it dried, after which time she could resume her ordinary duties at the nursing home. After the cast was removed he told her to "guard her activities." Two weeks later she complained of severe foot pain and the physician diagnosed acute muscle strain. Disapproving of the type of shoes she was wearing, the physician told her to get herself some "decent supportive shoes" to see if the shoes would relieve the complaints. He did not detail the type of "supportive" shoe she required, nor did he indicate that she should have an arch support molded to her foot. The foot pain persisted for several months. When the physician detected tenderness over the attachment of the plantar ligament to the calcaneus, he told her the supportive shoes were "not doing the job," and he mentioned that arch supports molded to her foot might be helpful. However, he did not give more explicit instructions, nor did he advise her that such supports were a special medical appliance.

The persistent foot pain prevented the patient from carrying on her job responsibilities at the nursing home. Therefore, she applied for Workmen's Compensation. The Compensation Commission's hearing examiner determined her foot strain was the result of failure to wear proper shoes, and thus was her own fault. When she was denied Workmen's Compensation benefits, she appealed to the court for judicial review.

The court pointed out that if further care were required, it was the duty of a physician, in the treatment of an injured patient, to furnish instructions as to the care of the injured part of the body. If a physician's failure to properly do so aggravates the original injury, his conduct would be negligent. In reversing the decision of the hearing examiner, the court concluded that the physician had not given his patient proper instructions as to the necessity for, and the type of, shoes she should have worn. Therefore, she could not be held responsible for the prolongation of her disability.

If ongoing or additional evaluation of a patient is necessary to effect a complete recovery, a physician is obligated to advise the patient of these further requirements. Thus an attending physician has the burden of establishing an understanding with the patient regarding the responsibility and details for follow-up care, including further visits if they are needed.

Barnes v. Bovenmyer. While a man was using a hatchet, a small piece of steel flew off and struck his eye. He went to a hospital emergency room where he was examined by an ophthalmologist. A red spot was noted on the sclera, which might have indicated a contusion or a point of entry of a foreign body. An injury to the lower eyelid was probed and a piece of steel was removed. The ophthalmologist thought that this was probably the only foreign body in the eye. A piece of steel imbedded in the orbit had gone unnoticed, however, and was not detected on the x-ray of the eye. The ophthalmologist told the patient he thought the foreign body was removed. When the patient asked the ophthalmologist if he should see him again, the ophthalmologist told him it was not necessary. He also told the patient there was no reason he could not go back to work the following day.

The next day the patient's eye pain became progressively worse. Because of the intensity of the pain, the patient returned to the ophthalmologist's office the following afternoon. An x-ray disclosed a sharp metallic 2 mm X 1 mm foreign body in the orbit. The patient was transferred to a university hospital for removal of the foreign body. The patient sued the ophthalmologist for failing to diagnose the foreign body sooner by means of appropriate follow-up.

Expert medical testimony established that it was part of the standard of care for treatment of such patients for the physician to direct the patient to see him the following day, so that further examination of the injury could take place. The court pointed out that it is an attending physician's duty to follow up on the case properly and to give proper instructions to the patient to accomplish this purpose. The failure to do so in this case was a negligent act.

Wells v. Woman's Hospital Foundation. The patient underwent a total abdominal hysterectomy. She experienced a wound dehiscence shortly after the sutures were removed. Her surgeon resutured the incision. After her discharge from the hospital, she returned to him on several occasions for treatment and finally for removal of the sutures.

Subsequently, she moved to another city. Because of pain in the area of the incision, she was hospitalized by a Dr. Moore who determined that the surgical wound had become infected. On July 7, he reopened, cleaned, and packed the wound with iodoform gauze. It was repacked and the patient was discharged from the hospital on July 9. The following day she returned to the hospital and the wound was again repacked. On her visit to the hospital on July 13, Dr. Moore told her that he had unpacked the incision and that she should "go home and take it easy."

Although the discharge summary of her medical records indicated that she was to "return to the clinic" two weeks after her discharge, Dr. Moore had not instructed her to return for further treatment. Approximately six weeks later she experienced abdominal pain and went to a different hospital. X-rays of her abdomen disclosed a foreign body. She underwent surgery and an iodoform gauze was removed from a site near her previous incision. The patient brought suit against Dr. Moore for having left the gauze inside her.

Expert testimony established that although it was customary procedure to place such gauze inside an infected incision, it was not customary practice to leave the gauze inside a wound for longer than one week. The court concluded that the physician was careless in explaining the nature and time of the postsurgical follow-up visits. This negligence made him unable to provide his patient with necessary and required aftercare.

A physician is expected to anticipate recognized complications and provide the patient with instructions which will signal the occurrence of these complications to effect early detection. The physician is expected to impart to the patient sufficient information to return if further care becomes necessary. The following case illustrates a situation where this duty was specifically fulfilled and the patient's attempt to prove insufficient instruction failed.

Reynier v. Delta Women's Clinic, Inc.   The patient's first trimester abortion by suction and curettage had been uneventful and uncomplicated. After a ninety-minute stay in the recovery room, she drove home. When she left the clinic she was given two printed documents which covered the course she would follow and what signs she should look for in the following weeks. One set of instructions entitled, "FOLLOW-UP INSTRUCTIONS," had a subheading, "THIS IS VERY IMPORTANT," which instructed:

> You may return to work the next day, but we recommend that athletics and strenuous activity be avoided for five days. You may experience light bleeding for some days after the procedure. During the next four weeks you may also have spot bleeding. . . .

Further down in the instructions, under the heading "IMPORTANT: WHAT TO DO ABOUT FEVER, BLEEDING OR PAIN," was the following instruction:

A small amount of bleeding occurs normally within the uterus (womb), and may cause a few cramps and brief increased bleeding as the uterus later pushes out some clots. You may need medication to help the uterus to contract. Continued heavy bleeding, severe cramps, and a high fever may indicate tissue retention which could require a repeat emptying of the uterus (this is a very rare complication).

PLEASE CALL THE CLINIC IMMEDIATELY IF:

1. You have more bleeding than your normal period.
2. You continue to bleed longer than two weeks.
3. You have a temperature of 101 degrees (or over 100 degrees on three consecutive readings).
4. You have severe cramps or pain.
5. You have a discharge with a particularly unpleasant odor. . . .

Cramps, even heavy cramping is normal for up to a few days, but sharp pain is not. Call at once if you're in doubt. For most women, the cramps you have right after the procedure will gradually subside over several hours. If yours are too severe to respond to the medication you've been given or do not improve after considerable rest or sleep, give us a call. The best way to handle even heavy cramps is to recline or sleep, allowing your body to relax. For most women, normal bleeding after the procedure will be the same as or not much heavier than your regular period, and will usually decrease gradually over a few days. Call us if you experience continuous heavy bleeding for more than 4 days, or have any fresh bright red bleeding after 48 hours. Nausea, headaches, dizziness, chills? Call us.

The other document entitled, "GETTING IT ALL BACK TOGETHER," stated the following:

DO: Get back to "normal" life as soon as possible—your usual work and exercise or return to school (except for physical education for two weeks).

Come back for a check-up at the appointment time arranged. Call us if you have or suspect any problems.

DON'T: Overtire yourself or take up unusual strenuous exercise in the next few weeks. (horseback riding, swimming)

Use Tampons until your next regular period, as to do so now could promote infection.

Swim or douche until the bleeding has completely stopped or preferably two weeks.

Avoid intercourse for FOUR WEEKS.

By the time the patient arrived home from the clinic she was in pain and bleeding. A neighbor called the physician who had performed the abortion. The physician prescribed Methergine and told the patient to call back if her problems persisted. After she took the medication, her pain subsided and the bleeding ceased for the next five days. Two days later when she went on vacation, she began bleeding heavily during the airplane flight. When she landed she was taken to a hospital and given a transfusion. Exploratory abdominal surgery uncovered a large peritoneal hematoma and a perforated uterus. A hysterectomy was performed immediately.

The patient sued the physician who had performed the abortion. She claimed that she had received confusing and inconsistent postoperative instructions that had urged her to resume a normal life as soon as possible and to avoid strenuous exercise for a few weeks, which had misled her. She attempted to demonstrate inconsistencies in the oral and written instruction. The court declared that a physician would be accountable if documents furnished to the patient as part of postoperative care were misleading and consequentially caused the patient subsequent problems. However, in this case, the court found no causal relationship between the document and the injuries sustained. The court pointed out that the written instructions contemplated mild cramping, but advised that if severe cramping continued, the patient was to call the clinic. The court determined that the patient had taken parts of the printed text out of context in an attempt to prove the instructions were conflicting. When read as a whole, the court concluded the overriding message was for the patient to call if there were any problems that seemed unusual to the reasonably prudent person. As proof that the patient had understood the import of the instructions, the court pointed out that a neighbor had called the clinic at the patient's request.

SECTION 3: THE DUTY TO DISCLOSE PHYSICIAN ERRORS

The attending physician's duty to make proper disclosures about the patient's condition encompasses the concomitant duty to disclose material errors in treatment made by treating physicians.

Duty to Disclose a Physician's Own Errors
A physician is required to make reasonable disclosure of errors in treatment, especially when the concealment of such facts would foreseeably have a significant and substantial deleterious effect on the patient's health.

Dietze v. King. During a radical mastectomy the patient's blood pressure dropped to 90/70. Realizing that the patient was in danger, the surgeon drastically curtailed the time of the operation. His primary purpose was to get the patient off the operating table as soon as possible. A sponge, sequestered in a small "pocket" in the axilla, went unnoticed and was not removed. Postoperatively, the patient continued to drain from the operative site for longer than would be expected. The surgeon made the following notation in her medical record:

The patient was seen daily in the hospital on the above dates and the wound was dressed as needed. She wishes to return to England. In view of the fact that there is still a slight drainage from the operative wound on the breast, the possibility of a foreign body in this wound must be considered and x-rays should be obtained. She states that she feels fine and is perfectly able to travel and is therefore going to England in spite of the fact that I would prefer that she stay here until she has fully recovered. She will have the ship's doctor check her and upon arrival in England will get in touch with a surgeon. An abstract of her record will be forwarded to the doctor there upon receipt of his name and address.

Two days later, on the patient's last visit to the surgeon's office, he changed her dressing and she picked up a letter written by the surgeon to the surgeon in London who would care for her there. The letter stated:

Dear Dr. Kimerling:

Mrs. Dietz has requested that I furnish you with an abstract from her recent record. She was found to have a mass in the upper outer quadrant of the right breast. A frozen section biopsy showed carcinoma and a radical resection of the breast was immediately carried out. The pathological diagnosis was comedo-carcinoma of the breast with no metastasis to the axillary lymph nodes.

Following the surgery, Mrs. Dietz has has persistent drainage which has been quite difficult to clear up. However, the prognosis in her case is very excellent and we do not believe that x-ray treatment is indicated. I would greatly appreciate a note from you in regard to this patient. She is a very delightful person and I do hope that her drainage clears up very rapidly.

When the foreign body was ultimately discovered, the patient sued the operating surgeon, charging that he had a duty to disclose his suspicions to her before he discontinued his treatment and she left the country.

The court pointed out that knowing of his patient's intentions to permanently leave the country made it all the more imperative that the physician act upon his suspicions. Although the physician contended that he was not required to act upon mere suspicion, his own expert witnesses testified to the contrary. The court pointed out that the letter to his patient's subsequent physician was evidence that the physician was not candid in disclosing all of his suspicions or beliefs as to the cause of the continued drainage. The court concluded that it was improper for a competent surgeon, suspecting that he had inadvertently left a foreign body in the operative wound, to permit a patient to leave the country without at least advising the patient of his suspicions.

If a physician becomes aware of an error in treatment, and acts to mitigate a resultant injury to the patient, his responsibility for a patient's injuries is limited to that which results from the error. If, however, the physician negligently fails to discover the initial negligent error, he may be liable for the damages that result from both acts of negligence. If the physician intentionally conceals his malpractice, he may become liable for the initial negligence and the negligence in failing to disclose the error. In addition, under such circumstances punitive damages may be awarded, as in the following case.

Dill v. Miles. After consultation with his physician regarding the diagnosis and treatment of vascular disease in his lower extremity, the patient was advised to undergo a lumbar aortogram to aid the physician in determining the nature and extent of the patient's condition. In attempting to perform the procedure, the physician made numerous insertions with a six-inch needle into the area of the spinal canal without aspirating for blood. In doing so, he made repeated injections of contrast media into the patient's spinal canal. The aorta was never located and blood vessels supplying the spinal cord were traumatized. Immediately upon regaining consciousness from the general anesthetic, the patient experienced excruciating pain and paresthesia in his lower extremities. When the patient asked the physician if his leg problems were caused by the procedure, the physician responded that the aorta had not been located or penetrated, and the aortogram had not been performed.

Within the seventy-two hours following the attempted aortogram the patient lost functional control of his bowels, bladder, and lower extremities. Although he specifically asked his physician about the nature of his condition, the physician did not respond or do anything. The patient's neurological status became progressively worse over the next few days, but the physician did not inform the patient of the seriousness of his condition and did not advise consulting another physician. Finally, the physician withdrew from the case. The patient sustained permanent injuries and sued the physician.

The court concluded that the physician knew or should have known that the patient's injuries were critical. Nevertheless, the physician negligently concealed these injuries from the patient by willfully representing to the patient that his condition was neither serious nor the result of the attempted aortogram. The court held that it was the physician's duty to advise and recommend to the patient the services of other physicians. The physician had reason to believe that concealment of his negligent act might injure his patient. Therefore, his conduct indicated a reckless disregard and complete indifference to the probable consequences of his wrongful acts, and was sufficient to charge him with wanton negligence and make him responsible for both compensatory and punitive damages.

A physician whose conduct is not negligent initially may commit a negligent act by trying to conceal an unfavorable result.

Taylor v. Milton. The patient suffered urinary retention because of a urethral stricture. His family physician inserted a urinary catheter to which was attached a filiform. During the procedure a portion of the filiform broke off from the catheter and ultimately passed into the bladder. When the physician removed the catheter and filiform, he became aware that part of the filiform had been retained in the bladder. Nevertheless, he did not inform the patient of this complication. Thereafter, the patient experienced intense suprapubic pain. Subsequently, physicians at the university hospital removed the filiform, which was seven inches in length, and presented it to the patient who then instituted suit against his family physician.

The court held that the physician was negligent, not because his placement of the catheter evidenced a lack of skill or judgment, but because of his concealment from his patient of the presence of the filiform in the bladder. The physician's failure to advise his patient of this event was a negligent act because it caused prolongation of the patient's pain.

Duty to Disclose Errors of Other Physicians
If an attending physician is clearly aware of the malpractice of another physician, in treating his patient, he may be legally obligated to disclose this information to his patient if it would be pertinent to the proper care of the patient. Nondisclosure or concealment of malpractice by the treating physician or any other physician who subsequently discovers the treating physician's error compounds the initial negligent act; it prevents the patient from obtaining medical treatment necessary to minimize the harm of the original malpractice.

One basis for this obligation of disclosure is the physician-patient relationship which establishes a special duty requiring a physician to disclose the clinical facts of the case to the patient. The silence or nondisclosure of a subsequent attending physician who has discovered a prior treating physician's errors may be sufficient to infer a form of negligent misrepresentation on his part.

Lopez v. Swyer. Mrs. Lopez underwent a radical mastectomy for metastatic carcinoma of the breast. Postoperative radiation therapy was recommended by her surgeon. He referred her to a radiation therapist who negligently administered an excessive dose of radiation. The patient's physical reaction to the radiation therapy was dramatic and calamitous. She experienced severe pain, nausea, and burning during treatment. Subsequently, she developed necrotic ulcers and spontaneous rib fractures which required reconstructive surgery. During the treatment, she and her husband asked her surgeon whether "malpractice" was occurring. He replied, "This was not malpractice. This sometimes happens." (Subsequently, the surgeon could not specifically recall what was said during the conversation, but recollected only that he was "mainly a listener.")

Several years after the radiation therapy, while Mrs. Lopez was hospitalized in a medical center for a phase of multiple reconstructive surgery she required as a result of the radiation complication, she was displayed to a group of physicians by a professor of surgery. After the physicians examined her they retired to an adjacent room and discussed her case. Through a door left ajar Mrs. Lopez heard the surgeon state, "Here is a woman who was on 300 milligrams of Demerol a day, and still couldn't stand the pain. And there you see, gentlemen, what happens when the radiologist puts a patient on the table and goes out and has a cup of coffee."

Thereupon Mrs. Lopez sued the radiation therapist and the surgeon who performed the mastectomy. As to the surgeon, she contended that he had intentionally misled her by giving her false reassurances which had the effect of keeping her from seeking proper medical advice relating to the effects of radiation. She also contended that the failure of her surgeon to come forth with proper advice concerning her radiation reaction constituted a wrong.

The court pointed out that the relationship between a physician and his patient is of such a vital nature that there exists an affirmative duty requiring the physician to disclose to his patient the full facts of the medical case. Therefore, silence in this regard may be sufficient to infer a wrongful misrepresentation. However, the court noted that judicial caution should be exercised in the application of such a rule in order to be fair to the physician who must often exercise clinical judgment relating to medical considerations of whether certain patients, such as cancer patients, should be "told."

As stated above, if an attending physician observes evidence of a negligent act committed by the patient's prior physician that has caused an injury to the patient, he may be obligated to disclose the fact of injury to the patient and to give advice as to the appropriate treatment in order to minimize the results of the other physician's malpractice. Failure to do so may constitute negligence. In jurisdictions which require physicians to act as their patients' fiduciaries, both the fact of injury and the fact of negligence may need to be disclosed. Thus, a physician may be liable for failure, without sound medical reason, to tell the patient about a foreign body which the physician did not leave in a patient, but knew or had reason to believe was left in by another physician.

Tramutola v. Bortone. Based on a bronchogram, the patient's family physician diagnosed "bronchiectasia and stenosis of the right middle bronchus." He referred her to a thoracic surgeon who performed a right middle lobectomy. Postoperative x-rays, taken while she was still in the hospital and under the care of her family physician, clearly disclosed part of a surgical needle in the right lung. After her discharge, the patient continued to receive regular postoperative treatment by her family physician. She continually complained to him of sharp right-sided chest pain. He performed radiological examination on most of the visits, but never informed the patient of the finding of a needle in the lung. Instead, he indicated that the pain was "muscular" and in time would clear up. For several years, she was treated by her family physician and was in constant pain and concern about her condition. Thereafter, she consulted another physician who took x-rays and informed her that there was a metallic object in her chest which was probably part of a surgical needle which had been used during the lobectomy; by now the needle had been encapsulated by scar tissue, and more difficult to locate and remove. The patient sued her family physician, charging him with negligent failure to disclose a retained foreign object.

The court pointed out that a physician, entrusted with the postoperative care of a patient and who has reason to believe that a foreign object was left in the patient's body by a surgeon, has a duty to disclose the facts to his patient unless there is sound medical reason for not doing so. Thus the family physician was negligent in having observed the needle in the patient's chest and in not informing the patient of its presence so that she could have it removed before it caused prolonged pain and became encapsulated.

The court pointed out that the physician's negligence was not related to technical matters peculiarly within the knowledge of a physician because there was no proof of any sound medical reason for nondisclosure. Therefore, the jury was competent to resolve the question of his negligence without the guidance of expert testimony.

If a physician not only conceals important information from the patient, but in addition knowingly and intentionally misleads the patient as to the patient's actual condition, thereby depriving the patient of an opportunity to remedy a medical predicament created by the physician's own negligence, his conduct is fraudulent.

Simcuski v. Saeli. Dr. Saeli excised a right posterior cervical lymph node. During the operation, he negligently injured the spinal accessory nerve. Following the operation, the patient told him that it was difficult and painful for her to raise her right arm and shoulder. Although Dr. Saeli was aware that as a result of his negligent surgery, his patient had sustained a potentially permanent injury, he told the patient that her postoperative problems would disappear if she would continue the regimen of physical therapy which he had prescribed.

Three years later while still undergoing physical therapy, the patient was first apprised by another surgeon that her condition had probably been caused at the time of her surgery. This surgeon also told her that reanastomosis of the severed nerve three years after the surgery would not bring about physiologically successful results.

The patient sued Dr. Saeli for fraud, charging that he had advised her that physical therapy would produce a cure even though he knew it was untrue and that she had to rely on his advice. She contended that this fraudulent misrepresentation deprived her of the opportunity for sucessful repair of the condition initially caused by his negligence.

The court pointed out that ordinarily a physician's concealment of his own malpractice does not give rise to a legal cause of action in fraud, which is distinct from the customary malpractice action. A legal action for fraud must establish that the physician knew (or had reason to know) that he negligently injured his patient; and thereafter he knowingly made material misrepresentation concerning his malpractice and the therapy appropriate to its cure. In addition, it must be established that the patient was diverted from undertaking an available, efficacious remedy in consequence of the misrepresentation.

The court pointed out that Dr. Saeli purposefully concealed and misrepresented the fact and consequences of his malpractice to the therapeutic detriment of his patient. Therefore, his misrepresentation to his patient was not merely negligent but intentional and fraudulent.

SECTION 4: COMMUNICATION AMONG PHYSICIANS AND OTHER HEALTH CARE PERSONNEL

The preceding three sections have dealt with the physician's duty to communicate with the patient about the patient's condition. Other requirements in the area of communications about treatment involve communication among health care personnel. For example, a physician may be required to notify another physician or other health care personnel of medical data concerning the patient. This duty may arise where there is a subsequent change in diagnosis or where such information would be helpful to other health care personnel in their evaluation and treatment of the patient.

Communication Among Attending Physicians

An attending physician has a continuing responsibility to assist other health care providers as long as the patient's condition requires it. Thus, if it is reasonable to assume that a subsequent treating physician will probably rely upon a former diagnosis, there is a duty to notify the physician who has assumed the care of the patient if subsequent developments cause a change in the basis of the original diagnosis and treatment.

Welch v. Frisbie Memorial Hospital.   While on an automobile trip, a woman was injured in an accident and sent to a hospital where Dr. Grigg examined her tender, swollen, and discolored leg. He suspected a fracture of the distal aspect of her leg and ordered an x-ray of her entire leg. Dr. Grigg was not aware of the fact that the x-ray technician did not include the ankle in the x-ray study. Therefore, when he received an oral report from the radiologist that no fracture was noted, he told the patient that she had a sprained ankle with no fracture. When he discharged her from the hospital the following day he instructed her to see her family physician when she arrived home from the trip.

Within a few days after the patient left the hospital, Dr. Grigg received the following typewritten x-ray report of his patient's leg: "Radiographic examination of the left knee and upper 3/5 of the leg show no evidence of injury from a radiologic standpoint."

Three months later, x-ray examination at another hospital disclosed a Potts fracture of the ankle. By this time the fractured bones had united in poor position, causing ankle deformity and dysfunction. Subsequent treatment provided only slight improvement. As a result the patient sued Dr. Grigg for negligent attention to her case.

She contended that it was the attending physician's duty to do what reasonable care required to ascertain that the x-rays were of the portion of the body which he suspected might be fractured. Dr. Grigg contended that his responsibility for the patient's case terminated when she left the hospital. With reference to the x-ray report he testified:

> PLAINTIFF'S ATTORNEY: And you didn't pay any attention to the report that came in later?
>
> DR. GRIGG: As the patient had been sent home when the report came in, I put it in my file without making a study of it.
>
> PLAINTIFF'S ATTORNEY: Did you write a letter or get any word to her in any way that the report of the hospital was different from what you had understood it to be previously?
>
> DR. GRIGG: Obviously not. I explained to her that she must be under the care of her family physician when she got home.

The court pointed out that originally Dr. Grigg diagnosed that the patient was suffering only from a sprained ankle. But when subsequent information demonstrated that the ankle was not shown in the x-ray, he should have reconsidered the basis of his original diagnosis. As long as the patient's recovery continued to be dependent on the accuracy of his diagnosis, his duty of care persisted. Having informed the patient of his diagnosis and directed her to call her own physician, he should have realized that the results of his own diagnosis would be projected into the future care of the patient. Therefore, when he subsequently received information indicating that the assumed basis of his diagnosis was lacking, he was required to notify the patient or her current attending physician of this new finding.

An attending physician may be obligated to communicate with a physician who previously has been responsible for the patient's medical care, especially if the prior treatment is likely to increase the risk of any proposed treatment. When the physician cannot reasonably obtain information about the prior treatment or is not otherwise aware of such treatment, this duty does not arise. However, if a physician's lack of knowledge of prior treatment results from failure to obtain an adequate medical history from the patient, liability might be imposed on that basis.

Langford v. Kosterlitz. The patient suffered from chronic asthma. Treatment by several physicians had provided only temporary relief. One physician had performed an operation on the patient's nose in which part of the middle turbinate bone and also some infected ethmoid sinus cells had been removed. This procedure likewise failed to provide satisfactory abatement of his symptoms.

Still seeking relief, the patient consulted another physician. He related to this physician the history of his asthmatic condition, including the treatment by other physicians and the facts of the prior operation as he knew them. The physician then examined the patient and told him that he could cure his condition by a procedure which he described as "deadening nerves," called the sphenopalatine ganglion. He told him it involved placing a needle deep inside the nose and injecting medication into a nerve plexus. The physician asked the patient if he wanted to have him "do it right now." The patient said he would like to consider it. He then told the physician that he thought it would be a good idea for the physician to call up his prior physician who had operated on his nose and ask him just what he had done. The physician told the patient that would be a good idea; however, he made no effort to contact the other physician.

When the patient returned for the procedure, the physician sprayed the patient's nostrils with a local anesthetic, inserted a four-inch metal tube into the nostril, and punctured a bony wall. He then inserted a hypodermic needle through this tube and infiltrated the area with a solution of alcohol and novocaine. Instantly, the patient had a sensation of a spark in his eye and immediately lost sight in that eye. Severe optic atrophy developed and the patient sued the physician.

Expert testimony established that the needle would have had to be in proximity to the optic nerve to produce the blindness and that the turbinate bone, if it had been intact, would ordinarily have protected the optic nerve from such injury. The court concluded that because the physician was aware that the patient's prior operation had been performed in the area where he planned to perform this procedure, he was negligent in not consulting the prior physician about the nature and extent of that operation before he proceeded with his proposed therapeutic procedure.

If certain information about a patient's medical condition would not have been necessary for proper evaluation or would not have made a substantive difference in treatment of the patient, failure of health care personnel to communicate it would not breach the standard of due care.

Brown v. U.S. A fifty-eight-year-old patient had severe diabetes mellitus, chronic obstructive pulmonary disease, cirrhosis, hypertensive cardiovascular disease, and arteriosclerotic peripheral vascular disease. He made regular outpatient visits to a Veterans Administration clinic. In April, on a regular routine visit, an atypical T-wave pattern was noted on his electrocardiogram. On another regular outpatient visit in October, a chest x-ray disclosed cardiomegaly and questionable mild pulmonary congestion.

On November 3, his wife called his Veterans Administration physician and told him that her husband was short of breath on exertion, sleeping all the time, and not eating. His physician suggested that he be brought to the clinic, but the wife did not feel that she was able to do so because of his weak condition. Therefore, the physician arranged for an ambulance to take him to the Veterans Administration emergency room for an evaluation.

At the emergency room he was examined by a physician who was familiar with the patient's poor health status. The physician noted that the patient was smoking and appeared comfortable. He was not pale, diaphoretic, or in acute distress. Although his cough seemed to be a little worse, he was breathing normally and his lungs were clear. His heart rhythm and pulse were normal. The physician called the outpatient clinic and obtained a verbal report that the patient's most recent chest x-ray did not show signs of pneumonia. The physician attributed the patient's status to his chronic illnesses. He detected no abrupt changes or acute distress. He did not feel hospitalization was warranted.

After returning home the patient gradually became worse over the next two days during which time he was seen by another physician. He was also taken to a private hospital, but was again sent home. On November 5, he was hospitalized, and died the next evening of an acute myocardial infarction. The widow sued the Veterans Administration, contending that its physicians were negligent in failing to send the electrocardiogram and the x-ray reports from the clinic to the emergency room. She claimed that these reports represented important medical information which, if communicated, would have led to hospitalization and an electrocardiogram which would probably have disclosed a coronary occlusion. The physician who declined to hospitalize the patient at the Veterans Administration hospital testified that, even with the benefit of the patient's prior x-ray and electrocardiogram, he would not have hospitalized the patient because these reports and his clinical status did not suggest evidence of an acute illness.

The court pointed out that the clinical findings were not indicative of a patient who was gravely ill and in need of immediate hospitalization. Because the clinic information would not have made a difference in the treatment which the patient received, the court concluded that the emergency room physician's failure to obtain the reports from the clinic was not a breach of the standard of due care.

Communications Among Attending Physicians and Other Health Care Personnel

An attending physician, as the preceding subsection indicates, may have a duty to consult with a former or subsequent treating physician as to a patient's condition. Likewise, an attending physician may have a duty to effectively communicate patient care information with nonprimary-care physicians and other health care personnel involved in the treatment of a patient. As the first case illustrates, communication in this area may simply require that an accurate medical record be available to appropriate personnel who are involved in caring for the patient. Liability may be established if a physician fails to provide such a record if inadequate treatment or disposition results.

Whitree v. State.   A patient was supposed to have been released from a state psychiatric institution in 1949. The psychiatrist in charge of the case, however, failed to make appropriate notations on the patient's chart so that his discharge could be processed. The psychiatric notes only indicated that the patient was severely disturbed. He was classified as "very hostile" and was disciplined by hospital personnel because he doggedly insisted that he was supposed to be released. When he was released finally in 1961, he sued the psychiatrist for failing to provide proper care while he was in the hospital.

The court held that it was negligent to fail to keep necessary health-related information and notes on a patient's case, and to fail to transmit them properly. The court concluded that a hospital record develops information for subsequent treatment of a patient. Information not properly recorded or transmitted would contribute to the inadequate and negligent treatment the patient received. The court further stated that the hospital record maintained by the state for the patient did not conform to the standards in the community, and that the inadequacies in the record militated against proper and competent medical care being given the patient while at the hospital. The court further found that lack of proper psychiatric care was the primary reason for the patient's inordinate length of incarceration and concomitant side-effects of physical injury and mental anguish.

A nonprimary-care physician, such as a radiologist, is also obligated to report significant diagnostic and therapeutic findings, even though such findings may have no connection with the primary consultative request and inquiry of the attending physician.

Capuano v. Jacobs.   The patient's chief complaint was low back pain. The attending physician ordered a lumbosacral series to assist in the diagnosis of this problem. A radiopacity was apparent in the area of the patient's right kidney, but the radiologist did not report it because it was outside the scope of the information requested of him by the attending physician. Several months later the patient developed hydronephrosis, secondary to a kidney stone. Ultimately the patient required a nephrectomy.

The patient sued the radiologist, alleging that earlier diagnosis of the presence of the kidney stone would have prevented the loss of her kidney. The court held that the radiologist was negligent in failing to transmit the finding of a radiopacity. His failure to report this finding caused a worsening of the subsequent kidney disease.

A physician may be obligated to communicate information about the patient's health status to other health care personnel who are also charged with the care and attention of the patient, especially if such communication is likely to avoid a preventable injury to the patient.

Thompson v. U.S.   The patient was admitted to the hospital for knee surgery. On his first day of hospitalization he was given Codeine at 3:35 P.M. and at 8:15 P.M. to relieve his knee pain. At about 9:00 P.M., he was given Seconal to help him rest. At 10:55 P.M., he awakened, having difficulty breathing, and complained of chest pain which radiated to his left arm. The physician on duty was notified of these complaints. At 11:05 P.M., the physician ordered an intramuscular administration of Vistaril and an aminophylline suppository. He did not give nor did he write an order to limit the patient's activities. All of the above complaints and medications were recorded in the "Nurses' Notes."

The following morning at 7:00 A.M., the nurse who came on duty examined the patient's records and noticed the drugs that he had been given. Because the patient was allowed to be fully ambulatory, she gave him a lab slip and instructed him to go downstairs to the laboratory for preoperative tests. He walked unassisted to the lab where he fainted while standing in line. The fall traumatized a finger, which subsequently required amputation. The patient sued the hospital for negligently causing his injury.

Expert medical testimony established that the conduct of the staff physician was negligent. Considering the mixture of drugs administered to the patient during such a short interval, and taking into account the possible potentiating effect of the drugs and the patient's symptoms, the physician should have specifically placed in the "Doctor's Orders" instructions limit-

activities. The court suggested that the physician should also have ordered that a warning sign to this effect be placed on the patient's bed, so that other health care personnel would be aware of the patient's condition. The court also determined that the nurse was negligent because she was aware of the patient's medication history, and yet she sent him to the lab unassisted and unaided. The court pointed out that had the patient been on a stretcher or in a wheelchair and lost consciousness, he would not have been injured.

Negligent miscommunications may lead to actionable legal consequences, especially where they involve diagnostic tests for conditions which should alert the physician and other health care personnel to take additional precautions in ordering and performing tests.

Favalora v. Aetna Casualty and Surety Co. A patient was hospitalized for evaluation of syncopal episodes. Skull x-rays were ordered. Neither the physician who ordered the x-rays nor the ward nurses indicated on the requisition form sent with the patient to the radiology department that the patient had a history of syncope. The radiologist did not take a history or inquire about her major complaint or the reason for the x-rays. While the x-rays were being taken, the patient fainted and injured herself. She then sued her attending physician.

The court found the attending physician negligent because he did not record a history on the space provided on the request form, pointing out that a loss of consciousness was a strong possibility since syncope was the cause of the patient's hospitalization. Thus, the physician's failure to inform the radiologist that the patient was likely to faint was a negligent cause of her injuries. In addition, the court concluded that the radiologist was negligent for not communicating with those in charge of the patient to determine the reason for the examination, or else not taking a rudimentary history, as such information was lacking on the form.

SECTION 5: DISCLOSURE TO THIRD PARTIES

Generally a physician has a duty to the patient not to disclose to a third party, whose interests are adverse to the patient's, information obtained during the physician-patient relationship. The physician essentially owes a duty of loyalty to the patient to keep their communications confidential. Thus it may even be wrongful for a physician to disclose confidential information about his patient during the litigation process. Nevertheless a physician's candid disclosure of confidential information and his opinion may be required through proper legal discovery procedures. Prior to that compelling point, however, courts usually expect that physicians will not respond to questions from persons whose legal interests may be adverse to the patient's. This viewpoint recognizes that the fiduciary aspect of the physician-patient relationship makes the attending physician an advocate of the patient, even in circumstances involving matters ancillary to medical treatment.

Alexander v. Knight. Mrs. Alexander was involved in a rear-end automobile collision. After the accident, she experienced headaches, neck and back pain. She was hospitalized by her physician and administered analgesics, neck traction, and physical therapy for several weeks. She wore a cervical collar for six months. Several months later, she was rehospitalized for low back pain and left-sided numbness. At the request of her attending physician, she was examined by Dr. Murtagh, a neurosurgeon. He concluded that she had sustained a moderately severe "whiplash" injury of the cervical spine and that she had pronounced muscular spasm. He was also of the opinion that a marked hysterical element made her symptoms more severe because the patient was emotionally unstable.

Mrs. Alexander brought a personal injury claim against the other driver involved in the accident. Dr. Erickson, a physician who was frequently employed by defense attorneys to interview physicians who had treated an injured plaintiff and to secure reports from them, requested a report from Dr. Murtagh. He paid Dr. Murtagh fifty dollars for a report on Mrs. Alexander's condition, which stated:

> It is my opinion that there was very mild musculoligamentous strain at the time of the accident, but no neurogenic involvement to suggest permanent neurologic sequelae, and that the prognosis for recovery of this mild strain should be very good. Her somatic symptoms, meaning joints and things, however, have been perpetuated by an underlying pre-existing anxiety neurosis and hysteria, centered about an hysterical personality.

Despite the fact he never received permission from Mrs. Alexander or her attorney to disclose such information, Dr. Murtagh gave this report to Dr. Erickson who gave it to the insurance company which employed him.

During the personal injury litigation, the propriety of Dr. Murtagh's conduct was raised. The court pointed out that members of the medical profession stand in a confidential or fiduciary capacity to their patients. Thus physicians owe their patients more than just medical care for which payment is exacted; there is also a duty of total care which includes a duty to aid the patient in litigation, to render reports when necessary, and to attend court when needed. The court concluded that this duty includes an obligation to refuse affirmative assistance to the patient's adversary in litigation. In qualifying this obligation, the court recognized that a physician owes a duty to his conscience to speak the truth. However, it noted that a physician need speak only at the proper and required time in the litigation process.

As the preceding case indicates, a physician is expected to exhibit a certain degree of loyalty to the patient. This allegiance may involve assistance in litigation or it may require that a physician not assist a patient's adversary. Thus ordinarily the physician should avoid a situation where to serve a third party's interests conflicts with the duty owed to the patient. The following cases explore this area, and as the first case points out, even the best interests of the children of a marriage may not be a sufficient reason for a treating physician to breach the duty of loyalty owed to the patient.

Schaffer v. Spicer. In 1965, a woman was granted a divorce from her husband and was given custody of their three children. Over the next few years, for various reasons, the father had custody of the children. Finally, the father brought a legal proceeding to require his ex-wife to show cause why custody of the children should not remain with him. Attached to the motions submitted in this proceeding was an affidavit written by the woman's former psychiatrist. In extensive detail, it divulged information that he had obtained while treating the woman over a two-week period in 1964. Many of the details of the information acquired by the psychiatrist from his patient during his treatment of her were transmitted in the presence of her then husband who had paid for the treatment.

The legal proceeding brought by the ex-husband was concerned with his ex-wife's mental condition and her fitness as a mother. Exposition of these issues was intended to enlighten the court in its task of awarding custody of the children. The psychiatrist responded to the ex-husband's request for information to be used ultimately in a custody proceeding. As a result of the psychiatrist's records and conclusions, the woman's ex-husband was awarded custody of their children. The woman then sued her former psychiatrist for breach of confidentiality.

The psychiatrist contended that information contained in the affidavit was published in the best interests of the children. The court, however, noted that the loyalty required of a physician to his patient establishes a duty to refuse affirmative assistance to the patient's legal adversary.

The court pointed out that it may be permissible for a physician to be examined and cross-examined as to information obtained in the course of a physician-patient relationship, by an attorney in a courtroom, in conformity with the rules of evidence, with the vigilant surveillance of the patient's counsel under the careful scrutiny of the trial judge. Nevertheless, the court concluded that it is quite another matter to permit an unsupervised communication of confidential information between the physician and his patient's legal adversary. Thus the court concluded that the information about the ex-wife's mental status had been improperly disclosed by the psychiatrist to her former husband.

In the preceding cases, the contractual duty of a physician regarding confidentiality has been illustrated. Another way in which the law protects the confidential nature of the physician-patient relationship is through the enactment of privileged communication statutes designed to prevent a physician from disclosing in court confidential information which was obtained from the physician-patient relationship. The following case illustrates the role of such a statute and its limitations. In this case it is important to note that, at least in this particular jurisdiction, public policy and the duty as to confidentiality arising from the physician-patient relationship are combined to effect a result in the patient's favor.

Hammonds v. Aetna Casualty and Surety Company. A defense attorney persuaded a patient's treating physician to surrender certain confidential information for use in litigation pending against the patient, on the false pretext that the patient was contemplating a malpractice suit against that physician. The patient subsequently sued the insurance company for inducing the physician to breach his duty of confidentiality to the patient, citing as a legal basis general principles of confidentiality recognized in the common law and the state's "privileged communication" statute, relating to testimentary disclosures.

The defendant insurance company contended that because there was no common-law privilege protecting communications between physician and patient, there could be no common-law action for the breach of confidence. Moreover, the company argued, the state's "privileged communication" statute merely precluded a physician from testifying in court as to communications received while treating a patient. Therefore, as far as the law and the statute were concerned, the physician could be uninhibited in private discussions about his patient.

The court recognized that when a patient institutes a personal injury suit it necessarily will lead to the ultimate waiver of the privilege of confidentiality on matters relevant to the claimed injury. Thus the privilege would not prevent pretrial discovery of medical evidence that would be placed at issue at trial. However, permission for an accelerated disclosure of the treating physician's opinion of the extent of a patient's injury does not permit a clandestine conference between a treating physician and the lawyer for his patient's adversary.

The court pointed out that when a course of conduct is shocking to the average man's conception of justice, it must be held to be contrary to public policy, even though such policy is unwritten. Any time a physician undertakes the treatment of a patient, and the consensual relationship of physician and patient is established, obligations are assumed by the physician. An implied condition of that contract is the physician's warranty that any confidential information obtained through the relationship will not be disclosed without the patient's permission. Moreover, the code of ethics adopted by the medical profession applied the confidentiality rule to private conversation with third parties. In addition, the public is aware of the promise of discretion and the safeguarding of patient secrets contained in the Hippocratic oath, and thus a patient has a right to rely upon this warranty of silence. Consequently, when a physician breaches his duty of secrecy, he is in violation of a public trust and his obligations under contract, his profession's ethical code, and his own sworn oath.

Disclosure of information obtained during the course of physician-patient relationship to third parties may, however, be acceptable and possibly even required under certain circumstances. In such situations the physician is usually not acting as a therapist, but as an examiner for the benefit of a third party. Although the following cases involve improper disclosures to third parties, fault is not found because of the physician's disclosure of information about the patient to an insurance company, but rather because of the failure to provide an objective report because of a conflict of interest on the part of the reporting physician.

Brousseau v. Jarrett.   A boy sustained a fractured femur when he was struck by an uninsured motorist. The boy was insured under his father's Allstate Insurance policy, which contained an "uninsured motorist provision." By the terms of that provision the boy was entitled to compensation for all damages for which the uninsured motorist would be legally liable, up to $15,000. His parents took him to an orthopedic surgeon to attend the injuries which he had sustained. The surgeon frequently prepared reports at the request of insurance companies regarding his examinations and findings of individuals injured in auto accidents.

In August and October of 1971, Allstate requested the attending surgeon to furnish reports containing his prognosis of the boy's injury. The first report was submitted by the surgeon on November 12, 1971, and stated that

> The above-captioned patient was struck by a car on 8–6–71, with a resultant fracture of the left femur in the immediate subtrochanteric area. He was placed in Buck's traction and did very well. On 9–11–71, he was discharged after the fracture had united securely enough to allow it to be placed in a one-and-a-half hip spica.
>
> X-rays throughout have indicated that the patient has had excellent healing. The patient has excellent configuration and good healing at the

fracture site. Particular mention was made by one of your agents regarding the possibility of injury to a growth cartilage. His growth cartilage was not injured, in that it was not close to the fracture site. It would be very unusual for the growth cartilage to permaturely close with a fracture at this level. At this stage, it would be highly unlikely likewise that the patient would show an avascular necrosis of the femoral head. This is still a possibility; however, I believe that it is rather remote. I do not believe that the patient will have further residual and I believe that shortly he will be ambulating without significant limp.

The second report, submitted on December 23, 1971, stated:

The above-captioned patient was last seen in this office on December 10. At that time he had no symptoms whatsoever. He still had a slight limp. I would expect his limp to disappear as he becomes more confident. . . . I do not believe he needs physiotherapy or any other means to treat the patient's limp or disability or for that matter residual from his accident in the future.

As to psychological implications, I believe that the patient is a very healthy young man coming from what appears to be a stable family and as near as I can determine I do not believe there will be major psychological difficulties which would be directly related to the accident.

The surgeon's records and reports relating to the nature and extent of the injury, impairment of function, disability and prognosis were used as a basis for settlement of the claim for damages arising out of the injuries sustained by the boy. Based upon the attending surgeon's reports of a favorable prognosis, Allstate offered $7,500 rather than the $15,000 limit requested by the parents for settlement. Dissatisfied with the offer, the parents retained an attorney to secure a more advantageous disposition of the claim. After retained counsel convinced Allstate that the medical reports were unduly conservative and inconsistent with the sequelae and residuals which are ordinarily known to follow injuries of the type sustained by the boy, the claim was then settled for the full policy limits of $15,000.

The parents subsequently sued the attending surgeon for $3,897.11, the amount incurred for attorney's fees and litigation costs. They charged that their son's injuries were known, or should have been known, to be of a potentially more serious nature with reference to future impairment and disability than the physician reported. They contended, therefore, that his conduct in drafting an unduly conservative report was negligent, and because of the nature of the report, Allstate offered less than the claim was worth. The surgeon contended that he owed no legal duty to the patient to prepare medical-legal reports in a fashion other than conservative.

The court pointed out that the parents contracted with the attending surgeon for the purpose, among others, of having the surgeon furnish to authorized persons medical-legal reports containing his prognosis as to re-

sidual disability from the accident. The court held that this contractual relationship was sufficient to create a duty to furnish an objective prognosis.
This duty arises from the physician's employment to perform the specific
professional service.

The court intimated that the attending physician's objectivity may have
been effected by a conflict of interest; he was frequently requested by insurance companies to conduct examinations and render reports because he traditionally prepared his reports in a conservative fashion favorable to the
insurance companies' position. The effect of such an approach was to minimize in each case the nature and extent of the residual disability, thereby
providing the insurance company with a better negotiating position. The
court also noted that a substantial portion of the physician's income from
his medical practice was derived from preparing such reports and testifying
in court on behalf of the insurance companies.

Kelley-Rickman, Inc. v. Hartford Life Insurance.   Mr. Rickman, who was
president of Kelley-Rickman, Inc., applied for a "key-man" life insurance
policy on July 25, 1972. The insurance company sent a request for medical
information to Dr. Kelley, the person whom Mr. Rickman had designated
on the insurance application as his private physician. This "attending physician's statement" was filled out on July 31, 1971 by Dr. Kelley who was
both Rickman's family physician and business partner. Dr. Kelley's carefully
worded statement purported to summarize the findings of various physicians and hospitals concerning Mr. Rickman's health. He represented that
there were no "absolute" findings of a coronary occlusion; and that "after a
thorough study at a medical center, it was determined that Rickman had not
had a coronary occlusion, and that there was nothing significant in Rickman's cardiovascular status." As worded, the statement was consistent with
Rickman's claim that he had never had any "heart trouble." Rickman thus
was approved for the insurance without any further investigation by the insurance company and the policy was subsequently issued at a standard premium. Eleven days after the policy was delivered to Rickman he entered the
hospital with complaints of chest pain, which he indicated to the admitting
physician had been progressive over a period of two months. He died three
weeks later as a result of complications of a myocardial infarction.

In processing the claim for death benefits on the policy, the insurance
company observed that entries in Dr. Kelley's own records contradicted his
"attending physician's statement." In addition, in a letter that was written
by Dr. Kelley in November 1964, in connection with a lawsuit involving
Rickman, Dr. Kelley represented to the court that Rickman had suffered an
acute anterior coronary occlusion and had suffered from angina pectoris
since that time. He also indicated that Rickman had been hospitalized on at
least three different occasions since then for sequelae of his original coronary

occlusion. He concluded that the emotional trauma of a court appearance would probably precipitate an attack of angina pectoris and, therefore, should be avoided "for the sake of the possibility of morbidity or mortality to this individual."

The court found that both Dr. Kelley and Rickman concealed, misrepresented, or falsified the medical facts to induce the insurance company to issue the policy without making further inquiry into Rickman's health status. The insurance company reasonably assumed that Dr. Kelley had fairly and truthfully stated all pertinent medical facts. On the basis of Dr. Kelley's statement, the insurance company could have reasonably assumed that no further investigation of Rickman's medical history was needed. Therefore, the court held that the contract for life insurance had been based upon a material misrepresentation of the facts and, therefore, could be rescinded by the insurance company.

5

CONSENT TO MEDICAL TREATMENT

Implicit in the physician-patient relationship is the expectation that a physician will obtain the patient's express or implied consent to treatment. A consent form signed by a patient is not conclusive evidence that the patient's valid consent was obtained. The physician must usually demonstrate that a voluntary and informed consent has been obtained from the patient or from another legally authorized to grant consent for medical treatment.

A physician is expected to sufficiently inform the patient of the nature and effect of the proposed treatment to allow the patient to personally decide whether to submit to it. Thus the physician must disclose material facts, risks, and alternatives of a proposed treatment unless there is a sound medical basis for concluding that it would not be in the patient's best interest to receive a full disclosure. Misrepresenting or misleading the patient as to the facts and circumstances of the condition, or of the treatment, may vitiate a patient's consent.

If the patient lacks the capacity to be informed of the nature and need for the treatment, or is unable to appreciate that a treatment decision should be reached, "substituted judgment" may be made with legal endorsement on the patient's behalf. If the patient has legal capacity to make an informed decision, even as to life-saving treatment, the patient may decline such care.

SECTION 1: DISCLOSURE OF INFORMATION FOR PATIENT DECISION

Questions of consent to medical treatment originate from, and are governed by, the contractual nature of the physician-patient relationship. Therefore, consent is given only in connection with what the physician and patient understood was to be done. A patient should be informed of material facts so that the patient can choose if he wants to undergo the proposed treatment, regardless of whether the choice is rational. This requirement is intended to give maximum effect to the patient's fundamental right to determine what medical treatment he will receive. However, the physician is not required to be a mind reader nor to disclose every possible risk in order to avoid liability for not having obtained adequate consent to treatment. A physician is only required to disclose to the patient those facts, risks, and alternatives which the physician knows, or should know, would be significant to a patient making a decision about the proposed treatment.

The cases in this section explore the required scope of the disclosure and illustrate legal requirements for valid consent to treatment. It should be noted, however, that there is a difference of opinion among the courts of various jurisdictions regarding standards of disclosure applicable in an informed consent dispute, especially with regard to the necessity for expert medical testimony. Requirements may vary from case to case, and the issue to be decided is whether the physician has met the standard of care for disclosure as established by the profession (in which expert testimony is required) or whether a reasonably prudent person would have acted as the physician did under similar circumstances (in which expert medical testimony is not required).

Generally, in order to obtain valid and informed consent from the patient for contemplated treatment, a physician is expected to determine what factors would be important in the decision-making process for a reasonable person in the patient's situation; that is, what does the patient need to know to decide whether to submit to the proposed treatment. Thus the physician necessarily is expected to determine to what factors, concerning the patient's condition and the proposed treatment, would the patient reasonably attach significance.

Canterbury v. Spence.   A young man was experiencing severe mid-dorsal back pain. When a myelogram disclosed a filling defect at the T-4 level, a neurosurgeon recommended a laminectomy, but did not inform the patient, who was a minor, or his mother that the procedure involved the risk of paralysis because it was not the custom of his fellow neurosurgeons to do so. At surgery, the neurosurgeon discovered that the patient's spinal cord was swollen and unable to pulsate. He also discovered an accumulation of large, tortuous, and dilated veins and a complete absence of epidural fat that normally surrounds the spine. He attempted to relieve the pressure on the spinal cord by enlarging the dura at the area of swelling. He also inserted a hypodermic needle into the spinal cord to aspirate any cysts, but no fluid emerged. During the postoperative period the patient became paralyzed from the waist down. The neurosurgeon reopened the surgical wound and created a gusset to allow the spinal cord greater room to pulsate. Although the patient's muscular control improved slightly, he was unable to void properly. Therefore he filed suit against the neurosurgeon, claiming the surgeon had failed to obtain his informed consent for the operation.

The surgeon testified that it was not good medical practice to inform patients of the risk of paralysis because the disclosure of this risk might deter patients from undergoing a needed laminectomy or such disclosure might cause an adverse psychological reaction that could decrease the probability of success of the operation.

The court noted that a physician's conduct is not necessarily measured by a customary professional standard when his conduct does not particularly involve his medical knowledge and skill. In such instances, the physician must conform to the general standard of care established by law; that is, he must exercise that care which a reasonably prudent person would have exercised under the same or similar circumstances.

The court pointed out that a patient has the right to decide what shall be done with his own body. However, a patient can effectively exercise this right to decide only if he has the proper information on which to base an intelligent choice. It is this right that determines the scope of disclosure that a physician must make, not necessarily the customary scope of disclosure dictated by the medical profession. The court concluded that the test for determining whether a particular fact or risk must be divulged is its materiality to the patient's decision. The patient must be informed of all material risks to which a reasonable layman would attach significance.

The type of information that must be disclosed to the patient includes the inherent hazards of the proposed procedure, the severity of the risk, the incidence of the risk, and the alternative methods of treatment available to the patient if he declines to consent to the procedure.

The court pointed out that disclosure need not be made in these situations: if the patient already knows of the risk; if the disclosure does not have any apparent materiality to the procedure or to the patient's decision; if a person of average sophistication would be aware of such risks; if as in an emergency situation the patient is incapable of consenting; and if the patient will become so emotionally distraught that he will not be able to make a rational decision.

In this case the court held that the testimony of the patient and his mother that the physician did not reveal the risk of paralysis from the laminectomy, made out a *prima facie* case of violation of the physician's duty to disclose. The court concluded that the physician's explanation did not suffice as a legal basis for withholding facts that were important to the patient's decision.

Sard v. Hardy. Prior to the birth of her third child (for which a Caesarean section was contemplated), the patient discussed the possibility of sterilization with her physician. She informed him that she did not want more children because she had "lost a lot of blood" during her pregnancies and could not "afford any more children." Subsequently, the physician stated on a routine sterilization consent form that "the patient has been personally examined by me and I feel that future pregnancies will endanger her life. Therefore, sterilization is recommended." The physician did not inform her of the various methods available for performing a tubal ligation because he felt it was good medical practice merely to inform the patient that a tubal ligation was to be done. Moreover, he felt that the final choice as to which technique to employ generally is made by the surgeon only after he has surgically entered the abdominal cavity and observed the condition of the uterus.

At the time the procedure was performed there were several methods in common use for sterilization by tubal ligation. The physican used the Madlener technique which was the simplest, but had a higher risk of failure when performed at the time of a Caesarean delivery than other available methods under similar circumstances. The rationale for the various methods were never discussed with the patient, nor was it explained that the failure rates for all the procedures diminished drastically when performed at a time other than when a Caesarean section is performed.

The sterilization procedure proved ineffective and the patient became pregnant with her fourth child. She sued the physician, charging that he failed to obtain her informed consent for the Madlener procedure and, therefore, was responsible for the damages sustained as a result of its ineffectiveness.

The court concluded that the information withheld from the patient was material to the decision of a reasonable person in her position. It pointed out that under the circumstances, a reasonable person with the patient's physical and financial concerns about having another child would have attached significance to the Madlener technique's projected risk of failure. Thus, the patient should have been informed of the relative risk of continuing fertility if certain techniques were utilized and if they were done under certain circumstances. The physician did not inform her about the increased risk of failure inherent in sterilization performed at the time of a Caesarean section. Therefore, the patient was denied the opportunity of deciding whether to undergo the sterilization at delivery or at a later date when the risk of failure would have been reduced significantly.

The court pointed out also that in order for the patient to recover damages under the doctrine of informed consent, there must be a causal relationship between the patient's lack of information from the physician and the patient's ultimate injury. If disclosure of material risks would not have changed the decision of a reasonable person in the patient's position, there is no causal connection between disclosure and damage. In this case, however, the court concluded that the patient's decision to undergo sterilization was prompted by the concern that a subsequent pregnancy might endanger her health and her family's financial security. Thus, the effectiveness of the operation would have been an important factor in her decision-making process.

Although a physician must disclose material risks that are known to be associated with the procedure proposed, a physician is not expected to forecast unknown or unreported risks, or risks which result from a negligent act or which materialize under urgent circumstances.

Haven v. Randolph. A pediatrician referred his two-year-old patient to a pediatric surgeon who diagnosed that the patient had an occlusion of his renal artery, and recommended that the child undergo surgical correction of the disorder. In preparation for renal surgery, the two-year-old child underwent a transfemoral retrograde aortogram for the purpose of localizing the renal artery occlusion. The surgeon injected 10 cc. of Hypaque contrast medium into the renal artery. Although this dosage was scaled down from the usual adult dose, it represented the upper limits of safe dosage for a child. Notwithstanding the high dosage, the injection of contrast medium failed to disclose the location of the stenosis. Considering the hazard to the patient of a second aortogram versus the life-threatening status of the patient's condition, the surgeon elected to repeat the test with the same dosage twenty minutes later. After completion of the procedure, the child was noted to be paraplegic.

The parents sued their pediatrician and the surgeon who performed the procedure. They alleged that the risks of the procedure outweighed the benefits and charged that the physicians negligently advised them in order to obtain their consent. They claimed that the pediatrician admitted no experience with the aortogram, but said it would probably be "no more harmful than taking an aspirin." They admitted that the surgeon explained the procedure and its risks, but they charged that he did not mention the risk of paralysis.

The court was persuaded that the reason the surgeon did not explain the risk of paralysis to the parents was that there was no known instance of a child under nine becoming paralyzed because of an aortogram. In addition, the child was believed to be in a life-threatening condition; therefore, the risks of administering an increased dose of the contrast material was justified under the circumstances. Because there was no prior recorded instance of such a reaction to aortography in a child under nine, the court held that the risk taken was not flagrantly unreasonable.

As the preceding cases indicate, a physician who proposes to perform a procedure upon a patient must disclose the nature and need for the procedure, and certain risks associated with its performance. In addition, the clinical alternative to the proposed treatment should be discussed as illustrated in the following case.

Pegram v. Sisco. A thirty-five-year-old mother of eight children began to experience fatigue and heavy intermenstrual bleeding. She was evaluated by Dr. Applegate who performed a Pap smear which was reported as showing moderate dysplasia. When conization of the cervix disclosed early invasive squamous cell carcinoma, Dr. Applegate advised the patient that she should undergo a radium implantation. With the patient in his office, he telephoned Dr. Sisco at the hospital and set up a referral to the radiation therapy department. The patient neither saw Dr. Sisco nor talked with him over the telephone.

On the first night of her hospitalization the patient was prepared for the procedure by nurses, but neither Dr. Sisco nor Dr. Applegate visited her. The next morning she was administered an injection. Although she remembered being wheeled on a stretcher to an elevator, the next thing she remembered was waking up after the implant procedure had been completed. That evening Dr. Sisco visited her and inquired how she was feeling. The first time she realized that radium had been implanted in her uterus was several days later when the nurse came to take her to the operating room, saying that Dr. Sisco would now remove the implanted radium. She only saw Dr. Sisco the evening of the implant, the day he removed the implant, and the day she was discharged from the hospital.

After discharge from the hospital, the patient experienced persistent vaginal burning and diarrhea. Several months later she began to pass fecal material through her vagina. She consulted a gynecologist who diagnosed a radiation-induced rectouterovaginal fistula. This condition required a radical hysterectomy and a bowel resection. Thereafter, the patient sued Dr. Sisco for failure to obtain her "informed consent" to the radiation therapy.

The patient testified that no one explained to her the basic nature of the procedure, that is, that radium capsules would be inserted into her uterus, allowed to remain there for several days, and then removed. In addition, she was not told of any of the unpleasant aftereffects or possible complications. Moreover, she established that neither Dr. Applegate nor Dr. Sisco explained to her that a hysterectomy was an alternative therapeutic modality to the radium implant procedure. Had she been so informed, she claimed she would have under the circumstances, elected to have a hysterectomy. Expert testimony established that a prospective implant patient should be informed by the operating physician of the unpleasant aftereffects, the possibility of radium burns and fistula formation, and the alternatives to radium therapy.

Dr. Sisco contended that he was only called into the case as a "consultant," and that Dr. Applegate was the patient's attending physician until after the operation; therefore, it was Dr. Applegate's responsibility to obtain an "informed consent" for the procedure. Dr. Sisco testified that when he was first contacted about treating the patient, he assumed that Dr. Applegate had fully discussed the procedure with his patient.

The court pointed out that Dr. Applegate and the patient contemplated that the patient would be placed under the care of Dr. Sisco when she entered the hospital, and that he would assume responsibility for the radium implant. Moreover, expert testimony established that the operating physician is required to obtain an informed consent before performing a radium implant. Therefore, Dr. Sisco did not adhere to the medical standards when he "assumed" consent had been obtained by the referring physician and failed to obtain the informed consent for himself. Thus the court held that because he negligently failed to obtain an informed consent for the procedure, he was responsible for the patient's injuries which occurred as a result of the procedure.

Where the risk of serious disease is high and routine tests to confirm its existence are inconclusive, a physician is obligated to disclose to the patient the existence of the abnormal condition, and of reasonably available additional tests capable of more definitively diagnosing it. The purpose of this obligation is to allow the patient to participate in the evaluation decision.

Gates v. Jensen. An elderly woman with severe myopia, consulted Dr. Hargiss, an ophthalmologist, because she experienced difficulty with her vision. Dr. Hargiss checked her intraocular pressure with a Schiotz tonometer and found it to be 23.8 bilaterally on the Goldman scale, which he felt was in the borderline area for glaucoma. Without dilating her pupils, he examined her with a direct ophthalmoscope. He did not observe any "cupping" of the optic discs characteristic of glaucoma. In response to the patient's inquiry about the pressure test, Dr. Hargiss said he had checked for glaucoma but found everything all right. He neither told her that he had found high borderline elevated intraocular pressure, nor that her risk of glaucoma was increased by this high pressure and by her myopia. He did not inform the patient of the diagnostic value of relatively simple and available procedures such as dilating the pupils to obtain a better view of the optic discs, or performing a visual field examination to detect visual field loss. Dr. Hargiss performed no further tests for glaucoma. He diagnosed that the patient's visual problem was the result of her contact lenses.

Shortly after this visit, Dr. Hargiss performed another tonometric intraocular pressure test on the patient, found pressures to be in the "high range of normal," and concluded that the initial borderline high readings were caused by the patient's tension at being subjected to having the tonometer placed directly on her eye.

Over the next two years, Dr. Hargiss adhered to his initial diagnosis that the patient's visual problems were the result of difficulty adjusting to contact lenses. He did not dilate her pupils for funduscopic examination nor did he administer a visual field test, even though she returned on multiple occasions complaining of gradually worsening "blurring and gaps" in her vision, and decreased visual acuity.

In 1974, when the patient was diagnosed by another physician as having open angle glaucoma, she sued Dr. Hargiss. She alleged that he failed to inform her that she had elevated pressure in her eyes; that she was in a high risk group for glaucoma; and that there were alternative diagnostic procedures available to determine conclusively if she had glaucoma. She contended that Dr. Hargiss had a duty to tell her these facts, so that she could make an informed choice about treatments she would undergo; and that if she had been informed of these facts, she would have requested additional tests and glaucoma would have been discovered earlier. Expert testimony established that these additional tests were simple, inexpensive, reasonably conclusive, and relatively risk free. It was also established that myopic patients had a higher risk of developing glaucoma. Dr. Hargiss contended, however, that the "doctrine of informed consent" did not apply to questions of appropriate diagnostic procedures.

The court pointed out that a physician has a duty, based on the trust inherent in the physician-patient relationship, to inform a patient of abnormalities that have been detected in the patient's condition. The basis of this duty is the patient's right to know the material facts concerning his condition, and risks presented by that condition, so that he may make an informed choice regarding the course which his medical care will take. The court added that a patient's right to know is not confined to the choice of treatment once a disease has been conclusively diagnosed. Because important decisions ultimately affecting treatment frequently must be made in many nontreatment situations in which medical care is given, and should be made with the patient's knowledge and participation, the physician has a duty to tell the patient what he needs to know in order to make these decisions. The existence of an abnormal condition, the presence of a high risk of disease, and the existence of additional or alternative diagnostic procedures to determine conclusively the presence or absence of that disease, are facts which a patient must know in order to make an informed decision about his future medical care. Thus, a physician's duty of disclosure arises whenever he becomes aware of an abnormality which may indicate a serious risk to the patient. The facts which a physician must disclose are those facts which he knows, or should know, the patient needs to have the requisite capacity to decide and to choose his medical course.

A physician may violate the duty to properly inform the patient prior to obtaining consent, if facts necessary to form an intelligent consent to proposed treatment are withheld without justification. Minimizing known hazards of a treatment to induce the patient's consent may be tantamount to withholding necessary facts from the patient. The following case illustrates that liability may be established when a physician knew, or should have known, that more serious risks were involved in the procedure than had been indicated to the patient, thereby minimizing the risks in such a manner as to mislead the patient into giving consent for the procedure.

Funke v. Fieldman. Unforeseen complications prior to the birth of Mrs. Funke's child resulted in her obstetrician, Dr. Cowles, recommending and subsequently administering a caudal anesthesia for the birth. Mrs. Funke had no reaction to the caudal anesthesia. She continued treatment with Dr. Cowles and subsequently entered the hospital for a scheduled hysterectomy.

On the evening prior to surgery, Dr. Cowles visited her in her room and advised her that Dr. Fieldman was her anesthesiologist and he would be in to see her. Dr. Fieldman visited her that same evening and asked her what kind of anesthetic she wanted. She replied that Dr. Cowles had recommended a spinal, to which Dr. Fieldman replied, "Well, those are the best, I like to give those." He then went on to state that, "The most you could get from them is a headache and we have medicine for that now." He did not mention any other possible adverse consequences from spinal anesthesia. Mrs. Funke did not have any questions as to the advantages and disadvantages of the anesthesia. She thought the physician chose the anesthetic because she was never asked before. She had always relied upon the physician to provide the information.

The next morning Mrs. Funke was placed on the operating table in a forward flexed sitting position with her legs straight out. When the spinal needle was first inserted at the L2-3 interspace, she felt a sharp pain down her left leg and her leg jerked. Soon thereafter she felt another pain and remarked that "Something's wrong, my legs aren't going to sleep." Dr. Fieldman responded, "Well, maybe we had better remove the needle." Shortly thereafter her legs went to sleep. When the anesthesia disappeared, paresis and paresthesia of her left leg remained.

Mrs. Funke sued Dr. Fieldman because of these neurological defects. She charged that he had not obtained her informed consent to the procedure because he did not mention the known risk of nerve injury associated with the procedure.

The court pointed out that the reasonableness of disclosure to obtain an informed consent depends upon the facts and circumstances of each case. Therefore, the crucial issue was whether Dr. Fieldman had made a reasonable disclosure of the nature and hazards incident in the spinal anesthesia he proposed. The court held that Dr. Fieldman either knew, or should have known, that spinal anesthesia carried with it more risks than mere headaches. For example, expert testimony had established that one out of twenty-five people have an abnormally low-lying conus medullaris, which makes the patient vulnerable to nerve injury if a spinal needle is inserted at L2-3 interspace, rather than at the next lower interspace. The court concluded that although Mrs. Funke consented to spinal anesthesia, Dr. Fieldman failed to warn her that the procedure he undertook involved significant risk of bodily injury. When Dr. Fieldman told Mrs. Funke that a headache was the only possible danger, he misinformed and misled her. Her consent, therefore, was not an informed consent, and was therefore null.

The court pointed out that a physician is not obligated to disclose any and all results that might possibly follow a medical or surgical procedure because there may be circumstances under which it would be poor therapeutic practice to disclose the nature of possible adverse results of procedures. However, in this case, there was not silence on the part of a physician or simply a failure to make a disclosure, but rather a misleading statement by Dr. Fieldman upon whom Mrs. Funke was relying when she gave her consent for the spinal anesthetic. As such, the misleading statement was equivalent to a false statement by Dr. Fieldman and vitiated Mrs. Funke's consent.

In addition to legal jeopardy for encouraging treatment by not alerting a patient to the risks of treatment, under certain circumstances a physician may be exposed to legal liability for the manner in which he discloses his clinical impressions of disease as an inducement to obtain consent to commence what he feels is needed therapy. In these situations the reasonableness and propriety of the physician's conduct under the circumstances is often determinative of the issue of liability for such disclosures.

Kraus v. Spielberg. The physician had treated his patient previously for long-standing pulmonary tuberculosis. When tubercula were detected in the sputum, he ordered chest x-rays, which he interpreted as showing evidence of a tuberculous cavity rather than representative of chronic bronchiectasis. He became convinced that the patient's inactive tubercular condition had become active once more, and that the patient required antituberculant therapy. In addition, his patient began to complain of abdominal pains for which he could not find an obvious clinical explanation. Therefore, he informed her of the possibility that the "germs" may have reached her intestines. He told her that this possibility was added reason why she must embark upon chemotherapy at once.

The patient, an anxious individual who was always apprehensive concerning her pulmonary tuberculosis, became exceedingly conscious of the possibility of the spread of tuberculosis to her intestines. This concern caused her mental anguish. When she was subsequently told that her chest x-ray had only demonstrated chronic bronchiectasis, and that tuberculosis had not "reached her intestines," she sued her attending physician, charging that his statements and misinformation caused her to suffer from a "tuberculosis phobia."

The court noted that the physcian's statement to the patient that the "germs may have reached your intestines," even though not verified medically at the time was a statement of the well-known fact that tuberculosis could affect the entire body. Thus, such disclosure did not constitute a departure from the standard medical practice. The court pointed out that regardless of whether the disease was active or inactive, or whether it had invaded intestinal tissue, chemotherapy was designed to be effective against tuberculosis. The patient was suffering from abdominal pains thought to be the result of tubercular invasion. Under the circumstances, it was not unreasonable for the physician to encourage the patient to undergo therapy. The court pointed out that had the physician not disclosed the possible existence of disease and the patient thereby was injured, he could have been subjected to suit. Therefore the court noted that based on the patient's reasoning of liability, the physician was in jeopardy both for making the disclosure and for withholding it. The court reasoned that if physicians could be successfully sued for honestly explaining their clinical impressions to patients for the purpose of effectuating a swift cure, they would tend to avoid such disclosures. The practice of medicine might then become a secretive practice with physicians remaining uncommunicative to patients, delaying therapy, and withholding information for fear that frightened patients might turn on them. The court explained that psychic injury suits based upon fright caused by medical advice from a diagnosing physician should be confined to gross negligence, as in cases in which information communicated to obtain consent is not well-founded and induces harmful therapy.

There are limitations on how much material information must be disclosed to the patient for an informed consent. A physician is not, for example, expected to disclose those alarming risks to the patient that in the physician's best clinical judgment would be harmful to the patient. The following case explores the issue of when the withholding of information might be acceptable.

Nishi v. Hartwell. The patient, a dentist, had a history of hypertension and chronic renal disease. Because of severe and recurring attacks of chest pain, he was referred to Dr. Hartwell, a cardiologist, who hospitalized him. His pain persisted after hospitalization and required frequent administration of Demerol for relief. When x-rays indicated that the patient might be suffering from an aortic aneurysm, Dr. Hartwell discussed with the patient a plan to send him for surgery to a renowned cardiovascular surgeon. Dr.

Hartwell felt, however, that it was inadvisable to send the patient on a long journey without a definite determination that he had an aneurysm. Therefore, after consulting with Dr. Scully, a cardiovascular surgeon, Dr. Hartwell recommended an aortogram to the patient and obtained his consent for its performance by Dr. Scully. Dr. Hartwell explained the procedure to the patient, relating that his femoral artery would be opened, a tube placed in the artery and dye injected through the tube. However, Dr. Hartwell said nothing to him about the attendant collateral risk of paralysis. Dr. Hartwell's reasons for the omission were:

> Each person is different. This man was well educated, but, in addition, he was very frightened about his condition, he was apprehensive, and this actually guided our hand in much of what we did because if a man has a serious heart disease, with hypertension, and you thereupon frighten him further, you have a problem which you have created . . .
>
> He had pain in his chest and if I had sat down with him and said, "We are about to inject something into you which has a remote chance of causing you to be paralyzed, you may get an immediate reaction which will cost you your life," I think it would have been a terrible mistake. . . . He is a professional man, he's a dentist. I would dare say he's given thousands of injections of novocaine and he knows, as well as I . . . that every time you inject anything into somebody, a hazard exists, so that it didn't seem necessary to tell this professional man. He knows it. And, therefore, not very much was said to him by me about the dangers of the procedure. I wished to reassure him that we were doing everything we could to find the cause of his pain and so I think in talking to him, I said, "This is a fairly simple procedure, it simply is an injection of material into your circulation so we can outline the swelling or widening of your aorta."

Dr. Scully also explained the procedure to the patient. In his explanation, he went into the technical aspects of the procedure in greater detail than he would have done with an average layman but, as in the case of Dr. Hartwell, omitted any mention of the attendant collateral risk of paralysis. Dr. Scully's reasons for the omission were that he thought that full disclosure would not be in the patient's best medical interest in view of the patient's psychological condition alluded to by Dr. Hartwell; that he was of the opinion that the chance of the collateral risk materializing was relatively minimal.

As a result of the procedure, the patient was paraplegic and died shortly thereafter. His widow sued claiming that neither her husband nor she had been properly informed of the risk of treatment.

The court declared that from the explanations given to him, the patient had an understanding of the general nature and purpose of the procedure.

He was not told, and did not make any detailed inquiry about the kind of dye that would be used because he relied on his physicians. The court noted that the physicians' omission to disclose the risk of paralysis was within the exception to the duty of full disclosure which excuses the withholding of information for therapeutic reasons. The medical standard applicable to this case was that a competent and responsible physician would not disclose information which was likely to induce an adverse psychogenic reaction in a patient highly apprehensive of his condition. The court went on to say that in some situations it would be bad practice to make full disclosure to an unduly apprehensive patient.

The patient's wife contended that if the patient could not be told, she should have been told about the risk of paralysis. The court pointed out that the physicians owed no duty of disclosure to the patient's wife. The duty of a physician to make full disclosure is one that originates from the physician-patient relationship and thus it is owed to the patient himself and not to his spouse or any other family member. The court pointed out that if, in situations in which the patient could not be told, a physician has to obtain consent from a spouse, the necessary corollary of that requirement would be that the spouse could refuse her consent to the proposed treatment. The court declared that such a situation would be incongruous because a spouse does not have the legal right or power to withhold consent to necessary medical assistance.

The patient's wife countered this argument by equating the circumstances in this case to a situation involving a mentally incompetent patient or a minor patient, where the consent of a person duly authorized to act for such person is required. The court pointed out, however, that because a mentally incompetent patient or a minor has no legal capacity to act, a duly authorized guardian must act for such a patient. In the case of a minor, the duly authorized person is the minor's legal guardian, or his parent who is his natural guardian. Thus, although a physician must secure the consent of the parent to operate upon a minor child, unless duly authorized by law, a wife is not the guardian of the husband, and her consent is not necessary before a physician is authorized to perform an operation upon him. Moreover, the court pointed out, the patient in this case had the mental and legal capacity to grant consent.

The court took special note that when withholding important information from a patient is called for by therapeutic considerations, full disclosure to the immediate family may help the physician in deciding his course of action, because of the family's knowledge of the patient's reaction patterns. Nevertheless a physician does not have a legal duty to make such a disclosure to the family.

SECTION 2: UNAUTHORIZED TREATMENT

In general, a patient's consent must be obtained for the treatment that the physician plans to provide. This requirement is based on the consensual nature of the physician-patient relationship. In the preceding section it was noted that proper disclosure was necessary to fulfill the requirements of informed consent. This section further explores the nature and scope of consent for treatment, and points out the conditions under which it is required.

Medical treatment which involves a "touching" of the body represents a technical battery and as such is excusable legally only when express or implied consent has been obtained from the patient. Thus, where a patient is mentally and physically capable of consulting about a medical problem, his consent is a prerequisite to treatment. When a physician fails to obtain consent for treatment, a technical battery has been committed and the physician becomes liable for any injuries resulting from the unauthorized contact, even if the treatment was not negligently administered.

Lloyd v. Kull. During a scheduled operation to correct a vesicovaginal fistula, the surgeon observed and surgically removed a mole on the patient's leg. The patient sued the surgeon for battery, charging that the removal of the mole was unauthorized. The physican contended that the removal of the mole during the fistula operation was authorized by the patient when she gave written permission to operate. The patient's written permission to operate stated in part:

> I hereby authorize the physician in charge of Evelyn Lloyd to administer any treatment or to administer such anesthetics and perform such operations as may be deemed necessary or advisable in the diagnosis and treatment of this patient.
>
> Signed, Evelyn Lloyd

The court held, however, that the patient's signature on the consent form did not constitute consent to an operation other than the one scheduled to be performed, unless a necessity for additional surgery arose during the authorized operation. The court concluded that removal of the mole was neither necessary nor authorized. Thus, the surgeon had committed a battery.

Consent forms themselves do not necessarily preclude liability for unauthorized treatment. For a consent form to be effective at all, its terms must be clear and unequivocal.

Bowman v. Davis. Prior to an elective bilateral tubal ligation, the patient and her husband signed a "Patient Sterilization Consent Form" which de-

clared that they: "fully understood that the purpose and effect of such surgical procedure will most probably result in a failure to ever again create,
conceive or bear any more children." The form also indicated that the patient
and her husband ". . . voluntarily consent to this operation and absolve the
attending physicians and the Miami Valley Hospital from responsibility for
any untoward or unfavorable results arising from this procedure." The tissue report from the tubal ligation stated that tubal lumen had not been
found in the submitted specimens. In fact, the round ligament had been ligated instead of the fallopian tubes. Three months after the operation the
patient became pregnant and delivered premature twins, one of whom was
born with serious congenital abnormalities. The patient sued the gynecologist for negligent performance of the procedure. The gynecologist contended that he was released from liability because the patient knowingly and
voluntarily signed a sterilization consent form relieving him and the hospital
for the unfavorable results.

The court pointed out that waiver agreements which purport to release
a physician from the consequences of his negligence, but fail to express that
intent in "clear and unequivocal" terms, are legally unenforceable. Although
the hospital consent form was not a waiver agreement, the court noted that
the form appeared to have been designed to release the hospital and attending physicians from the consequences of their negligence. However, the intent was not set out in "clear and unequivocal" terms. Nowhere did the
form mention release from liability or negligence. Instead, it merely spoke of
absolving hospital and attending physicians from responsibility for "unfavorable results" of sterilization and it did not clearly state the kinds of
"unfavorable results" it covered. The only result of sterilization described in
the form was the "failure to ever again create, conceive or bear any more
children"; therefore the court interpreted the form to apply only to the
effects of a successful operation, and not as a release of liability for a negligently performed procedure.

Even though a patient may have signed a surgical consent form, a physician
should not proceed with an operation which the patient has emphatically
refused, unless an emergency arises endangering the life of the patient, or
unless at a time when fully oriented, the patient has changed his mind and
consents to its performance.

Demers v. Gerety.   Several days after he had undergone an ileostomy and
colectomy in Boston, a forty-year-old patient moved to Albuquerque. There
he consulted a surgeon because he noticed a lump on his abdominal wall.
Although the surgeon was not able to perform an adequate examination of
the lump because of the patient's discomfort, he diagnosed a ventral hernia
and recommended surgery. The patient stated that if repair of the hernia in

any way involved surgery on the ileostomy, he wanted to return to Boston for that operation. The surgeon agreed not to touch the ileostomy.

On admission to the hospital the patient signed a surgical permission form which described the operation to be performed as "repair of ventral hernia." That evening, after he had been given Nembutal for sleep, he was awakened by a nurse and told that "something had been forgotten" and had to be completed. The nurse did not turn the lights on, but merely pointed to a paper where the patient was to sign. The patient complied by signing another "authority to operate" form which described the surgery to be performed as "repair ventral hernia and revision of ileostomy." The patient, who spoke only broken English and had a sixth-grade education, later could not specifically recall signing this authority to operate.

The next morning the patient was taken to surgery. After he was anesthetized, the surgeon manually examined the abdominal mass in a manner more thorough than he was able to do while the patient was conscious. During this examination he discovered that the hernia protruded from the same opening in the abdominal wall as the ileostomy. He concluded that the repair of the hernia would require relocation or revision of the ileostomy. Thus he proceeded to repair the hernia and revise the ileostomy. Postoperatively the patient developed complications which required additional surgery and a protracted course of treatment. As a result, he sued the surgeon for performing unauthorized surgery on his ileostomy.

The court pointed out that the patient had given only a consent limited to the surgery of the ventral hernia by making it clear to the surgeon that if ileostomy surgery appeared necessary he wanted to return to Boston for such treatment. When he consented to the hernia repair he was alert, but when he "consented" to the additional procedure he was not fully aware of what he was signing. Therefore the court held that his signing of the second consent form was performed under circumstances suggesting improper inducement through the use of a clandestine protocol.

Exceptions to the Requirement for Consent

Emergency or Unanticipated Conditions

Generally a patient's express consent is a prerequisite to a surgical operation. An exception exists for emergency situations requiring immediate action for the preservation of the life or limb of the patient. Under these circumstances, it may be impracticable to seek to obtain the patient's consent or the consent of a person authorized to assume such responsibility. Thus the law assumes that the imperiled patient would have granted consent if able to do so. Therefore, the consent to perform life-saving surgery is implied by the law.

A physician usually may not extend the performance of an operation to one different in nature from that for which consent was given, or to one involving inherent risks and results not discussed nor contemplated. As the next two cases indicate, however, it is often unclear where to draw the line between acceptable behavior (correctly responding to unanticipated conditions) and unacceptable behavior (going too far beyond what was consented to).

Rogers v. Lumbermens Mutual Casualty Company. Despite her and her husband's desire for children, Mrs. Rogers had been unable to conceive. She was distressed by her inability to bear children and was determined to overcome her sterile condition. One day she began to experience abdominal pain and consulted her physician. He advised her that she needed to undergo an appendectomy. She gave her consent for the removal of her appendix and signed the following hospital form:

> Authority to Operate:
> I hereby authorize the surgeon to administer such treatment as found necessary to perform this operation which is advisable in the treatment of this patient.
>
> Signed: ___Dolly Rogers___
>   Patient   or   Nearest
>   Relative
>   Witness _____
>   Witness _____

In addition to the appendectomy, the physician performed a total hysterectomy and bilateral salpingo-oophorectomy because he discovered at surgery unanticipated conditions adverse to the health and best interest of Mrs. Rogers, which required extension of the operation as a precautionary measure. On his first postoperative visit, when Mrs. Rogers discovered the extent of surgery, she charged the physician with "double-crossing" her. Thereafter she sued him for performing unauthorized surgery. The physician contended that Mrs. Rogers consented to the operation at the time of her admission to the hospital by signing the operative consent form. Furthermore, he declared that extension of the operation was in accord with good medical practice.

The court determined that the so-called authorization form was ambiguous and inadequate because it failed to designate the nature of the operation for which consent was given. Thus the court decided that the consent form had no possible evidentiary weight under the factual circumstances of the case. The court also pointed out that the extent of the operation to which Mrs. Rogers intended to submit, and to which she gave her consent, was the removal of her appendix. Expert testimony established that it was the usual practice to notify relatives of the patient in the event of any complications or the discovery of the need for surgery not originally contemplated. Mrs. Rogers's husband was in the hospital during the entire operation. At the time her surgeon made a midline abdominal incision in order to remove her uterus, Mrs. Rogers was under anesthesia and unable to give additional consent for this procedure. It would have been feasible and practicable for the physician to make immediate contact with the husband for the purpose of obtaining his consent. Failure to do so made the operation unauthorized.

Wheeler v. Barker. The patient had been treated by a surgeon for several months for persistent vaginal bleeding. Bimanual pelvic examination detected what appeared to be a small fibroid tumor on the anterior uterine surface. In succeeding months, additional examinations detected a mass in the area of the right ovary. When the mass was noted to have enlarged from the size of a walnut to the size of a lemon, the surgeon recommended surgery. The patient consented only to the removal of her right ovary. After entering the patient's abdomen, the surgeon located the mass, which on manual examination he thought was an enlarged ovary. In fact, it was a large fibroid tumor attached to the uterus, adjacent to the right ovary. The uterine wall was filled with multiple fibroid tumors. He performed a subtotal hysterectomy. The patient thereafter sued the surgeon to recover damages for a technical battery, contending that he had performed an unauthorized operation on her.

The court pointed out that the purpose of the operation was to stop the persistent vaginal bleeding and to remove the mass detected on physical examination. It was the physician's duty to do whatever was necessary to effect a cure. He was performing a professional service for which he had been employed to exercise his best clinical judgment as to the proper course to pursue. When a surgeon is confronted with a condition that could not have been reasonably anticipated, and that necessitates immediate action for the preservation of the life and health of the patient, and it is impracticable to obtain consent to an operation that is immediately necessary, he is expected to do what usually and customarily is practiced by similarly situated physicians under similar circumstances. Thus, the court concluded that in this case, extending the operation, removing the tumor, and curing the patient's medical problem was not a battery even though her express consent was not obtained.

Capacity to Consent—Mental Incompetence

A patient may be incapable of consenting due to mental incompetence. However, such a situation does not necessarily give the physician license to choose treatment for the patient. When a patient lacks the legal capacity to give consent, it should be sought from a person duly authorized to speak for the patient or from a court charged with the care of the incompetent patient. The following two cases focus on a patient's capacity to consent to proposed treatment.

A patient possesses legal capacity to make a decision concerning medical care if he has the ability to appreciate all relevant facts necessary to reach a rational (even though not necessarily reasonable) judgment. Where a patient elects both to live and to reject an operation which is vital for survival, the patient may be legally incompetent to consent to treatment because of an inability to appreciate that a choice between the two courses is necessary.

State Department of Human Services v. Northern.   An elderly woman was hospitalized for the treatment of advanced vascular gangrene of her feet. Her attending physician recommended amputation to preserve her life. Although she was generally lucid, on the subjects of death and amputation of her feet, her comprehension was dimmed to the extent that she was incapable of recognizing facts that would be obvious to a person of normal perception. The patient would look at her feet and refuse to recognize the obvious fact that the flesh was shriveled and rotting. She indicated that she wanted to live, but she also wanted to keep her necrotic feet; she refused to consider the impossibility of such a desire. The attending physician and other hospital personnel were concerned that they would not be able to obtain from the patient, valid consent for the life-preserving surgery. Therefore, they applied to the court for the appointment of a guardian who could consent to the amputation operation for the patient.

Expert psychiatric testimony established that to avoid the unpleasant experience of facing death and/or loss of her feet, the patient's mind had resorted to denying the existence of the unpleasant reality. This "delusion" rendered her incapable of making a rational decision whether to undergo surgery to save her life, or to forgo surgery and forfeit her life. Other medical testimony indicated that the patient only had a 50 percent chance of survival with surgery. Even if she survived, she would never be able to walk and might suffer severe mental and emotional problems. The patient's chances of survival without amputation were only 5 percent, and even if she should survive, she would never walk because the dead flesh would fall off the bones of her feet. The court recognized that the expression of such probabilities were opinions and not facts; however, the existence and expression of such opinions were facts the patient was unwilling or unable to recognize or discuss.

The court pointed out that if the patient was capable of giving evidence of some comprehension of the facts of her condition, and could express her unequivocal desire in the face of such comprehended facts, then her decision, however unreasonable to others, would be accepted and honored by the court and by her physician. However, the court concluded that she was incapable of comprehending the facts of her condition. Therefore, the court appointed a guardian for the purpose of granting the surgeon consent for the operation.

A patient who is subject to fluctuations in mental lucidity and to occasional loss of continuity of thought, may nevertheless be legally competent to reject a proposed vital operation if the patient is capable of appreciating the nature and consequences of the decision.

Matter of Quackenbush. The patient was seventy-two years old and lived as a semirecluse. He had no spouse or children, his parents and siblings were deceased, and he was unable to provide any information concerning relatives. A rescue squad brought him to the hospital emergency room at the request of his neighbors who felt he was in need of care and treatment. When he belligerently refused treatment, hospital officials attempted to send him home, but all available transportation agencies refused to transport him. As a last resort, he was hospitalized. It was then learned that he had been hospitalized two months earlier because of severe peripheral vascular disease of the lower extremities for which he was advised to have an operation. Instead, he refused the procedure and left the hospital.

Aside from that hospitalization, he had shunned medical treatment for the prior forty years. His attending physician described him as a "conscientious objector" to medical therapy. Physical examination disclosed bilateral gangrene of his legs, which was so severe that his left leg had partially mummified and the foot was about to fall off. There was also a draining lesion on his left leg, which exposed the tibia and tendons. Neither leg had a detectable popliteal or pedal pulse. Cultures of the blood indicated the presence of a gas-forming bacteria. The gangrene had induced high fever, dehydration, and anemia. After aggressive antibiotic therapy had been given, the patient's temperature gradually became normal. His attending physician described the antibiotic therapy as a heroic measure and indicated that concentrated use of one of the antibiotics, Gentamycin, ultimately could cause kidney failure.

The patient's attending physician carefully discussed with the patient, over a period of several days, the nature and extent of his condition and of the proposed surgery; the risks involved in the operation; and the risks involved if no operation took place. The patient signed a form consenting to the operation, but later that day he withdrew his consent. There was evidence that he was suffering from an organic brain syndrome with psychotic elements, possibly induced by the septicemia. He was not aware of when he was talking to a nurse or physician; he experienced visual hallucinations; and he responded inappropriately to the discussions on the gravity of his condition.

The attending physician felt that the patient needed the surgery for which the patient would not give consent. Therefore the hospital sought a court order to appoint a guardian for the purpose of granting consent to operate.

Expert medical testimony established that imminent death could be averted only if bilateral above-knee or possibly total amputations were performed, and that antibiotics could control the septicemia if the source of the infection was removed through amputation. His attending physician believed that the probability of recovery from the amputation was good and the risks involved were limited. The extent of the amputation required would dictate whether the patient would be confined to a wheelchair or be a candidate for rehabilitation. In either event, he would require nursing care.

A psychiatric interview with the patient disclosed no evidence of hallucinations, although he exhibited fluctuations in mental lucidity, a condition the psychiatrist felt was to be expected under the circumstances and was not a sign of mental incompetency.

During the interview, the patient expressed a desire to return to his trailer and live out his life. He was not experiencing any pain and indicated that if he did, he could change his mind about having the operation. Based on the facts and findings of the case, the court concluded that the patient had the mental capacity to make decisions regarding his treatment. He could understand the nature and extent of his physical condition, of the operation, and of the risks involved if he consented to or refused the operation. Therefore he had the capacity to refuse to consent to treatment.

In treating an incompetent patient, under limited circumstances, an attending physician may make treatment decisions without prior approval of a court. Thus, under certain prescribed circumstances, a physician may lawfully direct that resuscitation measures be withheld from a mentally incompetent, terminally ill, hopelessly suffering patient, in the event of cardiopulmonary arrest.

Matter of Dinnerstein.   A sixty-seven-year-old patient had Alzheimer's disease, a progressive and unremitting presenile dementia. The patient exhibited marked personality disorganization, and intellectual and motor function loss. The disease had left her in a vegetative condition with death imminent, and without the hope of treatment capable of arresting its course. She was dependent on intensive nursing care because she was unable to swallow without choking and barely able to cough. Although her eyes occasionally opened and appeared to fix on or follow an object briefly, she was otherwise unaware of her environment. Intravenous feeding was abandoned because it caused her pain. She was fed through a naso-gastric tube which caused discomfort due to ulceration and infection in her throat and esophagus, especially when it became necessary to remove the tube from time to time. Although her condition was hopeless, it would be difficult to predict exactly when she would die. She had severe arteriosclerotic coronary artery disease, which was expected to be the most likely immediate cause of her death. The precipitating event of death was expected to be cardiac or respiratory arrest.

The patient's family, consisting of a son and a daughter, concurred in the attending physician's recommendation that cardiopulmonary resuscitation should not be attempted in the event of cardiac or respiratory arrest. However, a recent legal case had created uncertainties in the minds of health care personnel as to whether it was acceptable legally for an attending physician to order a "no-code," even though he felt it was in the patient's best interests and he had concurrence of the family. Therefore, the family joined the physician and the hospital in petitioning a legal tribunal to determine whether a physician may enter a "no-code" order without prior legal authorization. The petitioners sought resolution of uncertainties spawned by the recent legal case that seemed to require judicial decision to withhold potentially life-prolonging treatment from a patient incapable of making his own decision. The petitioners contended that some medical professionals had interpreted this legal decision as casting doubt upon the lawfulness of an attending physician's order not to attempt resuscitation of an incompetent, terminally ill patient, except where the entry of such an order had been determined previously by a court to be in the best interests of the patient.

The court noted that judicial decisions implying that a physician attending an incompetent patient has a duty to employ lifesaving or life-prolonging treatments, in the absence of a court order allowing withholding heroic measures, referred to treatments administered for the purpose and with some reasonable expectation of effecting a cure or relief. The court pointed out that the legal duty to provide measures for the "prolongation of life" did not mean to provide treatment for the mere suspension of the act of dying, but contemplated a therapeutic effort toward the remission of symptoms enabling a turn towards a normal, functioning, integrated existence. The medical role is primary in those situations in which withholding extraordinary measures may be viewed as allowing the disease to take its natural course.

Although in cases involving treatment of incompetent patients courts have incidentally discussed the scope of the physician's duty to administer treatment, courts have been primarily concerned with the patient's right to refuse treatment and the manner in which the exercise of that right may be accomplished by patients unable to make the decision for themselves. The court pointed out that resuscitative measures involving cardiac massage, endotracheal intubation, intracardiac injections, defibrillation, intravenous cutdowns and pacemaker implantation, are highly intrusive and often pain-producing in nature. Therefore, the court held that the patient or someone authorized to speak for him should be allowed to exercise his right to refuse such measures, if the situation is appropriate for refusal. The court noted that this case did not offer a lifesaving or life-prolonging treatment alternative. Attempts to resuscitate, if successful, would do nothing to cure or relieve the illnesses that will have brought the patient to the threshold of death. The case does not, therefore, present the type of significant treatment choice or election which—in light of sound medical advice—is to be made by the patient, if competent to do so. Thus, the court concluded that what measures are appropriate to ease the imminent passing of an irreversibly, hopelessly and terminally ill patient, was a question peculiarly within the competence of the medical profession. Therefore, the patient management question is not one for judicial decision, but one for the attending physician.

Incapacity to Consent—Age of Patient

In addition to mental incompetency, another exception to the requirement of obtaining a patient's consent to treatment, is a patient's legal incapacity to consent due to age. The legal rationale and assumption is that many persons, because of youth, are incapable of intelligent and rational decisions. However, the decision as to treatment does not, as a result, become the attending physician's decision. Rather, a minor's consent must be coupled with consent of the minor's parents or guardians. An exception to this requirement is when the parents are unavailable, making it impractical to obtain their consent in time to accomplish proper results. In cases where the treatment is obviously materially necessary or is needed to save life and limbs, consent is implied by law. When a minor has been legally emancipated or is close to maturity; his consent alone may be legally sufficient to properly allow the proposed treatment.

A physician may be justified in relying upon and accepting the consent of a minor, if the proposed procedure is for the benefit of the minor and is done to save the minor's life or limb.

Bonner v. Moran.   A fifteen-year-old boy's cousin had been severely burned. A plastic surgeon advised the burned child's mother that a skin graft would help her, provided the blood of the donor matched. After a number of unsuccessful efforts to match her blood with that of her siblings, the mother persuaded her fifteen-year-old nephew to go with her to the hospital for the purpose of having a blood test. His blood satisfactorily matched his cousin's and the surgeon performed an operation on the boy's side, preparing a future donor graft site. The boy's mother lived in another state and knew nothing about her son's involvement in the arrangement.

After the operation, the boy returned home and advised his mother that he was going back to the hospital to have his side "fixed up." Instead, a tube of flesh was cut and formed from his axilla to his waistline, and at the proper time, one end of the tube was attached to his cousin. The result was unsatisfactory. The boy lost a large amount of blood and required prolonged hospitalization. On behalf of her son, the mother sued the surgeon for battery because he had operated on her son without proper permission.

The court pointed out that a surgical operation is a technical battery and is excusable only when there is express or implied consent by the patient. The consent of a fifteen-year-old boy does not dispense with the necessity of consent by his parents. The court reasoned that the circumstances of this case did not encompass an exception to the general rule that a minor lacks the capacity to consent to a medical procedure because the operation was: not for the benefit of the patient; involved intense pain and possible results affecting the minor's future life, and not an emergency situation. Therefore the court concluded that the surgeon had committed a battery, and the minor had a valid claim for resultant damages of the operation.

Whether medical treatment for a teenager can be properly consented to by parents over the objection of their minor child, is legally unclear. Although the following case indicates that the teenager's consent overrode her parent's wishes, it should be noted that a minor's consent to the medical care in question was statutorily prescribed in the particular jurisdiction of this case. Another state may not have such a statute. Moreover, the case involves the fundamental right of a woman to choose to terminate her pregnancy.

In re Smith. A mother requested that the juvenile court compel her sixteen-year-old pregnant daughter to submit to an abortion. On the grounds that her mother desired her daughter to be aborted, the court ordered that "Cindy Lou Smith shall obey her mother in submitting to the medical procedures to terminate her pregnancy and that the request and instructions from her mother shall be sufficient authority for any medical doctor or hospital to provide this treatment."

The legal representative of the minor appealed this ruling. The appellate court held that it was not the legislative intent that a parent have this power to compel a sixteen-year-old minor daughter to undergo an abortion. The court pointed out that a state statute expressly provided that no person shall be required to participate in medical procedures which result in the termination of pregnancy and the refusal of any person to do so shall not be a basis for any recriminatory action by the state or any person. The statute also provided that "a minor shall have the same capacity to consent to medical treatment as an adult" if one or more of the following designated conditions apply: the minor is married or the parent of a child; the minor seeks treatment or advice concerning venereal disease, pregnancy, or contraception not amounting to sterilization; in the judgment of a physician treating the minor, the obtaining of consent of any other person would result in such delay of treatment as would adversely affect the life or health of the minor; or the minor seeks treatment or advice concerning any form of drug abuse.

The court concluded that the statute contemplated giving the minor the same capacity to consent as an adult; therefore, it emancipated the minor from the control of the parents with respect to medical treatment within the contemplation of the statute. The court reasoned that if a minor may consent to medical treatment as an adult (particularly a minor over sixteen years of age), then the minor may not be forced, any more than an adult, to accept treatment or advice concerning pregnancy. The court declared that consent cannot be the subject of compulsion, because consent depends upon the patient's exercise of voluntary will. The court concluded that a patient who has the right of consent to treatment has to have the right to forbid treatment.

Section 3: The Patient's Right to Decline Medical Treatment

Generally a competent patient has the right to refuse medical care, even if it involves lifesaving treatment. In such a situation, a physician may apply to a court for an order to compel treatment based on the state's interest in the preservation of human life and health. The court may nevertheless balance this and other state interests with the right of the individual to be free from bodily intrusion; or if the refusal is based on religious tenets, the right of the individual to practice a religion which does not allow the proposed treatment. The following cases examine the scope of the patient's right to decline medical treatment.

Based upon the right of privacy, a competent, terminally ill adult patient's right to discontinue life sustaining treatment may be greater than various state interests in preserving life.

Satz v. Perlmutter. A seventy-three-year-old patient was confined to a hospital because of the progressive effects of amyotrophic lateral sclerosis, an incurable disease with a limited life expectancy, which he had suffered from for several years. The patient's disease had progressed to virtual incapability of movement and inability to breathe without a mechanical respirator. Even with the respirator, the prognosis was for death within a short time. Despite his medical disabilities, he remained in command of his mental faculties and was legally competent. While hospitalized, he sought, with full approval of his family, to have the respirator removed from his trachea. This act, according to his attending physician, would result in life expectancy of less than one hour. The patient was fully aware of the inevitable result of such removal, yet had attempted to remove it for himself; however, hospital personnel, activated by an alarm, reconnected it. He had repeatedly stated to his family, "I'm miserable, take it out."

The patient petitioned a judge to permit the removal of the respirator. At a bedside hearing, he told the judge that whatever would be in store for him if the respirator were removed, "can't be worse than what I'm going through now." After careful deliberation the judge ordered that the patient, in the exercise of his right of privacy, could remain in or leave the hospital, free of the mechanical respirator, and the hospital and staff were restrained from interfering with the patient's decision.

The state opposed the judge's order, contending that it had an overriding duty to preserve life, and that termination of supportive care, whether it be by the patient, his family, or medical personnel, was an unlawful killing of a human being. In addition, the state pointed out, because of the absence of state law on the subject, the hospital and medical staff feared both criminal prosecution and civil liability if they aided in removal of the mechanical device.

The court pointed out that the right of an individual to refuse medical treatment is tempered by the state's interest in the preservation of life, the protection of innocent third parties, the prevention of suicide, and the maintenance of the ethical integrity of medical practice. Because this case involved a competent adult patient, the court declared that none of these four considerations surmounted the right of this patient to discontinue treatment based upon his right to individual free choice and self-determination. However, the court intimated that the solution to the problem would be less easy if the patient was incapable of understanding the consequences of his action.

The court further explained that there is a substantial distinction in the state's insistence that human life be saved where the patient's affliction is curable, as opposed to the state interest where, as in this case, the issue is not whether, but when, for how long, and at what cost to the patient, his life may be briefly extended. Where the patient's condition is terminal, the situation wretched, and the continuation of his life temporary and totally artificial, the state's interest in preserving life is greatly lessened. The situation would be different also where the patient, by refusing treatment, is abandoning his minor child, which abandonment the state may legitimately prevent.

The court also pointed out that prevailing medical ethical practice does not, without exception, demand that all efforts toward life prolongation be made in all circumstances. Rather, the prevailing ethical practice seems to recognize that the dying are more often in need of comfort than treatment. Therefore, recognition of the right to refuse necessary treatment in appropriate circumstances is consistent with medical mores, and does not threaten the integrity of the medical profession in caring for such patients. Thus the court concluded that in this case it was not necessary to deny the patient's right of self-determination in order to recognize the physicians' interests in the attendance of patients.

Holmes v. Silver Cross Hospital.   A twenty-year-old married man was taken to the hospital after sustaining serious injuries in an accident. Surgery was required to treat his injuries. While he was fully conscious and competent, he informed his attending physicians that his religious convictions precluded his accepting recommended blood transfusions. The physicians were unable to persuade members of the patient's family, including his wife, brother, sister, and parents, that he should have a transfusion. The patient and his wife signed a form releasing the physicians from liability in performing surgery without the use of blood transfusions.

Approximately four hours later, when the patient became unconscious, the physicians sought to have the probate court declare the patient incompetent as a minor and to appoint a conservator for the purpose of authorizing a transfusion. Under the law of that state, an incompetent was defined as a person incapable of managing his person. The statute required a hearing to determine whether a patient was an incompetent minor and also whether the recommended, but refused treatment was a medical necessity.

Without affording the patient or his family notice or opportunity for a hearing, the magistrate declared the patient incompetent and appointed a conservator who consented to blood transfusions. The physicians gave the patient the transfusion, knowing this action was in violation of the patient's religious convictions. In spite of this treatment, the patient died. As administrator of his estate, his wife sued the conservator, the hospital, and the physicians, charging violations of the First Amendment guaranteeing freedom of religion. She contended that the defendants had conspired to deny the patient and his family the notice and hearing required by statute.

The court held that the patient's constitutional rights had been violated because the patient's religious beliefs had been restricted without a showing that such restriction was designed to prevent grave and immediate danger to a state interest which should be lawfully protected. The court pointed out that a physician must have more than a mere rational basis for providing treatment, in order to constitute a legally sufficient reason for restricting a patient's free exercise of religion. Therefore, the court held that the patient's constitutional rights had been violated.

In re Osbourne. A thirty-four-year-old patient was admitted to the hospital with serious injuries and internal bleeding, sustained when a tree fell on him. As the need for a blood transfusion became apparent his consent for the transfusion was requested. He and his wife refused to give consent. Both gave as reasons their religious beliefs which forbade infusion of whole blood into the body. The hospital sought a petition to appoint a guardian to give consent for the administration of blood to the patient. This request was taken to a judge's home on the night of the accident. The patient's wife, brother, and grandfather were present. They stated the views of the patient and expressed agreement with them, explaining that those views were based on strong religious convictions. The grandfather explained that the patient "wants to live very much, but that he wants to live in the Bible's promised new world where life will never end," and that "a few hours here would nowhere compare to everlasting life." The patient's wife stated, "He told me he did not want blood—he did not care if he had to die."

The judge became concerned with the patient's capacity to make such a decision in light of his serious clinical condition, and recognized the possibility that the use of drugs might have impaired the judgment and ability for choice. Counsel for the hospital advised the judge that the patient was conscious when spoken to by staff; knew what the physician was saying; was not under the influence of any medication; understood the consequences of his decision; and had, with full understanding, executed a statement refusing the recommended transfusion and releasing the hospital from liability. The judge visited the hospital and personally asked the patient whether he believed that he would be deprived of the opportunity for "everlasting life" if a transfusion were ordered by the court. His response was, "Yes. It is between me and Jehovah; not the courts . . . I'm willing to take my chances. My faith is that strong." He also stated, "I wish to live, but with no blood transfusions."

The judge concluded that the maturity of this lucid patient, his long-standing beliefs and those of his family did not justify legal intervention which would force his "consent" to the procedure.

The following case approaches differently the patient's right to the free exercise of religion in refusing to consent to a necessary blood transfusion than the prior two cases. In this case there was a serious question of the patient's capacity to refuse. Viewed together, the cases illustrate the different approaches taken by the courts in the balancing of interests of the patient, the attending physicians, and the state.

John F. Kennedy Memorial Hospital v. Heston. A twenty-two-year-old unmarried woman was severely injured in an automobile accident. She was taken in shock to the hospital, where it was determined by the attending physician that she would expire unless operated on for the removal of a ruptured spleen. It was determined further that if she were operated on she would expire unless whole blood was administered. She and her parents were Jehovah's Witnesses. A tenet of their faith forbade blood transfusions. The patient expressed her refusal to accept blood. In the judgment of the attending physicians and nurses, she was then, or soon would become, disoriented and incoherent. Her mother remained adamant in her opposition to a transfusion. Her father could not be located. The patient was unable to execute a release. The hospital and attending physicians transfused the patient and performed an emergency splenectomy. When the patient recovered, she sued the hospital and physicians for wrongfully treating her with blood transfusions.

The court pointed out that hospitals exist to aid the sick and the injured and that the medical profession is dedicated to the preservation of life. Therefore, failure to use a simple, established, lifesaving procedure such as a blood transfusion in the circumstances of this case, would be improper practice in the case of a dying patient. The court concluded that a surgeon should not be asked to operate under the strain of knowing that a transfusion may not be administered even though medically required to save his patient. Moreover, the hospital and its staff should not be required to decide whether the release tendered by the patient or a member of his family will protect them from civil liability. The hospital could not avoid the problem by compelling the removal of a dying patient in need of care. Thus the court recognized that the hospital staff were involuntary hosts whose professional interests were in conflict with the patient's beliefs. The court concluded that, under the circumstances, it was reasonable to permit the hospital and its staff to pursue their functions according to their professional standards.

A patient's decision to refuse proposed treatment may involve irrational and emotional factors that most people would consider unwise, and may demonstrate an impaired capacity to make a medically rational choice. However, if the patient is able to appreciate the consequences of the choice made, he will usually not be determined to be legally incompetent to refuse therapy. Thus a court will probably not appoint a guardian to consent to the treatment.

Lane v. Candura.   A seventy-four-year-old diabetic patient had a toe infection that became gangrenous and required amputation of the toe. Three years later part of her foot became gangrenous and required partial amputation. Although an arterial bypass procedure was performed to decrease the likelihood that vascular gangrene would recur, she was readmitted to the hospital because of progressive gangrene in the remainder of the foot. Her attending physicians recommended amputation of the leg without delay. She initially agreed to the operation, but she withdrew her consent on the morning scheduled for the operation. She was discharged and went to her daughter's home, but returned to the hospital a few days later. Two weeks later, responding to the persuasion of a physician whom she had known for many years, she consented to the operation. Soon thereafter, however, she reiterated her refusal. After some vacillation, she refused to consent to the operation and she persisted in that refusal. She discussed with the staff the reasons for her decision. She said that she had been unhappy since the death of her husband and did not wish to be a burden to her children. Although she expressed a desire to get well she indicated that she was resigned to death. She had made it clear that she did not wish to have the operation even though that decision would in all likelihood lead shortly to her death. She was lucid on some matters, but her train of thought would sometimes wander, and her conception of time was distorted. She was irascible and hostile to certain physicians, sometimes defensive and combative in her responses to questioning. Nevertheless, she exhibited a high degree of awareness and acuity.

While in the hospital, because of the progression of the gangrene, her daughter filed a petition in the probate court seeking appointment of herself as temporary guardian with authority to consent to the operation on behalf of her mother. She contended that her mother did not possess the legally requisite mental competence to make the treatment choice for herself because her degree of senility and confusion on some subjects prevented her from careful consideration of the medical alternatives; therefore she was unable to arrive at her treatment decision in a rational manner.

A psychiatrist who had examined her testified that the patient was incompetent to make a rational choice whether to consent to the operation. His opinion was based on her unwillingness to discuss the problem with him, which he inferred was because she was unable to face up to the problem. He characterized her unwillingness to consent to lifesaving treatment as "suicidal." He also based his opinion that she was incompetent on a possibility—which was not established by evidence as a reasonable probability—that her mind might be impaired by toxicity as a result of the gangrenous condition.

The court concluded that this psychiatrist's opinion did not represent incompetency in the legal sense. Instead, his opinion was concerned with incompetency in the medical sense because it indicated that the patient's ability to make a rational choice was impaired by her confusion which caused her to consider irrational and emotional factors. The court pointed out that until the patient had changed her original decision and withdrew her consent to the amputation, her competence was not questioned. It noted that the irrationality of her treatment decision did not justify a conclusion that she was legally incompetent, because the law protects a patient's right to make a decision to accept or reject treatment, whether or not that decision is wise. Similarly, the fact that she vacillated in her resolve not to submit to the operation did not justify a conclusion that her capacity to make the decision was impaired to the point of legal incompetence. Her reaction may have been understandable in the light of her prior surgical experience and the prospect of living the remainder of her life in a nonambulatory state.

The court further noted that, although senile symptoms in the abstract may justify a finding of incompetence, the inquiry into this determination must be more particular because a patient is presumed to be competent unless shown otherwise by sufficient evidence. The court concluded that such evidence was lacking in this case. Moreover, the evidence indicated that the patient appreciated the consequences of her choice. The most that the evidence showed was that her decision involved strong emotional factors; that she did not choose to discuss the decision with certain persons; and that occasionally her resolve against giving consent weakened. There was no proof of impairment of her ability to understand that in rejecting the amputation she was, in effect, choosing death over life. Thus, the court concluded that these findings cannot be construed as legal incompetence for the purposes of making a treatment decision. Although her decision may be regarded as unfortunate, it was not the uninformed decision of a patient incapable of appreciating the nature and consequences of her act. Therefore the law would not force her to undergo the operation against her will.

Even though an attending physician may consider a competent patient's beliefs about treatment unwise, foolish, or ridiculous, in the absence of an overriding danger to society, the law will not compel medical treatment that the patient has refused with full knowledge of the probable consequences.

In re Maida Yetter.   A sixty-year-old patient underwent a routine physical examination that disclosed findings indicative of breast carcinoma. The physician recommended a surgical biopsy along with any necessary corrective surgery. When this recommendation was made to the patient by her caseworker, the patient refused to give her consent, saying she was afraid because her aunt had died following such surgery. The caseworker indicated that the patient was lucid and appeared to understand the possible consequences of her refusal. In the months that followed, additional recommendations for surgery were made. The patient's reasons for refusing the surgery gradually became delusional. Ultimately, she was hospitalized in a state mental institution with the diagnosis of schizophrenia. The hospital brought a legal action to have a guardian appointed for the patient, who was authorized to give consent for the patient for diagnostic and corrective breast surgery.

The court pointed out that a patient's right of privacy against bodily intrusions of recommended treatment also encompassed the right to die. Therefore, where there were no overriding state interests such as minor or unborn children, or a clear and present danger to public health and welfare, a physician should not interfere with a competent patient's decision to refuse therapy. The patient had been competent when she first refused to consent, and had refused with full knowledge of the consequences. Although she had subsequently become delusional, her primary reason for refusal was her fear of dying. Therefore the court said it would not interfere with the patient's decision by compelling her to do something in the waning hours of her life to which she had not agreed. Even though her decision might be considered unwise, the court would not compel her to accept therapy.

A patient's right to privacy, and consequently the right to refuse treatment, may be preserved and applied even when the patient is incapable of directly exercising it. By applying the principle of "substituted-judgment," some courts have allowed the indirect exercise of this right by a duly authorized person acting on behalf of the incompetent patient.

In re Quinlan. For unknown reasons, this teenager stopped breathing for at least two fifteen-minute periods. As a result she suffered extensive brain damage and her condition was characterized as a "chronic persistent vegetative state." Although her brain was capable of primitive reflex-level functioning, she had no cognitive function or awareness of her surroundings. She did not, however, exhibit the signs of "brain death" designated by the Ad Hoc Committee of the Harvard Medical School. She was thus considered to be "alive" under controlling legal and medical standards. Nonetheless, it was the opinion of medical experts that there was no reasonable possibility that she would ever be restored to sapient life. Her breathing was assisted by a respirator, without which the experts believed she could not survive.

The patient's father petitioned the court for the purpose of obtaining authority to order disconnection of the respirator. The court pointed out that subsequent to her accident, the patient was totally incapable of knowing or appreciating life, was physically debilitated, and was pathetically reliant on sophisticated machinery to nourish and clean her body. Any other person suffering from similar massive brain damage would be in a similar state of total incapacity. Thus, the court concluded that it was reasonable to assume that there would be a general and consistent response to the situation by a similarly situated patient on the issue of whether the patient would choose to have the respirator disconnected. The court reasoned that most people in like circumstances would choose a natural death. In such circumstances, the central concern of the court would be to apply the doctrine of "substituted judgment," which requires that the guardian's decision regarding treatment conform with that which the patient would have made if competent. The court held that the father, acting as guardian, could exercise his daughter's right to privacy by authorizing removal of the artificial life-support systems, subject to certain qualifications.

It indicated that the decision whether to continue artificial life support belongs to the patient's guardian, family, attending physicians, and the hospital "Ethics Committee," and recommended the following approach: If the attending physician concluded that there was no reasonable possibility of ever emerging from the comatose condition to a cognitive, sapient state, and that the life-support apparatus should be discontinued, he was to consult with the hospital "Ethics Committee" or a similar group in the hospital. If that consultative body concurred with the attending physician's conclusions, the present life-support system could be withdrawn without civil or criminal liability on the part of the physician.

As *Quinlan* indicates, some courts have held that the right of the competent and the incompetent patient are the same: to decline potentially life-prolonging treatment as part of the right to be free from the nonconsensual invasion of the patient's bodily integrity. However, the courts have also recognized that society has an interest in the maintenance of the ethical integrity of the medical profession, as well as allowing hospitals the full opportunity to care for patients. Nevertheless, prevailing ethical medical practice does not demand that all efforts toward life prolongation be made in all circumstances. Some courts have declared that recognition of the right to refuse necessary treatment in appropriate circumstances is consistent with existing medical mores and does not threaten to undermine the integrity of the medical profession. Thus it is not necessary to deny a patient's right of self-determination in order to recognize the interests of physicians in attendance of their patients, especially when it does not involve the immediate institution of medical treatment.

Superintendent of Belchertown v. Saikewicz. A sixty-seven-year-old, profoundly mentally retarded man who had been a resident of a mental institution for fifty-three years, was diagnosed as having acute myeloblastic monocytic leukemia. Chemotherapy, the only effective, life-prolonging treatment, involved serious and painful intrusions into his body. Although some urgency existed with regard to beginning treatment, the physicians were not faced with the issue of institution of immediate lifesaving treatment. Because the patient was incompetent to make the necessary decision regarding treatment, the superintendent of the mental institution initiated court proceedings to obtain legal guidance in the therapeutic management of the patient.

The court concluded that the ultimate decision to withhold potentially life-prolonging treatment from a patient incapable of making his own decision should not be shifted away from the courts to any medical committee panel or group. The court pointed out that findings and advice of such groups, as well as the testimony of the attending physicians and other medical experts, simply assist the judicial resolution of the question of life and death. The court's rationale was that such a decisional process requires the detached but passionate investigation and determination of the judiciary and, therefore, should not be entrusted to any other group purporting to represent the "morality and conscience of our society."

The court addressed the question: at what cost to the patient may his life be briefly extended? The court determined that the factors weighing against administration of chemotherapy were the patient's age; the probable side effects of treatment; the low chance of producing remission; and the certainty that treatment would cause immediate suffering. The factor weighing in favor of administering chemotherapy was that most people elect chemotherapy and the chance of a longer life. However, the court pointed out that usually patients who request treatment know the risks involved and can appreciate the reason for the painful side effects when they occur. They know the reason for the pain and their hope makes it tolerable. However, this patient lacked the capacity to understand his present situation or his prognosis. If he were treated with toxic drugs he would be involuntarily immersed in a state of painful suffering and he would never understand the reason. Therefore the court concluded that the majority of patients would not choose chemotherapy if they were told merely that something outside their previous experience was going to be done to them that would cause pain, with the advantages of this treatment measured by concepts of time and mortality beyond their ability to comprehend.

An exception to the requirement that a court order be obtained to compel medical treatment is in an emergency situation where time does not permit such application. In such a situation, an attending physician may exercise the professional right to treat. Thus, if it appears that death will probably follow unless recommended medical care is administered, a physician is permitted to render that urgent service, because the law implies that the patient, if able, would have consented to the treatment under the circumstances.

In the Matter of Earle N. Spring.   This seventy-year-old patient had "end-stage kidney disease," which required him to undergo frequent hemodialysis. He also suffered from "chronic organic brain syndrome," which caused marked confusion and disorientation. When he had been competent, he had acquiesced in hemodialysis, and had received such treatments for several months before his incompetence became apparent. Both the kidney and the organic brain disease were permanent and irreversible; there was no prospect of a medical breakthrough that would provide a cure for either disease. Without hemodialysis, he would die; with it, in all probability, he would survive for only a few months even though it was conceivable that he could survive for years. Hemodialysis did not cause a remission of the disease or restore him even temporarily to a normal, cognitive, integrated, functioning existence, but simply kept him alive. He experienced unpleasant side effects, such as dizziness, leg cramps, headaches, from the treatment. On occasion he resisted transportation for treatment and pulled the dialysis needles out of his arm. This disruptive behavior required heavy sedation for control. If hemodialysis were terminated, he would not have suffered any discomfort.

Although there was no evidence that while competent he had expressed any wish or desire as to the continuation or withdrawal of treatment in such circumstances, his wife of fifty-five years and his son were of the opinion that if competent he would request withdrawal of treatment. Thus his wife and son filed a petition to a judge for the appointment of a guardian of the patient, and for an order that hemodialysis be discontinued. Because the governing law and its application to the patient's situation as presented were in serious doubt, the judge appointed a guardian who sought explicit judicial authorization for the proposed management of the patient.

The court pointed out that a patient's right of privacy may prevent an unwanted or nonconsensual infringement or invasion of the patient's bodily integrity. A competent patient's right to refuse medical treatment in appropriate circumstances is also extended to an incompetent person through the exercise of "substituted judgment." This involves the therapy decision that would be made by the incompetent patient if he were competent, taking into account his actual interests, preferences, and present and future incompetency. The court found in this case that the patient was incompetent, conscious, and suffering from an incurably fatal disease; that hemodialysis was intrusive and life-prolonging rather than lifesaving; that there was no prospect of cure, or even of recovery of competence; and that temporary continuation of hemodialysis would not greatly change the situation. Therefore it concluded that under the circumstances the patient would, if capable, refuse continuation of hemodialysis.

In addressing the issue of the legality of an action to continue or discontinue treatment without judicial authority, the court enumerated various circumstances to be taken into account in deciding whether there should be an application for a prior court order with respect to medical treatment of an incompetent patient. Important factors in this determination included:

the extent of impairment of the patient's mental faculties; the patient's level of understanding and probable reaction; the type (governmental or not) of institution having custody of the patient; the prognosis with or without the proposed treatment; the complexity, novelty, risk, and possible side effects of the proposed treatment; the urgency of the management decision; the consent of the patient, spouse, or guardian; the good faith of those who participate in the decision; the clarity of professional opinion as to what is "good medical practice," and the interests of third persons, such as dependent children.

6

TREATMENT DECISIONS

A physician is expected to make reasonable treatment decisions which are within the bounds of recognized medical standards in managing the patient's condition. A physician is also expected to keep up with the therapeutic advancements made by the profession, and to adopt appropriate new treatment methods as they are approved by the profession. If the physician chooses to use novel or experimental therapy instead of conventional or generally accepted therapy, however, he may be exposed to greater liability for resultant injuries, especially if the patient's clear and unequivocal informed consent is not obtained.

The physician may also be required to make treatment decisions in accordance with published guidelines such as medical texts and drug manufacturer's instructions, to avoid the inference of negligent treatment. The physician should also avoid providing unnecessary treatment, especially if the treatment is primarily rendered for his own economic benefit. Once treatment is administered, the physician is expected to be cognizant of recognized complications associated with the treatment and to take action to avoid them or to minimize injurious effect through timely identification and management.

SECTION 1: NOVEL AND EXPERIMENTAL TREATMENT

Although many considerations influence a physician's therapeutic decisions in any given case, the treatment administered is required to be within the bounds of recognized medical standards. Thus when a particular mode of treatment is the consensus among medical professionals, generally it should be followed by a physician. If a physician chooses to experiment with some other mode, he assumes a greater responsibility for any untoward effects of the treatment. While the law attempts to protect the public against reckless experimentation, it also recognizes that medicine as a progressive science must be allowed to adopt new remedies and modes of treatment when their benefits have been demonstrated.

Although a physician has a special duty to refrain from involuntary experimentation on patients, he nevertheless has a duty to keep up with the advancements made by the profession and may adopt new methods as they are approved by the profession. However, a physician who engages in drastic or experimental treatment which exceeds the bounds of established medical standards must always inform the patient of the experimental nature, and the foreseeable consequences of that treatment, to minimize exposure to liability. Thus in proposing innovative procedures, a more detailed explanation of the nature and effect of the treatment, and more developed advice concerning the need for such procedures are required of the attending physician than when conventional treatment is proposed. This includes the duty to inform the patient fully of special or unusual features of the proposed therapy. The following cases explore the issue of consent when novel or experimental treatment is proposed or administered by an attending physician.

Ahern v. Veterans Administration. The patient experienced progressive irregularity in his bowel movements. Examination by his physician disclosed a large tumor of the rectum. Upon his admission to the hospital, several examining and consulting physicians became concerned that the tumor would obstruct the rectum. Due to the large size of the tumor, it was considered nonresectable. Therefore, preoperative radiation was employed to reduce its size, so that it could be surgically removed. Because of the clinical presentation and circumstances, the attending physician determined that a total dosage of approximately 3,000 rads should be administered within a five-day period. The dosage was a drastic amount when measured by the relatively short time span in which it was administered. The only authority recommending 3,000 rads in a five-day period was a scientific paper which reportedly recommended such a dosage in this time span.

After the radiation treatments were completed, surgery was performed, and the tumor was removed. Thereafter, the patient developed serious complications, including extensive genitourinary, bone, and muscle necrosis as a result of the massive radiation exposure. The patient sued, charging that his attending physician administered excessive and experimental amounts of radiation to him.

Expert medical testimony established that the radiation dosage standards did not exceed 250 rads per day, or 1,250 over a five-day period. The attending physician testified that administering this dosage over a five-day period was experimental, but added that the patient was informed of the type of treatment that was to be administered and of the possible consequences which could arise from the treatment. However, the patient denied he was ever fully informed of the experimental aspect of the treatment or of the possible consequences of administering such large daily dosages. Although there was conflicting evidence, the court concluded that the attending physician did not fully inform the patient of the experimental nature of the proposed therapy, and therefore did not obtain an effective consent from the patient.

Blanton v. U.S. A pregnant patient's blood type was Rh-negative and her husband's was Rh-positive. The couple desired to have future children and they knew that if the patient had an Rh-positive fetus, a dangerous blood incompatibility to the fetus (erythroblastosis foetalis) might occur in subsequent pregnancies. They were also aware that this reaction could be avoided by administering anti-D antibody to the patient immediately after delivery.

There were, at the time, at least two proprietary names for anti-D antibody, Rho-Gam and Hyp-Rho-D. Prior to this pregnancy, the patient had given birth to an Rh-positive child and had received Rho-Gam. She knew it was effective in her case and took special precautions to advise her attending physician and the nursing staff of her condition and her desire to receive Rho-Gam again.

When she went into labor, the patient was asked whether she would be willing to take Hyp-Rho-D instead of Rho-Gam as part of an experiment then being conducted at the hospital to determine whether Hyp-Rho-D had effectiveness beyond its shelf life approved by the Food and Drug Administration. The patient refused to participate in the experiment. She insisted on Rho-Gam, and related this to her attending physician. Her chart was thus marked "Rho-Gam." When she received her shot the nurse said, "Here is your Rho-Gam." In fact, she received a shot of Hyp-Rho-D as part of the experimental protocol. Shortly thereafter, the patient learned that she had received Hyp-Rho-D and became fearful and angry.

It took approximately six months after the birth to conclusively demonstrate that the patient still had a negative anti-D titer and that there was no danger of erythroblastosis foetalis with a subsequent pregnancy. The preponderance of experimental evidence established that Hyp-Rho-D was as effective as Rho-Gam. Nevertheless, the patient sued the hospital charging that her involuntary inclusion in the clinical investigation caused her prolonged fear and anxiety that the drug she received would be ineffective in precluding antibody sensitization.

The court pointed out the patient was not simply given one drug that was inaccurately represented as another. The shelf life of the Hyp-Rho-D had been exceeded and the drug was of unknown effectiveness. It was, in effect, a "new drug" without the Food and Drug Administration's approval and thus presumed dangerous. Because it was administered over the patient's objections despite the availability of another drug known to be effective and proven reliable, the hospital violated accepted medical standards of due care.

The court pointed out that the only way in which the hospital could avoid liability was if the patient had validly consented to the experiment. The court noted that Section 505(i) of the "Food and Drug Act" allows experimentation on humans with the consent of those to whom the drugs are administered. In this instance, the patient had expressly withheld consent; therefore, the hospital was liable for breach of its duty to obtain consent and was liable for the injurious effects to the patient as a result of use of the experimental therapy.

When a physician contemplates a novel or investigational procedure, he must inform his patient of the novel or investigational nature of the procedure so that he may give an informed choice whether or not to submit to a proposed treatment.

Gaston v. Hunter.   Dr. Hunter diagnosed that Mrs. Gaston had an intervertebral disc herniation at two levels and suggested pelvic traction. When her condition did not respond to this conservative treatment, Dr. Hunter discussed with her the possibility of performing discography and chymopapain chemonucleolysis as an alternative to surgical removal of the herniated discs. He explained that chemonucleolysis was a procedure whereby chymopapain is injected into a herniated disc. The theory was that the chymopapain would dissolve the center part of the disc, relieve the pressure and contract the herniated disc, thereby decompressing the impinged upon nerve roots. When this procedure was discussed with Mrs. Gaston, chymopapain had not been approved for general use by the Food and Drug Administration. However, the drug could be distributed for use to selected physician investigators as an "investigational" drug. Because such a drug was still in the clinical testing phase, the investigators using the drug had to operate under close supervision of the drug's sponsor (manufacturer) and had to carefully monitor the results experienced in using the drug. An associate, who practiced medicine with Dr. Hunter in a professional corporation, was an authorized investigator for chymopapain at that time. Dr. Hunter was not so authorized.

Dr. Hunter explained to Mrs. Gaston that the procedure involved the insertion of a needle into the nucleus pulposus of each herniated disc, using a lateral approach. The insertion would be fluoroscopically monitored to insure proper placement. Radioopaque dye would then be injected into the discs and x-rays taken. By this procedure (discography) herniated discs would be identified through the leakage of dye. These x-rays would also show the placement of the needles in the disc space. Without moving the needles, chymopapain would then be injected into the affected discs to dissolve some of the nucleus pulposus. After she received this information about the procedure, Mrs. Gaston signed a surgery consent form for "discography and chemonucleolysis," and also a form entitled "The Use of Chymopapain in Disc Disease," which explained the investigational nature of the drug.

After the procedure was completed, Mrs. Gaston experienced fever, disorientation, difficulty in urination, back pain, and diarrhea. A blood culture subsequently grew out E. coli. A lumbar puncture was performed, and culture of the cerebrospinal fluid grew out E. coli. The diagnosis of bacterial meningitis was made. It was reasoned that the meningitis was the direct result of the discographic needle piercing the bowel and then the dura in the process of injecting the disc with chymopapain. As a result of the meningitis, Mrs. Gaston suffered residual neurological deficitis, including an abnormal gait, numbness in her feet, inability to control her bladder or bowels, and constant back pain. Mrs. Gaston sued Dr. Hunter, contending that he was negligent in operating on her without obtaining an informed consent because the procedure involved an investigational ultrahazardous activity.

The court pointed out that chymopapain was not a defective product (simply because it was a toxic substance that could injure human tissue), which would automatically subject the manufacturer to liability for any injury associated with its use. The court noted that the risks and benefits of new or experimental drugs are often imperfectly known. When a new or experimental drug turns out to be less valuable or more dangerous than initially thought, it would be unfair to hold a physician who uses it responsible for deleterious effects of the drug, *if* the distribution of the drug was justified in light of the facts that were known or that should have reasonably become known to those involved in the clinical investigation. Because chymopapain was designed to provide an alternative to disc surgery in cases where the patient has failed to respond to conservative, nonsurgical treatment, the court declared that its potential benefits were obvious. Moreover, the court found that the risks which should have been known to those involved in its clinical investigation were not so great as to outweigh the expected benefits from the drug. Thus the court concluded that the decision to distribute chymopapin for clinical investigation was not improper.

Once the justifiable decision to distribute an investigational drug has been made, the manner of distribution must also be proper. This requires, among other things, that a proper warning be given. For experimental drugs, a subject must be clearly advised that the drug is experimental, and must be warned of known risks (and those that should be known through the exercise of reasonable care). In the case of investigational drugs that can be prescribed only by selected physician investigators, duty to warn is ordinarily satisfied if a proper warning is given by the prescribing physician.

The law treats novel procedures, such as chemonucleolysis, differently from other hazardous activities. The use of chymopapain was not the type of "hazardous activity" that would make Dr. Hunter liable for any injury it caused if Mrs. Gaston voluntarily participated in the clinical investigation or agreed to be treated with chymopapain. The general law of medical malpractice requires, and federal drug law seeks to insure, that the physician investigator obtain an informed consent from the patient before administering an investigational drug. Under these circumstances the court concluded that the use of investigational drugs is not so hazardous that the law should impose absolute liability on the physician who dispenses such drugs under a properly established protocol. Although the court acknowledged that chemonucleolysis is a hazardous procedure, it concluded that the doctrine of informed consent is flexible enough to encompass such hazardous or novel procedures so that a patient's rights and safety were preserved. If a patient consents to a procedure while understanding substantially the nature and "probable results" of the procedure, then no battery occurs when such a procedure is performed. Although it may be difficult to determine the "probable results" of a procedure which, like chemonucleolysis, has been incompletely investigated, the court declared that absent unusual facts, it would be improvident to impose absolute liability on a physician who prescribes an investigational drug.

The type of information important to the patient's ability to give an informed consent includes the statistical probability of the risks associated with a proposed procedure, the treating physician's experience (or lack of experience) in performing that procedure, the treating physician's prior results (if significantly different from the norm), and the risks and benefits of alternative treatment. The court noted that the fact that Dr. Hunter had limited experience with the procedure and was not an authorized investigator of chymopapain would be relevant to Mrs. Gaston's informed consent to the operation.

Fiorentino v. Wenger. A fourteen-year-old boy had a moderate degree of thoracolumbar scoliosis. An orthopedic surgeon evaluated his condition and recommended correction by means of an innovative spinal-jack operation, rather than the customary spinal fusion and body cast treatment.

The spinal-jack operation involved bony excision of each of seven ribs and spinous processes, detachment of the aorta and the vena cava from the spine, and temporary displacement of other internal organs. Holes were drilled into vertebrae and filled with two screws. Then a four-inch metal bar with a turnbuckle was attached to the screws. First by manual pressure, and then by a wrench applied to the turnbuckle, the spine was straightened.

The surgeon claimed the advantage of the spinal-jack operation was that, if successful, it was more certain of achieving the desired result of straightening of the spine. Moreover, the patient would be ready for normal activity after a brief period of convalescence, rather than the much longer period involved in the conventional spinal fusion and body cast procedure. However, the procedure had not gained general medical acceptance. The surgeon himself had devised the operation and had written at length in medical journals on the nature of his operation. He was the only one in the country using the technique, and had performed it thirty-five times. Five of the operations had been followed by serious complications, including death and paralysis, and he had been forbidden to perform any more spinal-jack operations at one hospital because of a resulting postoperative paralysis. The surgeon, however, felt that his procedure had improved constantly.

The patient's mother executed a "Permit for Medical/Surgical Treatment" which provided only that "I hereby give permission to Dr. Wenger to do whatever operation in his judgment may be necessary on my son, Michael." The surgeon did not explain to the mother the hazards of this operation, the available alternative, or the fact that the procedure was not employed by anyone else in the country.

The surgeon performed the spinal-jack operation on the boy. Postoperatively the boy died of a massive hemorrhage, presumably as a result of manipulation of major blood vessels during the operation. The parents subsequently sued the surgeon for performing a radical procedure without obtaining adequate consent.

The court stated that the surgeon had been negligent not because the performance of the spinal-jack operation was itself a negligent act, but because the surgeon had failed to obtain informed consent from the boy's parents for the performance of an innovative procedure. The court concluded that the surgeon had not explained sufficiently to the mother the novel nature of the procedure, its attendant risks, and available alternatives to treating the patient's problem.

In the next case, more specific requirements for a legal cause of action based on experimentation are discussed. The court applied the standard negligence test, that is, how a reasonably careful and prudent physician would have obtained consent for the procedure under similar circumstances. It placed the burden on the patient to prove that adequate consent was not obtained, and that the physician's failure to obtain consent caused the patient's ultimate injury.

Karp v. Cooley.   A forty-seven-year-old man had serious and progressive cardiovascular disease. In 1968, he had a pacemaker implanted, but within six months he developed progressive and refractory congestive heart failure. When a left ventricular cine-angiogram disclosed a ventricular aneurysm, the patient's physician referred him to a renowned cardiac surgeon in another state. In early 1969, the patient, accompanied by his wife, was admitted to the surgeon's hospital.

After several weeks of hospitalization, the surgeon suggested that the patient could achieve a more active life-style by undergoing a heart transplant. The patient rejected the suggestion preferring to undergo ventriculoplasty, a technique developed by the surgeon, in which a wedge of the diseased left ventricle is excised so that the remaining myocardium can function optimally. The procedure was explained to the patient, and he was told there was a 70 percent chance of surviving the operation. The following three-stage treatment process was also explained in a specially prepared surgical consent form:

> I, Haskell Karp, request and authorize Dr. Denton A. Cooley and such other surgeons as he may designate to perform upon me . . . cardiac surgery for advanced cardiac decompensation and myocardial insufficiency as a result of numerous coronary occlusions. The risk of this surgery has been explained to me. In the event cardiac function cannot be restored by excision of destroyed heart muscle and plastic reconstruction of the ventricle and death seems imminent, I authorize Dr. Cooley and his staff to remove my diseased heart and insert a mechanical cardiac substitute. I understand that this mechanical device will not be permanent and ultimately will require replacement by a heart transplant. I realize that this device has been tested in the laboratory, but has not been used to sustain a human being and that no assurance of success can be made. I expect the surgeons to exercise every effort to preserve my life through any of these means. No assurance has been made by anyone as to the results that may be obtained. . . .
>
> Signature _____
>
> HASKELL KARP

WITNESSES:

/s/ _____

Mrs. HASKELL KARP (wife)

_____

HENRY C. REINHARD, Jr. (Administrator)

The patient gave verbal consent to surgery at that time.

According to the patient's wife, on the following evening the surgeon told her and her husband that his condition had taken a turn for the worse and that he would die of a "burst aneurysm" if the surgery were not performed soon. She said the surgeon was insistent and impatient for the patient to sign the specially prepared surgical consent; therefore, the form was signed. The surgeon subsequently denied the statement about a burst aneurysm, or that he told the patient his condition was without hope.

After the ventriculoplasty was performed, the heart began to fibrillate.

This condition was corrected, but cardiac contractility was insufficient to sustain life. Therefore, the surgeon removed the heart and implanted the mechanical substitute. The patient lived with the mechanical heart substitute for about sixty-four hours. The surgeon and the wife both made public appeals through the news media for a heart donor. They were successful and an operation was performed to replace the mechanical heart with a human heart. However, the patient developed renal failure and died on the day following the operation.

The patient's wife brought a legal action against the surgeon contending that the consent for the operation was fraudulently obtained because all the risks were not explained to her.

The court concluded that a reasonably careful and prudent physician would probably have acted as the surgeon did under the circumstances of this case. As to the requirement of informed consent, the court pointed out that the consent form signed by the patient and witnessed by his wife specifically referred to all three steps of the three-stage operation with their attendant material risks. The court found that the patient had expressly and validly consented to all three stages of the operation actually performed. In addition, the court decided that the allegation of experimentation, even if proven, would not be recognized by the law as the cause of death of this patient.

SECTION 2: TREATMENT DECISIONS NOT IN ACCORDANCE WITH PUBLISHED GUIDELINES

Guidelines and recommendations for patient care published in medical textbooks or on a manufacturer's labels may provide more information on a topic than the attending physician possesses. Thus it may be inferred that in treating a patient the attending physician should have known about and used such established statements as a guide or warning. When published hazards materialize, it may be negligent to disregard such published warnings. Thus, as the following cases indicate, under certain circumstances the printed information may represent evidence of whether the requisite standard of medical care was met.

Koury v. Follo. A nine-month-old infant was hospitalized with a diagnosis of acute asthmatic bronchitis and possible pneumonia. The pediatrician prescribed Strepcombiotic, a combination of penicillin and streptomycin. He ordered the administration of 75 percent of the recommended adult dose in the adult form. Although the recognized safe upper limit dosage for this infant would have been 400 mg. in twenty-four hours, the infant received 750 mg. in twenty-four hours. The bottle from which the injectable drug was taken for administration was labeled in red capital letters, "NOT FOR PEDIATRIC USE." The usual dosage for adults was also printed on the label. As a result of streptomycin induced ototoxicity, the infant sustained permanent deafness. The parents sued the pediatrician on behalf of the child.

Expert testimony established that ototoxicity is a known hazard of streptomycin administration and occurs frequently when more than the recommended dosage is administered. Also introduced into evidence was *Nelson's Textbook of Pediatrics*, which included a statement of "Clark's Rule" for estimating dosages for children when the recommended adult dosage is known. Under this rule, 13 percent of the adult dosage would have been proper, not the 75 percent used. The prescribing physician admitted that he was aware that streptomycin can cause ototoxicity, but contended that he did not consider the drug dangerous in the dosage prescribed and, therefore, did not warn the infant's parents of possible adverse effects. However, he also admitted that he was not aware of the statements printed on the manufacturer's labels or the warnings contained in the package insert.

The court pointed out that although such printed statements cannot establish the legal standard a physician must follow, they are relevant to the determination of whether the physician used reasonable care in prescribing a drug which was, in fact, dangerous to an infant. The court concluded that the physician was negligent because he prescribed a potentially hazardous drug without reading, or in disregard of, printed warnings upon the container and in the package insert.

Salgo v. Leland Stanford, Jr., University Bd. of Trust. The patient had occlusive arteriosclerotic vascular disease; therefore, a cardiovascular surgeon recommended that he undergo translumbar aortography to determine if he was a good candidate for surgical repair. During this procedure, the needle was inserted once and 30 cubic centimeters of Sodium Urokon were injected at a rapid rate without difficulty. The injection took only a few seconds and then a series of x-rays were immediately taken. The radiologist examined them. They demonstrated that the infrarenal abdominal aorta was occluded. In consultation, the radiologist and the cardiovascular surgeon thought it was desirable to take additional x-rays to determine the extent of the occlusion. They hoped that by changing the timing of the x-rays in relation to the time of making the second injection, they might be better able to delineate the vascular tree. During this consultative period, the patient was kept under anesthesia and the needle remained in place, which was the custom while physicians determined whether additional x-rays were necessary. Twenty cubic centimeters of Sodium Urokon were then injected without changing the position of the needle and additional x-rays were taken. The entire procedure seemed to proceed in an uneventful manner. However, when the patient recovered from the anesthesia his lower extremities were paralyzed. The patient sued all physicians involved in the care of his vascular disease. He contended that the drug package insert set the standard of use for the contrast medium, and the treating physicians deviated from its recommendations.

The drug package insert recommended 10–15 cubic centimeters of Urokon as adequate for the procedure. The patient contended that if a radiopaque substance was injected in an amount greater than recommended in the package insert, such injection constituted experimentation, and all of the physicians participating in the aortography would be negligent unless the patient was first warned of the "experimentation" and consented to it. Expert medical testimony established that under the circumstances a 50 cubic centimeter dosage was customary, noting that the drug package insert recommended the use of 50 cubic centimeters of Urokon in coronary angiography. The court noted that the mere departure from the manufacturer's recommendation, where such departure is followed customarily by reasonable and reputable members of the profession, does not make the departure an "experiment" requiring the physician to obtain a special consent to the procedure.

The drug package insert stated that translumbar aortography should not be repeated within twenty-four hours. Thus the patient contended that the second injection was prohibited. The physicians contended that this statement was ambiguous; that it only prohibited a second insertion of the needle, and that the second injection with the needle remaining in place after the first injection did not contravene the instruction. Uncontroverted expert testimony established that the second injection, if deemed necessary, was customary.

The treating physicians contended that the drug package insert did not establish the standard of care because drug manufacturer's recommendations are always conservative and are quickly outdated. Furthermore, the recommendations contemplate, and it was the custom, that physicians using the drug eventually rely primarily on their own experience and the published literature of colleagues concerning use of the drug in clinical practice. The physicians pointed out that the developments that have taken place in the effective use of antibiotics and other drugs might never have been accomplished if physicians were required to follow blindly the suggestions of the manufacturers who prepare but do not use the medications.

The court pointed out that the drug package insert was not conclusive evidence of standard or accepted practice in the use of the drug by physicians; nor was a departure from such directions negligent. As a caveat, however, the court noted that the drug package insert does represent fundamental evidence of a proper method of use, given by the maker who must be presumed qualified to give directions for its use and warnings of any inherent danger. Therefore, this information should not be ignored by clinicians without adequate and proper justification.

As the previous cases indicate, a drug package insert ordinarily does not establish the standard of care required of a physician in the use of a drug. However, if a drug manufacturer recommends to the medical profession, in writing, the conditions under which its drug should be prescribed, the disorders it is designed to relieve, the precautionary measures which should be observed, and the dangers inherent in its use, the court may find that a physician's deviation from such recommendation without clinical justification is a deviation of the required standard of care, even though other physicians may also deviate from the instructions.

Ohligschlager v. Proctor Community Hospital. The physician diagnosed that his patient was in acute distress because of marked dehydration, secondary to severe gastroenteritis. He telephoned the hospital, arranged for her admission, and ordered intravenous fluids. When the physician arrived at the hospital at 6:30 P.M., he started an intravenous line in the right antecubital area. He then ordered 50 mg. of Sparine, an antiemetic, added to the intravenous fluids. Although a nurse was present when he started the intravenous fluids, the physician did not give her special instructions for administering the drug or monitoring the intravenous site.

The nurse did not add the Sparine to the intravenous bottle, but instead injected it directly into the tubing approximately three inches from the needle insertion. At 8:30 P.M., the patient complained of severe pain in her right elbow to a nurse's aide, who said she would see what she could do; however, no one came to the patient's room to evaluate her condition. When the physician returned to the hospital at approximately 10:00 P.M., the patient was receiving a second 1,000 cc. bottle of intravenous fluids. This time the physician ordered 75 mg. of Sparine. Again the nurse injected a bolus of the Sparine directly into the intravenous tubing. When the second bottle of intravenous fluid was completed at 1:00 A.M., the patient asked for medicine for the pain in her elbow area. The following day the nursing supervisor recorded in an incident report that "Apparently the I.V. solution infiltrated as the next morning her arm at the site of I.V. injection was discolored. Ice bags applied per doctor's order." The area where the intravenous solution had been given had become swollen, discolored, and indurated. A physician examined the patient and recorded, "Medical findings—large ecchymotic area—extending over entire ulnar-volar aspect of arm 3 inches above elbow to 2 inches above wrist. Etiology-infiltration from I.V. medication."

The skin of patient's arm eventually sloughed. She required grafting and subsequently sued the attending physician. She contended that the manufacturer's instructions furnished with Sparine established the professional standard of care which her physician was required to exercise, and that evidence showed he had not met it. The physician testified that he was generally familiar with the manufacturer's instructions for use of the drug which cautioned that

> Sparine when used intravenously should be used in a concentration no greater than 25 mg. per cc. The injection should be given slowly. Suitable dilution of the more concentrated solution, 50 mg. per cc. with an equivalent volume of physiological saline is advised if used intravenously. . . . care should be exercised during intravenous administration not to allow perivascular extravasation since under such circumstances chemical irritation may be severe. Intravenous administration . . . in a concentration of 50 mg. per cc. has resulted in localized thrombophlebitis . . . . Injection should be made only into vessels previously undamaged by multiple injections or trauma.

The court pointed out that although expert testimony is essential to the setting and proof of the standard of professional care, the facts in this case were appropriate for applying an exception to the rule. The explicit instructions furnished by the manufacturer for the proper manner of intravenous injection of the Sparine and the warning of the hazards accompanying its improper administration provided evidence of the proper professional standards which would otherwise ordinarily be shown by expert medical testimony. The attending physician was familiar with the recommendation that Sparine be used "in a concentration of no greater than 25 mg. per cc.", and that intravenous administration "in a concentration of 50 mg. per cc. has resulted in localized thrombophlebitis." Nevertheless, he ordered or allowed concentrations of 50 mg. and 75 mg. to be injected directly into the intravenous tubing. Although he was also familiar with the manufacturer's caveat that "care should be exercised during intravenous administration not to allow perivascular extravasation," he did not instruct the nursing staff to watch more carefully than usual for signs of extravasation. Therefore, the court concluded that under the circumstances, the physician administered treatment in a manner which deviated from the required standard of care.

Departures from printed instructions may not necessarily be evidence of a deviation from the required standard of care in treating a patient. If the physician has relied upon other accepted and reliable sources to guide therapeutic decisions, disregard of such guidelines may be legally acceptable.

Haynes v. Baton Rouge General Hospital.   The patient had undergone surgery to repair her fractured hip. Three years after the operation, avascular necrosis of the femoral head was diagnosed. She was operated on a second time and administered parenteral Keflin postoperatively. Because a routine urinalysis and subsequent culture detected a urinary tract infection caused by E. coli, her attending physician switched her from Keflin to Keflex, the oral form of cephalothin. The laboratory's drug sensitivity tests indicated the organism causing the urinary tract infection was sensitive to cephalothin. Later, an infection caused by a strain of Enterobacter, was discovered at the surgical wound site. The drug package insert indicated the Keflex was not effective against most strains of Enterobacter. The drug sensitivity test indicated that this organism was, like the Escherichia coli that was causing the urinary infection, sensitive to cephalothin. In the physician's opinion the patient was already responding satisfactorily to Keflex, therefore he saw no reason to change the antibiotic. The long period of healing of the wound site prompted the patient to subsequently sue her physician.

The patient contended that her physician prescribed Keflex even though the drug package insert indicated that it was not effective against most strains of Enterobacter. The attending physician and the other physicians who testified on his behalf all indicated that they rely on the pathologist's drug sensitivity tests more than on the literature disseminated by the drug companies. In this regard the physician testified as follows:

Q. Now, Doctor, we have had a lot of talk here about this drug flyer. As a practicing physician what is your view of these drug flyers?

A. I read them and certainly take note of the indications and the contra-indications particularly. However, I depend much more on the laboratory, the hospital laboratory examination.

Q. What is this, Doctor, rather than the drug flyer?

A. Well, I think it is a little more specific than the drug flyers.

Q. In other words, the hospital lab is testing the bug you are dealing with?

A. They are testing that particular bug, that particular strain of species, and if they can demonstrate that the antibiotic is effective against that particular strain, I think that is very pertinent information and justification for utilizing that particular drug.

Q. And the next step, how was the patient doing with that particular drug?

A. The patient was responding.

The patient's own witness, recognized by the court as an expert in microbiology specializing in infections, admitted the organism causing the wound-site infection was probably sensitive to Keflex. He testified in the following manner:

Q. Now, Doctor, assuming that the Enterobacter infection was sensitive to cephalothin, would this definitely mean that the Enterobacter infection would be sensitive to the drug Keflex?

A. I can't make a positive statement on that. It is probably, yes.

The court held that the physician was not negligent in prescribing the drug because there was insufficient proof that he had deviated from the standard of care due this patient by prescribing medication and continuing to use the same, notwithstanding admonition in the drug package insert that Keflex had not been demonstrated to be active against most species of Enterobacter. His reliance on the drug sensitivity tests and the clinical course of the patient justified his deviation, in this case, from the manufacturer's published guidelines.

SECTION 3: UNNECESSARY TREATMENT

Inherent in the requirement that a physician make reasonable treatment decisions in the course of managing the patient's condition is the duty not to subject the patient to unnecessary treatment. Thus a physician may be liable for performing unnecessary treatment when, for example, a technique was used which was not generally accepted by the medical community and which resulted in no beneficial effect; or when the facts of or need for the medical treatment were misrepresented in order to induce the patient to consent.

There is no consensus as to the definition of "necessary services." Ordinarily, an attending physician is given great latitude to choose what medical care is required to manage the patient's condition. Thus, in many situations, the physician is certifier of the patient's necessity for medical services.

Breeden v. Weinberger.   An eighty-two-year-old patient, with a long history of arteriosclerotic hypertensive cardiovascular disease, was admitted to a general hospital by her attending physician on January 30, because she had suffered a stroke with resulting bilateral hemiplegia, mental confusion, aphasia, and incontinence. At the time of her admission to the hospital, her attending physician ordered routine laboratory tests, an edentulous diet, continuation of medication she had been receiving at a nursing home, catheterization, and an enema. She received routine medical care and supervision during her hospital stay of 111 days. Progress reports by the attending physician reflected a gradual deterioration in her condition. Her attending physician noted in his discharge summary: "While in hospital all therapy unavailing. Her condition has slowly but steadily deteriorated and cannot believe she will last long. She is sent home as is getting no further benefit from hospitalization."

When the patient applied for Medicare benefits to cover the cost of hospitalization, a physician reviewer of the claim indicated that the patient may only be partially eligible for benefits. Subsequently an administrative law judge decided that no benefits were payable for the period of February 20 to

May 21. He based his decision on his interpretation of Section 1862(a)(1) of the Social Security Act which provided that no payment may be made for any expenses or services which are not "necessary for the diagnosis or treatment of illness or injury." The factual evidence cited in support of his decision was that the medical records documented only routine care and conventional oral medication. Although the "Nurses' Notes" reflected close observation, notation, and evaluation of her condition until February 19, after that time notations were infrequent and sporadic; and documented only catheter care, problems with eating, and difficulty with positioning the patient. Although the attending physician stated that his patient required constant attention for the entire period of hospitalization for proper care, his medical opinion was not cited in the judge's opinion. In addition the physician reviewer's opinion was not directly relied on.

The patient sought judicial review of the administrative law judge's decision. The court pointed out that the statutory phrase "not necessary for the diagnosis or treatment of illness" is not defined in the Social Security Act or in the Regulations, nor had a study of the legislative history of the Act revealed its intended meaning or the criteria to be used in its application. The court noted, however, that several judicial decisions, dealing with the denial of Medicare benefits for services rendered in "extended care facilities" on the basis that such services amounted to "custodial care," were analogous to the present patient's situation. These decisions indicated that, in determining whether the services rendered to the patient are covered under the Act, treatment that might at any time be necessary must be considered together with treatment actually provided in determining whether extended care services are justified. Moreover, these cases held that the responsibility for determining what services the patient requires rests primarily with the treating physician. The courts recognized that there is significant divergence of opinion among individual physicians in respect to evaluation of medical necessity for inpatient hospital services; therefore they have concluded that the judgment of the attending physician should not be rejected except under unusual circumstances. Although an attending physician's opinion is not a binding conclusion, where there is no direct conflicting evidence, his opinion should be given great weight.

The court held that, in this case, the administrative law judge had ignored the opinion of the attending physician. In addition, the only other medical opinion, that of a physician reviewer, was not directly relied on. Therefore, the basis for the decision was the judge's own interpretation of medical records and reports, ignoring the principle that the treating physician has the primary responsibility of determining what services are needed. Other than the judge's interpretation, nothing else indicated that the services rendered to the patient after February 20 were any less necessary than those rendered during the first 21 days of the patient's hospitalization.

If a physician intentionally attempts to deceive the patient by misrepresenting the type of procedure to be performed in order to induce the patient to undergo the procedure, the physician's conduct would be fraudulent and the procedure would be held "unnecessary." However, it would not be fraud if the physician had not intentionally attempted to deceive the patient, but later felt it was advisable to perform a procedure that the patient had not previously agreed to undergo.

Suskey v. Davidoff. When the patient entered the hospital she signed a paper authorizing her attending surgeon to "perform such operations as may be deemed necessary or advisable in the diagnosis and treatment." Prior to the operation her surgeon represented to the patient that he would remove only an ovarian cyst and perform an appendectomy, which he claimed was necessary. The patient authorized the surgeon to remove the appendix and the ovarian cyst. During the exploratory phase of the surgery, the surgeon detected a diseased gallbladder. For reasons which he felt comported with good medical practice, he made a separate incision and successfully removed her gallbladder. The patient was notified promptly after the operation that her gallbladder had been removed. When she heard this she sued her surgeon claiming that he had fraudulently removed her gallbladder without justification of any necessity.

The court noted that ordinarily a patient cannot predicate fraud on a physician's unfulfilled promises unless the physician had a present intent to misrepresent his performance. The court determined that the surgeon's statement that he would only remove the cyst and appendix was not itself a representation of existing fact, but rather a statement of intention, because, at that time, the surgeon had not intended to remove the gallbladder. Therefore the statement was not made falsely with intent to conceal a different purpose. Thus the court held that the physician's conduct did not constitute fraudulent misrepresentation of fact, which would establish a presumption that the surgery performed was unnecessary.

In a legal action for malpractice based on unnecessary treatment, the patient must prove that a therapeutic procedure was one so palpably unnecessary that a physician of ordinary care and skill, in the honest exercise of the physician's best judgment, would not have advised it.

Fausette v. Grim. A twenty-five-year-old patient had a history of dysmenorrhea and of multiple spontaneous abortions. When she was two months pregnant she experienced severe right lower quadrant abdominal pain. Her physician diagnosed acute appendicitis and recommended surgery. She asked what effect an operation would have upon her pregnancy and told him that she would not submit to an operation if it would endanger the fetus. According to the patient, the physician told her the procedure would not create significant obstetrical problems. After undergoing the operation she had a spontaneous abortion. The pathology specimen reportedly failed to demonstrate evidence of acute appendicitis.

The patient sued the physician, charging that with the knowledge of her pregnancy, he carelessly diagnosed her condition as acute appendicitis and carelessly advised an operation which was not necessary to preserve her life and health.

The patient's expert medical witness testified that it was bad practice to operate for appendicitis upon a pregnant woman whose temperature was normal because the disease was no longer in an acute state. He also testified that an appendectomy on a woman from one-to-three-months pregnant had a high risk of abortion. The treating physician contended he told the patient the chances of an abortion following the operation would be about even, and that she said she wanted the operation performed anyway because she could not stand the pain of another attack like the last one. The physician stated he found the appendix contained pus, and the uterus was over on one side, adhered to the pelvis, and retroverted. He removed the appendix, lysed the uterine adhesions, and placed the uterus in its normal position. With her uterus in the condition it was, the physician's opinion was that the patient would have aborted again. In addition, he felt the pus-filled appendix would probably have caused problems prior to delivery because the expansion of the uterus as pregnancy advanced might have loosened the adhesions of the appendix, releasing pus and causing peritonitis.

The court pointed out that in order to prove the physician was negligent in advising an unnecessary operation, the patient must establish not only that the surgery was unnecessary, but also that her condition was such that the average skillful surgeon would have known that the surgery was not necessary. This required showing that the operation was one so palpably unnecessary that a reasonable surgeon would not have advised it. The court concluded that the patient had failed to establish that her condition did not require an operation, that is, the circumstances of her case would have led a reasonably careful and skilled physician to believe it was "unnecessary."

A physician who uses a mode of treatment not generally accepted, in the hope of assisting the patient, ordinarily would not be liable for providing unnecessary treatment if a reasonable and prudent physician would have provided the same treatment under similar circumstances. However, if this standard is not met, the law may conclude that the treatment was unnecessary.

Hood v. Phillips. In 1966, when Dr. Phillips first examined Mr. Hood, he diagnosed emphysema. In an attempt to reduce Mr. Hood's impairment in pulmonary function, Dr. Phillips surgically removed one of Hood's carotid bodies. The procedure did not result in any beneficial relief. When Hood became aware that the technique generally was not accepted by the medical community, he sued Dr. Phillips for subjecting him to unnecessary surgery.

Dr. Phillips testified that between 1962 and 1966 he had performed more than 1,200 carotid body excisions which, in his experience, produced beneficial results in 85 percent of his patients. He acknowledged that the use of this type of surgery was controversial and not generally accepted as a method for treating emphysema. Physicians testifying for Mr. Hood characterized carotid body surgery as an unaccepted mode of treatment for emphysema, the efficacy of which was not supported by medical data. They noted that the procedure had been proposed without adequate scientific rationale, tried by a number of physicians, found to be ineffectual, and abandoned. One medical witness stated that in his judgment the procedure was not only not beneficial, but potentially harmful.

The court pointed out that the physician who undertakes a mode of treatment which a reasonable and prudent physician would undertake under similar circumstances is not subject to liability for harm caused thereby to the patient. The burden of proof is on the patient-plaintiff to establish that the treatment was "outmoded" or "unnecessary." Circumstances to be considered in this determination include the expertise of and means available to the physician, the health of the patient, and the state of medical knowledge. In this case, the court held that expert testimony had convincingly established that Dr. Phillips's mode of treatment was ineffective and unacceptable.

Medical and surgical procedures which in retrospect turn out to be unnecessary but which represent a physician's good-faith effort at treatment are usually not indicative of fraudulent inducement of medical care, unless the physician knew at the time that the facts of the case were deliberately misstated. However, a physician who carelessly or recklessly distorts the medical facts, as to the urgency of the need for a particular procedure, may be charged with performing unnecessary and unauthorized surgery.

Nolan v. Kechijiah. The patient experienced left upper quadrant abdominal and hypochrondral pain. The physician she consulted took x-rays which he felt demonstrated that the spleen was "ptotic" when the patient was in an upright position. He told the patient and her husband that her spleen was "hanging by a thread," and that such a condition required an operation "to build up the ligaments" that held the spleen in place. Acting upon these representations and the physician's assurance that the operation was not a serious one, she consented to the proposed operation. During surgery the physician observed adhesions between the spleen and the stomach surface. In freeing the spleen from the stomach the physician tore the splenic artery at the hilum, thereby encountering massive hemorrhage, which had to be controlled by ligating the vessel and removing the spleen. When the patient learned that her spleen had been removed, she sued the physician for fraudulent misrepresentation leading to an unnecessary removal of the spleen.

At trial, the pathologist who examined the spleen testified that, except for a few fibrous adhesions on its inner surface, there was no evidence of disease. He stated, "It was an excised spleen, and that's all there was, no more, no less."

The court pointed out that unless an immediate operation is urgently and reasonably necessary, a physician has no right to perform such operation without the patient's consent. The court concluded that the physician's representations to the patient about the condition of her spleen were made in so reckless a manner as to be tantamount to misrepresentation. In relying on such representations the patient consented only to an operation that "would build up the ligaments" of the spleen. Although there may have been implied consent to lyse adhesions if it were necessary to attain the object of the operation, the excision of the spleen was not necessary nor reasonably incidental to the operation. Thus, extension of the procedure, regardless of its merits, was unauthorized.

A surgeon who knows that an operation is unnecessary but performs it to reap personal economic benefit, is acting outside the scope of professional practice. Therefore, expert testimony is not required to establish that his conduct is fraudulent.

Gonzales v. Nork. A twenty-seven-year-old man suffered from neck and back pain after being injured in an automobile accident. At the suggestion of his mother-in-law he consulted an orthopedic surgeon who promptly hospitalized the patient. Within a few days, the surgeon performed a laminectomy and spinal fusion. As a result of the procedure, the patient developed severe arachnoiditis that caused him constant back and leg pain. He sued, claiming the surgeon had fraudulently performed unnecessary surgery.

At trial, evidence was introduced which profiled the surgeon's professional conduct as it related to patients he had operated on. The surgeon made a practice of operating on the basis of inadequate and false preoperative findings. He produced false positive myelograms and falsified his progress records. Two medical experts who had reviewed twenty-six laminectomies that the surgeon had performed between 1966 and 1970 concluded that the surgeon's preoperative findings were statistically inconceivable. The surgeon induced patients to consent to surgery; some he actually terrorized, others he gulled or deceived. In those rare circumstances when he did obtain consultation with another physician prior to performing surgery, he often ignored the consultant's advice and sometimes lied to the patient about the consultant's recommendations. He falsified a consultation report in a patient's narrative summary and lied about the results of a patient's electromyogram.

The surgeon admitted to performing numerous other unnecessary operations over a nine-year period in order to satisfy financial obligations. His accountant testified that the surgeon performed unnecessary procedures to satisfy the demands of his creditors. The court concluded the evidence amply demonstrated that, under the guise of providing medical care, the surgeon had pursued a plan of purposeful fraud for his own economic benefit. Thus he was negligent for performing unnecessary surgery.

Section 4: Complications of Treatment

Some methods of treatment have attendant risks which may materialize into complications. The physician is expected to be aware of well-recognized complications associated with a treatment, and to act to avoid the occurrence of the complication if possible. However, as the first case illustrates, if a procedure is medically indicated, the mere occurrence of a complication is not necessarily indicative of physician negligence.

Johns Hopkins Hospital v. Genda.   A nine-year-old patient underwent cardiac surgery because of a congenital heart defect. During closing, a needle broke while the surgeon was suturing the chest wall fascia. The lost and imbedded fragment was intentionally left behind because time was of the essence, and it was not anticipated that it would be harmful to the patient. No perceived effects of the needle were noted by the patient during the postoperative and convalescent period. When the patient was x-rayed one year later in preparation for plastic surgery on his chest scar, the needle fragment was radiographically detected and his parents learned for the first time what had happened. Thereafter, the patient began to complain of chest pain and refrained from ordinary activities for fear of dislodging the fragment. The parents sued on behalf of their son, contending that the surgeon's placement of the needle was improper and an act of negligence.

The primary issue at trial was whether the breaking of the needle constituted an act of negligence on the part of the surgeon. The patient predicated his entire case on two things: first, that the needle broke; and second, that the surgeon, during deposition, stated that the needle broke because it was "put in at the wrong angle." He contended that the surgeon's own statement was expert testimony of his negligence.

The following transcript of the deposition was introduced at trial by the defendant surgeon's counsel.

PLAINTIFF'S COUNSEL:	You mentioned suturing and closing.
SURGEON:	Yes.
PLAINTIFF'S COUNSEL:	Did you follow the accepted surgical practice in carrying out this closure?
SURGEON:	Yes.
PLAINTIFF'S COUNSEL:	Did you use the accepted procedure in doing it?
SURGEON:	Yes.
PLAINTIFF'S COUNSEL:	Did you employ the accepted technique?
SURGEON:	Yes.
PLAINTIFF'S COUNSEL:	Even as to the insertion of the needle at particular angles, did you follow the accepted surgical practice in that respect?
SURGEON:	Yes.
PLAINTIFF'S COUNSEL:	In spite of the presence of all this, the needle broke. Is that what you mean?
SURGEON:	Yes.
PLAINTIFF'S COUNSEL:	Quite apart from just not sewing the child up at all, was there anything you could have done to prevent the needle from breaking?
SURGEON:	No.

On direct examination at trial, the surgeon gave the following explanation of his deposition testimony:

DEFENDANT'S COUNSEL:	Now in using that movement which you've demonstrated, you stated in answer to plaintiff's counsel when he deposed you, that it was the wrong angle. Do you remember that?
SURGEON:	Yes.
DEFENDANT'S COUNSEL:	Why did you say it was the wrong angle? What do you mean by that?
SURGEON:	I said it was the wrong angle because after the needle had broken, after the fact, I decided that I must have put it in at the wrong angle, but I have no way of knowing what the wrong angle is. I said I put it at the wrong angle because it broke after I put it in there.
DEFENDANT'S COUNSEL:	Was it, would you use the same angle today as you used then?
SURGEON:	Yes, I would use the same angle, I literally put thousands of these sutures in before and since this particular incident, and only occasionally the needle breaks. I really don't know why it breaks. Yesterday I tried to break this needle to demonstrate the angle, but I can't break it on purpose.

The court pointed out that the patient was requesting the court and jury to adduce from the surgeon's statement that he put the needle in "at the wrong angle," that at one and the same time a standard was established (a proper angle vis-à-vis a wrong or improper angle) and a violation of the same standard. That viewpoint placed a self-serving and artificial construction on the surgeon's explanation as to what he meant when he stated the needle was "put in at the wrong angle." The court concluded that the surgeon's testimony, explaining his statement, demonstrated that there was no way in which he could tell ahead of time whether he was inserting the needle at the wrong angle (rather than the right angle), other than from the after-the-fact knowledge that the needle broke. In other words, he could not tell prior to making the suture whether the needle was inserted correctly, other than by the successful carry through of the suture. Therefore his statement was not an admission of negligent application of skill. The surgeon stated that he used the motion and angle that he would use were he to insert the needle in fascia again, and that he had successfully put in a needle in the same manner in similar operations thousands of times without it breaking.

The patient further contended that the surgeon's act of putting in the needle was a singular act of negligence because it was analogous to carelessly dropping a scalpel on the patient, causing a cut, or dropping fluid on the patient, causing a burn. The court refused to accept the analogy because dropping a scalpel or acid on a patient is not a part of any operative technique, whereas the evidence in this case was uncontested that an accepted technique for closing the chest cavity is to suture the fascia of the muscle by using the same motion and angle which the surgeon was using at the time that the needle broke. Therefore the court concluded that sufficient evidence was not presented that the surgeon sutured in any manner other than with that reasonable degree of care and skill that a surgeon would ordinarily employ.

A physician is expected to anticipate and avoid the occurrence of recognized complications of a procedure, to monitor the patient to detect the occurrence of a complication early, and to plan for and execute effective management of the complication, once detected. Thus, prior to an operation, an anesthesiologist and a surgeon may be obligated to confer as to the advisability of surgery, the preoperative status and suitability of the patient for surgery, and to plan an efficient procedure for management of recognized complications.

Quintal v. Laurel Grove Hospital.   In May 1960, a ten-year-old boy underwent an operation to correct extraocular muscle imbalance. The procedure was not entirely successful in correcting his visual problems. Thus, in July 1960, he was again hospitalized and scheduled for another extraocular muscle operation. Prior to the operation, it was noted that he had a low-grade fever and an elevated white blood cell count. He also appeared to be unusually anxious and upset about undergoing a second operation; therefore, he was given twice as much preoperative sedation as he had received for the first procedure.

During the induction phase of general anesthesia, "vagal stimulation" precipitated a cardiopulmonary arrest. The anesthesiologist had not been closely monitoring the pulse and blood pressure; only after marked cyanosis was apparent did the anesthesiologist appreciate the problem and yell to the ophthalmologist, who had just been gloved, that the patient had arrested. The ophthalmologist rushed toward the table. The anesthesiologist squeezed the oxygen bag with one hand and with the other attempted external cardiac massage. This process was continued for about thirty seconds and was then stopped to ascertain if the boy's heart had started to function again. When it had not, the process was repeated for another thirty seconds, again without success. The anesthesiologist then asked the ophthalmologist to open the boy's chest for manual cardiac massage. The ophthalmologist stated that he did not feel qualified to perform such an operation, and left the operating room to get help. In the scrub room he encountered a general surgeon. At the ophthalmologist's request, the surgeon entered the room, was gloved and handed a scalpel. He opened the patient's chest and began cardiac massage. The heart began to beat immediately. Approximately four minutes had elapsed between the time the anesthesiologist notified the ophthalmologist that the heart had stopped and the time the heart was again started by means of open heart massage. By this time, the boy had sustained brain damage which left him blind, mute, and quadriplegic. On behalf of the boy, his parents sued the anesthesiologist and the ophthalmologist.

Expert medical testimony established that cardiac arrest, a known risk of general anesthesia, occurs rarely but persistently, and may not be caused by negligence. To determine whether negligence was a substantial causal factor of a cardiac arrest, the cause of it must be examined. If the physician should have, but did not, reasonably anticipate it; and if he should have prevented it, he may be held liable for the complication. In this case, either fever or significant apprehension were sentinel signals that might have increased the sensitivity of the boy's heart and made it more prone to cardiac arrest. The physicians, therefore, should have considered postponing the surgery or should have more closely monitored the patient for early signs of cardiac irritability, because early treatment was critically important to avoid brain damage.

The court was also critical of the management of the patient after the arrest had occurred. It noted that at the time of the incident, open chest massage was a customary method of managing such a problem, if external massage were not successful. The medical profession was so concerned about managing cardiac arrests that the medical association had furnished lectures, movies, and demonstrations on how cardiac arrest should be handled. Placards with directions on how to handle the emergency were placed in all operating rooms. The ophthalmologist was also aware that time was of the essence in such cases, and that the longer the brain was deprived of oxygen, the greater the probability of permanent brain damage. The court inferred that approximately one minute was consumed because the ophthalmologist was unable to manage the problem, and that these were brain-damaging seconds. All expert testimony admitted that the operating surgeon, regardless of his specialty, should be prepared to manage in some way the occurrence of a surgical cardiac arrest. The court held that if the ophthalmologist lacked the requisite skills for treating a surgical cardiac arrest, he should have had someone in attendance during the operation who could.

A treating physician is expected to expertly manage complications that occur as a result of treatment. The more urgent and life-threatening the complication, such as a cardiopulmonary arrest, the greater the need for proper execution and precision in management.

Daniels v. Hadley Memorial Hospital.   A forty-three-year-old patient went to a hospital emergency room for treatment of infected skin abrasions. The emergency room physician ordered an intramuscular injection of penicillin at 9:05 A.M. The patient departed the hospital at 9:25 A.M. At approximately 9:30 A.M., he was discovered in the hospital parking lot in a semiconscious state. At 9:35 A.M., when he was returned to the emergency room in a wheelchair, he was diaphoretic and obtunded. His pulse was forty and his respiratory rate was four. At 9:36 A.M., the physician who had prescribed the penicillin took over care of the patient. Within the first minute, oxygen was given through a nasal cannula. At 9:38 A.M., a subcutaneous injection of Sus-Phrine and Solu-Cortef was administered. By this time, the patient had stopped breathing, and external cardiac massage was initiated. A nurse rushed to the scene with an emergency "crash cart" that contained equipment for positive pressure oxygen, including an Ambu bag unit, oxygen tanks, tubing, masks, and airways. However, none of this equipment was used, nor was mouth-to-mouth resuscitation utilized to ventilate the patient. At 9:40 A.M., an anesthesiologist arrived, and immediately provided positive pressure respiratory assistance. By 9:42 A.M., the anesthesiologist had intubated the patient and established an intravenous line. Epinephrine, Solu-Cortef, sodium bicarbonate, and Aramine were pushed intravenously. At 9:43 A.M., the anesthesiologist noted that the patient's pupils had dilated. An intracardiac injection of epinephrine was then given. The patient's heart was still beating, though abnormally, and continued to beat until 10:00

A.M., when it began to fibrillate. Efforts at defibrillation failed. At 10:10 A.M., the patient was pronounced dead. Autopsy disclosed the death was caused by laryngeal and pulmonary edema which were consistent with an anaphylactic reaction.

A suit was brought against the physician and hospital. It contended that they caused his death by failing to give the patient adequate respiratory assistance during the resuscitation effort, and failing to give him an intravenous or intracardiac injection of epinephrine as soon as possible during the resuscitation attempt.

The court pointed out that the patient was in shock when he was rushed back to the emergency room. His respiration and his circulation were severely impaired and rapidly deteriorating. When the resuscitative effort began at 9:36 A.M., decisive and appropriate action was necessary if the patient's life was to be saved. Faced with this emergency, the physician had a duty to do three things without delay, to prevent irreversible brain damage. The first and most important action was to effectively deliver oxygen into the patient's lungs. This required giving the patient respiratory assistance by establishing an effective airway and by using positive pressure to force oxygen into the patient's lungs by means of mouth-to-mouth resuscitation, an Ambu bag, or an endotracheal tube and respirator. The second required action was to get epinephrine into the patient's circulatory system where it could begin to counteract the effects of the anaphylactic reaction. This necessitated either an intravenous or intracardiac injection of epinephrine, because, in a shock condition, the patient had no effective peripheral circulation; therefore, subcutaneous or intramuscular injections would be of little value. The third required action was to restore the patient's circulation so that both the oxygen and the epinephrine could be transported. This involved effective external cardiac massage to circulate the blood.

The court held that although cardiac massage was started immediately and was continued throughout the resuscitation effort, the physician made no attempt to provide proper respiratory assistance to the patient during the first four minutes of resuscitation (from 9:36 A.M. to 9:40 A.M.), even though the patient had gone into respiratory arrest. During these critical minutes, the patient's brain was not receiving enough oxygen. This was demonstrated when a physician recorded that the patient's pupils were dilated at 9:43 A.M. In addition, the physician did not administer an intravenous or intracardiac injection of epinephrine until 9:42 A.M.—six minutes into the resuscitation effort. The court concluded that the physician had a duty to get both oxygen and epinephrine into effective circulation as quickly as possible. His failure to do this effectively represented negligent management, and eliminated whatever chance the patient had of surviving; therefore it was a contributing causative factor to the patient's death.

An operating surgeon is expected to carefully monitor the patient for potential complications of the surgery so that timely identification of such complications can be made. Thus, for example, if a surgeon transects or ligates a duct during a cholecystectomy and does not identify this complication within a reasonable period, an inference of negligence is raised.

Guillen v. Martin. The patient consulted the surgeon with an abdominal complaint that ultimately led to a diagnosis of cholelithiasis. A cholecystectomy was performed on August 6. The operating surgeon was aware that he needed to expose and identify the cystic, hepatic, and common ducts, and to guard against damage to the latter two structures. After the operation, the patient continued to experience pain, developed a fever, was unable to retain food, and had abdominal distention. She did not have a natural bowel movement during her entire stay in the hospital. On August 15 the patient was discharged from the hospital; however, she continued to complain of pain to her surgeon and was readmitted to the hospital. Ultimately the surgeon called in a consultant who drained large amounts of bile-like fluid from the abdominal cavity and diagnosed bile peritonitis. Subsequently, the patient underwent an exploratory laparotomy which disclosed that during the cholecystectomy the common bile duct had been severed and partly ligated, causing bile to leak into the peritoneal cavity. One suture, imbedded in scar tissue, was lying loose and unattached near the severed end of the proximal common bile duct. The common hepatic duct had been severed about two centimeters from the juncture of the right and left hepatic ducts. The juncture of the common hepatic and the cystic duct was missing. When the patient learned of the complication, she sued her original surgeon for, among other things, negligent delay in the diagnosis of injury to her common bile duct.

The court held that the patient's postoperative course of fever, persistent pain, copious bile drainage were sufficient postoperative findings to alert the physician that he probably had damaged the bile duct. He should have known that an exploration of the area of the bile ducts was necessary to determine the reason for these findings. If he had done so, he would have promptly detected the occurrence of the complication of surgery, and lessened the ultimate injury to the patient.

Third parties who are indirectly involved with the care of a patient may have a duty to warn an attending physician about the complications of a treatment they recommend. This is illustrated by the following case which suggests that a physician may reasonably expect a drug manufacturer to warn of serious complications associated with the use of a drug or procedure, especially if the manufacturer is aware of greater dangers than those described in the official labeling of the drug.

Runnels v. Astra Pharmaceuticals. In 1968, a seven-year-old girl had a bike accident in which she sustained a deep laceration to her left leg. Her family practitioner determined that an emergency repair of the laceration was necessary and that local anesthesia would be inadequate. He telephoned the hospital to say that he was bringing the child, and he requested the services of an anesthesiologist. Because of the weekend schedule, an anesthesiologist was not available. Rather than transfer the patient to a neighboring facility, the physician decided to utilize intravenous regional anesthesia (IVRA), a technique he had not previously used. He based the decision to use it partly on recollections from *Blocking the Pathways of Pain,* an advertising booklet published by the pharmaceutical company which made Xylocaine.

In 1966, the pharmaceutical company sent the booklet to 141,000 general practitioners, surgeons, anesthesiologists, hospitals, and medical schools. At the time, the Food and Drug Administration had approved Xylocaine only as a local anesthetic. In order to enlarge its market the pharmaceutical company promoted Xylocaine for IVRA, a technique in which an entire limb is anesthetized, and a pneumatic cuff is applied to prevent the Xylocaine, which is injected into a vein, from flowing to other parts of the body.

In the operating room, the physician raised the patient's leg so the blood would drain away from the vein injection site. A nurse applied the cuff which was then inflated. The physician performed a saphenous vein cutdown, inserted a catheter, and injected 20 cc. of 1 percent Xylocaine over approximately ten minutes. A minute or two later the child had a seizure. The physician assumed the patient was having respiratory failure. In fact, she was exhibiting a toxic reaction to the Xylocaine. The surgeon's diagnosis of the complication was mistaken because he was unaware of the "flow-back" phenomenon associated with IVRA in which Xylocaine crossed the tourniquet barrier in children. Although the physician initially managed to control the seizures, when he removed the pneumatic cuff the seizures resumed. As a result, the patient sustained permanent brain damage.

On behalf of their child, the parents filed a lawsuit against the physician and the pharmaceutical company. They charged that the company had not made a reasonable effort to disclose to physicians the company's knowledge about the risk of serious injury from IVRA.* Both the pharmaceutical

---

* Shortly after the pamphlet distribution at an IVRA promotional symposium in 1966, an anesthesiologist reported cases of "flow-back" phenomenon in children. Anesthesiologists at the symposium warned the company that IVRA never should be used by anyone not specifically trained to use it. The company neither modified its brochure nor issued a warning to any of the physicians to whom it had distributed the pamphlet following the symposium.

company and the physician contributed to the settlement and satisfaction of the suit.

As a result of this malpractice case, the physician's insurer canceled his malpractice coverage, barring him from obtaining or maintaining staff privileges at reputable hospitals. He went bankrupt, neglected his family and practice, left town, and later was divorced. When he saw his children he was reminded of his brain-damaged patient. He sought and received psychiatric treatment for these problems. The physician then sued the pharmaceutical company, asserting that fraudulent inducements by the manufacturer prompted him to cause permanent injury to his patient. He contended that he had used IVRA because the company promoted it as suitable for solo use. In essence, he charged the company with laying a "malpractice trap" for him, by enticing him into undertaking an experimental treatment promoted by the pharmaceutical company which knew of, but did not disclose, any hazards associated with the treatment. He contended that the company was liable not only for failure to provide him with adequate warning but also for fraud. In support of his contention, he presented evidence that the company intentionally withheld important evidence about the substantial risks of IVRA, especially when used on children. He produced medical literature that reflected various opinions about the value and safety of the procedure. A 1965 editorial in a respected medical journal recommended the procedure not be generally used until more controlled studies were done. A 1966 study of electrocardiogram monitored cases emphasized the risk of Xylocaine leaking by the tourniquet with resulting cardiotoxic effects, and recommended the technique be abandoned.

In 1967, the company promoted Cetanest as superior to Xylocaine for regional anesthesia because it was safer. This Cetanest promotion involved the mailing of a brochure to 65,000 physicians. The Food and Drug Administration learned about this promotion after the mailing and directed the company to mail "Dear Doctor" letters stating the procedure was still regarded as experimental. At first this was to be a general mailing to all physicians in the United States, but because the Food and Drug Administration did not know about the previous Xylocaine brochure, they permitted the company to notify only the 65,000 physicians who had received the Cetanest brochure. Although the general practitioner recalled having seen the Blocking the Pathways to Pain brochure, he did not receive the Cetanest mailing and, therefore, did not receive a letter of warning about the experimental and hazardous nature of this mode of anesthesia.

The pharmaceutical company's central contention was that it owed no duty to physicians using their products to protect them from malpractice suits. However, the judge rejected this argument and instructed the jury that the physician was a "consumer" for purposes of fixing the company's duty.

On the facts of the case, the jury decided that the pharmaceutical company had committed fraud, and also had sold Xylocaine with insufficient warnings of known hazards from its use.

SECTION 5: TREATMENT DECISIONS FOR SPECIAL CONDITIONS AND CIRCUMSTANCES

A physician is expected to adhere to recognized and acceptable methods in the treatment of his patient, especially in the dispensation of medication. Although the law recognizes circumstances in which special conditions require that the physician adopt an individual approach to a patient's problem, that approach should be within the bounds of acceptable practice. There are also special circumstances which may affect a physician's therapeutic plan, especially if the means of treatment would constitute an invasion of certain constitutional rights.

A physician is expected to prescribe medication only in the course of a bona fide physician-patient relationship. Such a relationship presupposes at least rudimentary efforts at medical history taking, physical examination, and a determination that a particular drug is medically indicated and beneficial to the patient. Thus the prescription of a controlled drug that is issued to a habitual user, not for the purpose of curing the patient's habit, would not be issued in the "course of professional practice."

U.S. v. Moore. The physician conducted a large-scale operation of dispensing Methadone. Over a six-month period, three pharmacies filled over eleven thousand prescriptions that he had written. He often wrote over one hundred prescriptions for Methadone a day. In billing his "patients," he used a sliding fee scale, governed solely by the quantity prescribed rather than by the medical services performed. The fees ranged from $15 for a fifty-pill prescription to $50 for one-hundred-fifty pills. In less than six months, his prescription service receipts totaled more than $200,000. This activity eventually came to the attention of law enforcement authorities and he was prosecuted for violation of the Controlled Substances Act.

The physician's defense was that he had devised a new method of detoxification based upon the work of a British medical practitioner. Utilizing this method he prescribed large quantities of Methadone to achieve a "blockade" condition in which the addict became so saturated with Methadone that heroin would have no effect. The intent was to instill in the addict a strong psychological desire for detoxification. However, medical evidence at the trial established that the physician's therapeutic conduct was inconsistent with all accepted methods of treating addicts.

The physician also contended that his status as a "physician" registered to dispense controlled substances precluded prosecution as a drug trafficker. The court, however, held that only the lawful acts of registrants are exempted from prosecution. The court declared that the physician's conduct exceeded the bounds of professional practice: he gave inadequate physical examination or none at all; he ignored the results of the tests he did perform; he did not administer Methadone at the clinic and took no precautions against its misuse and diversion; he did not regulate the dosage at all, prescribing as much and as frequently as the patient demanded; and he did not charge for medical services rendered, but graduated his fee according to the number of tablets desired. The court concluded that, in practical effect, he acted as a large scale "pusher"—not as a physician.

A physician who indiscriminately dispenses controlled substances to patients at their request who he has not examined, would not be acting in the usual course of the medical practice or for a legitimate medical purpose.

U.S. v. Rogers. It became known to law enforcement authorities that Dr. Rogers routinely asked his patients what medication they wanted prescribed, instead of his prescribing what he thought they needed after examining them. A female agent, working in an undercover capacity with the police department, made an appointment to see Dr. Rogers. She filled out a medical history form, had her blood pressure and weight taken by the receptionist. When she went in to see Dr. Rogers, he had the form that she had filled out with him. He asked her what her problem was and she informed him that she was having trouble sleeping at night and was unable to stay awake in the morning. Dr. Rogers asked her what she wanted and she told him Quaalude and Desoxyn. Without examining her, he wrote her prescriptions for Quaalude, Desoxyn, and Valium. Subsequently, when the female agent returned to the office, she told Dr. Rogers that she was having the same problem as the last time. He again wrote her prescriptions for Desoxyn and Quaalude, but did not examine her. When Dr. Rogers asked for his fee, the agent told him that she had a male friend in the waiting room who had the money and also wanted to see him. The male agent was allowed into Dr. Rogers' office. Neither history nor blood pressure was taken. He received no physical examination of any kind. After the agent told Dr. Rogers that he was a truck driver who had turnaround routes which caused him insomnia at night and difficulty staying awake during the day, Dr. Rogers asked him what he wanted; the male agent replied that he wanted some Desoxyn. Then Dr. Rogers asked him, "What else?" and the agent replied that he also wanted some Quaalude. Dr. Rogers asked him if he wanted anything else, and before the agent could reply, Dr. Rogers said, "How about Valium or Librium?"

When the male agent made a second visit to Dr. Roger's office, the receptionist gave him a medical history form to fill out. The agent wrote on it that his problem was "drowsiness and staying awake." Dr. Rogers had the form when he saw the male agent on this occasion. Again Dr. Rogers asked the male agent what he wanted, and the agent responded that he wanted some Preludin. Dr. Rogers told him that Preludin was hard to get and suggested Desoxyn or Biphetamine. The male agent agreed to any one of them. Dr. Rogers then asked "What else?" and the agent responded that he wanted to try some Tuinal. Again, Dr. Rogers asked "What else?" and the male agent stated that that should do for the time being. But Dr. Rogers then asked him "How about some Librium or Valium for relaxation?" The male agent opted for Valium.

During the next visit of the male agent to Dr. Rogers' office, while waiting to see Dr. Rogers, a receptionist prewrote some prescriptions for him and when the male agent entered Dr. Rogers' office, all Dr. Rogers did was sign his name to the prewritten prescriptions for Tuinal, Biphetamine, and Valium.

On the basis of these documented activities the government charged Dr. Rogers with violating the Controlled Substances Act. Expert testimony established that the drugs which Dr. Rogers prescribed were often abused, causing physical dependence, and making individuals who acquire such addictions susceptible to overdose. Testimony also indicated that it was bad medical practice to prescribe a controlled drug before doing a physical examination of the patient to make sure that there was no organic cause of the patient's symptoms. Although the nurse might take the blood pressure, pulse, and weight of the patient, the rest of the examination should be performed by the physician. Furthermore, the physician should go into detail about the patient's past medical history in addition to what the patient or the nurse had written on the medical history chart.

It was also established that a physician who would prescribe an amphetamine, or Desoxyn, Quaalude, and Valium at the same time for the same patient, or who routinely prescribes these drugs in these combinations, would not be acting in the usual course of the medical practice or for a legitimate medical purpose.

Dr. Rogers testified that he would give his patients a mental status examination, because a physical examination was not necessary to diagnose and to prescribe for anxiety, stress, and depression. Thus the medications he had prescribed could be properly done with only a mental status examination and without a physical examination. Expert testimony indicated that in the usual course of medical practice, prescription of medications would be based on the results derived from a combination of the mental status examination and physical examination of the patient. Merely talking or conversing to a patient ordinarily would be an insufficient basis for the prescribing of a controlled substance. The court concluded that the evidence of Dr. Rogers' routine prescription practices demonstrated that he knowingly and intentionally distributed or dispensed controlled substances for other than a legitimate medical purpose in the usual course of his professional practice.

A physician is expected to individualize care and to avoid the adoption of a unitary "standard" pharmacological approach which the medical profession has established as unacceptable for a therapeutic approach to the treatment of a medical condition. A physician who treats all patients for obesity by dispensing controlled anorectic drugs would not meet the minimum medical diagnostic requirements, procedures, and standards for the acceptable practice of medicine.

U.S. v. Zwick.   A physician used order forms issued under a federal law to obtain over three million amphetamine dosage units between 1972 and 1975. He dispensed these anorectic controlled substances in his bariatric practice in unlabeled packets, each containing thirty dosage units. In this manner he prescribed a large number of anorectics to a large number of patients. In addition to the dispensation of amphetamines, the standard office visit consisted of taking a patient's pulse, blood pressure, weight, and a five minute interview in which a recommended written diet was delivered to the patient. This "standard" or unitary approach to the treatment of obesity was the only one used by the physician. Treatment was not geared to specific problems, habits, personality or life-style of each patient. The decision to use an anorectic drug was not made after an evaluation of the patient's needs and the risks which such drugs posed to the patient. A determination of the benefit of such drugs compared to their inherent risks was not made. The physician exhibited only a casual concern about possible dependency or addiction of his patients to anorectic drugs.

A federal regulatory agency requested the court to review the physician's treatment protocol and to declare whether it was outside the acceptable practice of medicine. Expert medical evidence established that the treatment of obesity was a complex therapeutic problem because it represented a spectrum, ranging from mildly inconvenient and/or unattractive "overweight" to massive and often life-threatening excess poundage. Its treatment likewise consisted of measures ranging from relatively modest dietary restriction to intestinal bypass surgery. In addition, obesity almost invariably involves a complex interplay between physiology and behavior. Thus, a physician must, perforce, combine physiologic measures with the skills of the psychologist and educator. Largely for these reasons, expert testimony concluded that there is no "standard" or unitary treatment that will serve to properly manage most obese patients.

After reviewing the opinions and publications of medical authorities in the treatment of obesity, the court concluded that none disagreed over the need to individualize the treatment of obesity. The court concluded, therefore, that in a practice where a large number of patients are treated for obesity, there ought to be significant variations in the approach to treatment. Thus the court declared that the minimum medical standards of practice for physicians treating obesity are not met where a single approach is used in which controlled anorectic drugs are dispensed to a large number of patients as a standard treatment.

Clinical decisions concerning the treatment of certain patients may violate their constitutional rights. For example, if a mentally incompetent patient or guardian refuses consent to an intrusive form of treatment, the decision to administer the treatment may require a formal legal balancing of the patient's medical needs and constitutional rights. In spite of this requirement, an attending physician is not expected to anticipate constitutional developments which might create newly recognized patient rights that thereby affect treatment choices.

Price v. Sheppard.   While he was hospitalized in a general hospital, an adolescent patient attempted to ·strangle a member of the hospital staff. Because the hospital was not equipped to handle dangerous patients, he was transferred to a psychiatric facility. His admission diagnosis was schizophrenia. Although he was treated with tranquilizers and antidepressants over the next several weeks, he continued to be assaultive to the staff and other patients, and therefore was confined to his room most of the time. His attending physician believed that this required confinement was a substantial obstacle to the patient's recovery and that the patient's assaultive behavior could be corrected by electroshock therapy (EST). He thereby sought consent from the patient's mother to administer EST. The mother arranged for an independent psychiatric examination to determine the advisability of the proposed treatment. The retained psychiatrist examined the patient and recommended that drug treatment be continued, but that if the patient did not respond favorably, EST be given. These recommendations were followed by the patient's attending physician. When the patient's condition did not improve, the attending physician administered EST to the patient without seeking the expressed consent of his mother. On behalf of her son, the mother sued the physician, claiming that he administered unauthorized treatment in derogation of her son's constitutional right of privacy.

The court noted that the right of privacy allows a patient the freedom of making certain personal and fundamental decisions. However, this right is not absolute; it may allow the state to assume the treatment decision of an incompetent patient, if necessity and reasonableness of the means of treating a patient are clearly demonstrated.

Expert testimony established that the techniques generally available to treat psychological disorders range in degree of severity and coerciveness from the least intrusive forms such as milieu therapy, to drug therapy, EST, and ultimately to psychosurgery. As the techiques increase in severity, so do the risks of serious alteration of personality and long lasting neuropsychiatric damage. The court, therefore, held that the necessity and reasonableness of the prescribed treatment should be determined by balancing the patient's need for treatment against the intrusiveness of the prescribed treatment. In accomplishing this goal, the court suggested the utilization of an adversary proceeding in which the following factors are considered before more intrusive forms of treatment may be utilized: the extent and duration of changes in behavior patterns and mental activity affected by the treatment; the risks of adverse side effects; the experimental nature of the treatment and its acceptance by the medical community; the extent of bodily intrusion and the pain connected with the treatment; and the patient's ability to competently determine for himself whether the treatment is desirable.[†] The court concluded that, although the more intrusive forms of treatment, such as psychosurgery and EST, would require this procedural hearing, therapies requiring the cooperation of the patient, or the use of mild tranquilizers, would not.

The court pointed out that in this case the attending physician acted in good faith. He also followed the recommendation of the psychiatrist retained by the patient's mother and continued the less intrusive forms of treatment for an additional period without success before commencing the EST. Given the definitional vagueness of the right of privacy, the court concluded that the treating physician could not reasonably have known that, under the circumstances, the manner in which EST was administered to his patient violated a constitutional right.

[†] This opinion represents a judicial approach to the treatment decision. In some states, similar treatment decisions are governed by statute, and in others the issue has not been addressed.

7

MULTIPLE HEALTH CARE PROVIDERS

Increasing medical specialization, improvement of medical credentials, and advances in communication technology have made consultation and referral among health care professionals more available than ever before. Given this widespread availability, the legal duty to consult or refer has gained greater recognition in the law. In general, such a duty arises whenever the patient's condition is beyond the physician's knowledge, ability, or capacity to treat. The clinical indications for consultation or referral include: continuing uncertainty about the diagnosis; ineffectual treatment (the patient is not improving); and situations where other therapy would likely be more beneficial, or appropriate facilities which would materially benefit the patient's condition are unavailable and inaccessible to the attending physician.

Inherent in the duty to consult is the requirement that the physician recognize his limitations of knowledge, ability, or capacity. Whenever a physician knows, or should know, his inability to treat the patient's condition with likelihood of reasonable success, he becomes obligated to advise the patient of the necessity for other treatment.

An attending physician who consults another physician is expected to coordinate effectively the ongoing care of the patient, but is usually not responsible for a consultant's malpractice unless the consultant is an associate of the attending physician, or unless the physician acts in concert with the consultant. Ordinarily a consultant establishes with the patient a separate physician-patient relationship and does not act under the supervision or control of the attending physician. However, if an attending physician knew or should have been aware of the consultant's incompetence or inability to properly care for the patient's specialized problem, but nevertheless selected the consultant; both the consultant and the attending physician may be liable for the consultant's negligent acts. When, however, an attending physician merely arranges, on behalf of his patient, for a consultation for a specific problem of his patient or casually assists in carrying out a consultant's directions, he does not become jointly responsible for the consultant's negligence.

A physician may be vicariously responsible for the negligence of other health care personnel, such as house officers and nurses under his control, even though such personnel may be in the general employ of the hospital. If their services are determined to be "loaned" to a physician by the hospital, as "borrowed employees" they become subject to the physician's direction, supervision, and control in connection with the work they are called upon to perform. Thus a hospital employee who is assisting a physician may be subject to the physician's control with regard to the work to be done and the manner of performing work in the service of the physician. Where a physician has the right to control an assistant in the details of a specific act, the physician may be liable for the negligence of the assistant in performing that act, even though the physician himself was not directly negligent in caring for the patient.

SECTION 1: CONSULTATION

Circumstances Requiring Consultation

A physician's duty to seek consultation or to advise the patient of the need for consultation is an inherent obligation of the physician-patient relationship. The standard by which the law determines whether a physician has a duty to consult in a specific situation is whether the attending physician knows or should know that the patient's condition is beyond the physician's knowledge, ability, or capacity to treat.

Manion v. Tweedy.   The patient fractured his tibia. A general practitioner set it, but knew that the bone was in poor alignment. Thus he attempted several times to set it in a better position. These maneuvers resulted in circulatory compromise to the lower extremity. When the bone healed with substantial deformity, the patient sued the physician because he failed to consult with an orthopedist.

The court concluded that no evidence was presented that the general practitioner should have known that the patient's fracture was beyond his ability to treat. The court pointed out that to adopt any other rule would impose upon every general practitioner the duty of consulting with a specialist on every conceivable complication that might arise, rather than when he knows or should know that consultation is indicated.

A physician is expected to seek consultation when he is unable to arrive at a working diagnosis, especially if it is clearly demonstrated that misdiagnosis would have been prevented if a specialist had been presented with the patient's clinical picture.

Cooper v. United States.   The patient worked in a meat processing plant, and became ill due to an apparent infection. He was admitted to a hospital for a diagnostic work-up, but the etiology of his illness was not diagnosed. No consultation or communication between the attending physician and consultants was attempted, even though specialists in infectious diseases were available. The patient's symptomatology persisted after discharge. Subsequently, he went to a clinic where brucellosis was diagnosed. The patient then sued his initial physician for failure to obtain consultation.

The court pointed out that when the attending physician recognizes that, after an evaluative effort, he does not know what is wrong with a patient, a consultation is required. The patient's clinical history, occupation, and the high incidence of cases of brucellosis in the area should have raised a high index of suspicion of that disease. Thus the court concluded that if brucellosis was not suggested by the clinical presentation, the physician should have realized that he was incapable of diagnosing the condition.

Inherent in the duty to consult is a physician's specific obligation to seek consultation in the treatment of conditions and matters of admitted unfamiliarity.

Largess v. Tatem.   An elderly patient injured her hip. Her general practitioner admitted her to the hospital for evaluation. X-rays disclosed a comminuted intertrochanteric fracture. The general practitioner concluded that the reduction of the fracture was beyond his training and experience, and called in an orthopedic surgeon. The specialist performed an open reduction and internal fixation of the fracture fragments with a Jewett nail. The fixation device was not designed to permit full early weight-bearing. The nail was packaged with a printed admonition that it could not be expected to withstand the unsupported stresses of full weight-bearing. The orthopedic surgeon directed the course of the patient's treatment for some time following surgery. He wrote on the physician's order sheet: "To P.T. for ambulation with no weight-bearing. . . . Doing fairly well with walker." His last entry on the patient's progress notes stated that the patient might go home when her family physician felt her general condition permitted. The patient remained in the hospital for three more weeks under the care of her general practitioner.

The general practitioner was not familiar with a Jewett nail or the management of patients who had been treated with this device. At the time of the discharge, he allowed the patient to walk out of the hospital unassisted by any person or weight-supporting device. Several weeks later, x-rays dis-closed that the Jewett nail and bone had fractured, necessitating a second operation to remove the broken device and insert a new one. The patient sued the general practitioner for failing to consult the orthopedist, and thus, for allowing her to bear full weight upon the device.

Expert testimony established that the device failed because it was sub-jected by the patient to prolonged and frequent full weight-bearing. The court declared that a physician is expected to be aware of what he does not know. Thus he incurs liability not so much for being ignorant about an as-pect of his patient's condition as for remaining ignorant. He is required to know enough to conduct a reasonable inquiry as to what he does not know. Thus he may require consultation in a matter of admitted unfamiliarity.

The court pointed out that the attending physician was aware of the instructions given by the orthopedist and was also aware that they had not been revised or countermanded. In spite of this, the general practitioner made no attempt to obtain advice from, or consult with the orthopedist about the advisability of the full weight-bearing which he knew was occur-ring. Despite his admitted personal lack of knowledge as to the limitations of internal fixation devices, the attending physician merely assumed, with-out inquiry, the strength limitations of the device, which were unknown to him. His admitted unfamiliarity with fixation devices and his knowledge of the hospital order prohibiting weight-bearing gave rise to an obligation to investigate by seeking advice or consultation on the question of weight-bearing before allowing or condoning full weight-bearing by his patient.

The requirement to consult also arises when the treatment of an injury or illness is known to be, or should be known to be, complex and fraught with complications strongly suggesting the need for specialized care. The need for consultation in such a situation is paramount.

Morgan v. Engles.   A four-year-old boy sustained a comminuted supracon-dylar fracture of the humerus, with epiphyseal displacement. On the day of the injury, a general practitioner performed a closed reduction of the frac-ture. He made a "mental note" of the possibility of epiphyseal damage be-cause of the severity of the fracture in such a young child, but did not feel that he should alter or modify his proposed closed reduction. The physician obtained an unsatisfactory result, and the boy experienced difficulty with the use of his arm. Although several corrective procedures eventually were required to be performed by an orthopedic surgeon, the patient was left with permanent disability of his arm. The patient sued the general practi-tioner, charging that his disability was caused not by the severity of the orig-inal fracture, but by the physician's failure to refer him immediately to an orthopedic specialist for proper initial treatment.

The orthopedic surgeon who performed the corrective operations testified that he could see evidence of epiphyseal injury in the x-rays taken by the physician who set the fracture. He further testified that a supracondylar fracture was a complex injury because it usually resulted in damage to the epiphyseal plate; therefore, treatment required immediate open surgical reduction in order to prevent deformity. The surgeon testified in the following manner:

Q. Doctor, is it your testimony then, that the standards of . . . medical practice . . . when a general practitioner runs into a fracture of the supracondyl, that this is an orthopedic problem and the standards of practice dictate he consult an orthopedic consultant before attempting to set this fracture?

A. Yes, that is the usual procedure.

Q. Doctor, are you familiar with the standards of medical practice wherein a fracture of the supracondyl also involves injury to the epiphysis?

A. I am familiar with it and I have had some experience with it.

Q. Doctor, is the standard of medical practice and treatment of a supracondylar fracture the same where you have a fracture of the epiphysis?

A. No, it is not the same.

Q. How does the standard of medical practice and treatment of such a fracture differ?

A. A fracture of supracondylar bone is usually longitudinal, or transverse, and therefore damage is done to the epiphyseal plate and an open surgical reduction is performed with the plate being tacked with noncorrosive pins.

Q. The surgery is done by whom?

A. An orthopedic surgeon.

The court concluded that because this type of injury required a major orthopedic procedure, the physician had not acted in accordance with good medical practice in treating the case alone. The physician should have called in a consultant, or referred the patient to the orthopedic specialist.

Whether a physician has breached the duty to consult is judged by reference to the standards and practices of the profession. If expert testimony fairly supports the conclusion that a reasonably careful and prudent physician would have sought consultation under the same or similar circumstances, the trier of fact is entitled to find that the physician was negligent in failing to do so.

Chasco v. Providence Memorial Hospital.   The patient was admitted to the hospital because he was nervous, tremulous, and hallucinating. His wife indicated that he had been drinking heavily. The patient was examined by a

general practitioner who diagnosed "Alcoholism; DT's" and ordered seda-
tives. The next day when the physician saw him at 8:30 A.M., he was slightly
obtunded. At 3:00 P.M., a nurse reported that the patient had not eaten. The
physician then ordered intravenous feeding. When the patient's pulse and
respirations became irregular, the physician consulted a neurosurgeon. The
patient, however, died at midnight before an operative intervention could be
accomplished. An autopsy disclosed an epidural hematoma of more than
forty-eight hours duration. The pathologist reported that the liver exhibited changes consistent with chronic alcoholism. The patient's widow sued
the general practitioner, claiming that he negligently failed to obtain
consultation.

The court noted that no evidence was presented that the physician had
violated any standard of care. Moreover, the physician sought consultation
when abnormality of the patient's vital signs became apparent. Thus the
court held that the plaintiff had failed to establish evidence of what the standard of practice was; and, therefore, there was no way for the court to determine whether the delay in consulting was negligent.

Ordinarily the standard of care required for seeking consultation must be
firmly established by expert medical testimony. However, courts have occasionally allowed an expert medical witness to retrospectively speculate as to
the need for seeking consultation.

Lab v. Hall.   An overweight, pregnant patient had a history of spontaneous abortions. When her labor pains began, her physician, a general
practitioner, ordered the nurse to administer an intranasal solution of
Pitocin at regular intervals for about three hours in order to induce labor.
Three hours after the drug was discontinued, the woman was given an injection of Demerol and scopolamine, as prescribed by the physician. Within
thirty seconds her face began to darken, her head hyperextended, and she
died. Up until this point, there had been no significant clinical indications of
anything unusual in her labor. The drugs prescribed and the manner of administration were in accordance with customary and acceptable practice.
The cause of death was reported to be an apparent amniotic fluid embolism
of undetermined etiology. The husband of the patient sued the physician.

The husband's medical expert witness testified that he thought that the
physician used "poor judgment" in not asking for obstetrical consultation
concerning the possibility of performing a caesarean section. However, he
conceded on cross-examination that the propriety of seeking consultation is
within the judgment of the attending physician, and that the physician was
in a better position than the testifying expert to make that medical judgment. Nevertheless, the court also questioned whether the physician exercised the necessary skill when he induced the patient with Pitocin without

obtaining an obstetrical consultation which might have resulted in a cae-sarean section, in light of the patient's weight problem and prior history of abortions. Therefore, the question of negligence in failing to obtain consul-tation became an issue for the trier of fact.

Consultation is required when the physician knows or should know that consultation is necessary. The test of this duty is determined by whether most physicians similarly situated would seek consultation. However, as the following case indicates, even if it is proven that most physicians would have sought consultation in a given situation, the physician may nevertheless be absolved of responsibility for a failure to consult if a physician's ample clini-cal experience was reasonably relied on in treating the particular condition. The courts view the clinical experience of an attending physician as an im-portant factor to be taken into consideration in determining the need for consultation.

Atkins v. Novinger.   The patient sustained a fracture to his ankle. His fam-ily physician set it in a cast and cared for it. Although an orthopedic special-ist was available, the physician did not seek consultation because he had un-dergone some formal training in orthopedics, and had extensive experience in treating fractures. The treatment result was unsatisfactory to the patient and he sued his physician, charging that his physician was under a duty to seek consultation with an orthopedic surgeon if one were available.

   An orthopedic surgeon testifying for the patient stated that the major-ity of general practitioners refer fracture cases to orthopedists. The court noted, however, that the duty to refer was not absolute and that proof had been introduced to show that the general practitioner was competent to treat ankle fractures. The court cautioned, however, that if a patient's recov-ery does not progress in a reasonable period of time, even an experienced nonspecialist has a duty to consult a proper specialist.

Experience to adequately manage a patient's problem may indicate that con-sultation is not required in a given situation. However, it cannot be assumed that a physician who is trained in a certain general area, such as surgery, has the knowledge and experience to adequately manage a patient's specific condition.

Wilson v. Gilbert.   A teenage boy sustained a gunshot wound in his thigh while on a hunting trip. His father took him to a hospital where he was examined by a general surgeon who determined that there was injury to his femoral artery. Although the surgeon had no specialized training in vascular surgery, he did not consult with a vascular surgeon about care of the pa-tient's injury. Instead, he anastomosed the severed femoral artery by grafting it with a portion of the saphenous vein. He did not perform a preoperative arteriogram to determine if a thrombus was obstructing circulation of the femoral artery. Circulation was not restored by the operation; the surgeon, therefore, performed a second vein graft which also was unsuccessful because of a preoperative arterial thrombosis. As a result of the surgeon's failure to perform a thrombectomy, amputation below the knee was required. The boy then sued the surgeon for failure to consult a vascular surgeon.

The court held that failure to discover the thrombus by use of an arteriogram or some other appropriate procedure was evidence of substandard care, and indicative of a lack of experience. Under the circumstances, the court inferred that the surgeon had a duty to consult a specialist, and failure to do so was negligent.

As with a lack of experience, a patient's repeated request for consultation is also a circumstance which tends to create an obligation requiring the attending physician to seek consultation.

Steeves v. U.S. An eleven-year-old boy was taken to an Air Force dispensary with abdominal pain, fever, nausea, and vomiting. Because the dispensary had no surgical facilities, the boy and his mother were sent to a U.S. Naval hospital with a report by the referring physician indicating that his clinical impression was acute appendicitis. The physician who examined the patient did not order any laboratory tests, and refused to call a surgeon for consultation even though one was available in the hospital. In spite of the mother's request and the fact that he had read the referring diagnosis report, the physician sent the child home. The mother took the child back to the hospital during the night. He was examined by an intern who likewise refused to order diagnostic tests or call a surgeon, in spite of repeated requests by the mother. When he also sent the child home, the mother then took the child back to the Air Force physician who this time arranged for surgical consultation at the hospital. The surgeon concurred with the diagnosis of appendicitis. By the time surgery was performed, however, the appendix had ruptured, and the patient developed peritonitis. On behalf of the child, the mother sued the government.

The court concluded that both physicians who had evaluated the child in the emergency room were negligent for failing to consult a surgeon because they knew the diagnosis of "appendicitis" had already been made by a physician, and the mother had made repeated requests for a consultation.

Requirement of Timeliness

The physician has an obligation to advise and inform the patient of the need for further specialized care in time to give the patient an opportunity to secure it. This is especially true whenever the beneficial aspects of consultative treatment will be lost if the patient is not treated within a certain period of time.

Doan v. Griffith.   The patient, an accident victim, arrived at the hospital with multiple fractures of his facial bones. The physician administered emergency treatment, admitted the patient to the hospital, and attended him there daily. He discharged him on the seventh day. The physician did not advise the patient at the time of his discharge that his facial bones needed to be realigned by a specialist before the bones became fused. Therefore, the patient did not seek further care. When informed that it was too late for effective treatment the patient sued the physician, contending that the physician was negligent in not advising him of the needed treatment before the broken bones became fused, thereby causing his face to be disfigured and his vision impaired.

Expert testimony established that customary medical treatment of a patient with such injuries would have been to surgically realign the fractured facial bones as soon as the swelling subsided, usually within ten days, in order to prevent bony distortion and its complications. On the seventh hospital day, when the patient was discharged, his face was still swollen and thus his fractured bones could not have been properly realigned prior to that time.

The court pointed out that if a physician knows, or should know, that a condition is more complex or serious than originally thought, he is obligated to inform the patient. The court concluded that the patient in this case should have been informed about the potential complications of his injury so that he would have had an opportunity to request or seek consultation. The court thus held that the physician failed to provide timely advice to the patient regarding his need for further medical treatment and that such failure was the cause of his deformed condition.

A physician is expected to monitor potentially serious clinical findings in order to be in a position to seek early consultation and effect a timely remedy.

Richardson v. Holmes.   The patient underwent an elective hysterectomy, performed by a general practitioner. On the day after the operation she had a fever, refractory vomiting, and a distended abdomen. On the second postoperative day, the radiologist reported that an abdominal x-ray demonstrated a paralytic ileus. Four days later the general practitioner's diagnosis was still paralytic ileus, although the patient had a markedly elevated white blood count, a high fever, a large amount of drainage on her wound dressing, and refractory vomiting. No further x-ray studies were performed. Two days later when a large amount of brown fluid with a foul odor drained from the incision, the patient was transferred to another hospital. When a surgeon at that hospital opened the incision, large amounts of fecal fluid escaped. A loop of gangrenous bowel was found between the separated fascia at the edges of the wound. There were indications that this condition had been present for some time. Subsequently her condition became further complicated and she died.

The patient's husband brought a malpractice suit against the general practitioner. He contended that the physician was negligent in delaying transfer of the patient longer than a physician of ordinary prudence would have under similar circumstances. The court concluded that if the general practitioner had exercised reasonable care, he should have known that such consultation was indicated. The court pointed out that the progression of serious and telling symtomatology should have alerted him to the need for earlier consultation, and therefore he had been negligent in delaying the patient's transfer to another hospital.

When a complication occurs, the attending physician is obligated to investigate and treat the matter himself or bring in a consultant without undue delay.

Lee v. Andrews. A thirty-eight-year-old patient underwent a hemorrhoidectomy. At 6:00 P.M. on the day after the operation, a medical student catheterized him because of urinary retention. The catheter tore the urethra and urine migrated into the scrotum. At 10:45 P.M., the surgeon who performed the operation was notified that the patient's scrotum was markedly swollen. He ordered the patient catheterized again. By midnight, the patient was complaining of severe pain, and the physician ordered application of an ice pack. The swelling persisted and the patient was catheterized again. On the following day, the patient's wife asked the surgeon about the possibility of a serious infection. The surgeon minimized the possibility, and undertook no investigation or treatment of the condition. Two days later, the patient had several syncopal episodes, and his blood pressure was erratic. Later the same day the physician consulted a second physician who diagnosed cellulitis of the scrotum and septic shock. He had the patient immediately transferred to the intensive care unit of another hospital, where shortly thereafter he died. The patient's widow sued the surgeon. The court found that the clinical facts demonstrated that the physician was negligent in not investigating the cause of the patient's problems or else consulting a specialist at an earlier stage.

The less knowledge or experience that a physician has in treating a certain condition, the greater the need to consult with knowledgeable and available resources. When appropriate resources are unavailable, a referral should be arranged without unreasonable delay.

Buck v. U.S. A fourteen-year-old boy was bitten on the anterior tibial aspect of his leg by a three-foot eastern diamondback rattlesnake. Fifteen minutes later he arrived at a hospital where he was evaluated by the emergency room physician. Examination disclosed two fang marks, one-inch apart, with surrounding erythema, corroborative of a large snake. The physician was aware that it was a potentially lethal situation. Because he had no prior training or experience in the treatment of a snakebite, he consulted by telephone with a staff surgeon who was "on-call" at home. The surgeon, who also had no special training or experience in snakebite treatment, did not come into the hospital to see the patient. Both of the physicians in the course of the conversation, informed each other of their inexperience in the treatment of snakebites; nevertheless, neither of them attempted to obtain consultation with a physician who was experienced in the treatment of a rattlesnake bite, even though a hospital with special facilities for the treatment of snakebite victims was located ten minutes away. In addition, the emergency room physician did not resort to reading medical literature which was available at the hospital library or any other literature to determine the manner to best treat a rattlesnake bite. The treating physician had only a vague familiarity of snakebite treatment, relying upon his memory of elective reading that he had done during his surgical rotation in medical school. After the telephone "consultation," the physicians determined that antivenom was the treatment of choice for the bite of a pit viper.

The emergency room physician referred to the drug package insert contained within a packaged ampule of antivenom (Antivenin). The insert provided the following clinical scheme for grading the severity of a snakebite, which was based on continuous twelve-hour monitoring of clinical signs and symptoms:

> Using subjective and objective criteria to evaluate the local and systemic response to poisonous snakebite, the clinical severity of envenomation has been graded:

> GRADE I   *Minimal envenomation.* History of suspected snakebite. Fang wound(s) usually present. Moderate pain or throbbing localized at fang wound(s), surrounded by 1 to 15 inches of edema and erythema. No evidence of systemic involvement *after 12 hours of observation.*

> GRADE II   *Moderate envenomation.* The signs and symptoms of Grade I rapidly progress *during first 12 hours*, with more severe and more widely distributed pain; edema spreading toward the trunk; petechiae and ecchymoses limited to

area of edema. Nausea, vomiting, giddiness and mild temperature elevation usually present.

GRADE III *Severe envenomation.* May resemble Grade I or II when brought under observation, but course is rapidly progressive. May arrive in shock within a few minutes of bite. *Within 12 hours* edema spreads up extremity and may involve part of trunk. Petechiae and ecchymoses may be generalized. Systemic manifestations may include rapid pulse, shock-like state, subnormal temperature.

GRADE IV *Very severe envenomation.* Seen especially after envenomation by large rattlesnakes. Characterized by sudden pain, rapidly progressive swelling, which may reach and involve trunk within a few hours, with ecchymoses, bleb formation, and necrosis. Systemic manifestations, often commencing within 15 minutes of bite, usually include weakness, nausea and vomiting, vertigo, numbness or tingling of lips or face. Muscle fasciculations, painful muscular cramping, pallor, sweating, cold and clammy skin, rapid and weak pulse, incontinence, convulsions and coma also may be observed; death may occur.

The insert recommended the following antivenom treatment schedules based on clinical staging and close observation, and also provided textual guidance for use and monitoring of the Antivenin.

	Suggested Guide for Initial Dosage of Antivenin	
Grade of Envenomation	*Administer Contents of*	*Preferable Route*
0	None	—
I	1 Vial	IM anterolateral thigh or buttock
II	2 to 4 Vials	At least 50% IV; balance IM
III	At least 5 Vials	IV
IV	10 to 20 Vials or more	IV

Virtually no limitation may be placed on the amount administered. Thirty vials have been used initially, with no untoward effects other than those types of delayed allergic reactions commonly observed after large doses of horse serum.

The smaller the body of the patient, the larger the initial dose required. Because children seem to have less resistance and less body fluid with which to dilute the venom, they may require twice the dosage of Antivenin that suffices for adults.

The need of subsequent doses must be based on the clinical response. Watch patient for three to five hours after the initial dose. Give additional injections of 1 vial of Antivenin every one-half to two hours if pain and active swelling progress.

The patient must remain under close medical supervision for several days. Recurrence of symptoms (shortness of breath, general weakness, failing pulse, faintness and vomiting, especially of blood-stained material is an indication that more venom is being absorbed and that additional Antivenin is required. The greatest danger is said to occur in the first twenty-four to forty-eight hours after the bite. The patient may rally and give false impression of recovery, then relapse.

The physician did not follow the instructions in the drug manufacturer's package insert accompanying the Antivenin, even though this was the only source that he consulted in the treatment of the patient. The boy was transported to the hospital ward at 8:15 P.M., approximately two hours after he arrived in the emergency room. Although the emergency room physician was the only physician who remained in the hospital all night, the patient was attended exclusively by nurses or orderlies until 3:45 A.M. During this time the physician did not evaluate the patient even though there was a systemic progression of manifestations of the seriousness of the rattlesnake bite. At 3:45 A.M., the emergency room physician responded to urgent calls by the nurse because the patient's left thigh was markedly swollen and had turned blue. The physician examined the patient but inadequately observed his signs and symptoms and prescribed one vial of Antivenin intramuscularly, which was contrary, both as to quantity and method of administration, to the drug package insert. The emergency room physician did not further observe the patient. At 7:00 A.M., at the end of his shift, he did not communicate the patient's status to any of his colleagues, nor did he confer with his surgical "consultant."

After approximately eighteen hours in the hospital, the patient was transferred to the nearby hospital in a seriously ill condition. There he was given large doses of intravenous Antivenin and eventually required anterior compartment fasciotomy with extensive debridement of his anterior compartment muscles. He sustained a permanent foot drop and sued the physicians and the hospital, charging negligent failure to obtain consultation.

Expert testimony, and the introduction of the drug package insert into evidence, established that "close" observation should be maintained of a serious snakebite victim during the first twelve hours. The court pointed out that the physicians' negligent failure to consult was compounded at various times throughout the night and early morning hours as the condition progressed. The court reasoned that even if initially such consultation need not have been sought, it was overwhelmingly indicated as the patient's symptoms progressed. The long delay after admission to the hospital before consultation was made was negligent, because there was sufficient progressive signs of worsening in the patient's condition that made earlier consultation essential.

In some cases, the law may infer a need for earlier consultation from the fact that the physician eventually requested consultation. Under such circumstances, courts may conclude that if the physician had called a specialist earlier, a less extensive injury to the patient would have occurred.

Valentine v. Kaiser Foundation Hospitals. An obstetrician performed a circumcision on a two-day-old infant. Several days later a dark area appeared on the infant's penis. The obstetrician was made aware of this finding, but he discharged the patient. The area continued to enlarge after he was taken home and he was taken back to the hospital and treated in the emergency room. The physician in the emergency referred the parents to a urologist to evaluate the child's condition. However, by the time the consultation occurred, an advanced gangrenous condition was evident. The parents, on behalf of their child, sued the obstetrician.

The court pointed out that when consultants are called in after a patient's condition has become progressively and materially worse, it may be inferred that it was negligent not to have called them in earlier. The court noted that, if the injury was the result of something evident prior to the infant's discharge, and if a urologist had been brought in to treat this condition, it was reasonable to infer that something might have been done at an earlier time to lessen the deleterious effects of the injury. The fact that consultants were later called in indicated that their services might have been required earlier. Thus in this case expert medical testimony was not required to set the standard for seeking consultations.

SECTION 2: LIABILITY OF ATTENDING PHYSICIAN IN CONSULTATION SITUATION

When a consultant is called in at the request of the attending physician and with the approval of the patient, an independent physician-patient relationship is established between the patient and the consultant. Even when the attending physician continues to participate in a case after a consultant has been called, the attending physician will ordinarily not be liable for the consultant's negligent acts if the attending physician has not assumed responsibility for the specific decision made by the consultant.

Floyd v. Michie.   A child treated by the family physician for tonsillitis later developed facial blisters. The family physician examined the child but refused to accept on-going responsibility for diagnosing or treating the child's skin condition. With the consent of the mother, he called in a dermatologist who initially diagnosed chicken pox. After a daylight examination, the dermatologist changed his diagnosis to impetigo and prescribed a topical treatment with a mercury compound. During the next ten days both the family physician and the specialist visited the child several times. The family physician did not take an active part in diagnosis or treatment, but did carry out the prescriptions of the specialist. On the eleventh day the child experienced severe vomiting episodes and died, presumably of mercury toxicity. On behalf of their child the parents sued both the family physician and the dermatologist.

The court pointed out that an attending physician is not liable for the negligence of a consultant whom he, in the exercise of reasonable care, recommends because he is unwilling to assume the responsibility of diagnosing and treating the malady. Once the patient accepts the services of a consultant, an independent contractual relationship is established between them. Thus there is ordinarily independence of diagnostic and therapeutic practice between the referring physician and a consultant.

The rule enunciated in *Floyd* above may apply to other situations in which the physician aids the consultant. For example, if the attending physician casually assists a surgeon in the preparation of surgery, but the surgeon determines, selects, and performs the surgical procedure, the physician would not be liable for negligence in the operation.

Harwick v. Harris.   A patient sustained a transverse subcapital fracture of the femur. In addition to engaging an internist who was a personal friend to take charge of her case, she also consulted an orthopedic surgeon who, after evaluation, recommended surgical repair. Three days after the operation, when the internist was in a position to reasonably assume that proper recovery was in progress, he saw no need to add to expenses by staying on and withdrew from the case. He remained ready to return to the case if needed. The surgery resulted in a worsening of the patient's condition. She sued the surgeon for malpractice and was awarded a judgment against him.

In a separate legal action she sued the internist, on the theory that he was in charge of the case and failed to inform the patient of the nature and risks of the operative procedure proposed and performed by the orthopedic surgeon. The court pointed out that the fact that the internist was asked to "take charge" did not make him responsible for the selection of the surgical procedures used by the orthopedic surgeon. Responsibility to obtain informed consent was not applicable to the internist because he did not

choose or advise which surgical procedures should be used by the orthopedic surgeon.

Ordinarily, an attending physician who refers the patient to a surgeon may
not be held liable for negligence in connection with the operation, even if
the physician is present at the surgery, because performance of the surgical
procedures are presumed to be under the control of the operating surgeon.

Smith v. Beard.   A family physician, caring for a patient who was severely
burned in an accident, recommended that she have skin grafting. He told
the patient, a Wyoming resident, that she could either go to Chicago or to
the Mayo Clinic. The patient chose Chicago. The physician then recommended that she have the skin grafts performed by his brother, who was a
surgeon. He accompanied the patient to Chicago, placed her under his
brother's care, and returned to Wyoming. Approximately two months later
she again came under the care of her family physician. The results of the
grafting were unsatisfactory and the patient sued both physicians.

The court pointed out that after the patient was placed under the care
of the Chicago surgeon she did not again come under the care of the Wyoming physician until long after the surgical procedure had been completed.
There was no evidence that the Chicago surgeon was an agent, partner, or
associate of the physician; or that he was not a competent surgeon. Therefore, the referring physician was not liable for negligence of the surgeon.

If a physician refers a patient to a specialist who recommends a procedure,
and the referring physician participates in that procedure to a material or
sufficient degree, he may be jointly liable, with the physician to whom he
referred the patient, for any injury negligently caused by the procedure.

Arshansky v. Royal Concourse Company.   A patient was referred by her
family physician to a podiatrist for consultation regarding her foot problems. After a diagnostic examination in which the referring physician did
not participate, the podiatrist decided that an operation was necessary. The
referring physician was present at the operation and provided manual assistance; but otherwise the podiatrist performed the operation. An unsatisfactory result occurred and the patient sued both the podiatrist and the
family physician, alleging that the operation was improperly performed.

The court stated that the referral itself would not render the physician
liable. It concluded, however, that the physician assisted at the operation to
a degree sufficient to present a question of fact for the jury about his personal liability in connection with the allegedly improper operation. If he had
been a participant in the surgical procedure, rather than a mere instrumentality of the podiatrist, he would be jointly liable with the podiatrist.

As the preceding cases indicate, an attending physician who obtains surgical consultation but does not participate in the recommendation for, or actual performance of, surgery; and merely continues to handle the medical aspects of the case, will not be responsible for the surgeon's negligence. Nevertheless, if the attending physician participates in the decision-making process; expressly or implicitly approves of the treatment administered; and continues to attend the patient on all phases of care; the referring physician may be held liable for the negligence of the consultant.

O'Grady v. Wickman. Because of chronic back pain a woman consulted Dr. Fabric, a general practitioner, whose name she obtained from the telephone directory. After a physical examination, he hospitalized her with a working diagnosis of muscular spasm. In the hospital chart he recorded, "The patient has a tumor of right ovary and retroflexed uterus. May have to do a suspension or removal of uterus." He requested Dr. Wickman, a gynecologist, to examine the patient. Dr. Wickman performed a pelvic examination and recommended a right salpingo-oophorectomy and ligation of the left tube. Dr. Fabric scheduled the surgery. On the day prior to the surgery the patient signed an operative consent form which stated, "I hereby authorize Dr. Fabric and Dr. Wickman to perform an exploratory laparotomy." The following day Dr. Wickman performed a hysterectomy and a right salpingo-oophorectomy. Dr. Fabric was in the operating room during the surgery and his name was listed as the attending physician on the hospital chart.

Following the surgery, the patient had leakage of urine from her vagina. After Dr. Fabric discharged her from the hospital, she consulted another physician who diagnosed a vesico-vaginal fistula and removed some silk sutures from the fistula site.

The patient continued to experience the type of back trouble about which she had complained prior to her surgery. She finally consulted an orthopedic surgeon who diagnosed her condition as a low back syndrome due to a limb length disparity and associated scoliosis. He prescribed a heel lift and exercises. This treatment relieved her back pain. The patient then sued Dr. Fabric, charging him with responsibility for Dr. Wickman's negligent diagnosis and treatment.

The court pointed out that the patient was admitted to the hospital by Dr. Fabric and that she was under his daily care and supervision. Upon his examination of the patient he recommended surgery, called in Dr. Wickman for further consultation, and scheduled the surgery. The court concluded that this was ample evidence to infer that common action and purpose existed between the two physicians. The court held that the facts and circumstances of the case justified holding Dr. Fabric responsible for Dr. Wickman's conduct.

Section 3: Referral To More Appropriate Facilities

In addition to the requirement that a physician be cognizant of personal limitations of knowledge and skill that may require him to consult with other physicians, a physician must also be aware of limitations of equipment and facilities that are available to him for care of his patient. A physician's recognition of such limitations in undertaking evaluation or treatment may, legally, be as important as·deciding proper care for the patient. If a physician discovers, or should discover, that the patient's illness is beyond his knowledge or technical skill to treat with a likelihood of success, a duty arises to disclose the situation and to advise the patient of the necessity for other treatment.

Wilson v. Corbin.   A man sustained trauma to his spine in an auto accident. The patient went to a physician's office for evaluation of the injury. At the time the physician evaluated the patient, it was agreed that, if any fractures were discovered, the patient would be referred to a medical center for care. In evaluating the nature and extent of the injury, the physician ordered anterior-posterior x-ray views of the vertebrae. Although a true cross-table lateral view could not be made because the physician lacked a special radiological device, he never suggested that the patient be taken to a hospital for the lateral x-ray. Instead, he told the patient that he could provide the proper and necessary examination, despite his awareness of the limitation of his facility. After reviewing the x-rays the physician advised the patient that he had no fractures. Three months later, because of persistent pain, the patient went to another physician for care. This physician ordered a series of x-rays of the patient's spine. The lateral x-ray disclosed several fractures of the vertebral bodies. Thereupon the patient sued the original physician for negligently failing to refer him for proper x-rays of his injury.

 The court pointed out that the physician should have recognized that his resources were limited under the circumstances of this case; therefore, he should have refrained from undertaking total care of the patient. Instead, he should have referred him to an available facility which was appropriately equipped to thoroughly evaluate the patient's problem.

Smith v. Mallinkrodt Chemical Works.   A woman complained of visual problems to her family practitioner who assumed that her symptoms were caused solely by the presence of a foreign object in the eye. He attempted to remove the object but could not actually locate it. In fact the symptoms were incompatible with his clinical impression and presented evidence of a detached retina. However, the physician did not have access to, nor training in, the use of an indirect ophthalmoscope to examine the eye properly and make the correct diagnosis. He did not inform the patient of his inability and incapacity to provide a thorough eye examination. By the time the patient consulted an ophthalmologist several weeks later, her vision was irretrievably damaged. She therefore sued her family physician for not referring her to an ophthalmologist.

The court held that the physician had been negligent in failing to refer her to a specialist who, by use of his specialized instruments, would have been better equipped and able to examine the patient and discover the nature of the eye problem.

A physician must inform the patient of the seriousness of his condition and make him aware of other available, accessible and appropriate treatment facilities that would be beneficial in the care and treatment of the patient's condition.

Tvedt v. Haugen.   A patient sustained a spiral fracture of the tibia and a transverse fracture of the fibula of the lower middle third of the leg. Specialists were not readily accessible in this small town. The family physician reduced the fractures, applied a cast, and x-rayed the leg. The patient was discharged from the hospital and instructed to stay in bed for thirty days. Approximately three months after the injury, the patient returned to the hospital for another x-ray which demonstrated no significant callus formation at the fracture site of the tibia, although the fibula had united. Nevertheless, the physician split the cast, examined the patient's leg, and told the patient that good callus was forming. During the next several months the patient saw the physician several times and complained of pain and inability to walk properly. The physician continued to assure him that he was coming along fine. Six months after the injury the patient consulted an orthopedist in another city who took an x-ray, discovered nonunion of the tibia, admitted the patient to a hospital, and performed an operation. The patient sued his family physician.

The orthopedic surgeon testified that the early treatment given by the physician, including application of a cast and instructions to the patient to stay in bed, was proper. He stated that the normal healing period for such fractures was from six to eight weeks. At the end of that time it was proper to remove the cast in order to examine the progress of the healing process. He further testified that the lack of callus at the end of three months indicated that there was either a delayed union or a nonunion. At that stage the chances of obtaining a bony union, except by operation, were speculative.

The court concluded that the physician deceived the patient by assuring him everything was coming along fine, although he should have known that there was no union of the tibia and that none was likely. When it appeared that union was unlikely, the physician was obligated to apprise the patient of facilities where he might obtain more specialized care for his complicated condition.

A physician may be negligent for referring a patient he knows to be in need of particular care to a specialist or facility which he should know cannot adequately or safely provide it.

Rise v. United States. The patient experienced recurrent syncopal episodes, was hospitalized and given a battery of diagnostic tests, but no definitive diagnosis was made. Six months later, the patient collapsed at her job and was again hospitalized. This time intracranial hemorrhage was detected. Because her attending physician felt he could not provide adequate diagnostic and treatment services for the patient's condition, he referred her to a board-certified neurosurgeon at a nearby accredited hospital. The neurosurgeon performed a carotid arteriogram, which disclosed a cerebral aneurysm. In attempting corrective surgery the neurosurgeon did not utilize an operating microscope because the hospital did not own such an instrument. In addition, the anesthesiologist, who lacked any special training in neurosurgical anesthesia, had difficulty in controlling the patient's blood pressure. This caused complications which resulted in the patient's death.

The patient's estate sued the referring physician, contending his referral was actionable negligence. The referring physician contended that his conduct was not improper because he determined only that he could not provide adequate treatment for the patient and referred her to a neurosurgeon at an accredited hospital.

During the course of pretrial deposition, expert testimony established that the referral hospital was not equipped to perform cerebral aneurysm surgery because it lacked an anesthesiologist trained in properly modulating blood pressure during cerebrovascular surgery, and also because it lacked the capability to utilize an operating microscope for the procedure.

The court declared that a referring physician may be negligent if he should have known that he was referring the patient to a hospital lacking the personnel, equipment, and resources ordinarily considered by the medical profession necessary to safely perform the cerebrovascular surgery. However, the fact that a physician refers a patient he knows to be in need of a particular type of care, to a facility that he should know is unable to adequately provide the service, does not necessarily establish that the referral was negligent. It may, however, represent evidence that the physician's conduct was negligent.

Section 4: Liability for the Negligence of Other Health Care Providers

Right to Control

A physician, usually a surgeon, may be vicariously liable for the negligent acts of other health care personnel who assist him in the treatment of a patient if he has the right to control the actions of his assistants, regardless of whether that right is exercised. As the following cases illustrate, however, courts interpret right to control situations differently. They may take into consideration different factors in determining whether a right to control existed. Sometimes courts of different jurisdictions consider similar factors, but reach a different result, thereby making it difficult to clearly ascertain the law's position in this area.

1. Associate Physicians

Vicarious or derivative liability for the negligence of an associate physician, who is also a specialist in a separate and distinct field, may be treated differently by the courts than vicarious liability for negligent acts of other health care assistants. The reason for this distinction is that some courts view the specialized associate physician as an independent actor, not under the control of the attending physician. This is exemplified by the surgeon-anesthesiologist relationship. The following cases examine this relationship in terms of the right to control issue. The first case treats the anesthesiologist as any other surgeon's assistant, that is, subject to the control of the surgeon; thus the surgeon is found to be vicariously liable for the anesthesiologist's negligence. The second and third cases, however, hold that the anesthesiologist is an independent practitioner; thus the surgeon is not vicariously liable for the anesthesiologist's negligent acts.

Rockwell v. Stone. The patient had chronic bursitis of his right elbow. His surgeon recommended surgery. The patient requested that the surgery be done with a local anesthesia, but due to the nature of the surgery, the surgeon advised general anesthesia. Although the surgeon ordered a general anesthetic, he did not specifically instruct the anesthesiologist, who was salaried by the hospital, as to the specific type of general anesthesia. In the induction room, a nurse prepared the patient and notified the anesthesiologist. Because he was busy at the time, the anesthesiologist directed a resident anesthesiologist to administer Pentothal. The resident inserted the needle into the patient's left arm. When he proceeded with the Pentothal injection, the patient instantly cried out because of the pain in his forearm and hand. This response was consistent with arterial spasm secondary to either an

intra-arterial injection or extravasation of the Pentothal. The resident removed the needle and summoned the anesthesiologist. When the anesthesiologist arrived, the patient's left arm was blanched and his radial pulse was
barely palpable. After discussion and deliberation, the anesthesiologist and
the resident proceeded to administer general anesthesia and took the patient
to the operating room, without telling the surgeon what had taken place in
the induction room. Surgery was successfully concluded within thirty minutes. The surgeon left the hospital without visiting the patient in the recovery room. Approximately two hours after the Pentothal injection, the surgeon learned of the incident that had taken place in the induction room and
returned to the hospital. The circulation to the patient's left arm and hand
was irreparably compromised, and amputation was required. The patient
then sued all involved parties.

The anesthesiologist testified that a surgeon could use the hospital's
anesthesiologist or bring in his own, and that the surgeon had the authority
to tell him what sort of anesthesia he wanted. The surgeon testified in the
following manner that he was "the boss of the surgical end of it":

> Q. Suppose you felt that anesthesia should stop and the anesthesiolo-
>   gist felt that it should continue and you felt that continuation would
>   create a critical condition for your patient?
> A. I would stop it immediately, regardless of what he had to say; if I felt
>   strongly that this should stop, I would stop it.
> Q. And you would tell the anesthesiologist to stop it, wouldn't you?
> A. I would.
> Q. And he would stop, wouldn't he?
> A. I think he would have to.

The court noted that the administration of anesthesia was an integral
part of the surgical procedure; that the surgeon chose the hospital in which
the anesthesiologist worked; and that the surgeon chose a general rather
than a local anesthetic. The court determined that the surgeon had the right
of control of what went on during the operation. It concluded, therefore,
that the anesthesiologist was the surgeon's agent for the anesthesia step in
the operative procedure because the surgeon had the right of controlling the
manner of the anesthesiologist's performance, irrespective of whether he actually exercised that control. Therefore, under these facts and circumstances
the court concluded that the surgeon was responsible for the anesthesiologist's negligence.

Marvulli v. Elshire.   A patient was scheduled to undergo a hemorrhoidectomy. The anesthesiologist administered "caudal epidural" anesthesia sup-
plemented by intravenous Pentothal. No consultation took place between
the surgeon and the anesthesiologist about the type of anesthetic agent to be

used. The surgeon did not know the content of the anesthesia used on the patient when he entered the operating room, because he felt that choice was the prerogative of the anesthesiologist.

A nurse who assisted at the operation observed that before the first incision was made, she thought that the patient's anus and rectum looked dark, indicating lack of oxygen. Although her impression was confirmed after the incision produced dark blood, she did not mention these matters to the surgeon immediately because he was "awfully sharp and I thought he would pick it up." The surgeon had placed a guide suture at the base of the hemmorrhoidal plexus to control bleeding. He then made an elliptical incision and noted duskiness of blood indicative of impaired ventilation and adequate oxygenation. The surgeon said nothing until he started to remove the second hemmorrhoid when the blood was still dark and he remarked, "Oh, my God, is she all right?" Her respiration became shallow for several minutes; her position was then changed from prone to supine; and her ventilation was assisted by an oral airway. Upon the anesthesiologist's assurance that it could safely be done, surgery was then continued and completed.

Postoperatively, it became apparent that the patient was severely disabled due to brain damage caused by a hypoxia during surgery. The patient sued the hospital, the anesthesiologist, and the surgeon, alleging that the negligent administration of anesthesia caused her brain damage.

A settlement was effected with the hospital and the anesthesiologist. Accordingly, they were dismissed from the case. The trial continued regarding the responsibility of the operating surgeon for the negligence of the anesthesiologist and the nurse who had assisted him during the operation.

The court pointed out that a surgeon is generally in command of an operation from the beginning to the end. However, it noted that because a surgeon and an anesthesiologist work in separate highly specialized fields, their legal responsibilities were not inextricably bound together. In this case, the surgeon did not have the right to control the action or inaction of the anesthesiologist or the nurse when problems involving respiration became manifest. These problems pertained to matters within the jurisdiction of the anesthesiologist, not the surgeon; therefore, the surgeon was not vicariously liable for their negligent failure to act.

Kennedy v. Gaskell.   The patient was hospitalized for diagnostic evaluation of abdominal pain. Test results obtained the following day indicated the need for immediate abdominal surgical exploration. The surgery was scheduled for 6:30 P.M. that evening. The physician suggested to the patient that an anesthesiologist from a certain partnership of such specialists be engaged, and the patient agreed to this arrangement. One of the members of the selected partnership responded and arrived at the hospital at 5:30 P.M.

The anesthesiologist and the surgeon decided to use an epidural block.

As was the custom in the medical community, the surgeon helped position the patient for the administration of Xylocaine by the anesthesiologist, and then went to the scrub room to prepare for surgery. After the anesthesiologist had administered the Xylocaine, he checked the patient, but could not obtain a blood pressure or pulse. He called for help and the surgeon immediately responded. Resuscitative efforts ensued. Although the patient's heart resumed beating, he subsequently expired as a result of complications of the cardiopulmonary arrest.

The patient's estate sued the surgeon, claiming that he was liable for the anesthesiologist's negligence because he selected the anesthesiologist, the type of anesthesia, positioned the patient on the operating table, and was present throughout the administration of the anesthesia.

The court decided that the facts indicated that the anesthesiologist, after being instructed on the type, nature, and purpose of the anesthesia desired, was in full control of the administration of the anesthesia. Although the surgeon actually engaged the anesthesiologist, there was created, by implication, between the patient and the anesthesiologist a separate contract for professional services. Under these circumstances, each physician was engaged to perform his separate and distinct service, each independent of the other. Even though the practice and custom may have required the presence or assistance of the surgeon in the operating room while the patient was being anesthetized, the court concluded that no material acts were performed in concert with the anesthesiologist for which the surgeon might be held liable for the anesthesiologist's negligence. The court also pointed out that if the surgeon were held responsible for the anesthesiologist's negligence, it would not only permit, but command the incongruous situation in which a health specialist in one field must supervise, direct, and control the precise manner of performance by a practitioner in another specialized field.

2. Other Health Care Personnel

In contrast to the issue of liability for the acts of associate physicians, in which there may be a legal question about independent professional conduct, surgical nonphysician assistants are generally considered to be under the control of some entity, either the surgeon or the hospital, or both. Thus the legal question is whether the surgeon or another third party, usually the hospital, has control over the assistant's actions.

A surgeon usually does not employ, select, or dismiss surgical assistants. However, the surgeon usually has the right of control of assistants during surgery; therefore, the surgeon is said sometimes to be "the captain of the ship" and thus legally responsible for his assistant's conduct. However, as mentioned above, because the surgical assistant usually serves two masters (the surgeon and the hospital), the court may find that the specific activity involved was performed not for the surgeon but for the hospital;

therefore, the hospital should be liable for the assistant's negligence. The following three cases illustrate the issues involved in this area.

The first case takes the position that the surgeon is vicariously liable, while the second case takes the opposite view. The third case questions the legal doctrine of subjecting the surgeon to vicarious liability simply because a right to control may exist, that is, whether "the captain of the ship" doctrine should be applied in determining a surgeon's liability.

McConnell v. Williams.   The patient's attending surgeon decided that she was going to require a caesarean section for the delivery of her child. He suggested that it be performed at a teaching hospital where he was on the obstetrical staff. He requested one of the hospital interns to be his assistant in caring for the baby at the time of the caesarean section, but was told that the intern would not be on duty. He therefore designated another intern to be his assistant. This intern, and a nurse employed by the hospital, were present at the operation.

During the procedure, the patient hemorrhaged and this required the surgeon's complete attention. When the infant was delivered he turned it over to the intern to tie the umbilical cord and apply a solution of silver nitrate to the infant's eyes. The intern squirted the solution once into the infant's left eye and put "a great many drops into the right eye." He did not irrigate the eyes for at least ten minutes. As a result of the prolonged application of this concentrated solution, the infant lost the sight of its right eye and its left eye was severely and permanently scarred. The parents sued on behalf of their child. They did not charge the surgeon directly or personally with any act of negligence, either of commission or omission, but sought to hold him vicariously liable for the negligence of the intern.

The surgeon admitted that he had complete control of the operating room and every person within it while the operation was in progress and that inserting the silver nitrate in the infant's eyes, although not a task that required any special skill, was part of the operation.

The court pointed out that a "borrowed employee" is one who, while in the general employ of the hospital, is subject to the right of the surgeon to direct or control details of the particular work and is not merely complying with suggestions of the surgeon. The court determined that for the purpose of and during the course of the operation, which included the immediate care of the infant, the surgeon "borrowed" an intern from the hospital; the intern thereby became a temporary assistant for the activity in which the surgeon was engaged.

The court reasoned that because the patient is helpless under the influence of an anesthetic and at the mercy of the surgeon performing the operation, the surgeon is charged with the duty to see that no preventable injury results to his patient. This relationship originates from: the conscious selection by the patient of a particular surgeon; the reliance by the patient on the skill and judgment of the surgeon; and the inability of the patient to control any of the actions occurring during surgery. The patient may reasonably expect that the surgeon selected will control the operation, require the operating room personnel to follow proper medical procedures, protect the patient from the negligence of the operating room personnel, and exclude unqualified personnel from the operating room. A surgeon who is in charge of an operation may thus be responsible for the negligence of assistants during the period when these assistants are under his control, even though the assistants are also employees of the hospital. Thus in this case the court held that until the surgeon leaves the operating room at the conclusion of the operation, he is in complete charge of and responsible for those present and assisting him, just as a captain is in charge of his ship. Thus, he will be held liable for any negligent acts of his assistants during this period.

Buzan v. Mercy Hospital, Inc.   A surgical sponge was inadvertently left in the patient's abdomen during a cholecystectomy. When a second operation was required to remove the sponge, the patient sued the hospital for the negligence of its nurse who assisted the surgeon in improperly counting the sponges. The hospital admitted that its employees did assist the surgeon in the operation, but contended that employees assisting the surgeon were under his orders and subject to his control during the operative procedure.

   The court pointed out that the nature of the type of service or act attributed to a hospital nurse assisting in an operation influences the determination of whether the surgeon had control over the nurse. Although the duties of an assisting nurse that involve professional skill or decision are controlled solely by the surgeon, services or acts not involving professional skill or decision, and which are ministerial in character, are controlled by the hospital. A sponge count by an assisting nurse is usually such a ministerial act. Counting the sponges to ensure that no sponge was left in the body of the patient did not require the special professional skill or discretion of the surgeon. Furnishing proper personnel and equipment for an operation are responsibilities of a hospital. Therefore, in this case the negligent act was the responsibility of the hospital because it was not an act requiring the exercise of a particular skill or judgment acquired or developed by special training, but instead, could have been done by an unskilled or untrained employee. The court pointed out, therefore, that the incorrect count was not a medical mistake; it was an administrative or nonprofessional mistake. The court concluded that although the surgeon is usually in sole command, with the right to control all the personnel present in performing duties in the operating room that are closely related to procedures being performed by the surgeon, and is in complete charge both of the operating room and the personnel assisting with the operation; all acts of nurses in the operating room are not the responsibility of the surgeon.

At issue in the two preceding cases was the "captain of the ship" doctrine, which holds that when a surgeon has the right of control, vicarious liability is imposed for a surgical assistant's negligence. This is a special and more onerous form of vicarious liability imposed on the medical profession than is assumed in similar relationships. Thus many courts have decided that this doctrine should not be applied.

In the following case the court applied the "borrowed servant" doctrine, holding that only if the surgical assistants were legally determined to be the "borrowed servants" of the surgeon, would the surgeon be liable for their negligence.

Sparger v. Worley Hospital, Inc. The patient underwent abdominal surgery. Near the completion of the procedure, the circulating nurse and the scrub nurse indicated that the sponge count was correct. The surgeon requested a second count. Again the nurses responded that the count was correct. As a result of the negligent miscount by the operating room nurses, a surgical sponge was not removed from the abdominal cavity. When this was discovered after the operation, the patient sought to hold the surgeon, Dr. Sparger, vicariously liable for the negligent sponge count by the nurses. The hospital contended that Dr. Sparger was solely liable because, for the purpose of surgery, the nurses were his exclusive employees.

The court analyzed the legal roles and responsibilities of the involved health care personnel. The nurses were hired as general employees by the hospital and were assigned solely by the hospital for the operation. They had established assignments including sponge counts in the operating room during the operation. The procedures for the sponge counts were intended for use regardless of the surgeon who was performing an operation. The circulating nurse prepared the operating room by laying out the necessary supplies and equipment. She remained in the nonsterile area of the operating room. The scrub nurse assisted the surgeon by handing him instruments, clamps and sponges. Before surgery began, the scrub nurse counted the sponges that had been laid out. The circulating nurse recorded that count. When Dr. Sparger was ready to close the peritoneum, the scrub nurse counted the unused sponges and the circulating nurse counted the used ones. The total was reported by the scrub nurse as tallying with the record. Dr. Sparger did not direct the scrub nurse and the circulating nurse to make the sponge count. The two nurses knew how to perform the sponge count because it was part of the hospital policy and regulations manual which detailed their duties. In that procedure manual, general instructions noted that

The nurse is responsible for all counts. All cases require sponge counts. This includes sponges, needles, drains, screws and any other similar articles which may be brought into the operating field. All counts are taken before the case begins and are recorded in writing on the operative record. All these must be accounted for before the closure of the operative incision. NO OTHER NEED IS MORE IMPORTANT!

If the counts are correct this is so written on the operative record and signed by the circulating nurse taking the counts. If there is a discrepancy in the counts, the surgeon is immediately notified and a search is made for the missing article. If the missing item is not found after a thorough search, an x-ray is mandatory and cannot be refused by the surgeon.

Counts are taken on each case; one before the case begins; one prior to the closure of the peritoneum or the first layer of tissue. Specific duties of the circulating nurse include sponge count to be taken before incision is made. Place dirty sponges where they can easily be seen by the scrub nurse and the anesthetist. Sponge count is taken as the doctor is ready to close the peritoneum.

With respect to his professional relationship with the nurses, Dr. Sparger testified as follows:

QUESTION: During the course of the operation the surgeon is in charge of the patient?

DR. SPARGER: In charge of all the medical aspects of the patient.

QUESTION: Now, in connection with an operation, a surgeon issues orders to the nurses during the operation, does he not?

DR. SPARGER: Correct.

QUESTION: And they are supposed to follow them?

DR. SPARGER: Yes, sir.

QUESTION: And you are supposed to tell the nurses what to do, and what not to do?

DR. SPARGER: Correct, in regard to the medical aspects.

QUESTION: Now, you have also told us that you did not ask either the scrub nurse or the circulating nurse for a sponge count, but that they voluntarily gave you one, is that correct?

DR. SPARGER: Correct.

QUESTION: Now, isn't it true that your judgment controls any surgical process from the beginning to end during an operation?

DR. SPARGER: The medical aspect of the operation.

QUESTION: If there is any conflict or disagreement in judgment between you and somebody else, including the nurses, or a surgeon who is assisting you, your judgment would control, would it not?

DR. SPARGER: If there is any conflict, that is true.

QUESTION: In other words, you are in charge of the operation, and everybody is supposed to do what you tell them?

DR. SPARGER: That's right, medically speaking.

Dr. Sparger also testified that he requested a sponge count after closing the peritoneum, but prior to closing the skin. With respect to the sponge counts the scrub nurse testified as follows:

Q. Do you know whether the hospital regulations required another count after the time that Dr. Sparger had begun to close the peritoneum?

A. No, I don't think they did. I am sure they didn't.

The scrub nurse also testified regarding the relationship between the nurses and Dr. Sparger:

Q. Are you instructed to follow the doctor's orders at all times?

A. Yes.

Q. Do you follow them?

A. Yes, I try my best.

Q. And he tells you what to do and what not to do?

A. Yes.

The circulating nurse testified as follows:

Q. When you made a second count after the peritoneum was closed, neither one of those doctors directed you to do that?

A. No, sir. It is accepted that you do that.

Q. Neither one of those doctors ordered you to do that?

A. You just know they expect it of you.

Q. Well, I am asking you, did either one of those doctors order you to do that?

A. No.

Q. All right, in fact, those orders and regulations that control you in that work come from your hospital regulations, don't they?

A. Well, the doctors just expect you to have a sponge count for them. It is just the way they expect it. . . .

Q. Now, in connection with the operating room, is the operating surgeon supposed to give you orders as to what to do, and what not to do?

A. Yes, sir.

Q. And you are supposed to follow those orders?

A. Yes, sir.

Q. Without question?

A. Yes, sir.

The patient contended that the testimony demonstrated that the operating surgeon had the right to control the actions of the nurses with respect to the sponge counts during the course of the operation. She argued that although the hospital had established standard procedures to be followed by operating room nurses, Dr. Sparger had the right to alter the procedures followed by these nurses because the nurses would not have refused to obey an order issued by the operating surgeon during the course of the operation, even if it conflicted with hospital policy and procedure. Moreover, the patient further argued that Dr. Sparger did in fact alter the procedures followed by these nurses by requesting a second sponge count.

The court refused to apply the "captain of the ship" doctrine and hold Dr. Sparger liable for the nurses's negligence. It referred to that doctrine as a "false rule of agency." Instead, the court stated that Dr. Sparger could be held vicariously liable only if the facts showed that legally the nurses were his "borrowed servants." After consideration of the facts, the court found that reasonable minds might differ as to whether the facts proved that the nurses were Dr. Sparger's borrowed servants. Thus, the trier of fact's decision on this issue would be decisive.

3. Preoperative and Postoperative Liability

The following cases explore the scope and extent of a physician's vicarious liability, particularly as to when the physician's right to control assistants begins and ends. They will also explore circumstances in which a physician can be found liable even though he is not physically present during the patient's treatment which was negligently performed by an assistant.

The first case indicates that a surgeon's right of control and legal responsibility begins with the start of the operative process. Therefore, he will incur liability if his authority to control activities in the operative process is actually exercised.

Benedict v. Bondi.   Dr. Bondi prepared to perform an emergency operation on a young patient who appeared to be in shock. A student nurse working in and about the operating rooms was requested by an unidentified person to get two hot water bottles and fill them with hot water. She filled them from a faucet in an instrument scrubbing room. Although the temperature of the water was near the boiling point, she did not test the temperature of the water. When she returned to the operating room she covered the bottles, not with flannel covers as was the proper practice, but with muslin pillow cases. As she was about to apply them to the anesthetized patient on the operating table, Dr. Bondi, who was standing near the operating table, told her to give the bottles to the operating room staff nurse. Then Dr. Bondi told the nurse to apply the bottles. She placed them on the lateral aspects of the feet of the anesthetized child. After the operation was over, the child was discovered to have sustained third degree burns of the feet. The father, as guardian, brought suit against Dr. Bondi for the negligence of the nurses.

The father contended that the surgeon was in control of the operating room and whatever went on in that room, insofar as the child's operation was concerned, was the surgeon's affair and concern. While he was in charge, he could give orders and they had to be followed even if the operating supervisor or his assistant objected.

Dr. Bondi contended that such control does not exist in regard to either preoperative preparation or postoperative care which is not administered in the operating room in the presence or direct charge of the surgeon. He contended further that a nurse's activities in cleaning the operating room, placing clean sheets on the operating table, preparing gowns and gloves, sterilizing the instruments to be used for the operation, preparing sterile drapes, and placing the patient on the operating table, are administrative or ministerial acts performed by the nurse as an employee of the hospital. In regard to those acts, Dr. Bondi argued that the surgeon has not yet "come into the picture."

The court decided, however, that the application of the hot water bottles to the child's feet was not merely a ministerial act of the nurse, but a medical or therapeutic act. Such an application was not a routine matter in all operative procedures, but sometimes was employed if the patient was in shock. It is, therefore, the surgeon's decision to determine and direct if, when, and how heat should be applied. His legal responsibility did not begin merely at the exact moment when he started to make an incision in the child's body. The operative process started with, and included, the application of the hot water bottles which were designed to assist in the restoration of the patient's well being. The court pointed out that Dr. Bondi not only had the complete authority and control in the operating room, but that he actually ordered the student nurse not to apply the hot water bottles to the child and ordered the staff nurse to do so. The court declared that even though the surgeon himself had not committed any act of negligence, if he had control over an assistant at the time of the occurrence, his own liability would automatically follow.

Benedict indicated that a surgeon's responsibility may begin with the inception of the operative process, not necessarily the actual surgery. Similarly, the following case illustrates that the physician's responsibility may begin before the start of the actual operation if the negligent act causing the injury was part of the previously discussed and proposed operative procedure. It also indicates that under certain circumstances responsibility may not end with the completion of the operative procedure, but may extend into immediate postoperative care and treatment.

Yorston v. Pennell.   Mr. Yorston was injured when a nail richocheted from a ramset gun, entered his leg, and fractured his fibula. When Yorston got to the emergency room he showed a note to a nurse and an intern, written by his family physician on one of the physician's blank prescriptions. It stated that because Yorston was allergic to penicillin, he should "never receive penicillin under any circumstances." Yorston's wife arrived at the hospital shortly thereafter. She also showed the note to one of the nurses and told another intern that there was a note about her husband's allergy that she had given to the nurse. In addition, she told the intern that her husband was allergic to tetanus antitoxin. Although Yorston was tested for an allergy to tetanus antitoxin, he was not tested for a penicillin allergy. A surgical resident was called to see Yorston. Subsequently, Dr. Pennell, the private attending staff surgeon, and the resident discussed the surgical procedures to be followed. The resident then ordered an intern to take Yorston's history. Yorston advised this intern that he was allergic to penicillin, but the intern forgot to include this in the history. Subsequently, the intern remembered this omission and went to the operating room. Because he was not gowned, he went to the door of the operating room and asked the nurse-anesthetist to make a notation on the patient's history that the patient was allergic to penicillin. She said she would.

The surgical resident extracted the nail in the operating room. As the operation concluded and while still in the operating room, he wrote postoperative orders and prescribed 600,000 units of penicillin to be administered intramuscularly every four hours.

Prior to the first administration of penicillin, Yorston advised the nurse that he was allergic to penicillin. Nevertheless, she administered it because she said there was no notation of a penicillin allergy on the chart. Despite his protests, the patient received penicillin on two more occasions. Because of his persistent objections, Dr. Pennell discontinued the penicillin and ordered tetracycline. After his discharge from the hospital, Yorston developed an allergic skin reaction and manifested signs of a cerebral vasculitis which were diagnosed to be the result of a delayed penicillin hypersensitivity. The patient sued all parties who had been involved in the care of his fractured leg.

The court held that the surgical resident had "borrowed" the intern from the hospital for the purposes of taking a medical history. Because the resident was an assistant of Dr. Pennell the intern became a subemployee of the surgeon, and the surgeon became liable for the negligent acts of his assistants that were performed in the course of the surgeon's employment. It pointed out that Dr. Pennell ordinarily would not be responsible for the acts of employees of the hospital, such as nurses who administered penicillin postoperatively at the insistence of other physicians. In this case, however, the penicillin was administered specifically at the direction of the surgical resident while he was in the operating room. Furthermore, because Dr. Pennell personally chose the surgical resident to perform the operation, other hospital employees assisting in the surgery became, during that operation, the employees of Dr. Pennell through the agency of the surgical resident. Thus the court concluded that, under the circumstances of the case, Dr. Pennell was responsible for the negligent acts of the resident, the intern, and the nurse.

A surgeon may be vicariously liable for operative negligence of his assistants, even if he has properly removed himself from the operating room at a time when his supervision was reasonably viewed to be unnecessary. The next case suggests that an operating surgeon may be responsible for the negligent conduct of surgical residents in closing the surgical field, even though the surgeon has already left the operating room.

Thomas v. Hutchinson. A patient underwent an operation to remove a herniated nucleus pulposus. The operating surgeon was a private orthopedic surgeon on the staff of the hospital. He was assisted by three orthopedic residents who were selected for this particular operation by the hospital. After the surgeon had removed the disc and completed the material and substantive aspects of the surgery, he left the operating room and allowed the residents to remove the remaining sponges and close the incision. Subsequently when the patient continued to complain of back pain, and his wound had not healed, another surgeon operated on his back and found a surgical sponge which had been used in the initial operation. The patient sued the first orthopedic surgeon, charging that he was responsible for the resident surgeons' negligence.

On pretrial deposition the surgeon described the residents as his assistants and himself as the one directing the operation. At trial, the patient contended that this was an admission that the residents were the surgeon's agents and therefore, the surgeon was vicariously liable for the residents' negligence. The court did not agree that the surgeon's statement definitively demonstrated an agency relationship between the surgeon and residents. The court felt that such a conclusion would penalize the surgeon for what might be "loose language" made during deposition. The court nevertheless noted that operating surgeons have been described as being in complete charge of assistants in the operating room. Therefore a surgeon becomes responsible for negligence of his assistants, even though the assistants were also employees of the hospital. In this case the surgeon "borrowed" the hospital employees to serve as his assistants to accomplish a service the surgeon had contracted to perform for the patient. Thus the court concluded that if the residents were negligent, the operating surgeon could be held vicariously liable for the residents' negligence.

The next two cases discuss circumstances in which a physician may be liable for the negligence of another even though he was not physically present during an operation or the administration of a form of therapy. In the first case, the physician was found to be vicariously liable for an assistant's negligence where a duty existed requiring his presence.

Pederson v. Dumouchel. A man injured in an automobile accident was placed in the hospital under the care of Dr. Dumouchel when it was determined that he had a fractured mandible. Dr. Dumouchel examined the patient and contacted a dentist to reduce the patient's fracture under general anesthesia. The anesthesia was administered by a nurse employed by the hospital. The dentist had no working knowledge of the use or administration of a general anesthetic and left the responsibility and control of the anesthetic to the nurse. On prior occasions when the dentist had reduced a fractured mandible under a general anesthetic in the hospital, a physician had been present. Hospital rules stated that patients requiring dental service could be co-admitted by a member of the medical staff and a local dentist qualified, legally and professionally, to practice there. The medical staff member was required to perform an adequate medical examination prior to dental surgery, and was responsible for the patient's medical care. Dr. Dumouchel left the hospital before surgery commenced and was not present during the surgery. While in the recovery room, the patient had seizures as a result of cerebral hypoxia due to inadequate ventilation of the patient during anesthesia or during the postoperative period. Dr. Dumouchel could not be located because it was his "afternoon off." No other physician was available in the hospital at the time. The patient sustained severe and permanent brain damage and sued Dr. Dumouchel for failure to supervise the surgery.

The court pointed out that Dr. Dumouchel failed to properly assume the responsibility "for the patient's medical care" while in surgery. It concluded that, in the absence of extraordinary or emergent circumstances, it was negligent to allow surgery under general anesthesia without the presence and supervision of a physician in the operating room.

In contrast to *Pederson*, the following case did not involve a physician's duty to personally supervise the acts of others who assist in the care of his patient. In this case, the physician referred the patient to another facility for a specific type of treatment. The court found that in this situation, the physician neither had a duty nor a right to control the actions of those who negligently administered the treatment.

Collins v. Hand. Dr. Hand prescribed electroshock therapy (EST) and arranged for his patient's transfer to a hospital where this mode of treatment was available. He was the only attending physician involved in her care and the only physician who wrote orders for EST. Dr. Hand, however, was not present nor did he direct the actual performance of these treatments, which were performed by a team of technicians headed by an experienced physician. As a result of the negligent administration of the EST, the patient sustained vertebral fractures. Thereupon, the hospital notified Dr. Hand and awaited his further orders. He ordered the treatments immediately stopped.

Because of the back injury, the patient then sued Dr. Hand, charging that he was vicariously liable for the EST team's negligence. Dr. Hand contended that he had no control over the terms of the employment of the personnel at the hospital where the therapy was administered and thus was not liable for their negligence.

The court noted that, in order to accord the anesthetized patient a high degree of protection, surgeons have been held liable for the negligence of those assisting in performing an operation. However, the situation was different in this case. Dr. Hand suggested the referral hospital as a place where EST could be administered to his patient because such therapy was not otherwise available. At the referral hospital, a group of employees, headed by a physician especially experienced in EST administered it. Dr. Hand did not choose the physician who was to administer the therapy. He could not hire or discharge any of the persons involved. He was not present when the treatments were given.

The court pointed out that in determining whether Dr. Hand had the right to control the manner of performance of the EST which caused the injury, it is insufficient to show merely that the therapy was ordered and stopped by Dr. Hand. Anyone who engages the service of a technician or specialist for the performance of a particular job must of necessity indicate the service that he wishes performed. The giving of such directions by Dr. Hand did not necessarily bring the EST team into Dr. Hand's employment and make him responsible for the performance of the EST services. The court concluded that Dr. Hand did not have any effective degree of control or the right to control the manner of performance of these treatments. The type of services involved were part of the routine procedures rendered by the hospital. Therefore the hospital was exclusively responsible for the negligence of its employee.

Joint Liability.   The preceding cases have indicated the scope of a physician's vicarious liability for the negligent acts of others who assist in the care of the patient. This subsection deals with shared or joint liability of health care personnel who independently provide services to the patient. (For example, when two physicians' separate acts of negligence combine to produce legal damage incapable of division; or when a hospital shares liability with the attending physician for the negligent acts of assistants it has provided.)

Where two or more negligent acts of physicians combine to produce a single damaging result, incapable of any logical division, and where each negligent act may be a substantial factor in bringing about the injury, each physician may be held solely responsible for all the consequences.

Gilson v. Mitchell.   The patient underwent stomach surgery. In order to monitor the patient effectively, Dr. Soria placed a central venous pressure catheter in his right external jugular vein. For some unexplained reason, Dr. Soria cut part of the catheter off, thereby inserting an unusually short central venous catheter. Subsequently the patient came under the care of his family physician, Dr. Mitchell, Jr., who removed the catheter and found it so short upon pulling it out that he, in conjunction with Dr. Mitchell, Sr., concluded that the missing length was adrift somewhere in the patient's circulatory system where it could produce a fatal consequence. X-rays were unable to identify the location of the "missing" part. Thus the patient was then flown to a medical center for evaluation by a heart specialist, where he underwent invasive diagnostic testing which was also inconclusive. The patient was then told that the fate of the missing length could not be medically determined.

The patient sued Dr. Soria and both Dr. Mitchells, charging that he was unnecessarily subjected to mental distress and to surgical procedures as a result of their combined negligence. He contended that the alleged "missing" length of catheter never existed, but was in fact cut off by Dr. Soria prior to insertion. He argued that the independent but concurring acts of negligence by the three physicians entitled him to a joint recovery against all of them. The physicians contended that they were not jointly liable because they had not acted in concert in the treatment of the patient.

The court found that the physicians were jointly negligent and therefore each responsible for the patient's damage. Dr. Soria, without telling the patient of the "experimental" nature of his procedure, inserted an unusually short catheter and subsequently did not follow the patient's progress through removal of the catheter. Dr. Mitchell, Jr., upon discovering the peculiarly short catheter, did not inquire of Dr. Soria the length he used, but instead jumped to the conclusion that a piece of catheter was lost and immediately subjected the patient to expensive and painful procedures to "locate" the missing part. Although the physicians' acts of negligence did not occur at the same time, the acts combined to create an urgent situation in which the missing portion of the catheter was thought to be in the patient's circulatory system. This required that he be subjected to further medical procedures. Thus the court concluded that the various acts of the Drs. Mitchell and Soria together produced the single legal injury to the patient of the needless medical procedures and mental distress. Physicians are jointly liable for concurrent and independent negligence if their actions produce a single indivisible result because under such circumstances a rational basis does not exist for an apportionment of damages among the physicians.

As previously mentioned, a physician rendering postoperative care to a patient may be responsible for injury to a patient when a resident physician negligently carries out the physician's orders. However, the physician may not be responsible for the resident's negligent act if such orders relate to procedures not potentially dangerous to the patient; such procedures fall within the ambit of the resident's training and qualification; and delegation of such tasks is the accepted standard of medical practice.

Strumper v. Kimel. The patient underwent a resection of an abdominal aortic aneurysm. On the seventh postoperative day he developed intestinal obstruction. To decompress the small intestine by extracting the intestinal contents, the surgeon inserted a Miller-Abbott tube (M-A tube) through the upper alimentary tract into the small intestine. The apparatus consisted of a rubber tube which surrounds two noncommunicating lumens, one for suction and the other for inflation of the balloon. The tube had a forked metal tip which communicated with their respective lumen. One fork had engraved in the metal "suction," the other "balloon." The suction lumen communicated with the interior gastric system through holes at the end of the tube so that gastric contents could be aspirated. The balloon lumen ended with a balloon attached to the end of the M-A tube. After the tube is inserted water, air, or mercury is placed in the balloon. The bulk and weight of the balloon allows the tube to be carried into the small intestine by the peristaltic action. Because the intestines may contact and plug the suction holes, it is necessary to irrigate the tube with fluid to maintain suction. This is accomplished by introducing a saline solution through the suction lumen.

After the surgeon had inserted the M-A tube, he entered orders on the hospital chart for the nursing staff to irrigate and advance it periodically. The nursing staff was trained and qualified to perform this task. Two days later, the surgeon was notified that the wrong lumen of the M-A tube may have been irrigated. He checked this report by examining the M-A tube and aspirating the balloon lumen, but found no fluid therein. Because x-rays of the tube appeared to be satisfactory, he ordered the M-A tube removed by a resident physician. When the resident attempted to remove it, he experienced difficulty. Further attempts to remove the M-A tube caused an esophageal perforation and a partial pneumothorax. When the balloon was removed clear fluid came out of it indicating that it had been improperly irrigated, and that was the reason which prevented its removal in the usual manner. The patient sued the surgeon and attempted to hold him liable for the resident's negligence, contending that carrying out the postoperative orders referable to managing bowel obstruction required a physician's expertise. Thus the surgeon should be liable for the resident's negligence.

The court noted that if the order given by the surgeon was such that the potential dangers incident to it were unduly great to the patient, then it would be a nondelegable duty, and the surgeon would be responsible for the resident's negligence. However, the court concluded that the delegation of such duty was an accepted medical standard because it was within the ambit of the resident physician's qualifications and training; therefore, the surgeon was absolved from responsibility.

Ordinarily a physician who has advised his patient of the need for an operation, and recommends the surgeon, is not liable for the surgeon's negligence even if he assists at the operation. However, a physician may be jointly liable with another physician when concert of action and common purpose exists between the two physicians. Thus, for example, liability may rest on the arrangements made by physicians for the care and treatment of each other's patients, as the following cases illustrate.

Watts v. Jankowski. A patient underwent a cholecystectomy on the advice of her family physician who recommended that she have the surgery done by a general surgeon. The physician did not actively participate in or control the surgical decisions, but instead acted as an instrumentality of the operating surgeon by holding a retractor, cutting sutures, and "just generally assisting." During the operation, the surgeon inserted a penrose drain in the patient's abdomen to expedite draining of blood, serum, or bile into the dressing. The drain was to be removed by the surgeon a few days after the surgery. The family physician, while making his rounds after surgery, read, dated, and initialed a notation on the patient's hospital chart: "Dressing changed. Moderate amount of light bloody type drainage present. Drain noted in suture line." On the sixth day after the surgery, a noted signed by the surgeon stated "All sutures and drain out." In fact, the drain was not removed and remained in the patient's abdomen. It had to be surgically removed several years later.

The patient sued the family physician and the surgeon claiming their joint venture had negligently caused her injury, and that both of them were liable for their own negligence as well as each other's negligence. The court declared that under the circumstances of this case, a joint and common duty did not exist between a family physician and a surgeon, because the family physician had not exercised control over the acts and decisions of the surgeon. Thus, the court concluded that the family physician was not responsible for the negligent omission of the surgeon.

Graddy v. New York Medical College. Both Dr. Street and Dr. Bell were otolaryngologists who shared a medical office, secretary, professional equipment, and office supplies. They used the office at different periods of the day. No medical partnership existed between them. Each had separate patients whom they billed as individual practitioners. A patient of one physician would, in the physician's absence, be treated by the other if the patient consented to the substitution. In such cases the physician would bill his own patient for the service and pay half of the fee to the substitute physician who had performed the service.

The patient had been treated by Dr. Street on two occasions for complaints referable to his nose and throat, for which Dr. Street had advised against surgical treatment. When the patient came back to the office, he was told that Dr. Street was ill and that Dr. Bell, who was then in the office, was caring for Dr. Street's patients. Although the patient recited the same symptoms he had previously given to Dr. Street, Dr. Bell advised surgery. Shortly thereafter, he performed the surgery in a negligent manner. The patient sued both Dr. Bell and Dr. Street, claiming Dr. Street was liable for Dr. Bell's negligence. He contended that the nexus of the professional relationship between Dr. Street and Dr. Bell was the financial interest that Dr. Street would have in the fee for the services performed by Dr. Bell. In this arrangement, the patient contended, Dr. Street had left it to Dr. Bell to exercise his own professional judgment upon Dr. Street's patient to the latter's economic advantage.

The court pointed out that in the absence of some recognized traditional legal relationship, such as partnership, employment or agency relationship, between physicians in the treatment of patients; the imposition of liability on one for the negligence of the other is usually limited to situations of joint action in diagnosis or treatment or control of the course of treatment of one physician's patient by the other. An act of negligence by one in the absence of the other, unless concerted, is ordinarily not attributed to the nonparticipant. However, where physicians actually participate together in diagnosis and treatment, each may incur liability for the negligence of the other, even though one of them may have taken a more active part in the treatment than the other.

Physicians employed by the patient to diagnose or treat the case together are both responsible to the patient and therefore may be jointly liable for any negligence. However, the court noted that referral of a patient by one physician to another competent and qualified physician, absent partnership, employment or agency, does not impose a liability on the referring physician. The court pointed out that a physician who is unable or unwilling to assume or continue the treatment of a case and recommends another unrelated physician to take over the care of the patient is not liable for injuries resulting from the latter's negligence unless the referring physician did not exercise due care in making the recommendation or selecting his replacement.

The court noted that the law has broadened the base of a physician's derivative liability for the professional acts of other physicians. In the past, even in situations when he might be regarded as being under control of another, a physician had been treated as an "independent contractor." As such, liability for his negligence was not always passed on to the other physician. However, in situations where one physician has submitted himself to the control of another physician, the limitation on liability does not apply. The court noted that the legal trend of broadening a physician's legal responsibility for the care of another physician's patient ought not to be extended to a situation where the physician has no control of the treating physician and the relationship between them is based simply upon a shared office and an agreement to cover each other's practice and service each other's patients for a shared fee.

The court concluded that this situation is different from an employment or an agency relationship, which is necessary to establish vicarious liability. The court concluded that the implications of such an enlarged liability would tend to discourage a physician from arranging to have another physician care for his patients in the event of his illness or absence and thus curtail the availability of medical services.

When the sole connection between two physicians is that each of them "covered" for the other on their respective days off, they are not responsible for each other's independent negligence.

Settoon v. St. Paul Fire & Marine Insurance Company. Mrs. Settoon was hospitalized for the delivery of her child. She signed the standard "Consent for Treatment" form which stated that she authorized and consented to any and all medical treatments as may be deemed advisable by her physician or "such other physician as he may designate." However, the patient crossed out the phrase, "such other physician as he may designate." That afternoon, Mrs. Settoon gave birth by caesarean section. After the delivery, her obstetrician told her that he was going home and that Mr. Settoon could select a pediatrician in the morning. In the meantime the obstetrician assigned Dr. Miller to be the attending pediatrician for the infant until the parents chose one. An attendant in the hospital nursery called Dr. Miller's residence an hour after the birth and advised him that a newborn infant had been assigned to him, and that the infant appeared normal and healthy. Dr. Miller's routine nursery orders for care of the infant were put into effect. Had the infant shown any signs of having problems Dr. Miller would have been notified and would have been expected to take care of the infant in person or by instructions to the nurses assigned to the nursery. If the infant appeared stable, the assigned pediatrician would ordinarily examine the infant within twenty-four hours, usually on his morning rounds at the hospital. The next day was Dr. Miller's regular day off. Dr. Miller and another pediatrician, Dr. Tyler extended to each other the professional courtesy of taking the other's calls and seeing the other's patients on their respective "days off."

The next morning Mr. Settoon returned to the hospital and talked to his wife with the infant present. Mrs. Settoon desired to breast-feed the infant; therefore, the usual signs were displayed indicating that the infant was being breast-fed and that no admittance was allowed by anyone. Mr. Settoon was required to leave the room and the curtain around Mrs. Settoon's bed was drawn. At this point Dr. Tyler abruptly entered the room while Mrs. Settoon was breast-feeding. Dr. Tyler was making his regular rounds at the hospital and, knowing it was Dr. Miller's day off, checked all the infants listed as Dr. Miller's patients in the nursery. The Settoon infant was so listed, and therefore Dr. Tyler had entered Mrs. Settoon's room to check her infant. That evening, Dr. Miller received a telephone call from Mr. Settoon advising him that he did not want him to treat his child.

The next morning, while making rounds at the hospital, Dr. Miller noted that the hospital chart still listed him as the Settoon baby's pediatrician. He thereupon went to Mrs. Settoon's room, accompanied by a nurse, informed Mrs. Settoon that the infant was still listed as being under his care, that under the hospital regulations the child could not be left without a pediatrician, and that he would be willing to care for the child until the services of another pediatrician could be obtained. He was told that his services were not desired. He thereupon instructed the nurses to obtain a written release from Mrs. Settoon.

Thereafter, Mr. Settoon sued both Dr. Tyler and Dr. Miller for invading his wife's privacy. He claimed that at the time of the allegedly wrongful intrusion, Dr. Tyler was acting as Dr. Miller's associate or agent, and thus Dr. Miller was liable for Dr. Tyler's actions.

The courted noted that Dr. Tyler and Dr. Miller had never been engaged in the practice of pediatrics as partners or associates. The arrangement between the two physicians was merely a professional courtesy of making themselves available to each other's patients during periods when one or the other was away from his practice. The patients of one were not obligated or required to use the services of the other.

Dr. Miller had never examined or even seen the Settoon infant. His only connection with this case is that the care of the infant was routinely assigned to him by the hospital without his previous knowledge. He never examined the infant and had only one harmless brief contact with Mrs. Settoon. Therefore, the court concluded that Dr. Miller could not be held accountable for any negligence allegedly committed by Dr. Tyler, because the sole connection between the two physicians was that each of them "covered" for the other on their respective days off. This type of professional relationship properly and commonly exists between members of many professions.

An operating surgeon may share responsibility for the negligence of operating room assistants with a hospital if it is determined that the assistant is simultaneously serving both the physician and the hospital in performing the same act.

Tonsic v. Wagner.   Dr. Wagner performed a colectomy. He was assisted by nurses and an intern who were employees of the hospital. The instruments were handed to him by the scrub nurse and were returned by the surgeon to this nurse. Neither the scrub nurse nor the intern kept count of the instruments to determine if any had been allowed to remain in the patient's abdomen. Because they did not call to Dr. Wagner's attention the fact that a clamp was missing, a Kelly clamp was left in the patient's abdomen. When it was subsequently discovered, the patient sued the hospital. She contended that although the nurses and intern in the operating room were subject to the control of the operating surgeon, they were also employees of the hospital and thus the hospital could be liable for their negligence.

The court indicated that under certain circumstances, an assistant may serve two masters. The court concluded that the hospital as well as the operating surgeon owed a duty of due care to the patient. If the hospital's duty to patients is breached by its negligent employee who was at the same time a "borrowed" employee of the surgeon, both "employers" may be liable for the employee's negligence.

Although a physician may "borrow" a hospital employee for use as an assistant for a particular procedure, the physician will not be primarily liable for the negligence of the assistant if the hospital has provided an incompetent or unqualified assistant.

Maybarouk v. Bustamante.   The hospital had furnished an unlicensed physician as a surgical assistant for an operation. During the course of the operation the assistant negligently failed to remove a hemostat from the patient's abdomen. The patient brought a malpractice suit against the operating surgeon for injuries resulting from the retained instrument, charging that the surgeon was responsible for the negligence of his assistants in the operating room.

The surgeon acknowledged that his status as the operating surgeon made him liable for the acts of his assistants, but he contended that he was at most passively negligent. He charged that the assistant's active negligence was the cause of the patient's injury. Therefore, the surgeon filed a cross claim against the hospital and the negligent assistant.

The court pointed out that primary liability rests upon the actively negligent party. Even if the assistant was determined to be the surgeon's "borrowed servant" rather than solely the hospital's employee, the hospital was primarily liable because of its failure to provide the surgeon with a qualified and skilled assistant. The hospital owed the surgeon that duty. Even if the surgeon had supervision and control over the assistant, and therefore was liable to the injured patient, the hospital was still responsible for the indemnification to the surgeon because it breached its duty to furnish him with a qualified assistant, and this breach was the primary cause of the injury.

8

PATIENT RECORDS AND REVELATION

A physician creates a medical record to preserve and transmit information about the diagnosis and treatment of the patient's problem. Although a medical record relates a clinical story of the patient's medical problem, it is more than a simple narrative. It also chronicles the physician's process of rational decision making, involving the formulation of an operative plan utilizing clinical data, for attending the patient. The significant components of a medical record reflect consideration of the fundamental elements of diagnostic logic: observation, description, interpretation, and verification.

As part of the contractual obligation to patients, a physician is expected to make and keep adequate medical records for the benefit of the patient. Although the law recognizes, in the absence of express agreement, that the physician owns the original medical record, it also recognizes that the patient has a property interest in the medical information in the record. Thus a patient or a patient's authorized representative generally has an access right to information in the patient's record.

As an implied condition of the physician-patient relationship, an attending physician is expected to safeguard the confidential information obtained in the course of treating the patient. However, this privilege of confidentiality is subject to certain exceptions, one being a superseding duty to certain private or public interests.

Another aspect of confidentiality, the right of privacy, is recognized in some jurisdictions by statute or judicial decision. The basis for such a right is the acknowledgement and presumption that a patient would resent and find harmful the disclosure of private personal matters. Thus a physician is expected to reasonably safeguard the feelings or sensibilities of patients. Failure to do so may result in liability for invasion of a patient's privacy.

Section 1: Recording Medical Events

Medical records are expected to evince and reflect a physician's professional analytical efforts performed in the actual treatment rendered the patient. If inconsistency in the physician's thought and action is apparent, an explanatory comment should be made in the medical records. Failure to reconcile the apparent divergence of thought and action indicated in the medical records may raise implications with adverse inferences referable to a physician's professional conduct. Thus a physician's records may cast suspicion on professional competence and credibility, two essential aspects of his professional conduct.

Accurate and complete medical records are often the best evidence of diligent and careful clinical formulation. If a physician's records indicate that a reasonably skillful formulation of the patient's problem was undertaken in the exercise of professional judgment, the records will help to absolve him of liability for a clinical judgment which in retrospect is erroneous.

Sinkey v. Surgical Associates. The mother of a five-year-old child called her family physician and related that her daughter had lower abdominal pain in her right side, vomiting, and fever. The physician met and examined the child at the hospital. His medical records disclosed that he had examined the abdomen and found no significant localized tenderness, referred pain, or rebound that would indicate an "acute abdomen." He noted that the tonsils were erythematous, and indicated that he felt the white blood count was more compatible with tonsillitis than appendicitis. Although a flat plate and upright of the abdomen disclosed a "reflex ileus," the physician noted that he believed this was more of a nonspecific finding than an indication of appendicitis. Based upon his clinical findings and reasoning, the physician diagnosed "tonsillitis," prescribed penicillin therapy and sent the child home. A few days later, the child was admitted to the hospital with a ruptured appendix and peritonitis. On behalf of the child the parents sued the physician for negligent misdiagnosis.

The court pointed out that a patient is entitled to a thorough examination conducted with reasonable and customary methods of diagnosis such as a history, physical examination, and confirmatory diagnostic tests. In this case, the court noted the physician's diagnosis of "tonsillitis" was based on a physical examination and laboratory findings. It was supported by other findings which were recorded in the medical records, and not based simply on intuition or careless assessment. Therefore, even though the clinical findings were consistent with other disorders, the court concluded that the physician's judgment was not negligent because it was predicated upon the application of careful and diligent methods of medical diagnosis as reflected by the physician's medical records.

Incomplete Records

The medical record in the preceding case absolved the physician of liability because, due to its completeness, it could reasonably be inferred that he had based his diagnosis on acceptable methods of diagnosis. The following cases, on the other hand, illustrate the legal implications involving incomplete records, which may work to an attending physician's detriment in the defense of his professional conduct because his inadequate medical records were incapable of providing sufficient evidentiary support of his contention that the care he rendered to his patient was not negligent.

Pigno v. Bunim. A neonate had hyperbilirubinemia because of a serious Rh blood incompatibility. An exchange transfusion was begun immediately. Her attending physician prematurely halted the transfusion when the infant became cyanotic, and did not resume the transfusion for four days. During the interim, the high level of bilirubin caused kernicterus and resultant brain damage. When the infant reached the legal age of majority she sued the physician, charging negligence in delaying the exchange transfusions.

At trial, which was more than twenty years after the incident, the physician contended that he was attentive to the patient's condition and did not unduly delay the transfusion. He testified that he was aware that the bilirubin level was vitally important in monitoring the care of this infant and that he ordered bilirubin levels every eight hours and constant clinical monitoring of his patient. His medical records did not corroborate his testimony because he had not recorded his clinical concerns or management plans in his progress notes. Moreover, at the time of litigation the "Doctor's Order Sheet" could not be located to corroborate his testimony. His scant progress notes did not indicate that the infant remained cyanotic, or that any tests to monitor the infant's course were actually performed. In addition, no results of such tests were recorded.

The court concluded that there was sufficient evidence from the facts and findings of the case to infer that the physician had not undertaken an adequate analysis upon which to exercise his professional judgment. The physician had not offered convincing evidence, because of the inadequacy of his records, to rebut the inference that his decision to delay the reinstitution of the transfusion was not based on careful analysis. Therefore, the court held that his conduct was negligent and that it was the cause of the infant's brain damage.

When information essential to warrant a clinical action is not documented or is missing from the record, evidence for the physician's justification for the procedure may be lacking.

O'Neill v. Kiledjian. The patient had a long history of medical problems related to thyroid dysfunction. In 1966, Graves's disease was diagnosed and she underwent a subtotal thyroidectomy. In 1971, she again manifested a hyperactive thyroid condition. A second operation was performed in which the thyroid remaining on the right side was removed. Within a year of this operation and soon after she had given birth to a child, the patient was again hospitalized because of a swollen, hyperactive gland. A surgeon removed the thyroid remaining on the left side. As a result of surgery all parathyroid glands either had been removed or had ceased to function, and, shortly after surgery, the patient went into hypocalcemic shock. She sued her attending surgeon for complications of the shock.

Expert testimony established that the parathyroid glands were difficult to identify and to isolate and that they could be damaged or even inadvertently removed in performing thyroid surgery. Therefore it was a recognized risk of the surgery. The patient countered that the surgical procedure was not indicated in the first place and the surgeon was negligent for advising it, and thus the surgeon was responsible for all resulting complications. The patient argued that radiation would have been a more appropriate method of treatment of her condition.

The court pointed out that a surgeon is not responsible for injury caused by a procedure if, in exercise of his professional judgment, he selected one method of treatment over another when both alternatives have the support of competent medical opinion. This doctrine, however, is predicated on the assumption that the physician has used ordinary care and skill in evaluating the patient and in arriving at a diagnosis. Therefore the court reasoned that the crucial question was whether the surgeon used due care in diagnosing his patient's condition, and not whether he was entitled to choose one of two or more approved methods of treatment.

On this issue, expert testimony established that a total thyroidectomy should be performed only when the gland is cancerous. Thus the court concluded that the dispositive question was whether the enlarged mass was thought to be cancerous. The patient's expert opined that it was probable that the thyroid swelling was due to the patient's pregnancy and consequently that she should have been treated by medication and kept under observation for several months. If her condition persisted, she should then have been treated with radioactive iodine when she was no longer pregnant.

On the other hand, the surgeon testified, as did other medical experts, that the patient's symptoms were indicative of cancer. They also testified that although various preoperative tests did not show conclusively the presence of cancer, they were not incompatible with the possibility that cancer existed. The surgeon's expert witnesses conceded, however, that nowhere in the medical record was there any mention that a malignancy was suspected.

On this basis, the court concluded the surgeon had not suspected cancer prior to surgery; therefore, there was no evidence of a justifiable clinical indication for surgery.

As *O'Neil* indicates, when the rationale for the treatment chosen cannot be reconciled with care recorded in the medical record, an inference of lack of due care may be made, and liability may result. The following cases explore this issue.

Sawyer v. Jewish Chronic Disease Hospital. A twenty-three-month-old child was scheduled to undergo surgery for correction of congenital deformities of the feet. The operation had previously been delayed two months because the child had a persistent upper respiratory infection, was poorly nourished, and underweight. While ether was being administered by the open drop method of anesthesia, the child died. As a result of her unexpected death, her parents sued the physicians and hospital. The "Clinical Abstract" and "Narrative Summary" in the hospital chart indicated that the procedure had been previously delayed because of her infection. It also noted she weighed only sixteen pounds, which was low for her age. The "Nurses' Notes" contained notations of nasal discharges on the days preceding the administration of ether, including one such notation made thirteen hours before the child was taken to the operating room. The child's attorney used the patient's medical record to support the inference that the anesthesiologist negligently failed to apply the required degree of care by not further delaying the operation.

The attorney maintained that the child died while ether was being administered, and that the evidence in the medical records suggested the procedure should have been further delayed. The court required the physician to explain and justify the appropriateness of his professional conduct in administering anesthesia under the circumstances. In effect, the court was requesting the anesthesiologist to reconcile the choice of action in proceeding with surgery in light of evidence of the child's acute and chronically debilitated clinical state.

A physician's medical records are expected to reflect his professional analytical mental process. As such, records may exhibit evidence of whether conduct was reasonably careful or diligent under the circumstances of a case by demonstrating that certain findings were known, or should have been known, to him. Failure to act on findings present in the record resulted in liability for the physicians in the following two cases.

Aurelio v. Laird. The obstetrician delivered a baby and attended him during his four-day hospitalization. On the morning of the infant's discharge from the hospital, the obstetrician examined the baby, observed a swollen red area on his right hip, placed a gauze on the lesion and told the mother it appeared to be a pinprick. He recorded, "Small red area" on a hospital form captioned, "Condition on Discharge." He instructed the mother to change the gauze pad periodically, but he did not prescribe any medication nor ask the mother to bring the baby back to have this lesion checked. In the "Nurses Notes," a nurse recorded: "Baby swollen area on Rt. hip no pustules reported." Just prior to discharge at 6 P.M. that evening, a different nurse recorded: "Baby had small red area on Rt. hip . . . opening about pinpoint size, small amt. blood and pus oozing. . . . Seen by the doctor—baby discharged with mother—in otherwise good condition." It was unclear if the 6 P.M. entry meant only that the obstetrician had seen the swelling in the morning, or that later he observed the precise condition recorded in that entry.

After the mother was home for a couple of days she observed that there was pus mixed with blood draining from the baby's hip. She called the obstetrician and described the baby's condition, but he only told her to use warm gauze pads. Two days later, when she spoke with him again, he told her the same thing and declined her request to examine the baby. A few days later, in response to another telephone call, the obstetrician told the mother to bring the baby to his office. There the obstetrician observed that the infant's buttock was "markedly discolored and swollen and had a red streak going up two or three inches to about the belt line." He referred the infant to a pediatrician who hospitalized him with a diagnosis of "disseminated cellulitis, secondary to hospital-type staphylococcus." On behalf of her infant the mother sued the obstetrician for negligently failing to treat the infection.

Expert testimony established that prudent medical practice would have required a culture and sensitivity test of the lesion, with antibiotic treatment commenced immediately or deferred, pending results of the culture. Medical experts also testified that, if this procedure had been followed, "it most likely would have" precluded the disseminated cellulitis which later developed.

The obstetrician testified that pus, as was recorded in the 6 P.M. hospital record entry, would indicate infection and that hospital-type staphylococcus was a common source of such infection of open wounds. He further testified that if "there was a pinpoint size wound which was infected, then the safest course would be to assume that there was a staphylococcus aureus condition in the wound and to treat it as such by using an antibiotic." However, he claimed that no such wound was evident prior to the infant's discharge from the hospital.

The court noted that the "Nurses Notes" indicated that there had been swelling and pus in and around the lesion; therefore, the physician should have been aware of the potential seriousness of the problem. The court pointed out that even if it assumed the obstetrician did not have knowledge of the appearance of pus by 6 P.M., such a finding was recorded earlier on the day of discharge. His own testimony as to the risk and likelihood of staphylococcus infection from open wounds in hospitals, and the redness and swelling about the wound described in the "Nurses' Notes" on the morning of discharge, indicated infection may have been expected to develop. Therefore, the importance of early treatment warranted a finding that he should have checked whether infection was developing, either by arranging to be notified immediately if any pus appeared, or at least by examining the infant when the mother initially reported obvious signs of infection which she had observed.

Alden v. Providence Hospital.   The patient had been hospitalized for several months with a diagnosis of bulbar poliomyelitis. The chief resident attending the patient had on numerous occasions examined the patient in the hospital. When he transferred the patient to a polio rehabilitation hospital for further care and treatment, the resident physician signed the hospital transfer form outlining the patient's physical condition on transfer and recorded the "chest, heart and lungs negative."

Medical evaluation, including a chest x-ray performed the day after the patient arrived at the rehabilitation hospital, disclosed that the patient had chronic empyema that had resulted in a right-sided pneumothorax. Therefore, he was transferred to a medical center for necessary treatment. As a result of the empyema, the patient's right fifth and sixth ribs had to be surgically removed. No diagnosis of empyema had been made prior to his arrival at the rehabilitation hospital. The patient sued the original hospital, charging that the staff physicians were negligent in failing to diagnose and treat the empyema while he was a patient in the hospital, and that his transfer from that hospital while suffering from this disease exacerbated his condition.

Expert medical testimony established that it was not good medical practice for a physician to transfer a patient with chronic empyema. The court noted that the patient's medical record showed that for several months prior to his transfer he had a persistent cough, fever, and a right pleural effusion. X-rays demonstrated persistent "opacity of the right lung field which could be due to excess pleural fluid and pleural thickening." A thoracentesis produced 600 cc. of cloudy yellow fluid. The record also showed repeated "dullness to percussion over the right lung lobe," indicating pleural effusion and pleural thickening.

The court concluded that the medical records indicated that the attending physicians knew or should have known that the patient had empyema. In either case, the failure to treat and the decision to transfer were negligent.

Related to the requirement that a record be reconciled with the clinical action taken by the attending physician is the requirement that a physician promptly make a report of an operation or a procedure. The reason for this is that reports that are not made contemporaneously are less reliable as to the accuracy of entries and, therefore, may impugn a physician's credibility in a subsequent lawsuit where his conduct is at issue.

Patrick v. Sedwick. The patient was advised to undergo a subtotal thyroidectomy. Immediately after the operation, the patient's left vocal cord was found to be totally and permanently paralyzed, indicating that the left recurrent laryngeal nerve had been severed. The following day the surgeon dictated the operative report. A pathologist reported that surgically excised tissue which was submitted as a tissue specimen of the patient's thyroid gland was three times normal size and exhibited evidence of chronic inflammation which was consistent with Hashimoto's disease. However, the specimen contained no trace of the recurrent laryngeal nerve. The patient sued the surgeon charging that he negligently severed a nerve which caused portions of the vocal cords to become paralyzed so that she had difficulty with speech and breathing capacity.

At deposition during the pretrial discovery phase of litigation, the surgeon expressed the opinion that surgical destruction of the nerve would be negligent unless disease in the thyroid gland made dissection difficult, or unless there were anatomical variations of the nerve through the operative area. The surgeon testified that he had no independent recollection of the operation. His assistants likewise had no recollection other than what their records disclosed. The operative report, dictated after surgery, did not refresh the surgeon's memory, and he could not identify it as being a transcript of his recollection. He could only say that the surgical procedures he employed in the patient's case would have been those he routinely followed in excising the thyroid gland. One of those procedures would have been to visualize the recurrent laryngeal nerve in the operative area where it is most vulnerable to surgically induced trauma, that is, where it comes in close proximity to the inferior thyroid artery. He admitted that it was good practice for a surgeon to note in his operative report when the nerve cannot be found, or when it is abnormal, such as scarred by disease or lying in an irregular course through the portion of the thyroid gland which is to be removed.

The "findings" of the surgeon's operative report merely stated: "There was symmetrical marked enlargement of both lobes of the thyroid gland. There were no hard nodules present in the gland. Gland was meaty and very vascular." The "operation" portion of the report consisted of nondescriptive sentences which simply stated the ultimate facts connected with each step of the operation commencing with the incision. No mention was made of any problems, variations, or difficulties encountered during the operation. After the operative steps, including visualization of the right recurrent laryngeal nerve through the dissection of the right lobe of the thyroid gland had been mentioned, the report then stated: "On the left, the same procedure was done." No mention was made of anything irregular in the appearance or course of the left recurrent laryngeal nerve or that the nerve or the gland presented any problem in connection with the operation.

The surgeon contended that the large size of the gland made it likely that the nerve was involved with the gland. However, the court countered that if there was such involvement and it made the surgery difficult, it seems reasonable that the surgeon would have mentioned the fact in the operative report. The court pointed out that it was incumbent upon the surgeon to describe accurately and fully in his operative report everything of consequence that he did and which his trained eye observed during the operation. In addition, to have maximum probative value, the report should have been dictated immediately after the operation. If these requirements had been met, the court concluded that the report would have been more likely to have refreshed his recollection and to have supplied sufficient facts to permit expert testimony on the question of negligence. Instead, the report was not dictated until the day following the operation, after the surgeon had visited and observed the patient's speech problems on the hospital ward.

The court also found it difficult to believe that a thyroid which was enlarged three times its normal size did not create particular operating difficulties worth mentioning in the report. Although the report did state that the recurrent laryngeal nerve was visualized while operating on the right side of the gland, no particular mention was made of any of the operative steps employed on the left side. The court noted that, even though the surgeon's report did not so state, the surgeon was asking the court to assume that the nerve was also visualized on the left side and that the operation was completed with faultless technique; the surgeon was also asking the court to rely on statistics that a small percentage of thyroidectomies result in damage to the laryngeal nerve in spite of all precautions. The court pointed out that usually the surgeon himself determines what actions he takes during an operation. Therefore, he is usually the only person who can prepare a full and accurate report of what was observed and done through the surgical incision. Thus the court declared that his obligation to his patient was to have prepared an accurate operative report. Having failed to do so, the court refused to permit the absence of personal recollection or recorded facts to serve as a defense for the surgeon under the circumstances of this case.

Altered Records

In the preceding materials, incomplete records which do not comport with the action taken or which reveal a lack of appropriate medical action demonstrate how record keeping affects the determination of liability in a malpractice suit. Another factor affecting liability is the alteration of records subsequent to the initial recording date. The following cases explore this issue.

As the first case indicates, suspicious entries in medical records may raise the inference that such records were altered to cover up for negligent conduct that caused the patient injury.

Foley v. Flushing Hosp. & Med. Center. On October 26, after a normal spontaneous delivery, an infant was examined and found to be in good condition. The "Doctor's Order Sheet" documented that on October 27, the pediatrician who was assigned to treat the infant prescribed "Acromycin 25 mg. I.M." A few days later, as the nurse was preparing the infant for home, she noticed an ecchymotic lesion on the infant's left buttock.

Several months later, the infant's father appeared in the pediatrician's office and raised the question of a sciatic injury to his son as a result of a buttock injection. Later that day, at the lower end of the original record, the pediatrician made another entry in the record which read "Acromycin given orally."

Subsequently, the hospital's medical record librarian wrote a letter to a physician at another hospital, where the infant was then being treated. The letter purported to summarize the treatment that the infant had received shortly after birth. It stated, "Acromycin, 25 mg. every eight hours, orally, was started on October 27, and discontinued on October 29." The word "orally" was in darker type and extended into the right margin of the letter, suggesting that it was typed in some time after the original completion of the letter. On behalf of the child, the father sued the pediatrician. The medical records librarian testified that the order slip for the Acromycin which might have shed some light on whether the Acromycin was to be administered orally or by injections, was not in the hospital record.

The court pointed out that suspicious entries in the hospital records and the testimony of the father about the black and blue mark on the infant's left buttock, established sufficient facts from which the negligence in administering the injection could be reasonably inferred.

Alteration of medical records after the occurrence of an untoward event casts doubt upon an attending physician's professional credibility and capacity. The following cases illustrate this point.

Rotan v. Greenbaum.   On June 6, at his office, a physician diagnosed that the patient had mumps. He gave an intramuscular injection of 600,000 units of penicillin. Approximately twenty minutes later the patient died. Autopsy disclosed that death was due to "anaphylactic shock—hypersensitivity—due to penicillin reaction." The coroner's report stated that "the history says she received it (the penicillin injection) for mumps." The police report stated: "Died suddenly about fifteen minutes after receiving an injection of penicillin, 600,000 units for mumps." The patient's estate sued the physician for negligently prescribing medication that caused the patient's death.

At the trial the physician was called as a witness. In conjunction with other medical expert witnesses, he testified that penicillin was not acceptable therapy for mumps. His medical record contained the following entry:

                               & pharyngitis
6/6/56. Expired after penicillin, 600,000 for ?mumps.
      Expired 2:15 p.m.

The expert testimony of a document examiner established that the question mark preceding the word "mumps" and the words inserted above the line, "& pharyngitis" after the word "mumps," were added by the use of a different pen from that used in the remainder of the entry. The physician testified that part of this entry was made immediately after the treatment and the other part sometime later, the exact time he could not specify. He testified that, as originally written, the entry on the card read, "Expired after penicillin for mumps. Expired 2:15 P.M." The insertions of the question mark before mumps and "& pharyngitis" were made at some time after the patient died.

Because of the alteration of the medical record, the court found as a fact that the penicillin injection was given for mumps alone, not for pharyngitis to which a later reference was made only after the patient had died. Expert testimony had established that penicillin therapy was not a clinically indicated treatment for mumps and, therefore, did not meet the requirements of standard practice. Accordingly the court held that the physician was negligently responsible for the occurrence of the complication of the drug therapy.

As *Rotan* indicates, if a physician alters a medical record after an untoward event has occurred, such an act may be construed as a deliberate attempt to evade liability because the physician had assumed that he had been negligent. If it becomes necessary to change a record, explanations for the change should be noted so that a suspicion is not raised that the record has been altered for ulterior purposes.

James v. Spear. A physician undertook to treat a patient's occluded right tear duct so that it would effectively drain lachrymal fluid from the eye. The patient visited the physician on numerous occasions for treatment of the duct. On the physician's final examination of the tear duct, as the patient sat in the treatment chair, she felt a severe pain in her right eye. The physician then applied a topical anesthetic and ointment to her eye, put dark glasses on her, and helped her to the outer office. Because her eye had swollen shut and the pain had become unbearable, she returned to the physician's office in the afternoon. He examined and washed out her right eye and told her "it looks like a piece of steel has taken a piece off the eye." He prescribed analgesics for her symptoms.

Five days after the incident the patient was taken back to the physician's office by her daughter, but because the office was closed, the daugher took her to another physician. An examination by this physician disclosed a corneal abrasion, necessitating two weeks of therapy.

The patient and her daughter then went back to see the patient's original physician. The patient's daughter questioned the physician about what had happened to her mother's eye. He responded that when he had looked in the patient's eye he "thought he saw something," so he took an instrument to look at it and "that was when it happened." The daughter, who was a nurse, asked to see the physician's record pertaining to her mother's treatment on the day of injury. After reviewing the office records, the daughter advised her mother to sue the physician for negligently injuring her eye.

At trial the daughter testified that the records she reviewed at the physician's office were materially different from those which the physician had produced at the trial. The records that the physician brought to trial documented only a morning visit and not the afternoon visit for the day that the eye incident occurred. No note was entered for the afternoon visit. The court indicated that this alteration of the record impugned the credibility of the physician as a witness. Therefore it could reasonably be inferred that he had attempted to conceal a negligent act.

As the preceding cases indicate, alteration of records may increase liability exposure for the physician. A more extreme case, creating a strong inference of the consciousness of guilt, is inevitable when the original record disappears entirely and the physician-defendant makes available only recopied ones as evidence of professional conduct.

Thor v. Boska. The patient consulted her family physician about a mobile cystic mass in her breast. The physician indicated that she had "nothing to worry about." He did not perform any tests, nor did he recommend that she see a specialist. Approximately one year later, the patient noticed that the lump had doubled in size. She again consulted her physician who neither performed any tests nor referred her to a specialist. Three months later, the patient consulted another physician who performed a biopsy which disclosed intraductal carcinoma with axillary metastasis, for which she underwent a radical mastectomy. She sued her family physician, charging that he had been negligent in failing to perform any diagnostic tests, in failing to refer her to a specialist, and in reassuring her that her condition was "nothing."

Pretrial discovery proceedings disclosed that the physician's original clinical records of his treatment of the patient had disappeared. All that was available were recopied records, which the physician said were taken verbatim from the now-missing originals.

The court said the fact that the physician was unable to produce his original records after he had been charged with malpractice created a strong inference of consciousness of guilt on his part. That evidence tended to corroborate the patient's case, and to discredit the physician's competence as a diagnostician and his credibility as a witness in his own cause.

SECTION 2: OWNERSHIP OF RECORDS AND ACCESS TO INFORMATION

Accurate and complete record-keeping is essential not only as proof of evidence of a physician's mental process and actions, but also to fulfill the physician's contractual obligation to the patient that the physician make and keep medical records.

Despite the fact that medical records are kept primarily for the patient's benefit, questions frequently arise of ownership of, and a patient's access to, medical records. Although the patient has a property interest in, and an access right to, the information in the records, the physician is generally considered to be the owner of the original record. The materials in this section discuss these issues. It should be noted that although the materials have been divided into access to a patient's records held by a hospital and access to a patient's records held by a physician, essentially the same issues and answers are involved in both categories.

Access to Hospital Medical Records

As mentioned above, a patient or authorized agent generally has the right of access to the information contained in his medical records. This right may be protected by statute that may establish a legal cause of action for breach of a statutory duty to furnish records.

Rabens v. Jackson Park Hospital Foundation. After his discharge from the hospital, the patient (an attorney) wrote to the hospital, demanding permission to examine and copy his medical records. The hospital medical record librarian replied that he could receive an abstract of his case history for a five dollar fee. He paid the fee, but received only a copy of his bill. Thereupon he discontinued his attempts to examine or obtain copies of his record. Instead, he brought a legal action against the hospital, seeking damages for severe mental and emotional anguish. The patient contended that he had a right to have his records produced for examination and copying. He cited the state statutory requirement relating to the inspection of hospital records which provided that

> Every private and public hospital shall, upon the demand of any patient who has been treated in such hospital and after his discharge therefrom, permit his physician or authorized attorney to examine the hospital records, including but not limited to the history, bedside note, charts, pictures and plates, kept in connection with the treatment of such patient, and permit copies of such records to be made by his physician or authorized attorney.

The court pointed out that the "fiduciary quality" of a physician-patient relationship requires the disclosure, upon request, of medical data to a patient. However, it does not compel that such information be given without charge. The court noted that the statute required the hospital, upon demand, to permit a patient's physician or attorney to examine and copy the records. However, the statute did not require the physician or attorney to physically appear at the hospital and be refused access to the records before there was a statutory violation by the hospital. A violation could occur when a demand pursuant to the statutory provision was refused by the hospital.

Some patients may not be entitled to direct access to their medical records if such access is likely to adversely affect the patient's well-being or breach the confidentiality owed to other people. This exception to the general rule allowing the patient or patient's representative access to medical records usually arises in the area of psychiatric treatment, especially if the request for access is not necessary to insure effective on-going treatment of the requestor.

Gotkin v. Miller. On several occasions between 1962 and 1970, a woman was a patient at several different psychiatric hospitals. The precipitating cause for many of these voluntary hospitalizations was a series of threatened suicides. After 1970, she had not been hospitalized or treated for any mental disorder. Several years later she began to write a book about her treatment experiences at the various institutions where she had been hospitalized for psychiatric care. In an attempt to verify some of her experiences for the book, and to compare her recollection of certain incidents with the hospitals' recorded version of what had transpired, she requested from the various hospitals where she had been treated, access to any medical records which might relate to her. Each of these hospitals, however, refused to grant her request. Therefore, in 1974, she instituted a legal action to compel the hospitals to allow her access to her psychiatric records. She sued on behalf of herself as well as on behalf of all other former mental patients who had similarly requested and were denied access to their hospital medical records. She contended that the hospital's refusal to grant such access of former patients to their medical records constituted a deprivation of property without due process of law because former patients had a property interest in their medical records.

The court pointed out that a patient's property interest in his medical records is not created by the Constitution, but must be based on some legitimate claim of entitlement under state law or contractual agreements. Therefore, the court reviewed the pertinent statutes, regulations, policies, commission recommendations, and judicial decisions in order to define a patient's property interest in his medical records.

The state mental hygiene law indicated that psychiatric patients were precluded from gaining direct access to their records. The pertinent section of the law provided that

> A clinical record for each patient shall be maintained. . . . The record shall contain information on all matters relating to the admission, legal status, care and treatment of the patient . . . clinical records shall not be a public record and shall not be released . . . to any person or agency outside of the department except as follows:
> —pursuant to an order of a court;
> —to attorneys representing patients in legal proceedings with the consent of the patient or of someone authorized to act on the patient's behalf;
> —to physicians . . . involved in caring for, treating, or rehabilitating the patient, when such information is kept confidential and used solely for the benefit of the patient.

The court concluded that this statute established a general rule of nondisclosure and only permitted access to a mental hospital's medical records in a limited number of enumerated situations.

The regulations and policy of the state mental hygiene department did not recognize the right of a former psychiatric patient to gain direct access to his medical records. Departmental policy, however, did permit a former psychiatric patient to designate a licensed physician to receive the records on behalf of the former patient. This procedure allowed a former patient to gain indirect access to his medical records, while it also insured that a physician would have an opportunity to review and screen the records before turning them over to the former patient. The department's rationale for not granting the patient direct access to this information was that medical records ordinarily include information stated in technical medical terminology, which might be misunderstood and misconstrued by an individual not medically trained. Thus the revelation of some information in a former patient's record could be detrimental to his current well-being. Moreover, information in a patient's psychiatric record often includes references to other individuals, such as relatives, friends, or fellow patients, which should remain confidential in order to protect the rights of those other individuals.

The court took note of the findings of a commission studying medical malpractice which reported that

> A medical record is far more than a series of entries reporting diagnoses, doctor's orders and actions taken pursuant to such orders. In the hospital setting the record is a complex of communications between health professionals, including a written history and physical, progress notes, nurses' notes, consultations, lab reports, operation summary, discharge summary and the like. During the course of a particular hospitalization the record may include a wide spectrum of speculation and observation as the various members of the health team contribute thoughts and observations that lead eventually to the final diagnosis. If not properly explained, many of these entries could be exceedingly disturbing to a patient already apprehensive. However, to deter such entries could often eliminate the very clues that lead to successful diagnosis and treatment . . . also, the health teams use a wide variety of abbreviations and phrases that can be both confusing and unintelligible to the layman. For all of these reasons, the patient, though he is entitled to information about his health and his care, needs guidance in understanding and using it. For reasons such as these, many physicians are reluctant to give copies of their records to patients.

The court further stated that many state statutes explicitly protect the confidentiality of the records of patients, especially in state mental institutions. Usually the disclosure of such records is prohibited by law unless it is necessary for the treatment of the patient; for the conduct of a legal proceeding; in situations where failure to disclose would be contrary to the public interest; or in hospitalization proceedings upon request of the patient's attorney.

Finally, the court pointed out that judicial decisions relating to the right to access of their records by former patients, have determined that such patients do not have a sufficient claim of entitlement to their record. Although some states have enacted special access laws which permit a patient to examine and copy his medical records without resort to litigation, such laws are the exception rather than the rule in the majority of states.*

The court concluded that neither the statutory, administrative nor deci-

Editor's Note
*At the time of publication there was a trend toward enactment of state laws granting patient access to information in their medical records.

sional law generally recognized a former patient's property interest to his medical records in the absence of pending litigation.

Although a hospital (or a physician) generally is required to allow a patient or a patient's authorized representative access to the information in its patients' medical records, it is required also to safeguard the patient's record from unauthorized scrutiny and to take necessary precautions to determine the propriety of a requested disclosure. However, a representative of the patient who has a valid interest in the contents of the record is not required to engage in legal proceedings to seek access to such information.

Emmett v. Eastern Dispensary and Casualty Hospital.   The patient had died while he was in the hospital. His son felt that the hospital and the attending physician had negligently caused his father's death. He made several demands for inspection of his father's medical records, but the hospital refused to allow his inspection of the records because, it said, he had no legal interest in this privileged information. Later he was appointed the administrator of his father's estate. In this capacity he filed a suit for wrongful death against the hospital and the physician. The statute of limitations applicable to a wrongful death action was one year, and suit was not filed within that length of time. In an effort to overcome this procedural obstacle to suit, the son contended that he was unable to file the lawsuit within the one-year period because of the attending physician's and the hospital's conduct in concealing the facts relating to his father's death.

The court pointed out that the responsibility of physicians and hospitals to protect their patients' medical information from extrajudicial exposure springs from the confidential nature of the physician-patient relationship. However, the court noted that the fiduciary or trust qualities of a physician-patient relationship also create a duty to disclose to the patient that which is in his interest to know. The court concluded that this duty of disclosure extends after the patient's death to his next of kin.

The court specifically declared that it was not necessary for the son to secure an appointment as administrator in order to have a legitimate interest in his father's medical information. The interest of the son as the patient's next of kin could defeat the hospital's claim that they had to protect the patient's privilege. A person to whom a duty to disclose medical data is already owed is not required to initiate legal proceedings to attain another, more legally explicit status.

Pyramid Life Ins. Co. v. Masonic Hospital Ass'n. of Payne Co.   An insurance company issued policies covering hospital and doctors' bills. The company, with the consent of its policyholders, requested permission from the hospital to inspect and copy hospital and medical records of patient-policyholders. The hospital denied permission to the insurance company on the ground that the medical records of the patient-policyholders were the property of the hospital; therefore, the hospital had discretion to permit or deny inspection, copying, or reproduction. The insurance company then sought legal process to restrain the hospital from denying them such permission.

The court noted that the hospital was required by statute to keep and retain "accurate and complete medical records" on its patients. It pointed out that records required to be kept and retained by the force of statute, regulation, or judicial decision are at least quasi-public. Therefore, the right to inspect such records is not one which may be exercised only by persons having a legal interest therein. Inspection may be made by any person who has an interest that would enable him to maintain or defend an action for which the document or record sought can furnish evidence or necessary information. Insurance companies have a legitimate interest in determining whether claims made under their policies are claims which they are obligated to pay and whether those already paid were in fact claims for which they were liable.

The court declared that the paper or other material on which the quasi-public medical records are maintained by the hospital pertaining to care and treatment of patients are the property of the hospital. However, the hospital, as keeper of the records, does not have the right to possess and use the information constituting the records to the exclusion of the patient or his representatives. The court also noted that the keeper of such information may not disclose it without the permission of the patient. Accordingly, the court concluded that the keeper of the records is only the custodian and not the owner of that information constituting the medical records of the patient. The patient has a property right in the information contained in the records and he, or those authorized by him, is entitled to inspect, copy, or reproduce the records without resort to litigation.

Access to Physician Medical Records
An attending physician also does not have the right to deny access to a patient's medical information to persons who have a legitimate interest in such information.

Cannell v. Medical and Surgical Clinic. The patient was treated by a physician associated with a clinic. Because the patient's physical condition had a bearing on an anticipated Workmen's Compensation hearing, the patient signed a form authorizing his attorney to obtain information from the clinic regarding his physical condition. This authorization form and a request for a medical report were sent to the physician who had treated the patient at the clinic. Another physician associated with the clinic informed the attorney that the clinic would not release any medical information about their patient without the consent of his employer. His attorney then advised this physician that the standards of practice governing the relationship between attorneys and physicians, approved by the county bar association and the medical society, required that a report be furnished promptly by the physician upon receipt of a written authorization from the patient. The clinic, nevertheless, refused to furnish to the attorney any medical information concerning the examination or treatment of the patient.

On behalf of his client, the attorney sought a legal order to compel the clinic to produce the necessary medical data. The clinic attempted to dismiss the order by charging that the patient was attempting to deprive the clinic of its property without due process of law. The clinic claimed that the records and information sought were in its private files; therefore, they were subject to production only in a lawsuit in which the patient's physical condition was in issue. Although the clinic conceded that the patient could subpoena the records for use at the Workmen's Compensation hearing, it contended that the patient had no right to a prehearing discovery of the content of the medical records.

The court pointed out that a medical record is an aid both to physicians and to other professional personnel, which enables them to have a detailed, current, and dynamic account of the patient's clinical status. It is an important document because it contains all pertinent information on the patient's past and present medical history, condition, and treatment. Although it is customary to obtain the attending physician's consent for release of information or for an examination of the record, the attending physician does not have the legal right to determine who shall have access to the record after a request to review the record is filed because the patient and other persons may have a legitimate interest in the information contained in the record. Therefore, the court held that a physician has a duty to disclose medical information to a patient on request, apart from any obligation which might be imposed on him by issuance of a subpoena or utilization of legal discovery procedures. However, the court noted that although information must be given on legitimate request, the physician's records themselves need not be turned over to the patient.

The following cases deal with the conflict that may arise when a physician's recognized ownership of the original record competes with the patient's right of access to the information in the record. This conflict may arise, for example, when a physician dies and provides by will that the patients' medical records are to be destroyed; or when a physician dies and another physician attempts to obtain the records from the physician's estate. Generally, in these cases, the physician's estate is allowed to retain the original records but the patients or their authorized agents are entitled to copies of the records, or pertinent medical information contained therein.

In re Culbertson's Will. When Dr. Culbertson died, some of his long-term patients sought to obtain their medical records from his estate. The executor of his will refused to deliver such records to the petitioners because of the following clause in Dr. Culbertson's will: "I direct my Executor to burn and destroy all of my office records and files without opening or examining same."

Dr. Culbertson's patients brought a legal action to compel the delivery to them of certain personal medical records which had been in the possession of Dr. Culbertson as their attending physician during his lifetime. In the alternative, they requested permission to examine and make copies of these records. They contended that Dr. Culbertson had conducted specific and general physical examinations of them including blood analyses, electrocardiograms, x-rays, and other diagnostic tests, and that such examinations and tests were made with the intent and understanding that they would be recorded and would always be available to them. They further contended that Dr. Culbertson had contractually agreed to make and preserve records, and to make them available at all times to his patients.

The court pointed out that records made by a physician in the evaluation and treatment of a patient become the property of the physician. In general, an individual does not seek out a physician for the purpose of having medical records established for the patient's personal use, but rather seeks the personal diagnostic and therapeutic services of his physician. Although the cost of performing and reporting x-rays, electrocardiograms, and other medical data is paid by the patient, these reports are supplied to the physician for his use in connection with the diagnosis and treatment of the patient. The records and notes in the possession of the attending physician constitute a history of the case, which is primarily of benefit as part of his clinical record concerning a particular patient. However, in those situations where the patient seeks the services of another physician, the best interest of the patient must be considered as foremost, and the patient should not be deprived of the benefit of whatever notes and records have been maintained by an attending physician. The court noted that the American Medical Association Canons of Medical Ethics regulate professional conduct with the underlying principle at all times, that the best interest of the patient be safeguarded.

Based upon general considerations of public policy and a recognition of the principles of procedure outlined by the American Medical Association, the court ruled that the provision in Dr. Culbertson's will was invalid. It noted that the records might be of extreme value to a subsequent examining physician, and their destruction could have grave consequences. Therefore, it ordered the executor of the estate to make available the patients' records to succeeding physicians for copying, upon the authorized request by the patients.

Estate of Finkle.   Shortly after a psychiatrist's death, the keys to his office, where his medical records were kept, were entrusted to another practicing psychiatrist. With the knowledge of the preliminary executor, the psychiatrist was permitted to notify the patients of the deceased psychiatrist's death, to administer urgent medical attention, and to preserve the practice. However, the psychiatrist was instructed that nothing was to be removed from the office because the executor intended to "sell" the practice. After the executor recovered the keys to the office from the psychiatrist, he discovered that eight of the deceased psychiatrist's patient files were missing. He demanded that the psychiatrist return these medical records to the estate. The psychiatrist refused to do so, even though the executor was willing to provide the psychiatrist with a copy of those records. Therefore, the executor, the widow, and her son sought a court order compelling the psychiatrist to return the records to the estate.

The court pointed out that records created by a physician in the examination and treatment of a patient become the property of that physician. The psychiatrist, even if authorized by the affected patients, is not entitled to the possession of the deceased psychiatrist's records of those patients. The patients themselves likewise are not entitled to their records. Thus if the estate does not wish to turn them over, it has the right to retain them. Although the estate may retain possession of the actual records, it must allow copies to be given to authorized persons. The court, therefore, ordered that the psychiatrist return to the preliminary executor the original records of the former patients of the deceased psychiatrist. Once he had done this, he would be entitled to a copy of those records based upon each patient's authorization.

The following case, in contrast to *Finkle*, involves the physician's retention of medical records he has made, rather than those of the physician who has died. In this case, although the medical records were technically the property of the estate which owned the clinic where the physician had been employed, the patients themselves were not considered to be property of the clinic.

Jones v. Fakehany.   Dr. Jones was employed by the Highland Medical Clinic, which was owned by Dr. Fakehany. When Dr. Fakehany died Dr. Jones continued to see patients at the clinic and was paid his salary by the executor of Dr. Fakehany estate. Subsequently, a dispute arose between Dr. Jones and Dr. Fakehany's widow and she fired him. Dr. Jones opened his own office in the same community. The widow refused to give him any records of the patients he had been treating, on the ground that they were part of her husband's estate. Persons who had been assisting Dr. Jones in the clinic removed certain current patient records, each of which contained the patient's medical history, a record of the treatment given, and the dates of each visit. Dr. Jones then sent to the patients of the clinic a notice which stated in part:

> Due to the death of Dr. Fakehany, the Highland Medical Clinic is being sold. Dr. Jones will continue your treatment at his new offices.

Eighty-six of these persons signed the following statement:

> We, the undersigned patients of Dr. R. F. Jones, M.D., do not wish to have our medical records sent to the Highland Medical Clinic. We are ordering Dr. Jones to retain our records in his possession.

Dr. Fakehany's widow wrote a letter to these patients which stated in part:

> There has been no interruption in the services of the Highland Medical Clinic and you can return for treatment anytime you desire. In this event, we will see that your medical records are made available.

The widow then sought a legal order which would require Dr. Jones to return all the records which he took from the Highland Medical Clinic. Dr. Jones returned all books and records which had been removed from the Highland Clinic except the medical records of approximately one hundred persons, which were in his own handwriting. Because he had cared for these patients since the death of Dr. Fakehany, he claimed he was their attending physician and that he was entitled to retain such records.

The court pointed out that the relationship existing between physicians and those who seek their services cannot be compared to the relationship of a merchant with his customer because the practice of medicine should not be treated as a commodity in trade. It is distinguished from commercial enterprises because of the extremely dependent and trusting role assumed by the patient. Often the patient is unable to fully understand the nature of his condition even after the diagnosis has been made and fully explained to him. His faith and confidence in the physician who prescribes treatment to alleviate his condition are often as contributive to his recovery as the medications or therapy prescribed. Therefore the court concluded that the patient may not properly be regarded as the subject of "ownership." His paramount right to seek and obtain treatment from a licensed physician of his own choice may not be denied him in order to protect the "property rights" of a competing physician or clinic. The court noted that although Dr. Jones acted wrongfully in removing the records from the clinic, adequate protection of the rights and interests of the patients who had selected his professional services required that he be allowed to retain such of the medical records of these patients as would be found necessary in order to enable him to render them proper care and treatment.

As illustrated by the preceding cases, in the absence of an express agreement or extraordinary legal circumstance to the contrary, a physician is not obligated to release to the patient or to others the entire or component parts of the original medical record. This principle also applies to the original representation of a test as is illustrated in the following case.

McGarry v. J. A. Mercier Co. An employee strained his back in the course of his employment. His employer engaged a physician to provide the injured employee with professional care. The physician rendered the necessary services; however, the employer refused to pay for the services because the physician refused to deliver to the employer x-rays taken incident to treating the employee. The physician, who was willing to allow the x-rays to be inspected by other physicians if the x-rays were not removed from his clinic, then sued the employer for payment of the professional services he had provided the patient.

The court pointed out that the physician did not refuse to report the employee's condition to the employer when requested. In the absence of a specific understanding to do otherwise, the reports which were made to the employer were all that was required of the physician. He was justified in refusing to surrender possession of the x-rays because they were his property. He had made them incident to treating his patient. The court noted that retention of the x-rays by the physician was reasonable because the x-rays constituted an important part of his clinical record in this particular case. In the aggregate, these x-rays could embody and preserve much of the value incident to a physician's experience. They were as much a part of the history of the case as any other record made by a physician. They differed little, if at all, from other diagnostic representations, such as microscopic slides of tissue that are made in the course of diagnosis or treatment of a patient. The court pointed out that such microscopic slides could not be claimed to be the property of the patient. In addition, retention of the x-rays was important to the attending physician because in the event of a malpractice suit against a physician, the x-rays might often constitute the unimpeachable evidence that would fully justify the treatment of which the patient was complaining. The court concluded that, in the absence of an agreement to the contrary, x-rays are the property of the physician rather than of the patient or party who employed such physician; even though the cost of taking the x-rays may have been charged to the patient or to the one who engaged the physician as part of the professional service rendered.

SECTION 3: DISCLOSURE OF CONFIDENTIAL INFORMATION

An implied obligation of the physician-patient relationship is the physician's obligation to safeguard confidential information that is gathered pursuant to providing treatment within the context of that relationship. Not only does the physician-patient relationship require such safeguarding but also, pursuant to certain licensing statutes, improper disclosure may represent unprofessional conduct.

The legal protection given to physician-patient communications has two distinct components. One is statutorily determined and is referred to as "privileged communication." The other is a doctrine that has evolved through the common law and is recognized as "confidential communication." Their respective applications are distinct. The purpose of a privileged communication statute is to prevent disclosure *in court* of certain types of confidential information. Because it is the patient's privilege, its effect is to prohibit a physician from disclosing in a judicial proceeding certain information obtained from a patient. A confidential privilege between a physician and the patient may also be asserted under the common law "doctrine of confidential communication." This doctrine is intended to preclude a physician from disclosing confidential information about his patient, except for compelling reasons, in circumstances other than a judicial proceeding.

Even when protection of a patient's confidential communication is legally recognized, it is never deemed absolute. It is not applied legally in cases covered by Workmen's Compensation, for example; nor cases which arise under laws requiring, for example, the reporting of communicable diseases, child abuse, or the unlawful procurement of narcotics. In addition, use of the privilege of confidentiality in criminal prosecutions, insanity proceedings, and will contests is limited.

Generally, before a physician-patient privilege of confidentiality is recognized legally, the existence of a "confidential communication" must be demonstrated. A "confidential communication" usually involves information which is acquired through the physician-patient relationship and is needed to professionally treat the patient.

The Privilege

The cases in the subsection illustrate how the privilege of confidentiality becomes at issue in litigation and what it means in terms of the everyday interactions between physicians and their patients.

The first case illustrates that a physician who enters into an agreement with a patient to provide medical attention, impliedly promises and is legally required to keep in confidence all disclosures made by the patient concerning the patient's physical or mental condition, as well as all matters discovered by the physician in the course of examination or treatment.

Doe v. Roe.   A woman and her late former husband were, for many years, patients of a physician and her husband, a psychologist. Eight years after termination of treatment, the physician completed writing a book that reported verbatim the patients' thoughts, feelings, and emotions; their sexual and other fantasies; their most intimate personal relationships; and the disintegration of their marriage. Interspersed among the footnotes were the physician's diagnoses of the illnesses suffered by the patients and by one of their children. Consent to publish this work was sought while the woman was in therapy, but it was never obtained in writing. In the physician's own words, "consent was there one day and not there another day. That was the nature of the illness I was treating, unreliable." The therapists, however, were aware that they had failed to obtain the patient's unequivocal consent to publication. When the physician published the book the patient brought suit to enjoin its distribution.

In support of her case, she cited the violation of a state statute which provided:

> Unless the patient waives the privilege, a person authorized to practice medicine . . . shall not be allowed to disclose any information which he acquired in attending a patient in a professional capacity, and which was necessary to enable him to act in that capacity.

The patient also cited a state healing arts regulation which provided that:

> Unprofessional conduct in the practice of medicine shall include . . . the revealing of facts, data or information obtained in a professional capacity relating to a patient or his records without first obtaining the consent of the patient.

The patient also argued that the contractual aspect of the physician-patient relationship encompasses an implied promise that the physician will obey the Hippocratic oath which states in part:

> Whatever, in connection with my professional practice, or not in connection with it, I may see or hear in the lives of men which ought not be spoken abroad I will not divulge, as reckoning that all such should be kept secret.

The court held that the statutes providing that physicians shall not disclose information acquired while attending the patient in a professional capacity are not confined to trials and other formal hearings. In finding for the patient, the court gave the law a broad and liberal construction, evidencing a public policy of prohibiting physicians and other health care providers from disclosing, without the authorization of the patient, information discovered in attending the patient.

The following case exemplifies another protective use of a privileged communication statute. This case held that where a former patient turned litigant attempts to obtain information about some of the physician's other patients whose privacy is at stake, a physician may be obligated to protect these patients' interests.

Marcus v. Superior Court of Los Angeles County. A patient sought to recover damages from Dr. Marcus for injuries allegedly sustained by him when Dr. Marcus performed an angiogram upon him. By deposition, interrogatories, and a motion to produce documents, he sought to force disclosure of the names and addresses of other patients to whom Dr. Marcus had given angiographic testing. Dr. Marcus sought protective orders. After a hearing, the trial court made the following order:

> Dr. Marcus is ordered to disclose to plaintiff by letter or otherwise, and within 10 days of receipt of notice of this Order from Plaintiff, the names and addresses of the eight patients of Dr. Marcus receiving the same type of tests as Plaintiff, next prior to the angiogram of Plaintiff, and the names and addresses of the eight patients of Dr. Marcus receiving the same type of tests as Plaintiff, next subsequent to the angiogram of Plaintiff, including (or, if not included, then also) the names and addresses of the two patients of Dr. Marcus who developed complications from said testing.

On appeal, in defense of this order, plaintiff's counsel explained that the purpose for seeking the information was the need for the discovery, through the investigation of other patients, of the type of information related by Dr. Marcus to determine his veracity as to his normal practice prior to performing this type of serious procedure. The attorney contended that patients of Dr. Marcus so identified could, upon contact by plaintiff's counsel, claim the privilege and refuse to discuss their particular experience. However, he argued that at least in the first instance, discovery should permit the exposure of names and addresses for proper investigation.

The court pointed out that the purpose for giving the patient-plaintiff this information was to enable his investigators to seek out and interrogate Dr. Marcus's other patients and try to persuade them to discuss their experiences with the physician. The court cited the statutory provision that governed the issue of confidentiality in such matters. It provided that: ". . . the patient, whether or not a party, has a privilege to refuse to disclose, and to prevent another from disclosing, a confidential communication between patient and physician." Moreover, the statute required the attending physician to claim the privilege on behalf of his patients. Furthermore, it defined "patient" to include a person who submits to an examination for the purpose of securing a diagnosis. The court noted that persons do not ordinarily consult physicians from idle curiosity. A person who received the specific test (an angiogram) from Dr. Marcus probably communicated to the physician facts about himself indicating the need for such testing. If Dr. Marcus was required to list persons receiving such tests as required by the court's order, he necessarily would reveal this confidential information. Therefore, such a disclosure would violate the physician-patient privilege.

The court recognized that the disclosure of a patient's name does not necessarily violate the privilege. An example would be a case where the context of information disclosed revealed nothing of any communication concerning the patient's condition or the physician's diagnosis. However, in this case, the court pointed out it is not merely the disclosure of the name and address, but the joining of that information with the fact that these were patients who had received angiographic tests. Therefore, the court prohibited the enforcement of the trial court's order requiring the disclosure of the names and addresses of Dr. Marcus's patients.

Generally, to come within the ambit of the privilege, the communication must involve information, acquired through the physician-patient relationship, needed to treat the patient professionally. If the communication involved satisfies this requirement, absent waiver or exception to the privilege, the confidential communication will be protected from disclosure.

Vaughan v. Martin.   Mr. McIntosh was an elderly but active farmer until he suffered an infection which curtailed his physical activity. Because he practiced the Christian Science faith, he refused medical aid during this illness. However, he recognized the need for continued nursing care because of his failing physical condition. Therefore he made preliminary arrangements to enter a nursing home.

After he discovered that a physician's permission was required for admittance into the nursing home, he asked Dr. Derhammer, a physician he had known socially, if he would satisfy this requirement. Dr. Derhammer conducted an examination by observing and by conversing with McIntosh. After this evaluation, Dr. Derhammer determined that McIntosh should be placed in a nursing home. He signed the necessary admission papers and was paid by McIntosh.

After being placed in a nursing home, McIntosh's health failed rapidly and he survived only a month. Because of his religious beliefs, he had received no medication or medical attention while in the nursing home. His will, which provided for a series of charitable bequests, was contested by relatives who charged that he lacked the testamentary capacity to make a valid will. At a hearing concerning his testamentary capacity, in order to demonstrate that McIntosh's condition was impaired at the time he made the bequest, his relatives sought to introduce into evidence a document entitled "Physician's Sheet" that had been filled out by Dr. Derhammer for purposes of admitting McIntosh to the nursing home. The proponents of the will sought to block introduction of this document by contending that it was the product of a physician-patient relationship and that confidentiality barred the attending physician from testifying as to his patient's condition. As a legal basis for their contention, the proponents cited a statutory provision that purported to preclude an attending physician from testifying "about matters communicated to him by a patient in the course of professional business."

The opponents of the will conceded that Dr. Derhammer was acting in his professional capacity when he evaluted McIntosh. However, they contended that he was not in a physician-patient relationship because that relationship required a more intimate traditional diagnostic and therapeutic contact than simply providing a utilitarian service.

The court pointed out that the issue in this case was whether a physician-patient relationship existed. It held that the words "matters communicated" to the physician by the patient, as used in the statute describing privileged information, related to information heard or observed by the physician that he obtained from the patient in order to make some evaluation, perform some duty, or to apply his medical expertise to benefit the patient. Thus the court concluded that the determination of the existence of a physician-patient relationship should be made on a qualitative basis rather than a quantitative basis.

The court pointed out that Dr. Derhammer's professional efforts were for the direct benefit of McIntosh. He was called at McIntosh's request to perform a duty which required a physician. He examined him in his professional capacity and was paid by him for his services. Therefore, confidential matters were communicated to him within the statutory definition, and a physician-patient relationship existed. His record was, therefore, protected from disclosure.

Exceptions to the Privilege

A physician's duty to safeguard confidential information may be subject to an exception that could allow or even require disclosure. As illustrated by the following materials, if the communication involved did not originate from the physician-patient relationship, it is not privileged; likewise, if the patient raises an issue in litigation, the privilege is considered waived as to information on that issue. Moreover, a physician may be allowed or even required to disclose confidential information if an important private or public interest demands it.

1. *Communication not Related to Treatment*

As illustrated in the preceding materials, a confidential communication, to be protected from disclosure, must usually involve information acquired through the physician-patient relationship needed to professionally treat the patient. The following case exemplifies this requirement and holds that when a communication is not related to diagnosis or treatment of a patient, it is not privileged.

State v. Bedel.   While operating his motor vehicle, a man lost control and struck a tree. As a consequence he sustained injuries and was taken to the hospital. He was also placed under arrest for operating a motor vehicle while under the influence of intoxicants. A nurse at the hospital called the physician who was "on-call" to the emergency room. He directed the nurse to administer intramuscular injections of Demerol and Tetanus Toxoid. The physician was not present at the hospital when the drugs were administered, nor had he known the man prior to his admission to the hospital.

A written request for a chemical test of the man's blood was made by the arresting officer and the man executed a written consent to the withdrawal of a speciman of his blood. A second call was made to the "on-call" physician who then authorized a laboratory technician at the hospital to perform a venipuncture and collect the blood specimen. The blood was withdrawn and later submitted for chemical analysis by a laboratory regularly performing such service. It contained .15 milligrams percent of alcohol, an amount equal to the state's statutory definition of intoxication.

Subsequently, when the man was tried for driving while intoxicated, he sought to suppress the blood alcohol test results, despite his consent to the test, contending that such tests represented a confidential by-product of his relationship with his physician. He cited as authority for his contention a statute which recognized a physician-patient privilege by providing that:

> No physician who obtains such information by reason of his employment shall be allowed, in giving testimony, to disclose any confidential communication properly entrusted to him in his professional capacity, and necessary and proper to enable him to discharge the functions of his office according to the usual course of practice or discipline.

The court found that essential elements of this privilege concerned the necessity and propriety of the information to enable the physician to treat the patient skillfully in his professional capacity. The court concluded that the necessary elements to create a physician-patient privilege did not exist in this case. Although a physician is not necessarily required actually to see and examine the patient for the privilege to exist, it is essential that the communication sought to be held confidential be related to the medical diagnosis or treatment of the patient. In this case, the court noted that the certification to withdraw the blood and the test itself were not related to either medical diagnosis or treatment of the patient, and therefore were not privileged. The court pointed out that there was no showing that any communication concerning the blood test was necessary to enable the physician to treat the man. In fact, the physician did not see the man personally until the next morning, and the nurse who contacted the physician had not done so at the request of the man. Therefore, the court concluded that the results of the blood test were not protected from disclosure.

2. Issues Raised by the Patient

When the patient raises the issue of his medical treatment during litigation, a waiver of the privilege of confidentiality may be implied. The following case illustrates this and also the limitation of the treating physician's "right" to withhold information during the course of litigation on behalf of the patient.

Caesar v. Mountanos. On December 4, 1969, a patient was involved in an automobile accident. Thereafter, she experienced persistent cervical pain. Later in December she was referred by her physician to Dr. Caesar for psychiatric examination and treatment. Dr. Caesar saw her approximately twenty times for psychotherapy. In 1970, she filed a legal action to recover damages from the accident. She alleged that the accident caused her pain and suffering which were not limited to her physical ailments but included psychological injury also.

During the pretrial discovery phase of her case, the patient indicated that some of the treatment she had received from Dr. Caesar might involve relevant issues in her lawsuit. In a deposition, a psychiatrist who was acting as an expert for the defense, testified that the patient's attending physician had recommended referral to Dr. Caesar because he felt there was "an emotional overlay" to her problems which was "magnifying her distress." When Dr. Caesar's deposition was taken he indicated that he had an opinion with respect as to whether his patient suffered from any emotional distress as a result of the accident, and that he had given his medical notes on his patient to her counsel. Refusing to respond to specific inquiries by the defense counsel concerning the possible relationship of the patient's symptoms to her emotional state, Dr. Caesar stated that in his judgment, answering further questions and revealing his patient's confidence could be psychologically detrimental to her future well-being.

Dr. Caesar also indicated that he had not received a "valid consent" from his patient which would permit him to testify on her mental state. His patient's lawyer then told him that, although there had been some prior confusion about her consent, she had authorized Dr. Caesar to testify. Nevertheless, Dr. Caesar refused to accept this consent and stated further that even if written consent had been given, he would still refuse to testify because such disclosure would violate his and his patient's right of privacy.

At a legal hearing to decide whether Dr. Caesar had to disclose his opinions concerning his patient in a deposition, the judge determined that the information disclosed by the patient to Dr. Caesar was a "confidential communication," and that the state statute allowed the therapist to claim the privilege for his patient when information about a confidential communication was sought. However, it was ruled that there was no privilege as to communications relevant to an issue concerning the mental or emotional condition of the patient when such an issue had been tendered in litigation by the patient. Dr. Caesar appealed the ruling.

The appellate court construed the statute to require disclosure only of information directly pertinent to issues raised by the patient in a lawsuit. It held that in applying the statute, the psychotherapeutic privilege should be liberally construed in favor of the patient. The court noted, however, that the fundamental right of privacy provided a conditional, not absolute, privilege for therapeutic communications. Even though the nature of the relationship depended on the patient's complete confidence in the psychotherapist, the court concluded that limited intrusion into the psychotherapist-patient privilege was permitted upon the showing of a "compelling state interest."

The court pointed out that the statute neither contemplated a complete waiver of the psychotherapeutic communication privilege nor sought to deter psychotherapy patients from instituting lawsuits. Therefore, disclosure was to be strictly limited to that information placed in issue by the patient-plaintiff and about which the patient and the psychotherapist have practically exclusive knowledge. Communications which are not directly relevant to those specific conditions did not fall within the terms of the statute's exception, and therefore remained privileged.

In this case, the court concluded that the patient had clearly raised before the court the issue concerning her mental and emotional condition; she sought damages for mental and emotional injuries resulting from the accident; and she was examined and treated by Dr. Caesar for emotional distress and depression following the accident. Dr. Caesar testified that he had an opinion with respect to whether his patient suffered from emotional distress of any kind as a result of her having been in the accident; but he declined to state that opinion to questions clearly relevant and directly related to the issue of her mental and emotional condition, which the patient herself had raised. The court therefore held that the privilege did not apply to the psychiatrist's withholding of information.

3. Private Interest

The patient's right to prevent an attending physician from disclosing confidential information is not absolute. The responsibility of the physician to keep information confidential may be outweighed by a higher duty to disclose information if there is a sufficiently important interest to protect. If, for example, the vital private interest of another person is at stake, a physician may, under certain circumstances, have a "conditional" right to make a disclosure that is reasonably necessary to protect such an interest. Some circumstances involved in such a conditional privilege are illustrated in the following cases.

Clark v. Geraci.   In the course of the treatment of his patient, a family physician learned that the patient consumed excessive amounts of alcoholc beverages as a means of dealing with his social problems. The patient required repeated treatments for pulmonary problems that the physician opined were secondary to chronic alcoholism. At the behest of his patient, the physician had issued several medical certificates indicating that the patient's pulmonary condition was responsible for his frequent absences from work. Sometime thereafter, the physician informed his patient that the latter's employer had requested an explanation of the underlying cause of the patient's condition that was causing his frequent absences from work, because this information had not been specifically set out in the medical certificates. The physician related that he intended to respond to the employer's request, and showed the patient the letter which he, the physician, had written which established that the absences were due to alcoholism. The patient told him not to send the proposed letter. The physician ignored the request and sent the letter. Upon receipt of the letter, the patient's employer formally notified the patient of his discharge. The employer listed the employee's repeated absences, recited the physician's letter, and rejected the patient's attempt to attribute the absences to a series of misfortunes.

The patient sued the physician, contending that he had improperly divulged confidential information. The physician contended that he had an overriding duty to disclose the underlying cause of his patient's absences because he had previously supplied incomplete medical information to the patient's employer.

The court pointed out that the delicate balance of a physician's conflicting duties to a patient and an involved third party must be weighed to determine the physician's paramount duty. The court reasoned that the prior incomplete medical certificates requested by the patient and supplied by the physician to explain the former's absences, gave the physician a right to make a full disclosure of those medical facts, which superseded his duty to the patient to remain silent. The requested certificates constituted, in effect, the patient's waiver of the privilege of confidentiality to the extent that they told the reason for the employee's absences. The patient's specific request not to dispatch the letter was invalidated because he had previously asked for and permitted incomplete disclosures as to the nature of his illness. Although the patient knew that his illnesses had been set out in the certificates requested by him, he insisted that their underlying cause, alcoholism, could not legally be disclosed. Under such circumstances he was aware that the certificates were true only as far as they went. Having placed the physician in the position of telling but part of the truth, he was precluded from preventing disclosure of the remainder by putting limitations on the waiver of privilege.

The patient also contended that the physician was liable because the letter sent to the employer set forth more than was required. However, the court held that a narration of less than all the facts requested would have tended to further mislead the employer. In addition, the physician was specifically asked by the employer to clarify the dubious information previously supplied.

Horne v. Patton. A family physician was asked by his patient's employer to certify the patient's good health. The patient had instructed his physician not to release any medical information to his employer. The physician disclosed to his patient's employer that his patient suffered from a longstanding "nervous condition," which was manifested by feelings of anxiety and insecurity. Although the physician acquired this information in the course of a physician-patient relationship, he assumed the employer had a reasonable interest in his patient's health condition. As a result of the disclosure, the patient's status as an employee was jeopardized. He, therefore, sued his physician for breach of confidentiality.

The court pointed out that, although the physician had not generally circulated this information about his patient, nor had he frivolously gossiped about his patient's health, he had disclosed confidential information about the patient. The court noted that even though an employer may have an interest in his employee's health, he does not necessarily have a legitimate interest in knowing specific details because there are many conditions about which a patient might consult a physician which have no bearing or effect on employment. The court held that if a physician feels he has a legitimate reason for making the disclosure under the particular facts of a case, then the burden is upon him to present this as a defense to his act of disclosure.

Berry v. Moench. Dr. Hellewell wrote a letter to Dr. Moench, with whom he was unacquainted, requesting information concerning an ex-patient, Mr. Berry, and asking for his impression of the man. The expressed purpose of this request was to pass this information on to Mr. and Mrs. Williams, the parents of Mary Boothe, who was then engaged to Mr. Berry. Dr. Moench supplied Dr. Hellewell with information that had been obtained seven years earlier in connection with his treatment of Mr. Berry. He had not seen Mr. Berry since that time. Dr. Moench wrote a letter which set forth the following information:

Dear Dr. Hellewell:
Since I do not have his authorization, the patient you mentioned in your last letter will remain nameless. The patient was attempting to go through school on the G.I. Bill, but instead of attending class he would spend most of the days and nights playing cards for money.

Because of family circumstances, we treated him for a mere token charge (and I notice even that has never been paid). During his care here, he purchased a brand new car without even money to buy gasoline. . . . He was in constant trouble with the authorities during the war and did not do well in school, nor did he ever really support his wife and children. . . . Since he was here, we have repeated requests for his record indicating repeated trouble.

My suggestion to the infatuated girl would be to run as fast and as far as she possibly could in any direction away from him. Of course if he doesn't marry her, he will marry someone else and make life hell for that person. The usual story is repeated unsuccessful marriages and a trail of tragedy behind.

Dr. Moench's source for most of the information in the letter was Mr. Berry's ex-wife and his sister-in-law.

The letter was related by Dr. Hellewell to Mr. and Mrs. Williams who became violently opposed to the marriage. When, over their protests, their daughter married Mr. Berry, they disowned her. Mr. Berry sued Dr. Moench for breach of confidentiality. Dr. Moench contended that writing the letter was justified because the disclosure was made under a "conditional" privilege for the benefit of a person other than the patient whose welfare would be endangered if she did not receive the information.

The court pointed out that a "conditional" privilege to disclose confidential information may be allowed in various situations. For example, where a patient has gone to a second physician for treatment and the latter requested information from the first physician to assist him in the diagnosis, professional custom and comity require that disclosure be permitted for the help and protection of both physician and patient. However, the court noted that this was not such a case. Dr. Hellewell, the requesting physician, had never seen Mr. Berry and had no concern with him as a patient. The court stated, however, that a "conditional" privilege could extend to the protection of the interests of persons other than the physician's patient under proper circumstances. Thus, where such a person's safety, well-being, or other important interests are in jeopardy, a physician who possesses information that could protect against a potential hazard may have a "conditional" privilege to disclose confidential information for such purpose. The court cautioned, however, that this "conditional" privilege does not arise automatically or become absolute merely because there is a persons' interest to protect. A physician who transmits such information about his patient to protect another is obliged to consider the likelihood and extent of benefit to the recipient, compared with the likelihood and extent of injury to the patient, if the information proves to be false or improper for disclosure.

The court concluded that the circumstances in this case came within the framework of "conditional" privilege in that Mary Boothe's well-being was a sufficient interest to protect. It was within the generally accepted standards of decent conduct for the physician to disclose the information that might have an important bearing on her well-being. However, the court pointed out that the privilege of disclosure is referred to as "conditional" because it must be exercised with certain precautions.

The privilege is unavailable as a defense against a breach of confidentiality if the physician passes on derogatory information without exercising reasonable care and diligence to ascertain the truth of the information. Dr. Moench was uncertain as to what information came from which source: the referring physician, Mr. Berry, or Mr. Berry's then wife and her sister. Although an estranged spouse is not usually an impartial source of information as to the conduct and character of her mate, Dr. Moench relied upon such statements without attempting to test their veracity.

The physician must also communicate the information fairly. He should not report information as facts if the source of his information is gossip or hearsay, or there are other circumstances which would render it open to suspicion. Fairness requires him to report such circumstances along with the information. The court made special note that this is an especially important obligation for an attending physician because his professional status and his well-known duty to keep the confidence of his patient tend to endow information he discloses with more than ordinary credibility. Dr. Moench disclosed unverified information obtained seven years earlier, which he stated as fact, without stating the source.

The physician should also disclose only such information as is necessary to accomplish the proper purpose and only to such persons as are necessary to accomplish that purpose. Dr. Moench published to more persons than reasonably necessary to afford protection to Mary Boothe. Dr. Hellewell was not acting as a physician to Mr. Berry, Mary Boothe, or her parents. His only objective was to do what he regarded as a favor to the Williamses who had been his patients. He functioned as a conduit to pass the information to intermediaries, the Williamses, rather than to Mary Boothe, the person directly concerned. Dr. Moench did not take into account the likelihood that the concerned parents would talk to others about the matter. Thus, conceding that Mary Boothe had such an interest that Dr. Moench properly thought she should be given information, a more direct method of getting the information to her should have been employed than to relay it through others, even though they had initiated the inquiry to her interest.

4. Public Interest

Another exception to maintenance of confidential communications between physician and patient is disclosure of information in the public interest. In this area, disclosure may not only be allowed but may be required whenever the public interest involved is sufficiently strong. For example, when the physician has reasonable grounds to base a diagnosis of a contagious disease, disclosure of that fact to those who are endangered by the disease is allowed, as long as the physician acts in good faith.

Simonsen v. Swenson. A man was traveling on business. While he was staying in a small hotel, he developed skin lesions, and consulted the hotel physician about the cause of this problem. After taking a history and performing a physical examination, the physician informed the patient that he believed the patient had syphilis. He stated, however, that it was impossible for him to be positive about the diagnosis without making certain tests that he was incapable of performing. Because he felt that there was a danger of the patient transmitting the disease to others in the hotel, he requested the patient to leave the next day. The patient promised to do so. The following day, while the physician was in attendance at the hotel, he learned that the patient had not checked out. Therefore, he warned the hotel manager that he thought the patient had a "contagious disease," and instructed her to carefully disinfect the patient's bedclothing and to wash her hands in alcohol afterwards. Acting upon this warning, the hotel manager placed all of the patient's belongings in the hallway, fumigated his room, and forced him to leave the hotel. After leaving the city, the patient consulted a physician who performed a test for syphilis that was negative. He then sued the hotel physician for breach of confidentiality.

The patient contended that the law absolutely prohibited disclosure of any confidential communication at any time or under any circumstances. In addition, he cited a state statute which provided that a physician's license may be revoked when he is found guilty of the "betrayal of a professional secret to the detriment of a patient."

The court pointed out that it is often necessary for the patient to give information about himself that would be embarrassing or harmful to him if given general circulation. This information the physician is bound, not only by his professional ethics to keep secret, but also by reason of the affirmative mandate of the statute. However, the court stated that such a rule of secrecy is subject to qualification or exception. The physician's duty does not necessarily end with the patient, because the medical condition of his patient may be such that an affirmative duty of disclosure may be created for the welfare of the public. The court reasoned that when a physician, in response to such a duty, discloses to public authorities confidential information about his patient, in the manner prescribed by law, he has not breached his duty of confidentiality to his patient, and has betrayed no confidence. A patient cannot reasonably expect that if his condition is found to be dangerously contagious, he can still require a physician to keep it secret from those to whom, if there were no disclosure, such disease could be transmitted. Confidential information given to a physician must be given and received subject to the condition or qualification that if the patient's disease is determined to be so contagious that it will necessarily be transmitted to others unless the danger of contagion is disclosed to them, and there are no other means of protection possible; a physician should be allowed to make as much disclosure to such persons as is necessary to prevent the spread of the disease. The court concluded that such a disclosure would not be "betrayal of the confidence" of the patient because the patient must know, when he imparts the information or subjects himself to the examination, that, in the exception stated, his disease may be disclosed.

The word "betrayal" as used in the statute was intended to signify a wrongful disclosure of a professional secret in violation of the patient's trust. In making such disclosure for the welfare of the public, a physician must demonstrate that a disclosure was necessary to prevent the spread of disease; that the communication was to one who it was reasonable to suppose, might otherwise be exposed; and that he acted in entire good faith, without malice, and with reasonable grounds for his diagnosis. The court concluded that the facts of this case showed that the physician had reasonable grounds for his belief, that he made no further disclosure than was reasonably necessary under the circumstances, and that he acted in good faith.

Hague v. Williams. Five months after his infant daughter's birth, her father purchased a $1,500 life insurance policy for her. The father, who was the beneficiary of the policy, represented to the insurance agent that the baby was in good health to the best of his knowledge and belief. He did not report any abnormality or the existence of possible heart trouble, in spite of the fact that a pediatrician had examined the child approximately eleven times during the first four months of her life for evaluation of a possible cardiac abnormality. At the age of eight months the child became seriously ill, was rushed to the hospital, and died a few hours later. An autopsy disclosed a congenital heart defect. During the investigation of the claim under the insurance policy, the insurance company requested information from the attending pediatrician and he told the company that the child had suffered from "heart trouble from birth." On the basis of this information, the company decided that had this preexistent medical condition been disclosed, the child would not have been issued a policy. Therefore, the company denied the claim on the policy. The father filed suit against the company, but he collected less than the full policy amount. He then sued the pediatrician for the remainder of the policy limits, claiming unlawful disclosure of confidential information had jeopardized his insurance claim.

The court pointed out that although a physician is obligated not to disclose confidential information, this duty is subject to exceptions where the interest of society demands disclosure. The court concluded that this case involved such an exception because of the public interest in an honest and fair resolution of legal claims. Therefore, the disclosure of the physical condition of a patient was justified because the condition was a significant factor in a just and fair claim disposition.

Virgil v. Rice. A thirteen-year-old girl developed a serious fungus infection on her foot. She was taken to a physician for diagnosis. Treatment required confinement to her home; therefore, her parents asked the school for a home teacher. Under the established procedure, a report form was sent to the attending physician to obtain information about the illness which prevented school attendance and justified a home teacher. The form was returned, signed by the physician, stating that the girl was pregnant. The parents learned about this when they inquired about the delay in obtaining a home teacher. After several unsuccessful attempts to obtain the report from the school or to have it destroyed, the parents telephoned the physician and asked him to correct or retract the report. He told them that he had checked his files and found nothing that would indicate that he had made such a report, but if they would bring in the report he would do what he could to correct an error, if any had been made. Several times thereafter, telephone calls were made to the physician's office asking that the report be corrected and the school be notified, but all requests were to no avail. Finally the physician's nurse told the parents that no call had been made to the school and none would be made. As a result of the physician's conduct, the patient brought suit against the physician for breach of confidentiality.

The court pointed out that a false statement that an unmarried girl is pregnant is defamatory without the necessity for proof that the disclosure caused actual injury. In this case, however, the court concluded that the physician had a "conditional" privilege to disclose information about his patient's condition. Nevertheless, the physician's persistent refusal to correct or retract the false report was evidence that he acted with a reckless disregard of the effect of his action on the patient. Therefore, he lost this "conditional" privilege to disclose his patient's confidential information.

As discussed previously, situations in which the safety and welfare of the public demand protection may not only permit, but may require disclosure. Thus a physician may have a public duty to breach a patient's confidentiality by warning a specifically named person whom the patient has threatened to harm.*

---

*See chapter 2, section 2, which discusses a physician's duty to nonpatients.

Tarasoff v. Regents of University of California.   While receiving outpatient psychotherapy at a campus clinic, a student disclosed to his therapist his intent to kill his girl friend. The therapist, in conjunction with other therapists at the clinic, had the conviction that the patient was a danger to his named victim. The director of the clinic requested the campus police to detain the student. When the police talked to the student, he replied, "Oh, I talk about killing, but I don't mean anything by it." He was released because he appeared rational to the police and promised not to bother the girl. The psychiatrist in charge then ordered that no further action be taken. Two months later the student carried out his threat. The parents of the victim sued, charging that the physicians had a duty to warn them or their daughter about their patient's threat. The therapists contended that such a disclosure would have breached their patient's confidentiality.

The court held that the psychiatrist was liable for failing to warn the intended victim of the possible danger. It stated that the protective privilege of confidential communications ends when public peril begins. If a physician has a reasonable conviction that his patient might carry out the threat against a specifically named person, he should warn the intended victim.

Under certain circumstances, the privilege of confidentiality may justify a physician's nondisclosure of information to a person who is foreseeably endangered by his patient's conduct.

Shaw v. Glickman.   A man, his wife, and another man received group therapy from a psychiatrist. Sometime during the course of therapy, the woman left her husband. Subsequently, she and her estranged husband had two sessions of marriage counseling, directed by their psychiatrist's assistant. During the first session the wife told her estranged husband that she was interested in the man who was in their therapy session. Her husband did not seem distraught over that revelation. Subsequently, the man who was the object of the woman's interest expressed concern to the psychiatrist about the possibility of violence from the woman's husband. The psychiatrist, even though he was aware that the husband possessed a gun, brushed aside the man's expression of concern with the remark, "We have got to get on to other things. We don't have to be concerned about that." A week after their last group therapy session, the woman's husband broke into the other man's home where he found his wife and the man asleep in the same bed. Believing he had been cuckolded, the estranged husband discharged several bullets into the body of the other man seriously injuring him.

The injured man sued this psychiatrist for malpractice, alleging that he had a duty to warn him of the estranged husband's unstable and violent condition which presented a foreseeable and immediate danger to him.

The court declared that once an attending physician determines, or under applicable professional standards reasonably should have determined, that a patient poses a serious danger of violence to others, he may have a duty to exercise reasonable care to protect the foreseeable victim of that danger. The court noted that other courts have found that a physician may become sufficiently involved in the therapy of some patients to assume some responsibility for the safety not only of the patient himself, but also of a third person whom the physician knows to be threatened by the patient. In those cases, however, there was no question of a missed diagnosis or failure to predict the future conduct of the patient, because the patient told the therapist of the plan to kill an identifiable person; and the therapist, while correctly predicting the event, negligently failed to warn the victim.

The court pointed out that a physician has a competing duty to keep his patient's secrets, partially based on the Hippocratic oath taken by physicians in the state, which in pertinent part, stated: "All that may come to my knowledge in the exercise of my profession or outside of my profession or in daily commerce with men, which ought not to be spread abroad, I will keep secret and will never reveal." The court noted that many courts have held that when a patient informs his physician of the patient's plan to kill another person, and the physician is convinced that the named party is endangered, such disclosure of information is not forbidden by the Hippocratic oath, but rather "ought to be spread abroad" to prevent injury or loss of life. In this case, however, the court reasoned there was no threat revealed by the estranged husband to kill or injure the other man; and there was no confiding by the husband in the physician, concerning any animosity or hatred toward the other man. Although the husband was known by the psychiatrist to possess a gun, that fact does not give rise to the inference that the husband did so for the purpose of harming the other man. Moreover, his intent to kill or injure was not disclosed to the psychiatrist.

The court, however, went on to declare that had the husband confided in the psychiatrist, that he planned to shoot the other man, the psychiatrist would have faced a dilemma, that is, to breach the patient's confidence and "tip off" the other man, or keep the patient's confidence and, figuratively speaking, "throw the man to the wolves." The court noted that resolution of this dilemma had legislative guidance in the state because of a statute which provided that: "Unless otherwise provided, in all judicial, legislative, or administrative proceedings, a patient has a privilege to refuse to disclose, and to prevent a witness from disclosing, communications relating to diagnosis or treatment of the patient's mental or emotional disorder." The statute provided the patient with the privilege of preventing disclosure of that information by his psychiatrist. The court reasoned that inasmuch as the statute conferred a privilege of confidentiality on the communication between patient and psychiatrist in judicial, legislative, or administrative proceedings, no lesser privilege existed when the matter is not judicial, legislative, or administrative. Thus the court concluded that with the exception of those instances where the privilege of confidentiality is expressly prohibited by the statutory provisions, the lips of the psychiatrist have been statutorily sealed shut, subject solely to being unsealed by the patient. The court held, therefore, that under the current law of that state, it would have been a violation of the statute for the psychiatrist to have disclosed to the other man the propensity on the part of the estranged husband to shoot his wife's lover.

As an example of acceptable disclosure of confidential information in the public interest, the law requires reporting such information in certain specific circumstances. In making such reports, the physician is protected by law from liability for breach of confidentiality if such disclosures conform to the law's specific requirements.

Felber v. Foote.   A state statute required physicians to report the names of, and other information about, "drug-dependent" persons to the State Commissioner of Health. It specifically required that:

> Each practitioner of the healing arts shall report to the commissioner of health the full name, address and date of birth of every person who, in his opinion, is dependent upon controlled drugs. Practitioners making such reports in good faith shall be immune from any civil or criminal liability that otherwise might be incurred from the making of such report. No such report of the information therein shall be admissible in any criminal prosecution or used for other than rehabilitation, statistical or medical purposes, and each such report shall be held confidential by the commissioner.

A physician resisted enforcement of the law, contending that the statute unreasonably invaded the constitutional right to his and his patient's privacy. He claimed his right of privacy was invaded because the statute interfered with his private practice of medicine by creating a conflict between his professional duty toward his patients to keep communications confidential and the requirement of the statute that he disclose information about them. He contended that the statute placed the attending physician in the position of an "informer," unless the physician advised the patient of the statute, in which event the patient may refuse to submit to treatment. In addition, he claimed that the statute required licensed physicians to violate professional standards of conduct or ethics.

The court pointed out that it is unwarranted to assume that the special nature of the physician-patient relationship affords an attending physician a constitutionally protected right to privacy in the conduction of his relationship with his patient. The court noted that there is no "general constitutional right to privacy" that would protect that aspect of the physician-patient relationship. Moreover, the court concluded that the conception of privacy which the physician sought to protect bore no analogy to those spheres of privacy that have previously won constitutional protection.

The court held that a privilege of confidentiality is not legally recognized as to information which the physician or the patient is required to report to a public official, unless the statute requiring the report specifically provides that the information shall not be disclosed. The court pointed out that other statutes which require physicians to report information, such as cases of communicable diseases, are outside the scope of any privilege of confidentiality.

SECTION 4: INVASION OF PRIVACY

In addition to asserting breach of confidentiality, if a patient claims information has been wrongfully disclosed, the aforementioned cases illustrate that invasion of the right of privacy may also be alleged in appropriate situations and circumstances. Some states have recognized that a patient has a right to be free from the wrongful intrusion into private matters where such intrusion would cause mental suffering or humiliation to a person of ordinary sensibilities. In addition to public disclosure of private facts, the law of privacy may also encompass invasion of other distinct interests of a patient's right "to be left alone," including a physician's medically related activities that are not for the therapeutic benefit of the patient, and that encroach upon the patient's physical and mental solitude or seclusion.

Bazemore v. Savannah Hospital. A baby had been born with an extracorporeal heart. Hospital personnel took pictures of this condition and sold them to the local newspaper which published them. All this was done without the consent of the parents who then sued the hospital for invasion of privacy.

The court stated that the publication of the photographs could possibly subject the patient to humiliation. Thus the patient was entitled to protection from general disclosure of such information. The court then held that the patient's right of privacy had been improperly invaded because the hospital had appropriated a sensitive aspect of the patient's life and had published it solely for the hospital's benefit.

Griffin v. Medical Society of the State of New York. A plastic surgeon took two pictures of the patient's nose prior to the performance of a rhinoplasty and two pictures after the operation had been completed. These four photographs were published without the patient's consent in a medical journal as part of an article entitled, "The Saddle Nose," which was written and prepared by, and bore the byline of the operating surgeon. When the patient became aware of the publication she sued the surgeon for invasion of privacy.

The court noted that in this case, the use of the pictures was not strictly and solely for medical and scientific purposes. It pointed out that an article, even in a scientific journal, may be published as the physician's advertisement in disguise, rather than for the patient's benefit, or the advancement of medical science. Therefore, under these circumstances, if the appropriation of the patient's likeness is not authorized by the patient's consent, it would constitute an invasion of privacy.

The law recognizes that medical science may benefit by the addition of a photograph to the medical record of a case, to better evaluate and treat other patients who are similarly afflicted. However, courts are unwilling to declare that a physician has a right to make such a photographic record of the patient without the patient's consent or over the patient's objections.

Estate of Berthiaume v. Pratt.   A surgeon performed a laryngectomy and later a radical neck dissection on a patient with cancer of the larynx. During this period of medical attendance, many photographs of the patient's neck were taken by or under the direction of the surgeon. The sole use of these photographs was to make a medical record of the case for the surgeon's use. Although the surgeon did not receive any written consent for the taking of photographs, the patient had never objected to having such photographs made.

Later, during the terminal phase of the patient's illness, he was hospitalized and attended by an internist. Shortly before the patient died, the surgeon who had performed the radical neck dissection and a nurse appeared outside the patient's hospital room with a camera. Before entering the room to take the pictures, the surgeon was intercepted by the patient's wife who told the surgeon that she did not think her husband wanted his picture taken. Nevertheless, the surgeon proceeded to enter the room and in the presence of the patient's wife and a person who was visiting the patient in the next bed, the surgeon lifted the patient's head and placed blue towels under it for the purpose of obtaining a color contrast for the photographs which he proposed to take. The patient protested the taking of the pictures by raising a clenched fist and moving his head in an attempt to remove it from the camera's range. Despite this, the surgeon proceeded to take several photographs. After the patient died, his estate sued the surgeon and claimed that taking the photographs without the patient's consent constituted an invasion of privacy, and violated the patient's right "to be left alone."

The court noted that a physician's mere taking of photographs of his patient is not an invasion of privacy, especially when they were not published or used for any purposes other than the record keeping process of the care rendered the patient. It reasoned that, although taking photographs is not necessarily a treatment, it is part of the overall medical relationship between the physician and his patient. However, the court pointed out that consent to such an intrusion is implied, based upon the premise that a physician-patient relationship existed at the time of the alleged intrusion. In this case, however, the patient was then under the care of another physician. The surgeon's visit to the patient's room on the day of the alleged invasion of privacy was not for any purpose relating to the treatment of the patient, but merely to conclude the making of a photographic record of the case. The court held that under certain circumstances, a physician's intrusion upon the patient's physical and mental solitude may be a legally actionable invasion of privacy. In this case, the patient was dying and desired not to be photographed in his hospital bed in that condition and manifested such desire by his motions. Thus, taking pictures without his consent or over his objection was an invasion of his legally protected right to privacy.

9

THE PATIENT'S CONDUCT

Legal expectations for a physician's conduct based on the nature of the physician-patient relationship have been explored and discussed. However, the law also has certain expectations for conduct required of patients. A patient is expected to cooperate and comply with the physicians's diagnostic and therapeutic efforts. Failure to do so may bar the patient from holding the physician legally responsible for a medically related injury, especially when the patient's negligent conduct is a substantial factor in causing the injury. However, the law realizes and expects the physician to recognize that an ill or injured patient may be unable to act as reasonably as someone who is well. In some instances, the treatment itself may impair a patient's ability to cooperate with a treatment plan. In other situations a patient's age, mental capacity, education, or cultural background may interfere with the patient's ability to comply with the care prescribed.

Another expectation for the conduct of a patient involves the situation when he feels he has received improper treatment from his physician and is considering instituting legal action for compensation of his perceived damages. Under such circumstances a patient is expected to have a reasonable basis for bringing a malpractice suit against his attending physician. As a corollary to that requirement, the patient (and his attorney) must not pursue unjustifiable, malicious, or improper legal action against a physician.

SECTION 1: PATIENT CONDUCT AS A CAUSE OF INJURY

A patient's own negligent conduct may be an adequate defense in a malpractice suit brought against a physician by his patient, especially if the patient's negligence substantially contributed to the patient's injury. A patient, like his physician, also has a duty to use the same degree of care concerning his health and welfare as a prudent person would use in similar circumstances. Ordinarily a physician is not accountable for the consequences of a patient's own lack of ordinary and reasonable care in the treatment process. A patient's negligent conduct may consist of failing to follow the physician's instructions, refusing recommended treatment, or giving the physician false, incomplete, or misleading information.

A patient's physical condition and emotional condition are among the factors and circumstances to be considered in determining whether the patient has contributed to, or caused the injury for which he seeks compensation. Although a patient is expected to cooperate and comply with his physician's care and treatment efforts, certain aspects of a patient's traits, characteristics, and circumstances may impair his ability to cooperate in the treatment process. A physician is expected to detect obvious impairments and to appreciate the effects they are likely to have on the patient's ability to assist in his own medical care. Thus a physician may be required to become reasonably convinced that important medical information has been understood by the patient. If the patient has serious cognitive or communicative impairments, clinical information and instruction must be presented in a form that is likely to be understood by the patient or his lay caretaker. Instruction to children, even to adolescents, must usually be given to the parents as well, to minimize the chance for misunderstanding.

Where the physician has been negligent and causes a patient injury which is simply compounded by *subsequent* negligence on the part of the patient, legal damages will be awarded against the physician even though they will probably be mitigated. Not only must a patient's negligence be demonstrated, but it also must be shown to be an active and efficient contributing cause that occurred *simultaneously* with the treating physician's failure, and acted in *concert* with it. If the patient's negligence did not occur until after the physician's, then the physician cannot contend that the patient's conduct alone directly caused the injury.

The cases in this section explore the scope of a patient's responsibility in the physician-patient relationship. They also illustrate how the patient's misconduct may become part of a physician's defense in a malpractice action. For example, although a physician ordinarily has a duty to take whatever steps are reasonable to notify patients of significant test results, a patient also has a corresponding duty not to intentionally interfere with the physician accomplishing his duty.

Ray v. Wagner. In June the patient remarried and moved to an apartment on Lake Street. Her children by a previous marriage remained with her mother at her former address. In August, she selected Dr. Wagner from a telephone directory and consulted him for the purpose of obtaining a contraceptive device. The patient told Dr. Wagner that she and her husband both worked at a local university. As a routine matter in assessing her for the contraceptive device, the physician took a Pap smear and sent it to a laboratory. It was returned about two weeks later with a report that it was "suspicious for malignancy."

The physician attempted on numerous occasions to reach the patient by telephone to advise her of the report and to recommend further procedures. He tried to reach her through the university, identifying her as a secretary and her husband as an accountant, but was unsuccessful because she had never worked at the university. He also attempted several times to reach her at her Lake Street address without success because she had moved to another address where she had no telephone. In December, Dr. Wagner finally was able to get in touch with the patient's mother and asked that the patient call his office. The patient, however, did not communicate with him until January when she paid the bill for his medical services. He then informed her of the test result, and took another Pap smear which again was "suspicious of malignancy." A biopsy disclosed a cancerous lesion. The patient sued the physician for failing to notify her promptly of her condition, which she alleged caused her to undergo more drastic surgery to prevent further progression of the cancer than would have been required if she had been promptly notified of the result. The physician contended that the patient's negligence was the cause of the delay in definitive treatment.

The court pointed out that, ordinarily, a patient can rely on being informed of positive test results by the attending physician. In this case, however, the patient gave the physician misleading information as to her status. In addition, she had no telephone at the address where she lived and did not live at the address where she previously had a telephone. Furnishing misinformation to the physician about her occupation, and failing to promptly notify the physician of a change of address, were inconsistent with the conduct expected from an ordinarily prudent patient. Therefore, the court decided that it was the patient's own negligent conduct which, under the circumstances, contributed to the delay in her needed treatment.

The patient has a duty to be reasonably truthful in describing symptoms to the physician. Thus intentional deception by the patient may bar recovery from the physician for any harm which results from the misinformation supplied by the patient.

Rochester v. Katalan. The patient and a companion were taken into custody by a police officer. Both men claimed to be heroin addicts suffering withdrawal symptoms and requested medication for their discomfort. They were taken to an emergency room for treatment of their complaints. The patient told the emergency room physician that he was a "junkie" and had a habit requiring four or five bags daily. The physician asked the patient whether he had attended the methadone clinic and the patient responded that he had participated in the program for four months, but had dropped out because he had found a new supply source of heroin. Both the patient and his friend manifested signs and symptoms consistent with their claimed withdrawal syndrome. The patient rolled his head, clutched his abdomen, and complained of severe abdominal pains. His eyes appeared glassy, his body was shaking, and he seemed agitated. After hearing their stories and noting their behavior, the physician ordered 40 mg. of methadone for each of them. Although his companion calmed down thereafter, the patient became violent, and beat his head against a wall. He told the physician that he was still sick and needed more methadone. Consequently, thirty minutes after the initial dose, the physician ordered a second 40 mg. dose of methadone to be given to the patient. Shortly after receiving the second dose, the patient calmed down. Shortly thereafter, he was taken to the jail by the police officers. The following morning he was found dead in his jail cell. The autopsy disclosed that he had died as a result of multiple drug intoxication.

It was subsequently determined that the patient had never been an addict, nor had he participated in a methadone program; although his companion was, in fact, a heroin addict. Shortly before being taken into police custody, the patient had consumed beer and Librium capsules. He did not give such information to hospital personnel. When his family learned of the manner of the patient's death, they sued the physician, alleging that his negligent treatment of the patient caused the patient's death.

The court pointed out that the critical issue in this case was not the physician's conduct, but the patient's own conduct. If the patient's conduct contributed to his death, his estate could recover no damages, even if the physician was assumed to be negligent by not doing more to determine the truth of the patient's assertions. The court noted that for unexplained reasons, the patient put on an effective act in the emergency room which induced the physician to do what the patient wanted, that is, to provide relief from heroin withdrawal discomfort. The patient demonstrated clinical symptomatology associated with addiction withdrawal and confirmed the clinical presentation by insisting that he was an addict. He continued to contribute to his own destruction by failing to tell the medical personnel present that he was not an addict, and that he had been drinking alcohol and taking Librium. He took the medication offered and continued to act out a deception to obtain another dose. Thus, he causally and materially contributed to his own death.

Another expectation for a patient's conduct is to reasonably follow and comply with the attending physician's instructions or advice. When the patient materially fails to do so and an injury results from such noncompliance; the patient, not the physician, ordinarily will be held to have been the determinative cause of the patient's legal damages.

Brown v. Dark. A six-year-old boy had fractured his arm. The physician set it in a cast and strongly urged the father to hospitalize the child. The father, who was from a neighboring community, refused to leave the child at the hospital and took him home. Neurovascular complications occurred which ultimately required amputation of the child's arm.

The father sued the physician, claiming that he had abandoned his patient. The court held that because the father had refused to do what the physician had strenuously and repeatedly advised, the father, and not the physician, had deprived the child of necessary attention. Thus, the physician was not liable for the resulting harm.

Although it is the patient's responsibility to follow the physician's advice, in some situations the patient may be unable to comprehend what he is being told. When the patient is incapable of full comprehension, but urgently requires a proposed treatment; and the physician knows (or should know) of the patient's impaired cognition, the physician's obligation to inform the patient of the necessity for the treatment does not end by simply advising the treatment. Depending on circumstances, such as the seriousness and the urgency of the situation, or the patient's mental incapacity, a physician may be obligated to take whatever steps are necessary to bring about a patient's understanding of the care and treatment required. This may necessitate that the physician communicate with and advise the spouse or other responsible persons who are available, competent, and in a position to speak for the patient.

Steele v. Woods. A thirty-three-year-old patient underwent a varicose vein operation under general anesthesia in which the great saphenous veins were injected with a sclerosing agent. Immediately after recovery from the anesthetic, impairment of circulation to the patient's lower extremity caused her intense pain. Her physician recommended a paravertebral sympathetic block to improve the compromised circulation. Because of her suffering and the administration of drugs, she was unable to comprehend the seriousness of her condition from the conversation with her physician. The physician tried to explain things to her, but indicated that "she was pretty much hysterical at times." As a result of her confused condition, she refused to undergo the sympathetic block. The husband, who was present in the hospital, was not consulted about the need for the procedure. Eventually vascular gangrene developed requiring amputation of her toes. The patient sued the physician charging that his negligent inaction caused the partial loss of her foot.

The physician contended that the patient's vascular gangrene and subsequent disability resulted from her refusal to submit to a postoperative paravertebral block; therefore, she contributed to her own injury. The patient countered this contention by charging that the physician negligently failed to advise her of the need for such a procedure. She testified that she did not even remember her physician asking her about a sympathetic block.

The court stated that the patient's testimony indicated that the physician did not discuss the block with her at any time when she was capable of understanding him. The treatment was needed, and a reasonable, careful physician should have advised it. The court concluded that the physician had failed to discuss a sympathetic block with the patient at any interval when the patient was sufficiently in possession of her mental faculties; therefore the physician did not advise the procedure at a time when the patient was capable of understanding, remembering, and heeding that advice.

The court cautioned, however, that a physician would not necessarily become liable because he could not convince or persuade a temporarily incompetent patient to accept his recommended treatment. Nevertheless it declared that a physician's duty to advise and treat requires him to make further effort to communicate with such a patient at a more propitious time or to communicate with the spouse or someone in a position of authority, as the circumstances demanded or opportunity permitted.

A patient's lack of ability to understand given advice or instructions (and therefore effectively comply with them to avoid injury) may also be predicated on the physician's failure to give advice or instructions in a clear and unambiguous manner.

Martineau v. Nelson.   Because of the patient's chronic tension state, which was exacerbated by her fourth pregnancy, her family physician certified that it would be "medically unwise" for her to have future pregnancies. Therefore, he referred her to a surgeon who, at the time of delivery of her child performed a bilateral tubal ligation. The pathologist reported that one section of tissue submitted as a specimen of the right salpinx was in fact a cross section of an artery. The family physician and the surgeon concluded from the pathology report that the ligation was unsuccessful, but decided that a hysterosalpingogram was necessary to determine whether the right tube had nonetheless been effectively blocked by the surgical suturing. After that study was completed both physicians concluded from a review of the x-rays that both Fallopian tubes were blocked.

The physicians then arranged a conference to discuss this situation with the patient. The family physician told the patient that he felt, based on the hysterosalpingogram, that both tubes were blocked. Although he neither recommended nor advised against a second operation, he did comment on the disadvantages of a second operation, such as additional expense and risk of injury. He also stated that he "preferred not to do this if he did not have to." In addition, he offered a free vasectomy for her husband as an alternative because it could be done in his office without any risk or expense.

The surgeon, on the other hand, advised the patient that he saw no need for a second operation or a vasectomy unless she and her husband had "any qualms or uneasy feelings about it, or there was any doubt in their minds." The physicians then asked the patient what she wanted to do. The patient replied that, although she wanted to think and talk about it, she thought she was going to "decide to go with the way things are."

The patient had a different recollection of the conference. She perceived that the physicians told her that they felt the tubal ligation had been successful and that she would not be able to get pregnant. It was her understanding that the free vasectomy was offered if she and her husband felt uneasy in their marital relations.

No operation or sterilization procedure was performed. Subsequently, the patient became pregnant. She and her husband then sued the physicians for negligently causing an unwanted fifth pregnancy. The physicians responded that the patient and her husband negligently contributed to causing the pregnancy by failing to use contraceptives or to undergo further sterilization procedures. After hearing the evidence at trial, the jury apportioned causative negligence on a fifty-fifty basis between the physicians and the patient. This determination led to an appeal by the patient.

The appellate court pointed out that ordinarily a patient is not considered to be negligent if the patient refuses to submit to a second procedure which is intended to correct the result of the physician's negligent initial treatment. Thus, the relevant issue became whether, and to what extent, the patient and her husband acted unreasonably in the face of certain statements and advice of her physicians. The court noted that the only evidence of the husband's conduct was that he concluded his wife could not become pregnant and he elected not to have a vasectomy. He did not receive any advice directly from the physicians nor did he act unreasonably in arriving at his conclusion. Moreover, the court found that it would be unreasonable for the law to compel a husband, who might possibly remarry and later change his mind regarding more children, to undergo sterilization because of a surgeon's negligence.

The court concluded that the following factors contributed to the unwanted pregnancy: the surgeon's failure to properly perform a tubal ligation; the physicians' equivocal statements to the patient regarding her tubes being blocked (with one physician encouraging vasectomy while the other encouraged further procedures if she and her husband would feel uneasy about marital relations); and, the patient's election not to undergo further sterilization procedures. Focusing on the patient's conduct, the court noted she was confronted with evidence indicating the removal of a segment of an artery rather than Fallopian tube and with equivocation by her physicians about the success of the operation and the necessity of further procedures. Under such circumstances, she might have acted unreasonably in failing to suggest that her husband have a vasectomy or in failing to continue a regimen of birth control. However, the court concluded that she was not negligent in failing to have a second operation because neither of her physicians were affirmatively recommending additional surgery. Moreover, neither physician directly informed her that she was capable of becoming pregnant again. The court held that under these circumstances, the patient could not be held equally negligent with the physicians because the subject matter of the negligence was the interpretation of medical matters about which the physicians owed a greater duty to the patient than she owed to herself. The superior knowledge and skill of the physicians should have been reflected in straightforward, accurate information and advice to their patient. Thus the court concluded that the patient should not be completely denied recovery for her legal injury because she could not sift from their equivocation this kind of information and advice.

A patient's conduct may remotely affect or contribute to a medical condition which eventually requires medical treatment. If a physician's subsequent supervening negligence causes a complication of that medical condition, the patient's prior negligent conduct is not usually a legal cause of the patient's ultimate injury, and therefore is not available as a defense in a malpractice case against the physician.

Matthews v. Williford. In 1960 the patient had a myocardial infarction and was advised by his physician to discontinue smoking and to lose weight. In spite of this advice and warning, he continued to smoke and he remained overweight. In May 1970 he began to experience chest pains and shortness of breath, and consulted his physician. An EKG did not demonstrate evidence of active cardiac disease. His symptoms increased in frequency and severity, and in late October he telephoned a physician, who had not previously cared for him, to arrange for a checkup because of progressive and persistent chest pain. The physician said he would make arrangements for the patient to be evaluated in the hospital. Within two hours of this conversation, the patient telephoned back asking the physician to wait until the following week to admit him to the hospital. The following week, the man's wife telephoned the physician requesting medication for the chest pain, nausea, and abdominal discomfort her husband was experiencing. No mention was made of shortness of breath. Three days later, the wife called the physician advising him of her husband's chest pain, shortness of breath, and prior heart attack. The physician immediately arranged for the hospitalization of the patient, but he did not order continuous monitoring in the Coronary Care Unit, nor did he come into the hospital and examine the patient. In the early morning hours of the following day, the patient died of a myocardial infarction. Thereupon, the patient's wife sued the physician for malpractice in the management of a myocardial infarction, and the resultant wrongful death of her husband.

Expert medical testimony established that the physician did not meet the requisite standard of care under the circumstances because he did not make an admitting diagnosis by taking a detailed history and performing a timely examination of the patient. Under the circumstances the physician should have assumed on admission that the patient was having a myocardial infarction, or that one was imminent. Expert testimony indicated that the patient should have been placed immediately in the Cardiac Care Unit; an intravenous line should have been established; a cardiac monitor should have been installed; cardiac medications should have been commenced; and the defibrillator, ready to be utilized, should have been alongside the bed, with trained nurses available to utilize it in the event of a life-threatening arrhythmia.

The physician contended that the negligence of the patient played a part in the patient's death, and therefore constituted a defense to the malpractice suit against him. He argued that noncompliance and violation of the prior physician's instructions given to the patient in the course of treatment was misconduct, which contributed as a cause of the patient's death. The court pointed out that the wife's malpractice suit was not claiming legal damages for the patient's heart attack. The damages claimed were for the loss of life expectancy of the patient if he had survived, together with damages for the wrongful death, not for the occurrence of the heart attack. Thus, any conduct on the part of the patient contributing to the heart attack was not a legal cause of the damages sought by the wife.

The court noted that the patient's negligent conduct occurred prior to the patient's coming under the care of the physician. Conduct of the patient prior to an injury is not significant in a lawsuit for damages unless it is a legal cause of the injury, as distinguished from a cause of the remote conditions (such as cigarette smoking), which set the occasion for the later negligence of an attending physician. Thus, a patient's conduct may have contributed to his medical condition, for which he subsequently receives negligent medical treatment and resultant injury. However, that conduct is unavailable as a defense to a physician's negligence which causes a distinct subsequent injury, as in this case, the ultimate injury—death of the patient.

Although the patient has a duty to comply with the attending physician's instructions about follow-up care, as the following cases illustrate, failure to do so may not necessarily bar recovery for the physician's negligence, unless the noncompliance is concurrent with, and contributive to, the physician's negligence.

Blair v. Eblen.   A man severely injured his hand in an industrial accident. He was given emergency treatment by a general practitioner and kept under the physician's care for a week. When an infection developed, the patient was eventually referred to an orthopedic surgeon, and the infection was controlled, but not before it became necessary to amputate several fingers. Both physicians then recommended rehabilitation therapy, but the patient did not perform the recommended exercises and, therefore, was left with a poor functional result. The patient then sued both the general practitioner and the orthopedist for loss of the use of his hand.

The physicians contended that rehabilitation and functionally restorative efforts were unsuccessful because the patient did not perform the recommended exercises. Thus they charged that the patient thereby negligently contributed to the dysfunction of his hand.

The court pointed out that a patient's negligence which occurs *after* a physician's malpractice does not bar recovery by the patient, but only mitigates the nature and scope of the damages. In order to bar recovery a patient's negligence must be *concurrent* with the physician's negligence, and must aggravate the condition by such behavior as walking on a cast when specifically instructed not to do so. Therefore, the physicians were responsible for the damage caused the patient by their negligence.

Bird v. Pritchard.   The patient lacerated the palmar aspect of her hand, injuring the ulnar nerve. She was taken to a community hospital where she asked to be treated by a certain surgeon. Because the surgeon was unavailable, she agreed to be treated by a general practitioner. Although she complained to the physician that the fourth and fifth fingers of the injured hand were numb, he simply cleaned the wound and instructed her to return three days later. The patient did not return for the follow-up appointment. Several weeks later, she consulted the previously sought surgeon and he diagnosed the nerve injury. A surgical repair was undertaken, but the patient was left with permanent dysfunction of her hand. She sued the general practitioner and charged that he had been negligent in failing to properly treat the injured nerve.

The physician contended the patient's failure to return for the follow-up appointment had negligently contributed to her injury. The patient countered this contention by presenting the testimony of the surgeon who attempted to repair the nerve that the surgical repair should have been performed within six to eight hours after injury in order to be fully effective. On the basis of this testimony, the court found that her failure to return in three days could not have contributed to the injury. The court pointed out that, by failing to operate or refer immediately, the general practitioner had insured the repair could not be performed until after the swelling and edema around the wound had resolved, thus preventing complete restoration of nerve function. Thus, by asking the patient to return three days later, the general practitioner precluded an effective repair. Therefore, the court concluded the patient did not contribute to the injury by her failure to keep her appointment.

The physician-patient relationship assumes the patient's confidence in the capacity and skill of the physician. Because a patient is not expected to distrust the attending physician, the patient is not required to set his judgment against that of the medical expert who has been employed for treatment, or to appeal to other physicians to ascertain if the physician is properly performing his duty to the patient. The law requires an extraordinary set of facts to hold a patient, possessed of no medical skill, contributorily negligent for an injury simply because the physician's word is accepted and the prescribed treatment followed.

Los Alamos Medical Center v. Coe.   Mrs. Coe underwent a hysterectomy. During her convalescence, she experienced severe pain and therefore was administered morphine frequently. Because she continued to complain of severe pains after her discharge from the hospital, her family asked the physician about the possibility of having pain-relieving medication administered to Mrs. Coe at home. This arrangement was agreeable to the physician. Therefore, her husband, children, and Mrs. Coe herself, all administered morphine to her by hypodermic injections in order to alleviate her pain. Over a three-month period her physician did not visit or treat her except to perform two follow-up pelvic examinations. During this period, when Mrs. Coe would complain of pain, her family would telephone the physician and he would issue a prescription for morphine to be administered for relief of pain as needed. The family was to be the judge of the need. Mrs. Coe received prescriptions for morphine or Demerol on many occasions; each time the quantity ranged from ten to thirty doses. At some point, Mrs. Coe began to use the medication for "nervousness" and "just to feel good." To obtain a prescription, she frequently complained of pain when none was present. Her family became apprehensive of her behavior and discussed the possibility of addiction with her physician. He assured them that they had no cause for alarm because, as he stated, her pain was so severe it would "counteract the effect of the morphine." He explained, moreover, that he felt since she was improving physically, she would have less future need for the medication.

Finally, her family decided that she was not recovering properly from her illness and consulted a surgeon to seek his advice concerning her clinical progress and the cause of her persistent abdominal pain. This physician performed an exploratory operation, which disclosed adhesions and partial intestinal obstruction. After corrective surgery, Mrs. Coe's tolerance to pain was so low that it aroused the surgeon's suspicion about her use of narcotics. When he determined she had been using morphine about every three hours, day and night, he confronted Mrs. Coe with the issue. Mrs. Coe then confided in him the amount of morphine she had taken over the past several months. At his request, she undertook a program of withdrawal from the narcotics.

The patient then sued her family physician for causing her addiction. She charged that, instead of attempting to discover the cause of her pain and relieving it, he continually gave her morphine to palliate her discomfort, with the result that she became an addict. The family physician contended that all morphine prescribed or administered by him was made upon the insistent demands of her family who were responding to the patient's pretenses. He argued that if he were negligent, Mrs. Coe and her family were contributorily negligent and a substantial cause of her injuries.

The court pointed out that the family had a right to rely upon the physician's instructions and his superior medical knowledge. Neither the family nor the patient was obligated to determine at what point addiction would begin. Nor were they obligated, at any time before addiction became a fact, to cease to rely upon the attending physician's knowledge regarding the amount of the drug that could safely be taken over a given period of time. They were not required to consult other physicians to determine if the physician really possessed the requisite knowledge and skill because they had not become fully aware that the physician had not been providing proper treatment.

SECTION 2: PHYSICIAN REACTION TO NONCOMPLIANT PATIENT

As previously mentioned, the law recognizes that a patient, by virtue of his illness or injury, is not expected to comport himself in the same reasonable manner as when he is well. A physician is expected to appreciate this aspect of illness and the effect it may have on the patient's ability to cooperate with his physician's therapeutic efforts. Therefore, even when a patient's unacceptable behavior impedes his own clinical recovery or disturbs other patients, a physician is not allowed to react to the patient's noncooperation by disciplining him in a manner that constitutes a battery.

Magma Copper Co. v. Shuster. While Mr. Shuster was a hospital patient receiving rehabilitative therapy, he had several quarrelsome meetings with Dr. Hicks, the medical director of the hospital, regarding his (Shuster's) behavior. Shortly thereafter Shuster was moved from the room he shared with other patients to an unoccupied room because he kept causing disturbing commotions. The following day, Dr. Hicks went to Shuster's room to dis-

cuss the fact that the patient had not been cooperating with hospital personnel and had been violating hospital regulations. During a heated exchange,
while Shuster was sitting propped up in his bed, Dr. Hicks spontaneously
struck Shuster on the mouth. He gave the following reasons for striking
Shuster:

> I didn't like the language that Mr. Shuster was using, particularly in
> front of the nurse . . . I thought if Shuster was acting like a child, if I
> treated him like a child, like I would my son, if I popped him in the
> mouth, he would not use the words again. Shuster was startled. He set-
> tled down. He quit swearing. We finished our conversation and I left.

Dr. Hicks stated that he bore no hostility toward Shuster other than "his
using four-letter words in front of the nurses."

Two days later in the hospital physical therapy department, Dr. Hicks
applied painful pressure with his thumb to Shuster's injured knee during
the course of a physical examination. Thereafter Shuster brought a legal action against the physician seeking compensatory and punitive damages for
battery.

Dr. Hicks contended that there was no evidence of malice to support
the submission of the punitive damages. The court, however, noted that
malice may be implied from the nature of the acts of the physician and the
circumstances in which they occurred. The court held that even if this act
were spontaneous, it represented a battery performed while carrying out his
professional duties; as such, it was subject to punitive damages.

A physician cannot reasonably expect even a well patient to act with a high
degree of responsibility regarding treatment decisions unless he is informed
of the consequences of acceptance or rejection of treatment proposed by the
physician. Although a patient must ultimately decide which treatment to undergo, he is not expected to shoulder the burden of refusal unless adequately
informed of the consequences. Thus, a physician who recommends an appropriate test but fails to inform the patient of the risks entailed in refusing
to follow his advice, may be liable for an injury resulting from the patient's
refusal to take the test, if a reasonably prudent person in the patient's position would not have refused the test had he been adequately informed of the
significant perils of refusal.

Truman v. Thomas.   Between 1963 and 1969, a young woman frequently
sought medical advice and often discussed personal matters with her family
physician, Dr. Thomas. During this period when Dr. Thomas told the
woman that she should have a complete physical examination, particularly
a Pap smear, she either declined by saying she just "didn't feel like it," or in
other ways would put off his suggestion, limiting her requests for medical

attention to her most immediate health problems. Dr. Thomas never explained or specifically informed her of the purpose of the Pap smear or of the risk involved in declining to undergo the test. He believed that any intelligent woman of childbearing age was aware of the purpose of a Pap smear.

In April 1969, the woman consulted a urologist about the persistence of symptoms referrable to a urinary tract infection which had been treated previously by Dr. Thomas. While examining the patient, the urologist became concerned about the condition of the patient's cervix, and advised her to see a gynecologist as soon as possible. When the patient did not make an appointment with a gynecologist, the urologist made an appointment for her. In October 1969, the gynecologist consultant diagnosed carcinoma of the cervix, too far advanced to be removed by surgery. The tumor was unsuccessfully treated by other methods and the patient died in 1970.

The patient's two children sued Dr. Thomas for failure to perform a Pap smear test on their mother between 1964 and 1969. Expert testimony indicated that if the patient had undergone a Pap smear, cervical carcinoma probably would have been detected in time to save her life. Expert testimony indicated that the standard of medical practice required a physician to explain to women patients that the importance of having a Pap smear each year is to pick up early lesions that are treatable, rather than have to deal with more advanced tumors that often are not treatable. Dr. Thomas conceded at the trial that it was the accepted standard of practice for physicians in his community to recommend that women of childbearing age undergo a Pap smear each year. Dr. Thomas also testified that on at least two occasions when he performed a pelvic examination on the patient, she refused him permission to perform a Pap smear, stating that she could not afford the cost of the test. Dr. Thomas said he offered to defer payment, but the patient said she wanted to pay cash. He testified that he did not "go through all of the different lectures about cancer" because he felt that such information was widely known, and that the generally accepted manner of treatment was to expect the patient to act with a high degree of responsibility. Dr. Thomas contended that practicing physicians were not enforcers, but advisors of medical care.

The court pointed out that the scope of an attending physician's duty to disclose medical information to a patient in discussing proposed medical procedures is determined by the following basic characteristics of the physician-patient relationship and the presumption that a patient is unlearned in the medical sciences: first, except in rare cases, the patient and physician are not in parity in the knowledge regarding medical science; second, an adult patient has the right to determine whether to submit to medical treatment, and therefore his consent to treatment must be secured; third, to be effective, a patient's consent must be informed; and fourth, a patient has abject dependence upon and trust in his attending physician for the information upon which he relies during the decisional process, thus raising an obligation in the physician that transcends "arm's-length" transactions common in conventional contractual relationships.

In light of these factors, the court concluded that an integral part of the physician's overall obligation to the patient is to reasonably disclose the available choices of a proposed therapy and the dangers inherently and potentially involved in each. The physician should give all information that he knows, or should know, would be regarded as significant by a reasonable person in the patient's position when deciding to accept or reject the recommended procedure. Ordinarily, a fact that is commonly appreciated is not required to be disclosed to the patient; however, if the physician knows, or should know, of the patient's lack of familiarity with medical procedures, the physician's scope of required disclosure may be expanded. Thus, a patient must be apprised not only of the risks inherent in the proposed procedure, but also the risks of a decision not to undergo the treatment. Thus, when a patient indicates that he is going to *decline* a risk-free test, a physician may have the additional duty of advising the patient of material risks a reasonable patient would want to be informed about before deciding not to undergo the procedure; and also of explaining the potential consequences of declining to follow the recommended course of action.

Dr. Thomas contended that the physician's duty of disclosure applied only where the patient consents to the recommended procedure, because a physician's advice may be presumed to be founded on an expert appraisal of the patient's medical needs and, therefore, no reasonable patient would fail to undertake further inquiry before rejecting such advice. He argued therefore that a patient who rejects his physician's advice should shoulder the burden of inquiry as to the possible consequences of his decision.

Disapproving Dr. Thomas' contention, the court pointed out that the duty of disclosure was imposed so that a patient might meaningfully exercise his right to make treatment decisions. Thus, the need for disclosure is not lessened because a patient rejects a recommended procedure. Moreover, a decision to reject a physician's advice does not alter the "fiducial qualities" of the physician-patient relationship, because patients who reject a procedure are as unskilled in the medical sciences as those who consent. The court concluded that if a patient who rejects his physician's advice had the burden of inquiring as to the potential consequences of his decision regarding medical care, the duty of disclosure would be contradicted.

The court reasoned that in advising treatment, Dr. Thomas was not engaged in an "arm's-length" contractual transaction with his patient, and thus was obligated to provide her with all the information material to the decision of whether to undergo a Pap smear test. However, he never specifically informed her of the purpose of a Pap smear, even though she was not aware of the serious danger entailed in refusing to undergo the test. Thus, she was not truly informed of the important potential consequences when she declined the test because of its cost, or because she "just didn't feel like it." Therefore, the court concluded that when the patient refused the test, Dr. Thomas had a duty to inform her of the danger of that decision, because it was unreasonable for him to assume that she appreciated the potentially fatal consequences of her conduct.

A physician may be legally justified in striking a patient in self-defense. Even in that situation, however, he is expected to reasonably anticipate and avoid the possibility that an uncooperative patient reaction might place him in a position where he is required to strike a patient in self-defense.

Mattocks v. Bell. A twenty-three-month-old child was taken to the hospital by her mother for treatment of a lacerated tongue. As the physician attempted to examine the child's mouth, the child clamped her teeth on his finger and bit hard enough to draw blood. The physician shouted to the child to open her mouth, but she retained her grip on the finger. He twice unsuccessfully attempted to extricate his finger by forcing a tongue depressor into her mouth. He then slapped the child on the cheek with his other hand. This caused her to open her mouth and release the finger. The child, through its mother, sued the physician for battery.

The mother of the child contended that when the physician, without authorization, intentionally slapped the child, a battery was proved which entitled the child to a recovery unless justification was established. She further contended that there was not evidence of a justification. The physician contended that although his action may have been rash, it was not malicious; and the blow was not severe.

In analyzing the facts of the case, the court cited a similar case in which a four-year-old child sued a physician who slapped her leg severely several times in an attempt to make her lie still in order to remove sutures from her toe. In that case, the child was allowed to recover damages because the physician had used "exceedingly bad judgment." However, the court found that case distinguishable because in the present case there was "poor or hasty judgment" instead of "exceedingly bad judgment," and an emergency situation existed. In the other case the slaps were in the nature of *discipline*, whereas, in the present case, the single slap was more a protective or *defensive* measure and, therefore, was justifiable under the circumstances.

SECTION 3: COUNTERSUITS AGAINST THE PATIENT

The patient (and the patient's attorney) is expected to have a reasonable basis for a legal action against an attending physician. If, however, there is no reasonable basis for the suit, several options may be available to the physician as illustrated by the following materials. First, the physician may attempt to have the suit dismissed at the trial by proving that it is frivolous or fraudulent. Second, the physician may attempt to sue the patient's attorney for negligence in bringing a groundless suit. Third, the physician, usually following the conclusion of the malpractice suit against him, may countersue the patient (and the attorney) for malicious prosecution or abuse of process.

Defense to Suit
When charged with a frivolous or fraudulent malpractice suit, a physician may elect to present evidence to prove his contention at the trial for malpractice.

Sanden v. Mayo Clinic.   A patient sued her attending surgeon alleging that he had negligently performed a radical hemorrhoidectomy on her; and that as a result her anal sphincter was irreparably injured, causing her permanent incontinence of the feces, as well as other disabilities. At trial the surgeon introduced evidence that the patient, who was a nurse, and her attorney (who was also her boyfriend) had planned to bring this lawsuit even before she had submitted to surgery; that she had faked the disabilities purportedly resulting from that surgery; and that she had attempted to introduce at trial fraudulent evidence to substantiate those disabilities. The surgeon contended that the evidence proved that the patient-plaintiff's injuries were feigned and that the lawsuit was no more than a scheme for financial gain.

In order to test the validity of the surgeon's contentions, the court ordered the patient-plaintiff to submit to an examination including an electromyographic study of her anal sphincter. After the tests had been completed, an expert witness testified that the electromyograph indicated that the muscles and nerves in question were normal, and that any abnormal reactions displayed by the patient-plaintiff were the result of her purposeful efforts to determine the outcome of the test. As a result of this evidence, the court rejected all of the patient-plaintiff's allegations that surgery had been negligently performed on her.

Malicious Prosecution
When a physician has successfully defended what is shown to be a wholly groundless suit, he may be able to establish a countersuit for malicious prosecution. It should be noted, however, that it is difficult for a physician to prevail in a suit for malicious prosecution because of the public policy against deterring free access to legal remedies. Subjecting a patient to suit for bringing a malpractice suit against the physician would, arguably, deter patients from using the court system to seek relief.

In a suit for malicious prosecution, the physician must prove that the malpractice suit was initiated without probable cause and brought with malice—that is, that the primary motive in bringing the suit was ill will, and that there was a lack of belief in any possible success of the action. In some jurisdictions, the countersuing physician must prove that "special" damages were incurred as a result of the malicious prosecution.

The cases in this subsection explore the issues of probable cause, malice, and special damages.

1. *Probable Cause*

Whether the facts in a particular malpractice case are sufficient to constitute a reasonable basis to sue, or "probable cause," is sometimes determined by a "reasonable man test"; that is, given the appearances of the facts which were presented to the patient (and his attorney), would a reasonably prudent person have sued the physician for malpractice.

Carrol v. Kalar. Mr. Kalar, while in the course of his employment, sustained an injury to his right wrist that was diagnosed as traumatic synovitis by his personal physician. Treatment of the condition did not bring about a satisfactory result. Eventually Kalar consulted an orthopedic surgeon who treated the wrist as a possible fracture of the navicular bone. After several weeks of treatment without demonstrable improvement, Kalar was referred to the "Hand Board" of the state Industrial Commission. This board consisted of physicians specializing in the treatment of hand, wrist, and arm injuries who advised the Industrial Commission about the injured worker's condition, and also determined the percent of disability from an injury.

Dr. Carroll, one of the specialists advising the board, examined Kalar and reviewed x-rays of his wrist that had been taken six months earlier. He concluded that Kalar had degenerative joint disease and synovitis. Based on Dr. Carroll's opinion, the board recommended surgery and, depending upon the findings at surgery, the removal of the synovium and/or a fusion of the wrist. Surgery was performed in which part of the navicular was removed, and a piece of bone taken from Kalar's iliac crest was fused with the lunate and distal radius. The fusion was unsuccessful and two additional operations were required. As a result, Kalar consulted an attorney to represent him in a malpractice suit.

The attorney discussed the case with Dr. Martin, a physician practicing in the area. Dr. Martin examined Kalar's medical records and his x-rays, including those examined by the "Hand Board." He indicated to the attorney that he believed that in recommending surgery, Dr. Carroll had deviated from the required standard of care. Kalar's attorney then filed a malpractice suit against Dr. Carroll.

When Dr. Carroll received notice of the suit he countersued both Kalar and his attorney for malicious prosecution. He contended the malpractice case against him was initiated without probable cause. During the pretrial discovery phase of the countersuit, Kalar's expert witness, Dr. Martin, was deposed by Dr. Carroll's attorney and asked the following questions:

Q. Were you asked to state any opinion concerning the care and treatment given by Dr. Carroll, and whether or not that treatment fell below any applicable standard of care?

A. I felt that from the standards that I know in the practice of medicine, that if it were a navicular fracture, it was not treated properly.

Q. When you said "not treated properly," in other words the fusion was not indicated?

A. Not only that, the radiologist recommended another diagnostic x-ray study which was not done and which could have determined whether or not aseptic necrosis or a fracture actually did exist. Tomographs of the wrist could have determined bone density and whether or not there was a fracture. Six months ensued from the time the last series of x-rays were made. At that time it was equivocal in the radiologist's mind whether or not a fracture existed. I think that is not acceptable medical practice that the man had six months worth of no treatment. The fracture, if it were there, could have healed during that time without subjecting him to surgery and fusion of the wrist. That's the basis for my opinion.

Mr. Kalar's attorney asked Dr. Martin the following questions:

Q. Do you recall my telling you at the time Dr. Carroll made the recommendation for surgery on Mr. Kalar's wrist, it had been six months since x-rays had been made?

A. Yes.

Q. And my asking you whether under those circumstances it would be good medical practice to make a recommendation for surgery without having current x-rays?

A. My opinion was it was not good medical practice.

The court pointed out that a medical expert in this case indicated that there was a possibility that a bony union could have occurred during the time between the last x-rays and the board's recommendation for surgery. This suggested the possibility that conservative therapy could have been used which would, in the opinion of Dr. Martin, have made surgery unnecessary. When these opinions are coupled with Dr. Martin's opinion that Dr. Carroll's reliance on x-rays six months old was not proper practice, they demonstrate that Kalar and his attorney had probable cause to believe that a medical malpractice suit would properly lie against Dr. Carroll. The court concluded that a reasonable man faced with such facts could and probably would have brought suit.

Although a patient (and his attorney) must have probable cause for bringing a malpractice suit against a physician, they need not be certain of the propriety of proceeding with the suit to establish reasonable grounds for instituting the suit. Sufficient probable cause exists if the suit is based on the honest belief there are reasonable grounds, even if such belief turns out to be unfounded.

Ammerman v. Newman. A neurosurgeon recommended that his patient undergo a pneumoencephalogram. He informed his patient on several occasions of the risks inherent in the procedure and obtained the patient's written authorization. In addition, a physician who was not professionally affiliated with the neurosurgeon also informed the patient of the attendant risks of the pneumoencephalogram. Shortly after the patient underwent the procedure he died while still under the neurosurgeon's care. His widow retained two attorneys, one of whom was her son-in-law, to determine if there were any grounds for a malpractice case against the neurosurgeon. The attorneys requested a physician to review the adequacy of the care which the patient had received. The reviewer informed them that death could occur as a result of a pneumoencephalogram without malpractice. He did not address the issue of the neurosurgeon's duty to disclose certain information to the patient to obtain an informed consent for the procedure. A recent appellate case in the jurisdiction had addressed the issue of the physician's duty of disclosure inherent in the doctrine of informed consent. The judicial decision declared that the legal adequacy of a physician's communications to his patient must be measured by the patient's need for the information to make an informed choice regarding the proposed procedure. Under this reasoning, expert testimony was not necessary on the question of a physician's duty of disclosure; lay witness testimony could establish a physician's failure to disclose both specific risk information and the patient's lack of knowledge. Relying on this case, the widow and her attorneys did not heed the reviewer's opinion that a malpractice suit against the neurosurgeon was unwarranted. They believed the rationale of the recent appellate case would sustain them even where the facts of the case indicated a disclosure of risk had been made. They reasoned accordingly because it was unclear whether the patient had given a knowing acceptance of the risks of the procedure. Therefore, they brought suit against the neurosurgeon, alleging that he had negligently failed to obtain an informed consent for the performance of a pneumoencephalogram.

At trial, the surgeon obtained a directed verdict in his favor. He then brought a malicious prosecution suit against the widow and her attorneys. The court pointed out that in order for the surgeon to prevail, he must show that there was no "probable cause" to bring a malpractice action against him. The court defined "probable cause" as "reason supported by facts and circumstances that will warrant a cautious patient to believe his legal action, and the means taken in prosecuting it, are legally just and proper." The court noted that "probable cause" does not mean the patient has to have a legally sufficient cause to bring a malpractice action against his physician. Probable cause does not depend on the actual case in fact, but upon the honest and reasonable belief of the patient instituting the suit, even if that belief turns out to be unfounded. The court concluded that although the widow and her attorneys did not prevail on the issue of informed consent, their position was not patently unreasonable in light of the evolution and development of the informed consent doctrine at the time the suit was filed.

The courts have not recognized that an attorney who represents a client who is suing a physician for malpractice has a duty of due care to the physician in instituting and maintaining a malpractice suit against him. Notwithstanding this, an attorney's failure to exercise prudence in commencing a suit may constitute evidence that he lacked probable cause to bring the suit against the physician.

Drasin v. Raine. In July 1975 Mr. Browning suffered a massive heart attack at his home. He was taken, unconscious, to the hospital. Following resuscitative treatment, he was examined in the emergency room by Dr. Fitzpatrick, who discovered an injury to Browning's shoulder. He ordered x-rays of the shoulder. Dr. Drasin, a radiologist, read the x-rays and reported that the shoulder was fractured. Dr. Fitzpatrick then called in Dr. Fadel, an orthopedic surgeon, to treat the shoulder.

After his discharge from the hospital, Browning contacted an attorney, Mr. Raine, regarding a possible malpractice suit for the fracture of his shoulder. In September 1975 Raine visited the hospital and reviewed Browning's medical records which clearly showed that the shoulder fracture occurred before Drs. Drasin and Fadel were involved in the care of Browning.

In November 1975 a complaint was filed against the hospital for allegedly "breaking Browning's shoulder." Raine prepared the complaint, but because he represented a local hospital he did not want to sign the complaint. At Raine's request an attorney associate, who rented space in Raine's office, signed the complaint without reading it or investigating any of the facts.

In March 1976 the attorneys served interrogatories on the hospital, the answers to which revealed that neither Dr. Fadel nor Dr. Drasin was an employee of the hospital, and that the physicians became involved in the case of Browning after the shoulder injury was discovered. In May 1976, when the deposition of Dr. Fitzpatrick was taken, he clearly told the attorneys that the injury occurred before he saw Browning in the emergency room, and that after he discovered the injury, he then called in Drs. Fadel and Drasin.

In spite of this clear and cumulative evidence, in July 1976 Raine filed an amended complaint (signed by his associate), in which Dr. Fadel and Dr. Drasin were joined as defendants, charging them with malpractice for "negligently and carelessly breaking Browning's shoulder." When they received the summons, Drs. Fadel and Drasin contacted their liability insurance carrier, who employed a local attorney to defend the two physicians in the lawsuit. Based on the information given to Raine by this defense attorney (which was similar to that already in Raine's possession), Raine voluntarily entered an order which dismissed the malpractice suit against Drs. Fadel and Drasin. This dismissal did not involve or include any compromise or settlement of the lawsuit.

As soon as Drs. Fadel and Drasin were dismissed from the malpractice suit, they filed a countersuit against Raine charging him with malicious prosecution and abuse of legal process. At the trial both physicians testified as to their embarrassment, humiliation, mortification, and mental anguish at having been publicly accused of malpractice. Dr. Fadel testified that he suffered an acute anxiety reaction. Both physicians stated that the malpractice accusation (even though specious), became a permanent part of their professional and insurance records. It was established at trial that there was no evidence to implicate Drs. Fadel and Drasin, and that Raine had access to and was aware of this fact before he filed the malpractice action against these two physicians.

The deposition of a member of the Ethics Committee of the local Bar Association was introduced to the jury to show a key element of a malicious prosecution action, namely, lack of "probable cause." In the opinion of this bar member, the actions of Raine did not comply with the standard of care for an ordinary and prudent lawyer because he brought a suit without probable cause, that is, without grounds that would induce an ordinarily prudent attorney to believe that the person sued for malpractice had committed the act charged.

The court pointed out that the attorney's failure to investigate the facts and law prior to filing of the malpractice suit was material to the determination whether the attorney had "probable cause" to bring the suit. The court declared that prior to filing the malpractice action, an attorney is obligated to act in a prudent manner. In addition, an attorney is obligated not to file a suit without probable cause. The court concluded that a physician who countersues an attorney who has brought a malpractice suit against him cannot recover damages unless the attorney breaches *both* duties: the prerequisite duty of "probable cause" in addition to the requirement of "prudence or ordinary care." The duty of ordinary care is not owed to the physicians in the sense of a negligence case, but rather is owed in establishing probable cause (or lack thereof) for bringing the suit against the physician.

2. *Malice*

In instituting a malpractice suit against a physician, the patient-plaintiff's attorney must show that the physician was at fault. If the attorney prosecutes a malpractice suit knowing the charge of fault is false, or with reckless disregard as to whether it is false, it may be inferred that the attorney acted with malice toward the physician. If, in addition, the attorney's theory underlying the malpractice suit is so improbable that merely bringing the suit indicates malice, the physician may have grounds for a successful countersuit against the attorney. Notwithstanding these principles, courts vary in their determination of the sufficiency of evidence necessary to establish malicious conduct.

Spencer v. Burglass. The surgeon performed an indicated operation on a child in February 1968. The procedure was successful and no complications were noted. In February 1969, several days before the statute of limitations period would have ended for a claim based on the surgery, an attorney filed a malpractice suit against the surgeon, charging her with "negligence in operating upon the child and in causing damage to the child's body."

In April 1971, at the malpractice trial, the plaintiff's attorney called only two medical expert witnesses; neither of these witnesses was fully apprised of the facts of the case by the attorney prior to trial. In addition, the attorney had not determined whether the child had any demonstrable damages prior to trial. Both experts testified that the surgeon's treatment was proper, and that they could detect no injury to the child. Thereupon, the trial ended in judgment for the surgeon, who then countersued the attorney, charging that she was damaged by the attorney's failure to interview and consult with his expert witnesses prior to the filing of suit and prior to trial. She contended that the attorney had both filed and tried the medical malpractice suit against her without ever having established any medical expert evidence of malpractice, or any evidence of damage to the child's body. Moreover, she contended that the attorney's allegations of "negligence in operating" are of a kind that require some sort of expert medical testimony, unless the operation produced some self-evident anomalous result, such as amputation of the wrong leg. Although the surgeon allowed that the allegation of "damage to the child's body" might have been proved without medical evidence, she countered that the attorney did not even inquire into the child's alleged but nonexistent bodily damage. She argued further that although the attorney had no medical or nonmedical evidence of medical malpractice, he not only filed the suit but also tried the case. Thus she contended that the attorney had violated his duty to refrain from filing suits that have no basis in law or in fact. She claimed that he owed an affirmative duty to her and to the public to refrain from filing groundless litigation, and that he breached this duty by filing a frivolous suit.

The court noted that the gist of the surgeon's complaint was that three years had passed between filing and trying the suit, during which time the attorney should have informed himself of the facts of the case by obtaining medical or lay evidence which tended to support his claim. Had he sought evidence, he would have learned that there was no evidence of negligence or damage to the child. Had he learned this, he would have known that he was obligated by the general legal duty not to injure another, to withdraw from proceeding against the surgeon.

The court pointed out that, although the surgeon suggested the attorney breached a duty to her, her allegation really implied that the attorney had acted with malice and, therefore, her legal action was one for malicious prosecution. In such an action the surgeon had to show that the attorney had acted with malice. The court declared that malice can be found from the lack of concern with which an attorney prosecutes a malpractice action when no evidence exists that the physician was at fault. It may also be inferred by proving a lack of "probable cause" or arguable justification to bring the malpractice action. The court pointed out, however, that in order to charge an attorney with bringing a malicious malpractice suit, his theory underlying the suit must be so improbable that malice is indicated by the mere action of bringing or trying the unfounded suit. "Malice" for purposes of malicious prosecution exists where the malpractice charge against a physician is made with the attorney's knowledge that the charge is false, or with a reckless disregard as to whether it is false. The court noted that the surgeon's allegations were that the attorney simply did not know enough about the case at the time he filed and, therefore, he acted with malice. The court concluded that the attorney's failure to interview his witnesses or to obtain "competent medical advice" prior to trial did not constitute malice under the circumstances of this case. Therefore, it did not provide a basis for a malicious prosecution claim.

If an attorney institutes a meritless malpractice claim against a physician for the ulterior purpose of securing a nuisance settlement, he may be liable to the physician for abusing the legal process.

Bull v. McCuskey. In May an eighty-six-year-old woman was hospitalized following an automobile accident in which she had sustained fractures of the wrist, the patellas, and femur. She was also senile and uncooperative as a result of cerebrovascular and cardiac arteriosclerotic disease. Dr. McCuskey, an orthopedic surgeon, was called to take care of the woman's fractures, while other physicians managed her other disabilities. In August she was transferred to an extended care hospital, where she continued to be uncooperative and uncommunicative. When she developed bed sores on her hips and heels, her nephew, who had been appointed her guardian, dismissed Dr. McCuskey and replaced him with a Dr. Sargent. Soon after the substitution, the nephew asked Dr. Sargent whether his aunt's bed sores had been the result of malpractice by Dr. McCuskey and was told that Dr. McCuskey had not committed malpractice, and that her bed sores had resulted either from the patient's refusal or inability to follow directions, and were not traceable to any conduct by Dr. McCuskey.

In October the nephew contacted an attorney who then filed a legal action charging Dr. McCuskey with malpractice, and the extended care hospital with negligence. The complaint was filed on the basis of the nephew's statement that the condition of his aunt had greatly deteriorated, and upon photographs showing bed sores, which were taken by the attorney's assistant. Before filing suit, the attorney did not examine or obtain medical records from either hospital, nor did he confer with a physician to determine whether Dr. McCuskey deviated from the requisite standard of care. Neither did he submit his client's claim to a malpractice screening panel, established pursuant to an agreement between the county medical society and the county bar association, to obtain a determination of the merits of the case.

After filing suit, the attorney did not secure the deposition of Dr. McCuskey or of any physician. Furthermore, he did not even attempt to retain an expert witness for trial. Shortly before trial, the claim against the extended care hospital was settled for $750. Even though Dr. McCuskey also could have settled the claim against him for $750, he refused to authorize his malpractice insurance carrier to settle for any amount.

During trial, the attorney called Dr. McCuskey an incompetent "fumble-fingered," "liar," "scoundrel," and a "damned idiot." He also stated that Dr. McCuskey "will lie under oath, steal an elderly woman's redress, cheat if he can get away with it, and all that is left for him is to make a pact with the devil and murder those who would oppose him." The jury quickly returned its verdict for Dr. McCuskey. Then Dr. McCuskey commenced a countersuit against the attorney for abuse of the legal process, charging that he suffered emotional and mental distress.

Dr. McCuskey contended that the legal process (complaint and summons) charging him with malpractice was misused for the ulterior purpose of coercing a nuisance settlement. The court declared that abuse of process hinges on the misuse of regularly issued legal process in contrast to malicious prosecution which rests upon the wrongful *issuance* of legal process. The court pointed out that the two essential elements of a legal action for abuse of process are an ulterior purpose and a willful act, in the use of the process not proper in the regular conduct of the proceeding. The court noted that "malice" and want of "probable cause" necessary to a claim of malicious prosecution are not essential to recover for abuse of process.

The court concluded that it was permissible for the jury to conclude that the attorney had utilized an alleged claim of malpractice for the ulterior purpose of coercing a nuisance settlement. His offer to settle the case for the minimal sum of $750 when considered in the light of his failure to investigate adequately before deciding to file suit, and the total absence of essential expert evidence, supported such a conclusion by the jury. Thus, the court reasoned that it was permissible for the jury to conclude that the malpractice suit was filed against Dr. McCuskey and an offer to settle was made with the intention to force a nuisance payment, and that this occurred intentionally and in reckless disregard of possible consequences.

The court pointed out that Dr. McCuskey may recover punitive damages if the attorney has been guilty of oppression, fraud, or malice, expressed or implied. Malice may be established by showing that the attorney's conduct in filing a malpractice suit against Dr. McCuskey was intentional and in reckless disregard of its possible consequences on Dr. McCuskey. In seeking punitive damages, Dr. McCuskey introduced the attorney's denigrating comments concerning him during the trial of the malpractice case, as evidence to establish malice on the part of the attorney. The court pointed out that generally an attorney at law is absolutely privileged to publish defamatory matter concerning another in communications in connection with a judicial proceeding in which he participates as counsel, if his remarks have some relation to the proceeding. The privilege rests upon a public policy of securing to attorneys as officers of the court the utmost freedom in their efforts to obtain justice for their clients. The malpractice complaint placed in issue Dr. McCuskey's competence as a physician. When Dr. McCuskey testified in that case, he placed in issue his credibility; the attorney's comments pertained to either Dr. McCuskey's competence or his credibility and, therefore, were privileged. Although the denigrating comments of the attorney were privileged, and alone would not supply a legal basis for liability in damages, the court concluded that an attorney who behaves that way may subject himself to discipline. The oath taken by a licensed attorney in the state provided that an attorney will "abstain from all offensive personalities, and advance no fact prejudicial to the honor or reputation of a party or witness, unless required by the justice of the cause with which I [the attorney] am charged." The court concluded that this oath commanded that a lawyer should not be unfair or abusive to adverse witnesses or opposing litigants. The court declared that an attorney's obligation to present his client's cause vigorously does not contemplate violation of the attorney's oath or of the standards of conduct.

3. Special Damages

In some jurisdictions a physician who countersues a patient (and/or attorney) for maliciously prosecuting a groundless medical malpractice action must prove "special" damages. In particular the physician must present evidence that he sustained a "special injury" consisting of more than the inconvenience, cost, and other consequences usually associated with defending oneself against unfounded legal charges.

O'Toole v. Franklin. In July 1974 an attorney commenced a medical malpractice action against several physicians on behalf of a client, Mr. Mathis. The core of the case involved the allegation that the physicians had administered certain drugs to Mathis in 1972. Upon learning of this legal action, the physicians informed Mathis and his attorney that they had not even treated Mathis during the period in question. Although they repeatedly requested that the action be dismissed, the attorney did not dismiss it for nearly six months. As a result the physicians countersued the attorney and Mathis. They charged that the legal action had been maliciously prosecuted and had injured their professional reputation in such a way as to cause emotional anguish.

The court pointed out that an important element of a malicious prosecution claim is the existence of "special injury" to the physician as a result of institution of a malpractice claim against the physician without probable cause. The direct injury or extraordinary harm contemplated by this "special injury" requirement must involve more than the kind of secondary consequences that are a common and often unavoidable burden of a physician in a malpractice case. The court noted that the claim of "special injury" to a professional reputation as a result of an unfounded charge of malpractice is one that would be common to most professional malpractice actions and, therefore, not the type that would usually satisfy the "special injury" requirement. The court noted that some jurisdictions have recognized that exceptionally sensitive legal proceedings (such as maliciously instituted insanity proceedings) would be sufficient to establish a "special injury." However, under these special circumstances, the court declared that it must also be shown that a physician who was wrongfully subjected to a malpractice suit was uniquely vulnerable to being harmed by the proceeding beyond the ordinary hardships of similar cases.

Some states have specifically rejected the requirement of some "special injury" or interference with the physician's person or property to maintain a malicious prosecution suit.

Nelson v. Miller. In April 1976 Dr. Nelson, a board-certified neonatologist, and four other physicians were named as defendants in a suit alleging that their negligent treatment of a pregnant woman had damaged the mother's infant. The plaintiff contended that while the mother was pregnant with her son a "dilation and curettage" (D & C) was performed without a prior examination to rule out pregnancy and that as a result the undetected fetus was injured. It was also contended that the decision to deliver by cae-sarian section was premature, and therefore constituted negligence on the part of the treating physicians. In October 1977, the malpractice action against Dr. Nelson was dismissed, subject to the discovery of new informa-tion in the case. Thereafter, extensive discovery was conducted by plaintiff's counsel of the remaining parties in the case. In April 1978 the trial judge granted summary judgment in favor of all of the remaining defendants be-cause he felt that their actions, upon which the plaintiff had based his claim, dealt only with questions of medical judgment, and not professional negligence.

Following the entry of summary judgment in the medical malpractice action, Dr. Nelson filed his action for malicious prosecution against the at-torneys for plaintiff in the prior malpractice action. Dr. Nelson commenced the discovery process by filing requests for admissions, interrogatories, and production of documents. All these discovery procedures were opposed and never answered by the defendant attorneys who filed motions to dismiss Dr. Nelson's claim. When the trial judge sustained these motions for the de-fendant physicians, Dr. Nelson brought his contention before an appel-late court.

Dr. Nelson contended that the attorneys had broadly and publicly al-leged in the prior malpractice suit that he was "guilty of gross and wanton negligence and recklessness in his medical treatment of the infant," and that he caused the infant "severe, permanent and progressive worsening brain damage and a lifetime of shame, embarrassment and indignity." Plaintiff's attorneys had asked for large punitive damages against Dr. Nelson and the other physicians. Further, he contended that at the time the attorneys filed the malpractice complaint it was known or should have been known by de-fendant attorneys that all of the allegations made against Dr. Nelson were false and that the defendant attorneys instituted and continued to prosecute the medical malpractice proceeding against him without probable cause, and with malice. The defendant attorneys contended that in order for Dr. Nelson to recover in an action for malicious prosecution, he had to prove that he suffered "special damages" as a result of their conduct.

The court pointed out that the requirement of alleging "special damages" in a malicious prosecution action is not recognized in many courts, and that in this court's jurisdiction, it may be maintained if a person can demonstrate that he has sustained any damage over and above the taxa-ble costs in the case, even though there has been no attachment or other special interference with the person or his property. The court declared that damages occurring in the course of the medical malpractice suit which are recoverable if a malicious prosecution action is proven include: the harm to a physician's reputation and professional standing by any defamatory mat-ter alleged as the basis of the medical malpractice suit; expense a physician reasonably incurred in defending himself; specific financial pecuniary loss resulting from the suit; emotional distress caused by the proceedings; hindrance, harassment and humiliation in the operation of a physician's practice; diminished earning capacity; and, anxiety and mental anguish.

Attorney Negligence

A physician may contest a groundless suit by countersuing the attorney for negligent initiation of a malpractice suit against him. However, in most jurisdictions a physician is not permitted to countersue an attorney on these grounds.

Lyddon v. Shaw.   While an orthopedic surgeon was acting as a consulting surgeon in a hospital emergency room, he assessed a patient for an injured ankle. After x-rays were examined, the orthopedist diagnosed a sprained ankle, applied an elastic bandage, and instructed the patient to seek further medical attention from his family physician if the symptoms persisted for more than seven days. It was the only occasion on which he treated the patient. One year later the surgeon was sued by the patient for malpractice. The surgeon felt that there was no reasonable basis for the suit against him, and therefore wanted to countersue the patient immediately for malicious prosecution. One legal requirement for a malicious prosecution action was that the countersuit not be filed until the medical malpractice case was decided in the surgeon's favor. Thus the surgeon countersued on the theory that the attorney was negligent in filing a suit without evidence to support allegations of malpractice. The surgeon charged that the attorney had not examined the relevant x-rays and records, nor had he obtained the opinion of a qualified expert as to the required standard of care before filing suit. Thus he contended that the attorney failed to exercise that degree of skill or care required of an attorney, in that he brought the suit without reasonable cause to believe that the physician had committed malpractice, and that as an officer of the court, he had a duty to refrain from filing suit without evidence to support the allegations of malpractice.

Although the court acknowledged the seriousness of the effect of the medical malpractice problem on the practice of physicians, it concluded that a more basic and important consideration of public policy prohibited enlargement of the potential liability incurred by those who file even groundless lawsuits. According to the court, public interest was against the extension of liability for the wrongful filing of a lawsuit beyond the ambit of a malicious prosecution suit. The court pointed out that the purpose of a court of law is to determine whether a lawsuit filed by a patient has merit. Therefore, it refused to recognize a rule which would render a patient-litigant and his attorney liable for negligently failing to determine in advance whether their case had merit. The court's rationale was that only courts could dispositively make that determination. The court concluded, therefore, that a physician who believes that he has been wrongfully sued by his patient, and who thereby seeks to countersue, cannot sue the attorney for negligence in bringing the suit.

The court also noted that in addition to the availability of a legal action for malicious prosecution, a physician who is required to defend a patient's groundless lawsuit, may have available the remedy of a motion in the original lawsuit for an award of attorney fees; and in an appropriate case, he may be able to institute disciplinary proceedings against the offending attorney.

An attorney may be liable in a legal action by a nonclient that originates in the context of legal work (for example, drafting or execution of wills) because of the foreseeable reliance of such third parties upon the proper performance of the attorney's service. However, between plaintiff and defendants, there is usually no relationship other than that of adversaries; therefore, an attorney owes no duty of care to a physician he is suing.

Friedman v. Dozorc. When Dr. Friedman's patient died, his estate charged that his death was caused by Dr. Friedman's medical malpractice. The lawsuit was tried by a jury and the judge directed a verdict for Dr. Friedman on the grounds that the plaintiff had not demonstrated a legal cause of action. Dr. Friedman then commenced a lawsuit against the attorney alleging that he had negligently initiated and prosecuted an unjustifiable medical malpractice suit against him.

The court pointed out that ordinarily an attorney is responsible only to his client for any negligent acts done during the course of the attorney-client relationship. An attorney does not, by giving bad advice to a client as to the feasibility of a malpractice action against a physician, render him liable to a physician-defendant who is affected by the client's actions in reliance upon his attorney's advice. In the absence of fraud or collusion, an attorney's duties are owed only to his client; therefore he cannot be found liable to physicians for acts or effects which arise out of his representation of his client. Thus, a physician-defendant usually has no remedy for the negligent performance by plaintiff's attorney—even if the physician is thereby injured in some manner.

The court pointed out that the rationale for this policy is that an attorney has a duty to zealously represent his client seeking a lawful objective through legally permissible means. The court concluded, therefore, to allow an attorney's adversaries to sue him, would establish an atmosphere that would put the fear of being sued by his client's adversaries in the minds of attorneys, and thereby prevent attorneys from representing bona fide legal causes of action.

An attorney generally is not responsible to the physician for having negligently brought a suit against him. Although the Canons of Legal Ethics reflect an attorney's duty to the legal system to stay within the bounds of the law when representing clients, it does not create, for a sued physician, a private legal cause of action for attorney negligence. The effect of such a code, however, does not overcome the general rule that a physician who is negligently sued by the attorney, does not have a legal cause of action against the attorney.

Bickel v. Mackie. Acting on advice of her attorney, the patient initiated a malpractice suit against her physician, Dr. Bickel. When the court summarily dismissed the suit for failure to state a legal cause of action, Dr. Bickel countersued his patient's attorney. He contended that the attorney's negligence in advising the patient to commence and prosecute the malpractice suit, and his failure to comply with the Lawyer's Code of Professional Responsibility, constituted reckless disregard of the duty that the attorney owed him. Dr. Bickel claimed that as a result of the malpractice suit against him, he suffered mental anguish, damage to his professional reputation, and expenditures of time to prepare a defense to the meritless claim against him.

The court pointed out that an attorney may have a legal duty to a person who is not his client if he knows that such a person is reasonably relying upon his effective professional performance. Therefore, under certain circumstances even a person who has employed an attorney may have a legal cause of action against the attorney because of the latter's negligence. However, where an attorney's negligent conduct in an adversary process injures his adversary, a physician; the physician is presumed not to have relied upon the nonnegligent performance of the attorney. The nature of the adversary process precludes such reliance. The court declared that although an attorney also owes a general duty to the judicial system, breach of this type of duty also does not translate into liability to a physician who is his adversary in a legal proceeding, because again there is no foreseeable reliance by that physician on the attorney's professional conduct.

The court explained that, in general, the law does not recognize an attorney's duty of due care to nonclients, such as physicians whom he has sued for malpractice at the behest of his client. There is no duty analogous to the duty of a physician, who knows his patient has an impairment affecting his ability to safely operate a motor vehicle, to the public which requires him to warn his patient about the hazards of driving. The rationale for the physician's duty is that the public reasonably relies on other drivers being reasonably fit to drive.

Thus the court decided that an attorney cannot be held liable for heedless disregard or indifference of the consequences to a physician who is an adverse party resulting from his client's malpractice suit; except when the attorney's disregard amounts to malicious prosecution, or where there is reasonable reliance by the physician, or a specific duty owed by the attorney to the physician. Thus the court concluded that there may be no effective remedy by which physicians can vindicate themselves after being subjected to an unreasonable malpractice suit which does not constitute malicious prosecution. It noted that the public policy in favor of encouraging primary access to courts and discouraging retaliation by defendants against plaintiffs' attorneys, creates a gap in the law which if it is to be remedied, should be done by legislative action.

Dr. Bickel also contended that the attorney's failure to comply with the Lawyer's Code of Professional Responsibility (Ethical Considerations and Disciplinary Rules) provided a legal cause of action for the physician against the attorney because the code established a specific duty owed him by the attorney prescribing adequate preparation and proscribing participation in suits to harass or maliciously injure another. The physician analogized the professional code and rules to drivers' rules of the road, which if a driver violated and an injury resulted, constituted "negligence per se," or proof that the driver was negligent.

The court pointed out that an attorney's violation of a professional code was not tantamount to a legally wrongful act, particularly with regard to an attorney's liability to an adversarial nonclient. Although the code speaks of a general duty to the legal system to stay within the bounds of the law when representing clients, the court concluded that it did not create a private legal cause of action for a physician. The court indicated that its conclusions were supported by the preliminary statement of the Code which stated in part:

> The Canons are statements of axiomatic norms, expressing in general terms the standard of professional conduct expected of lawyers in their relationships with the public, with the legal system, and with the legal profession. They embody the general concepts from which the Ethical Considerations and Disciplinary Rules are derived.

The court reasoned that although the Disciplinary Rules (unlike the Ethical Considerations) are mandatory statements of the minimum level of conduct below which no lawyer can fall without being subject to disciplinary action, the Code made no attempt to undertake to define standards for civil liability of lawyers for professional conduct. Therefore, it could not be the legal basis for a duty owed by the attorney to a physician adversary.

PART II
CLINICOLEGAL TEACHING CASES

INTRODUCTION

These teaching cases are intended to represent the various roles, tasks, and events an attending physician regularly encounters in the practice of medicine. In general, they have been drafted from clinical occurrences and situations that have culminated in legal disputes. The clinical content and flavor in each case study has been preserved to enhance identification with the problems and concerns of the attending physician.

The case studies describe the type of professional conduct expected of an attending physician under varying clinical circumstances. In particular, they emphasize the general scope of knowledge or awareness expected of a physician and the degree of clinical skill he is expected to exercise. Moreover, the cases illustrate the legally acceptable manner (in terms of due diligence and due care) required of a physician in attending to the specific needs of his patient.

The case studies were designed to highlight and make vivid the significant medicolegal factors and events an attending physician confronts in the performance of his clinical activities. These medicolegal tasks or events include issues involving: consent to proposed procedures; collection and selection of diagnostic and therapeutic data; disclosure of medical information; consultation and referral; supervision of assisting personnel; complications of disease and medical care; and recordation of medical information. In addition, in this section of the book, reference is more often made to the issue of "causation" as a factor in professional negligence lawsuits.

The case studies, especially the *discussion* segments, were developed to stimulate thought, dialogue, and debate, utilizing fundamental information acquired in Part I. In this manner, individual and collective attitudes of physicians will surface and thus can be assessed. It is assumed that this attitudinal approach will provide an effective means of establishing greater convergence between a physician's internalized sense of reasonable conduct and society's evolving expectations of such conduct.

For ease of use in a clinical-teaching setting, a brief descriptive sum-

mary of the cases is provided to assist the reader, or an instructor, in selecting cases appropriate to specific individual education goals and objectives.
In addition, the cases are inventoried by clinical condition and management
issues, and cataloged by the clinical specialty that is most directly connected
with the facts and circumstances that led to the dispute.

SUMMARIES OF
CLINICOLEGAL TEACHING CASES
(Correlated Supplement to Chapters in Part I)

CHAPTER 1

1. Hospital personnel refuse to accept ineligible patient with developing *myocardial infarction* when other facility was reasonably available.
2. Physician refuses to evaluate patient with suspected mumps, thus patient's *lymphadenitis* goes untreated and requires surgical excision.
3. Physician does not readily respond to child in respiratory distress from terminal *tracheal stenosis* whose parents requested that child be treated at home.
4. Attending physician, against family's wishes, decides "not to resuscitate" patient with *amyotrophic lateral sclerosis*.

CHAPTER 2

5. Psychiatrist keeps patient who was referred to hospital for evaluation on psychiatric ward after discovery that she was mistakenly admitted there.
6. Physician does not inform job applicant of suspicious *lung lesion* detected on preemployment chest x-ray.
7. Nurse prepares a patient for *C-section* by shaving pubic area despite objections. Patient also claims that she felt pain during surgery.

CHAPTER 3

8. Physician does not inquire about medication patient had been given by parent and thus prescribes aspirin which exacerbates her *salicylism* causing death.
9. Physician does not perform tests to rule out cancer in a middle-aged smoker with *hemoptysis*.
10. Physician does not diagnose *seizure disorder* in a patient with alterations in consciousness; patient is not advised to limit activities and has automobile accident during a seizure.
11. Physician does not diagnose *subarachnoid hemorrhage* in a patient who presents in emergency room with severe headaches.

12. Physician evaluates sibling of child with documented *meningococcal meningitis* for an illness, but child is sent home and dies of meningococemia.

13. Physician does not initially diagnose *subacute sclerosing panencephalitis* in an adolescent patient because of nonspecific behavioral aberrations.

14. Pathologist misdiagnoses *thyroid biopsy* specimen because of microtome contaminated with breast cancer.

15. Physicians mistakenly diagnose psychogenic basis for patient's upper abdominal pain rather than *laceration of liver*.

16. Physicians do not diagnose *rubella* in gravid patient nor do they obtain rubella titer on initial prenatal visit and patient delivers child with rubella syndrome.

17. Physicians only diagnosed intrauterine pregnancy in *combined tubal intrauterine pregnancy*; gravid patient given Valium and IUD, and delivers child with marked developmental defects.

18. Physician reviews normal mammogram and examines patient complaining of a *breast lump* but cannot palpate dominant breast mass which later turns out to be breast cancer.

19. Physician's assistant diagnoses *"hyperdefecation"* without performing routine tests despite changes in bowel habits of a middle-aged patient.

CHAPTER 4

20. Surgeon does not clearly disclose probable need for *arthotomy* in an infant with septic arthritis, and anesthetist does not take precautions usual in a prolonged procedure; thus, the child becomes *hypothermic* and sustains cardiopulmonary arrest.

21. Otolaryngologist and resident physician do not effectively communicate about potentially catastrophic complications of a pulsating *tracheostomy tube* caused by erosion into innominate artery which ruptures and patient exsanguinates.

22. Surgeon performs *sigmoidoscopy* on child with hematochezia, does not tell parents that he plans to cauterize *colonic polyp*, and perforates bowel causing peritonitis.

23. Pathologist unequivocally diagnoses *scirrhous cell carcinoma* of the breast on a "frozen section" biopsy, and surgeon performs radical mastectomy, but lesion turns out to be *myoblastoma* on permanent section.

24. Radiologist reports ambiguous mammographic findings, and pathologist reports inconsistent breast biopsy finding, inappropriately reassuring the attending surgeon that *cancerous breast lesion* was benign.

25. Renowned orthopedic knee surgeon does not tell patient that resident surgeon is going to operate on knee, and *popliteal artery* is *transected.*

CHAPTER 5

26. Resident surgeon and anesthesiologist fail to report patient's deteriorative postoperative status and marked changes in chest x-ray findings caused by *central venous catheter* perforation and *hydrothorax.*

27. Gynecologist, without explaining to the patient his intended use of a stapler, performs abdominal *hysterectomy* with metal sutures which cause complications.

28. Surgeon, without explaining the nature of the procedure, uses thoracic (rather than abdominal) approach for repair of *hiatus hernia* and injures spleen and ribs. ˙

29. Plastic surgeon does not disclose to patient with mastodynia the incidence and materiality of risks associated with *subcutaneous mastectomy* and patient sustains breast tissue loss.

30. Physician gives patient exposed to relative with tuberculosis choice of *INH* which patient accepts and patient gets *hepatitis.*

31. Attending physician seeks to remove *life-support respirator* from his adult patient in *chronic vegetative state* who had convincingly expressed, when he was competent, his desire to have such life-support measures withdrawn.

32. Attending physician, despite the patient's mother's request for discontinuation of such therapy, seeks to administer *blood transfusion* to lifelong incompetent with mentality of child who has exsanguinating bladder cancer.

CHAPTER 6

33. Cardiologist does not advise patient with valvular heart disease, complicated by *embolization*, of complications of disease or alternative therapy to heparinization.

34. Physicians and surgeons recommend and perform *colectomy* on patient with long history of relatively stable *ulcerative colitis* and patient dies.

35. Orthopedic surgeon performs *internal fixation* with intramedullary rod on patient with compound *fracture* of *tibia*, and complications of nonunion and osteomyelitis necessitate amputation.

36. Surgeon does not detect *transection* of *common bile duct* in timely fashion despite persistent and progressive postoperative drainage.

37. Physician continues to infuse chemotherapeutic agent (5-FU) despite patient's complaint of extreme pain as a result of extravasation which causes *skin slough.*

38. Psychiatrists do not rule out that psychotic patient may have *acute intermittent porphyria*; patient manifests findings of *akathisia* secondary to antipsychotic medication, elopes, and drowns.

39. Resident obstetrician does not appreciate and document response to findings of *fetal distress* during monitoring in labor of patient with complicated pregnancy.

40. Physicians perform preoperative pulmonary assessment of patient with pulmonary disorder who develops intraoperative *pneumothorax*.

41. Anesthesiologist does not undertake special precautions for anesthesia for children and child experiences refractory *laryngospasm* and consequential brain damage.

42. Physicians and surgeons recommend and perform *gastrectomy* on patient with slow healing gastric ulcer, but no definitive *ulcer* is found on examination of stomach specimen.

43. Physician performs *"trigger-zone injection"* on patient with paravertebral *myositis* and pneumothorax results when patient jerks as injection is given.

44. Urologist performs *transurethral prostatectomy* with significant complications, and the medical record provides evidence that the procedure was not skillfully performed.

45. Neonatologist uses *umbilical artery catheter* in treating infant with *respiratory distress syndrome* and infant develops paraparesis.

46. Anesthesiologist elects not to transfuse a pale infant who has undergone surgical repair of a *craniosynostosis*, and blood loss causes hypovolemic shock.

CHAPTER 7

47. Physician who orders hospitalization of combative and disoriented alcoholic patient does not perform evaluation of patient's condition and nurses do not follow physician's order, and patient *aspirates* gastric contents and dies.

48. Family practitioner does not obtain consultation before accepting a complex *femoral fracture* or after patient's condition deteriorates; patient eventually requires amputation.

49. Pediatrician, although he was unfamiliar with patient's condition, ignores consulting surgeon's recommendation that *eventration* of diaphragm should be repaired, and patient develops fatal *volvulus*.

50. Pediatricians do not refer patient with *intractable diarrhea of infancy* to another hospital with facilities and personnel to provide adequate and life-sustaining nourishment.

51. Neurosurgeon elects to clinically manage his *post-cervical fusion* patient's *depression* without consultating a psychiatrist, and patient kills himself.

52. Orthopedic surgeon treats child with a *septic hip* (H. Flu) but is unaware of complication or sequela of meningitis and thus fails to provide adequate antibiotic coverage to preclude meningitis.

53. Emergency medical technicians respond to accident in which patient sustained *fractured femur*; the nature and severity of the injury is not detected nor communicated to other healthcare personnel and timely definitive critical care is not implemented.

CHAPTER 8

54. Vascular surgeon does not read Nurses' Notes record indicating *postoperative bleeding* in a heparinized patient who has undergone major aorto-femoral by-pass vascular surgery; patient develops resultant hypotension precipitating a myocardial infarction.

55. Anesthesiologist's chart reflects that he properly detected and managed intraoperative *pneumothorax*.

56. Physician relies on patient's outpatient records as justification for not performing *EKG* on a patient with chest pain who suffers *myocardial infarction*.

57. Physician requests his nurse to relay test result to patient and in crowded waiting room she tells college student that *"V.D. test* was negative"; this information gets back to his fiancee's parents.

CHAPTER 9

58. Physician fails to diagnose *pneumonia* and *gastrointestinal bleed* in a woman whom he sends home with her husband; husband fails to bring *alcoholic* wife back to hospital for reevaluation after she progressively deteriorates and subsequently dies at home.

59. Physician does not tell parents of serious consequences of not performing definitive surgical procedure on their child who has suspected *Hirschsprung's Disease*, they take the child home and he subsequently develops enterocolitis and its complications.

60. Physician fails to detect radiological evidence of air under diaphragm as a result of *perforated duodenum*, a type of injury commonly inflicted in the course of parental *abuse*.

61. Physicians do not perform thorough examination in a patient with recurrent rectal pain because patient refuses to undergo painful recto-sigmoid examinations, and patient dies of metastatic *rectal carcinoma*.

INVENTORY OF
CLINICAL CONDITION ISSUES

30. Hepatitis
31. Chronic Persistent Vegetative State—Respirator
32. Bladder Cancer—Hemorrhage
33. Mitral Stenosis—Arterial Embolization
34. Ulcerative Colitis
35. Compound Fracture of Tibia—Non-Union
36. Transected Common Bile Duct
37. Skin Slough of Arm
38. Acute Intermittent Porphyria—Psychosis—Akathisia
39. Complicated Maternal Pregnancy, Fetal Distress and Injury
40. Intraoperative Pneumothorax
41. Intraoperative Laryngospasm
42. Gastric Ulcer
43. Paravertebral Myositis
44. Benign Prostatic Hypertrophy
45. Infant Respiratory Distress Syndrome
46. Craniosynostosis—Hemorrhage—Hypovolemia
47. Acute Alcoholism—Aspiration of Gastric Contents
48. Fracture of Femur—Tight Cast
49. Eventration of Diaphragm—Volvulus of Intestine
50. Intractable Diarrhea of Infancy—Malnutrition
51. Post-Cervical Fusion Depression—Suicide
52. Septic Hip—H. Flu Meningitis
53. Fracture of Femur and Pelvis—Exsanguination
54. Aorto-Femoral By-Pass Surgery—Hemorrhage—Hypovolemia
55. Intraoperative Pneumothorax
56. Myocardial Infarction
57. Genital Lesion—Disclosure
58. Chronic Alcoholism—Gastritis—Pneumonia
59. Hirschsprung's Disease—Enterocolitis
60. Child Abuse—Rupture of Duodenum—Peritonitis
61. Rectal Cancer

INVENTORY OF CLINICAL MANAGEMENT ISSUES

30. Prophylactic INH Therapy
31. Surgical Cardiac Arrest—Artificial Life Support
32. Blood Transfusions
33. Anticoagulation—Cardiac Valve Replacement
34. Colectomy
35. Internal Fixation of Tibia Fracture with Intramedullary Rod
36. Cholecystectomy
37. Chemotherapy Injection
38. Psychotropic Medication
39. Fetal Monitoring
40. General Anesthesia—Ventilation
41. General Anesthesia—Endotracheal Intubation
42. Subtotal Gastrectomy
43. "Trigger-Zone" Injection
44. Transurethral Resection of Prostate
45. Umbilical Artery Catheterization
46. Craniosynostectomy Blood Transfusion
47. Restraints—Precautions
48. Traction Splint of Extremity
49. Upper Gastrointestinal Series—Surgical "Tacking" of Stomach
50. Hyperalimentation—Referral
51. Cervical Fusion—Anti-depressants—Psychiatric Referral
52. Arthrotomy—Antibiotics
53. Emergency Assessment ("Packaging")—MAST Trousers—Institution of IV Fluids
54. Aorto-Femoral By-Pass—Anticoagulation
55. General Anesthesia—Ventilation
56. EKG
57. VDRL
58. CBC—Chest X-Ray
59. Rectal Biopsy—Barium Enema
60. Abdominal X-Ray Series
61. Anuscopy—Recto-sigmoidoscopy

CATALOG OF CLINICAL SPECIALTIES

(The numbers following the specialty refer to the teaching case number)

Anesthesia 7, 20, 25, 40, 41, 46, 55
Emergency Medicine 1, 2, 8, 11, 12, 53, 58, 60
Gynecology 27
Internal Medicine 4, 5, 6, 9, 10, 13, 15, 19, 30, 31, 32, 33, 34, 37, 38, 42,
    43, 47, 56, 57, 58
Neurosurgery 46
Obstetrics 7, 16, 17, 39
Orthopedics 20, 26, 35, 43, 48, 52
Otolaryngology 21
Pathology 14, 24
Pediatrics 2, 3, 12, 13, 22, 23, 45, 49, 50, 60
Psychiatry 5, 10, 13, 38, 47, 58
Radiology 18, 24
Surgery 18, 22, 24, 28, 29, 34, 36, 42, 49, 51, 54, 59
Urology 44

CLINICOLEGAL TEACHING CASES *

(1) The Physician-Patient Relationship

1: *Facts*

The fifty-eight-year-old self-employed house painter began to experience substernal pressure which lasted one hour and spontaneously abated. However, that evening the pain recurred and persisted. He went to bed, but awoke at 2:00 A.M. with severe substernal pain which radiated through to his back and was associated with diaphoresis. By 3:00 P.M., when he could no longer stand the pain, his wife called the ambulance. After the rescue squad arrived, oxygen was administered. His wife ordered the ambulance driver to take her husband to a local military hospital, even though a civilian hospital was located approximately the same distance, because her husband was a "veteran" and because they did not have insurance coverage for hospitalization. She indicated that she would follow the ambulance with her husband's discharge papers. But in fact, the husband was not eligible for care at the military hospital. En route, the ambulance crew radioed the emergency room at the military hospital and related that they had a possible heart attack victim who appeared stable. The military corpsman on duty in the emergency room inquired if he was "retired military." The ambulance attendant asked the patient if he had been retired from the military. The patient responded, "No, I am a World War II veteran." The patient was then asked if he had ever been treated at the military hospital, and he replied that he had not. When this information was relayed to the corpsman, he told the ambulance driver, "Use your own judgment." The ambulance driver assumed that when he was told by personnel at the military hospital to "use his own judgment," it meant that they would not accept the patient at the hospital. Thus, he decided to transport the patient to the nearby civilian hospital. According to the wife, when her husband was informed of this

---

* These clinicolegal teaching cases were drawn from actual lawsuits, and were specifically designed for classroom use. Their clinical content is authentic, and their analytical discussion is intentionally provocative. Although each case contains variegated and multifaceted clinicolegal issues, the cases have been categorized into groups which roughly correspond to chapters in Part I that addressed related legal issues and topics. Thus, clinicolegal teaching cases 1–4 are included under the heading Chapter 1, "The Physician-Patient Relationship"; and so forth with succeeding chapters.

change he became worried, thinking that it would be "that many more" minutes before they would be able to get to a hospital and have his condition treated.

When the patient arrived at the civilian emergency room he was diaphoretic and his pulse was 76, respiration 22, and blood pressure 150/110. CPK was 2250 units, SGOT was 228, and his EKG showed evidence of an acute inferior myocardial infarction. He was given lidocaine and morphine and was admitted to ICU. He overhead a nurse say that he should not be there because he did not have health insurance.

During his hospitalization he had an S-3 and S-4 gallop and required diuretics intermittently. He had persistent tachycardia which eventually responded to digitalization. However, serial EKGs demonstrated persistent S-T elevation. Serial chest x-rays were not performed. He was anticoagulated initially with heparin and subsequently with Coumadin. Throughout his hospitalization, he experienced stress regarding what he would do after he got out of the hospital, and how, as a self-employed individual, he would "make ends meet." He was discharged in fair condition three weeks after admission and was given Valium for sedation.

One week after his discharge he suddenly died while at home. Autopsy disclosed recent myocardial infarction and a perforated aneurysm of the left ventricle with hemopericardium. Cause of death was ruptured left ventricular aneurysm secondary to the myocardial infarction.

Allegations

The patient's widow sued the military hospital, alleging that her husband had a right to be treated there. She contended that her husband became anxious about the expense he was incurring at the civilian hospital, and that this caused his second and fatal heart attack. As support for her claim, she submitted a letter from his attending cardiologist indicating that the patient had been "unusually concerned about finances" during his convalescent period.

Discussion

The patient was neither eligible for nor entitled to care at the military facility. He was not already a patient of that facility; thus, the hospital did not have a duty to accept him as a patient or to render him care, especially since there was another available and accessible emergency facility. The wife's decision to go to the military hospital rather than the civilian institution was based on economic considerations. Moreover, there was no "undertaking" on the part of the military facility to provide him care that might establish a duty to care for the patient.

Even if a duty to accept him under emergency circumstances existed, the failure to admit him to the military hospital was not a causative factor in his death. The contention that financial responsibility for the patient's hospitalization made his cardiovascular situation worse is unpersuasive. Had he been admitted to the military hospital as "a civilian emergency," he would have been required to pay for care. Moreover, his future employability and lack of "sick care" benefits would be a more significant source of stress. The letter written by his attending cardiologist, suggestive of the deleterious aspects of the patient's stress related to his finances at the civilian hospital, is couched in terms of concern for his patient. However, this physician failed to consider the possibility and/or probability of a ventricular aneurysm despite persistence of ST elevation. The patient was discharged and subsequently died as a result of the aneurysm, a complication of the original myocardial infarction. Under such circumstances, the physician is more implicated in the causative chain leading to the patient's death than the military hospital's refusal to accept the patient.

2: *Facts*

In early October, a three-and-one-half-month-old boy began to be irritable and seemed to have a cold. On the evening of October 8, his parents took him to an outpatient clinic because the father had noticed a lump below and behind the left ear. A nurse examined the infant, recorded a temperature of 100° F., and noted "edema" under the left ear. When the nurse related her diagnosis of "mumps" to the father, the father requested that a physician evaluate the child. The nurse consulted with the clinic physician who responded that he would not examine the child because he had not previously contracted the disease. Therefore, the nurse prescribed Tylenol, and told the parents to bring the child back if his temperature rose higher than 101° F.

On October 10, the parents brought the child back to the clinic because they were concerned with his persistent irritability and an increase in the size of the neck mass. He was examined by another nurse who also diagnosed mumps. The father asked to speak to the physician on duty, who happened to be the one present two days earlier. The father explained to the physician that he felt his son did not have mumps. The father himself had a history of recurrent lymphadenitis. In spite of this request, the physician refused to evaluate the child and suggested that the parents use home treatment for lowering the temperature if it became excessively high. He also indicated to the father that he should not bring the child back to the clinic because he might infect other people. Although the physician was a general practitioner, he did not suggest the possibility of a consultation.

One week later, on October 17, the father telephoned a pediatric clinic and explained his son's condition to a pediatric nurse clinician, who asked that he bring the child in for evaluation. A pediatrician detected a 6 X 5 cm. indurated mass in the area of the left parotid gland, and diagnosed salivary duct blockage. An immediate ENT evaluation was arranged. The otolaryn-gologist detected bilateral, posterior cervical lymphadenopathy. He noted that there was no history of an exanthem or exposure to other children with a similar illness. He diagnosed cervical lymphadenitis, probably secondary to staphlococcus or streptococcus. He started the child on Oxacillin, and reevaluated the child at two-day intervals. The mass became more fluctuant. By October 19, the lymphadenitis was nontender and the child was not irritable. On October 21, the size of the mass made surgical incision and drainage necessary. Approximately 10 cc. of purulent material was drained. By November 3, the mass was gone; however, a residual 3.0 cm. scar persisted.

Allegations

A malpractice claim was filed by the father on behalf of his son. The gravamen of his claim was that, on two occasions, his son had been refused medical care and treatment and that this refusal resulted in pain, suffering, and a surgical scar.

Discussion

The general practitioner's conduct in this case was unprofessional and negligent. The father's request to have a physician review the nurse's diagnosis was reasonable. If the physician was concerned about exposure to mumps, he could have arranged a referral for the child. However, his concern about exposure lacked professional medical foundation under the circumstances, and his refusal to see a patient was unreasonable.

Because the physician did not consider the history from the father that might have suggested cervical lymphadenitis, the diagnosis is negligent for this reason also. He simply presumed "mumps" without an adequate diagnostic basis. Although in the early stage mumps and cervical lymphadenitis simulate each other, the physician should have consulted someone, especially the second time the father brought the child back to the clinic. His instructions not to come back, until the child was no longer contagious, were careless.

The child's damages are not extensive. Even if his condition had been timely diagnosed, it may have still required a surgical incision and drainage. However, the benefit of this doubt should not be given to mitigate professional misconduct. Therefore, it is likely to be presumed that earlier diagnosis and drug treatment would have prevented the surgical excision, which caused additional discomfort, prolongation of the treatment course, and the residual surgical scar.

3:    *Facts*

An infant was born at thirty-four weeks gestation by emergency C-section and admitted to the intensive care unit because of respiratory distress syndrome, pulmonary dysplasia, subglottal stenosis, and feeding intolerance. On the second day of life, a patent ductus arteriosus was diagnosed. Congestive heart failure was noted and he was treated with digitalis and diuretics. The patient developed seizure activity and became acidotic. Hydrocephalus was diagnosed by CAT scan. The fourth ventricle was normal size, suggesting aqueduct stenosis with massive dilation of the lateral and third ventricles which was treated by a ventricular peritoneal shunt. The following day he developed bilateral pneumothoraces and pneumomediastinum which were successfully treated with chest tube. One month later a tracheostomy was performed. A marked delay in development, particularly in gross motor functions, was noted. Three weeks later the patient developed an aspiration pneumonia after being fed by his mother. He became septic, and antibiotics were instituted. Tracheal aspiration grew out staphylococcus and pseudomonas. He was maintained on 30 percent oxygen, with heat mist, frequent vigorous suctioning, and irrigation with normal saline.

After six months of intensive neonatal care, the patient was transferred to a regional medical center for placement in a custodial institution. There he was diagnosed as having Klebsiella and Staphylococcal pneumonia, and was treated with Methicillin. His condition stabilized. His parents decided not to place him in a custodial care institution. They signed the following statement, indicating their willingness to accept the care of their son in their home and their realization of the seriousness of his illness. In addition, they acknowledged that a chronic care facility and not an acute care facility, was the only care facility available for the custodial care of their son.

> We understand that our son has tracheal stenosis which is scarring his airway and in the opinion of his doctors will eventually close off his airway and choke him. There is no way to know when this will be, but is expected to occur sometime this year. We understand that his chances of living a long time are very small, and that his many medical problems, his tracheostomy shunt, and oxygen requirement will require a great deal of care at home and will be a hardship on us. We still wish to have our son returned from the chronic care center which is the only nursing home available for him and wish to keep him home at all times except when he needs hospital care for brief illnesses like pneumonia or shunt repair.

Two weeks later the mother called the pediatric ward at the hospital where her son had received his treatment and requested emergency transportation for her son because she felt that he was showing signs of respiratory distress. The mother felt that her son's shunt was knotted up in his abdomen, and that this was why he had stopped bottle feeding. She was told that there was no one on the pediatric ward who could help her. When she talked to the attending pediatrician concerning her son's condition, he told her that it was all right to "tube" her son until his appointment, which was scheduled for ten days later. Thereafter, she dozed off. When she awoke, she found her son not moving or breathing in the crib. She notified her husband who attempted unsuccessfully to resuscitate the child.

Misconception existed between the mother and hospital personnel. The mother felt the hospital personnel would not accept their son back into the hospital after she had signed for his release.

Allegations

The mother sued the pediatrician and hospital, alleging negligent refusal to send an ambulance to pick up her son. She contended that her child was not given proper attention in getting emergency transportation for him to the hospital.

Discussion

This child had multiple serious congenital anomalies, which despite proper treatment, offered little prospect for long-term survival. The life-threatening defects could only have been held at bay temporarily. It was not unreasonable for the parents to choose to care for him at home for what was known to be a foreshortened lifespan. The parents were counseled on the patient's care and cautioned that care at home might not be as easy to provide as it would be in a chronic care facility. While at home, the infant's condition worsened predictably.

If the mother's contention is accepted that when she called the hospital to report her son's signs of distress, the hospital personnel did not respond; the personnel should have ascertained whether the help she sought was immediately necessary, and if so, to connect her to a source in the hospital for that help. However, at that point, the danger created by the parents in taking the child home for care had materialized. Even if negligence is assumed, there are no legally recognizable damages because there was no prospect for any outcome other than this child's eventual demise. The health care personnel's conduct was not "outrageous" under the circumstances. Had an ambulance been sent on the first call by the mother, or had she been instructed to bring the child to the hospital, the best outcome that could have ensued was that of a brief postponement of the inevitable process of dying. The parents had earlier indicated that they wished their son to spend his last days with them. If there were any chance to save the child by sending an ambulance or by advising the parents to bring their child in, hospital personnel's response may have prevented that small opportunity. However, considering the parents' choices in the matter and the lack of probable success in treating this child, the parents do not have an actionable claim.

4: *Facts*

A forty-eight-year-old man experienced progressive shortness of breath, diaphoresis, and chest pain. A chest x-ray performed in the emergency room demonstrated a left pneumothorax and fluid level above the diaphragm. Amyotrophic Lateral Sclerosis (ALS) had been diagnosed fourteen years prior, and the patient had been kept alive by the meticulous twenty-four-hour home nursing care of his wife and children. He had been on a respirator with a permanent tracheostomy for eight years. The patient was well known to the hospital staff because of multiple admissions, primarily for the treatment of pulmonary infections. Although completely paralyzed except for eyelid and extra-ocular muscle movement, his intelligence was intact, and he had been able to develop a means of communication by blinking his eyes.

The patient was admitted to the Medical Intensive Care Unit (MICU). A chest tube was inserted, resulting in reinflation of the left lung and drainage of 30 cubic centimeters of purulent material. He was started on intravenous ampicillin and gentamycin. He had a pulse rate of 170 and a cardiac monitor pattern consistent with ventricular tachycardia. A 100 mg bolus of lidocaine was administered followed by a lidocaine drip at 2 mg. per minute. Shortly thereafter, he went into sinus bradycardia, became acutely hypotensive and went into cardiopulmonary arrest. He was administered intravenous epinephrine, atropine, sodium bicarbonate, and calcium chloride. He was defibrillated repeatedly over forty-five minutes and a transthoracic pacemaker was inserted.

Finally, a pulse was maintained with the support of intravenous Dopamine, and his cardiac status stabilized. He had reactive pupils, positive corneal reflex, and volitional lid control on command. The neurologist's assessment was that he was not "brain dead." He noted that the patient "shifted his eyes towards verbal stimulus, remains pale and apparently non-communicative. Mouth and facial jerks however, would not make eye contact. Recommend: follow-up neuro exams only. Discussion with family Re: termination of support."

Several days later the patient experienced frequent transient episodes of asystole which were treated with atropine. There was no mention whether the patient had circulatory compromise sufficient to cause further neurologic injury. Two days later the attending physician's note stated, "Appears to be base-line status—responds to deep pain, but not to commands." The neurologist surmised that the patient was "not clinically dead." He added, "There is little reason to expect return to his cognitive function." The neurologist advised that the family should be counselled regarding "loss of the sole remnant of an already catastrophically devastated individual. And support removed as soon as possible."

The patient remained unresponsive to verbal stimuli and showed no signs of eye contact or other communication, although he was occasionally responsive to painful stimuli. Nevertheless, his cardiac and ventilatory status stabilized.

When the attending physician decided that the patient had received full benefit from the MICU, the patient was transferred to the ward. The attending physician's note stated that only supportive care would be given to the patient, including continuation of the ventilator, nutrition via a feeding tube, decubitus care, chest-tube drainage, chest x-rays, and "routine labs." He wrote an order on the same date stating, "No heroic measures if patient's condition worsens." A following order read, "No blood cultures."

Although there were frequent notes in the chart concerning support and discussion with the family, the family never actually was told that "no-code" orders were written. The family repeatedly made known their desire that all possible medical care be rendered to the patient. In two family counselling sessions, the family expressed a desire of having second opinions from consultants as to the management of the patient. The physician noted, "The family's request will be honored." However, no consultant ever saw the patient.

The patient was maintained on the ward for one week in his stable vegetative condition. Brown fecal-like liquid began leaking from the gastric feeding tube and leaking around its insertion into the neck. The abdomen was tense, and there were no bowel sounds. A bowel obstruction was diagnosed, and the patient was placed on low Gomco suction. Shortly thereafter, the patient became pale, diaphoretic, and died.

The family was notified of the patient's death. When they arrived on the ward they viewed the body with the ventilator, intravenous lines, nasogastric tube, and chest tubes still in place. There was also staining of the patient and bedsheets from various fluid and discharge. The family was outraged by having to view the patient in such a condition. The attending physician had ordered the apparatus left in place as evidence to the family that essential care had not been withdrawn contrary to the family's wishes.

Autopsy disclosed that the cause of death was severe bilateral pneumonia with a right pulmonary abscess, contributed to by ALS. The fixed brain showed normal gray and white matter with the exception of the atrophic and cystic area in the right cortex, and a grossly normal brain stem and spinal cord. Microscopically, the cerebellum showed an atrophic cortex with loss of Purkinje cells and the granular layer. The spinal cord showed loss of anterior horn cells with marked gliosis of the lateral corticospinal tract. The cerebral cortex was normal with the exception of a cystic area in the right hemisphere.

Allegations

The family filed a malpractice suit against the attending physician, consultant neurologist, and hospital, charging multiple negligent actions including: the patient's removal from the MICU against the family's wishes; the issuance of a "no-code" order over the objections of the family; the "outrageous witnessing of the body after the patient's death, with IV fluids and with other tubes that were still connected with IV fluid continuing to drain into the patient's uncleansed body or bed."

Discussion

Several issues of professional conduct are raised by this case. Although there are many philosophical and moral issues involved in the care of a severely debilitated patient, often these may be different from the generally accepted medical standards, which an attending physician is required to follow. When the diagnosis of left pneumothorax and empyema were made, the patient was promptly admitted to the MICU where standard medical therapy was effectively begun. However, at the time the patient was transferred to the general medical ward, the attending physician had given up any intentions to treat the patient's infections or a subsequent cardiac arrest. He was unable to clearly communicate his intentions to the family, who expressed their desire to have all efforts made to keep the patient alive. The family was not notified that the patient had "no-code" orders written or that serious infections would not be treated. Even though the physician could not reach a common understanding with the family as to the appropriate clinical management, his intentions not to treat should have been disclosed and documented. This miscommunication was compounded by the rather blunt and insensitive notes of the neurologist, who recommended withdrawal of life support even though at the time the patient apparently possessed normal cognitive ability. The attending physician also failed to obtain a "second opinion" as the family requested and he had promised. The AMA Code of Ethics, while not legally binding, suggests that the attending physician has a fiduciary duty to seek consultation when the patient (or his family) formally requests it. This ethical duty may provide a matrix for the evolution of a legal duty under certain circumstances.

The family experienced emotional distress and shock when they viewed the patient's body because they had invested much time, effort, and emotion in the care and welfare of the patient. On the other hand, it would be expected that they would also be accustomed to witnessing the patient in a debilitated and pathetic state. Moreover, they had seen him in the hospital when he was comatose with the intravenous lines and gastric tubes. It was not unreasonable for the staff to leave all tubes hooked up for the family's viewing, to demonstrate to them that all standard life-support measures were given to the patient up to the time of his death. However, if the body and the bed were filthy at the time of the family's viewing, there may be some colorable argument that the staff negligently or recklessly caused the family emotional distress, which might be compensable. Such conduct would border on insensitivity and is unacceptable for a professional health care provider.

Although there are serious philosophical questions concerning the attending physician's failure to treat the patient aggressively, failure to communicate properly clinical management decisions to the family, and failure to obtain the requested consultation as he agreed to do; under the circumstances, these findings are probably insufficient to provide a legal remedy. Most respectable physicians would have used a similar management plan for the care of this "terminal" patient; and the patient had received maximal benefit from the MICU, raising questions of allocation of health care resources. Although the insensitivity or inexpertise in clinically managing these sensitive matters is suboptimal, the choices and insensitivity were not wanton, malicious, or outrageous.

(2) Variations of the Physician-Patient Relationship
5: *Facts*

A thirty-two-year-old mother had been treated for recurrent headaches with various narcotic medications without significant relief. Skull films, lumbar puncture, brain scan, and EEG were within normal limits. A neurologist diagnosed her condition as "severe suboccipital tendinitis, secondary to occipital neuritis and severe anxiety which was possibly situational." Several months later she was admitted to the community hospital for a headache that was thought to be due to tension. She underwent psychiatric interviews, but a functional basis for the headaches was not detected. Therefore her attending physician decided to send her to a university center for neurological consultation. Because of a clerical coding error, the transfer note designated her a neuropsychiatric patient requiring intensive care, rather than a neurology patient. She arrived at the university hospital on a stretcher and was sent to a psychiatric ward. When she discovered that she was being admitted to a psychiatric ward, she became fearful and indicated to the nurses and the physician that she had been transferred to the medical center primarily to have a CAT scan performed.

The psychiatrist threatened to put her in the seclusion room if she did not calm herself. He said, "If you have to shit or pee, you will have to bang on the door." She thought she might not be able to see her children or her husband again if she did not calm down. She was admitted to an open mixed psychiatric therapeutic community.

On the day following admission, the psychiatrist discovered that she was not really a psychiatric patient and that she required a medical work-up. However, he told the patient that she would have to stay on the ward because there were no other beds available on the hospital. He indicated that she could be adequately cared for on the ward during the pendency of her medical work-up. She was advised that she would have to abide by all the rules of the ward while she was there. Although she disagreed with this arrangement, she went along with it out of fear that she would be put in a seclusion room and not be released to return to her family.

During her ten days on the ward, the patient was subjected to several humiliating experiences including being made to wear a robe which identified her as a psychiatric patient; not being allowed to leave the ward without an escort; and being forced to participate in group therapy programs and occupational therapy programs, including group dances. During such dance sessions she was required to dance with an attendant who made suggestive sexual remarks to her; and subsequently threw a deck of cards on the floor, and demanded that she pick them up. After she received a "gig" for failing to make her bed, she lived in fear of getting more gigs for anything she might do wrong. There was some censoring of information when she attempted to communicate with her husband. She began to participate in the milieu activities, including recreational and occupational therapy, while her medical workup was in progress. After initial reluctance she appeared to become involved in the group therapeutic processes, and shared her insight with the seriously ill psychiatric patients. According to her attending physician's discharge summary, at no time during her hospitalization did she evince psychopathology nor did she receive psychotherapeutic medication Ultimately, the medical work-up demonstrated that her headaches were related to hormonally induced retention of fluids.

Allegations

Since her discharge she has experienced nightmares and dreams of trying to run to escape, only to find that her legs would not move. She contended that these emotional disturbances adversely affected her marital and maternal roles and relationships. She filed a malpractice claim alleging that she was kept in a psychiatric ward for a ten-day period against her will.

Discussion

As a result of a typographical error, this patient was involuntarily incarcerated on a psychiatric ward. After she informed the psychiatrist of the mistake, he chose to conclude that the patient was incorrect despite the fact that she manifested no obvious need for "intensive psychiatric confinement." Contacting the referral physicians to clarify the situation would have been a more reasonable and prudent course. This mismanagement was compounded when it became apparent that she did not require psychotherapy, let alone intensive psychotherapy, and the psychiatrist failed to transfer her to another ward. His motives for such decisions were questionable and manifested poor professional judgment. Even if there were no other available hospital beds, other arrangements should have been made because the patient had already demonstrated stress at being placed on a psychiatric ward. The psychiatrist was also aware of her prior psychosocial problems. He should have been aware that she would be intimidated by this loss of self-control and, therefore, may have complied out of fear and not volition. She was, in effect, falsely and improperly "imprisoned" and deprived of her fundamental right to liberty during the entire hospital stay. On this theory, the physician involved will be exposed to substantial liability.

6: *Facts*

A thirty-eight-year-old man underwent a preemployment physical examination at the shipyard of his prospective employer. A chest x-ray was taken and sent to a nearby hospital for interpretation. The radiologist noted a 3 X 2 centimeter soft tissue abnormality in the right lung and suggested that further diagnostic studies be undertaken to delineate the nature of the lesion. Because of a clerical error, both the x-ray report and the x-ray film were filed at the shipyard medical office without being seen by the physician who had performed the preemployment examination of the man. As a result, the prospective employee was found fit for employment and hired.

After having worked at the shipyard twenty months, the man experienced persistent chest pain associated with shortness of breath and coughing. He consulted his private physician who obtained a chest x-ray which disclosed a large mass in the right lung, which at surgery was found to be an undifferentiated large cell carcinoma. Postoperatively, the patient received radiation therapy, resulting in marked shrinkage of the tumor.

Allegations

The man brought suit against his employer, alleging that the company physician breached his duty to notify him of the abnormal chest x-ray when the lesion was first noted. He asserted that earlier diagnosis and treatment of the tumor would have significantly increased his chance of survival.

Discussion

Ordinarily an employer owes no duty to prospective employees to ascertain whether they are physically fit for the job they seek. However, when an employer assumes that duty, and the examiner relies upon proper performance that is not achieved; the employer may be liable to an employee if the duty is negligently performed. Thus a duty of due care may exist even if technically no physician-patient relationship existed at the time of the examination. The legal rationale for imposing such a duty is that an employee may be foreseeably harmed if he relies on the false interpretations and results of a negligently performed examination. This duty is distinguishable from one in which a patient relies to his detriment on the report of an examining physician where the employee is seeking compensation for a work-connected disability. In such a case the physician generally owes no duty to the examinee (claimant) because the physician is employed by the insurance carrier to examine the claimant in order to evaluate and rate the injury. Therefore, the physician usually is in an adversarial relationship to the claimant, and thus has no reason to expect that the claimant would rely on his report.

Even if there was a breach of duty in this case, it is arguable that the tumor was less undifferentiated at that time than when finally diagnosed. Nevertheless, the man may have lost an opportunity to receive treatment for a less aggressive tumor. Thus the delay in diagnosis may have been deleterious, and therefore partially compensable. If so, he might also receive compensation for mental anguish secondary to the awareness of this lost opportunity.

7: *Facts*

A twenty-four-year-old female, gravida 4, para 0, was concerned about having another problem with her current pregnancy. Therefore, she had an amniocentesis performed for chromosomal analysis. She was assured that the status of the fetus was normal. The patient's estranged husband did not know about the pregnancy. At thirty-three weeks gestation she was admitted to the hospital in premature labor and treated with Terbutaline. She was discharged two days later. At thirty-five weeks gestation she was rehospitalized in active labor. Pelvimetry and ultrasound examinations demonstrated that the patient had a contracted outlet. The fetus was in a breech presentation. In preparing the patient for caesarean section, the labor room nurse shaved the pubic area of the patient against her protests. The patient had no preoperative medication and was taken to the operating room at approximately 5:00 P.M. and placed in the right lateral position for induction of spinal anesthesia. The lumbar puncture was accomplished with a 25 gauge spinal needle, using an introducer, and Tetracaine 5 mg. in dextrose and water was introduced in the lumbar subarachnoid space. An anesthesia level to T-8 was achieved. Approximately five minutes later, the blood pressure and pulse fell rapidly. The patient was given intravenous Ephedrine and the blood pressure and pulse rate rapidly climbed to 130/80 and a pulse rate of 100. Five minutes later surgery was initiated and a healthy, viable infant was delivered through a low caesarean section. The procedure was completed 40 minutes later. Ten minutes after that, the patient complained of pain and received 5 cc. of Fentanyl and 10 mg. of Valium. On arrival in the recovery room, the patient's blood pressure was 120/80, and pulse rate was 112. One hour later she was transferred to her room with stable vital signs. She still had weakness in her lower extremities. The patient subsequently had an uncomplicated postoperative recovery.

Allegations

The patient sued her attending physicians and the hospital for assault and battery. The patient alleged that shaving her pubic area in preparing for caesarean section was improper and against her wishes, and that the administration of her spinal anesthetic was improperly and inadequately performed. The alleged malpractice is contained in the patient's following statements.

> Prior to the delivery of my baby, the doctor determined that it was necessary for me to have my child by caesarean section. I was informed that it was unnecessary to have my pubic area shaved. Shortly prior to being taken to the operating room, I was prepped by a nurse. I advised her that I did not wish to have my pubic area shaved since I was delivering by caesarean section. Over my protests, she completed shaving my pubic area.
>
> A short while after receiving a spinal anesthetic, the surgeon began to operate on me. I advised him that I could feel a burning pain as he proceeded to cut. He paused for a moment and then proceeded to cut. I experienced excruciating pain throughout the entire procedure. Afterwards, while I was in the recovery room, the person who administered the anesthetic came to see me, apologized for the pain that I went through, and explained that possibly some fluid may have leaked out. She informed me that ordinarily no pain was involved with the procedure.

Discussion

The preparation of a patient for obstetrical surgery is designed to prevent or minimize serious postoperative complications, such as postoperative vaginal, uterine or urinary infections. The propensity for infection is high because of the bleeding and the unprotected uterine wall, which is at risk to harbor infective organisms. Thus it is standard operating procedure to shave and prepare the pubic area to reduce the amount of bacteria, and the opportunities for infection to develop, by removing as much superficial contamination as possible. The patient should have known that in a caesarean delivery, the pubic area had to be cleansed for her own safety in preventing serious postdelivery infections. She attempted to prevent hospital personnel from preparing her surgically in order to hide the fact of her pregnancy and delivery, even though it is unlikely she could conceal the surgical scar.

The choice of regional spinal anesthesia was not negligent. Elective caesarean sections may be performed under general anesthesia, or under spinal anesthesia utilizing a subarachnoid or epidural technique. The obstetrical patient is considered at high risk of anesthesia because of the complication of aspiration of stomach contents. Therefore, the choice and technique of anesthesia is designed to prevent this usually fatal complication. General anesthesia requires preparation of the patient's intestinal tract with antacids and oral ingestions in the preoperative period. During induction of anesthesia, a rapid sequence utilizing a short-acting induction agent and short-acting muscle relaxant are used to accomplish rapid tracheal intubation to prevent aspiration of abdominal contents. Ordinarily in the patient in active labor, intestinal peristalsis is inhibited, thus any secretion or ingestion will remain in the stomach until delivery. Therefore, endotracheal intubation is a protective device to prevent aspiration of these contents during the caesarean section.

Regional block anesthesia is appropriate in nonemergency caesarean sections, because the anesthetic level utilized is low and the upper chest muscles and upper respiratory reflexes are maintained so that the patient may protect her own upper airway and prevent aspiration of stomach contents. Properly performed, such anesthesia can provide requisite and satisfactory comfort to the patient. Following injection of drugs in the subarachnoid or epidural spaces, there is a five to ten minute delay in achieving loss of sensation. In this case, a successful block was obtained because the blood pressure and pulse rate rapidly decreased over the first five minutes after the anesthetic injection and required vasopressor agents to restore the blood pressure and pulse rate to preanesthetic levels. In the early phase of a subarachnoid or epidural block, the initially affected nerve is the sympathetic, because it requires the least amount of anesthetic concentration and results in the lower extremities becoming engorged with circulation as the vessels relax. This condition causes a fall in blood pressure, which is restored by rapid treatment with intravenous fluids and vasopressor agents. The next nerve group affected are the sensory nerves. There is evidence in this case that the patient had a sensory level well above the umbilicus which equates to a skin anesthesia level between the breast nipple line and the umbilicus. This level is adequate to perform the delivery of the infant through a lower uterine incision. The next group of nerves affected by the anesthetic are those which control the lower abdominal, pelvic and lower extremity muscles. It is not necessary in a caesarean section to completely block the motor nerves. Loss of feeling and surgical anesthesia is accomplished by anesthetic concentrations less than those required for muscle paralysis. The patient's anesthetic level was T-8. However, such anesthesia would not alleviate all painful stimulation of an intraabdominal procedure because the peritoneum may be innervated from a level as high as T-4. Therefore, retraction on the lower abdominal excision may cause the patient to experience unpleasant sensations during surgery. Thus it is the usual technique, as was done in this case, to sedate the patient after the infant is delivered to alleviate this mild discomfort. Ordinarily, the existence of discomfort is not evidence of negligent anesthesia practice. The operative or anesthesia notes did not reflect that the patient was experiencing excruciating operative pain. Had the anesthetic not been adequate at the time of surgical incision, a patient without adequate preoperative medication would have reacted strongly to this stimulus. With the subarachnoid block at T-8, the sedative and analgesic drugs were adequate to provide the patient with anesthetic comfort for the remaining forty minutes of surgery. When the patient arrived in the recovery room, the patient had a low extremity weakness at this time, which indicates that cutaneous anesthesia was still present and indicating that the block had been satisfactorily performed.

(3) Diagnostic Considerations

8: *Facts*

An eighteen-month-old infant female was well until her mother noted a left postauricular mass which was associated with a low-grade fever. Over the next three days, the mother gave the infant one aspirin every two hours. When the postauricular mass, which the mother thought might be "mumps," did not decrease in size, the mother took the child to an emergency room. There the infant's temperature was 100° rectally. The infant was tachypneic and appeared groggy. The physician listened to the infant's chest and told her mother there was a "little" congestion. His clinical impression was "R/O mumps." He then asked her what she had been giving her. She replied aspirin. Aspirin (strength not recorded) every four hours and Dimetapp were prescribed. She was asked to see her pediatrician in the morning.

The following day the infant visited her pediatrician. She appeared so dehydrated to the pediatrician's nurse that she was immediately seen on a priority basis. The pediatrician noted that the infant had been seen in the emergency room the day before because of "deep breathing and listlessness." His examination disclosed a toxic, obtunded, and markedly dehydrated child with Kussmaul respirations. Salicylate level was 77 milligrams percent. Initial arterial blood gases showed a pH 7.28 and pCO_2 40; the bicarbonate was 18.7 with a base deficit of 6.2.

She was treated with IV fluids, sodium bicarbonate, and acetozolamide. Twenty-four hours after admission, she had a cardiopulmonary arrest. Salicylate levels at the time of the unsuccessful cardiopulmonary resuscitation was 19.2. Autopsy disclosed pulmonary edema and lymphocytic laryngitis. Examinations of the gastrointestinal tract demonstrated no errosive hemorrhages.

Allegations

A malpractice claim for wrongful death was filed alleging that "the emergency room physician negligently prescribed additional aspirin, while already aware of the infant's symptoms," and that this act of negligence caused her death.

Discussion

Careful history-taking from the parents is required for proper evaluation of pediatric patients. This usually includes specific inquiry as to the nature and amount of medication taken for the present illness. If the history that one baby aspirin had been given every two hours for three days had been obtained, it should have alerted the interviewer to the probability of acute and/or chronic salicylism. Strict adherence to that dosage schedule would be excessive for the average eighteen-month-old infant. Under those circumstances, it would be imprudent to prescribe continued usage. Moreover, if any doubt existed as to the possibility of salicylate overuse, an alternative antipyretic medication (e.g. acetaminophen) should have been prescribed. Moreover, the indication for continued scheduled prescription of an antipyretic was not strong because the rectal temperature was 100° F. The absence of the dose strength of the aspirin in the record could also create an inference that adult strength aspirin might have been inadvertently prescribed. This tends to reinforce the notion that due care was not exercised in this case.

Primary health care personnel are obligated to carefully investigate clinical problems. A minimum level of clinical skill and competence to treat patients requires enough knowledge to conduct an intelligent inquiry as to what is not known about the patient's illness. In this case the health care provider who assessed the infant's degree of toxicity lacked certain fundamental knowledge concerning both the degree of toxicity of an infant and the side effects of aspirin overdose. Notwithstanding this, consultation with a more knowledgeable person was not obtained. Instead, the provider unreasonably acted on ignorance.

9: *Facts*

On January 15, 1975, this sixty-three-year-old patient was evaluated in an outpatient clinic for arthralgias. A physical exam was unremarkable. A chest x-ray demonstrated cardiomegaly. He was referred to an internist for cardiovascular evaluation. On January 24, 1975, the internist found his chest clear bilaterally with no rales or rhonchi. The cardiomegaly was thought to be secondary to heavy cigarette smoking. The recommendation was to discontinue all smoking. There was also a plan to review his chest x-rays and chart when they became available in order to determine if further evaluation was necessary, however no such review was ever accomplished.

In October 1975, the patient was evaluated at an emergency room with a chief complaint of coughing up blood. He gave a past medical history of epistaxis; however, no nasal bleeding site was noted. The emergency room physician did not feel that the hemoptysis was a result of the epistaxis, and therefore, referred the patient to an internist.

In November 1975, a preappointment chest x-ray was taken and subsequently interpreted by the radiologist to show interstitial fibrotic changes in both lower lung fields, unchanged from the chest film taken on January 15, 1975. The internist noted that the patient had experienced epistaxis for several years. After taking a history, the internist opined that the patient did not, in fact, have hemoptysis; but instead his coughing up blood was secondary to epistaxis. Bronchoscopy was not offered. The patient incidentally admitted to a weight loss of more than twenty pounds. The patient was then referred to an otolaryngologist in December 1975, and a vessel over the right septum was cauterized.

On January 2, 1976, the patient was seen by an ophthalmologist because he complained of poor vision. The ophthalmologist noted that the patient seemed "out of it" and was "shabbily dressed." The exam showed 20/20 corrected visual acuity bilaterally. No visual field testing was performed and no additional history of associate symptoms such as headaches was made.

On January 5, 1976, the patient arrived at the emergency room complaining of memory lapse and poor coordination. On January 12, 1976, a neurological evaluation disclosed a history of recurrent right-sided weakness. A left homonymous hemianopsia to gross confrontation testing was detected. Left-sided incoordination and poor balance were also noted. A CAT scan demonstrated a cerebral lesion. He underwent a right craniotomy for a subtotal resection of a right parietal occipital tumor of bronchogenic origin. The chest x-ray was "suggestive of carcinoma of the left side."

Several months later the patient was readmitted to the hospital with widespread metastasis and died. The death certificate estimated the duration of the cancer was approximately eighteen months, that is, since approximately January 1975. The estimated duration of symptoms from metastases was approximately ten months since approximately October 1975.

Allegation

The patient's widow filed a claim alleging that her husband died of carcinoma of the lung because of the failure of his physicians to make a timely diagnosis.

Discussion

In retrospect, the patient probably had carcinoma of the lung in January 1975. This was probably not apparent on the chest x-ray taken at that time. Nevertheless, the lack of follow-up in reviewing the x-rays and re-evaluating the clinical state of the patient was substandard care.

In October 1975, when the patient presented with hemoptysis, a bronchoscopy was clinically indicated because of the patient's age and history of smoking (even though metastasis as manifested by headaches and progressive hemiparesis had already developed). Thus there is no effective causative link between the negligent delay in diagnosis and the damage suffered by the patient. Therefore the issue is whether the disease should have been diagnosed in January 1975. The normal chest x-ray at that time indicates that a failure to make that diagnosis was not negligence.

Although this case also illustrates the problems of multiple incomplete consultations, little or no liability will be established because the tumor would not have been diagnosed at a curable time.

10: *Facts*

On October 11, a twenty-four-year-old female went to her physician because she had "felt weird" for approximately one week and wanted to know if something was physically "wrong" with her. She described episodes of "unawareness," and complained of headaches. She also related that she had become "frustrated" at work and upset because her husband's job was not going well. She had no serious prior medical illness, and her family history was unremarkable. Physical evaluation disclosed a healthy appearing female. Gross neurological examination was normal. A CBC and chest x-ray were within normal limits. The clinical impression was "probable anxiety." Several days later, she returned to her physician because of "nervous tension." She stated that she had multiple emotional and physical problems which seemed to be related to her husband's job situation, which required frequent trips away from home. Again, no positive findings were noted. The physician's diagnosis was "tension and anxiety" and he prescribed Librium.

On November 20, she again saw her physician in order to recheck her "nervous tension." Her physician requested an EEG, recording on the consultation sheet that the patient experienced "nervous tension, explosive headaches, and emotional instability." Approximately one week later, the EEG was reported as "normal"; however, a repeat EEG was recommended. On the front sheet of the EEG recording, notations were made by the technician which referred to "abnormal left frontal-central activity." A follow-up EEG was not performed.

On February 16, she again consulted her physician because of "nerves." She stated that her neighbors have stated that she "talks to herself," and she is unaware she is doing this. She indicated that she was seeing a psychiatrist at that time but had not been taking any medication. Her physician prescribed meprobamate.

On March 17, she was again seen by her physician. She indicated that she had "spells of mumbling" and would sit through traffic stop lights. She thought she might be having seizures because she would drift away in a trance. Her physician did not make a diagnosis or diagnostic plan nor did he give her a warning about the hazards of driving an automobile.

Two days later the patient sustained a flexion-extension injury of the cervical spine and a sternal contusion as a result of an automobile accident in which she struck another car in the rear. The accident was caused by an episode of unconsciousness.

On April 10, she was evaluated by a neurologist who detected that she experienced multiple daily transient episodes, which occurred without warning or provoking factors. Each episode was characterized by a sudden feeling of detachment and associated with automated behavior. She experienced no loss of postural tone. After each episode she was fully alert and oriented.

The neurologist concluded that the clinical history was compatible with temporal lobe automatism or a closely related type of seizure disorder. He indicated that on the basis of its clinical presentation alone, her condition required a therapeutic trial of anticonvulsive medication. An EEG disclosed a localized abnormality of the left frontal temporal region with epileptiform activity superimposed on a semirhythmic dysrhythmic abnormality. The neurologist felt that the EEG findings correlated closely with the patient's clinical history. After reviewing the initial EEG done on the patient, he also opined that the EEG which had been performed four months earlier was strongly indicative of the abnormality.

Allegations

Subsequently, the patient filed a malpractice claim alleging that epilepsy should have been suspected and diagnosed from the patient's presenting clinical symptoms and the initial EEG. She requested legal damages for injuries sustained as a result of the automobile accident, and the emotional suffering of being continually told that her condition was caused merely by nerves due to marital problems. She also contended that the delay in diagnosis forced her to discontinue her employment and interfered with her ability to obtain employment.

Discussion

This case represents an example of a physician not adequately suspecting a serious, yet treatable, condition before complications of the illness occur. The episodes of "unawareness" and headache should have suggested a neurologic etiology despite the subjective symptoms of feeling "weird" and being "frustrated." The preliminary evaluation and initial request for an EEG were timely and appropriate. However, later the physician's diligence and care were lagging.

The first significant error was not repeating the EEG as requested, even though it was reported as "normal." If the report seemed self-contradictory, the physician should have contacted the electroencephalographer to explain the need for a repeat. The electroencephalographer also erred in reporting the EEG "normal." If the tracing was suspicious or borderline abnormal, the report should have stated this.

When the patient returned in February and March complaining of trancelike states, her physician was under a duty to continue the prior evaluation. The prescription of meprobamate and failure to warn the patient not to drive is not within the standard of acceptable care under the circumstances of this case. If the physician were at a loss for a diagnosis, he should have referred the patient to a neurologist because her symptoms were compatible with a seizure disorder or a neuropathic condition.

This case demonstrates lack of diligence in the diagnosis of a treatable condition and lack of care to prevent foreseeable complications. The physician's casual and careless attitude in failing to warn the patient about driving will make him liable for those consequential damages in addition to loss of wages referrable to the improper delay in the diagnosis for the injuries secondary to the automobile accident.

11: *Facts*

In January, a twenty-nine-year-old female began to experience recurrent headaches. In February, a neurologist was consulted. The patient related that the headaches often began suddenly, late in the day. They were frequently associated with her menses and were becoming most severe. The headaches were throbbing, usually left-sided, but spread to involve the entire head. They were almost always terminated by nausea and vomiting. Occasionally the headaches were associated with uncontrollable trembling of the left leg, but were not associated with an aura. After the headache, her vision would usually "blur out." Demerol provided significant relief. Skull x-rays, brain scan, and EEG were normal.

The neurologist's clinical impression was "migraine-type headache." A cervical spine series and a repeat EEG were within normal limits. On his advice, the patient stopped taking birth control pills. He instructed her to take Cafergot only for relief of severe headaches. Thereafter she had the headaches sparingly, and they were adequately controlled by the Cafergot.

One evening in June, the patient excitedly told her husband that something had "snapped in her head and that she was in terrible pain." He took her to an emergency room. When they arrived, she appeared to be incoherent and sleepy. She was placed in a wheelchair. Her husband told the clerk that his wife had a history of headaches. When the intern in the emergency room asked the husband what was the nature of the problem, the husband was belligerent and demanded that his wife be given Demerol. The intern elicited that the patient had a history of migraines, that the headache had been "on and off" during the day, and not associated with vomiting or an aura. Cafergot tablets had not provided relief. The discomfort which led her to come to the emergency room had been of sudden onset and localized at the top of her head and was constant and throbbing in nature. She gave no history of extremity complaints.

Initially the patient was agitated and hyperventilating. Her blood pressure was 182/112. The neurological exam was within normal limits except for bilateral hyperflexia and bilateral clonus on quick flexion of the ankles which the intern attributed to anxiety and hypertension. Although the patient related that it hurt to bite or wrinkle her forehead, there was no meningismus or neck pain. Her optic discs were flat. No focal neurological deficits were detected.

The intern consulted with a staff physician. They discussed the possibility of a subarachnoid hemorrhage, but they felt that the lack of neck pain made the diagnosis unlikely. Their clinical impression was "probable vascular headaches and hysterical reaction to pain." The intern ordered the administration of Vistaril intramuscularly and placed the patient in a dark room. Shortly thereafter her diastolic blood pressure went from 112 to 92. Over the next thirty minutes of observation she became calm. The intern discharged the patient and told the husband that if his wife was not feeling better to come back to the ER. He requested that they consult a neurologist in the morning for follow-up.

Because she continued to complain of pain and vomiting an hour after she arrived home, the husband called the emergency room and related that his wife was still in pain. He was told to come to the hospital and get sleeping pills for her, which he did. The intern told the husband that if the sleep medication did not work within an hour, he should bring his wife back to the hospital. Although the pills did not cause her to sleep, the husband decided to wait until morning and see the neurologist.

When the patient saw the neurologist, her condition seemed to be unchanged. The neurologist felt that she probably had a migraine headache; however, because he was impressed with her degree of discomfort, he decided to hospitalize her.

The patient's admission blood pressure was 100/60. The rest of her vital signs were within normal limits. Admission work-up disclosed a mild left hemiparesis, terminal posterior neck stiffness on forward flexion, questionable left homonymous hemianopia, flaccid paresis of her extremities, sustained ankle clonus on the left, and decreased sensation to light touch on the left. No papilledema was noted. Her reflexes were normal.

A lumbar puncture was then performed. The opening pressure was 265 and the closing pressure 160. The cerebral spinal fluid was pink and xanthochromic. The patient was transferred to the Intensive Care Unit. A brain scan disclosed increased uptake to the right parietal area consistent with a hemorrhage of the right middle cerebral artery. A cerebral arteriogram disclosed a posterior temporoparietal lesion with spasm in the distal middle cerebral vessels, and slight shifting of the mid-line vessels from right to left. A CAT scan performed five days later was suggestive of an intracerebral hematoma in the right posterior superior parietal region with evidence of superior extension into the subarachnoid space.

Hospital therapy consisted of Decadron and phenobarbital. After gradual development and improvement of strength on the left side, the patient began physical and occupational therapy. She was largely spared the defects usually associated with a subarachnoid hemorrhage.

Allegations

Subsequently a malpractice claim was filed, claiming damages for partial paralysis due to a failure to properly diagnose and treat the patient's condition. This failure allegedly caused the patient partial paralysis, pain and suffering, loss of wages, and future medical problems.

Discussion

Although it is not possible to ascertain if the patient was leaking from an aneurysm when she presented in the emergency room, the findings were consistent with a subarachnoid hemorrhage. The usual procedure after a diagnosis of subarachnoid hemorrhage is made is to institute bed rest, lower the blood pressure with medication, and do an angiogram as soon as reasonable for clarification and definitive treatment of the process. Because the patient had a nonlocalizing neurological examination, either the signs of a subarachnoid hemorrhage were not recognized on the initial exam, or she developed the hematoma from a re-bleed after she was sent home.

The patient's initial attending neurologist was critical of the care the patient received. A significant factor that may have colored his opinion was his own inability to diagnose the existence of a cerebrovascular problem prior to the hospitalization. The patient gave him a history on her first visit that she experienced a left-sided deficit associated with her headaches. He did not actively pursue the cause of this symptom. In retrospect, the findings probably heralded her subarachnoid hemorrhage.

In general, there is insufficient evidence to establish a lack of requisite care or diligence on the part of the emergency room physician. The early diagnosis of a subarachnoid hemorrhage may be difficult, especially where there are no objective neurological deficits nor posterior neck pain. The subtlety of her injury probably accounts for the sparing effect of the injury. If the patient's subarachnoid hemorrhage were caused by an aneurysm (rather than, for example, an arteriovenous malformation), and if her initial presenting symptomatology were the manifestations of aneurysmal dilatation, rupture of the aneurysm may have been preventable. However, such conditional assumptions are unwarranted. Because of her past history of headaches and the absence of focal neurological defects, it was reasonable for the emergency room intern and resident to conclude that the etiology of the patient's headache was "vascular." Although in retrospect the nature of the headache was peculiar, it was clinically consistent with a "vascular" headache.

Even if a hemorrhage had been diagnosed in the emergency room, her injury would not have been substantially altered. Treatment would not have significantly differed from what she received. Under the circumstances, her legal damages would not be significant.

12: *Facts*

The brother of this eight-year-old girl was admitted to a medical center with a tentative diagnosis of meningococcal meningitis, subsequently confirmed by culture. The patient was placed on penicillin, 250 mg. QID for five days, by their family physician.

Four days later, in the evening, the girl arrived at the emergency room with a four-hour history of headache, neck and leg aches, and fever. She was evaluated by her family physician who noted that she was toxic, but alert and oriented. Her rectal temperature was 104.5°. No rash or stiff neck were noted. CSF disclosed three polys, a glucose of 55, and protein of 34. No organisms were seen on gram stain of the spun sediment. WBC was 4,000 (61 percent polys).

The family physician inspected the hospital bacteriology laboratory log but could not obtain a final report of the patient's nasopharyngeal or throat culture that had been taken four days earlier when her brother was hospitalized. Five days was required for Neisseria to be positively identified.

Two hours after arrival in the emergency room the patient told her physician that her symptoms had lessened. The physician's clinical impression was "probable Flu Syndrome." He sent the patient home with instructions to return if a rash appeared, or if her condition worsened, but definitely to return to his office the next morning.

The patient had a restless night. Early in the morning her parents noticed an abdominal rash and took her to the emergency room. She arrived in a toxic, tachypneic, and tachycardic state. She had signs of meningeal irritation and ecchymoses over her body. CSF disclosed two cells and a glucose of 16. Smear of the spun sediment disclosed gram negative diplococci. She was hospitalized, given 1,000,000 units of aqueous penicillin, followed shortly thereafter by 3,000,000 units by IV push.

Two hours after admission, she became comatose and had a seizure that was initially controlled with IV Valium. Shortly thereafter, she had a gastrointestinal hemorrhage, went into shock, and died.

An autopsy disclosed evidence of meningococcemia (Neisseria meningitidis) with bilateral adrenal hemorrhage. There was scant evidence of meningitis.

Allegations

The patient's parents filed a wrongful-death claim alleging negligence in diagnosis and treatment of their child.

Discussion

More than one-half of the patients with meningococcemia die within six hours after coming under medical observation. Clinical evidence of meningitis is usually muted because the fulminant course of the disease causes death before there is opportunity for marked meningeal involvement. In terms of legal liability for delay in diagnosis, the recognized fulminant nature of meningococcemia "cuts both ways." On the one hand, the poor likelihood of survival is evident. On the other hand, when the presenting clinical constellation is compatible with the diagnosis of meningococcemia, anticipation by the attending physician is obligatory.

In this case, clinical evidence of meningococcemia was present: a recent exposure history, appropriate incubation period, suggestive and compatible clinical and laboratory data, and knowledge that the patient was receiving antibiotic treatment which might mask or alter the clinical presentation. Sufficient knowledge of the disease process should have induced greater anticipation and caution.

The attending physician was presented with the following choices: hospitalize and immediately commence intravenous antibiotic therapy; hospitalize and closely monitor; or send home with instructions to return. Under the circumstances, the third course was not reasonable.

Although the attending physician carefully evaluated the patient, he failed to apply his medical knowledge skillfully. He did not adhere to the principles of a differential diagnosis in arriving at a diagnosis of "Flu Syndrome." Under the circumstances, his diagnosis cannot be easily reconciled with his patient's clinical presentation. Moreover, a physician is expected to exclude or rule out life threatening or serious conditions which demand urgent intervention. This was not done in this case, as evidenced by the patient's clinical history, toxic appearance, WBC and CSF. Therefore, the attending physician's judgment was not founded on proper application of clinical skills.

The argument that treatment would have been futile is speculative and does not break the legal chain of causation. At the time of initial evaluation, there was no convincing evidence that adrenal hemorrhage, the direct cause of death, was present or inevitable.

13: *Fact*

A sixteen-year-old female was brought to the emergency room because of a history of attempted suicide by ingestion of Librium, Tylenol, and Actifed. The apparent precipitant was a fight with her father regarding her boyfriend. She was noted to be depressed, lethargic, and unsteady, but coherent and oriented. Although she giggled inappropriately, there was no evidence of psychosis. The diagnosis was "Drug overdose secondary to adolescent reaction." She was admitted to the hospital on the medical service. Four days later, after psychiatric consultation, she was discharged as "improved."

Three days after discharge, her parents took her to their family physician because of dizziness, confusion, and transitory dissociative staring. A neurologic examination was within normal limits, and a drug screen was negative. The clinical impression was "Psychological reaction."

One week later, she again was taken to her family physician complaining of jerky movements of her legs, which had been increasing in severity and frequency. She also related that it was difficult for her to concentrate. Neurological examination and skull x-ray were within normal limits. She was referred to a psychiatrist for further evaluation. After an evaluation, the psychiatrist referred her to a psychologist for psychometric testing. The psychologist determined that the cause of her symptomatology was probably organic. Therefore, he referred her to a neurologist. An EEG disclosed a grossly abnormal pattern.

Her parents became impatient with this pattern of multiple referral. Before the family physician could coordinate and complete the evaluation, they took their daughter to a university medical center for evaluation. There, the physician elicited a history of progressive myoclonic jerks, associated with labile personality and expressionless affect. There was no family history of neurologic disorders. It was noted that she had measles and chicken pox at age five. The suspected diagnosis was progressive encephalopathy, probably secondary to Subacute Sclerosing Panencephalitis (SSPE). Subsequently, measles titres (CSF 1:64; serum 1:128) confirmed the diagnosis.

After her discharge from the hospital, gradual neurologic deterioration became evident. Out of desperation, her parents secured various forms of medical and quasimedical aid, including extensive chiropractic treatment. When she was reevaluated at the university medical center, her parents were told that she had a progressive and incurable disease.

Allegations

A claim was filed alleging that, while under the care and supervision of the family physician, and while suffering from SSPE, she continued to deteriorate due to the physician's failure to diagnose her condition and treat her;

and that as a result, she suffered irreversible brain damage causing her to be totally and permanently disabled.

Discussion

The patient clinically presented to her physician as manifesting an aberration in behavior that simulated a functional psychological disorder. When these findings persisted, she was appropriately referred to behavioral specialists for evaluation, with the intent to reevaluate her for organicity, if functional disease was not established. Her symptomatology was insidious and masked by common behavioral aberrations; therefore, the etiologic diagnosis was not suggested earlier. In addition, SSPE is sufficiently rare that it would be unreasonable to expect a physician to make a definitive diagnosis in its nascent state.

Even if a delay in diagnosis or misdiagnosis is assumed, there is no causal connection between the alleged negligence and the patient's injury. SSPE is a progressive and incurable disease that does not respond to any specific therapy. Thus failure to diagnose it in its early stage would not represent a legally recognized causal relationship between the alleged negligent act and the patient's disability.

14: *Facts*

A nodule in the right inferior pole of the thyroid gland of a fifty-eight-year-old woman was first noticed when she went to her physician for a health evaluation. Ultrasound of the thyroid gland, and thyroid function tests were within normal limits. However a thyroid uptake scan demonstrated a solitary "cold" nodule in the location where the nodule was palpable.

The patient was given a therapeutic trial of synthetic thyroid hormone in an attempt to shrink the nodule. However, the nodule did not change in size. Her physicians felt that the physical findings, laboratory studies, and the unresponsiveness to suppressive thyroid therapy raised a strong possibility that the nodule was malignant. Accordingly, surgery was scheduled for diagnostic and therapeutic reasons.

Under general anesthesia, the patient underwent excisional biopsy of the nodule, which on frozen section was reported as undifferentiated carcinoma. Accordingly, a right subtotal thyroidectomy and modified radical neck dissection was undertaken. Because of difficulty in locating certain anatomical landmarks, the surgery took much longer than expected. The anesthesiologist lost interest in the progress of the operation and began to doodle on the anesthesia record. In the "REMARKS" column, he wrote "Boredom."

Postoperatively, the patient developed a hoarse voice as a result of injury to the recurrent laryngeal nerve and a right shoulder drop, secondary to injury to the brachial plexus. Furthermore, a Foley catheter was incorrectly inserted preoperatively, thereby allowing excessive bladder distention and resulted in difficulty in normal urinary function.

On permanent pathology sections of the thyroid tissue, the pathologists could identify only benign disease (Hashimoto's thyroiditis). The error in frozen section diagnosis was found to be due to an artifact (floater) contaminating the fixing solutions or the microtome employed in the frozen section procedure. The pathologist had actually examined a specimen from a prior patient who had adenocarcinoma of the breast.

Allegations

When the patient was informed of the error in diagnosis, she filed a claim alleging medical malpractice in the unnecessary and negligent performance of radical neck dissection, caused by the mistaken diagnosis of carcinoma of the thyroid gland. As a result, she claimed, among other things, physical and mental pain and suffering, prolonged healing, permanent hoarseness, loss of the use of her right arm, facial paralysis and numbness.

Discussion

When a patient has a solitary thyroid nodule, confirmed as "nonfunctioning" by radioactive uptake and scan, the possibility of carcinoma must be considered. The preoperative work-up and evaluation was entirely appropriate, including the trial to determine the responsiveness of the nodule to suppressive thyroid therapy. Therefore, thyroid excisional biopsy for diagnostic purposes was clinically indicated.

However, liability must be conceded on the issue of the erroneous pathologic diagnosis of the thyroid nodule as malignant. A medically related task, as critical as this, requires scrupulous technique, careful controls and appropriate procedures to insure against contamination of the material used for frozen section examination. Such an error is inexcusable and indefensible.

Once the surgeon was informed of the frozen section diagnosis of undifferentiated carcinoma, his decision to perform a modified radical neck procedure to look for local spread of the lesion to adjacent lymph nodes or soft tissue of the neck was the treatment of choice. However, the patient will be able to recover damages for all adverse results of the surgery. Even though the surgery may not have been negligently performed, damages for all direct consequences of the surgery are recoverable because the surgery itself was not clinically indicated. Compensation for treatment of hypoparathyroidism, weakness and edema of the right arm, ptosis, anisocoria, and the appearance of the scarred and sunken neck contour will amount to substantial damages.

The unexpected complications of surgery, the improperly inserted Foley catheter, and the anesthesiologist's doodling will be perceived by a court of law as evidence of a generalized casual and unprofessional attitude by hospital personnel. Even if these events are not compensible in themselves, they will help to assure a substantial verdict for the patient.

15: *Facts*

A female dock worker was struck below the breast by a heavy three-inch rope. A fellow worker drove her to a physician who evaluated job-related injuries for the company. According to the patient, the physician "touched her on her ribs," reassured her that nothing was broken, and told her that she was "scared." She was given Darvocet and sent back to work. There was no record made of this physician's evaluation.

The following morning, the patient reported back to the physician, and was evaluated by his partner. The patient related the injury that she had sustained on the day before. She complained of pains under her right breast, right shoulder discomfort and bilateral mid-dorsal backache. She also related that she had "spit up" some blood during the night. The physician recorded that he felt the patient had a "voluntary reaction" to his abdominal examination and noted that she was a "difficult patient." He ordered a chest x-ray that did not disclose a fracture. Although the patient told the physician that it was painful for her to lie down on the x-ray table, the physician concluded that the patient had, "chest trauma by history, but without any clinical findings." He suspected a "moderate hysterical reaction" to the incident, and prescribed Valium. Although he provided her a medical explanation of her condition (which the patient said she did not understand), he gave no instructions to return to the clinic and placed no limitations on her activities.

Immediately after returning to the waterfront to work, she felt more ill and was transported to a local emergency room. Physical examination disclosed exquisite left upper abdominal tenderness with positive shake, and referred rebound to the left upper quadrant. The hematocrit was 38, and the hemoglobin was 12.5. SGOT and amylase were elevated. Peritoneal lavage was positive for blood with an elevated amylase content.

An exploratory laparotomy disclosed intraperitoneal hemorrhage secondary to laceration of the left lobe of the liver and the superior subdiaphragmatic surface. The patient experienced nausea and diarrhea in a protracted convalescence and lost a substantial amount of work time as a result.

Allegations

The patient filed a malpractice suit alleging negligent examination and treatment by the first two physicians. She asserted that had they properly discovered her injury earlier, she would not have suffered such a prolonged and painful convalescence.

Discussion

This case represents a failure of physicians to formulate a careful differential diagnosis. The first diagnosis arrived at was plausible; however, a more careful analysis and collection of data would have modified the physicians' diagnostic thinking and placed a "hysterical reaction" further down on the scale of possibilities. Moreover, in cases of trauma in particular, there is a medical priority to identify the more serious potential complications. The legal standard of care for the diagnostic process recognizes this medical priority. Medical conduct appropriate and reasonable under the circumstances may later be found mistaken; however, adherence to the standard diagnostic process will usually effectively refute allegations that a misdiagnosis was negligent.

The initial physician's avoidance of specific findings in the recording of his physical examination of the abdomen indicated that he was either unfamiliar or unconcerned with customary medical model methodology. The fundamental physical diagnostic approach of inspection, palpation, percussion and auscultation, would have (as it did subsequently in the emergency room) elicited point tenderness and referred pain consistent with abdominal trauma. The partner's evaluation may be more pertinent to the patient's allegation of negligent misdiagnosis because her condition had progressed on the following day to the point where signs and symptoms were more indicative of the diagnosis of intraabdominal trauma. His evaluation was deficient because he made no inquiry or examination of abdominal injury although the patient complained of trauma in the hypochrondrial area, hematemesis, and shoulder pain. The inference will be made that this second physician leaped to the conclusion that the patient was having a "hysterical reaction." This bias discredited his diagnostic analysis because it suggests that he did not arrive at this diagnostic conclusion after carefully going through the differential diagnostic process. The lack of a recording of blood pressure and pulse further suggests that he did not consider the possibility of intraperitoneal hemorrhage, nor was he even diligent or careful enough to take vital signs in the course of examining the patient. In addition, a history of abdominal trauma should have caused him to consider internal injuries to the intraabdominal organs in his differential diagnosis. A CBC would have been a useful early indicator of hemorrhage or significant peritoneal irritation. Moreover, normal serum transaminase and amylase tests offer some assurance that significant injury has not occurred to the liver and pancreas. A urinalysis would have helped to evaluate kidney damage. A flat plate and upright x-ray of the abdomen would also have been indicated, as a perforation of a visceral organ was a possibility, especially with a complaint of hematemesis and shoulder pain. None of these tests were performed. If they were unavailable at his office, arrangements with a hospital could have been made.

The two physicians based their diagnosis on incomplete history-taking and examinations. If they were unsure of the diagnosis, they may have had a duty to seek consultation, or perhaps simply to have the patient observed and monitored for change in symptomatology. Instead, consistent with their mistaken diagnosis of "hysterical reaction," they sent her back to work without instruction for limitation of activity or for returning for follow-up. Moreover, they allowed the patient's personality ("difficult patient"; "poor historian") to make them less diagnostically objective. Although they did not completely forsake the differential diagnostic process, they did fail to apply it carefully.

Although there is evidence of negligent conduct on the physician's part, the causal link between the negligent acts and a legally compensable injury is not clear. Had the patient's condition been properly diagnosed during her first visits, it is unlikely that the course of her disease and treatment would have been substantially different. She probably would have been admitted to the hospital, observed, and her condition explored as her symptoms progressed. Notwithstanding this, it is also possible that sending the patient back to work could have caused some aggravation of her condition. At any rate some aggravation is likely to be found because of the physician's negligent conduct.

16: *Facts*

A nineteen-year-old gravida o female was seen three times between June 7 and 9, 1978 because of tender nodes, fatigue, and malaise. The physician diagnosed "probable viral syndrome." On her initial visit for these problems, she told the physician she had had a rash that had already gone away.

Five weeks later, after missing two menstrual periods, the patient went back to a clinic. A pregnancy test was positive, and at the first obstetrical visit twelve days later, it was recorded that her last menstrual period had been on April 21, 1978. Physical examination suggested a gestational age of fifteen weeks. The risk of "minimal x-ray exposure, BCP (birth control pills), phenobarbital and Dalmane" were discussed with the patient. There was no note concerning the risks of the "probable viral syndrome" and no inquiry concerning rubella; nor was a rubella titer drawn.

On January 15, 1979, the patient delivered a 5 lb., 12 oz. male. The hospital summary reported the mother's rubella titer as 1:256. The infant was jaundiced during the first week of life, with a bilirubin as high as 11. On January 31, 1979, he experienced seizures and was admitted to a children's hospital the next day. During that hospitalization a patent ductus arteriosis was demonstrated by echocardiogram. In addition, the child had bilateral cataracts, microphthalmia, and a platelet count of 81,000, all consistent with congenital rubella syndrome. The mother's and infant's rubella titers were 1:160. Thereafter, the child manifested signs of congestive heart failure and hepatitis. These findings were also thought to be part of the congenital rubella syndrome. A cardiac catheterization showed a patent ductus arteriosis and mild bilateral pulmonary branch artery stenosis. The patient then underwent a ligation of the patent ductus without difficulty. Subsequently the child underwent cataractectomy, and an audiologist detected a severe hearing loss. When the child was twenty months old he was able to sit alone but would not pull to a standing position or crawl.

Allegations

The mother and child each sought damages alleging that because of negligent prenatal care, the child was born with serious handicaps and would require lifelong special education and medical care.

Discussion

The facts described above outline a relatively new cause of action that has been variously termed "wrongful life" or "wrongful birth." For the sake of clarity the parents' legal claim of delivering an afflicted infant will be referred to as "wrongful birth," and the infant's legal claim for being born in an afflicted state as "wrongful life." The rationale of these legal causes of action is that if the mother had been properly informed of the risk of delivering an afflicted child, she would have chosen an abortion. From the facts presented, the mother would likely assert that if the diagnosis of rubella had been properly made during her first trimester of pregnancy, she would have opted for an abortion and thereby avoided the possibility of delivering an affected infant.

Most courts have denied the afflicted infant a legal cause of action for wrongful life. The reason for this stems from the difficulty in determining damages. If the mother had been properly informed and had opted for an abortion, the child would have no life at all. Courts have presumed that the infant is in a better position being alive, even though handicapped, than in not being born at all.

On the other hand, a few courts in recent years have allowed the parents of an afflicted child a cause of action for wrongful birth. These courts have maintained that if the parents had been properly informed of the risk of having an affected child, they would have opted for an abortion, thereby avoiding the special burden of caring for the child's abnormalities. Some courts have allowed the parents damages only for pain and suffering; others have allowed parents damages only for the cost of rearing the afflicted child.

It is likely that this child was in fact born with a congenital rubella syndrome. Patent ductus arteriosis, pulmonary artery stenosis, hepatitis, deafness, cataracts, and microphthalmia form a persuasive constellation for the

diagnosis of congenital rubella syndrome. However, certain factors confirming the existence of the syndrome are absent. There were no follow-up
rubella titers on the infant showing sustained immunity. It is the usual procedure to repeat the titer several months after birth to substantiate whether
or not the child is actively producing antibodies against the virus. Furthermore, the rubella virus was not cultured from the infant.

Nevertheless this woman did have a diagnosed viral infection in June
1978. She also gave a history of an associated rash. It is the generally accepted standard of care that a woman of childbearing age who has such a
history, be carefully evaluated for rubella. Apparently, the attending physician did not even suspect this diagnosis. Acute and convalescent titers for
rubella should have been taken on the patient at that time. A fourfold or
greater rise in titer after one month would have established the diagnosis of
rubella. At that time, her attending physician would have been required to
advise the patient of the risk of delivering an afflicted child. Therefore, the
facts of this case establish the physician's negligent failure to diagnose
rubella.

Moreover, on her first two prenatal visits, the woman was neither questioned about having a prior rubella titer nor was a rubella titer taken at that
time. It is the generally accepted standard of care among obstetricians that a
woman on her first prenatal visit have a rubella titer done. It would be even
preferable to have a titer done long before the first pregnancy so that vaccine
could be used if necessary.

17: *Facts*

The twenty-seven-year-old para 1001 woman's last normal menses began on August 14. On October 10, she was hospitalized because of hypovolemic shock. Emergency laparotomy disclosed a ruptured tubal pregnancy, which was treated by salpingectomy and blood transfusion. At the
time of the surgery, her uterus was noted to be "enlarged." She was given
Valium, for its sedative effect. Confirmation of the tubal gestation was made
by the hospital pathologist. The patient's postoperative course was unremarkable. At a follow-up outpatient visit on November 9, a copper IUD was
inserted. A few days later the patient moved to another city, and was lost to
follow-up.

Over the next month, when symptoms of pregnancy and amenorrhea
persisted, the patient consulted a physician. The physician referred the patient to a hospital where on December 19 an intrauterine pregnancy was
confirmed. The IUD could not be located on vaginal examination. "Moving
B-mode" ultrasound placed the gestational age at eighteen weeks, but could
not locate the IUD because of the advanced state of the pregnancy. A pelvic
x-ray demonstrated that the IUD was intrauterine mid-pelvic. The patient

elected to continue the pregnancy. Thereafter, the patient experienced intermittent vaginal bleeding, which on March 26 became associated with premature labor with breech presentation culminated in a Caesarean section delivery of a 1,672 gram male consistent with thirty-two weeks gestational age. The IUD was located in the mid-portion of the placenta.

The premature infant was born with the following anomalous formations involving all four extremities: ectrodactyly (split hands, "lobster claws") four digits on the left hand and two on the right, and bilateral absence of both lower legs (peromelia) with stump formation. These congenital anomalies have defied etiological classification. There was no family history of congenital defects. The infant overcame initial respiratory distress and demonstrated progressive growth.

Allegations

The mother sued the original obstetrician, on behalf of her child, alleging that his negligent failure to diagnose the intrauterine pregnancy and his subsequent placement of an IUD caused her child's abnormalities.

Discussion

The failure to diagnose the uterine pregnancy under the circumstances of this case may have been negligent, even though combined intrauterine and ectopic twin gestation is a rare occurrence. Failure to consider the possibility of another pregnancy coexisting with a newly discovered tubal pregnancy can lead to a continuum of problems. Although slight enlargement of the uterus at the time of surgery for an ectopic pregnancy is expected, and failure to consider the possibility of an intrauterine pregnancy at the time of surgery is not unreasonable; in suspicious instances, prudent postoperative follow-up pregnancy tests or sonographic evaluation of the uterus would be appropriate to rule out an intrauterine pregnancy. At such a follow-up examination, uterine size should be noted. Persistent or progressive enlargement would require evaluation, especially prior to insertion of an IUD. In addition, an increased rate of spontaneous abortions, previable, and premature delivery has been documented to be associated with "inert" IUD pregnancies. Much lower rates for these untoward events occur when the IUD is removed during early pregnancy. For these reasons, the third trimester complications that occurred in this case should have been anticipated and the patient should have been alerted to their possible occurrence.

Even if negligence is assumed in failure to diagnose the intrauterine pregnancy, the cause of the infant's anomalies is unclear. Although the rare combination of congenital deformities have defied a syndrome assignment, variations resembling such a constellation have been observed and some investigators have proposed its recognition as a distinct genetic syndrome unrelated to prenatal events. However, there was no family history of congenital defects. Except for Valium, the anesthetic drugs used during the first trimester emergency laparotomy are commonly used for surgery in early pregnancy. Acute hypovolemia, such as the patient sustained from rupture of the tubal pregnancy, has not been described as a cause of limb defects.

The insertion of a copper-containing IUD late in the first trimester places it beyond the expected time for causation of limb bud deformities. The assertion that the incidence of anomalous births with inert IUD pregnancies is no greater than is found in non-IUD pregnancies would be difficult to validate because of the high abortion (spontaneous and induced) rate associated with IUD pregnancies. Nevertheless, the index of suspicion probably rises with the pharmacologically active IUDs, such as those containing progesterone or copper. There have been some reports of anomalous births, manifesting primarily limb reduction defects, in association with copper-containing IUDs. However, as the following table demonstrates, the expected development of the extremities preceded the insertion. The use of Valium, however, may be implicated as a cause of some of the anomalies because of the time in the gestation period when it was given, and because of its reported tetratogenicity.

Dates and Events

Day	Date	Event	Development
0	August 13	Last Menstrual Period	(Expected Date of Confinement: May 20)
1	August 27	Fertilization	
9	September 4	Implantation	
14	September 10		
28	September 24		Arm Bud
34	September 30		Leg Bud
38	October 4		Hand Plate
44	October 10	Surgery (Valium)	
45	October 11		
51	October 17		Finger Rays
56	October 22		Finger/Toes
74	November 9	IUD (Cu-7)	Tubular Bone
112	December 19	Scan (18 weeks)	
210	March 26	Delivery	

18: *Facts*

In July 1977, the forty-three-year-old female underwent a routine "GYN cancer check." No breast masses were detected. In August 1977 she presented to an emergency room with a history of left chest pain, of a type she had experienced for several years. Examination of her breasts detected a small tender nodule in the left breast. She was referred to the surgical clinic where it was noted that she had developed a breast mass just prior to her menses. The physical examination disclosed bilateral, ill-defined nodularities without a dominant lesion. The clinical impression was "fibrocystic disease." A diuretic was prescribed on a trial basis. Thereafter she performed regular breast self-examinations. In May 1978, when she was evaluated for vaginal bleeding, she did not mention any problem with her breast. In January 1979 she was seen in the emergency room because of a one-day history of left chest pain which radiated to her scapula and axilla. Her chest wall was markedly tender, and the clinical impression was costochondritis and anxiety. In June 1979 she was evaluated in the emergency room for chest pain which radiated to her back. Her chest wall was tender to palpation and costochrondritis was again diagnosed.

On December 3, 1979 she underwent a preemployment examination. She related to the physician's assistant who examined her that she had noticed two lumps in her left breast and requested that he examine her breasts. The physician's assistant did so and also ordered a mammogram. The history on the request form indicated a "questionable mass in the superior lateral quadrant of the left breast." The radiologist reported the mammogram demonstrated fibrocystic disease, but not a dominant mass. The radiologist, who lectured frequently on breast examination, also examined the patient, but could not detect a dominant palpable mass. He reassured the patient. In May 1980, while the patient was being evaluated in the emergency room because of a swelling of her arm, she also indicated to the examining physician that she had a breast mass, which she had noticed several weeks before. He examined her, confirmed the mass, and referred her to a surgeon, who detected a 2.5 cm. indurated breast nodule in the left upper outer quadrant. Diffuse fibrocystic disease of the breast was also noted. A 1.5 cm. nontender, movable, irregular mass was also noted in the left upper outer quadrant. She was hospitalized with a history of a breast mass of six weeks duration. The patient underwent a modified radical mastectomy for medullary carcinoma of the breast. A 3 X 2 cm. lesion was excised. Seventeen of twenty-three lymph nodes were positive for malignancy. Subsequently, when she indicated to her attending surgeon that the breast mass had actually been present for five months, he told her that *if* a dominant mass had been palpated in December 1979, she should have been referred to a surgeon for a needle aspiration or biopsy.

Allegations

The patient sued the radiologist, alleging that evidence of her cancerous condition was confirmed by studies in November 1979, but she was not referred to a surgeon until June 1980. As a result, she claimed that her survival has been jeopardized.

Discussion

This patient probably had latent breast cancer for several years prior to its diagnosis, which was not manifested in a clinically detectable manner until after December 1979. In August 1977, when she was evaluated, a discrete dominant lesion could not be palpated; thus, fibrocystic disease was a reasonable diagnosis. Thereafter, breast self-examination did not alarm the patient, nor was a dominant mass detected when she was evaluated on several occasions for chest pain—pain which was correctly diagnosed to be of musculoskeletal origin. When the patient underwent an examination by a physician's assistant for employment, she related a history of breast masses which had been detected one week earlier. Although the mammogram did not demonstrate a dominant lesion, one of the masses she described at that time was the carcinoma which was diagnosed six months later. However, the mammogram was negative, and a physician with documented skill in evaluating breast lumps was unable to detect a suspicious lesion. Thus his failure to refer her to a surgeon was not unreasonable.

It would be syllogistic to reason that if the physician had sent the patient to a surgeon at that time, the mass would have been detected and definitively diagnosed before lymph node involvement occurred. Notwithstanding, it would have been prudent to have advised her to arrange for follow-up evaluation in three to six months. Even if this had been done, however, it would not have changed the course of her treatment or the overall outcome of her disease. The statement by the surgeon that the patient should have been referred to a surgeon earlier, might represent evidence of the required standard of care under the circumstances. However, he qualified his opinion by stating that she should have been referred *if* a dominant mass was demonstrated. Because no such lesion was detected and there was evidence of an adequate and proper examination, there was no significant deviation from the standard.

19: *Facts*

This fifty-four-year-old man made an appointment to see a physician because he had been experiencing a four-month history of frequent bowel movements. He was evaluated by a physician's assistant to whom he stated that he had five stools a day and associated increased flatulence, without a significant change in his diet. The physician's assistant examined the patient's abdomen and noted that it was soft, nontender, and tympanitic. No rectal exam or stool guaiac test was performed. The assessment was "hyper-defecation anxiety," and the plan was to perform stool examinations for ova and parasites, and to obtain a stool culture and sensitivity. The patient was prescribed Mylicon and asked to return "as needed." The patient made a return visit to the physician's office and was again seen by the same physician's assistant approximately fifteen months later. The patient complained of frequent diarrheal stools of three months duration, and gave a history of unexplained 26 lb. weight loss. No physical examination was performed; the assessment again was "hyperdefecation." An SMA-12, CBC, urinalysis, stool analysis, ova and parasites, and stool culture and sensitivity were ordered. A physical exam was not performed. The patient was prescribed Gaviscon. The assessment was "hypermotility," and the patient was asked to return to the office as needed. The patient returned to the physician's office two weeks later complaining of frequent stools and loss of appetite. The physician's assistant's objective findings were recorded as "work-up normal," and "hyperdefecation" was again diagnosed. The patient was prescribed Lomotil. None of the physician's assistant's notes were cosigned by a supervising physician.

Three weeks later, the patient consulted an internist who diagnosed a rectal lesion and referred the patient to a surgeon. The surgeon staged the tumor as Dukes C and performed an abdomino-peritoneal resection for a rectal carcinoma. The pathologist reported that the rectal specimen demonstrated an eight centimeter mucinous undifferentiated adenocarcinoma infiltrating the muscularis of the rectal wall.

Allegations

The patient sued the physician's assistant and his physician employer for negligent delay in the diagnosis of the patient's rectal carcinoma. He contended that had the rectal tumor been detected on initial evaluation he would have had a much improved life expectancy.

Discussion

A fifty-four-year-old man complaining of a four-month history of frequent soft bowel movements, increased flatus, and a change of bowel habits, is suggestive of a partial colonic obstruction, making malignancy rank high on the differential diagnostic list. A reasonably prudent practitioner would have performed a rectal examination and stool guaiac test on the initial visit. Although the patient had seemingly nonurgent symptoms on initial presentation and the multitude of nonserious problems, which could have caused his symptoms, rectal examination and stool guaiac testing are routine and important screening tests, especially for a middle-aged man who has experienced a change in bowel habits. Although detection of the tumor at that time may have been difficult, the failure to perform these routine tests would be negligent conduct under the circumstances. The assistant's conduct on return visits also lacked due diligence and care. Notwithstanding this, the physician's assistant is only responsible for damage caused by his negligent conduct.

Determining causative damages in this case is difficult. Although the rate of growth of a rectal cancer is variable, the existence of such a large tumor at the time of diagnosis (and retrograde extrapolation, using a doubling time of thirty to sixty days) would suggest the presence of the tumor at the time of initial clinical presentation, in April 1979. The damages are related to the spread of the tumor which may have occurred during the intervening fifteen months. Because the patient had no evidence of metastatic disease, it is difficult to assess damages. Even if the patient is unable to demonstrate metastatic disease, it is likely that the patient will successfully be able to argue that he deserves compensation because his "five-year survival" rate with a Duke's Stage C undifferentiated rectal carcinoma is less than 50 percent.

Because the physician's assistant's work was not cosigned by a supervising physician, it suggests that he was practicing without direction and supervision; this will create a major weakness in the defense of this suit. Moreover, if a physician was responsible for his direction, supervision and control (as most state laws require), he would be vicariously liable for the physician's assistant's negligence. That is, if it could be proven that the physician's assistant was negligent in not properly applying diagnostic procedures, his physician employer would also be indirectly liable, even though he was not directly negligent. The result might be the same whether or not he was negligent indirectly in supervising them. This is because of the legal doctrine which holds that the master must answer for his servant.

(4) Communications About Treatment

20: *Facts*

An infant was the product of a normal spontaneous delivery at thirty-six weeks gestation with APGAR scores of 8 and 9 and a birth weight of 1,950 grams. He remained in the nursery for fifteen days, primarily for weight gain. His nursery course was apparently unremarkable. Three days after discharge, his mother noted that he seemed to be in pain when he moved his right arm, and that his appetite had decreased.

One week later, during a routine postpartum evaluation, the examining physician's attention was called to the infant's right arm problem. An orthopedic surgeon was consulted who detected swelling, tenderness, decreased range of motion of the right arm, and a decreased grasp of the right hand. The clinical impression was "septic joint." The infant was hospitalized to perform tests to confirm the diagnosis. His white blood count was 19,700, hemoglobin was 11, hematocrit was 33, and sed rate was 57. The treatment plan was to perform an arthrotomy, unless serosanguineous fluid could be aspirated by needle from the joint, in which case only a lavage would be performed. On the second day of hospitalization the surgeon precipitously telephoned the infant's mother and urged that the surgery be performed in the morning. Although he explained the purpose of the surgery, he did not disclose the risk involved in administering anesthesia to an infant.

The surgery consent form indicated that the operation was a "right shoulder arthrotomy, that is, opening the right shoulder joint to get pus out." The surgeon specially recorded on the chart that "any possible suspected harm to this young child from an arthrotomy would be less than the residual from a septic shoulder." Anesthesia was provided by a nurse anesthetist. The surgeon advised the anesthetist that he was going to aspirate the right shoulder for suspected septic arthritis. On the preanesthetic summary the anesthetist indicated that the operation proposed was an "I & D" of the right shoulder.

The operation began at 9:00 A.M. with the use of Halothane anesthesia. Precordial stethoscope (pulse and respiration) and EKG monitoring with an oscilloscope screen were utilized. The patient was not intubated because the anesthetist anticipated a short procedure involving only aspiration of the shoulder joint. The anesthetist did not use temperature monitoring during the course of the surgery, also because he thought the surgery would be brief. He used a radiant heat lamp focused on the infant, but did not use a heating pad. The operating room used the standard hospital ventilation system, which did not allow regulation of the operating room temperature. At 9:15 A.M., the surgeon aspirated 0.25 cc. of yellow, gluey fluid from the right shoulder and placed it in a blood culture bottle. At 9:30 A.M., the shoulder was surgically prepared and draped for an arthrotomy. A one-inch incision was made over the delto-pectoral groove on the anterior aspect of the right shoulder, and the joint was exposed and opened. No evidence of infection, synovial hypertrophy, or abnormal-appearing fluid was detected. Aspiration of the proximal humerus was performed; the wound was irrigated with normal saline and closed.

At this time the pulse rate fell from 140 to 100, and the respiratory rate dropped from 50 to less than 10. Shortly thereafter, at 10:15 A.M., after the dressing had been applied, the patient experienced a cardiopulmonary arrest. Resuscitative measures were undertaken. At 10:30 A.M., the infant was intubated. When the attending pediatrician arrived five minutes later, the heart rate was less than 100, spontaneous respiration was absent, and the infant's temperature was 95.2° F. At 11:08 A.M., the temperature was 94° F. Post-cardiopulmonary arrest arterial blood gases (on oxygen) were pH 7.2, PCO_2 54, PO_2 57. By the time he was extubated at 11:45 A.M., his temperature had increased to 96° F. Arterial blood gases at 11:50 A.M. were pH 7.36, PCO_2 39, PO_2 31.

Although the patient's condition remained stable for the next thirty minutes, he again became cyanotic and had irregular respirations. He was sent to the ICU Nursery. IV fluids were given at a rate 10 cc/hr. Subsequent x-rays indicated evidence of osteomyelitis. He was treated appropriately, and a satisfactory orthopedic result was obtained.

Thereafter, the infant began to have head-banging episodes and was placed on phenobarbital. Developmental delays, and left hemiparesis were noted. These findings were thought to be causally related to a focal right-sided brain insult, secondary to the surgical cardiopulmonary arrest.

Allegations

On behalf of their child, his parents filed a malpractice claim, alleging that "all the complications involving the cardiac arrest were the direct result of hypothermia, secondary to the anesthesia."

Discussion

The surgical cardiopulmonary arrest was preventable. The cardiopulmonary arrest resulted from hypothermia and postoperative anesthesia arousal apnea, secondary to cold stress with anesthesia as an aggravating factor. A small infant who is scheduled to have Halothane/oxygen maintenance should be intubated for more effective ventilation while under anesthesia. Because small infants have a relatively increased amount of CO_2 and a decreased lung volume, postanesthesia arousal apnea may rapidly lead to hypoxia. A temperature monitor should be routinely utilized in conjunction with a blanket in order to prevent hypothermia. In addition, the postoperative IV fluid therapy of 10 cc/hr was probably excessive for post-cardiopulmonary arrest care, and may have caused cerebral edema.

Brain damage was the result of a complication of anesthesia. The occurrence of the complication was the result of negligence. The anesthetist and surgeon failed to communicate adequately concerning the nature and extent of the intended procedure. Consequently, the anesthetist failed to take the proper precautions necessary for a small infant who is scheduled to undergo general anesthesia (temperature control, ventilation, and monitoring). Thus, hypothermia, hypoventilation, and metabolic depression of the infant were not identified in a timely fashion. Once the arrest occurred, management was improper (acidosis persisted, the temperature remained down, and there was probable fluid overload) due to a lack of anticipation and preparation to handle an arrest.

In addition, the arthrotomy, although indicated, was not an emergency. Since the child lacked capacity, the informed consent of the parents was necessary for the surgery and anesthesia. The telephone consent, which was obtained, may have been vitiated by the surgeon's misrepresenting the urgency for the procedure.

21: *Facts*

A forty-seven-year-old woman had a history of diabetes mellitus complicated by progressive renal failure, for which she was admitted to a medical center for renal dialysis. A bovine heterograft arteriovenous shunt was placed in the right femoral area. Several minutes after the beginning of the first dialysis with this shunt, the patient had a cardiac arrest. She was successfully resuscitated. An endotracheal tube was inserted and then removed several days later.

One month later, she went to the emergency room, complaining of shortness of breath. X-rays of the chest and neck disclosed a soft tissue lesion below the vocal cords. Otolaryngoscopic examination disclosed a subglottic polyp, probably secondary to the placement of the endotracheal tube during her previous cardiac arrest. She was admitted to the hospital for excision of the lesion.

Direct laryngoscopy disclosed a "cauliflower-like mass," located below the left arytenoid and true cord. This lesion was excised, and bronchoscopy was also performed. Ten minutes after the procedure was completed, the patient experienced respiratory distress. She was given intravenous Decadron and monitored. Because of continued airway difficulty, she was intubated. Approximately ten minutes later she became alert and cooperative, and was extubated. Within five minutes, respiratory difficulty recurred. She was reintubated and returned to the operating room where a tracheostomy was performed under general anesthesia. The operative note described the tracheostomy incision as located over the third tracheal ring.

Posttracheostomy laryngoscopy disclosed edema of the false cords and airway obstruction when the tracheostomy tube was occluded. On the sixth postoperative day she was able to tolerate occlusion of the tracheostomy tube. Indirect laryngoscopy did not disclose an obstruction below the tracheostomy site; however, visualization of the subglottic area was inadequate. Therefore, repeat direct laryngoscopy was scheduled for five days later to determine the etiology of her post-laryngoscopy stridor. This procedure was postponed because the patient's hyperkalemia necessitated further dialysis, and her anemia required blood transfusion. The tracheostomy tube was left in place to assure an adequate airway during and after the proposed procedure.

The next day pulsatile movement of the tracheostomy tube was noted on rounds. This prompted a staff discussion of tracheostomy complications, including the danger of hemorrhage from erosion of the innominate artery. As a result, the senior staff otolaryngologist indicated to the senior resident, that the tube should be removed. The resident interpreted this remark to mean that the tube should be removed "as soon as possible after the scheduled laryngoscopy was performed." He felt it would be a good precaution to leave the tracheostomy tube in place while doing the laryngoscopy, in case of an episode of acute respiratory obstruction such as occurred when the original procedure was performed.

The following day, massive hemorrhage occurred. Inflation of the balloon on the tracheostomy tube and pressure on the innominate artery could not control the hemorrhage, and the patient exsanguinated.

Autopsy described the location of the tracheostomy site as below the sixth tracheal ring. Because of the discrepancy with the operative report that indicated that the tracheostomy site was at the level of the third tracheal ring, an independent evaluation was obtained from a forensic medical examiner. He concluded that post-tracheostomy x-rays of the patient and color slides taken at autopsy supported the conclusion that the tracheostomy tube was placed below the third tracheal ring and probably below the sixth tracheal ring.

Allegations

The patient's estate filed a malpractice claim which alleged that as a result of negligence the patient suffered massive hemorrhage and death.

Discussion

In a tracheostomized patient, infection and pressure from the tube are recognized as possible causes of hemorrhage of the innominate artery. Because this major artery is usually located at the level between the fifth to eighth tracheal rings, there is an increased likelihood of injury to the artery if a tracheostomy site is substantially below the third tracheal ring. Although the surgeon noted in his operative report that the tracheostomy was made at the level of the third tracheal ring, the pathologist's opinion that the tracheostomy site was lower is more persuasive.

Even if erosion caused the tube to "drift" lower, the otolaryngologist is not relieved of liability for the hemorrhage because he should then have anticipated the dangerous possibility of erosion into the artery. A pulsatile tracheostomy tube is a manifestation of arterial wall pressure and a harbinger of hemorrhagic erosion. Under the circumstances, it was unreasonable not to remove the tracheostomy tube as soon as persistent pulsations became evident. Due care required that the surgeon be aware of this recognized complication and take difinitive action to prevent its occurrence.

In addition, an external pressure balloon to regulate endotracheal cuff pressures automatically was not used in this case. Although many physicians believe that a soft cuff on an endotracheal or tracheostomy tube adequately protects the trachea from pressure injury, recent evidence suggests that even soft cuffs can exert great pressure on the tracheal mucosa, producing tracheal wall necrosis promotive of erosion into adjacent structures if the pressure used to inflate the cuff is greater than 30 mm. Hg for a prolonged period. There is increasing evidence that major complications from prolonged tracheal intubation in the treatment of acute respiratory failure can be greatly decreased by utilizing an external pressure pilot balloon to regulate. endotracheal cuff pressure automatically. This method utilizes a compliant cuff which is easily inflated to a diameter larger than the adult trachea at pressures below 30 mm. Hg, thereby maintaining pressure within the cuff below this level.

Such a technique may become the standard of care for prolonged tracheal intutation. If so, when such a technique is not utilized, it may be deemed that any pressure induced complications were preventable because a specialist is obligated to keep abreast of new developments that improve the quality of patient care.

22: *Facts*
A two-year-old female went to her physician with a three-day history of rectal bleeding. Her stool guaiac was negative; a rectal exam was unremarkable, and hematocrit was 38 percent. Several days later, she had a positive stool guaiac. On rectal examination, a questionable polyp was palpatated at 4 centimeters.

Two weeks later, she was evaluated in a surgery clinic. The parents consented to a "procto." No specific mention of a polypectomy was made. At 11:00 A.M., she underwent proctoscopy. A 1.5 cm. polyp on a small stalk was located at 10 cm. and removed by electrocautery. No description of the procedure was recorded in the chart. The specimen was lost, and no pathology report was made. She was sent home after the procedure. Home care instructions were not documented in the record.

At 5:30 A.M., the next morning, the child awoke with abdominal pain. She returned to the clinic later that day, with a temperature of 101° F, generalized abdominal tenderness, and absent bowel sounds. An abdominal x-ray demonstrated free air under the diaphragm. Laparotomy disclosed a perforation of the sigmoid colon on the anterior wall at the approximate polypectomy site. Purulent and fecal material were removed from the peritoneal cavity and a colostomy was performed. Subsequently, the colostomy was closed.

Allegations
The parents sued on behalf of their child, claiming that the cauterization was negligently performed without consent, and that abdominal surgery, pain, and suffering resulted.

Discussion

The eighteen-hour delay between the procedure and the initial symptoms of perforation suggests cautery-related injury to the bowel wall. Perforation of the sigmoid colon after polypectomy is a recognized complication of the procedure. Adequate information is unavailable from the record to determine whether the polypectomy was properly performed. There is no description of the method or technique of removal, how the patient tolerated the procedure, and a specimen was not sent to pathology for examination. Therefore, because of the injury an inference arises that it was negligently performed.

A standard consent form was signed by the parent for a "procto." This form, however, did not secure consent for other procedures such as a polypectomy, even though it may have been determined to be desirable in the physician's judgment. Moreover, the risks of a polypectomy were not described to the parent. If a biopsy was anticipated by the physician, the parents should have been so counselled. There was no urgent situation that would allow the procedure without specific consent. Thus, the consent obtained was legally insufficient for performing a polypectomy.

Substantial liability exposure for negligence exists because of the questionable documentation of the procedure. It may also be established that the polypectomy amounted to a battery because no consent either express or implied was given. Legal damages consist of residual abdominal scars and associated pain and suffering related to the abdominal surgery.

23: *Facts*

When the physician discovered a lump in his patient's breast which strongly suggested a malignancy, he arranged for an excision biopsy. After the mass had been excised, the hospital pathologist studied a frozen section of the specimen and reported to the patient's surgeon, who was standing by in the operating room, that the diagnosis was "scirrhous carcinoma." The surgeon immediately performed a modified radical mastectomy. The next day, the pathologist examined the permanent paraffin section and determined that the tissue was not scirrhous carcinoma but rather granular cell myoblastoma, a nonmalignant tumor. The distinguishing features between scirrhous carcinoma and granular cell myoblastoma are the tiny granules in nonmalignant conditions. Although these tiny granules were apparent on the permanent paraffin section, they were not visible on the frozen section.

Allegations

The patient sued the pathologist, claiming that it was negligent to use a cryostat rather than a freezing microtome for cutting sections. The pathologist contended that it was standard procedure for the pathologist to report his findings based on the frozen section as soon as possible to the surgeon to reduce the risk that a malignant growth would spread. Therefore, it was customary to proceed to surgery based on the diagnostic report of a frozen section because delay is undesirable and because it is beneficial to the patient that everything be done in one operation rather than two.

Discussion

The law recognizes that in clinical medicine there are many considerations involved in most treatment decisions. Although medical science can make this process easier, it cannot automate it to the point where a physician is alleviated of the decisional dilemmas. Because the procedure for diagnosis of frozen sections is uncertain and inconclusive, paraffin sections are subsequently made and viewed. The imperfections of medical science alone which cause an erroneous diagnosis are not the basis for establishing negligence on the part of the pathologist. However, both the surgeon and the pathologist knew that on a frozen section what may look like scirrhous carcinoma may be the benign myoblastoma. Therefore, it would have been prudent for the pathologist to report that information to the surgeon rather than a definitive diagnosis of carcinoma. A pathologist is relied on to distinguish the rare as well as the commonplace. The rarity of myoblastoma means only that it is improbable; it does not mean that issuing a definitive misdiagnosis was reasonable. In view of the seriously disfiguring surgery that would result from his unequivocal diagnosis, the pathologist should not have returned an unequivocal diagnosis. Thus, an inference arises that the patient underwent a mutilating operation unnecessarily.

24: *Facts*

A thirty-four-year-old woman was seen in the general practice clinic and surgery clinic at a medical center because of a painful "cystic area" of the left breast accompanied by a greenish discharge of the left nipple. A mammogram performed reported:

> An area of increased density . . . in the lateral aspect of the left breast. There are also some very fine calcifications in a small area. . . . with no specific characteristics of benign or malignant lesions. Suggest clinical correlation.

A surgical clinic note three days later recorded:

> Agree with fibrocystic disease and mammograms concur. No treatment needed. Patient reassured. Return to Clinic PRN or one year.

Approximately one year later, the patient returned to the same surgery clinic because of a bloody discharge from the left nipple. A left breast biopsy was performed. The pathologic diagnosis of the tissue specimen was intraductal papilloma of the breast with an undifferentiated pattern and extensive luminal necrosis. The patient was asked to return for follow-up in one year.

Six months later, the patient again complained of a lump in her left breast. An examination at another medical center confirmed a tender area in this location. The physician diagnosed probable fibrocystic disease and released the patient without follow-up.

Six months later, the patient returned because of a large lump in the left breast. A biopsy confirmed the preoperative diagnosis of carcinoma. The patient underwent a mastectomy and a bilateral salpingo-oophorectomy. The final pathologic diagnosis was poorly differentiated infiltrating duct cell carcinoma. Left axillary lymph nodes were positive for tumor. A bone scan demonstrated metastatic disease. Following a rapid downhill course, the patient died of metastatic disease.

Subsequently, a review of the initial biopsy slides by two independent pathologists confirmed that the slides demonstrated evidence of carcinoma.

Allegations

The husband claimed damages for the wrongful death of his wife due to the failure to diagnose cancer.

Discussion

The undifferentiated pattern of cells with luminal necrosis is suggestive of malignancy, and should have at least prompted the original pathologist to seek an outside opinion of the diagnosis of the initial biopsy slides. In any event it was unreasonable to confuse the lesion with an intraductal papilloma.

Furthermore, the mammogram, which disclosed a soft tissue density with fine calcifications, was also highly suspicious of cancer. The opinions of the radiologist and surgeon at that time, which downplayed the significance of these findings, were lacking in due care. Although the radiologist should have known the findings were suggestive of cancer, the surgeon improperly used the ambiguous nondiagnostic interpretation ("no specific characteristics of benign or malignant lesions") to support his clinical impression of fibrocystic disease.

The opinions of the radiologist and surgeon concerning the mammograms, and of the pathologist concerning the biopsy suggest that each had inadequate medical knowledge of the clinical significance of the demonstrated objective findings. If the physicians claim that they were aware of the possibility of cancer and ignored it, they are left on the horns of a defense dilemma. Their lack of due care to biopsy early and refer questionable microscopic findings to experts in the field is equally negligent.

25: *Facts*

The sixty-year-old woman was hospitalized after adenocarcinoma of the rectosigmoid colon had been diagnosed. The following morning at 7:45 A.M., she underwent a bowel resection. During surgery, the central venous pressure (CVP) catheter, which had been inserted through an antecubital vein, was believed to be malfunctioning. Therefore, the anesthesiology resident withdrew the catheter and inserted a different catheter in the right internal jugular vein. The placement was tested by aspiration of blood during surgery; it appeared to function well. The surgery was completed by noontime. Shortly thereafter the patient was extubated and ventilated spontaneously. During the next several hours in the recovery room, her vital signs were stable. The hematocrit, arterial blood gases and electrolytes were within normal limits.

At 5:00 P.M. the patient's central venous pressure dropped to two cubic centimeters of water and her urine output diminished. The resident surgeon and anesthesiologist who were caring for the patient ordered a bolus of fluid infused through a peripheral vein and this increased the central venous pressure. At 9:30 P.M. when it was noted that urine output had decreased to 20 milliliters per hour, fluids were given at a faster rate, including through the central venous catheter. At 11:00 P.M. the patient was noted to be tachypneic and tachycardiac. Over the next thirty minutes the CVP rose from 6 to 18 cubic centimeters of water. This latter reading was discounted as being erroneous. During this time three liters of 0.45 percent normal saline solution and 5 percent dextrose and water were infused through the CVP line. At 1:30 A.M. the patient's blood pressure rose, tachypnea and tachycardia persisted. Arterial blood gases on 40 percent oxygen by mask were PO_2 89, PCO_2 83, and PH 7.23. The resident physicians interpreted these findings as "acute respiratory acidosis." At 2:15 A.M., the first chest x-ray obtained since surgery was interpreted as a "whiteout" of the right lung, secondary to a "mucous plug" obstruction. Nasal tracheal suction was ordered. A repeat chest x-ray at 3:00 A.M. disclosed progression of the "whiteout." Diffuse rhonci and diminished breath sounds in the right lower lobe were noted. Vigorous suction resulted only in slight transient improvement in her clinical state. The patient's pulse rose steadily to 160 and respiratory difficulty increased. At 4:10 A.M. arterial blood gases were PO_2 61, PCO_2 83, PH 7.08. These findings were interpreted as "progressive severe hypoventilation with respiratory acidosis." At 4:20 A.M. the surgical resident transferred the patient to the Intensive Care Unit (ICU) for intubation and placement of a Swan-Ganz catheter. She was intubated at 4:30 A.M. and an attempt at ventilation was made. She became bradycardic, however, and developed cardiac standstill. Cardiopulmonary resuscitation was unsuccessful, and she was pronounced dead.

After the patient's demise, the two postoperative chest x-rays were read by the radiologist. He reported that the first x-ray (taken at 2:15 A.M.) demonstrated a massive right hydrothorax, shift of the mediastinum to the left, and catheter in the superior mediastinum. He reported that the second x-ray (taken 3:00 A.M.) was similar to the first, but added that the catheter was intrapleural in location and that the presence of a mediastinal shift had caused left lung obstruction with resultant collapse.

Autopsy disclosed that cardiopulmonary collapse had occurred from a massive right hydrothorax (fluid compatible with IV fluids), compressive collapse of the right lung, and obstructive collapse of the left lung.

Allegations

The patient's estate sued the two resident physicians and their supervising staff physicians for failure to detect in time and to properly manage the complication caused by the central venous catheter. They contended that such negligence caused the patient's death.

Discussion

Several errors in the postoperative management occurred in this case and constitute a constellation of negligent care. A postoperative chest x-ray was not taken immediately to verify the proper positioning of the CVP catheter and to rule out the existence of a pneumothorax. After the patient experienced distress, postoperative x-rays were delayed. Once taken, they were misinterpreted. The medical attention to the patient's immediate postoperative clinical care was inadequate, and the interpretation of the diagnostic studies undertaken was incorrect. Collectively, these acts were negligent. Proper diagnosis and chest tube placement for drainage and cessation of the administration of fluids through the CVP catheter may have precluded death. Consultation should have been sought when the patient's clinical deterioration was not responding to management. The resident physicians, as trainees, were obligated to consult or confer with those physicians who were more experienced and who were charged with supervision of their clinical conduct. At the very least the residents should have communicated the patient's atypical recovery course to their supervising physicians or some more experienced physicians.

(5) CONSENT TO MEDICAL TREATMENT

26: *Facts*

The thirty-four-year-old athletic male sought medical attention from a prominent knee surgeon because of a history of pain, swelling, and stiffness in his knees. The surgeon diagnosed "chronic bilateral synovitis and bilateral internal derangement of the lateral meniscus," and recommended a trial of conservative treatment. When the patient's condition did not improve, he recommended surgery. Although the surgeon had a faculty appointment at a university hospital, he admitted the patient to a nearby private hospital. The patient signed the usual hospital permit which stated that he consented to the "performance of surgery by the orthopedic surgeon and his assistants."

The surgeon operated on the patient's right knee, removed a torn lateral meniscus and performed a chrondroplasty. On the left knee, the surgeon made the initial incision, but his resident assistant (who had not previously seen the patient) performed the meniscectomy. When the surgery was completed, and the leg tourniquet was released, blood was observed to be coming through the dressing around the left knee. Pulses did not return in the left foot which remained white. An arteriogram disclosed that there was no vascular passage in the popliteal artery which directly filled the popliteal vein. An arteriovenous fistula was diagnosed. A vascular surgeon, who was called in, found the vein lacerated and the artery transected. He repaired the vein and did a saphenous vein graft on the artery. At the conclusion of this surgery, the patient had a bounding pulse in the popliteal artery. However, no pedal pulses were detected and the lower leg remained cold. Arterial spasm was suspected, and the patient was given Papaverine. Nevertheless, absence of pulses and coolness of the leg persisted. Adequate circulation in the foot could not be reestablished in spite of excision of the distal anastomosis which opened both branches of the artery down into the foot and the placement of another graft. The foot now seemed warm with good pulses, but no sensation returned. Thereafter, the patient experienced progressive pain in his left leg.

The patient asked if the resident had done the surgery on his left leg. He was told that the surgeon was present throughout the surgery. The surgeon told him that the surgery was a combined job; that the resident had assisted him in the right leg, and he assisted the resident in the left leg. The surgeon stated that he was right there and could have stopped him from doing anything he thought he was doing wrong and that he did not see him doing anything wrong in the course of that surgery. He said that somewhere or another, the artery had been cut. He told him that he had never seen it happen before. The surgeon told the patient his leg was "looking better all the time." The patient seemed to understand and said to the surgeon, "Anybody can make a mistake. I was sure all along that you hadn't operated on my left knee."

Thereafter, the patient's temperature rose to 104°, and his leg had to be debrided. Several days later, the surgeon talked to the patient's wife and informed her that the patient might need an amputation. The patient was seen in consultation by another orthopedic surgeon because state law required a second opinion when an amputation is planned. He recommended amputation because the leg was not salvageable and infection might spread elsewhere. An above the knee amputation was soon performed.

The patient subsequently suffered from ghost pains and experienced withdrawal from narcotic addiction.

Allegations

A malpractice suit was filed which alleged that as a result of medical negligence during surgery the patient lost his leg. He contended that he had not given consent to have surgery performed by any assistant of the orthopedic surgeon. He further alleged that he was not told that the resident had performed the surgery until several weeks after the operation.

Discussion

Because the resident never saw the patient, before surgery, it may be argued that the patient did not give consent for him to have such an important role in surgery. Consent for assistants is usually implied, especially in a teaching institution; however, this situation is different. The patient was a private patient, and the surgery occurred in a private hospital. Furthermore, he sought the skill of a renowned surgeon, whom he expected to perform the surgery.

The procedure itself involved passing a sharp hooked knife "blindly" along the edge of the lateral meniscus to cut the posterior horn with a forward, pulling motion. Apparently, the resident had inserted the knife too deeply, thus cutting the popliteal artery and vein. Because the technique is "blind," it is questionable that the attending surgeon could actually supervise the resident. Thus the resident may be portrayed as a ghost surgeon operating without the consent of the patient. Certainly, the average patient would not expect that such a difficult part of the procedure would be performed by a resident in a private hospital. For this reason, the patient may have a viable claim for negligent supervision of surgery or for battery because of lack of consent.

27: *Facts*

On October 28, 1971, this twenty-eight-year-old gravida III, para III, female, underwent a total abdominal hysterectomy and bilateral salpingo-oophorectomy. The apparent indication was a several year history of irregular spotting and bleeding, which had not responded satisfactorily to several D & C's and to a course of hormonal therapy. This dysfunctional uterine bleeding was felt to be related to cystic disease of the ovaries and/or uterine fibroids. The attending surgeon did not disclose to the patient that he planned to use metal staples in the procedure. He reasoned that she "possibly would not understand the technique." However, he did indicate to the patient that dissolvable sutures would be used. The extent of staple usage is unclear from the operative report which simply states that "staples were used to close off the upper part of the vagina."

In September 1972, the patient experienced pain and swelling in the vagina, and consulted another physician. The medical record documented complaints of pelvic pain, dysmenorrhea, and dyspareunia. This physician opted for symptomatic treatment.

In November of 1972, the patient experienced increased pelvic discomfort, particularly in the right lower quadrant. This clinical episode resulted in a laparotomy and an appendectomy. The pathological report described the appendix as "fibrotic." At this time the patient first became aware that staples had been used during her hysterectomy. Apparently, abdominal x-rays ordered for diagnosis of her acute abdomen disclosed the presence of staples in her pelvic cavity.

Over the next six weeks the patient continued to experience dyspareunia, and her husband complained of penile discomfort during coitus. On January 3, 1973, a revision of the vaginal cuff was performed and several malpositioned superficial staples were excised. On January 15, 1973, more staples were removed through an abdominal incision, although those encapsulated near the bladder were left in place. The patient continued to complain of the dyspareunia.

Allegations

The patient filed suit alleging that she required two additional operative procedures and experienced additional pain and suffering because metal staples had been negligently used during the October 1971 hysterectomy. She contended that had she been properly informed of the nature of this "novel" procedure, she would have withheld her consent. Her husband also sought damages for loss of consortium.

Discussion

Although a hysterectomy may be an aggressive approach to dysfunctional uterine bleeding in a young married female, the physician's judgment and the patient's consent for the operation justify the operation itself. However, the use of staples for closing the vaginal cuff without the informed consent of the patient led to a malpractice award against this gynecologist.

At the time of surgery, staples had been used by some gynecologists during the course of an abdominal hysterectomy to seal the vaginal cuff. However, this was considered by many gynecologists to be a "novel technique," thus requiring specific informed consent. When a physician uses a new procedure not generally accepted by the profession, the patient should be specifically informed of the nature and acceptance of the technique.

Furthermore, the physician in this case lacked special training in the use of the staple gun. Improper loading and application of the stapler resulted in incomplete closure of the vaginal cuff. Because the physician's lack of experience may materially effect the outcome of the surgery, his inexperience with this technique should also have been disclosed as part of the informed consent.

The fact that the patient was young and sexually active probably played a significant role in the adverse results of surgery. The physician should have anticipated that sexual activity may put a special strain on staples and make the technique inappropriate for this particular patient. The manufacturer's guidelines contraindicated the use of staples on young females for A-P repairs.

For these reasons, the court concluded that a reasonable young female would not consent to the use of staples for an abdominal hysterectomy. This would constitute a causative link between the negligent disclosure on the part of the surgeon and the patient's injuries. The husband may recover on his claim, which is derivative to his wife's successful suit.

28: *Facts*

A forty-two-year-old man had a long history of a symptomatic hiatal hernia, manifested by pyrosis, pain, and nausea. He was hospitalized for an intensive evaluation of these symptoms. An upper GI series disclosed an esophageal lesion. A thorough work-up ensued, including multiple esophageal biopsies and esophagoscopy that disclosed only chronic inflammation. When conservative therapy was unsuccessful in providing reasonable relief, surgical repair of the hiatal hernia was considered. However, after a conference and discussion of the case, the hospital surgical staff advised against surgery. The patient was disappointed because he hoped that surgery would definitely relieve him of his symptoms.

Approximately two months later, the patient was contacted by a member of the hospital staff and asked to come into the hospital for surgery the next day, if he still desired it. The reason for the sudden offer of surgery was that it coincided with a visit to the hospital by a nationally recognized thoracic surgeon. A transthoracic approach to the hiatus hernia, which the surgical consultant had developed, was performed to allow the thoracic surgeon to demonstrate a new technique used in heart surgery because no heart patient was available for surgery. The initial incision, although appropriate for heart surgery, was high for the purpose of a hiatal hernia repair. Therefore, it necessitated additional muscle stripping and rib breaking. In the process, the spleen was lacerated, thereby requiring a splenectomy.

Prior to the surgery, the patient was not informed of the nature of the surgical approach to the hiatus hernia. He was never told that he was going to have a thoracic incision. He assumed he would have an abdominal incision because in the previous month when he was on the hospital ward, those patients with hiatal hernia repairs had abdominal incisions. In addition, no one discussed with him the risks or complications of a thoracic approach. In particular he was not told that he might have ribs fractured during the operation.

Since the operation the patient has had persistent severe left-sided chest wall pain.

Allegations

The patient filed a malpractice claim, alleging that the nature, extent, and risks, of a transthoracic repair of a hiatal hernia were not explained to him prior to surgery. He sought recovery for fractured ribs, removal of the spleen, and persistent chest wall pain.

Discussion

A physician has a duty to inform his patient of the nature of the proposed treatment of the patient's injury or illness, and alternative methods of treatment. Moreover, a physician is obligated to discuss the nature of a reparative procedure, including its inherent risks and recognized complications that have significant frequency and materiality. This is necessary for a reasonable patient to decide freely whether to submit to the procedure.

In this case, the patient will be able to demonstrate a causal connection between the surgeon's negligent failure to obtain the patient's informed consent and the patient's injury as a result of the procedure because complications arose that were known to be related to the type of surgery (lacerated spleen and the fractured rib). A court would probably assume that this patient might have reasonably elected an abdominal repair approach if these complications referable to a transthoracic approach had been explained to him. If he had, he would not now have the injuries for which he is seeking compensation.

In addition, if the surgeon had led the patient to believe he would use an abdominal approach during the first hospitalization, the patient could attest that the thoracic approach was done with no consent at all. This would also give the patient a legal cause of action for battery.

In this case, another factor that weighs heavily against the surgeon was the breach of a fiduciary relationship in that the procedure was performed primarily for demonstration and teaching rather than treatment.

29: *Facts*

This thirty-six-year-old female had long-standing mastodynia, secondary to chronic cystic mastitis. Treatment with Esidrix, Methotestosterone, and narcotics did not provide reasonable relief of her symptoms; however the pain was relieved by field block. The surgeon recommended a subcutaneous mastectomy to permanently relieve the patient's discomfort. He did not disclose or explain the inherent risks and complications of the proposed procedure to the patient. Relying on the surgeon's recommendation, the patient signed the operative consent form. She underwent bilateral sub-cutaneous mastectomy through intralateral 90° quadrant incisions. Ten days later, two 235 cubic centimeter round silastic mammary prostheses were in-serted. The immediate postoperative course was uncomplicated, and the pa-tient experienced relief of breast pain. The patient was discharged with in-structions to wear a firm supportive brassiere and keep her elbows down to her sides for two weeks.

Several days later, a left areolar cellulitis developed, and Staphcillin, hot compresses, and bed rest were prescribed. A needle aspiration of the fluc-tulant area produced no fluid or purulence. One week later the patient's breast was tense, struted, edematous, and superficially ulcerated along the left aerolar, with surface slough of the nipple. She was hospitalized for in-tensive antibiotic treatment and observation. All cultures of the area of ul-ceration were sterile. Observation during the hospitalization did not dis-close the presence of active infection. The clinical impression was a fibrous capsule contracture around the prosthesis and loss of full thickness of skin in the area of the nipple.

Thereafter, she consulted another plastic surgeon who detected an es-char of the left breast and clear fluid exuding from her breast, even though the implant was not exposed. The plastic surgeon excised the eschar, re-moved the left breast implant, widened the breast pocket beneath, and inser-ted a smaller prosthesis. A release of fibrous capsule contracture of the right breast was also performed. Postoperatively, the left breast became indu-rated, erythematous, and tender. Additional surgery to correct the thinness and breakdown of skin was required.

Allegations
The patient sued the original operating plastic surgeon for failing to ob-tain a proper informed consent for the procedure. She alleged that if she had been made aware of the risks and complications of the procedure, she would never have granted consent to have it performed on her.

Discussion
Elective subcutaneous mastectomy for severe mastodynia secondary to chronic cystic mastitis may have been clinically indicated in this case. Nev-ertheless the surgeon had a duty to obtain informed consent for the proce-dure. The scope of the surgeon's duty was to adequately disclose and ex-plain to the patient, the nature, frequency, and materiality of risks of the procedure. Because postoperative infection is a commonly recognized atten-dant risk of surgery, ordinarily the patient may be presumed to be aware of it. Therefore, no specific detailed disclosure as to the possible occurrence of a local postoperative infection was required.

Capsular contraction is a frequent but relatively immaterial complication of mammary implantation procedures. Correction of the contracture through surgical release, readjustment, or replacement of the prostheses is usually achievable. Thus failure to specifically disclose this complication may not necessarily be negligent because the information is unlikely to strongly influence the patient's decision to accept or reject the proposed procedure.

Negligence in disclosure may be inferred if concealment or misrepresentation is used as an inducement to secure patient "consent." Evidence in this case may be sufficient to allow such an inference because the surgeon did not disclose any pertinent information to the patient concerning the procedure except that it might relieve her pain. Moreover, skin breakdown or sloughing of surface breast tissue is a frequent and material complication of subcutaneous mastectomy for cystic mastitis, and specific disclosure of this risk to the patient is usually required. In this case, the patient was not properly informed of these risks. If she had been, she may have reasonably declined surgery. Under the circumstances, failure to properly disclose this information creates an inference of negligent conduct of the attending surgeon in obtaining the patient's consent.

In addition, the following aspects of this case may raise separate and collective inferences of improper application of medical knowledge and skill by the attending surgeon: the failure to specifically instruct in, and warn of, the use of heat over an area of surgically undermined skin that should have been anticipated to be relatively insensitive as a result of surgery (this inattention was probably a substantial factor in causing a surface burn which significantly contributed to breast tissue loss); the performance of this two-stage procedure with only a ten-day hiatus; and the needle puncturing of the implant.

30: *Facts*

During a routine checkup appointment for her chronic asthma condition, this forty-one-year-old registered nurse advised her physician that she had been in close contact with relatives who were being evaluated for possible tuberculosis. The physician performed an intermittent strength PPD that was subsequently read as "negative," and a chest x-ray that was reported as "within normal limits." Ten days later, the patient reported to her physician that active tuberculosis had been diagnosed in her relatives, and that her daughter had converted to "positive" on a second PPD. Her physician advised her that she had the option of starting on INH with retesting with intermediate strength PPD in three months; and if the PPD was still negative, stopping the INH or repeating the PPD in three months, and commencing the INH therapy at that time if the PPD converted to "positive." The physician documented in the record this option disclosure. The patient chose the second course of treatment because of the possibility of developing hepatitis from INH. However, three days later, she telephoned her physician and requested a prescription for INH. She indicated a desire to take the INH for three months, after which time it would be stopped if the PPD was still negative. She pointed out that her supervisor at the hospital where she worked as an intensive care unit nurse was concerned about the possibility that the patient would develop active TB and spread it to critically ill patients. The physician honored her request and wrote a prescription for INH, with instructions to see him in one month for a follow-up examination.

Seven weeks later, her physician hospitalized the patient with a diagnosis of hepatitis. Her initial elevations of SGOT, LDH, and alkaline phosphatase showed serial decline during her eleven days as an inpatient, and she was discharged with the recommendation that the INH be discontinued and that serial liver function tests be conducted every four weeks. A liver biopsy was planned in twelve months if the liver function studies were still abnormal. Her posthospital convalescence was unremarkable except that she complained of fatigue, nausea, and fatty food intolerance.

Allegations

The patient sued her physician, alleging that he prescribed INH for prevention of tuberculosis without warning her of its possible side effects, and as a result she suffered liver damage, which caused her nausea, vomiting, and fatigueability.

Discussion

Although mild hepatic dysfunction, evidenced by elevation of liver function tests, occurs in approximately 20 percent of persons taking INH, in most cases these tests return to normal range without necessity to discontinue medication. Occasionally progressive liver damage occurs, necessitating immediate cessation of the drug.

In this case the risks and benefits of the disease process and its therapy had to be balanced by the attending physician. The use of INH therapy was reasonable despite its risk, considering the overall risk of tuberculosis to the patient. INH is generally the most effective medication for preventive therapy of tuberculosis. In this patient's age group, the incidence of INH-induced hepatitis is approximately 1 percent (the risk increases with age). However the risk of contacting tuberculosis in an individual exposed to a close relative with active tuberculosis is 2.5 percent. Moreover, the risk of developing INH-induced hepatitis exists only during the course of preventive therapy, whereas the risk of developing tuberculosis is present for as long as the exposure exists. Furthermore, the patient, a medical professional, was made aware of the risk of hepatitis and of her therapeutic options, and nevertheless still chose to receive such therapy. Thus she assumed the risk of occurrence of hepatitis under the circumstances.

In considering preventive therapy, priorities must be set which take into consideration not only the risk of developing tuberculosis compared to the risk of INH toxicity, but also the likelihood of infecting others. INH therapy may also be indicated for the purpose of diminishing possible transmission of the disease or infection, especially among household members, other close associates of persons with recently diagnosed tuberculosis, and positive tuberculin skin test reactors with radiologic findings. As an ICU nurse, this patient may have created a significant risk of serious infection to her already debilitated patients.

Although an allergic hypersensitivity theory has been postulated as a mechanism for INH-induced hepatitis, the patient's allergic diathesis (although perhaps it should have been taken into account in considering the use of INH) would not contraindicate the use of INH. As previously mentioned, the medication was clinically indicated under the circumstances. However, if the medicine had been contraindicated (as distinguished from not being clinically indicated) the prescribing physician would have incurred substantial liability exposure simply by prescribing it for his patient.

Although it might be argued that the attending physician should have recalibrated the balance of risks versus benefits (tuberculosis versus hepatitis) of INH therapy because of patient's allergic history, it is speculative to *retrospeculatively* assume, after the development of a complication of therapy, that the balance would have been tipped in favor of withholding therapy. Moreover, his disclosure to the patient concerning her therapeutic options was medical judgment based on possession of appropriate medical knowledge and exercise of skill and care under the circumstances.

31: *Facts*

A seventy-two-year-old clergyman had publicly discussed the moral implications of a celebrated legal case involving disconnection of the respirator of a patient in a chronic vegetative state. His religion permitted the termination of extraordinary life support systems when there was no reasonable hope for the patient's recovery, and church officials had concluded that use of the respirator for a patient in a chronic vegetative state constituted an "extraordinary measure" under the circumstances. The clergyman expressed agreement with those views and stated that he would not want his life prolonged by such "extraordinary measures" if his condition were hopeless.

Two months after such a declaration, he was hospitalized for the elective repair of an inguinal hernia. During the hernioplasty, he had a cardiac arrest, resulting hypoxia, and consequential serious brain damage. As a result, he lost his cognitive ability and was unable to breathe spontaneously and was placed on a respirator which maintained him in a chronic persistent vegetative state. His attending physician informed the director of his religious order that there was no reasonable chance of recovery and that the patient would die in that vegetative state. After retaining a consultant who confirmed the prognosis, the director requested the hospital to remove the respirator. When the hospital refused to disconnect the respirator without court authorization, the director petitioned, pursuant to a state statute, to be appointed guardian of the patient, with authority to direct removal of the respirator.

At the hearing to determine whether the respirator should be discontinued, the medical experts agreed that there was no reasonable likelihood that the patient would ever emerge from the vegetative coma or recover his cognitive powers.

Discussion

A competent adult patient has a fundamental right to determine what should be done with his own body, and thus the right to control the course of his medical treatment. In cases of emergency where a patient is unconscious and where it is necessary to treat him before his consent can be obtained, the law will usually assume that consent would have been granted had the patient been able to do so. Even in emergencies, however, consent will not be implied if the patient has previously stated that he would not consent to treatment under such circumstances.

When the treatment is life saving, a patient's right to refuse to consent to medical treatment *may* have to yield to the state's superior legitimate interest in protecting the lives of its citizens. Thus under certain circumstances a patient may be prohibited from declining necessary medical treatment, or a physician may be precluded from honoring the patient's decision to decline necessary treatment. In general, however, courts have consistently supported the right of a competent adult patient to make his own decision about treatment. Absent superior state interests, civil liability has been imposed on physicians who perform medical treatment without consent, even though the treatment may be necessary to preserve the patient's life, because a patient's right to determine the course of his own medical treatment is paramount to the physician's obligation to provide needed medical care. Thus a physician who respects an adult patient's right of self-determination would not be responsible for violating the state's interest in preserving life.

The state may also assert additional legitimate interests (such as prevention of suicide or protection of dependent children) that may outweigh a patient's refusal to undergo necessary treatment. In this case, those concerns are inapplicable because the patient's condition was not self-inflicted and he has no dependents.

Although the patient's right of self-determination is personal, it is not lost when the patient becomes incompetent. There is no consensus, however, of the mechanism of how such a personal right is to be exercised by a third party. In this case, however, the question of whether or how a decision to discontinue life sustaining medical treatment may be made by someone other than the patient is not the issue because the patient made the decision for himself before he became incompetent.

Where it is claimed that an incompetent patient who has no hope of recovery left instructions to terminate life sustaining procedures when he had been competent, the law usually requires "clear and convincing" evidence (the highest standard of evidence applicable to civil cases) to honor the patient's instructions. Loose, equivocal, or contradictory evidence would not meet this standard and thus not provide a basis for the court to act. In this case the evidence of what the patient's decision would have been if he had been competent, was compelling. There was no suggestion that the petitioner seeking to discontinue treatment had any motive other than to see that the patient's stated wishes were respected. The patient's thoughtfully expressed conclusion not to have his life prolonged by extraordinary means if there were no hope of recovery, was supported by his religious beliefs and was consistent with his life of unselfish religious devotion. The patient's pronouncements were solemn, and not casual remarks made at some social gathering. The patient was not too young to realize or appreciate the consequences of his statements. His commitment to such views was persistent in that he reiterated the decision only two months before his final hospitalization. In addition, there was no need to speculate whether he would want the respirator discontinued under these circumstances, because what occurred to him was identical to what happened in the celebrated legal case that he had discussed with others and which had originally prompted his decision that he would want to have extraordinary measures discontinued in his case. In sum, the evidence clearly and convincingly shows that the patient did not want to be maintained in a vegetative coma by use of a respirator. Thus, the court would allow the respirator to be disconnected by the patient's guardian.

32: *Facts*

The fifty-five-year-old lifelong resident of a state mental facility, had a mental age of eighteen months. His mother resided near the facility and visited him frequently. His attending physician noticed blood in his urine and asked the mother for permission to conduct diagnostic tests. She initially refused but after discussions with the facility's staff gave her consent. The tests disclosed cancer of the bladder. Radiation therapy was recommended. When the hospital refused to administer the treatment without the consent of a legal guardian, the patient's mother applied to the court and was appointed guardian of her son. With her consent he received a course of radiation therapy which put the disease in remission. However, nine months later, blood was again observed in his urine. Bladder lesions were cauterized in an unsuccessful effort to stop the bleeding. At that point his physician diagnosed the cancer as terminal, concluding that after using all medical and surgical means then available, the patient would nevertheless die from the disease.

The attending physician asked the patient's mother for permission to administer blood transfusions as needed. She initially refused but the following day withdrew her objection. After several weeks of blood transfusions, his mother requested that the transfusions be discontinued. The director of the facility, pursuant to a state statute, sought legal authorization to continue the transfusions, claiming that without them the patient would die within weeks. The patient's mother petitioned for a legal order prohibiting the transfusions. The court appointed a guardian to represent the patient in the litigative dispute and signed an order temporarily permitting the transfusions to continue, pending the determination of the proceeding. At the hearing, all the medical experts concurred that the patient had irreversible metastatic bladder cancer. His life-span was estimated to be less than six months. They also agreed that he had an infant's mentality and was unable to comprehend his predicament or to make a reasoned choice of treatment. In addition, there was no dispute that he was continuously losing blood as a result of his bladder cancer, and required two units of blood every eight to fifteen days to replace the blood lost. The attending physician explained that without the transfusions the patient's circulation would be insufficiently oxygenated. To compensate for this blood loss, his heart had to work harder and he breathed more rapidly, which caused fatigue, strain, and lethargy. After the transfusions, he had more energy and was able to resume his usual activities—feeding and cleaning himself, taking walks, and running. The attending physician recognized that at some point the rate of blood loss might increase to such an extent that transfusions would be an ineffective replacement.

There was testimony that suggested that the patient found the transfusions disagreeable and was distressed by the blood in his urine, which increased immediately after a transfusion. He could not comprehend the purpose of the transfusions and on occasion displayed initial resistance. His mother testified that she wanted the transfusions discontinued because she wanted her son to be comfortable, and she believed that he would want them discontinued.

Discussion

The patient had never been competent in his life. He was always totally incapable of understanding or making a reasoned decision about medical treatment. Because he always had been an infant mentally, it would probably be unrealistic to attempt to determine whether he would want to continue potentially life prolonging treatment if he were competent.

Although a parent (or guardian) has a right to consent to medical treatment on behalf of a minor, the parent may not deprive the child of life-saving treatment (even when the decision to decline treatment is based on good intentions or such constitutional grounds as religious beliefs), because the state is required to protect the health and welfare of minors. However, when parents have chosen a course of treatment for their child among reasonable therapeutic alternatives, it is not the role of courts to determine the most "effective" treatment. Nevertheless, the law will not permit a parent to deny his child any or all treatment for a condition which threatens his life, such as the case of a child who may bleed to death because of the parent's refusal to authorize a blood transfusion.

The case involved two threats to the patient's life: first, cancer of the bladder, which was incurable and would in all probability claim his life; secondly, the blood loss, which posed the risk of an earlier death that up to a point could be prevented by the replacement of blood. Although the transfusions would not cure the cancer, they could help to preclude the risk of death from a treatable cause. Although the patient did not like the transfusions (as might be expected of one with an infant's mentality), the procedure did not involve excessive pain. Moreover, without the transfusions, the patient's mental and physical abilities would not be maintained at the usual level; whereas with the transfusions he was able to function essentially in his usual state. Thus, under the circumstances of this case, a court would probably grant the application for permission to continue the transfusions because it would be improper to allow an incompetent patient to bleed to death simply because someone (even someone as close as a parent) feels that this is best for someone with an incurable disease.

(6) Treatment Decisions

33: *Facts*

A thirty-five-year-old man had rheumatic fever and consequential valvular disease. In 1971, he complained of arthralgias, chest pain, dyspnea, and fever of three weeks duration. His cardiologist described a grade III systolic regurgitant murmur radiating into the axilia, an opening snap and diastolic rumble, and a soft diastolic murmur at the sternal border. The EKG showed left atrial enlargement, and a chest x-ray demonstrated a prominent left ventricle and a straight left heart border with elevation of the left main stem bronchus. The cardiologist diagnosed inactive rheumatic heart disease and continued the patient on prophylactic penicillin.

In July 1972, the patient was hospitalized because of abdominal pain radiating to the back. Atrial fibrillation was detected. An IVP demonstrated nonfunctioning right kidney. An arteriogram showed multiple emboli to the right kidney. Subsequent pyelograms indicated only minimal function of the right kidney. His condition improved on heparin and he was discharged on digoxin .25 mg. q.d., Quinidine 300 mg. t.i.d., Pen V-K 250 mg. b.i.d., and Coumadin 7.5 mg. q.d. A follow-up prothrombin time was 30 with a control time of 12. The patient was asked to return in two weeks.

Two weeks later, the patient was rehospitalized because of left flank pain and hematuria. His blood pressure was 120/72, and his pulse was 90 and regular. A hematocrit was 39, and a prothrombin time was 46 with a control time of 12. When he developed massive hematuria and severe left flank pain, and his hematocrit had dropped below 30, he was given Aquamephyton, and transfused with two units of packed red blood cells. An emergency IVP showed a nonfunctioning left kidney consistent with a massive renal bleed. A follow-up IVP two days later demonstrated restoration of left renal function. The BUN returned to normal in a few days. Subsequently, the patient improved and was discharged on penicillin, Quinidine, and digoxin. He was never again prescribed Coumadin.

Between 1972 and 1976, the patient had recurrent episodes of ectopia and atrial fibrillation for which he frequently visited his cardiologist. In April 1976, he went to the physician because of chest tightness and dyspnea on exertion. His physician diagnosed borderline congestive heart failure. The Quinidine was discontinued, and the patient was started on hydrochlorothiazide. An echocardiogram demonstrated enlargement of the left atrium and left ventricle, mitral stenosis, and a thickened aortic valve. On April 13, 1976, the cardiologist considered cardiac catheterization, but no date was set.

In July 1976, he went to the emergency room complaining of abdominal pain. An examination of the abdomen was normal. An x-ray of the lower abdomen was normal. EKG showed atrial fibrillation. Urinalysis and CBC were normal. He was released and was next seen by his cardiologist three days later with no complaints. Physican examination and urinalysis were normal. The physician doubted recurrent emboli and noted his hesitation to resume anticoagulants. The patient was requested to return to the clinic in three months. Two weeks later, the patient suffered a severe stroke resulting in a permanent right hemiparesis and loss of speech.

Allegations

The patient and his family filed suit seeking legal damages for permanent neurologic deficits, contending that due to negligent medical care he suffered this stroke, which would otherwise have been preventable.

Discussion

The treatment this patient received during his first hospitalization in July 1972 for renal emboli and in the second hospitalization in August 1972 for control of the bleeding episode was appropriate. However, in light of the patient's previous massive embolization, a reasonably prudent physician would have done more after that time. Because he was excessively anti-coagulated and poorly monitored prior to the bleed, more consideration should have been given to reanticoagulate with a lower, and yet effective, dose of Coumadin. If, however, it was decided not to reanticoagulate the patient, the physician should have undertaken a more thorough cardiological evaluation, including evaluation for possible cardiac surgery. A patient who frequently goes in and out of atrial fibrillation, as this patient did between 1972 and 1976, is at great risk of embolization. Because of this special risk and his past massive embolus, more should have been done during the subsequent visits to prevent a recurrent embolus. The echocardiogram in April of 1976 showed moderate valvular damages; therefore, the patient may well have been a surgical candidate, in light of his past embolization, his poor response to anticoagulation, his recurrent bouts of atrial fibrillation, and his poor cardiac reserve manifested by symptoms on that visit.

Although the stroke that he suffered may not have been preventable, anticoagulation or surgery would have decreased the chance of the embolic stroke; and, therefore, should have been more diligently pursued.

34: *Facts*

A twenty-nine-year-old female had a ten-year history of chronic ulcerative colitis, which had required multiple hospitalizations and extensive drug therapy with steroids, antibiotics, and tranquilizers. She exhibited no evidence of arthritis, hepatitis, iritis, or skin changes. However pancolonic strictures effectively precluded the use of colonscopy for monitoring progression and transformation of her disease. Her internist discussed and advised elective colorectal surgery because of the duration of the disease, extent of involvement, severity of onset, and stricture of the colon which impeded effective monitoring. He referred her to a colorectal surgeon for consultation.

The surgeon discussed the surgery with the patient and her husband and cited as an indication for surgery the fact that ulcerative colitis for longer than ten years in a young woman created a greater likelihood of developing cancer. He explained the nature of the operation and the possible complications, including hemorrhage, infection, anesthetic risk, and death. He also discussed the management of an ileostomy, and advised her to contact the Ileostomy Society for further information. Approximately two weeks later the patient called the surgeon and informed him of her desire to undergo surgery.

One month later, the patient was admitted to a medical center for an elective proctocolectomy. She underwent the usual preoperative evaluation. Physical examination and laboratory data, including PT, PTT, and platelet count were within normal limits. She was specifically questioned about a history of bleeding problems and replied in the negative. The following day, a senior resident noted on the medical record that he "explained the procedure to the patient and the possible complications of hemorrhage, infection, urinary tract problems, splenic injury, and ileostomy dysfunction," and that she understood and granted her consent.

On entering the abdomen during the surgery, the surgeons noted the presence of large veins in the pelvic area, especially the ovarian veins. However, surgery proceeded smoothly. Shortly thereafter the perineal aspect of surgery was started by a second team of surgeons. Before the bowel was resected, bleeding occurred from the right parasacral vein and was controlled by suture ligatures. After the colon was resected and removed, significant bleeding was noted in the pelvis, which was initially controlled by suture ligature. The sacrum was then packed.

When the packing was removed, multiple areas of profuse bleeding occurred from the sacral plexus. Suture ligation, cautery, and repeat packing controlled the hemorrhage. However, upon removal of packs, hemorrhage recurred. Bone wax was also used to pack the sacral foramina, but hemostasis was not achieved. Although the patient was being vigorously transfused, she went into shock. When an estimated blood loss of ten units had occurred, the aorta was cross-clamped, and the surgeons decided to perform a ligation of the internal iliac vessels. As this procedure was begun, the patient experienced a cardiac arrest. External and subsequently internal cardiac massage was performed. The patient was transfused with whole blood, packed cells, fresh plasma, and other purified clotting factors through multiple intravenous routes. She was packed with Kerlex dressing soaked in sulfamylon.

Cardiotonic drugs were administered. The urine output ceased and dilated fixed pupils were noted. In spite of base replacement, metabolic acidosis remained uncorrected. A neurologic consultant reported absent corneal reflex and absent oculocephalic reflex which indicated brain stem damage. When an epicardial pacemaker, attached to the apex of the heart, failed to improve cardiac output, resuscitative efforts were discontinued, and the patient was pronounced dead.

Allegations

A claim was filed alleging negligence in inadequately advising the patient of the hazards of surgery and securing informed consent for the operation; inadequate preparation for the operation; improper operative procedure; and unnecessary surgery, because the patient's condition was controlled medically and she was asymptomatic and free of pain at the time of surgery.

Discussion

Although the patient was relatively asymptomatic for several years prior to the surgery, she had at least a ten-year history of persistent active ulcerative colitis despite adequate medical treatment. The colon stricture made colonscopic follow-up impossible; therefore, concern for the development of cancer in this young woman was justified. She had no history or evidence of a bleeding diathesis. In view of the above factors, there were legally sufficient indications for colectomy.

The patient was counseled regarding the nature of her disease, the reason for the procedure, and the benefits and risks, including possible death. She gave an informed consent for the surgery.

The bleeding which occurred began despite proper surgical technique and no warnings of unusual bleeding tendencies. An adverse occurrence such as this is not negligent without evidence of technical error or an overlooked risk factor.

Heroic efforts were made to control the bleeding and replace the loss, and at times seemed to be succeeding. When it was apparent that these methods were not going to succeed, a ligation procedure was attempted. However, a cardiac arrest intervened. It is speculative to assume that the ligation would have saved the patient's life because it was not reasonably foreseeable that the initial methods of hemostasis would have invariably failed. Thus failure to commence the ligation at an earlier time was not negligent.

35: *Facts*

A twenty-two-year-old man was injured when the motorcycle he was riding was hit broadside by a taxicab. He was taken to the emergency room where physical and radiological evaluation disclosed a transverse compound fracture of the midshaft of the right tibia with slight posterior displacement, and a nondisplaced fracture of the midshaft of the right fibula. He was given Demerol 75 mg. IM, Phenergan 25 mg. IM, and Hypertet 250 units IM. There is no documentation that the wound was cleaned or debrided, that a splint or dressing was applied, or that antibiotics were administered.

The patient was subsequently transported to another hospital and arrived there five hours after the injury occurred. Marked swelling of the right leg and knee, and crepitis over the lateral border of the knee were noted. Neurovascular function of the lower extremity was intact. The open fractures of the middle right tibia and fibula were observed as well as a nondisplaced fracture of the lateral aspect of the tibial plateau that extended into the knee joint.

Seven hours after the injury, the patient underwent debridement in the operating room. Fascial layers of the anterior compartment were opened, and the wound over the right tibia was irrigated with normal saline and Keflin solution. Thereafter the relatively inexperienced orthopedic surgeon decided to internally fix the tibia. The operative report indicated that the surgeon decided to internally fix the bone because of the "marked swelling of the muscular structures." An intramedullary Lottes nail was inserted for internal fixation of the tibial fracture. All wounds were closed primarily and a long-leg cast was applied. Intravenous Keflin was continued for six days, followed by a six-week course of oral Keflex. Sutures were removed approximately two weeks after surgery.

During the third postoperative week, a wound slough was noted, followed by purulent drainage and eventual exposure of the bone. Debridement and local wound care were instituted. Two weeks later, a skin graft was placed at the site of the wound slough resulting in a partial take. Cultures of the wound drainage initially grew Staphylococcus aureus, coagulase positive, sensitive to cephalothin. The patient was continued on oral Keflex.

He was discharged ten weeks later in a long-leg walking cast, with an infected nonunion of the tibia, and skin slough of the right anterior tibial area. Examinations at two-week intervals were required because of persistent drainage. Culture of the wound was taken the next month and again grew Staphylococcus aureus, coagulase positive, sensitive to cephalothin. Radiographically, a nonunion with involucral bone was noted. The following month, the Lottes nail was removed, and suction irrigation with Keflin and Alevaire was performed for twelve days. Thereafter, all drainage sites were successfully closed. The patient was discharged in a short-leg walking cast, and Keflex was prescribed. Over the next year the patient spent much time in hospitals where he sought relief of leg pain by narcotic medication. The nonunion persisted, and osteomyelitis continued on an insidious and relentless course, necessitating a below-the-knee amputation.

Allegations

The patient sued, alleging negligent care by the orthopedic surgeon in the treatment and aftercare of his injury, which caused him extended pain and loss of his lower leg.

Discussion

The surgeon's decision to openly reduce and internally fix the tibia deviated from the standard of care for management of compound fractures of the tibia. Although a general consensus does not exist among orthopedic surgeons as to one acceptable mode of management of such injuries, the majority support a more conservative, closed reduction method because such an approach is less likely to result in nonunion and infection.

Although a developer of this internal fixation technique has reported good results with internal fixation and a lower incidence of infection than with a closed approach, his results appear to be an indication of his unusual competence and experience in this area. In less experienced hands internal fixation of open fractures of the tibia is a marginially acceptable method of management. In the past decade, medical literature has extolled the virtues and advantages of closed care, and highlighted the risks and complications of open reduction and internal fixation. At some hospitals, the latter method of management is prohibited by departmental policy.

When a controversial and disreputed method is selected, justification for it is required to overcome the charge that it represents a deviation from the requisite standard of care. The surgeon hints at his recognition of the management controversy in his operative note which stated that he "decided" to internally fix the tibial fracture because of the "marked swelling of the muscular structures." Unfortunately, he provided no further explanation for his choice. He did not disclose his professional thinking concerning the clinical significance of the relationship of swelling to the choice of management. His reasoning would appropriately account for the anterior compartment fasciotomy that he performed. It can only be speculated that perhaps the fasciotomy allowed relatively easy access for open reduction. Even if it did, this would not seem to be sufficient indication for the internal fixation.

In addition, controversy exists as to the need to treat this injury on an emergency basis. Some orthopedic surgeons who internally fix tibial fractures prefer to delay the fixation for several days to determine if antibiotic therapy will effectively preclude a wound infection. This moratorium allows the physician to monitor the wound while the patient is immobilized in a cast and to consult with more experienced surgeons, if necessary. Because this surgeon elected not to wait, he will therefore have to demonstrate that he possessed adequate experience, training, and skill to manage such an injury in the manner he chose. If he cannot convincingly demonstrate that he was aware of the complications associated with open reduction and internal fixation, and took reasonable precautions to avoid them, it will be difficult to defend his conduct.

The causation relationship between the internal fixation and the patient's injury is unclear. The occurrence of infection and nonunion in an open fracture of the tibia is possible even with proper management. However, medical experts will probably testify that the incidence of infection and nonunion is higher with internal fixation of a tibial fracture. Thus it may then be argued that this patient was unreasonably subjected to this additional risk, and therefore the surgeon's selection was a material factor contributing to the complications.

36: *Facts*

A thirty-seven-year-old male patient was referred for surgical evaluation because of radiological evidence of multiple gallstones and chronic right upper quadrant pain, which caused an inability to sleep on his right side.

The surgeon who performed the cholecystectomy recalled no problems during the procedure. The operative report did not suggest any difficulty.

The common bile duct did not appear dilated prior to closure of the abdomen. The gallbladder contained one large stone. An operative cholangiogram was not performed because no small stones were noted in the gallbladder, and, therefore, the surgeon felt that the probability of residual stones in the common duct was remote.

On the first postoperative day, copious bile drainage from the penrose drain was noted. On the following day, the drainage had increased. The amount of drainage concerned the surgeon, but because the patient was afebrile, nonicteric, and had experienced only noncolicky pain at the operative site, he decided to continue monitoring the drainage and the patient's clinical course.

On the fourth postoperative day, less drainage was noted; however, on the sixth postoperative day, the patient's stool was clay-colored. An intravenous cholangiogram was performed to detect whether or not common duct obstruction might have caused a cystic duct suture "blow out"; however, the liver was unable to concentrate enough dye to visualize the biliary tree.

When on the seventh postoperative day the patient's stool was still clay-colored, the surgeon made an informal telephonic "consultation" with a surgeon who was not on the hospital's staff, and thereafter had a hallway "consultation" with another staff surgeon. Neither "consultant" examined the patient or his record. On the basis of these "consultations," the surgeon decided to continue to observe the patient in the hope that the bile drainage would spontaneously abate. The surgeon stated that he did not order a fistulogram because he was concerned that it might introduce an infective organism into the biliary system.

When copious drainage persisted through the ninth postoperative day, the surgeon discussed the drainage problem with the patient. He did not suggest transfer to a facility that would be better able to handle this problem. Although the surgeon had performed many cholecystectomies, he had little experience in dealing with this specific postoperative complication of the procedure.

On the seventeenth postoperative day, the surgeon indicated to the patient that further surgery was necessary to determine the cause of the drainage. The patient, however, requested referral to another surgeon who had been recommended by a relative. The surgeon's referring diagnosis was "persistent biliary fistula." Referral was accomplished three weeks postoperatively.

A fistulogram disclosed the proximal, but not the distal and of the common bile duct. Abdominal exploration disclosed complete transection of the bile duct. A primary anastomosis of the common duct could not be accomplished because of morphological changes in the drainage area and the resultant inability to identify and locate the distal common duct. Therefore, a Roux-en-Y choledochojejunostomy was performed. Subsequently, the patient experienced recurrent episodes of ascending cholangitis.

Allegations

The patient asserted that the surgeon transected the common bile duct creating a fistula between the hepatic duct and peritoneal cavity, which necessitated the performance of a choledochojejunostomy and resulted in extensive liver damage.

Discussion

The mere occurrence of a recognized complication such as operative transection of the common duct is not necessarily negligent, if the cholecystectomy was indicated, and if the surgeon was aware of the complication and took reasonable action to avoid its occurrence. In this case, the procedure was indicated, and the surgeon was aware of important anatomical relationships. Because the mechanism of injury to the common duct is undetermined, it is difficult to comment upon the care exercised by the surgeon during the procedure. Although an inference of negligent surgery is raised by the mere fact of transection of the common duct, evidence of a negligent surgical act could not be adduced from the record.

Detection of transection of the common duct must be made as soon as reasonably possible, because early corrective treatment decreases the likelihood of serious and irreversible injury. Therefore, monitoring and diagnostic formulation must be diligent. In this case, the finding of persistent and excessive bile drainage was identified, but an effective differential diagnostic investigation was not undertaken, despite recognized serious consequences of delay. An intravenous cholangiogram was not performed until the sixth postoperative day. Moreover, this procedure did not exclude the existence of a serious complication. Nonvisualization should have suggested the need for further investigation.

Although the surgeon's experience with postcholecystectomy complications was limited, liability is not predicated upon his inexperience, but upon his delay in necessary evaluation. He should have known at least his professional limitation in managing with this type of postoperative complication and then diligently sought helpful information from competent sources. Under the circumstances, there was a need for timely and effective consultation. It was not until the seventh postoperative day that he sought consultation. Moreover, the consultation he sought was inadequate. Effective consultation requires that the consultant examine the medical record as well as the patient. Casual opinions are insufficient.

In this case, the negligence involved in the management of the complication is legally inseparable from its detection. The surgeon's ultimate admission that he could not effectively manage the complication is further evidence that he was dilatory in not seeking earlier consultation.

The longer the delay, the more distortion and destruction of anatomical structures decreased the possibility of a primary anastomosis and increased the probability of serious persistent and progressive liver damage sequelae.

37: *Facts*

A fifty-two-year-old man underwent an abdomino-perineal resection for cancer of the rectum. Thereafter, he underwent several courses of chemotherapy, prescribed by an oncologist. On the occasion of his last course of chemotherapy, his attending physician administered 600 mg. of 5-Fluorouracil through the intravenous tubing that was connected to a butterfly needle in the antecubital fossa. The physician then slowly injected the Adriamycin and repeatedly aspirated for blood return, to test that the needle was still in place in the vein. After administering two-thirds of the full dose (30 cc.), the patient suddenly complained of a painful burning sensation in his arm. The physician stopped the injection, aspirated, and received a blood return. He therefore continued the injection even though the patient continued to complain of pain. Because of the patient's protests and exclamations of pain, the physician consulted an oncologist concerning the possible extravasation of the drug. As a consequence of the oncologist's advice, the physician injected steroids subcutaneously into the area of extravasation and applied ice packs to the region. In spite of this treatment, necrosis and sloughing of the skin in the antecubital space occurred. This necessitated multiple debridements and eventual grafting, resulting in a permanent limitation of flexion and extension of the elbow.

Allegations

The patient filed a claim for compensation alleging that he did not give an informed consent for the procedure and as a result of improper administration of a chemotherapeutic agent, he could no longer engage in certain activities, such as playing golf, and therefore was depressed.

Discussion

The patient had previously been counseled about the usual adverse effects of these potent chemotherapeutic agents, including alopecia and bone marrow depression. Although he was not specifically warned of possible extravasation of drug and necrosis of tissues, it is doubtful that he would have refused the treatment for his grave illness had he been specifically counseled regarding this risk. Therefore, under the circumstances, he does not have a persuasive claim that he did not give an informed consent for the therapeutic procedure.

The patient's skin slough was caused by extravasation of the toxic chemotherapeutic medication into subcutaneous tissues. Such an extravasation may occur in the absence of negligent conduct. The resident was aware of the hazard of extravasation because he repeatedly aspirated blood between successive small injections. When the patient complained of burning in the antecubital area, the physician checked again for blood return. When he received it, he again proceeded cautiously. When the discomfort persisted, he terminated the procedure, sought consultation, and instituted therapy as advised.

A burning sensation may be indicative of extravasation, or it may simply represent the reaction of a chemically induced phlebitis. The latter is common in an individual such as this patient who had received multiple intravenous injections of toxic agents.

Notwithstanding the above factors, the patient's injury was aggravated by the physician's conduct in not exercising a greater degree of caution or in heeding the patient's complaints of burning and assuming for the moment that it represented extravasation. However, even assuming that the patient's initial burning sensation represented extravasation, some unavoidable and probably irreversible tissue injury may already have occurred when the patient uttered his initial complaint. Thus, assuming that the physician negligently failed to heed the patient's warnings, causative damages would be limited to only aggravation of the eventual injury.

38: *Facts*

An eighteen-year-old male's behavior abruptly changed. He became suspicious and withdrawn. He experienced auditory hallucinations with threatening racial and homosexual undertones and felt that there was a plot against his life. He was referred to a psychiatrist who treated him with trifluoperazine, which provided control of his symptomatology. However, he soon developed a skin rash, and the medication was discontinued. Approximately two days later, hallucinations and delusions recurred. He became agitated and uncontrollable. Antipsychotic medications were reinstituted, but were ineffective. He was referred to a medical center and admitted to the psychiatric ward. Although his affect was blunted, he was generally oriented. Calculating ability and recent memory were intact. A history was obtained that a brother, an uncle, and a first cousin had also experienced psychotic illnesses. Subsequently it was learned that the brother had an elevated twenty-four-hour porphyrin level (coproporphyrin and uroporphyrin). A screening test for porphyria was considered for the patient but not performed.

Initially, all medication was withheld to insure that his symptoms were not the result of medication. The patient's motor activity was slow and verbal production sparse. He began to develop symptoms of "waxy flexibility." He was treated with trifluoperazine, benztropine mesylate, and group psychotherapy. His condition improved, and he was discharged two weeks later with a diagnosis of: "Schizophrenia, paranoid type in partial remission, characterized by auditory hallucinations, delusions of persecutions and agitated, withdrawn behavior, affective lability, and disoriented thinking." He was referred to a mental health clinic for follow-up care; however, his parents did not follow through with this recommendation by making an appointment.

Three weeks later, his behavior again deteriorated, and he was readmitted to the psychiatric ward. He was treated with Thorazine, trifluoperazine, and benztroprine mesylate. Because of mounting agitation, the dose of Thorazine was increased to 1,000 mg. a day. However, this did not result in clinical improvement; instead, he became increasingly paranoid and anxious. He also experienced intermittent episodes of vomiting; therefore a medical consultation was obtained to "rule-out organic disease." Although it was not high on his differential diagnosis list, the medical consultant recommended a urinary screen for porphyria. The patient was uncooperative and refused to provide urine samples. His behavior became fearful, suspicious, and bizarre around other patients; nevertheless he discussed these suspicions with staff members and continued to take increased dosages of Thorazine.

One week later when he struck a staff member, he was given Thorazine 100 mg. every two hours until sedated. Despite doses of Thorazine of 2,000 mg. a day, he was still noted to be extremely anxious, preoccupied with sexual and aggressive concerns, and exhibited profound thought disorder with blocks in association. Therefore it was decided to further increase the Thorazine dose.

Several days later, he eloped from the ward, jumped in a river adjacaent to the hospital, swam away, and drowned. The attending psychiatrist concluded that his sudden elopement and suicide were secondary to his belief that his life was in danger because he was to be the victim of a homosexual assault.

Allegations

A wrongful death claim was filed alleging that his attending physicians failed to diagnose his organic brain disorder, caused by acute intermittent porphyria, while he was under their care. It was asserted that with proper treatment, his death would have been prevented. It was contended that Thorazine was used indiscriminately by giving the patient "massive doses although his condition worsened while on the drugs."

Discussion

This case involves the clinical differentiation between functional and organic psychosis. A diagnosis of functional psychosis was adequately supported by the patient's poorly organized and illogical communication;

psychomotor behavior (waxy flexibility); his long-standing paranoid delusions; his thought disorder; his illogical abstractions, and his poor judgment. This patient's early clinical presentation, especially his disturbances of thought, mood, and behavior, was characteristic of schizophrenia. His initial impaired sensorium cleared in several days when his medication was discontinued, and was reasonably attributed by his physician to medication effect. Moreover, his cognitive ability, memory, and calculating ability remained intact.

Consideration of an organic basis for his behavioral aberration was made because of his vomiting. However, other findings compatible with organicity were not evident. The medical consultant's recommended screen for porphyria was thwarted by the patient's lack of compliance.

Acute intermittent porphyria is thought to be inherited as an autosomal dominant trait, but penetrance is often incomplete. It usually becomes manifest in the third decade of life. The pattern is one of recurrent attacks, which may be precipitated by a variety of drugs. Abdominal pain, vomiting, and hypertension are commonly present at the outset. Psychiatric manifestations of the disease are most prominent during an attack at which time confusional psychosis, which may even be clinically indistinguishable from schizophrenia, may be present. Because some psychiatric patients have acute intermittent porphyria as a basis of their illness, this disease entity should be suspected in patients with psychiatric illness, to avoid exacerbation of the disease by such factors as drugs, oral contraceptives, infection, and starvation.

In this case the following factors were suggestive of acute intermittent porphyria: a familial history of psychiatric disorders, a history of emesis in association with behavioral aberrations, and appropriate age range. In addition, his brother's elevated urinary porphyrin levels are also suggestive, although not conclusive of the diagnosis.

A second layer of liability exposure involves the escalation of Thorazine doses in the face of mounting agitation. It may be argued that the restlessness that led to the elopement was the manifestation of an extrapyramidal side effect of the high level of Thorazine that he was receiving. Akathisia is an extrapyramidal drug side-effect characterized by restlessness, which is difficult to distinguish from anxiety or hyperactivity. As a result, afflicted patients may be given increased doses of Thorazine to relieve anxiety, only to exacerbate the akathisia, and increase the patient's fear and restlessness.

When a patient's behavior, as in this case, worsens with increased doses of Thorazine, the physician must take necessary steps to prevent the adverse affects of the drug. The restless behavior which compelled this patient to run off the ward and "escape" to his death may well have been due to the drug side-effect because large doses of antipsychotic drugs were given even though the patient's hyperactivity was worsening.

39: *Facts*

A seventeen-year-old primagravida was followed in the complicated obstetrics clinic because of a history of chronic pyelonephritis and nephrotic syndrome. At a recorded date of twenty-four weeks gestation, she was hospitalized because of progressive elevation of her blood pressure. Ten weeks later, she was readmitted to the hospital because of excessive weight gain, increasing blood pressure, progressive edema, and proteinuria. Four weeks after this she was again hospitalized for similar reasons. At that time the cervix was long and closed with fetal vertex floating. The biparietal diameter (BPD) by ultrasound scan was consistent with thirty-four-weeks gestation. The BUN was elevated to 33. The patient was not evaluated for the clinical significance of this laboratory finding nor was she referred to an internist.

Two weeks later, at forty weeks gestational age, she was hospitalized again for evaluation of maternal and fetal well-being. The BPD suggested gestational age to be thirty-six weeks. Urinary estriols were collected, and referral for an amniocentesis determination of fetal maturity was planned but not accomplished, due to intervention of labor. The next day, at approximately 10:00 A.M., the latent phase of labor spontaneously ensued. The cervix was recorded to be 2 cm. dilated, 50 percent effaced, and the vertex was at -2 station. Maternal blood pressure was 150/110. The labor chart recorded the following:

4:00 P.M. FHR - 120   Cervix: 4 cm, 100% effaced
5:00 P.M. FHR - 130   Cervix: 6 cm, vertex almost engaged (maternal blood pressure 150/120)
5:30 P.M. FHR - 130   Cervix: 7 cm

The labor chart recordation of an FHR of 120 at 4:00 P.M. was inconsistent with the progress note of the resident physician who recorded at 4:00 P.M. that fetal monitoring disclosed "variable deceleration down to 60 to 90 beats per minute." Meconium stained fluid was also noted, and the clinical impression was "fetal distress." It was further recorded that the patient was turned on her side, given oxygen, and blood was sent for a cross-match in preparation for an emergency caesarean section. The next progress note was not till 6:30 P.M., and it noted that there was a "spontaneous delivery at 6:03 P.M. over a median episiotomy with local anesthesia."

The birth weight was 2,270 grams. The placenta was small and meconium stained. The neonate had an APGAR score of 1 and 2. She was initially resuscitated with oxygen, endotracheal intubation, and tracheal suctioning. Her color and respiration improved after resuscitative efforts. She was placed in the intensive care nursery. The infant developed seizure activity caused by hypoxic brain damage.

Allegations

On behalf of her child, the mother filed a malpractice claim alleging that her infant's severe brain damage was the result of the negligent management of labor.

Discussion

Because high prenatal morbidity and mortality has a recognized association with severe maternal disease, the infant's condition may have resulted from the mother's basic disease process, and not medical negligence. Inferences may be drawn, however, that the infant's injuries were aggravated, or conversely, not minimized, by casual inattention to the signs and significance of maternal and fetal findings.

The BPD, which was determined to be consistent with thirty-six weeks gestation, may have been misleading because of intrauterine growth retardation, an expected finding in an infant whose mother had severe prenatal disease. Therefore, it was an unreliable criterion for estimating gestational age, especially when the history by dates was consistent with near term gestation. A more precise determination of fetal maturity was indicated and necessary under the circumstances, and should have been promptly obtained by the attending physician. In addition, a more thorough evaluation of the mother's renal status should have been undertaken. Casual neglect of these factors may have deprived the infant of the chance of having an elective caesarean section to terminate on-going fetal insult.

The resident physician's progress note at 4:00 P.M. documented "fetal distress." Thereafter, the clinical record failed to indicate the nature of action taken to prevent or minimize fetal injury. A record of the resident physician's activities during labor to substantiate that appropriate care was given during the two hours prior to delivery is unavailable. Fetal monitoring records were not retained; therefore, no record is available to reconcile the discrepancy between the progress note and labor record. This provides a foundation for inferring negligence in failing to alleviate a recognized problem. In a mother compromised by significant prenatal complications, fetal distress should be anticipated and treated promptly. Under these circumstances, monitoring fetal heart tones every hour during labor is inadequate. It indicates either a lack of awareness of prenatal complications, or a lack of attention to patient needs. In either case, it represents a deviation from the required standard of care. Under the circumstances, consultation with a qualified and experienced physician was indicated.

Although nonnegligent causes of the infant's injuries may have been operative, expert medical witnesses (obstetrician, neonatologist, and neurologists) will be able to persuasively testify that intrauterine fetal distress was a significant and substantial factor in causing the infant's injuries.

40: *Facts*

A nineteen-year-old obese female with symptomatic cholelithiasis was hospitalized for a cholecystectomy. She had a past medical history of poor dental hygiene and asthma. Several months prior to surgery when she was examined by a pulmonary specialist for her asthma, her pulmonary function studies demonstrated significant pulmonary disease, and she had been treated with Quibron and Metaprel inhalers.

Because intraoperative bronchospasm and other pulmonary complications secondary to anesthesia were anticipated by her attending physicians, she was preoperatively treated with bronchodilalators, steroids, and pulmonary toilet. During her surgery she had a reaction to succinylcholine, but no rapid increase in temperature, tachycardia or tachypnea. The procedure proceeded without incident until Renografin was injected into the common duct for an operative cholangiogram. At that time she developed bronchospasm and, shortly thereafter, cardiopulmonary arrest. She was rapidly resuscitated, the operative procedure completed, and she was taken to the recovery room. Subsequently she was discovered to have bilateral pneumothoraces and evidence of acute cerebral hypoxia. Bilateral chest tube insertion restored her pulmonary function; however, she developed spastic quadriplegia and lost the ability to speak.

Allegations

The patient, through a guardian, sued the anesthesiologist claiming that he negligently administered the anesthesia, thereby causing her brain damage.

Discussion

This case illustrates the multifaceted treatment decisions that a physician has to make in the care of a patient. It points out that each choice takes into account a multitude of factors, all adjusted for the medical need and condition of the patient.

In the preoperative preparation of this patient, the anesthesiologist was required to anticipate the risk of anesthesia in a patient with documented pulmonary disease. The pneumothoraces may be related to asthma, emphysematous blebs, or other intrinsic pulmonary disease. They probably were the result of ruptured emphysematous blebs during high pressure ventilation for her laryngospasm and/or bronchospasm. Once the condition was recognized, prompt management prevented severe and permanent damage to this patient.

The patient's long preexisting history of pulmonary disease, particularly asthma, was known to health personnel, and her preoperative preparation was a combined effort of the departments of general surgery, anesthesia, and inhalation therapy. Because the anesthesia department was aware of the patient's preexisting pulmonary disease, agents were selected for their known bronchodilating effect, to maintain adequate ventilation in a patient with a bronchospastic diathesis. Such bronchospastic tendencies are common in patients with asthma, and anesthetic agents that produce bronchodilation are the agents of choice.

Although injections of succinylcholine have been implicated in triggering malignant hyperthermia, this patient did not have such a typical reaction to succinylcholine (tachycardia, tachypnea, muscle rigidity or flaccidity, and rapid increase in temperature). This patient's temperature increased only 0.6 C over 75 minutes. Her tachycardia is probably explained as a result of increasing pCO_2, due to her development of bilateral pneumothoraces and hypoxia. A small dose of succinylcholine was given to this patient to facilitate endotracheal intubation. Usually dosage in the range of 80 to 100 mgs. are used to provide a brief period of total body relaxation in order to facilitate endotracheal intubation. However, the use of larger dosages of succinylcholine provide a longer period of relaxation than a smaller dose. In this patient, the use of spontaneous ventilation utilizing the patient's own muscle power was desired to achieve surgical plane anesthesia by allowing the patient to breathe mixtures of oxygen, nitrous oxide, and fluothane. Therefore the small dose of succinylcholine was appropriate to provide a short period of relaxation for rapid intubation and return of spontaneous ventilation to continue with the anesthetic program. The problem with such a small dose of succinylcholine in patients who have bronchospasm, is the tendency to develop bronchospasm after insertion of the foreign object (the endotracheal tube). Although this might have happened in this patient, the use of the small dose of succinylcholine was within the appropriate standard of care.

The use of sodium pentothal in asthmatics may cause intrapulmonic release of histamine, a known precipitant of bronchospasm. However, its use was probably more appropriate than long-acting secondary anesthetic agents in protecting this patient from bronchospasm during the period following intubation. Although the decision to use pentothal in this patient may be subject to some criticism, its use did not deviate from the appropriate medical standard of care.

The bradycardia hypotensive reaction to the injection of Renografin into the biliary ducts may have been the result of acute dilation of these structures, stimulation of the vagus nerve, causing a vasovagal response and consequential drop in heart rate and blood pressure. Appropriate treatment at this time would have been the use of atropine, although such stimulation is usually transient and will correct itself. It is also possible that the injection of Renografin caused a histamine type release within the lungs, causing a bronchospasm. Nevertheless, the use of Renografin under the circumstances was indicated and not contraindicated.

The short delay in diagnosing the patient's pneumothoraces is understandable because at a time of complications, a differential diagnosis had to be considered by the surgical and anesthesia team. Appropriate considerations in this patient included a malignant hyperthermia, reactions to light anesthesia, allergic drug reaction, airway obstruction, pulmonary bronchospasm, and pneumothoraces. As each one of the considered diagnoses was ruled out, another was considered until the most likely diagnosis was made. Once the diagnostic impression was confirmed, the management of the pneumothoraces by the surgical and anesthesia team was prompt and proper and led to a successful resuscitation.

41: *Facts*

A two-year-old, twenty-six pound child was hospitalized for repair of an umbilical hernia. His past medical history, physical examination, and laboratory findings were within normal limits. Prior to admission to the operating room at 7:30 A.M. he was premedicated with 0.15 mg. atropine and 15 mg. Demerol. After preoxygenation with three liters of oxygen, anesthesia was started at 8:00 A.M. Anesthesia was induced with fluothane 1.5 percent, nitrous oxide, and oxygen, utilizing a mask system. The patient was not intubated; an oral airway was inserted. The patient received approximately seven minutes of fluothane, nitrous oxide, and oxygen before surgical incision. The pulse remained at 140 from the time of incision through the first fifteen minutes of surgery, but then decreased over a twenty-minute period. When it reached 100, the patient was given atropine and succinylcholine intramuscularly, and the pulse rapidly returned to 140. Intubation was attempted at this time. Gastric distention was noted and a nasogastric tube was inserted to deflate the stomach. Shortly after gastric decompression, there was a rapid decrease in heart rate to 80 and then cardiac arrest at 10:10 A.M. Attempts at resuscitation were unsuccessful, and the patient was pronounced dead. Autopsy disclosed brain and lung changes consistent with anoxic changes.

Discussion

Laryngospasm, inadequate ventilation, bradycardia and hypotension are recognized complications of anesthesia which must be promptly recognized and properly managed to prevent serious and permanent injury to anesthetized patients. Although the mere occurrence of these complications is not conclusive evidence of negligence, in this case there is evidence that these conditions occurred because of inadequate preparation of the patient for surgical anesthesia. Moreover, there is also evidence of substandard practice in failing to recognize and properly manage the complications in a timely fashion when they did occur. Thus, on balance there is substantial evidence that the provision of anesthesia in this case was negligent.

In establishing proper surgical plane anesthesia, a patient must be rendered insensitive to pain without inducing detrimental reflexes, while at the same time maintaining necessary and adequate physiological function (pulse rate, blood pressure, respiration, temperature, and urinary output). This is accomplished by using parenteral and inhalational drugs and closely monitoring the patient's vital signs. In providing adequate anesthesia to children, drug doses higher than adults are required, because a child's metabolic rate is much higher.

Before initiating anesthesia, it is important that the patient is in a cooperative and relaxed state. This is particularly important in children because the foreign and frightening surroundings and absence of parents tend to cause more excitement and nervousness than in adults. Therefore, patients are premedicated usually an hour to an hour and a half prior to transport to the operating room. In children, combinations of drugs are routinely used to provide hypnosis, analgesia, and areflexia. Morphine and atropine are a recognized combination which usually insures a cooperative and relaxed child. Other drugs may be substituted or added to this combination (such as one mg. per pound of Demerol) in the place of morphine. When either a narcotic or barbiturate alone is used with atropine, a proportionate increase in dose is required to provide the same level of cooperation. In this case the patient was given 15 mg. of Demerol and 0.15 mg. of atropine prior to surgery at 7:30 A.M. This amount of Demerol may have been insufficient to compensate for the omission of a hypnotic drug such as Nembutal to provide the desired level of cooperation and minimization of excitement. Atropine is also used preoperatively to decrease the probability of a vagovagal response (bradycardia and hypotension of syncope) which may occur when the upper airway is stimulated or when the surgical incision is made. Atropine is also used to decrease airway secretions which are particularly troublesome in children in maintaining proper ventilation during surgery. Another purpose of preoperative medication in children is to help insure an uncomplicated induction of anesthesia, particularly when an inhalation technique is to be used. In this case it is doubtful that the patient's preoperative medication was adequate to provide easy and uneventful induction.

The induction of anesthesia in children is usually accomplished by an inhalation method, utilizing a mask and spontaneous respiration. After pre-oxygenation, which is designed to replace nitrogen with oxygen in the lungs, anesthetic agents such as halothane and nitrous oxide are delivered into the system in varying concentrations and dosages until the patient is rendered unconscious. The concentration and dosage of inhalation agents required to maintain anesthesia in adults following induction with Pentothal is much less than that required to induce and maintain children. The induction of anesthesia in children usually requires a much higher percentage of halothane than this patient received, unless a prolonged period of inhalation of lower percentages is given. Seven minutes of 1.5 percent halothane in a two-year-old male who is inadequately premedicated is probably insufficient time to achieve surgical plane anesthesia.

The foreseeable danger of making a surgical incision prior to surgical plane anesthesia is that the stimulation is likely to precipitate detrimental reflexes such as a vagovagal response and/or laryngospasm. In this case, no change in pulse was noted at the time of incision, which indicates that either the patient was in surgical plane of anesthesia, or that a change in pulse was not recognized. Because of evidence of inadequate preparation of the patient for surgical anesthesia, it is more probable that the patient was not in surgical plane anesthesia at that time, and that the surgical incision manipulation triggered a laryngospasm which made ventilation difficult.

In this case a mask system with an oral airway was used to insure that the upper airway was unobstructed by the patient's tongue. As the heart rate decreased over a sustained period, an injection of atropine and succinylcholine was used to facilitate ventilation and the patient was then intubated. As a result of the succinylcholine injection, the patient relaxed and adequate ventilation was accomplished by use of the endotracheal tube, and the heart rate returned to the preoperative level of 140. At this point either the endotracheal tube became dislodged, thereby causing gastric distention from ventilation of the esophagus, or the biochemical effects of the succinylcholine dissipated and the patient redeveloped laryngospasm, thereby causing distention of the stomach on forced ventilation. The patient's heart rate rapidly decreased to 80 and cardiopulmonary arrest occurred. In addition, the nasogastric tube used to decompress the stomach may have been inserted in the trachea prior to effective gastric decompression. If so, suction may have removed oxygen from the patient's lungs. Other possibilities include that the nasogastric tube dislodged the endotracheal tube. If the endotracheal tube had been dislodged, the nasogastric tube may have stimulated upper pharyngeal reflexes resulting in a recurrence of laryngospasm.

The patient's cardiopulmonary arrest resulted from lack of oxygen, secondary to improper ventilation. It is probable that the patient received brain damage during the initial laryngospasm, as the heart rate was noted steadily decreasing over a twenty-minute period. During episodes of hypoxia, hypotension, and bradycardia, brain damage may occur prior to cardiac injury from hypoxia. During the initial phases of anesthesia, laryngospasm probably occurred secondary to light plane of anesthesia and cerebral hypoxic changes occurred. Efforts to improve ventilation were complicated by the recurrence of laryngospasm and resultant inadequate oxygenation which led to irreversible cerebral and cardiac anoxia.

42: *Facts*

A sixty-one-year-old man had a past medical history which included Laennec's cirrhosis and adult onset Diabetes Mellitis. Two years earlier he injured his knee and underwent a meniscectomy. Postoperatively he continued to complain of discomfort. His orthopedic surgeon prescribed daily doses of Naprosyn for more than two months. He began to experience abdominal pain, tarry stools, and dizziness. On May 18, 1974, he was hospitalized with the diagnosis of gastric bleeding. Naprosyn was discontinued. Esophagogastroscopy disclosed a 15 mm. gastric ulcer. He was placed on a bland diet in which coffee, tea, or alcohol were prohibited. However, he did not comply with this conservative regimen. During this time his ulcer was monitored with endoscopy and biopsy. On June 14, the ulcer was 5 mm. but on June 25 it was 10 mm. Because the ulcer was healing slowly and inconsistently, on June 28 his case was presented and discussed at a medical-surgical conference. It was concluded that surgery was indicated and necessary because of the danger of rehemorrhage (particularly in an older man with cirrhosis of the liver, attendant enlarged vessels, and gastritis); the patient's noncompliance with the conservative therapeutic regimen; the patient's excessive alcohol consumption; and his diabetic condition.

Thus, when on July 9 endoscopy disclosed that the ulcer had become slightly smaller, the surgeon nevertheless decided to proceed with surgery. His decision was also influenced by the fact that the possibility of underlying cancer in the muscle wall of the ulcer could not be ruled out because this area was not accessible by biopsy forceps through a gastroscope. The nature and risks of surgery were discussed with the patient and his family, and accepted by the patient. The operation was performed without complications.

The surgical specimen did not contain an ulcer, but disclosed only gastritis. It was opined that the ulcer may have become obliterated by the clamps in removing the stomach. Postoperatively, a pleural effusion and a wound infection developed. Both complications responded slowly to treatment, and required protracted hospitalization.

Allegations

The patient sued his orthopedist, alleging that the bleeding ulcer was caused by Naprosyn. This claim was settled in his favor. He then sued the surgeon who performed the gastrectomy, alleging that the surgery was unnecessary.

Discussion

The clinical decision to perform a gastrectomy was neither unnecessary nor unreasonable under the circumstances of this case. Colorably, the contention of unnecessary surgery may be predicated on the fact that the ulcer partially responded to conservative therapy, and that an ulcer was not located in the surgical specimens. However, both qualitatively and quantitatively, the evidence indicates that the medical judgment to operate was not unreasonable. Moreover, a conservative trial was undertaken but did not lead to a reasonable clinical response. Although reasonable and respectable surgeons would have disagreed as to the need for surgery, as long as a respectable minority would have recommended surgery under the circumstances, the law will not declare that the surgery was unnecessary.

If an unusually effective drug in the care of peptic ulcers had been in customary use at the time of the decision to operate, and the patient had not been given a clinical trial with such medication, the patient's contention would have taken on greater force.

43: *Facts*

A thirty-five-year-old chronically anxious woman visited an outpatient Family Practice Clinic, complaining of persistent left-sided back pain. Her family practitioner recorded the following information and findings referable to the patient's complaint:

March 13, 1980
Problem - Myofascial Syndrome
S - Pain in left thoracic paraspinous area, T 8–10 region, with no history of trauma. Makes patient even more anxious.
O - Marked tenderness over left paraspinous muscles.
A - Myofascial Syndrome
P - Discontinue Motrin. Start Malate. Return to clinic in two weeks if not improved.
March 20, 1980
Problem - Myofascial Syndrome
S - Patient upset because pain unrelieved by Norgesic or Motrin. Pain still localized in the T 8–10 region over left paraspinous muscles.
O - There is point tenderness over the paraspinous muscle, T 8 and T 9 region.
A - Myofascial Syndrome
P - Attempt to inject the area with 2 percent Xylocaine, using a 22 gauge, one-inch needle.

The attending physician had experience utilizing a local anesthetic technique for a patient with similar problems, and recommended it to this patient. She agreed to undergo the procedure for the relief of pain. He placed the patient on a table in the prone position and advised that she should not move. When the 22 gauge, one-inch needle was inserted into the "trigger point" and Xylocaine injected, excruciating pain radiated to the anterior aspect of the patient's chest and she suddenly jumped upwards. Immediately thereafter, air was aspirated into the syringe. When the physician auscultated her chest and noted left-sided wheezes and rhonchi, he sent the patient to the Radiology department for x-rays.

The radiologist read the chest x-ray, observed a 30 percent pneumothorax on the left, and asked the patient how she had gotten to the clinic.

When she replied that she had walked, he looked at her in disbelief, became excited, and called for a wheelchair, exclaiming, "We have a pneumothorax here!" When the radiologist heard how the pneumothorax had been caused, he appeared to shake his head in disgust. The radiology technician who had taken the x-ray, commented, "This is unbelievable. I have never heard of this happening before." In this setting, the patient became alarmed about suffocating, and experienced progressive dyspnea. Subsequently, in preparation for the placement of a chest tube, she overhead the surgeon ask the attending physician, "Are you sure this was your fault, maybe she was going to pop anyway?" Whereupon the attending physician responded, "No, it was my fault. I punctured the lung."

After the patient was discharged from the hospital she requested and was allowed to examine her medical records. The report of the incident was not placed in chronological sequence, and she was able to locate it only after a search of the entire record.

Allegations

The patient sued the physician, alleging that his treatment caused a pneumothorax and attendant pain, suffering, and mental anguish. The patient also contended that the attending physician made an effort to subsequently "cover up his mistake" by hiding the medical report of the incident in an inconspicuous part of her medical records.

Discussion

This case involves a complication (pneumothorax) of a therapeutic procedure (anesthetic infiltration of a "trigger zone") for myofascial syndrome. Under the circumstances the procedure was clinically indicated, and not contraindicated. The main issue is whether or not the procedure was performed in a reasonably competent and careful manner. No substantial evidence is suggested that the attending physician did not possess the requisite training and experience to perform this relatively straightforward procedure. However, evidence might be adduced that the procedure was not done with due care to prevent injury from the procedure. It is unclear whether the attending physician was aware of this complication or took reasonable precautions to avoid its occurrence. Although he placed the patient on a table, cautioned her not to move, he knew that she was unusually anxious, and he used a needle that was longer than necessary. Even in large patients, a 1.4 cm. 25 gauge needle provides sufficient shaft length to reach chest wall trigger points. The procedure involves searching for the trigger area with the needle point until the area is identified by the patient experiencing pain. Pain with radiation will occur if the needle is correctly placed. To obtain the sought for relief, the injection must be placed directly into the trigger point, within muscle and ligament parenchyma. Movement of a patient is not unexpected because of the sensitivity of the trigger-zone area. Thus it might be inferred that the physician unreasonably failed to properly anticipate and avoid the occurrence of sudden movement.

The alleged "admission of error" by the attending physician to the surgeon is the clinical expression of remorse after the occurrence of the complication, and not probative of a negligent deviation from the required standard of care. Moreover, the allegation of a "cover up" as evidence of guilt of the physician is a meritless misconception by the patient.

Although the patient was not specifically informed of the risk of a pneumothorax, she was cautioned to remain still to preclude injury. Specific disclosure of that risk may not have been required because of the relative infrequency and unlikelihood of a material effect of this complication. Moreover, judgment is reserved for the physician to not unduly alarm an anxious patient with a catalog of risks.

44: *Facts*

A fifty-four-year-old man had a history of progressive prostatism, and was hospitalized for a transurethral resection of the prostate (TURP). After performing a cystoscopy, the surgeon estimated that the prostate weighed 25 grams. The surgeon recorded that bleeding and incontinence were mentioned as possible complications of the TURP, and that the patient gave his consent. The surgeon did not mention impotence because he felt it was an unusual complication.

During the TURP severe bleeding from the prostatic fossa occurred. Two units of blood in the operating room and two more immediately in the recovery room were required. The estimated blood loss was 2,500 cubic centimeters, and when the hematocrit was noted to have dropped from its preoperative level of 32 to 28, an additional unit of blood was administered. The operation took nearly four hours. The removed prostate weighed 60 grams. After the Foley catheter was removed, the patient complained of urinary incontinence.

Six days later, cystoscopy disclosed that residual tissue in the prostatic fossa was preventing adequate closure of the bladder neck. The surgeon, therefore, advised resection of this tissue. Two days later he resected the tissue. When the Foley catheter again was removed two days later, the patient was still incontinent. Subsequently, the patient underwent a reconstructive procedure by another surgeon to help relieve his incontinence.

Allegations

The patient sued his original surgeon, alleging that the complications that resulted from surgery were due to negligent incompetence in performance of the operation.

Discussion

Several factors raise the inference of negligent lack of requisite skill on the part of the surgeon in the performance and after-care of the TURP. The surgeon's estimation of prostatic weight was inaccurate. The gland weighed 60 grams, rather than the 25 grams he estimated preoperatively. Ordinarily a 50–75 gram prostate is considered too large to remove by a transurethral approach. This raises suspicion as to the skill of the surgeon. Worse, it might be inferred that underestimation of the size of the gland was intentionally done to allow the performance of the TURP for the surgeon's personal economic benefit. However, there is no direct evidence to support such an inference.

The length of the operation, four hours, was excessive. Although the standard "60-minute rule" (a surgeon should complete a TURP in less than an hour) is only a "rule of thumb" because modern anesthesia and isotonic saline minimizes complicating hemolysis, a surgeon is usually expected to complete the procedure in less than two hours. Failure to do so without adequate justification raises an inference of negligence.

The blood loss, 2,500 cubic centimeters, was excessive. By computing 10 cubic centimeters of blood per gram of prostate tissue, only 600 cubic centimeters blood loss was expected with this procedure. The heavy bleeding was probably caused by obliteration of the verumontanum, a classical surgical landmark. As a result, the surgeon probably got "lost" and damaged the sphincter neck. When heavy bleeding occurred, it would have been more prudent of the surgeon to put in a catheter traction and close up.

45: *Facts*

After a pregnancy complicated by prolonged leakage of amniotic fluid, this patient was born at 29 weeks of gestational age by elective low forceps delivery after a frank left footling breech presentation. Delivery was complicated by separation of the umbilicus from the placenta. The birth weight was 1100 gms, and APGAR was 1/4. The infant required immediate resuscitative care. His initial arterial blood gas determination after two hours of resuscitation showed a pH of 7.15. Because of prematurity and respiratory distress, he was intubated and placed on positive pressure breathing with 100 percent oxygen. A 3.5 umbilical artery catheter was inserted in order to monitor his respiratory status. Subsequently this was withdrawn and replaced with a larger catheter in order to make aspiration of blood easier. The umbilical cord had the usual two arteries and one vein. When the catheter was radiographically documented at T-3, it was pulled back until it was at the T-9 level. No extremity blanching or cyanosis was noted, nor was there any inability to withdraw blood from the catheter. The catheter was utilized for six days.

The infant was severely depressed for the first week of life. During this time he responded only to painful stimulation. He had a hypotonic (floppy) character, probably because of his prematurity and birth asphyxia. At age ten days, nurses first noted absence of left lower extremity movement. The flaccid paralysis was first noted when the nurses could not reverse apneic episodes by stimulation of the feet, but only by stimulation of the hands. Prior to that time, his lack of movement was thought to be due to the immaturity and asphyxia.

Prior documentation of movement of this extremity was not made in the medical records. Although the infant's parents maintain they observed movement of their infant's legs during this period, during his first week of life his legs were restrained as a precautionary procedure.

On his sixteenth day of life, the infant manifested occasional jerky movements. On the following day, the left leg was noted to be flaccid and unresponsive to noxious stimuli. Although the right leg was responsive to noxious stimuli, a foot drop was noted. Deep tendon reflexes were active and equal bilaterally without clonus, but areflexia was noted and there was no response to perianal pinprick. The differential diagnosis was "flaccid congenital diplegia versus traumatic induced diplegia." X-rays of the lumbosacral area and of the lower extremities disclosed no gross abnormalities. Several weeks later, electromyographic studies were compatible with a lower motor neuron involvement. Ultimately the infant manifested permanent bilateral paralysis of his legs. His medical records were replete with references that the impairment was "secondary to the prolonged use of an umbilical artery catheter."

Allegation

A suit was filed, alleging that improper usage of an umbilical artery catheter caused his paralysis.

Discussion

Possible causes of paralysis included: spinal cord or nerve trauma secondary to the breech delivery; hypoxic damage to the lower spinal cord secondary to birth asphyxia and ischemia; embolization from the umbilical arterial catheter; and hematoma of the spinal cord. The most likely cause was hemorrhage and hematoma formation in the lower spinal canal secondary to breech delivery and the tendency of small premature infants to bleed. These hematoma formations damage nerves by compression or ischemia.

The umbilical artery catheter functioned well during the six days it was in place; therefore, complications such as clot formation or embolizations were unlikely. The high placement of the tip between T-7 and T-10 is an acceptable position for such catheters, although some neonatal centers prefer a low location with the tip at the aortic bifurcation. Neonatologists are evenly divided as to their preference of low versus high placement. Although clot formation on the tip of the line has been shown to occur in as many as 50 percent of the cases, the incidence of clinically apparent complications from embolization is less than 5 percent. One such study concluded the incidence of embolization to be lower in high placement as compared to low placement.

Reinsertion of an umbilical artery line is common because the original catheter may be in an undesirable location, may become clotted, may be accidentally dislodged, or be of an inadequate size. In this patient's case, the small 3.5 F. catheter was withdrawn because of its small size, and a larger 5 F. catheter reinserted. A small lumen makes withdrawal of blood samples difficult, and there is a greater tendency to clot.

There is no generally accepted method of monitoring umbilical catheters. Radiographic location is empirical and was appropriately utilized in this case. Conditions which signal a complication include blanching or cyanosis of an extremity and inability to withdraw or infuse blood or fluid through the catheter. If any of these events occur, the catheter is immediately removed. None of these signs were apparent in this case.

There is no convincing evidence that the placement, reinsertion and monitoring of the catheter was negligently performed. Moreover, if the paraparesis resulted from the catheter, there is no reasonable way that it could have been prevented under the clinical circumstances of this case. Radial artery catheterization was not a reasonable alternative, and it is also associated with serious complications. This procedure has only been extensively used in the past few years, but even now only a few neonatal intensive-care units utilize it and then only after an umbilical artery line has been removed for some specific reason, or if catheterization was unsuccessful.

The notes of some physicians indicate the etiology of the paraparesis was from "prolonged" use of the umbilical artery catheter. Evidence is insufficient to verify such conclusions. Using an umbilical artery catheter for six days in such a critically ill neonate is not *prolonged* use. The length of time for its use was appropriate considering the status of the infant.

Umbilical artery catheterization has known risks. Postmortem evaluations have demonstrated that a high percentage of all umbilically catheterized patients have thrombosis (most of which is latent and clinically insignificant). Vascular compromise to the spinal tract has been suggested but not well documented. In spite of these hazards, when the procedure is clinically indicated, it is of such value that the risks are generally considered acceptable. Even if the neurologic deficits were caused by the catheter, the risks were outweighed by the need to monitor and care for this seriously ill infant.

46: *Facts*

This six-week-old infant was hospitalized for the elective correction of sagittal craniostenosis, which was felt to be clinically indicated by his neurosurgeon. The infant's preoperative hematocrit was 36. No preoperative blood coagulation tests were performed. At surgery, the sagittal and lambdoidal sutures were released and Silastic binding was implanted on the bone edges. Blood pressure was not monitored during the procedure because a Doppler was unavailable. Pulse rate was in the 140–180 range. Twenty cubic centimeters of albumin and 350 cubic centimeters of D5W were infused during the operation. The anesthesiologist estimated 13 percent blood volume loss. When the procedure was completed at 11:30 A.M. the infant appeared so pale that the neurosurgeon asked the anesthesiologist to consider administering a blood transfusion. The anesthesiologist declined to transfuse the infant, explaining that the patient had an adequate circulatory volume and noted that his vital functions in the immediate postoperative period were satisfactory. At 1:00 A.M., while the infant was in the surgical intensive care unit, the neurosurgeon again suggested to the anesthesiologist the need for blood transfusion because of the patient's persistent pallor. The Nurses' Notes indicated that the patient was "extremely pale and cool during the postoperative period." A hematocrit was ordered to be done on a routine basis at 4:00 P.M. No blood recordings were made during the recovery phase because again a Doppler was unavailable. At 3:00 P.M. the patient went into cardiorespiratory arrest. He was intubated and ventilated. Cardiac monitoring disclosed a normal sinus tachycardia of 200. His hematocrit was 20. The nurse obtained a blood pressure device from another ward, and recorded a blood pressure of 40/10. After 50 cubic centimeters of packed red blood cells were transfused through an intravenous catheter, the systolic pressure increased to 90. Three hours later his hematocrit was 22 and he was transfused with additional 80 cubic centimeters of packed cells. Initial arterial blood gases demonstrated marked acidosis. Seven hours after his arrest, symptoms compatible with hypoglycemia were observed and treated. Three hours later, he developed seizures and died shortly thereafter. The cause of death was hypovolemia and cardiovascular collapse. Hypovolemic shock was secondary to intraoperative blood loss.

Allegation

The parents sued the hospital, neurosurgeon, and anesthesiologist for the wrongful death of their child.

Discussion

This patient had sustained a significant intraoperative blood loss which was not adequately replaced. This resulted in hypovolemia, cardiovascular collapse, and subsequent brain damage. In the immediate postoperative period, no blood determination was made or recorded, although the patient was pale. Although a hematocrit determination was ordered for four hours postoperatively, the intraoperative blood loss was unrecognized and unanticipated. The child was essentially unmonitored. Intraoperative blood loss was a recognized complication of this procedure. There was failure to anticipate, identify, and manage a recognized complication of surgery. The anesthesiologist knew or should have known that any blood loss in an infant may be a serious threat to life. He therefore should have monitored blood loss closely by doing such things as weighing sponges, observing surgical drapes, and exploring hidden areas under the patient. Blood should have been replaced one cubic centimeter for every cubic centimeter lost. This patient should not have been allowed to lose more than 10 percent of his blood volume, and transfusion should have been started before this much loss. This duty became imperative when the infant manifested persistent pallor. The clinical management of this patient was negligent because the anesthesiologist and neurosurgeon did not exercise due care to avoid a recognized complication of the procedure. In the immediate postoperative period, no blood determination was made even though the patient was obviously pale to several observers. A hematocrit was ordered for four hours postoperatively on a "routine" basis. The infant was essentially unmonitored during the recovery phase, thus postoperative blood loss was negligently unrecognized in addition to being unanticipated. Intraoperative blood was a recognized complication of a craniectomy in an infant because blood loss is unavoidable, especially in young infants. Moreover, such loss is likely to be greater than the surgeon suspects; therefore, whole blood transfusions should be given and hematocrits checked carefully during the postoperative period.

(7) MULTIPLE HEALTH CARE PROVIDERS

47: *Facts*

A forty-eight-year-old male had a history of recurrent alcoholic intoxication, belligerent behavior, and situational depression. One evening his wife brought him to an emergency room, relating a suspicion that he had been on a drinking "binge." She reported, however, that his behavior seemed "unusually strange," and that he had been experiencing tactile hallucinations. No history of trauma was elicited.

In the emergency room, the patient threatened to kill his wife. He was combative and required restraints. Because of slurred and incoherent speech and vomiting, the possibility of organic disease was entertained. The emergency room physician did not record an evaluation of the patient but simply notified the patient's family physician, who decided to admit the patient and obtain a neuropsychiatric consultation. The family physician was not present in the hospital at the time of admission, which was near midnight, therefore he gave telephone admission orders to the emergency room nurse which included: "Thorazine, 50 mg. IM for combative behavior; restraints on a PRN basis; positioning of the patient on his side; close observation of the airway; vital signs every hour; and CBC in the morning."

The patient was transported to the ward and arrived in four-point restraints. The nurse noting that the patient was belligerent, profane, and intoxicated, positioned him on his side with the support of a pillow. Thirty minutes past midnight, the patient vomited a large amount of dark brown material. The ward nurse administered Thorazine, 50 mg. IM, to control the vomiting. She then assigned a recently trained attendant to "monitor" the patient. The nurse applied a tight chest restraint in addition to the usual wrist/ankle restraints. The sequence of recorded vital signs and Nurse's Notes were as follows:

Time	Vital Signs	Nurses' Notes
1:00 A.M.	BP 130/80 P 120	
2:00 A.M.	BP 136/74 P 130	
3:00 A.M.	BP 100/60 P 140	Sleeping soundly, but thick mucus cleared from mouth with tongue blade
3:40 A.M.	BP 100/50 P 140	
4:00 A.M.		Gurgling breath sounds, position changed, dark thick mucus from mouth & nose. Suction machine set up, not utilized
4:10 A.M.	BP 100/60 P 140	
4:50 A.M.		Skin pale, respirations labored
4:55 A.M.		Apparent arrest, supervisor notified, resuscitation unsuccessful.

An autopsy disclosed a blood ethanol level of .23 mg. percent, acute focal hemorrhagic gastritis, and hemorrhagic gastric contents in the esophagus, trachea, and bronchi.

Allegations

The wife sued the physician and hospital personnel alleging that they were negligent in "strapping down the patient without adequate supervision and permitting him to choke to death on his own vomit."

Discussion

The patient required hospital admission to evaluate a probable organic psychosis. There is little demonstrable evidence that the patient was medically evaluated in the emergency room. Documentation of the nature of his medical status prior to admission to the ward is lacking. The admitting physician's orders for restraint and positioning of the patient properly anticipated the complications that ensued. However, their effectuation was not reasonably assured through the use of reasonably detailed standards or qualified monitoring personnel. On the ward he was "monitored" by an inexperienced attendant and without adequate supervision. Moreover, the ward nurse negligently failed to recognize and act on the alarming changes in the vital signs which signaled impending shock and danger of aspiration from gastrointestinal hemorrhage. Gastrointestinal hemorrhage was a serious, and not unexpected, complication of acute alcoholism, and thus should not have been ignored, unanticipated, or unappreciated. The physician who gave orders to monitor the patient should also have been contacted when the vital signs heralded the hazardous complications. The gastrointestinal hemorrhage caused shock, emesis, aspiration of gastric contents, and resultant death. On balance, there is substantial evidence of a lack of careful analysis and anticipatory monitoring of this patient's clinical problem. Moreover, there is indication that the fatal complication may have been prevented if due care and skill had been applied.

The physician should be criticized for not examining the patient on admission or requesting the emergency room physician to medically evaluate the patient. Such an evaluation may have detected evidence of alcoholism and gastrointestinal hemorrhage. This would have caused the physician to write more specific orders and commence supportive and sustaining management of the patient's problems. On the other hand, this might not have altered the patient's course. The orders given for the patient's care would probably have been adequate if properly carried out. The patient was injured by inadequate execution of the orders by the nursing staff.

48: *Facts*

The patient was involved in an automobile accident and sustained a serious leg injury. She was taken to a community hospital where she was attended by a general practitioner who was on the hospital staff emergency room "on-call" roster. X-rays disclosed an oblique spiral fracture of the tibia and the fibula. The patient was anesthetized, and the physician reduced the fractures. A circular plaster cast was then applied. It was separated from the skin by four to six thicknesses of sheet wadding down the leg and over the dorsum of the foot. Ordinarily this type of cast takes approximately 10 hours to dry. The physician then returned to his home where he was spending the weekend holiday with his family. He saw the patient that evening when she complained of nausea and leg pain. Over the next two days he visited the patient twice a day. That night he asked the nurse to examine the patient because she was complaining that the cast felt tight. The nurse reported that the patient's toes were warm. Because of his experience with fractures while serving in a M.A.S.H. unit when he was in the Army, the physician was aware that retention of position of oblique spiral fractures is difficult because of the tendency of the ends of the bones to slip past and override one another. A bivalved cast is less efficient for the purpose of immobilization and retention than an unsplit one. Having in mind the importance of maintaining immobilization and retention of position, and because he felt the patient's symptoms did not indicate circulatory impairment, he decided not to bivalve the cast that night even though the patient's complaints of leg pain were progressive.

The next day the physician noted cyanosis of the toenails, and leakage of serum from the abrasions was discoloring the cast. Because the toes were still warm, he decided to wait 24 hours before making a decision about bivalving or removing the cast. That night the patient herself called the physician at home and told him that the medicine she was being given was not relieving her pain. The physician called the nurse and told her to increase the amount of morphine the patient was to be given.

The next day the cast had become soft from the seepage; the physician feared that this would allow the bones to slip out of alignment, and so he decided to bivalve it. When the cast was bivalved, the bones at the site of the fractures slipped out of place and became overriding. The following day he removed the cast entirely because of its soiled condition and because it was no longer useful with bones not in apposition. He substituted a padded posterior wire splint so that the leg would be more accessible for treatment of the skin lesions. Shortly thereafter, large sloughing areas appeared on the foot and leg. The condition of the leg continued to worsen, despite vigorous attempts to arrest the tissue deterioration. Two days later, the physician removed some necrotic tissue from the lower leg. Four days after that he had to perform a below the knee amputation.

Allegation

The patient sued the general practitioner for malpractice contending that the physician should not have undertaken the care of the patient's leg without seeking consultation.

Discussion

The following enumerated aspects of the general practitioner's conduct are suggestive of a lack of requisite, clinical skill and care:

—Knowingly undertaking the orthopedic care of a difficult and complicated fracture even though he possessed inadequate training and skill to effectively manage such a condition;

—Failure to consult an orthopedic surgeon in the initial treatment and after care of his patient;

—Premature placement of the patient's leg in a plaster cast at a time when the tissues were swollen and subject to further traumatization from application of the cast;

—Failure to bivalve or remove the cast when it became apparent that the tightness of the cast had compromised circulation to the patient's lower leg;

—Failure to adequately monitor the development of infection and gangrene under the cast, and to take adequate steps to treat such conditions;

—Failure to adequately manage the complication (he merely split the cast and failed to remove it in order to treat the infection adequately) when it became apparent that the patient's leg was infected.

49: *Facts*

A two-year-old child was brought to her pediatrician because of rhinorrhea and fever. The parents also related that the child seemed to strain on bowel movements. On physical examination, the physician thought that he palpated a left upper quadrant abdominal mass. Chest x-rays were ordered and disclosed bowel in the left upper chest and marked elevation of the anterior portion of the left diaphragm, compatible with eventration. The child was hospitalized for a "work-up and possible surgical correction."

An upper GI series disclosed "eventration of the left diaphragm with stomach and large and small bowel under the diaphragm." It was noted that the stomach was inverted and did not empty well. A surgical consultant agreed with the radiographic diagnosis. He recommended that they "rule-out congenital diaphragmatic hernia" with another radiologic study, and then "repair from above if eventration, or from below if Bochtalek diaphragmatic hernia." Because the child was asymptomatic, the attending physician elected a "conservative," nonsurgical approach even though he had not previously evaluated or treated either an eventration or Bochtalek hernia.

Several months later, the patient visited the emergency room with "difficulty catching her breath, and constipation." The clinical impression was upper respiratory infection, constipation, and eventration on the diaphragm by history. Glycerin suppositories were prescribed. Two weeks later, the patient developed a gastric volvulus which resulted in her death.

Allegations

The parents filed a wrongful death suit alleging that the physician negligently delayed treating their child for a diaphragmatic abnormality. They asserted that if the problem had been treated more promptly, the gastric volvulus and subsequent death of their child would have been prevented.

Discussion

The patient's congenital defect was difficult to diagnose definitively. The uncertainty of diagnosis made the actual risk to the child an unknown factor. Under the circumstances, the attending physician was obligated to investigate more diligently the nature and significance of the disorder and the degree of potential hazard represented by the condition. The physician's failure to make this determination was negligent. Liability is predicated not upon his ignorance of a condition he had not previously treated, but upon his remaining ignorant by not seeking additional information. He was expected to have become knowledgeable about the nature and consequences of eventration and then to have acted upon this enlightenment.

Although the physician appropriately sought surgical consultation, he either ignored or rejected the recommendation without further investigation of the propriety of his action. In effect, this nullified the value of the consultation. He did not consult any other specialists nor did he investigate the literature concerning the serious complications of the putative diagnosis. Good medical practice would have dictated a more active and reparative course, or a management plan to monitor, learn about, and treat the condition.

His passive approach set the course for further negligent care. Therefore, when the child subsequently visited the clinic with symptoms referable to her basic disease process, they were unappreciated and once again ignored. Thus, additional opportunities for successful surgical correction were lost, and the fatal complications were not prevented.

50: *Facts*

This 7 lb. infant was the product of a full-term, uncomplicated delivery. During the first week of life he was exclusively breast fed. At one-week of life, he was hospitalized for three days for a "fever work-up." The cause of the fever was not determined. During this time, his mother's milk diminished and he required supplementation with formula. Thereafter, he experienced mild, persistent diarrhea. His mother and an older sibling had a history of "milk sensitivity," manifested by diarrhea and rash.

At five weeks of life his loose stools became watery. His mother tried several formula changes and Pedialyte, all without success. His stools became even more watery and he experienced severe postprandial emesis. At his six-week "well-baby" check, his weight was 9 lb. 6 oz. His mother reported diarrhea, to the examining physician. When the loose bowel movements persisted for the next two weeks, she consulted another physician who recommended that the infant be hospitalized for rehydration. On January 21, when the infant was eight weeks old, he was hospitalized. His weight was 8 lb. 5 oz. and he was poorly hydrated. However, he was afebrile and in no acute distress. The specific gravity of his urine was 1.008. His hemoglobin was 9.7 and hematocrit 29. WBC was 18,200 with a normal differential. His electrolytes were within normal limits, and an abdominal x-ray series was negative. While on IV fluids, his stools decreased in number. When he was started on half-strength Enfamil, however, he vomited most feedings. A Barium swallow and UGI series with cinematography were negative. During the first four days of hospitaliation, he was moderately edematous.

By January 26 his stools were guaiac positive. Gavage feedings were started the next day, but were followed by emesis. Stool smear demonstrated numerous white blood cells but none were in sheets, and multiple cultures did not grow out enteric pathogens. He was started on ampicillin 100 mg/kg/day. On January 29 the infant was started on breast milk feedings which he tolerated without vomiting; however, he still had approximately ten stools per day. On January 31, Hirschsprung's disease was suspected, but not confirmed by radiological studies.

By February 1, he had become more edematous. His total protein was decreased, and he continued to lose fluid. On February 2, his fluid loss was greater than his gain, and he was 10 percent dehydrated despite IV rehydration at twice the rate of maintenance. The diagnosis of "intractable diarrhea of infancy" was made. The treatment plan was to transfer his intake to breast milk, keep fluids stable, and monitor closely. On February 3, the breast feedings were discontinued because of increasing diarrhea and guaiac positive stools. On February 4, his hemoglobin was 8.1 and he was transfused with 112 cubic centimeters of packed red blood cells. On February 5, his weight was 8 lb. 8 oz. Erythematous lesions on his body were noted and thought to be due to nutritional deprivation. He continued to be managed by IV hydration, electrolyte monitoring, and supportive care for his dermal condition. At this time, his attending physician considered transferring him to a tertiary care center for total parenteral nutrition and further diagnostic studies. On February 6, the day prior to his scheduled transfer, multiple erythematous hemorrhagic lesions appeared on his body. He became lethargic and then moribund. Cultures of the lesions were taken and antibiotics instituted. He was transferred to a Special Care Nursery. His platelets were 16,000; PT was greater than 60; PTT was greater than 120; and WBC was 3,000. Later that day he had episodes of hypotension, agonal respirations, and bradycardia. He went into congestive heart failure. Resuscitative measures were unsuccessful. Antemortem cultures grew out Pseudomonas.

Autopsy disclosed that the cause of death was gram negative septic shock. Superficial gastrointestinal mucosal hemorrhagic and necrotic lesions; and hemorrhagic necrotizing bronchopneumonia were noted. The gastrointestinal tract showed multiple elongated superficial hemorrhagic ulcers. No anatomic defects were seen, such as malrotation or pyloric stenosis, and the large bowel was not dilated or ulcerative. The liver was markedly enlarged without accompanying splenomegaly. Microscopy showed the ulcers to be surrounded by necrotic gastric and small bowel mucosa and to be overlying marked lymphofollicular proliferation in the submucosa of the small bowel. The skin showed full thickness coagulative necrosis of the epidermis and dermis. Special stains for organisms showed gram negative bacilli in the bowel, but not in the lungs or skin. The liver showed uniform diffuse fatty change as a consequence of the malnutrition.

Allegations

The child's mother sued the attending pediatrician, alleging multiple occurrences that she suspected represented negligent clinical management of her child.

Discussion

The immediate clinical cause of death was acute necrotizing bronchopneumonia secondary to Pseudomonas sepsis. Although not immunologically debilitated, the infant was nutritionally compromised by the refractory diarrhea. This condition made his gastrointestinal tract vulnerable to Pseudomonas infection. Infants who die from neonatal sepsis often have necrotic avascular gastrointestinal ulcers. The mucocutaneous lesions probably represented erythema gangrenosum, a common finding in Pseudomonas sepsis. The gastrointestinal tract was anatomically normal and the ulcers were most likely a consequence of the Pseudomonas infection rather than diarrhea. Malnutrition was secondary to marked gastrointestinal tract irritability, manifested by refractory diarrhea.

Infantile diarrhea may be self-limited and responsive to routine supportive measures and/or secondary to an easily identified microorganism responsive to antibiotic treatment. However, intractable diarrhea of infancy is a distinct clinical entity, which is either secondary to recognizable but difficult to treat pathologic entities; or as in this case, precipitated by relatively trivial causes evolving into an ominous self-perpetuating, "non-specific enterocolitis." Characteristically, this condition occurs before three months of age, and is manifested by stunted growth and hypoproteinemia. The condition is refractory to standard measures, and changes in the gastrointestinal tract may become irreversible. The clinical management challenge is to devise adequate therapy to break the self-perpetuating, life-threatening cycle. Although the efficacy of steroids, colostomy, and antibiotics is undetermined, an adequate caloric and nutritional support by a parenteral route is essential to overcome the life-threatening sequelae of malnutrition. If only routine supportive measures, periods of "bowel rest," and dietary substitution are used, such as were used in the management of this case, high mortality is expected.

The attending physician did not recognize or appreciate the gravity of the illness, and he failed to expeditiously transfer the patient to a more appropriate treatment facility once he did or should have recognized that he and his facility were incapable of effectively treating the condition. In the alternative, he should have conducted a more organized and aggressive approach to the clinical management of the illness, including obtaining appropriate consultation either when diagnosis was not clear or when his treatment was ineffective. This lack of knowledge, diligence, and care was negligent. It also denied the child a chance for appropriate therapy and survival.

51:    *Facts*

This thirty-two-year-old patient was admitted to the Neurosurgery Service of a medical center because of a three-month history of numbness and weakness of his hand, and stiffness in both legs. Bilateral triceps weakness and spastic extremity hyperreflexia were detected on physical examination. Myelographically, a block at C6−7 was demonstrated. He underwent an anterior cervical discectomy at C6−7. Operative complications included nerve root irritation during dissection, CSF leakage, and trauma to nerve root. One week postoperatively, he was discharged from the hospital and scheduled for follow-up therapy. Even after multiple physical therapy treatments, weakness remained in the left upper extremity. When he was seen by his neurosurgeon six weeks postoperatively, he complained to the surgeon of difficulty maintaining an erection, sleep disturbances, apathy, listlessness, and poor appetite. The neurosurgeon diagnosed "situational depression." He explained this condition to the patient and started him on antidepressant medication, Imipramine and Elavil. The patient was instructed to return to the clinic in one month. The surgeon felt that the patient appeared to be handling his depression satisfactorily because he did not communicate any suicidal ideation to him, nor did the surgeon receive any communication from the patient's wife to the effect that there was any serious problem with her husband. The neurosurgeon decided not to refer the patient to a psychiatrist but to initiate psychological counsel on his own because he felt that the depression did not seem that severe at the time and because the patient was reticent about seeing a psychiatrist. The surgeon felt that this was an acceptable course of management because it seemed obvious to him from the frequent telephone conversations he had with the patient after his discharge from the hospital that the patient understood the problem and was willing to work with it. Two weeks later, the neurosurgeon had a conversation with the patient in which the patient stated that he was doing quite well. The next day the patient shot himself in the right temple, following an argument with his wife. At the time of death, the patient had a high level of blood alcohol. The medical records did not indicate recordation of the surgeon's telephone conversations with the patient.

Allegations

The widow stated that the patient had threatened suicide many times since his surgery, and she sued the neurosurgeon for not referring her husband to a psychiatrist for treatment of his depression. The neurosurgeon contended that he had not been made aware of the patient's self-destructive behavior.

Discussion

It may be acceptable and even customary for cases of mild postoperative situational depression to be handled by the operating surgeon. Even if it were acceptable for a neurosurgeon to make a diagnosis of situational depression in a postsurgical patient and to begin that patient on antidepressant drug therapy, the follow-up and reevaluation of such a patient without expert guidance and solely by telephone would be substandard. Although the wife did not communicate to the neurosurgeon that her husband was threatening suicide, she was not trained to fully recognize potentially significant emotional problems. The neurosurgeon's initial diagnosis of depression was reasonable and within the scope of his expertise; however, his subsequent management of the case was suboptimal. Moreover, his poor documentation of encounters with his patient will make it difficult for him to justify his medical judgment for not seeking a psychiatric consultation. There may have been circumstances that made his conduct reasonable: the unwillingness of the patient to undergo psychiatric counseling; the lack of notice of severe psychological problems in the patient's prior mental status; his and his wife's failure to relate suicidal ideation to the surgeon; and the difficulty in differential diagnosis and prediction between situational depression and suicidal intent. Had he properly recorded the events, the surgeon may have been able to reasonably foresee self-destructive ideation or preparation that would have supported the need for hospitalization, thereby decreasing the likelihood of a suicidal act at that time.

52: *Facts*

This two-year-old child was brought to a pediatrician's office with symptoms of a "cold." Examination by a nurse practitioner did not disclose a focus of infection. The child was treated for nasal congestion. One week later, on March 6, the child was taken back to the physician's office because of inability to use her left leg. There was no history of trauma. Except for coryza, no significant physical findings were noted in the physician's examination. X-rays of her leg and hip were within normal limits. "Muscle strain" and possible "respiratory infection" were diagnosed. The following day the child returned to the physician's office because of fever and inability to support weight on her left leg. She was referred to an orthopedic surgeon who admitted her to a community hospital. An arthrocentesis of the left hip produced scant fluid with a few WBC, but no bacteria were noted on gram stain or culture. The next day the patient spiked a fever and her WBC was 13,000. The following day she again spiked a fever and vomited twice. The day after that a repeat arthrocentesis produced 40 cubic centimeters of purulent material. When the orthopedic surgeon surgically drained the hip, he noted that the head of the femur and the articular surface appeared normal, and x-rays did not disclose destructive joint pathology. He established an ingress/egress irrigation system with Keflin in dextrose and water. When gram stain of the joint demonstrated gram positive cocci, intravenous Keflin was started. The culture ultimately grew out Hemophilus influenzae. The following day it was noted that the egress tube had not been removing the irrigation fluid. As a result, the child's hip and leg had become markedly swollen. Shortly after this discovery, the child vomited and had a seizure which was controlled with phenobarbital and Valium. The patient was transferred to the Intensive Care Unit of a medical center. It was noted that the serum sodium was 119. Proper sodium levels were restored. A lumbar puncture disclosed purulent cerebral spinal fluid from which Hemophilus influenzae was demonstrated on gram stain. The diagnosis of meningitis was made and the patient was started on ampicillin, Chloromycetin, gentamycin, and Oxacillin. Despite vigorous therapy, the infant was left with neurological deficits as a result of the meningitis.

Allegations

On behalf of the infant, the mother filed a malpractice suit against the orthopedic surgeon, charging him with failure to diagnose meningitis, and failure to consult a pediatrician.

Discussion

On March 7, the child was properly hospitalized and an arthrocentesis was appropriately performed. Although the embarkation of a "sepsis workup," including blood cultures, might have provided an earlier suspicion of meningitis, its omission was not necessarily a deviation from the required standard for diagnostic investigation for what appeared to be a localized problem at the time. However, when the surgeon's lack of diligence is combined with his failure to consider the possible coexistence of a meningitis, an inference of negligence is raised.

In a two-year-old patient, Hemophilus influenzae is a likely causative agent of septic arthritis. Moreover, an association between this condition and meningitis is recognized in pediatric care. Thus gram staining should not be relied upon to dictate initial drug therapy of septic arthritis. It may be argued that an anticipatory assessment of the peculiar problems of septic arthritis in a young child should have been considered in the clinical management. The orthopedic surgeon should have obtained a pediatric or infectious disease consultation to better inform himself of recognized complicating factors of septic arthritis in young children. When this association is recognized, the more rational approach to drug therapy would likely involve initiating a combination of drugs to help prevent the serious complication of meningeal involvement or progression. From a practical standpoint, Keflin cannot be given in high enough doses to achieve a blood level capable of effectively eradicating Hemophilus influenzae, thereby preventing meningeal involvement.

53: *Facts*

A man who was drunk and driving recklessly was being pursued at high speed by the police. As he rounded a corner, he ran into the left side of a small automobile. The driver of the small car and his thirteen-year-old sister, a front seat passenger, each sustained head trauma. Another sister, a sixteen-year-old, was pinned in the left rear seat. This sister's boyfriend was in the right rear seat and also sustained a head injury. The collision occurred at 2:41 A.M.; the police arrived within minutes and called the city ambulance dispatcher, who then requested an ambulance from a nearby community hospital. However, the hospital's ambulance had just been dispatched for another emergency. Because the city had an agreement with a larger private hospital to provide ambulance service when a city ambulance was not readily available, the dispatcher then called the emergency room at that hospital, and requested that an ambulance be sent to pick up the people injured in the automobile accident. An ambulance was dispatched with two emergency medical technicians (EMTs). At 2:48 A.M., the fire department arrived on the scene of the accident. Shortly thereafter, efforts to extricate the sixteen-year-old girl from the car commenced. The girl's feet protruded from a tear in the side of the small car. She was removed from the car by police and firemen with the use of a backboard, and then placed on a stretcher next to the car.

When the ambulance arrived at 3:05 A.M. the accident scene was chaotic; the driver of the small car was fighting with the drunken driver, and the police were in the process of arresting both of them. The small car was on the roadside, under a large tree that shielded the streetlight and darkened the area. One of the EMTs assessed the sixteen-year-old girl's condition and noted that she appeared confused and had poor color. Her pulse was weak and rapid, and her blood pressure was 100/60. She was wearing slacks. There was no sign of bleeding. She was placed directly in the ambulance. This information was transmitted to the private hospital which had dispatched the ambulance. Her boyfriend was evaluated and also placed in the ambulance by the other EMT, who also functioned as the ambulance driver. The younger sister insisted on going with them in the ambulance. At 3:15 A.M. the ambulance left the accident scene for a community hospital located approximately five minutes from the scene.

The light inside the ambulance allowed the EMT to more adequately assess the sixteen-year-old's condition. The EMT then noticed a deformity of the patient's leg and suspected leg injury. He attempted to apply a femoral traction splint; however, there was not enough room to accomplish this task in the ambulance because of the presence and the activity of the two other patients, especially the unruly conduct of the boyfriend. Anticipating a short trip to the community hospital, the EMT elected to give oxygen and splint the girl's leg with his own arms and body to prevent further injury. In this position, however, the EMT was unable to take vital signs.

When the ambulance arrived at the hospital at 3:20 A.M., hospital attendants opened its doors to assist in removing the injured patients. Along with the driver, they helped the boyfriend and the younger sister out of the ambulance. The attendants peered into the ambulance, observed that the remaining patient was responsive and moving her extremities, but seemed anxious. The sixteen-year-old's boyfriend argued that she be taken to the private hospital which had dispatched the ambulance because it was a larger and better equipped hospital to treat an accident victim than the small community hospital. Because she did not appear to be critically injured, the driver decided to take her the longer distance to the private hospital. During this time, the attending EMT caring for the girl in the ambulance remained at the girl's side to reassure her. Although the EMT felt that the girl was more seriously injured than her younger sister or boyfriend, he did not feel that a frank emergency existed at that time. In addition he was aware that another ambulance had just arrived at the community hospital, and this might overload the emergency physician on duty there. Therefore, when the driver decided to transport the girl to the private hospital, the EMT acquiesced. Rather than debate the advisability of the decision, he urged the driver to get there as fast as possible. The EMT was also aware that at the private hospital an emergency physician had earlier been alerted to the condition of the injured girl's leg; thus he concluded that this course was the best and least disturbing choice for the girl's condition. However, en route, the patient became more pale and clammy.

At 3:35 A.M., when the ambulance arrived at the private hospital's emergency room, a nurse and the physician on duty were at the emergency entrance. Once in the hospital, the physician immediately observed that the girl was pale and diaphoretic. Although she had a weak carotid pulse, blood pressure could not be recorded. Her left thigh was swollen and deformed. His clinical impression was hemorrhagic shock. He therefore directed that the girl be kept on the stretcher and that a call be made for helicopter transportation to the regional Shock/Trauma Center. He asked the patient if her leg hurt and she said it did. Her blood pressure was unobtainable; her pulse was rapid and weak; her skin was cold and clammy. He instructed the EMT to start an IV. While the other attendants cut her clothes away, the physician and the ambulance driver placed the girl's left leg in a femoral traction splint. The EMT was unable to start an IV; the physician then made several attempts to start an IV. Before he was able to establish one, he was informed that the helicopter had arrived. He therefore took several intravenous catheters and a bag for intravenous infusion and accompanied, along with the EMT, the patient back into the ambulance, with the intention of establishing an internal jugular or a femoral intravenous line en route to the helicopter. In the ambulance, shortly after embarkation, as he turned the patient's head to locate the internal jugular vein, he noted that she was flaccid and had no carotid pulse. She began to vomit copiously. He immediately started mouth-to-mouth respiration and ordered the EMT to perform closed cardiac massage. The girl did not regain spontaneous cardiopulmonary activity. At 3:38 A.M. the ambulance arrived at the heliport. Two minutes later the helicopter took off. Eight minutes later it landed at the Shock/Trauma Center.

When the patient was received into the Shock/Trauma Center, her pupils were fixed and dilated and her abdomen was grossly distended. She was intubated and taken to the shock room where ankle and groin cutdowns were performed and subclavian IV placed. External cardiac massage and later open-chest aortic compression massage was performed. Although idioventricular electrical activity was noted, she only transiently developed a recordable blood pressure or a palpable pulse. At 4:24 A.M. her hemoglobin was reported to be 5.8 and her hematocrit was 17. Attempts at resuscitation were terminated at 4:45 A.M. Autopsy determined that she had exsanguinated from a hemorrhage as a result of a fractured femur and pelvis.

Subsequently, the emergency physician charged that the EMT/driver did not alert him that the patient was in shock. If he had been alerted, he indicated that he would have rerouted the ambulance directly to the Shock/Trauma Center. Police and fire personnel who were on the scene of the accident were openly critical of the emergency aid that was rendered by the EMTs.

Allegations

The parents of the deceased patient sued the automobile insurer of the drunken driver and obtained a settlement. They then sued the EMTs and emergency physician, alleging that negligence in the emergency transportation and treatment of their daughter caused her death.

Discussion

Several aspects of the conduct and performance of the emergency medical technicians create significant liability exposure. Standard practice required them to perform an interview at the scene of the accident. Nevertheless, they did not obtain information about the nature of the accident from the first responders (police and firemen) which might have guided their subsequent evaluation. They were also required to perform a field examination consisting of a "primary" and "secondary" review. Although they properly performed a primary survey designed to discover conditions which are immediately life-threatening (assessment for adequate breathing, circulation, and bleeding), their "secondary" survey was inadequate. Such a survey is designed to discover injuries that do not pose an immediate threat to life, but which may eventually become life-threatening problems if they remain uncorrected. It involves a comprehensive hands-on check of an injured person's body and usually requires exposing injured sites. This includes palpating for pelvic fractures by gently compressing the pelvis in order to elicit pain suggestive of a fracture. It also includes checking each leg for injury or paralysis. If a deformity is detected, the limb is immediately immobilized. Although every injured person does not require an in-depth survey, auto accident victims should usually be surveyed, even when they are conscious and coherent. Often less-than-obvious injuries are masked by pain and paralysis, and therefore will be discovered only during a comprehensive secondary survey. Under most circumstances an experienced EMT should be able to conduct a primary survey in a matter of seconds, and a secondary survey in several minutes.

In this case, the EMT elected to forego a comprehensive secondary survey. Two reasons may have influenced that decision. He may have determined that a crowded ambulance was unsuitable to effectively treat the type of injury that a secondary survey is designed to discover (e.g., traction splint for a fractured femur). He was also aware that the destination, the community hospital, was nearby, and that a comprehensive survey by a physician under more optimal conditions could be performed there. Therefore, he may have decided that time should not be lost by performing a survey under the adverse conditions of the accident scene.

Although understandable under the circumstances, this course of action failed to achieve an EMT's fundamental mission in responding to accident, that is, to properly "package" an accident victim in a manner designed to prevent further injury. In this case, routine "packaging" would have included stabilizing or immobilizing the injured leg with a femoral traction splint, or cloth wrap around the backboard with a blanket or pillow wedged between the victim's legs, using the uninjured leg as a splint. Comprehensive "packaging" would have also included the application of MAST trousers to stabilize the leg injury, and to provide an "auto-transfusion" to treat impending or suspected shock. Although in some jurisdictions, an EMT is not permitted to inflate the MAST trousers unless he is in communication with a physician, other jurisdictions permit inflation if certain clinical criteria are met (for example, blood pressure less than 100/60). However, if the trousers had been applied, the EMT would have been justified in inflating them when the girl subsequently went into frank shock en route to the private hospital. MAST trousers would have been the most effective initial emergency aid to combat shock in this case, and was designed for the type of injuries she sustained. Proper "packaging" would usually also include the establishment of an intravenous fluid route. Training of EMTs usually includes providing such therapy in communication with a supervising physician. However, an IV might have been difficult to establish under the circumstances and multiple attempts might waste valuable time; therefore, considering that the destination community hospital was nearby, the failure to establish an IV was not unreasonable. However, once the decision to make a relatively more distant trip to the medical center was made, it became critically important to provide fluids for the initial treatment of shock.

EMTs are also required to effectively monitor injured victims in transit to a hospital. Only one blood pressure was taken in this case. Although the EMT felt the patient's color was poor even at the outset, he did not monitor or reevaluate her clinical condition in a manner that would allow rational decision-making concerning the necessity for emergency measures, such as direct transportation to the Shock/Trauma Center.

The decision to go to the private hospital represented poor clinical judgment under the circumstances. At that time, it should have been recognized and appreciated that an urgent or emergency situation existed and that the girl was already in shock.

An inference can be drawn that the emergency room physician's conduct contributed to the patient's demise. His failure to establish an intravenous administration route is subject to criticism. When he recognized hemorrhagic shock, his priority task was to establish an intravenous route to infuse life-prolonging fluids and medications. He should not have delegated this task at this time to the EMT. When attempts at establishing an intravenous line in the extremities failed, he should have performed a "jugular stick" or a "cutdown." Rather than establish an IV under the optimal circumstances of the hospital, he inadvisedly chose to move the patient to the ambulance. This movement delayed the infusion of vital fluids and may have increased the hemorrhage and precipitated the cardiac arrest. Moreover, it made the institution of an intravenous route less likely. In addition, the physician also did not attempt to intubate the patient. This would have provided better ventilation and oxygenation of her ischemic tissues, as well as prevented aspiration of vomitus.

Other problems in the defense of this case include the anticipated (and perhaps self-serving) testimony of police, firemen, and health care personnel from the community hospital, which can be expected to be critical of the care rendered by the EMTs. In addition, the hostility of the emergency physician, because of the EMT's failure to adequately warn him of the nature of the emergency, will add to willingness on his part to shift the blame and indict the performance of the EMTs as the cause of the patient's death. In addition, because of media exposure, societal expectations for emergency care have created an "expectation gap" between what the public expects in terms of saving accident victims, and what health care personnel can reasonably be expected to provide. It might also be anticipated that physicians who specialize in critical care would be willing to testify to a higher standard of what should have been done in such an emergency situation.

Notwithstanding the liability exposure created by the judgment and skill of health care personnel caring for this patient, other factors and circumstances of this case indicate that health care personnel may not have significantly deviated from the requisite standard of care. The following circumstances are significant factors in assessing whether the patient received an adequate care.

The police and firemen extricated the patient and placed her on a stretcher, but did not put her on a backboard although one had been used for extrication. Usually, extrication is performed under the supervision of an emergency medical technician. The girl's injuries were probably aggravated by the extrication. In spite of the use of flashlights, the darkness at the accident scene made it difficult to perform an adequate overall evaluation of the patient. Her initial vital signs were not alarming (100/60), even though her pulse was rapid and weak. The girl was wearing slacks and had no external signs of bleeding, therefore her injuries were not obvious. Chaos and commotion were caused by the drunken driver's and the girl's brother's combative behavior. Her boyfriend's and younger sister's injuries were initially competitive with the girl's injuries for the medical attention. A single ambulance was insufficient to handle all the victims of the accident. Only triage technique could be effectively employed. The girl's boyfriend had sustained head injury. This, plus the emotional upheaval of the event made his behavior inappropriate and unruly, and critically interfered with the EMT's evaluation and care of the patient in the ambulance during the transportation to the community hospital. Moreover, his insistence that his girlfriend be taken to the larger hospital created a dilemma which had to be immediately resolved. The community hospital emergency room was apparently overloaded with incoming patients and the private hospital had already been alerted and prepared to receive the girl. At that time it was difficult to discern that the girl was in critical distress because she moved her hands and communicated. Although the EMT was concerned that the girl was injured more seriously than the two other people in the ambulance, he wanted to get somewhere and felt that action rather than debate was needed. Moreover, time is not usually of critical essence in the type of injuries suspected. Therefore, he acquiesced to the driver's decision, knowing the private hospital was prepared for arrival and would give immediate attention.

The emergency physician's dilemma was that he had to make a choice to get the patient to the shock unit for life-saving surgery as soon as possible. He tried to expedite this by attempting to perform the IV in the ambulance. Although his decision was retrospectively erroneous, it was not necessarily unreasonable because of the circumstances under which the decision had to be made.

Under certain circumstances, immunity might be raised as a defense under the state's Good Samaritan statute if it can be shown that the second hospital agreed to provide a humanitarian health care service to the visitors and residents of the city as an emergency "back-up," not as a regular replacement. It would be the city's responsibility to see that the back-up system was not overtaxed as it was in this case. The nature of the agreement is important. The hospital agreed to provide its emergency medical technicians for coverage. This agreement may have required highly trained paramedics.

Even if negligence of the EMTs and emergency physician is conceded to have contributed to this patient's death, the legal damages are mitigated or limited by several factors. It is likely that the girl was in shock by the time the ambulance arrived. Given the time at the scene during which she received no medical aid, there was perhaps a 25 percent probability that she would die from direct complications of her injuries. This figure may be higher where a specially trained shock trauma unit is not readily accessible. The community hospital did not have such a unit, nor was it likely to have had an adequate supply of blood to timely replace the patient's blood loss. The extrication procedure traumatized the girl's fractured femur and pelvis, causing accelerated hemorrhage. Moreover, the extent and nature of the patient's injuries played a causative role in her demise. Most pelvic and femoral fractures do not involve these injuries and do not result in fatal hemorrhagic shock. She may have had an unusual type of pelvic and femoral fracture involving a significant tear or transection of the obdurator artery or the femoral artery. Both types of injury are likely to cause massive and perhaps uncontrollable hemorrhage.

It can be concluded that the patient's death was the result of a chain of complicating circumstances. Each individual event and erroneous decision was insufficient in itself to cause the fatal result. The erroneous judgments were made in the interest of getting the most appropriate treatment for the patient. Each decisional point, however, further delayed care in favor of the next, more expert level of medical attention. The confluence of the accident, the extrication, the dark scene, multiple injured persons, multiple assistance persons, other accidents requiring medical attention, subtle masking of unusual injuries, and finally, the extraordinarily rapid deterioration of the patient's condition, left no room for even reasonable misjudgment or delay.

(8) PATIENT RECORDS AND REVELATIONS

54: *Facts*

This fifty-six-year-old man had a history of progressive gangrene of his lower extremities. Two months after the onset of the symptoms, he consulted a vascular surgeon. Although he had adequate bilateral aortic, femoral and popliteal pulses, he had no pedal pulses in either foot, and the tips of two toes on the right foot had gangrenous changes. The surgeon recommended conservative therapy. The patient was a known insulin resistant diabetic, under poor control. He also had a history of arteriolosclerotic cardiovascular disease manifested by a positive stress test.

When vascular gangrenous changes progressed, the surgeon hospitalized the patient for a vascular bypass procedure. Arteriograms disclosed 50 percent stenosis of the left renal artery, atherosclerotic changes in the infrarenal abdominal aorta, narrowing of the right hypogastric artery, narrowing of the left profunda femoris, and marked narrowing of the right superficial femoral artery. There was poor runoff to both legs, with evidence of severe disease in the trifurcation. The patient underwent a staged, bilateral femoral-popliteal bypass procedure. The estimated operative blood loss was 200 milliliters.

Early in the postoperative period the patient did well and was given heparin. The Nurses' Notes indicate that at 7:00 P.M. on the night of surgery there was "some bright, bloody drainage from the right drain incision." The notes indicated further that the dressing became saturated with drainage and that the attending surgeon was made aware of these findings. The patient received one unit of blood at 10:00 P.M. the night of the surgery, but no specific reasons were given for this blood transfusion. The physician's progress notes did not give any indication of postoperative bleeding or a need for blood. The hematocrit on the evening of surgery was 33.5, and a repeat hematocrit the following day was 32.5, after the patient had received one transfusion. The next day, the Nurses' Notes also showed evidence of bleeding. Three days postoperatively the patient developed hypovolemic shock, severe chest pain, and then cardiac arrest and subsequently died of an acute myocardial infarction. At the time the patient went into shock his hematocrit was 22.

Allegations

The patient's estate sued the attending surgeon and hospital for negligently monitoring his postoperative course.

Discussion

There was a lack of diligence in monitoring his postoperative course. The patient's anemia was a substantial factor in the causation of his myocardial infarction. This patient was at high risk to have a myocardial infarction in the postoperative period if adequate oxygenation of his tissues was not maintained. Lack of follow-up of the persistent oozing and bleeding from the operative site led to a significant drop in hematocrit, which was a causative factor in the patient's myocardial infarction. With proper anticipation, monitoring, and management, this complication would have been avoided.

The medical records lack adequate documentation of the patient's clinical progress. The Nurses' Notes indicate that there was persistent oozing and bleeding from the leg wound, a situation not unexpected in a heparinized patient after vascular surgery. The laboratory reports also documented a dropping hematocrit, which is a significant finding because the patient had received one unit of blood transfusion, and his hematocrit had decreased rather than increased or stabilized following that transfusion.

The Nurses' Notes documented that the attending surgeon was notified of this finding by the nurses. However, there is no evidence in the record that the attending surgeon properly responded or investigated the cause of the complication. The physician's progress notes did not demonstrate any attention to the problem. Thus, the available factual evidence in the record leads to the conclusion that there was negligence in attention, and miscommunication between the surgeon and nurses involved in the treatment of the patient; and that this negligence substantially contributed to the patient's demise.

55: *Facts*

This forty-two-year-old moderately obese woman was hospitalized to determine the nature of a right adnexal mass. She was scheduled for an exploratory laparotomy, possible elective hysterectomy, and bilateral salpingo-oophorectomy. A preoperative chest x-ray indicated the presence of chronic pulmonary disease. No preoperative pulmonary function tests or arterial blood gases were performed. There was no information recorded for previous anesthetics, complications, or present drug therapy. The patient's preoperative orders included Demerol, 75 mg, Phenergan 25 mg, and Robinul 0.3 mg on call to the operating room.

The patient was taken to the operating room at 10:00 A.M. and an intravenous line was started. Shortly after induction doses of fentanyl, curare, and Pentothal, the pulse was 175. No blood pressure was recorded for the first fifteen minutes of surgery. At 10:15 A.M. the patient received Anectine and was apparently intubated without difficulty, using a Mac #3 laryngoscope blade and a size 7.0 endotracheal tube with a cuff, after use of a topical anesthetic. The patient was then given more fentanyl and Inderal to lower the rapid pulse rate. At 10:25 A.M. the blood pressure was 180/95 and the pulse rate was 140. Shortly thereafter, the blood pressure and heart rate decreased. Chest sounds were noted to be distant. Subcutaneous emphysema was observed over the neck and side of the face to such an extent that one eye was closed by the swelling. The possibility of bilateral pneumothoraces was suspected. The patient was given more Pentothal, fentanyl, Benadryl, and atropine. The EKG demonstrated ectopic heart beats. Severe end-expiratory wheezing was observed. A chest x-ray demonstrated bilateral pneumothoraces. Bilateral chest tubes were rapidly inserted. Aminophylline drip was begun at a rapid rate and the patient's respiratory difficulties resolved. The patient was maintained with mechanical ventilatory support for the next two days and then extubated. She made an uneventful recovery after removal of the chest tubes. Although bronchoscopy failed to disclose a perforation of the upper airway or large bronchi, there was evidence of blood in the distal bronchioles. No untoward effects of cerebral hypoxia were observed.

Subsequently the patient had abnormal pulmonary function tests and arterial blood gases. Three months later when the patient underwent general anesthesia and excision of a fibroid, bronchoscopy did not demonstrate evidence of bronchial or tracheal scarring or airway abnormalities.

Allegations

The patient sued the anesthesiologist, claiming that the pneumothoraces occurred during the induction of anesthesia because the endotracheal tube was negligently placed.

Discussion

The development of iatrogenic tension pneumothoraces is a well-known complication of general anesthesia that may occur in the absence of negligence. The occurrence of airway complications is inherent in the practice of anesthesiology and is not necessarily evidence of substandard medical practice. However, an anesthesiologist would be negligent if he was unaware of the possibility of a complication, or failed to act to reasonably prevent the occurrence; or if he inadequately monitored the patient and thus did not detect the occurrence of a complication in time to prevent serious injury. In this case, pneumothoraces occurred shortly after induction of anesthesia. The immediate cause of the bilateral pneumothoraces was not known. However, the surgical and anesthesia team rapidly detected the developing complication and appropriately managed the condition so that the patient recovered rapidly and without serious sequelae.

It is probable that this patient's bilateral pneumothoraces and subcutaneous emphysema occurred during the intubation of the patient. The laryngoscope blade probably tore the posterior pharyngeal wall, allowing air to dissect along the tracheal fascia into the subcutaneous areas of the neck, face, mediastinum, and intrapulmonary spaces, thereby causing a tension pneumothorax. Another explanation is that the copper wire stylet used in intubation to guide the endotracheal tube may have protruded through the tip of the endotracheal tube and perforated or tore the upper trachea. The endotracheal tube itself may have directly perforated the upper airway. Although the patient's subsequent successful intubation and general anesthetic is not evidence that negligence occurred during the previous anesthetic, it tends to make the explanations of airway injury from iatrogenic causes more persuasive.

Notwithstanding these plausible and probable mechanisms, a preexistent intrinsic pulmonary problem cannot be excluded as a cause of the complication. Occasionally forcible ventilation causes intrapulmonary pressure to increase to a point where pulmonary blebs or other weakness within respiratory tissue may rupture, causing tension pneumothoraces and subcutaneous emphysema. However, there is no evidence on the anesthesia chart that the patient was preoxygenated or was forcibly breathed by bag and mask technique prior to intubation.

Although not recorded on the preanesthetic summary, a preoperative chest x-ray disclosed evidence of chronic pulmonary disease. There were no arterial blood gases or other pulmonary function tests to clinically correlate this finding. The preanesthetic summary records the lungs as being "clear" and chest x-ray "negative." The patient had insidious pulmonary disease which was not appreciated on physical examination or was not fully clinically investigated. Whether this information would have been valuable to the attending anesthesiologist in preventing the complication is speculative.

The choice of a general anesthetic was appropriate in view of the surgery contemplated (even though in retrospect, a regional anesthetic would have probably been the safest choice if the patient's intrinsic pulmonary disease had been recognized). Whether a regional block would have been more appropriate in this situation is also speculative, because the selection of the type of anesthesia is usually a matter of clinical judgment of the combined surgical and anesthesia team and is dependent on the patient's personality, medical condition, and desires during operative procedure.

56: *Facts*

On May 10, 1980, this fifty-one-year-old man was evaluated by a physician in a hospital outpatient department because of a five-day history of intermittent midsternal, nonradiating chest pain, precipitated by drinking coffee. He admitted to smoking three packs of cigarettes a day for many years. At the time of examination he was asymptomatic. His blood pressure was 148/90. The medical records available to the examining physician for review contained the following information:

March 10, 1975	Complaint of chest pain, dull ache lasting 1–2 minutes, not related to exercise or eating, without nausea or sweating. Pain occurs while coughing. Patient 3 pack a day smoker. Signs: Pulse 78, BP 120/76. Chest, few scattered rhonchi. Chest x-ray, interstitial marking; EKG normal. Impression chronic bronchitis. Do not feel patient has heart disease.
March 29, 1975	EKG normal as compared to March 10, 1975. Lingular infiltrate noted, obscuring left cardiac border. Chronic sputum production, patient feels

tired and weak. Exposure to TBC. EKG—
normal.

September 19, 1977   Chest discomfort, "heart fluttery" several times a
day. EKG WNL.

September 8, 1979   Complains of sharp burning in stomach for one
week, occurring immediately after eating, especially after rich foods. Not worse on recumbency.
EKG—within normal limits. Impression: Gastrointestinal problem. Prescribe Donnatal.

The attending physician reviewed the patient's medical record and
noted that the patient had experienced similar chest pain many times in the
past and that previous electrocardiograms had been normal. He noted that
the patient currently had a nonproductive cough and that examination of
his lungs and chest was within normal limits. Based on the patient's past
medical history and his present illness, the physician's clinical impression
was "Possible Hiatal Hernia." He prescribed Mylanta and planned to order
an upper GI series if the pain persisted.

The following morning, while at work, the patient experienced severe
chest pain, which remitted spontaneously. He returned home from work because he felt he "needed to relax." At noontime, he experienced retrosternal
chest pressure which was so severe that he called the Rescue Squad. An electrocardiogram demonstrated an acute anterolateral myocardial infarction.
An xenon ventilation study demonstrated generalized reduction in ventilation, suggestive of pulmonary emphysema. Serial electrocardiograms demonstrated resolving changes of the myocardial infarction and no evidence of
aneurysmal formation.

Allegation

The patient sued his attending physician, claiming that he failed to diagnose and treat the patient's myocardial infarction, and therefore his heart
suffered additional injury.

Discussion

For the patient to establish that the attending physician negligently
failed to diagnose his myocardial infarction and that such negligence caused
his present damages, the following facts must be established convincingly:
first, that the patient was suffering, or had suffered, a myocardial infarction
at the time of his outpatient visit on May 10, 1980, or that clinical indications were evident that he would suffer a myocardial infarction if no preventive measures were untaken; second, that if the physician had undertaken
proper care measures, the patient would not have suffered the myocardial
infarction or would have been less damaged by its occurrence; and third,
that the patient acted reasonably under the circumstances.

The physician noted the patient's complaints, examined the patient, and reviewed his medical record before arriving at the diagnosis of a gastrointestinal cause of the patient's chest pain. The patient did not clinically present in acute distress; he complained of intermittent chest pain which was similar in nature to prior episodes. He had documented chest pain presentations since 1975, some of which were attributable to gastrointestinal problems. He also had chronic bronchitis as a result of heavy smoking. Previous electrocardiograms were within normal limits. In addition, his chest pain was not associated with radiation, nausea, shortness of breath, diaphoresis, or other indicia of an acute myocardial injury. The patient's existing medical history and physical findings were not sufficient, under the circumstances, to prompt a more aggressive clinical investigation of the cause of his pain.

The professional conduct of the attending physician was not unreasonable under the circumstances. The index of suspicion for acute heart disease was not sufficiently heightened because the patient's past medical history, present symptoms, and lack of acute distress state were factors which served to allay the suspicion of myocardial infarction.

It is conjectural whether, had the patient presented at the hospital outpatient clinic the previous day with the symptoms he subsequently exhibited in the emergency room, he would have been hospitalized and given the same supportive care. The record supports the clinical impression that he was suffering noncardiac chest pain on May 10, 1980, and his myocardial infarction occurred only after he went to work on May 11, 1980. In general, the facts of this as adduced from the medical records fail to convincingly demonstrate negligence in the evaluation, diagnosis, and treatment of this patient.

The patient's conduct was not a substantial causative factor in delaying the diagnosis of the myocardial infarction. Although the patient might have returned to the outpatient clinic if and when his symptoms had not resolved, and although it is arguable that with his pain continuing he should not have gone to work, his conduct was not unreasonable. In defending his own conduct in this case, the attending physician cannot reasonably assert that the diagnosis of a gastrointestinal disturbance was reasonable, and at the same time argue that the patient should have acted more diligently in seeking care or refraining from work. The patient acted on the supposition that his condition was not serious, and relied on the May 10, 1980 diagnosis.

57: *Facts*

A twenty-one-year-old male college student consulted his family physician because of a genital sore. The physician was confident from inspection that the lesion was representative of an infected hair follicle and was not the manifestation of a venereal disease. Nevertheless, to be cautious, he drew a blood sample to test for syphilis, and asked the patient to return for the results of the test.

When the patient returned, the physician was having a busy office day and the student waited for nearly two hours in a crowded waiting room. Because the physician was running behind schedule and because the test was negative, he asked his nurse to give the test results to the patient. The nurse went into the waiting room and briskly exclaimed to the patient, in the presence of several other patients, "Your test for syphilis was negative." Embarrassed by this, the patient quickly left the office. An acquaintance of his fiancée's mother, who was in the waiting room at the time of the nurse's pronouncement, transmitted the information to the student's prospective mother-in-law who became upset. When the patient's fiancée was told of the student's visit to the doctor for a syphilis test, she broke off the engagement.

Allegations

The patient brought a suit against the physician and his nurse, alleging they breached their duty of confidentiality, thereby causing him mental anguish and the loss of his prospective spouse.

Discussion

The bases for a legal action for a breach of confidentiality stem from several sources. The Hippocratic oath requires a physician to promise not to divulge his patients' secrets. The state Healing Arts statutes declare that it is unprofessional conduct for a physician to improperly disclose certain information concerning his patient. The physician-patient relationship incorporates an implied warranty of confidentiality as part of the physician's fiduciary duty not to embarrass, humiliate, or unnecessarily invade his patient's privacy. Thus, even though the care provided by a physician for his patient's illness is properly carried out, the physician may be liable to the patient in damages if he fails to properly safeguard from unauthorized disclosure information he has obtained from the patient, which he needed to properly treat the patient. When a physician violates this trust, without proper justification, he breaches his duty of confidentiality to the patient and may also invade the patient's privacy.

Under the circumstances, the nurse's "public" announcement of the sensitive information that the patient was being evaluated for syphilis was a breach of confidentiality. Although the test result was negative, the mere knowledge that the test was performed would create foreseeable suspicions and innuendos of illicit sexual activity about the student, among those who overhead the announcement. Once this breach of confidentiality is established, injuries to the patient, caused as a direct result of the breach, become the basis of monetary compenation. Although the facts in this case illustrate an *indirect* dissemination of the confidential information to the most damaging source, the patient's fiancée; the consequence was foreseeable that persons who might be acquainted with friends of the patient would relay the information.

The nurse's professional conduct in disclosing information to the patient was so careless or reckless that a court might infer that it was intentionally designed to harm the student patient. Although the nurse who made improper disclosure would be personally liable for damage that her act caused the patient, the physician would probably be vicariously liable for his nurse's professional misconduct, because he is responsible for errors committed by employees under his supervision, direction, and control, *if* such errors are made during the course of, or within the scope of, their employment. In this case, he directed his employed nurse to inform the patient of the test results. This act was clearly within the scope of her employment.

(9) THE PATIENT'S CONDUCT

58: *Facts*

This forty-year-old woman experienced difficulty breathing. Her husband thought that in light of her prior history of alcoholism, her condition was due to drinking. That evening when the wife's breathing became worse, the husband decided to seek medical care for her. Because of her fear of doctors, his wife resisted going to the emergency room and became abusive and agitated. This increased her breathing difficulty. By the time her husband got to the clinic, she had calmed down, but her breathing still seemed to be "poor." When they reached the emergency room, she was placed in a wheel chair. Shortly thereafter, when she was seen by a physician, the husband mentioned that he thought his wife might have pneumonia or the "flu." The husband was not in the room when his wife was examined. After the physical examination, the physician told the husband that there was no evidence of pneumonia and that his wife's difficulties with breathing were due to hyperventilation secondary to her drinking.

On the way home, the husband gave his wife back her cigarettes because he felt he had been assured by the physician that his wife did not have pneumonia. When they returned home, they had a series of arguments; his wife wandered around the house during the night. In the morning she was still agitated. Her husband attributed her worsening physical condition to additional drinking throughout the night. He stayed home to take care of her. He did not detect her drinking alcoholic beverages. In the afternoon she complained of the inability to produce urine. When she refused to eat, the husband noticed that her abdomen was distended, and he put her to bed.

Because her condition continued to deteriorate, her husband felt the need to contact a physician again. He did not call the clinic because he did not know the physician's name. Instead, he telephoned his wife's psychiatrist, and related his wife's shortness of breath, agitation, and nervousness.

He did not convey a sense of alarm to the psychiatrist because he did not realize the seriousness of his wife's situation. The psychiatrist did not suggest further examination by another physician, but telephoned a pharmacy for a prescription of Dalmane. The husband picked up the prescription. Upon returning home from the pharmacy, he gave his wife two pills and a couple sips of water. Almost immediately she became unconscious. A dark red fluid came from her nose and mouth. He turned her over on the floor to allow it to flow out, tried to keep her air passage open, and called an ambulance. When the rescue squad arrived she was not breathing. They could not resuscitate her in the ambulance. Because she was "dead on arrival" at the hospital, no record of the patient's illness was made.

The autopsy indicated that the patient had multilobular pneumonia, and blood in the intestinal tract. Aside from "erosions," no significant gastrointestinal pathology was evident. No evidence of Dalmane or other drugs was found at postmortem examination.

The physician indicated that his standard procedure on examining a patient complaining of shortness of breath was to listen to the patient's lungs and heart, and to do a general physical examination. He would also review the vital signs taken by the nurse or technician, and then record the pertinent findings. However, the medical record relating to the patient's visit to the clinic could not be located. The physician who attended her there could not recall any of the details of his encounter with the patient without the aid of the missing record. On the night he evaluated the patient he was the only physician in the emergency room, and a check of the clinic log indicated that she was one of forty-four patients that he had seen that evening.

After the patient's demise, the following information became apparent. The patient had had two episodes of pneumonia in the past, and smoked excessively. She demonstrated little self-concern for her condition and exhibited a fear of physicians. The death of an infant daughter was a psychologically traumatic event for her. Her alcohol problems started thereafter and negatively affected her marriage. The marriage was marred by fighting and squabbling.

Allegations

The husband contacted an attorney immediately after his wife's funeral and then sued the physician, alleging negligent failure to diagnose and treat pneumonia. He contended that if she had been hospitalized at that time, she would have survived.

Discussion

The existence of chronic and acute alcoholism with attendant behavior problems complicated this patient's illness and made it difficult for the attending physician to provide timely and adequate care. Like many patients who abuse alcohol, she elicited inappropriate responses from her spouse and physicians. In addition, she may have had deficiences in host defense mechanisms as a result of her psychophysiologic debilities. The combination of a compromised host, an antipathetic spouse, and an incomplete medical evaluation, was sufficient to allow combined effects of pneumonia and gastrointestinal hemorrhage to cause her death.

It cannot be determined with precision how long the pneumonia had been present in a readily recognizable clinical form because the clinical data is undocumented, and x-ray evidence is unavailable. Nevertheless, it is reasonable to assume that the dyspnea the patient experienced the day before her death was a manifestation of pulmonary disease because it is an uncommon symptom of uncomplicated alcoholism. There is also an inference that her clinical signs and symptoms were sufficiently advanced to merit the word "toxic" eighteen hours before death, and thus invoke the need for a thorough medical work--up (e.g., temperature, pulse, respiration, BP, auscultory pulmonary findings, chest x-ray, CBC, arterial blood gases, and recordation by the examiner of personal observation of the patient). Because such data is unavailable (either from records or recollection), it is unlikely that a reasonable person would assume that she was not toxic at the time she came to the emergency room. It is likely that there was some evidence of pneumonia at the time of her evaluation in the clinic.

Although retrospective reasoning from static postmortem findings to re-create what a living patient looked like is speculative, most patients with this patient's postmortem pulmonary findings would have had detectable signs and symptoms eighteen hours earlier, especially if they were carefully looked for in a patient complaining of dyspnea. Moreover, the multilobe involvement was clinically consistent with one to two days' duration of pneumonia. In addition, a careful history, physical examination, and a CBC would probably have detected evidence of anemia (in addition to infection), and stimulated a search for its cause. Gastrointestinal bleeding would have been an indication for hospitalization.

The husband's conduct also contributed to his wife's demise. Although he was aware that his wife's condition had worsened by the next day, he did not bring her back to the clinic. His reliance upon the physician's "reassurance" the night before is unpersuasive under the circumstances. The husband's behavior was probably influenced by his ambivalence toward his wife's self-destructive behavior. However, the husband was not trained to be a diagnostician or prognostician of his wife's condition. This mitigates the effect of his faultworthy conduct in not seeking medical attention for his wife.

The professional conduct of the patient's psychiatrist was also faultworthy because he made an incomplete assessment of the patient's problem by telephone. This falsely reassured the husband and perhaps prevented him from seeking more appropriate help. A reasonably prudent physician would have recommended that a patient with respiratory problems be personally evaluated by a physician. If this had been done, perhaps the patient might have been saved. However, considering that her demise occurred shortly after the "telephone consultation," it is unlikely that she would have survived. In addition, the husband's ambivalence may have caused him to perceptually distort the information he provided the psychiatrist regarding the severity of his wife's condition. Thus the information related to the psychiatrist may have been inaccurate and unalarming.

59: *Facts*

This neonate was the full-term product of an uncomplicated vaginal delivery, but fed poorly at one day of age and began vomiting the next day. Because he had not passed meconium after two days, a barium enema was performed, which demonstrated recto-sigmoid narrowing with distal colon dilation consistent with Hirschsprung's disease. Following this procedure, the infant fed well. A repeat barium enema at seven days of age again demonstrated the narrowed recto-sigmoid colon with dilation of the descending colon. A large bowel biopsy was planned; however, the father and the mother (who was a perinatal nurse) rejected the biopsy proposal and also further hospitalization. They took the infant home on the following day. He was given a follow-up clinic visit for one week after discharge.

Four days later, the parents brought the infant to the emergency clinic because of a one-day history of abdominal distention and poor feeding. However, the parents claimed that the child was stooling. The physician, noting the abdominal distention, diagnosed "constipation." He prescribed Pedialyte and glycerin suppositories and discharged the infant to the parents.

The infant was hospitalized three days later with marked weight loss and appearance of illness. He had abdominal distention, a low-grade fever and a history of poor feeding. Feces were evacuated from the colon by warm saline enemas and initial electrolyte abnormalties were corrected with IV therapy. A full thickness rectal biopsy was performed on the fourth hospital day. The final pathology report six days later confirmed a diagnosis of Hirschsprung's disease. The next day the infant went to surgery while weighing one and one-half pounds less than his birth weight. An exploratory laparotomy was performed through a midline abdominal incision. Frozen sections of muscle biopsies from the descending and transverse colon were read as normal. A loop colostomy on the transverse colon was performed through a separate stab wound. The final pathology report noted chronic inflammation of the transverse colon.

Postoperatively, the infant experienced a wound infection of the abdominal incision resulting in a dehiscence. The wound was debrided and closed with retention sutures. Despite hyperalimentation, the child lost weight and appeared lethargic. Although cultures from a sepsis workup were negative, he was empirically begun on ampicillin and amikacin on the fifteenth postoperative day, and thereafter had steady weight gain. He was discharged at fifty-six days of age.

Thereafter, he was treated for a suture abscess at three months of age, and an intra-abdominal abscess under the midline incision at five months. At seven months, the infant underwent definitive surgery with a "pull through" procedure. A month later, the infant underwent closure of the colostomy site.

Allegations

The parents allege that they were inadequately informed of the potential risks of Hirschsprung's disease, the diagnosis of which had been suggested by x-rays, when they took their child from the hospital at eight days of age. Because of this allegedly negligent care, the child suffered enterocolitis, a wound dehiscence, wound infection and excess scarring.

Discussion

The physicians involved in this case had strong indications during the first eight days of life that the infant had Hirschsprung's disease. The difficulty of passing meconium, abdominal distention, and the abnormal barium enema were adequate indications for a rectal biopsy during the initial hospitalization. The complications of a potentially lethal toxic megacolon and enterocolitis should have been clearly explained to the parents and specifically documented in the chart. If the parents were still unwilling to permit a rectal biopsy, the physicians should have applied for a court order to keep the infant in the hospital. To simply discharge the child to the parents, without allowing a third party to intervene on behalf of the welfare of the child, was lacking in due care.

When the child was rehospitalized at fifteen days of age, his illness was already complicated by enterocolitis. The abdominal distention, foul smelling stool, electrolyte imbalance, fever, and chronic inflammation in the excised transverse colon support this conclusion. The three-day wait prior to the rectal biopsy was understandably slow because of the need to stabilize the child's condition. However, the additional week before the bowel resection and colostomy were performed was excessive. The weight loss during this delay suggest that the infant became more weakened.

The infant's injuries were also caused by the parents' conduct when they rejected medical advice. As a result of their unreasonable behavior, the infant developed enterocolitis. Only after the infant was ill did the parents agree to the rectal biopsy and surgery. Although the physicians should have sought a court order earlier, it is questionable whether there is a legal duty to do so. The parents were sufficiently educated to have the primary duty to seek other medical care if they were dissatisfied with the advice they received. Therefore, the wound dehiscence, which was probably due to abdominal distention and a weakened nutritional state, was caused by parental neglect.

The injuries which the child experienced are the development of enterocolitis, a wound dehiscence and its repair at surgery, a wound infection, and accentuated abdominal scarring. Since most of the scarring would be the same even if the infant received ideal treatment for his Hirschsprung's disease, only that part caused by the wound dehiscence and infections is compensable. Whether a court will find the physician primarily liable for the child's injuries will depend on the weight given to the fact that he did not specifically warn the parents about possible complications.

The physician would be liable for any damages resulting from the delay in surgery following the rectal biopsy. However, these would be small compared to the liability for damages flowing from the enterocolitis itself.

60:   *Facts*

The two-year-old child was brought to the emergency room at night by her mother, who said the child had been vomiting material with black specks, had a fever, and a hard, black stool. Several family members had experienced symptoms consistent with gastroenteritis the preceding week. The physician who examined the patient noted that the child appeared uncomfortable, and he observed grunting respirations. The abdomen was distended with increased gas tympany, and bowel sounds were decreased. There was no tenderness or guarding. During the examination, the patient vomited green material with black particles. The emesis was slightly positive for occult blood. A rectal swab was negative for occult blood and the chest x-ray, upright and flat plate of the abdomen were interpreted by the physician as demonstrating increased bowel gas.

The emergency room physician called the on-call pediatrician and recommended that the child be hospitalized for observation and treatment of mild dehydration. The pediatrician agreed with the plan of treatment, and stated that he would see the child in the morning. A pediatric Fleets Enema given on the ward returned a small amount of clay-colored stool and flatus, after which, the child's abdomen seemed to be less distended. Six hours later, the child suddenly stopped breathing. Cardiopulmonary resuscitation was begun immediately, but was unsuccessful. The following morning, when the hospital radiologist read the x-rays which were obtained on admission, he detected air under the diaphragm, and diagnosed a ruptured viscus.

An autopsy was performed. The pathologist attributed the death to generalized peritonitis due to a rupture of the third part of the duodenum (at the point where it crosses anterior to the vertebral bodies) caused by gastroenteritis. Subsequently, a forensic pathologist opined that the child's death probably resulted from a blow to the abdomen inflicted by a "battering parent." The mother was a twenty-six-year-old "exotic dancer" who had been married six times, and had received extensive psychiatric treatment. The ten-year-old stepchild stated that he saw his father beat the deceased stepdaughter. A pediatrician had treated three other children of the mother's current husband for injuries consistent with child abuse. Records at the hospital where the child died indicated that the three other children in the step-father's family were seen on several occasions for various injuries which were reported to local police as suspected child abuse. He was described as a violent and physically abusive person.

Allegations

The child's natural, but divorced, parents asserted that the emergency physician was negligent in his care of their child. They alleged that he was not qualified to read x-rays and that he failed to diagnose a rupture of the duodenum. They contended that their child died as a result of this alleged negligence.

Discussion

Perforation of the duodenum is usually the result of a blunt force injury. Although perforation of the intestine can occur from a number of natural causes (regional enteritis, shigellosis, salmonellosis, tuberculosis) which rarely affect the duodenum, the probable cause of perforation of the third part of the duodenum was blunt force injury to the abdomen, most likely intentionally delivered. It is probable that the perforated duodenum was the result of child abuse. The injury was a substantial factor in causing peritonitis and the child's death. However, the emergency physician was negligent for failing to diagnose the bowel perforation because air under the diaphragm indicative of bowel perforation was not identified.

The history was consistent with an intestinal disorder. Although gastroenteritis was statistically the most likely cause, more serious conditions requiring urgent treatment had to be ruled out, especially in a child who is less likely to be able to provide helpful history. The physician recognized this when he ordered an abdominal x-ray series. However, he failed to detect the important finding of air under the diaphragm. Had he done so, the child's urgent clinical condition would have been appreciated, and proper surgical and medical management may have then saved the child's life.

The physician's failure to diagnose a ruptured viscus, not his failure to diagnose "battered child syndrome," exposed him to liability in this case. However, if he had diagnosed the duodenal perforation and not further questioned the parents or investigated the cause of the perforation he would have been liable for failing to reasonably suspect and report child abuse.

The pediatrician who treated the other siblings would be criminally liable for failing to report reasonable suspicion and evidence of child abuse to appropriate authorities.

61: *Facts*

When this 48-year old woman was evaluated by her family physician for a nontender lump in her anus, she expressed fear that the lump was "cancer." Physical evaluation disclosed external hemorrhoids. Sitz bath and Anusol suppositories were prescribed. Ten months later she again complained of a painful lump in her rectum which had receded after several sitz baths. The clinical impression was thrombosed hemorrhoid. Continued sitz baths were recommended.

One year later she visited her physician because of incapacitating rectal pain. He noted that the patient had hemorrhoids and had received only transitory symptomatic relief from multiple and varied medical treatments. The physician recorded that he observed a large external hemorrhoid, but that the patient "would not tolerate a reasonable examination." His clinical impression was "hemorrhoids." He prescribed Anusol, Colace and Dibucaine, sitz baths, and arranged for surgical consultation.

One week later the patient related to the surgical consultant that she had a long history of painful and protruding hemorrhoids. On rectal examination, both external and internal hemorrhoids were noted. The surgeon did not perform an anuscopic or sigmoidoscopic examination because the patient refused to grant permission for an additional uncomfortable procedure.

Two months later the patient was admitted to the hospital for evaluation of a periumbilical lesion. Under general anesthesia, the umbilicus was explored. The nodular lesion proved to be a benign enfolding of the umbilical skin. At the time of the "admission workup," the patient had refused to undergo a rectal examination because of her past painful experiences. There was no indication in the records that the patient had refused an offer for such examinations. Two months later the patient was referred by her family physician to a surgeon for excisional biopsy of a breast lesion. This also was performed under general anesthesia. There was no indication in the record that a rectal examination or sigmoidoscopy was performed at any time during the hospitalization. The patient was discharged and asked to return to the surgeon in one week for follow-up.

The following week she was unable to have a normal bowel movement because of severe rectal pain. Her husband took her to a different surgeon who noted induration and "tenderness over the entire anus which barely permitted the insertion of one finger." The patient was then hospitalized for further evaluation. She refused to have any additional rectal examination without anesthesia. She underwent sigmoidoscopy under general anesthesia, and a large rectal mass was biopsied. It disclosed adenocarcinoma of the rectum, with infiltration into the vagina.

Three days later she underwent an abdominal-perineal resection. Exploration of the abdominal cavity disclosed metastatic lesions to the liver and vagina. Three months she died of widespread metastases.

Allegation

A malpractice claim was filed by her husband for negligent failure to diagnose cancer.

Discussion

Standard medical practice required careful evaluation into the cause of persistent hemorrhoids in a patient her age. Under the circumstances, this requires the performance of a digital, anuscopic, and proctosigmoidoscopic examination. Although the physician alleges that he attempted to digitally examine the patient's rectum but she refused to allow this procedure, the records do not show that such an examination was offered, but refused. Moreover, the patient's reluctance to undergo additional painful procedures is understandable. Under such circumstances it became incumbent on her attending physician to fully inform her of the need for such examinations or to provide a less painful investigation, if he believed that such an examination was important.

In addition, health personnel had the means and opportunities available to thoroughly examine and diagnose the patient's condition, but failed to do so despite the multiple occasions she complained of rectal pain. She underwent general anesthesia twice during this period, at which time a thorough rectosigmoid examination could have been performed in a painless manner, thereby overcoming the patient's objection to the examinations.

TABLE OF CASES
GLOSSARY
INDEX

TABLE OF CASES

GLOSSARY

Abandonment. Unilateral termination of a physician-patient relationship by the physician without the patient's consent at a time when the patient requires medical attention and without the physician's making arrangements for appropriate continuation and follow-up care.

Abuse of process. A civil action for damages that alleges that the legal process has been used in a manner not contemplated by law. It has been invoked by health practitioners attempting to countersue patients and their malpractice attorneys and by psychiatric patients alleging wrongful confinement.

Action. See *Lawsuit.*

Administrative law. Public law designed, not to prohibit certain conduct, but to advance certain objectives which a representative society has determined to be valid public goals. However, sanctions may be brought against those who fail to abide by promulgated rules or regulations.

Affidavit. Sworn statement that is usually written.

Affirmative defense. Used in an answer to a complaint to plead facts that do not deny the behavior alleged but rather attempt to excuse it. Pleading "Good Samaritan" immunity or a statute of limitations defense are examples.

Agency. Relationship between parties in which one authorizes the other to act for or represent him, usually including the exercise of an element of personal discretion.

Allegation. Statement that a person expects to be able to prove.

Appeal. Complaint to a superior court of an injustice done or error committed by an inferior court, whose judgment or decision the court above is called upon to correct or reverse.

Appellate court. Court with the power to review the decisions made in the trial court or a lower appellate court. The appellate court will not make a new determination of facts, but will only examine the law as it was applied in the case.

Assault. Intentional and unauthorized act of placing another in well-founded fear, which produces apprehension of immediate bodily harm.

Authority to act for another. Lawful permission as a result of delegation of power by one person to his agent.

63

B

Battery. Intentional and unauthorized touching of a person, directly or indirectly, without his consent. For example, a surgical procedure performed upon a person without express or implied consent constitutes a battery.

Bona fide. Made in or with good faith, that is, without deceit, fraud, simulation, or pretense.

Borrowed servant. Employee temporarily under the direction, supervision and control of another. For example, an operating room nurse employed by a hospital, who may be "borrowed" by a surgeon in the operating room to perform certain tasks. The temporary employer of the borrowed servant under the doctrine of respondant superior.

Breach of contract. One party asserts that the other party had an obligation which it failed to perform. It gives rise to an action to compel performance of the obligation or adequate compensation for failure to perform.

Breach of warranty. Failure to deliver something specially promised to be undertaken as part of a contract although the contract remains binding; however, damages are recoverable for the breach. A breach of warranty cannot also or at the same time be characterized as fraud because a warranty rests upon contract, while fraudulent misrepresentations are essentially a tort.

Burden of proof. Rule of practice fixing which party to a lawsuit has the responsibility of proving certain facts, or else letting the other party prevail.

C

Captain of the ship. A doctrine of agency by which vicarious or derivative liability is fixed. Initially used on an analogy, in some jurisdictions the phrase has grown into a separate and independent concept of agency that is especially applicable to medical malpractice cases, in asserting that the surgeon in the operating room has total authority and full responsibility for the performance of the operating crew and the welfare of the patient. Thus, the surgeon may be held vicariously liable for the negligent act of any member of the surgical team.

Case law. Body of law developed as the result of decisions made by the courts. It is distinguished from statutory, constitutional, or other types of law.

Causation. Existence of a reasonable connection between the act or omission of the defendant and the injury suffered by the plaintiff. In a suit for negligence, the issue of causation usually requires proof that the plaintiff's harm resulted directly from, or was a substantial factor of, the negligence of the defendant.

Cause of action. Set of facts that gives rise to a legal right to redress at law.

Civil action. Action invoking a judicial trial either at law or in equity, which is not a criminal lawsuit.

Civil rights. Inalienable rights of all citizens guaranteed by the 13th and 14th amendments to the U.S. Constitution and any acts of the Congress pursuant thereto.

Class action. Court action instituted by one or more persons on behalf of others in a similar situation.

Code. Collection, compendium, or revision of laws scientifically arranged and promulgated by legislative authority. A code implies compilation of existing laws, systematic arrangement into chapters, subheads, table of contents, and index, and revision to harmonize conflicts, supply omissions, and generally clarify and make a complete body of laws designed to regulate completely subjects to which they relate. A code is to be distinguished from a "digest." Digests of statutes consist of a collection of existing statutes while a code is promulgated as one new law covering the whole field of jurisprudence.

Common law. Body of rules and principles based on Anglo-Saxon law, derived from usages and customs, and developed from court decisions based on such law. It is distinguished from statutes enacted by legislatures and all other types of law or bodies of law, including equity law.

Compensation. Money equivalent for the injury sustained directly and proximately caused by a breach of contract or duty, which is necessary to restore the plaintiff to his former position. Permits recovery for an imponderable and intangible thing for which there is no real money equivalent.

Complaint. The initiatory pleading on the part of the plaintiff in filing a civil lawsuit. Its purpose is to give defendants plain and concise information of all material facts constituting the cause of action, which plaintiff relies on to support his demand.

Conclusion of fact. Logical deduction supported by the facts in evidence.

Conclusion of law. Decisive application of rules of law to the facts in evidence.

Confidential communication. Information transmitted during the course of a physician-patient relationship that is necessary for treatment of the patient.

Consent. Voluntary act by which one person agrees to allow another person to do something. Active acquiescence, rather than "assent," which is silent acquiescence. Every consent involves submission, but every submission does not necessarily involve consent. "Express consent" is that directly and unequivocally given, either orally or in writing. "Implied consent" is that manifested by signs, actions or facts or by inaction and silence, which raises a presumption that the consent has been given. It may be implied from conduct (implied-in-fact), for example, when someone rolls up his sleeve and extends his arm for vein puncture; or by the circumstance (implied-in-law), for example, in the case of an unconscious person in an emergency situation.

Consultation. Formal request by an attending physician of a specialist in a field for which information is sought. Ordinarily a duty to consult arises when, after a reasonable length of time and effort on the part of the attending physician, the diagnosis is unusually difficult and uncertain; the therapy is ineffective, or the patient requests a consultation. To be legally sufficient, a consultation requires that the consultant personally examine the patient and his records. A referral is to be distinguished from a consultation because it involves the transferral of prior responsibility for the care of the patient to the specialist. In a consultation, the attending physician retains primary responsibility.

Contention. Earnest and vigorous assertion, debate, and dispute over the legal significance and interpretation of a legal issue in controversy.

Contract. Obligation that binds the involved parties to perform the terms of the agreement that they have reached, providing that there was a mutual meeting of the minds and a quid pro quo. A legally cognizable contract carries with it the legal means of enforcement.

Contributory negligence. Affirmative defense in most states to a successful action against a defendant where the plaintiff's concurrent negligence contributed to his own injury, even though the defendant's actions may have been mainly responsible for the injury.

Counterclaim. Defendant's countersuit against a plaintiff.

Covenant. Agreement, convention, or promise of two or more parties, by which either of the parties pledges himself to the other that something is either done or will be done.

Covenant not to sue. Covenant which involves the relinquishment of a claim or right of action by a person against another. Ordinarily it does not purport to release all persons causing the injury and does not expressly recognize the consideration paid thereunder as full satisfaction for the injury; therefore, it does not bar actions against others for causing the situations where the injury has not been fully compensated.

Criminal law. Body of laws established to promote "public order" deemed injurious to a legitimate public interest, which defines prohibited conduct and provides punishment for those who are determined to have engaged in such conduct.

D

Damages. Money receivable through judicial order by a person sustaining harm, impairment, or loss to his person or property as the result of the accidental, intentional, or negligent act of another. "Compensatory" damages are awarded to reimburse a person for his pecuniary losses due to the injury (e.g., lost earning and medical expenses), and nonpecuniary losses (e.g., pain and suffering) due to the injury. "Nominal" damages are awarded to demonstrate that a legally cognizable wrong has been committed. "Punitive" damages are awarded to punish a defendant who has acted maliciously or in reckless disregard of the plaintiff's rights.

Day in court. Opportunity afforded a litigant to appear in court and to have his claim heard.

Decedent. Person who has died.

Defamation. Willful and malicious communication, either written (libel) or spoken (slander), that is false and injures the reputation or character of another. It is to be distinguished from "criticism," which involves things that invite public attention or comment, and does not follow a person into his private life or pry into his domestic concerns. Defamation does not attack the individual, only his works.

Defamation per se. Defamation in which the defamed person is presumed to have been damaged because of the nature of the publication. An example is a case in which a professional person is defamed in his capacity as a professional.

Deposition. Component of the pretrial discovery process, consisting of an oral, sworn, out-of-court statement taken in preparation for trial in which a witness is asked questions and cross-examined. The statement may be admitted into evidence if it is impossible for a witness to attend in person.

Disability. Want of legal capability to perform an act. Incapacity for the full enjoyment of ordinary legal rights, usually because of a prior demonstrated impairment.

Disclaimer. Document purporting to repudiate or renounce a claim of injury by a plaintiff against a defendant or potential defendant. Ordinarily, a disclaimer of future negligent conduct is not recognized by the law and thus would be an ineffective defense.

Disclosure. Revelation of information.

Discovery. Pretrial activities of the parties to litigation to determine what evidence the opposing side will present if the case comes to trial, in order to prevent surprise during trial and to facilitate out-of-court settlement.

Due care. Required degree of reasonable or ordinary observation and awareness that a person has and owes to another person by virtue of a special relationship or circumstance, such as a physician's attendance of his patients. Such care is expected to be sufficient to avoid or minimize the deleterious effects of known, expected, or obviously emergent complications of the patient's disease or treatment.

Due diligence. Required degree of reasonable or ordinary effort and thoroughness that a person has who owes a duty to another person by virtue of a special relationship or circumstance, such as a physician's attendance of his patient. Such diligence is expected to be commensurate with the medical needs of the patient.

Due process. Course of legal proceedings according to those rules and principles which have been established in systems of jurisprudence for the enforcement and protection of private rights.

Duty. Obligatory correlative of a right. For example, a patient has a right to be attended and treated by his physician according to the requisite standard of care, and the physician has a correlative duty to provide such care. It is often the expression of the sum total of those considerations of policy that lead the law to conclude that a particular plaintiff is entitled to protection. In general a defendant owes a duty of care to all persons who are forcibly endangered by his unreasonably dangerous conduct, if the defendant bears some special relationship to the person to be protected (such as a physician-patient relationship).

E

Enactment. Creation of statutory law through a legislative process.

Enforceable. Alleged obligation that can be put into execution, or caused to take effect.

Enjoin. Court order commanding a person or entity to abstain from performing a given act, or directing that the person or entity perform the act.

Equity. System of jurisprudence or branch of remedial justice, administered by certain tribunals, differing in its origin, theory, and methods from the common law. It is collateral to, and in some respects independent of, "law" in that its object is to render the administration of more complete justice by affording relief where courts of law are incompetent to give it.

Error. Mistaken judgment or incorrect belief as to the existence or effect of factual matters. Negligence is not necessarily implied.

Estate. Convenient phrase to identify the subject of litigation in certain types of proceedings and courts, for example, "the deceased's estate sued the physician."

Ethics. Consensus of expert opinion as to the necessity of professional standards. It is to be distinguished from etiquette, which is a code agreed on by mutual understanding and tacitly accepted by members of a profession.

Evidentiary facts. Facts necessary to prove an ultimate fact.

Executor. Person appointed by a testator to carry out the directions and requests in the testator's will. An "administrator" is a person who has been granted limited authority by a proper court to administer a deceased's estate.

Expert witness. Person who testifies at a hearing or trial, usually for a fee, and who has special training, knowledge, skill, or experience in an area relevant to resolution of the legal dispute, that is beyond the average person's knowledge, and who is allowed to offer an opinion as testimony in court.

F

False imprisonment. Intentional and unjustified detention of a person against his will, which deprives him of his liberty and he is aware of such deprivation.

False arrest. Illegal confinement or physicial restriction of a person's freedom of movement.

Fiduciary. Person in a position of confidence or trust who undertakes a solemn duty to act for the benefit of another under a given set of circumstances.

Finding of fact. Specific conclusion by the court concerning a fact in dispute either between the parties, or as indicated by the evidence.

Foreseeability. Reasonable anticipation that harm or injury is a likely result of acts or omissions.

Fraud. Intentionally misleading another person in a manner that causes legal injury to that person.

Future earnings. Element of damages involving the specific "loss" of earnings that would probably have been made during a given future time had it not been for the injury that is the basis of the lawsuit.

G

Good faith. Honest intention to abstain from taking unconscientious advantage of another, even through technicalities of law; together with absence of all information, notice, benefit, or belief of facts that render transaction unconscientious.

Good Samaritan statute. Statute established to encourage physicians to stop by roadside and assist victims of accidents, by granting immunity from liability for negligence to a person who responds and administers care to a person in an emergency situation. Statutes vary among the states as to the persons covered, the scene and type of emergency, and nature of conduct immunized.

Guardian. Persons appointed by a court to manage the affairs and to protect the interests of a person who is adjudged incompetent by reason of age, or physical, or mental status, and is thereby unable to manage his own affairs.

H

Harm. Wrong or injury done to another's rights or property.

Held. Decision of the court rendered upon a legal dispute of facts and/or issues.

Homicide. Lawful or unlawful killing of one human being by another.

I

Immunity. In civil law, protection given certain individuals (personal immunity) or groups (institutional immunity) that may shield them from *liability* for certain acts or legal relationships. Ordinarily, the individual may still be sued, because immunity can be raised only as an affirmative defense to the complaint, that is, after a lawsuit has been filed. Some nonprofit hospitals have been granted immunity under the doctrine of "charitable immunity." Many governmental agencies have been held to inherently possess immunity under the doctrine of "sovereign immunity." Such governmental groups may allow themselves to be sued by statutorily creating a specific exception to the doctrine.

Impairment. Measurable dysfunction of a person's organ system or mental apparatus.

Imputed negligence. Negligent acts of another person are assigned to the party charged, because of a legal relationship with the other person.

Incapacity. Inability and preclusion of exercising an inherent right or carrying out a transaction because of a legal impediment or impairment. The medical and legal determination of this status or condition may be varied and irreconcilable because the purpose and test of determination may be different.

Incompetency. Inability of a person to manage his own affairs because of mental or physical infirmities. If this status or condition is legally determined, a guardian will usually be appointed to manage the person's affairs.

Indemnity. Agreement whereby a party guarantees reimbursement for possible losses.

Independent contractor. Person who agrees to undertake the performance of a task for which the person is not expected to be under the direct supervision or control of the employer. Ordinarily this arrangement and relationship shields the employer from liability for negligent acts of the independent contractor that occurred during the performance of the work he contracted to perform.

Indicia. Obvious signs or situations that would lead an observer to make inferences.

Informed consent. Patient's voluntary agreement to accept treatment based upon his awareness of the nature of his disease, the material risks and benefits of the proposed treatment, alternative treatments, or the choice of no treatment at all.

Injunction. Court order commanding a person or entity to perform or to refrain from performing a certain act, or otherwise be found in contempt of court.

Injury. Damage or harm done to an individual by violating his legally protected person or property.

In loco parentis. Assignment by a court of a person or legal entity to stand in the place of parents and possess their legal rights, duties, and responsibilities toward a child.

Insurance. Written agreement (the insurance policy) wherein, for premium payments, the insurance company (the insuror) promises to compensate the policy holder (the insured) for losses which occur as defined in the agreement.

Intent. Voluntary function of a person's mind in purposely performing a perceivable act.

Interrogatories. Component of the pretrial discovery, consisting of a series of formal written questions submitted to the opposing parties to be answered before and in preparation for the trial, formulated for the purpose of obtaining written answers under oath from a party or witness in a law suit.

Invasion of privacy. Violation of person's right to be left alone and free from unwarranted publicity and intrusions. It may consist of the unauthorized dissemination of private information about the person or the publication of his likeness without his consent.

J

Joint and several liability. Several persons who share the liability for the plaintiff's injury can be found liable individually or together.

Judge-made law. Law established by judicial precedent.

Judgment. Official and authentic decision of a court of justice upon the respective rights and claims of the partiers to an action or suit therein litigated and submitted to its determination. Although the term "judgment" is also used to denote the reason which the court gives for its decision, this is more properly denominated as "opinion."

Judicial opinion. That portion of a court's summation of a case that presents the legal reasoning supporting the decision.

Jurisdiction. Authority by which courts and judicial officers take cognizance of and decide cases.

Jury. Certain number of persons selected according to law, sworn to inquire of certain matters of fact and declare the truth upon evidence to be laid before them. In trying issues of fact, they function under supervision of a judge who is empowered to instruct them on the law and advise them on the facts. Their verdict may be set aside if in the judge's opinion it is contrary to law or evidence.

K

Knowledge. Organized information about a medical condition that a physician who is treating that condition is required to possess, so that he may function as a "learned intermediary." If a physician does not possess such knowledge, he is expected to acquire it or else refer the patient to more appropriate available and accessible resources for medical care. Also used in the law to refer to a person's awareness of a fact or circumstance.

L

Law. Documented guide to conduct, based on the expression of how society views the responsibility of each individual to other individuals. It includes an amalgam of principles that provide a basis for dispute resolution, in addition to the ultimate resolution itself, if necessary.

Lawsuit. Civil legal action or adversarial proceeding by which a plaintiff seeks enforcement of his rights or redress for the transgression of them by a defendant.

Leading case. Case decision wherein the judicial opinion had definitively determined the law on all issues involved, and as a result the case is viewed as being determinative of the same issues in subsequent cases.

Liability. Obligation that a person has incurred or might incur through any act or omission. In civil matters, liability for damages is for a definite amount, ascertained by a final judgment or preponderance of the evidence that demonstrates that the defendant was responsible for the plaintiff's legal injury and, therefore, is bound to compensate him. Failure to do so would subject the defendant to judicial enforcement.

Libel. Defamation of a person's reputation or character by any type of publication, including pictures or written word.

License. Permit from an appropriate governmental agency allowing certain acts to be performed, usually for a specific period of time.

Litigation. Trial of a dispute in a court of law to determine factual and legal issues, rights, and duties between the parties to the litigation.

Loss of consortium. Element of damages sought by the spouse of an injured party for the loss of conjugal relations because of spouse's injury.

M

Malice. The performance of a wrongful act without just cause or excuse, with an intent to inflict an injury, or under such circumstances that the law will imply an evil intent.

Malicious prosecution. Countersuit to collect damages that have resulted to a person from a civil suit filed in bad faith and without probable cause. Ordinarily, it may not be brought by a person until the initial suit against him has been judicially decided in his favor.

Malpractice. Professional misconduct in improperly discharging of professional duties, or failing to meet the standard of care of a professional. Professional negligence is the most common legal cause of action subsumed under this concept.

Material. Influential and necessary effect. Having to do with matter, as distinguished from form.

Matter of fact. Point that must be decided on the factual testimony of witnesses regarding their perceptions, or by other direct evidence acceptable to the court.

Matter of law. Point that must be decided on the basis of either applicable statute or decisions of case law.

Medical act. Act which in general requires professional training and skill, and the exercise of clinical discretion, to be properly performed.

Medical judgment. The utilization of sufficient medical knowledge through the exercise of the mind. The requirement that a physician use his best judgment in the formation of a diagnostic or therapeutic opinion is predicated or grounded on the possession of some knowledge referable to the medical condition in question; and the exercise or application of skill in a careful and diligent manner.

Ministerial act. Act which is controlled by administrative policy and does not require skill or discretion (e.g., counting surgical sponges during an operation).

Ministerial duty. Obligation or responsibility that is defined and imposed by law and leaves nothing to personal discretion in its performance.

Minority. Person who has not yet reached the statutorily determined age of legal transactional capacity. As a result of this presumed legal incompetence, minors ordinarily cannot consent to their own medical treatment unless they are "emancipated," that is, substantially independent from their parents, supporting themselves, married, or otherwise on their own, or unless a statute provides otherwise.

Misrepresentation. Manifestation by words or other conduct by one person to another which, under the circumstances, amounts to an assertion not in accordance with the facts. An incorrect or false representation of a condition other and different from that which exists. A "fraudulent misrepresentation" is made by a person with a knowledge of the falsity of the representation, which causes the other party to enter into an arrangement or an agreement. A "negligent misrepresentation" is made by a person who has no reasonable grounds for believing that the representation is true, even though he does not know that it is untrue, or even believes it to be true. An "innocent misrepresentation" is made by a person who had reasonable grounds for believing that the representation was true.

Motion. Request to be a judge for an order or a ruling.

Motive. Rationale that induces a person to perform an act. It is to be distinguished from intent.

N

Negligence. Legal cause of action involving the failure to exercise the degree of diligence and care that a reasonably and ordinarily prudent person would exercise under the same or similar circumstances, and the result of which is the breach of a legal duty, which proximately causes an injury which the law recognizes as deserving of compensation.

Negligence per se. Finding of negligent conduct that is established by showing that a statute that generically prohibits such conduct was violated. For example, if a nurse injures someone by performing a medical act beyond the scope of her license, the nurse's act be held to be negligent per se because it is a statutory violation.

O

Opinion evidence. Type of evidence that a witness gives based on his special training or background rather than on his personal knowledge of the facts in issue. Generally, if the issue involves specialized knowledge, only the opinions of experts are admissible as evidence.

Opinion of the court. Legal reasons for an appellate court decision. One judge writes the opinion for the majority of the court. Judges who agree with the result but for different reasons may write concurring opinions explaining their reasons. Judges who disagree with the majority may write dissenting opinions.

Order. Direction or command entered on the record by the officiating judge.

P

Pain and suffering. Element of "compensatory" nonpecuniary damages that allows recovery for the mental anguish and/or physical pain endured by the plaintiff as a result of injury for which he seeks redress.

Parens patriae. State's sovereign power of guardianship over persons under a disability who are presumed to lack capacity to properly care for themselves, such as minors or incompetent persons.

Partnership. Contractual state resulting from the agreement of two or more associates (partners) to engage in a commercial enterprise for the benefit of all co-partners, and to share the profits and losses proportionally. Each partner acts as a principal in his own behalf as well as an agent for his copartners. Thus where losses occur each partner is personally responsible for the payment of all partnership debts.

Perjury. Willful giving of false testimony under oath.

Plaintiff. Party who files or initiates a civil lawsuit seeking relief or compensation for damages or other legal relief.

Police power. Power of the state to protect the health, safety, morals, and general welfare of the people it is charged to govern.

Possibility. Improbability without excluding the idea of feasibility. Bare chance that something occurred, or might occur.

Presumption. Legal inference drawn by the jury on the basis of other facts that are proven. A "presumption of law" is a legal inference that a judge draws from the facts or evidence.

Prima facie case. A complaint which apparently contains all the necessary legal elements for a recognized cause of action and will suffice until contradicted and overcome by other evidence.

Privilege. Particular benefit, entitlement, or immunity enjoyed by a person or class beyond the common advantages of other citizens. An exceptional or extraordinary power of exemption.

Privileged communication. Communication made within a certain trust relationship, such as from patient to physician, which is privileged in the sense that the person making the communication may be statutorily granted the qualified power to prevent the other from divulging the nature of the communication in court. This privilege is conditional and usually subject to several exceptions. Although this physician-patient privilege of confidentiality is recognized by statute in most states, it was not recognized as common law.

Probability. Reasonable ground of presumption because there is more evidence in favor of the existence of a given proposition than there is against it.

Probable cause. Evidence that would lead a reasonable person of ordinary intelligence to conclude that a cause of action is supportable in a civil lawsuit or that an accused is guilty of the offense charged in a criminal prosecution.

Probate court. Court having jurisdiction over wills and the supervision of a decedent's estate. In some states the probate courts also have jurisdiction of the estates of minors, including the appointment of guardians.

Proximate causation. Essential element in a legal cause of action for negligence, that is, it must be shown that the alleged negligent act proximately caused the injury for which legal damages is sought. The dominant and responsible cause, the one that necessarily sets other causes in operation. It represents a natural and continuous sequence, unbroken by any efficient intervening cause. It is not merely incidental or instruments of a superior or controlling agency. It is to be distinguished from "immediate" cause, that is, the nearest cause in point of time and space.

Proximate cause. Act of commission or omission that through an uninterrupted sequence of events directly results in an injury that otherwise would not have occurred, or else becomes a substantial factor in causing an injury.

Publication. Oral or written act (including dictation to a stenographer) that makes defamatory material available to persons other than the person defamed.

Public law. Law dealing with interaction of private parties and the government.

Q

Qualified. Term implying that which is limited, confidential, restricted, confined, modified, credentialed. It also refers to the credentials or presumed capability of a professional to perform a task.

Quasi. Term used to indicate two analogous subjects which resemble each other in certain characteristics, but which have intrinsic and material differences between them.

R

Real evidence. Evidence furnished by tangible objects, such as x-ray and equipment.

Reasonable. Fit and appropriate to the end in view; not immoderate or excessive.

Reasonable act. An act which may fairly, justly, and reasonably be required of a person.

Reasonable certainty. Term implying more than mere conjecture or likelihood or even a probability of an injury. Permits recovery of damages only for such future pain and suffering as is reasonably certain to result from the injury.

Reasonable person. Hypothetical person used as an objective test or standard against which a defendant's conduct in a negligence suit will be judged, by the lawyer asking the question whether a reasonable person, under the same or similar circumstances, would have reacted in the same way as the defendant.

Regulation. A rule or order prescribed by a competent authority to fix, direct, or establish the conduct for action of those under its control.

Release. Statement signed by a person relinquishing a right or claim against another person or persons usually for a valuable consideration. It raises the presumption that the person's alleged injury has been fully satisfied. It is to be distinguished from a covenant not to sue.

Rescind. To nullify a contract by the act of a party declaring the contract void in its inception and to put an end to it as if never were. It is to be distinguished from termination which releases the parties to a contract from any additional or ongoing responsibilities.

Res ipsa loquitur. "The thing speaks for itself." A doctrine which may be invoked in a negligence action when the plaintiff has no direct evidence of negligence but the injury itself leads to the inference that it would not have occurred in the absence of a negligent act. The doctrine applicable to cases where the defendant had exclusive control of the thing which caused the harm to the plaintiff, and where the harm ordinarily could not have occurred except as a result of negligent conduct, and where the plaintiff did not contribute to his own injury. It raises an inference of the defendant's negligence, thereby altering the order of proof so that the defendant must produce evidence that he did not commit a negligent act.

Respondeat superior. "Let the master answer." A doctrine of vicarious or derivative liability in which the employer (master) is liable for legal consequences of the breach of duties by his employee (servant) that the master owes others, if the breach of duty occurs while the servant is engaged in work within the scope of his employment. For example, a hospital is liable for the negligent acts of a nurse it employs, if the acts occurred while the nurse was working within her job description.

Right. Power or demand, inherent in one person, which that person is entitled to have, or to do, or to receive from others within the prescribed limits of the law.

S

Settlement. Agreement made between the parties to a lawsuit, which resolves their legal dispute before a court judgment is rendered.

Shall. When used in legal documents or statutes, a term operating to impose a mandatory duty.

Skill. Clinical ability, as a result of knowledge, to perform a task or procedure in a professional and competent manner.

Slander. Method of oral defamation in which the false and malicious words are published by speaking or uttering in the presence of another person, other than the person slandered, which prejudices another person's reputation and characater.

Speculative damages. Conjectural damages that depend on the occurrence of developments, however, are anticipated to result from the same facts involved in the legal action.

Standard of care. Measure against which a defendant's conduct is compared, involving those acts that an ordinary prudent person would have performed or omitted.

Stare decisis. "Let the decision stand." The application by courts of previous decisions to subsequent cases involving similar facts and legal questions. When a point of law has been settled by decision, it forms a precedent that is not afterwards to be departed from. Although it should be strictly adhered to, there are occasions when departure is rendered necessary to vindicate obvious principles of law and remedy continued injustice.

Statute of limitations. Statutes which specify the permissible time interval between the occurrence, giving rise to a civil cause of action and the actual filing of the lawsuit. Thus failure to file the suit within the prescribed time limits may become an affirmative defense to the action. These legal limits on the time allowed for filing suit vary among the states even as to the same legal causes of action. Most statutes recognize "exceptions" that if accepted by the court, have the effect of tolling the statute. In malpractice actions, the measuring time for bringing suit is tolled, or does not begin to run until the party claiming injury first discovers or should reasonably have discovered the injury. In some states "fraudulent concealment" by the defendant of the injury or nature thereof tolls the statute. In addition, in some states, the statutes do not begin to "run" until the treatment for the condition involved in the alleged negligent act has been completed ("continuing treatment" exception).

Statutory law. Formal written enactments and declarations by a legislative branch of government which have the force of law, as distinguished from case judge-made law handed down by a court.

Strict liability. Liability without fault, in which neither due care, requisite knowledge, or good faith constitute adequate defenses to preclude recovery for damages sustained by the plaintiff in connection with his relationship with the defendant.

Subpoena. Court order requiring a person to appear in court to give testimony.

Subpoena duces tecum. Subpoena that requires a person to personally present to the court for use during a trial a specified document or property in his possession or under his control.

Substantive law. Law which creates, defines, and regulates legal rights, as distinguished from adjective (procedural) law, which prescribes the procedures under which substantive law is administered.

Suit. See *Lawsuit.*

T

Testimony. Oral evidence presented under oath during a judicial proceeding by a competent witness in order to prove a fact. It is to be distinguished from non-oral types of proof, such as types of physical evidence (documents, etc.).

Tort. Civil wrong in which a person has breached his duty to another, which must allege the following: that a legal duty was owed to the plaintiff by the defendant; that the defendant breached that duty and that the plaintiff was damaged as a result of that breach. It includes legal causes of action, such as negligence, false imprisonment, assault, and battery.

Trial. Judicial examination, before a proper court having jurisdiction of issues of law or fact between the litigating parties in accordance with the governing law.

Trier of fact. Jury, or in the case of a juryless trial, the judge.

U

Undertake. To unilaterally engage in, or attempt, a task such as to lay oneself under obligation to perform or to execute. An example is to accept responsibility for the care of or attendance to a patient.

Undue influence. Improper or wrongful constraint, machination, or urgency of persuasion whereby the will of a person is overpowered and he is induced to do or forbear an act. Consists of the use, by one in whom a confidence is reposed by another, or who holds a real or apparent authority over him, of such confidence or authority for purposes of obtaining an unfair advantage over him; in taking an unfair advantage of another's weakness of mind; or in taking a grossly oppressive and unfair advantage of another's necessities or distress. It does not necessarily involve physical injury or threat of it, but is a species of duress.

Unethical. Not according to professional standards.

Uniform act. Model act concerning a particular area of the law created by a non-legislative body in the hope that it will be enacted in all states to achieve statutory uniformity in that area of the law.

Unprofessional conduct. Unethical behavior by a member of a profession, that constitutes neglect of a professional duty.

V

Verdict. Formal, unanimous and binding declaration and findings made by a jury regarding all matters of fact submitted to them for their consideration and determination.

Vicarious liability. Derivative or secondary liability predicated not upon direct fault, but by virtue of the defendant's relationship to the actual wrongdoer, in which the former is presumed to hold a position of responsibility and control over the latter. The "borrowed servant" doctrine and the "captain of the ship" doctrine are predicated on the agency concept of derivative liability.

W

Waiver. Intentional and volitional renunciation of a known claim or right, or a failure to avail oneself of a possible advantage to be derived from another's act. For example, a waiver might allow a person to testify to information that would ordinarily be protected as a privileged communication.

Wanton. Conduct which by its grossly negligent, malicious, or reckless nature evinces a disregard for the consequences or for the rights or safety of others.

Warranty. Express or implied statement of something undertaken as part of a contract but collateral to its object, as or shall be as it is stated or promised to be. It is to be distinguished from a "representation" in that a warranty must always be given contemporaneously with, and as part of, the contract, whereas a "representation" precedes and induces to the contract. For example, a physician who has a contractual relationship with a patient may specially warrant a particular undertaking (sterility from surgery) as part of but collateral to the physician-patient relationship.

Willful. Term descriptive of conduct that encompasses the continuum from intentional to reckless.

Witness. Person who is called to give testimony in a court of law.

Written authorization. Consent given in writing, specifically empowering someone to do something.

INDEX